SUBCOMMITTEE ON COMMERCE, CONSUMER PROTECTION, AND COMPETITIVENESS

CARDISS COLLINS, Illinois, *Chairwoman*

EDOLPHUS TOWNS, New York
JIM SLATTERY, Kansas
J. ROY ROWLAND, Georgia
THOMAS J. MANTON, New York
RICHARD H. LEHMAN, California
FRANK PALLONE, JR., New Jersey
JOHN D. DINGELL, Michigan
(Ex Officio)

CLIFF STEARNS, Florida
ALEX McMILLAN, North Carolina
BILL PAXON, New York
JAMES C. GREENWOOD, Pennsylvania
CARLOS J. MOORHEAD, California
(Ex Officio)

DAVID SCHOOLER, *Staff Director/Chief Counsel*
BRADFORD ROSS KANE, *Counsel*
MARY-MOORE HAMRICK, *Minority Counsel*

AF767821

CONTENTS

HEALTH CARE REFORM
Testimony of HHS Secretary Shalala

TUESDAY, OCTOBER 5, 1993

House of Representatives, Committee on Energy and Commerce, Subcommittee on Health and the Environment, and the Subcommittee on Commerce, Consumer Protection, and Competitiveness,

Washington, DC.

The subcommittees met, pursuant to notice, at 9:40 a.m., in room 2123, Rayburn House Office Building, Hon. Henry A. Waxman, chairman, Subcommittee on Health and the Environment, and Hon. Cardiss Collins, chairwoman, Subcommittee on Commerce, Consumer Protection, and Competitiveness, presiding.

Mr. Waxman. The meeting of the two subcommittees will come to order.

For the first time in over a decade we have a President who is personally committed to universal coverage for basic health care. Two weeks ago, he came to the Congress and outlined his proposal for reform. Last week, the First Lady appeared before our full committee and responded to members' questions. This morning, we begin an extensive series of hearings on President Clinton's health care reform proposal.

Both the Subcommittee on Health and the Environment and the Subcommittee on Commerce, Consumer Protection, and Competitiveness will be holding hearings throughout the fall in order to prepare the members for markup on the President's proposal next January. Today's hearing is being held jointly with the Commerce Subcommittee, chaired by my colleague from Illinois, Mrs. Collins.

I share the President's commitment to universal coverage, and I intend to work with him to achieve this goal. All Americans need to know they are always assured of basic benefits and preventive care whether they are employed by large or small employers, whether they earn a lot or a little, whether they live in isolated areas or inner cities, whether they have lost their job or taken a new one and whether they are sick or healthy.

The President will soon be sending to the Congress his legislation. It is the responsibility of the Congress to examine this bill carefully, to debate it fully and to make the needed changes. I intend to do all I can to assure that this Congress sends health care reform legislation providing universal coverage to the President for his signature before adjournment next October.

I would like to now recognize the distinguished Chair of the Subcommittee on Commerce, Consumer Protection and Competitiveness, Congresswoman Cardiss Collins. I know that she also intends to be brief in her opening remarks, and we both encourage our colleagues to be brief so that we will have ample time available to us for questions to the Secretary.

I want to call on Mrs. Collins and also ask unanimous consent that the full opening statement of all members be included in the hearing record. Without objection, that will be the order.

Mrs. COLLINS. Thank you very much. I am also pleased today to co-chair this joint hearing of our two subcommittees on the President's health care reform proposal.

In the coming hearings, the Subcommittee on Commerce, Consumer Protection and Competitiveness will be focusing on the proposed insurance reforms as well as the consumer protection issues contained in the proposal. I look forward to close working relationships with Chairman Waxman and his subcommittee as this legislation progresses.

We are honored today to have Secretary Shalala here to continue our hearings which began with the First Lady last week, and I want to commend the Secretary and the entire administration for their very hard work in bringing this important issue before the Congress. I know that both subcommittees are planning extensive hearings during this session, and members will have ample opportunities to express their views on a variety of health care issues.

With that in mind, I will conclude my opening remarks. And they are brief so that we can maximize our time for questions for the Secretary. I yield back the balance of my time.

Mr. WAXMAN. Thank you very much, Mrs. Collins.

Mr. Bliley, I would like to call on you.

Mr. BLILEY. Thank you, Mr. Chairman.

Secretary Shalala, welcome to the committee. We await your testimony and comments on the administration's health care proposal and look to your insights as the top administration official on health care.

Let me say, first, Dr. Shalala, I would have strongly preferred that your testimony be based on an introduced bill so that all members could work off actual legislative language and not just the unofficial September 7th draft document.

Because we are working from a "moving vehicle," both Congress and the public are told different and sometimes contradictory things about the plan on a daily basis. Today's Washington Post, for example, reports that the administration has now raised the estimate for the small business subsidy to $16 billion.

Another example is that in the last several days Mrs. Clinton has stated in congressional testimony that the early retirees' health benefit will cost $4.5 billion annually, while during the same week Hour Magazine has said that this benefit will cost an estimated $6 billion annually.

We have also not seen any of the administration's working papers concerning the assumptions and quantitative analysis of the plan's financing, cost containment and economic impact.

Since I am not aware of one independent health care expert or economist who has found your financing and cost containment proposals credible, it is critical that this documentation be made public so that Congress, the experts and the public look at the validity of your analysis.

This administration's proposal is built on vast new Federal and State bureaucracies. Every American's health care would be changed. As the Secretary of HHS, however, you have a special responsibility for the integrity of the Medicare and Medicaid programs. These programs take an unprecedented cut of $238 billion over 5 years, according to the draft. These cuts could devastate these programs, and during this hearing I hope we hear your insights concerning these potentially devastating cuts in these programs.

I thank you, Mr. Chairman.

Mrs. COLLINS. Mr. Chairman, now it is my pleasure to call upon the Ranking Member of the Subcommittee on Commerce, Consumer Protection, and Competitiveness, Mr. Cliff Stearns, the gentleman from Florida, for brief opening remarks.

Mr. STEARNS. Thank you, Madam Chairwoman.

I also want to welcome the Secretary to our committee hearings.

I want to echo my colleague from Virginia, Mr. Bliley's, comments that, while we are hearing your comments, we don't have the detailed legislation. It is a little difficult to basically understand the assumptions, and I think that is one of the key aspects about this whole legislation. What are the key assumptions that you made, the models that you created to develop this piece of legislation? So, without that, we are forced to just hear general comments, so I am hoping today we get into specifics.

And, Madam Chairwoman, I would like to have my—be able to extend on my opening comments, and make it part of the record.

Mrs. COLLINS. Without objection.

Mr. WAXMAN. Thank you, Mr. Stearns.

[The prepared statement of Mr. Stearns follows:]

STATEMENT OF HON. CLIFF STEARNS

Thank you, Madam Chairwoman: As legislators, we have a lot of important issues facing us during this Congress, but none is more important than the future of the health insurance and health care industry. The President has not submitted a detailed plan to the Congress which we can evaluate in this series of hearings. However, the Clinton plan can be described qualitatively. It is not the only approach to the question of health care reform, and I sincerely hope that the Majority will not sacrifice the free and open debate which is usually the rule in this committee simply for the sake of expediency.

In survey after survey, when people are asked about their preferences for a new health insurance system, they make two points: first, they want to feel more secure about their health insurance, and not have to worry that they will lose it because they lose their job or get sick; and secondly, they want to have *choices* when it comes to their health insurance. They want choices of plans, choices of doctors, and choices of hospitals.

I have serious concerns about the Clinton Plan's ability to deliver to the American people in those areas. That is why I will shortly be introducing "The Health Care Consumer Choice and Security Act of 1993." The goals of the legislation are similar to those of the President: allowing Americans to feel more secure about their health insurance and provide them with a greater choice of plans; making the health care delivery system responsive to consumer needs and fostering competition; and assisting low-income and otherwise uninsured Americans in purchasing health insurance and medical care. The difference is that my legislation seeks to achieve real reform through reforming the health insurance market from the bottom up, while the President's plan wants to manage the health care industry from the top down.

Because the Chair has limited the time for opening statements, I cannot discuss my plan in detail. However, I will be discussing this issue in greater depth during the coming weeks of hearings and would ask unanimous consent that the full text of my opening statement be included in the record.

I look forward to engaging our many witnesses over the coming weeks in a debate about these issues. I particularly look forward to hearing Secretary Shalala's ideas about how to minimize the negative effects of government bureaucracy on the individual citizen.

Thank you, Mr. Chairman.

Mr. WAXMAN. Mr. Synar.

Mr. SYNAR. No.

Mr. WAXMAN. Mr. Wyden.

Mr. WYDEN. Mr. Chairman, just very briefly.

First, we have heard some comments from the other side of the aisle about the policy-making process. I think it is important to note—and I want to commend you for this, Dr. Shalala—that on this issue there has been an unprecedented inclusion of Members of Congress on both sides of the aisle on executive branch policy formulation.

I don't know of another instance in the time that I have been in Congress where there has been this much effort prior to the introduction of a bill to reach out across the aisle and involve members. I think it is going to make it easier for us to get a bipartisan bill on the President's desk, and I want to commend you for it and look forward to questions, Mr. Chairman.

Mr. WAXMAN. Thank you, Mr. Wyden.

Mr. Moorhead.

Mr. MOORHEAD. Thank you, Mr. Chairman.

I would like also to join my colleagues in welcoming Secretary Shalala to the committee to start the hearings on this important piece of legislation. I understand that you, unfortunately, are on a very short string this morning, so I won't make my talk very long.

I do want to emphasize the importance of getting an actual bill to us. We have heard all the comments. Most commentators don't believe the figures match up in the legislation. We have to be able to see whether they match up or not. We have to see that, the actual bill. Until we do, it is very difficult to ask Congress to get all the hearings over before the end of this congressional session unless we have a bill in time to do it. It is going to take a lot of study because this is a very, very complicated piece of legislation.

I would join with Mr. Wyden in saying that the President's wife has been very generous with her time and a lot of people have been consulted, but very few people know, other than the summary we have got, what this bill is going to do and how the figures are going to come together. So I would urge you to get a concrete bill before us in the very near future.

Thank you.

Mr. WAXMAN. Thank you, Mr. Moorhead.

Mr. Rowland.

Mr. ROWLAND. Mr. Chairman, I have an opening statement that I wish to submit for the record. I do want to welcome the Secretary here this morning. We do appreciate you coming.

Mr. WAXMAN. Thank you, Mr. Rowland.

[The opening statement of Mr. Rowland follows:]

STATEMENT OF HON. J. ROY ROWLAND

Thank you Chairwoman Collins and Chairman Waxman. I commend you for holding this series of hearings on President Clinton's health care proposal.

All of us know from meeting with constituents that health care is the number one domestic issue facing us. And, our constituents want to know what we are going to do about our current health care problems and how it will affect them. They already pay hundreds even thousands of dollars every year and are tired of their costs going up every year. In addition, millions of Americans are either uninsured and underinsured.

Currently, health care expenditures are about $900 billion per year and take up approximately 14 percent of GNP, yet we have not been able to provide high quality, affordable health care coverage to every American.

I appreciate the administration's willingness to tackle this tough issue and bringing it to the forefront of the domestic agenda. I look forward to continuing our dialogue on this issue in the months ahead.

Mr. WAXMAN. Mr. McMillan.

Mr. MCMILLAN. No opening statement.

Mr. WAXMAN. Mr. Upton. Mr. Greenwood.

Mr. GREENWOOD. I will pass.

[The opening statements of Mr. Greenwood and Mr. Richardson follow:]

OPENING STATEMENT OF HON. JAMES C. GREENWOOD

Thank you, Mr. Chairman. I also would like to welcome Secretary Shalala.

I think that we all agree that it is time for the Congress to take action on comprehensive health care reform. Too many Americans do not have adequate health care through no fault of their own.

It is time for us to provide families with health care security. We have to control spiralling health care costs. We need to make our health care system more efficient; to cut down on the paperwork burden of the billing process; to provide portability; and to address the denial of access to insurance for those who have pre-existing illnesses.

I also believe we need to remain mindful of what most Americans don't want. They don't want more bureaucracy. They don't want higher taxes. They don't want small businesses closing their doors because they can't afford additional Federal mandates. Finally, they don't want unrealistic financing mechanisms.

I would like to take a moment to read an excerpt from a letter which I received yesterday from Bob Griffith, president of Woods Services in Langhorne, PA, which provides residential care to mentally retarded clients.

"As a nonprofit, we have worked hard to keep our service rates low and still be a responsible employer. And we do make health coverage available to each full time employee, although that is typically single coverage, and there is a small co-pay required of most employees. But if we had to come up with sufficient funds to pay for family coverage for all eligible employees, the cost would be horribly burdensome and, frankly, I don't know where the money would come from."

I have heard similar stories from many employers throughout my district. It seems inevitable that when you impose a mandate such as this on employers, you have to create a downward pressure on employment.

I fully realize that there are many individuals in this country who have jobs, but no health insurance. This is, indeed, unfortunate and needs to be rectified. It would be equally unfortunate if the Congress enacts health care reform legislation which creates an environment in which people have health insurance, but lose their jobs.

I hope that when it comes time to report a bill from the subcommittee that I, as a Republican, can vote yes. I recognize that we have a lot to hammer out and many compromises to make before we can got to that point.

I am confident that working together we can enact comprehensive health care legislation which is good for this country and which provides American families with the security they deserve.

I look forward to working with you towards that goal.

Thank you.

STATEMENT OF HON. BILL RICHARDSON

Mr. Chairman and Madam Chairwoman, I would like to thank you both for holding this very important joint hearing on The American Health Security Act of 1993. I would also like to welcome someone who has very quickly become one of the most well-respected members of the Cabinet, Secretary Shalala.

Thank you, Madam Secretary, for taking the time to answer questions about some of the more specific details of the administration's health reform plan.

As so many of us stated here last week and have stated in previous forums, the problems of the American health care system are numerous and complex. The number of uninsured people varies from one estimate to the next but we can say with relative certainty that the number continues to climb.

Furthermore, the costs of health care are excessive for almost all: the costs to the Federal government keep us from effectively reducing the Federal deficit; the costs of health care for large businesses prevents them from competing well internationally; the exorbitant costs for small businesses, of which there are so many in my district, prevents them from being able to provide insurance to their employees; and the catastrophic costs to individuals and families can cause bankruptcy in a very short period of time.

It's time to tackle the difficult issues of the uninsured and health care costs because to do anything else would be to neglect problems that directly affect nearly all members of this society.

It's high time for us to return security to the minds of so many members of the public who are currently frightened. Frightened of losing their health insurance. Frightened of becoming ill. Frightened of losing their jobs because for so many losing their jobs means losing their health insurance.

I believe that if we had to sum up the message of the administration's health care plan, it would be this: "MAKING SURE PEOPLE HAVE PEACE OF MIND."

People should simply not be living in fear of an illness to themselves or a loved one. This is a terrible burden for any individual or family head to have to shoulder.

Granted, all of us clearly realize that there is plenty that is good about the American health care health care system. But Madam Secretary, when I return to my district, I see a tremendous amount of unfairness and inequity.

As we reform our current health care system, what I would like to see more of instilled in a new system is fairness and equity.

Some parts of my district in New Mexico have high rates of insured people with ready geographical access to health care. However, more parts of my district have extremely high rates of uninsured people with a severe shortage of health care personnel to meet their needs.

Almost without exception, these areas are rural ones.

If you talk to people in these areas, many can remember days gone by when there were more primary care personnel in their midst. But we have built far too many perverse incentives in our system for people to become specialists and to practice medicine in urban areas.

The American Health Security Act of 1993 reverses that trend and proposes to return some of the lost resources to rural areas through efforts to attract more personnel and provide financial assistance to areas in need of capital improvement.

I look forward to working with Secretary Shalala on this very critical issue of returning fairness and equity to our health care system. For without doing this, we truly are not reforming our existing system.

Mr. WAXMAN. Mr. Hastert.

Mr. Sharp has joined us. If he would like to make an opening comment.

Mr. SHARP. Just to thank you, Mr. Chairman and Chairwoman Cardiss Collins, for letting me sit in and compliment the Secretary for the extraordinary amount of work that has already preceded on this issue.

Mr. WAXMAN. Our witness this morning is Secretary of Health and Human Services, Donna Shalala.

The Secretary is responsible for the $248 billion Medicare and Medicaid programs. The department has expertise in establishing quality standards, providing access to care and implementing cost containment. And, of course, under the President's health reform plan, these responsibilities will only expand as the department works in conjunction with the national board and States and the regional alliances to implement health reform.

Secretary Shalala, we are delighted to have you with us. We look forward to your testimony and our opportunity to ask you some questions as we explore the President's proposal and try to work through this legislative process.

STATEMENT OF HON. DONNA E. SHALALA, SECRETARY, DEPARTMENT OF HEALTH AND HUMAN SERVICES

Secretary SHALALA. Thank you, Mr. Chairman and Madam Chairwoman and members of the committee. It is indeed an honor to appear before you this morning to discuss President Clinton's comprehensive plan for health system reform.

I am of course aware, as noted, that you do not have the bill before you, so this is an opportunity for us to explore some of the ideas in the plan. My colleagues and I will, of course, be back for detailed testimony before your subcommittees when the bill is sent to the Hill.

Chairman Waxman, you have devoted your entire career in public life to the improvement of our health care system and the protection of our people. But for too much of that time you have had to work against the current of indifference that has flowed from the White House. Today, the President and I stand ready to work with you to achieve real change.

Chairwoman Collins, I applaud the work you have done to ensure that our government and our health care system does not forget those who are most needy. We have a historic opportunity to enter all of our people into a high quality, accessible health care system.

I know that Chairman Dingell will come here at some point, and it is not often that a son is able to fill the legacy of his father. In so many ways he has already done that with his own remarkable career of public service. And now, 50 years after Chairman Dingell's father offered our Nation his wise counsel on national health insurance, all of us together can make that dream a reality.

At Health and Human Services, we are enthusiastic about the promise of the President's plan for health reform. We have worked many months on the details of this plan and believe it will deliver what the President has promised, a system that provides every American with the security of health care that is always there.

Our enthusiasm is tempered by the knowledge that when this legislative process is completed it will be HHS as well as other agencies that will share the responsibility of implementing this program in rapid fashion so that the benefits we promise today quickly become the reality of American life tomorrow. It is a daunting task, but we look forward to the challenge.

Before I begin my formal remarks, I would like to pay special tribute to the members of these committees who have worked so hard to keep the issue of health reform alive and well during the many years of national debate. We in the administration know that we did not discover the issue of health reform, and I believe that together we can make it happen.

Over the coming months we will consult with you, work with you, and, yes, sweat with you over the details of this plan. And I commit to you now that we will listen to your comments, your criticisms and your ideas so that together we can fashion the best health care system for our people. And when we are done, I promise you that my department will share in the responsibility of implementing the new law with all the urgency that it will require.

Six principles. In his speech to the joint session of the Congress, the President laid out six principles that have guided our work: security, simplicity, savings, quality, choice and responsibility. As long as we adhere to these guideposts, we can create a system of health care delivery and financing that provides the kind of protection for the American family that all of us desire. It has been heartening to hear the level of agreement on these six points. If we can agree on where we want to end up, the task of getting there will be made all the easier.

We offer a plan that will guarantee Americans the security of health insurance that is both affordable and reliable.

We promise consumers and providers of health care a system that is simplified so that all players will know what is due them and what is expected of them.

We offer savings for individuals, for business owners and, yes, for government, too.

We will protect the quality of a health care system that is, for many, the best in the world, and we will make sure that it is now available to all our citizens.

We will cover all Americans a choice of health care plans that will compete—not on the basis of who can craft the slickest marketing plan but on the basis of who can offer the best policy to meet the needs of communities, families and individuals. And we will protect our citizens' right to choose from among the thousands of talented health care professionals who stand ready to care for them in their time of need and who might prevent or forestall that need.

And, finally, we will ask everyone—employers and employees, hospitals and nurses and physicians, insurers and pharmaceutical companies, rich, poor and middle class—to take responsibility for their health, be it financial or physical.

Today I would like to talk a bit more about this last point, responsibility, because I believe it is at the core of what the President proposes. One of the key tenets of our Nation is that those of us who prosper in our society owe something to the rest.

President Kennedy told us to ask what we could do for our country, and President Clinton's health security proposal asks all Americans to contribute something to the betterment of our health system.

We ask employers to provide every worker and their families with a health plan that provides comprehensive coverage of their health care needs. In return, our plan provides small businesses and all low-wage firms Federal premium discounts to make the cost of that coverage affordable.

We create an even playing field on which all businesses compete for workers and profits on the same terms. And the overall effort to reduce the cost of care will produce significant savings for all businesses, large and small, in the years ahead.

We ask our doctors and hospitals to reduce the rate of growth in their costs so that health care is affordable to all. In return, the plan offers millions of additional paying patients the virtual elimination of charity care and a significantly simplified system of administration.

If we do this right, we will do away with a system in which the first question a health care provider staff must ask a patient is "Are you covered?" rather than "Tell me where it hurts."

And we provide flexibility in our antitrust laws to enable our practitioners to cooperate instead of compete with each other.

We ask our drug manufacturers to curb their double-digit price increases while promising them millions of newly insured consumers of their products. At the same time, we will advance the government's efforts to fund biomedical research.

We ask our academic health centers, the vanguard of our health care system, to shift their training programs toward primary care.

In return, we promise an increased flow of funding from both the Federal and the State governments. And we will increase funding from the National Institutes of Health for support of research conducted at these vital institutions.

We ask the Governors, the mayors and the legislators of our great States to maintain their current commitments to health care and to act with wisdom and speed to craft this new system so that Americans can enjoy its benefits.

In return, we offer States and cities the opportunity to shape health reform to fit the unique needs of their rural and urban communities and those peoples. We will provide them with relief from the seemingly unending upward spiral in Medicaid acute care costs and from the burden of uncompensated care.

We will protect the critical safety net providers in our inner city and rural areas and assist them financially so that the quality and availability of care will be greater under this plan.

We realize, of course, that simply handing every American an insurance card will not achieve universal coverage if there is not a sufficient supply of doctors, nurses and other health professionals. We will strengthen our commitment to community and migrant health centers and the National Health Service Corps to guarantee that promised benefits reach all of the people whether they live in Harlem, N.Y., or in Waycross, Ga. And we will use creative new technology to link physicians practicing in isolated areas to care networks that can guide treatment decisions from many miles away.

For the consumers of health care we offer the greatest benefits of all—guaranteed coverage that goes with them from job to job, from employment to unemployment, from mother to child and from generation to generation.

We will remove the stigma from Medicaid beneficiaries and enter them and others of lesser means into a unified health care system that sees no difference in patients be they poor or rich, working or unemployed.

We will create a system in which a woman on Medicaid no longer has to explain to her child why they must travel by train, bus or on foot to a doctor many miles away because the doctors nearby won't accept their kind of insurance. And we will create a system that permits elderly patients and others with disabilities to receive desperately needed long-term care services where they need and want it most—in their own homes.

Here, too, we ask for something in return.

We ask parents to immunize their children against preventable disease. We ask working men and women to contribute to the cost of their coverage. We ask the elderly to contribute toward the cost of prescription drugs.

And we ask all Americans to be conscious not only of the cost of their care but the savings possible from a change in their behavior. Government cannot dictate the life-styles of its people, but it can encourage its people to be healthier.

The comprehensive benefits package includes an array of preventive benefits with little or no cost sharing. In addition, the President proposes a significant increase in the Federal cigarette excise tax not only to raise funds for reform but to encourage citizens to quit what is a singularly destructive habit.

We all know the expression "an ounce of prevention is worth a pound of cure." Well, until now, we have been a country that is all too ready to spend a pound while conserving our ounces. Under the President's plan, that will change.

Together, we have taken important steps towards ensuring all of our children access to needed immunizations. In the months ahead, we will complete that task by improving our infrastructure and our outreach and our education efforts.

The President's health reform plan adds important new instruments to our national prevention effort. Women over age 50 will be entitled to a regular mammogram, and those who are at risk will get them at an earlier age. Children will have coverage for their preventive dental care. Women of childbearing age will have greater access to family planning, prenatal care and to well-baby care. Our vital network of mental health benefits will be enhanced. And all Americans will have coverage for an annual physical examination.

By taking these steps now, we will not only lower our health bills tomorrow, but we will ensure a healthier and more responsible Nation.

Finally, there is the responsibility of each of us as public officials. Health reform gives each of us—legislators and administrators, Democrats and Republicans—an opportunity to provide our constituents with tangible evidence that their government works and cares.

Health reform asks us to take a chance that change is better than standing still and that bipartisanship is worth more than an extra soundbite on the evening news.

Mr. Chairman, Madam Chairwoman, we share a common vision, one of a health care system that is secure but not stagnant, simple but not simplistic, saves rather than saps our resources, gives us choice not chance, guarantees quality for all, not for just a few, and asks for responsibility instead of risk.

None of this will come easily, not here on Capitol Hill, not at my department, not in our State legislatures and certainly not in the boardrooms and the family rooms of this country. But we believe that we can work together to make change work and to make reform work.

Each of us has come here to our Nation's capital to improve the lives of the people we represent. Too often, our efforts to achieve change are necessarily at the margins. Health reform presents all of us with a chance to be part of history, to be able as we end this century to leave behind us tangible evidence of our ideas and our work.

It allows us to keep the promise of America. Health care reform is about those that each of you represent. It is about our own children, it is about our friends, and it is about our neighbors. It is about big dreams, big steps and big changes.

I began my testimony by saying we will listen to your ideas, and, right now, I would be pleased to respond to your questions. Thank you very much.

Mr. WAXMAN. Thank you very much, Secretary Shalala, for that outstanding statement.

Mr. WAXMAN. Let me set out the ground rules.

Members will be called under the rules in the order in which they showed up at this hearing. At the time of the gavel those that were present will be recognized in order of seniority.

Each member will be permitted 5 minutes to ask questions, and we will use the little timer that will indicate a red light and a green light. When the red light flashes, we would request the members complete the question and then the Secretary will have an opportunity to respond to that question even if the red light is still on.

If I might start with the questioning myself, Secretary Shalala. Our job now is to see how well this plan lives up to the promises that are being made to the American people. One of the promises is that people will have a choice not only of plans but of providers, and that choice will be for everyone to make, no matter what their economic status may be. On paper, at least, everyone will have a choice of at least three plans, one of which will be a fee-for-service plan.

I don't think we would want to see a situation in which low-income families ended up only in managed-care plans. So my question to you is do you believe that low-income people, workers or nonworkers, will have meaningful access to fee-for-service coverage and not just a choice that will lead them to one option, the lowest-priced managed-care plan?

Secretary SHALALA. Mr. Chairman, as you know, the President's plan is committed to choice, and we are, in fact, providing subsidies for those that are low income and folding the Medicaid recipients into the plan at the average of the premiums. That may or may not, depending on where the fee for service plan is set, give every low-income American who comes off the welfare system into the new system access to fee for service, but it is not at all clear that fee for service will necessarily be the highest cost plan, will be over the average.

It is true that everyone, including those that are subsidized through Federal subsidies, particularly welfare recipients, will have a choice of plans, and that those choices will include managed care or managed-care networks, and certainly they will have some flexibility within the plan. But you have, both in private sessions with me and with my colleagues, noted that we need to look again, which we are prepared to do with you, at the subsidy scheme for whether low-income workers actually have access to every plan.

Mr. WAXMAN. I realize all the details haven't been worked out for this legislation, but I would hope that when the details are put on paper and submitted to us that we will, in fact, give every American a choice to say that low-income people may or may not have a choice or they have a choice but they can't afford—and, therefore, it is really not a choice at all doesn't seem to me a very satisfactory answer.

Secretary SHALALA. Mr. Chairman, low-income people will have a choice. The question is, how many choices will they have within the plan. We believe that they will have choices within the plan, but I cannot assure you that every low-income person will have a choice of the highest cost plan if it be fee for service or any other plan. But certainly they will have a choice.

Mr. WAXMAN. Let me move on to another topic because this first one is one of great concern.

One of the reasons I have concern about the size of the Medicare cuts is the effect such reductions might have on the quality and accessibility of services for Medicare beneficiaries who are the disabled and the elderly. As you know, Medicare payments to providers currently lag behind what most private insurers pay for similar services. My question is, are the recommended Medicare cuts likely to make this payment differential worse and increase the likelihood that Medicare beneficiaries will have difficulty finding providers who will serve them?

Secretary SHALALA. We don't think so, Mr. Chairman. We think that the alliances will receive from the Federal Government appropriate payments. We will be blending those payments in with other premium payments. Even where we are paying the premiums we believe that when you see our final numbers that you will be assured that low-income people have been well taken care of in the integration procedures we have for the plans.

Mr. WAXMAN. In the budget bill we just enacted we reduced Medicare spending by $55 billion and Medicaid by about $7 billion over the next 5 years to help finance health reform. The administration is proposing to use about $125 billion of Medicare savings and $230 billion of Federal Medicaid savings between 1996 and the year 2000. These are very large numbers, even by budget reconciliation standards. My question is, will the administration be submitting a request for Medicare and Medicaid cuts as part of the President's fiscal year 1995 budget next January?

Secretary SHALALA. No.

Mr. WAXMAN. Thank you very much.

Mrs. Collins.

Mrs. COLLINS. Thank you.

Secretary Shalala, one of the objectives of health care reform is to eliminate the practice of insurers seeking to find only low-risk health customers. I think the practice is known as "cherry picking." While your proposal requires that plans be open to all, how do you propose to eliminate more subtle efforts to target certain populations and neighborhoods within their specific areas, within their service areas, such as by perhaps targeted marketing schemes?

Secretary SHALALA. We will vigorously enforce civil rights laws in relationship to the plans. We will look at the design and the lines drawn for the alliances to make sure that there is not redlining. If necessary, we will recommend additional changes in laws to make certain that we have the tools necessary to assure that there is not targeting and we don't continue the kind of cherry picking or the selection by the plans or by the alliances of certain groups of people.

The other thing is there will be no benefit for individual plans because of the way we are doing the risk adjustment for selecting out certain groups. So I think that we are—through our strategies, we are actually overcoming some of those issues that are currently existing in the systems in the new system.

Mrs. COLLINS. In light of the greater power the health plan is going to have in the new system due to their increased market share, consumers need increased protection when they believe that their insurer has been acting improperly toward them.

You had proposed an ombudsman within each health alliance as an impartial party to resolve the disputes. But I am concerned that may not be adequate because if there is just, for example, one ombudsman per health alliance, then there may be insufficient resources or staff. Also, the range of problems might be just unbelievable. And so, my question is, have you considered other mechanisms for resolving disputes between consumers and the health care plans, such as when a health care plan refused to pay for a service by a doctor?

Secretary SHALALA. Madam Chairwoman, we have. And, obviously, we think that the centerpiece of the plan is the consumer protections that are built in. And the quality assurance system that we intend to put in place will do more than simply look at the quality of the health care provided but at the satisfaction of the customers. And so at a data quality assurance level we will have one check.

We will also have due process and an appeals process within the plans as well as the ombudsperson that you referred to.

In addition to that, these plans and the alliances are basically governed by consumers and employers so that at different levels we have, in fact, turned this from a seller's market to a buyer's market and empowered consumers as the governance part of the plans themselves, and I think that there will be checks up and down the system to protect both individuals as well as employers concerns.

Mrs. COLLINS. Well, this month being National Cancer Awareness Month, I just happened to wonder—I know under the plan women over the age of 50 would be entitled to a free mammogram without any copayment or deductibility every second year. Yet, on the whole, women over the age of 65 are especially at high risk for breast cancer, and it has been said that these women should receive annual mammograms. So I wonder if there is going to be some kind of additional automatic coverage for annual free mammograms for women over the age of 65.

Secretary SHALALA. We will—there are new standards coming out from the National Cancer Institute and from the medical societies, and we will adhere to those standards for all of our programs for the President's new health care reform program as well as for the Medicare program. There will be—I think numerous groups will have different points of view on how much should be free. But let me assure you that every woman in this country who needs a mammogram, whether they are in a high-risk group and under 50 or over 50 in a group in which the recommendations are that they should have a mammogram every 2 years, will have them available to her.

Mrs. COLLINS. But every year would be a little bit much for those over the age of 65?

Secretary SHALALA. I don't actually know the scientific evidence on those over 65, but I would be happy to provide it. I would be happy to provide it for you.

[Testimony resumes on p. 30.]

[The information follows:]

The Health Security Act would cover biennial screening mammography for women over age 65, which is the same as current Medicare policy. Our policy to encourage women over age 65 to have regular mammography on a biennial basis is based on extrapolation of data from clinical trials in the United States, Sweden, and England, all of which have shown about a one-third reduction in breast cancer mortality with screening every 1 to 2 years. These results were affirmed by the recent (February 1993) International Workshop on Breast Cancer Screening held by the National Cancer Institute (NCI), the National Institute on Aging, and the Health Care Financing Administration in July-August, 1990. The Forum concluded that screening approximately every 2 years would yield a substantial reduction in mortality. For the record, I am including the key summary reports of the Forum as well as the recent NCI statement on mammography.

NATIONAL CANCER INSTITUTE

Office of Cancer Communications Building 31, Room 10A24 Bethesda, Maryland 20892

National Institutes of Health

For Response to Inquiries

December 3, 1993

NCI Press Office
(301) 496-6641

Breast Cancer Screening

The National Cancer Institute (NCI) today released the following statement concerning breast cancer screening:

> **There is a general consensus among experts that routine screening every 1 to 2 years with mammography and clinical breast examination can reduce breast cancer mortality by about one-third for women ages 50 and over.**
>
> Experts do not agree on the role of routine screening mammography for women ages 40 to 49. To date, randomized clinical trials have not shown a statistically significant reduction in mortality for women under the age of 50.

The statement represents a summary of scientific fact about effectiveness, that is, the ability of mammography, coupled with appropriate treatment, to reduce the mortality from breast cancer. It summarizes scientific knowledge derived from two decades of clinical trials research. The statement is a successor to a "working guideline" formulation drafted in 1987 and will be revised as new information is developed.

Background Information

The National Cancer Institute is the lead federal agency for research on the causes, prevention, diagnosis and treatment of cancer. NCI conducts ongoing evaluations of the results of cancer research, and in late 1991 began the process of examining clinical trial evidence of the value of screening mammography.

NCI convened an International Workshop on Breast Cancer Screening in February 1993. The results from eight randomized clinical trials were reviewed. The workshop conclusions reinforced the advisability of screening for women ages 50 to 69, and stated that the effects of screening in women ages 40 to 49 do not demonstrate a statistically significant reduction in mortality to date.

Between May and December 1993, scientific data from clinical trials, including the workshop results, were reviewed by a number of scientific organizations, health groups, and advisory boards.

###

Press documents can be downloaded from Compuserve®. They are located in the SciNews-MedNews library" which is located in the Journalism forum (GO JFORUM).

The Journals of Gerontology
1992; Vol. 47 (Special Issue):1-3

In the Public Domain

— 1 —

Breast Cancer Screening in Older Women: Overview

Mary E. Costanza

University of Massachusetts Medical Center.

BREAST cancer is the most common cancer in American women, affecting one in nine (1). An estimated 155,000 women will be diagnosed with breast cancer in 1991. Almost 50,000 women will die from it, the majority of whom will be 65 and older. Incidence rates have increased steadily (1% per year) since 1976 (2). Overall, mortality rates have not changed in spite of apparent advances in detection and treatment.

The potential to decrease mortality is available to us. With widespread and regular use of screening mammography and clinical breast exam, experts estimate that breast cancer deaths could be decreased by 30% (3–6). However, the majority of women are not getting regular screening. Moreover, older women are less likely to get screened, in spite of the fact that they are at greater risk for developing breast cancer than younger women (7,8).

Of specific concern to all in health care is the tremendous demographic shift in the health and longevity of Americans. Compared to the beginning of the century, relatively few deaths are occurring in childhood and in midlife. We are experiencing a dramatic revolution in longevity as the oldest group within our society is now the fastest growing segment. With growing numbers of older people, health care costs are estimated to increase significantly (9,10).

By 2,010, 15% of the population will be over 65. The implication of this in terms of breast cancer incidence and mortality is staggering: breast cancer is already of epidemic proportions; the incidence rises sharply with age; the oldest segment of our society is increasing at the fastest rate. What can health care providers and regulators do about screening women aged 65 and over for breast cancer?

The published breast cancer screening guidelines are not always helpful for clinicians treating older women. Existing guidelines fail to address the 65-and-older age group specifically, or they recommend different age cutoffs (10–17) (see Figure 1).

Recent studies (7,8,18–22) have amply documented the current low utilization of breast cancer screening modalities

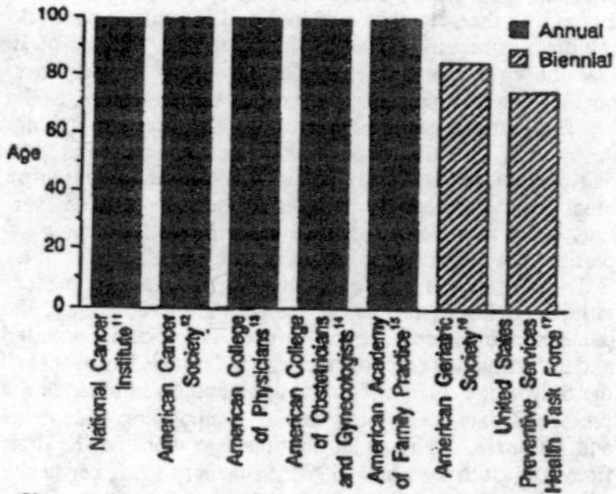

Figure 1. Breast cancer screening guidelines for mammography.

by women aged 65 and over. Various barriers such as lack of physician recommendation; lack of awareness that mammography is necessary in the absence of symptoms; cost; or access have been described in the literature. This noncompliance with published guidelines suggests a lack of understanding on the part of both provider and consumer.

Practicing primary care physicians, family practitioners, internists, geriatricians, and gynecologists are faced every day with difficult decisions in recommending screening to individual elderly women. Critical issues which might influence their decisions are: whether age itself should be a reason for not screening, what intervals are appropriate, what is the impact of a specific comorbid disease on the cost effectiveness of screening, and what is the evidence that screening in older women is effective in decreasing mortality or morbidity from breast cancer.

Such questions prompted the establishment of the Forum

on Breast Cancer Screening in Older Women, sponsored by the University of Massachusetts Medical School through a grant from the National Cancer Institute with additional support from the National Institute on Aging and the Health Care Financing Administration. The Forum was convened to study, in depth, the issues surrounding breast cancer screening in women aged 65 and over through a careful review of ongoing research and existing data. Based on this scientific review, the Forum was charged with the task of developing reasonable screening guidelines for women over 65. Secondary goals included: compilation of background papers to serve as a state-of-the-art review, and development of a research agenda for unanswered questions in breast cancer screening in women aged 65 and over.

The credibility of recommendations is based not only on the science and the reasonableness of the guidelines but also on the credibility of those who issue them. Accordingly, the panel members are listed in the Appendix and the process by which the panel arrived at its conclusions is detailed below.

The first Forum session was held in Sturbridge, Massachusetts, on July 30–August 1, 1990, for the purpose of examining the scientific evidence and formulating a working draft of recommendations for screening. A panel of 10 was chosen to represent expertise in a variety of disciplines: oncology, gerontology, primary care, law, economics, health services, ethics, consumer advocacy, and decision making. A group of scientific experts was commissioned to prepare and present scientific papers summarizing the research on breast cancer screening in older women. In addition, various panel members presented perspectives from their expertise: law, ethics, and provider disciplines.

The first day of the Forum meeting was spent in presentation and discussion of the papers. The second day, the panel met in closed session to discuss the data presented and to formulate screening recommendations. The panel left the Sturbridge meeting with assignments to summarize the presented data and discussion as "supporting statements and rationale." The panel continued to work on the draft from August to December 1990. In January 1991, key health care, consumer, and scientific advisers were invited to a discussion of the draft. The meeting was held at the National Institutes of Health in Bethesda, Maryland. We acknowledge the interest, comments, and concern of the invited guests. Further work on the draft continued until September 1991. This special issue of *The Journals of Gerontology* contains the panel's recommendations and supporting rationale as well as the background papers.

We hope the recommendations and rationale presented here will guide primary health care providers in making sense of the various screening recommendations for women 65 and over. We hope that additional research will be forthcoming and will increase our understanding of the efficacy of breast cancer screening in this older age group.

Organization

This special issue is arranged in the opposite order as the panel worked. That is, originally the panel worked from the background papers to the supporting statements and rationale to the recommendations. For the readers' interest, the recommendations are presented first, followed by the 13 statements and rationale.

The background papers are arranged in sections. The first section deals with the *nature of breast cancer in older women*: its biological nature; whether it is more or less lethal than in younger women; the nature of comorbid diseases among breast cancer patients; and the effect of screening on mortality, incidence, and prevalence.

The second section addresses the *impact of breast cancer in the elderly on the health care system*: To what extent health status and function are related to the use of mammography, the implications of implementing a screening program, and the economic consideration of such a program.

The third section reviews what is known about the use of the three *screening modalities* (mammography, clinical breast exam, and breast self-exam) in older women and an analysis of their efficacy in reducing breast cancer mortality.

The fourth section details the *current knowledge, attitudes, and practices* of primary care providers, older women, and minority older women.

The last section, entitled *Perspectives*, presents a summary of expert reflections about legal and ethical aspects of decision making, and about the realities of provider and consumer concerns.

Finally, the panel and interested observers developed a research agenda for the 1990s. This list grew out of unanswered questions generated by the written reviews of and discussion about existing data. Readers of the background papers will no doubt generate even more areas needing research. Indeed, a motivating force for the Forum was the responsibility of highlighting neglected areas of potential research.

References

1. American Cancer Society. Cancer facts and figures—1990. Atlanta, GA: American Cancer Society, 1990.
2. National Cancer Institute. Division of Cancer Prevention and Control. 1987 annual cancer statistics review. Including cancer trends: 1950–1985. Bethesda, MD: 1988; NIH publication no. 88-2789.
3. Shapiro S, Venet W, Stranx P, Venet L. Periodic screening for breast cancer—the health insurance plan project and its sequelae, 1963-1986. Baltimore, MD: The Johns Hopkins University Press, 1988.
4. Shapiro S, Strax P, Venet L, Rosen R. Ten-to-fourteen year effect of screening on breast cancer mortality. J Natl Cancer Inst 1982;69:349–55.
5. Baker LH. Breast cancer detection demonstration project: five year summary report. Cancer 1982;32(4):194–225.
6. Tabar L, Gad A, Holmquist U, et al. Reduction in mortality from breast cancer after mass screening with mammography. Randomized trial from the Breast Cancer Working Group of the Swedish National Board of Health and Welfare. Lancet 1985;8433:829–32.
7. Centers for Disease Control. Trends in screening mammograms for women 50 years of age or older—Behavioral Risk Factor Surveillance System, 1987. MMWR 1989;38:137–40.
8. Breast Screening Consortium. Screening mammography—a missed clinical opportunity? Results of the NCI Breast Cancer Screening Consortium and National Health Interview Survey Series. JAMA 1990;264:54–8.
9. Brody JA, Brock DB, Williams TF. Trends in the health of the elderly population. Annu Rev Public Health 1987;8:211–34.
10. Lonergan ET, ed. Extending life, enhancing life: A national research agenda on aging. Washington, DC: National Academy Press, 1991.
11. Early Detection Branch. Working guidelines for early detection. Bethesda, MD: National Cancer Institute, 1987.
12. American Cancer Society. Summary of current guidelines for the cancer-related check up: Recommendations. Atlanta, GA: American Cancer Society, 1988.

13. American College of Physicians. Screening for breast cancer. In: Eddy DM, ed. Common screening tests. Philadelphia: American College of Physicians, 1991.
14. American College of Obstetrics and Gynecologists. Committee on Professional Standards. Report of Task Force on Routine Cancer Screening. In: Standards for obstetric/gynecologic services, 7th ed. Washington, DC: American College of Obstetricians and Gynecologists, 1989:97–104.
15. American Academy of Family Physicians. Positions on the clinical aspect of medical practice. Kansas City, MO: American Academy of Family Practice, 1991.
16. American Geriatrics Society. Screening for breast cancer in elderly women. J Am Geriatr Soc 1989;37:883–4.
17. U.S. Preventive Services Health Task Force. Guide to clinical prevention services: an assessment of the effectiveness of 169 interventions. Baltimore: Williams and Wilkins, 1989.
18. Zapka JG, Stoddard AM, Costanza ME, Greene HL. Breast cancer screening by mammography utilization and associated factors. Am J Public Health 1989;79:1499–502.
19. Berg MA, Lane DS, Polednak AP. Age group differences in the use of breast cancer screening tests: the effects of health care utilization and socioeconomic variables. J Aging Health 1990;2:514–30.
20. Rimer BK, Ross E, Cristinzio CS, King E. Older women's participation in breast screening. Presented at the Forum on Breast Cancer Screening in Older Women. July 31, 1990, Sturbridge, MA. J Gerontol 1992;47(Special Issue): 85–91.
21. Fox SA, Murata PJ, Stein JA. The impact of physician compliance on screening mammography for older women. Arch Intern Med 1991;151:50–6.
22. Harris RP, Fletcher SW, Gonzalez JJ, Lannin DR, Degnan D, Earp JA, Clark R. Mammography and age: are we targeting the wrong women? Cancer 1991;67:2010–4.

The Journals of Gerontology
1992; Vol. 47 (Special Issue):5

In the Public Domain

— 2 —

Screening Recommendations of the Forum Panel

Clinical Breast Exam and Mammography Recommendations for Women Aged 65–74 Years

Clinical breast examination should be performed annually and mammography should be performed approximately every two years for women aged 65–74.

Although there is no separate direct evidence in the 65–74-year-old age group, there is direct clinical evidence that screening by annual clinical breast exam and mammography is effective in reducing breast cancer mortality in women age 50 to 74 at the start of screening. Methods of screening that have been proven to be effective are clinical breast exam plus mammography and mammography alone. The schedules of screening for breast cancer that have shown to be effective have varied from approximately yearly to every 33 months.

Clinical Breast Exam and Mammography Recommendations for Women Aged 75 Years and Over

Screening mammography and clinical breast examination should be encouraged at regular intervals of approximately every two years for women age 75 and over whose general health and life expectancy are good.

For a substantial minority of older women, those with decreased life expectancy or quality of life, mammography screening may not be indicated. This decision can be made by the woman herself or in conjunction with her physician and family.

There are no data that indicate mammography is less effective in women aged 75 years and older than it is in women 75 years and younger. The incidence of breast cancer continues to increase after age 75, and then positive predictive value for mammography is improved in older women. However, there is no direct experimental evidence of the effectiveness of screening for breast cancer in women age 75 and over.

Recommendations for Breast Self-Examination (BSE)

It is prudent to recommend that women age 65 and over perform monthly breast self-examination (BSE) to identify clinical lesions and seek professional care.

BSE should be used in conjunction with, but not as a substitute for, a program of clinical breast examination and mammography. Many breast cancers are found by women themselves between scheduled screenings. There is no direct evidence that BSE can reduce mortality from breast cancer. There are, however, several large ongoing trials that will provide mortality-based data related to BSE.

The Journals of Gerontology
1992; Vol. 47 (Special Issue):7–16

In the Public Domain

—3—

Supporting Statements and Rationale

Mary E. Costanza, Chair; George J. Annas, Martin L. Brown, Christine K. Cassel, Victoria Champion, Harvey Jay Cohen, Paul S. Frame, Lou Glasse, Vincent Mor, and Stephen G. Pauker

THE following statements summarize the panel's consensus regarding important topics relevant to the screening guidelines. Each statement is followed by a brief review of the evidence, whether presented to the panel in the Forums of 1990, 1991, or from the panel's own review of the literature. These 13 statements provide the rationale for the panel's screening recommendations.

1. The Incidence of Breast Cancer Rises With Age

The incidence rate of breast cancer according to age in U.S. women is shown in Table 1. The incidence rate rises with age through the eighth decade, although the rate at which the incidence increases varies somewhat with age. It is important for physicians and women to realize the extent of the rising risk of disease in older women. Women 65 years of age and older represent 14% of the female population but account for 43% of invasive breast cancer.

In addition to the rise with age, the incidence rate of breast cancer has risen strikingly with time (1,2). Although the data are not entirely consistent, it seems likely that the increase has been concentrated in women over 45 years of age, and has been particularly strong in women over 60 years of age (3). Possible reasons for the increase include changes in the distribution of the causes of breast cancer, increasing frequency of screening and of diagnostic mammography, and changes in pathologic diagnostic practice (3–6). The relative contributions of those influences to the increasing rate are uncertain.

2. The Biology of Breast Cancer in Older Women Is Probably No Different From That in Younger Women

The biologic behavior of breast cancer in older women is characterized by a number of complexities creating a seemingly paradoxical situation. On the one hand, relative survival for older women with breast cancer, especially those over age 75 (7,8), is lower than that for younger women. It is not clear if this is a function of the tumor per se, or of other intrinsic host factors, such as immune surveillance, which may decline with age (9). This would be consistent with what appears to be an increasing tendency for older women to present with more extensive disease, although this has not been uniformly observed (7,10–12).

Table 1. Age and Incidence of Breast Cancer

Age (year)	Cases/100,000 Person-Years
25–29	7.4
30–34	26.7
35–39	66.2
40–44	129.4
45–49	159.4
50–54	220.0
55–59	261.6
60–64	330.7
65–69	390.7
70–74	421.8
75–79	461.4
80–84	451.3
85+	411.9

Source. Data from the Surveillance, Epidemiology and End Results (SEER) Program (1984–1988) (1).

Note. The numerical value of the rate expressed as cases per person-year is approximately equal to the one-year probability of having a new diagnosis of breast cancer.

Although breast cancer experimental tumor models have not been studied directly, such models of other tissue types have revealed that there may be variable age relationships, with some tumors behaving less aggressively and others more so in the older host (9). To some extent this may depend on the antigenicity of the tumor, the type of immune response needed to control it, and how that aspect of the immune system is affected by age. On the other hand, breast cancer in older women has some features that would suggest that it ought to have a better prognosis. Thus, there tends to be a much higher rate of estrogen and progesterone receptor positive tumors, which usually correlates with better tumor response to hormonal therapy (13,14). There is a lower proliferative rate (by thymidine labeling index), a tendency toward more diploidy (by flow cytometry), and a tendency toward more well-differentiated histologic tumor grade (which also correlates with estrogen receptor positivity), which suggests that older women would have slower growing, more indolent tumors (10,15). Yet, while in some cases there is increased hormonal response and even increases in disease-free intervals, relative survival is not improved (see Table 2) (8,11). The 20-year relative survival data of Adami et al. (7) show poorer relative survival for older women.

In spite of the fact that the prognostic features of breast cancer are generally better (which supports the prevalent notion that the disease is more indolent in older women and screening may be unnecessary), survival from breast cancer is, in fact, poorer in older women. Therefore, from a biologic perspective, the notion that screening is needed less in older women is erroneous.

3. Breast Cancer Detection by Mammography Is Enhanced in Older Women

Mammography detects breast cancers as shadows denser than normal fibroglandular breast tissue, and/or as calcific particles. Some cancers, however, have radiologic attenuation properties that are similar to normal breast tissues. Since these shadows cannot be seen, the mammographic exam is falsely negative. Approximately 10% of cancers may be palpable but not detectable by mammography (16,17). This is the reason why clinical breast exam should be performed.

In older women, the breast changes from predominantly fibroglandular to fatty tissue (18,19). Fat has a much lower radiologic attenuation. Therefore the contrast between fat and tumor is usually much clearer, and smaller tumors can, in fact, be detected (19). Note that older women on estrogen replacement therapy have breasts that are dense and radiologically more like premenopausal, younger women.

The positive predictive value for mammography and physical exam is higher in older as compared to younger women (Table 3). As reported in several studies (19–22), the biopsy to cancer ratio is lower in older women. This is both due to the increased incidence of breast cancer and to the fact that there are less noncancerous causes of abnormal mammograms and breast lumps in older women (19) (Table 4). Mammography and clinical breast exam should be at least as effective or may well be more effective in finding breast cancer in older women.

4. Life Expectancy in Older Women Is Longer Than We Thought

Female babies born in 1991 in the United States have an average life expectancy of 78.5 years (23). This number is increasing, and there is no sign that increase will stop at least before average life expectancy reaches the age of 85 (24,25). Regardless of the upper limit of average life expectancy, a specific statistical concept, there is no doubt that mortality rates among the elderly continue to decline and that women can expect to live longer. Thus a women who reaches age 65 will live, on the average, to age 83 (Table 5).

These average life expectancies represent great variance, so in each group approximately a third can expect to live substantially longer than the average life expectancy for that age. At a present age of 80, substantial numbers of women will live in relatively good health to be 100 or even 100+ years old. A recent publication by the Census Bureau shows the dramatic increase in centenarians in the United States. Of the currently 15,000 people over the age of 100, only 40% were seriously disabled and dependent (26). Thus, measures which can prevent premature death, such as screening for breast cancer, could be justified well into old age. There is some consensus that if life expectancy is less than five years, there is little to be gained with screening mammography. However, clinical breast exam may continue to contribute to decreased morbidity.

The complication, of course, arises in that as people are living longer, they become more susceptible to chronic disease. Many people live in a quite functional state with numerous chronic diseases such as diabetes, hypertension, and arthritis, while others often are completely disabled from neurological disorders such as Alzheimer's disease or stroke (27). Thus, any policy question about the recommendation of breast cancer screening has to include some acknowledgment of the heterogeneity of this population, of the competing causes of death, the concurrent causes of disability, and the increasing numbers of women who, if they survive breast cancer, could live for many years or even decades after their 80th birthday.

Table 2. 5-Year Relative Survival and Extent of Disease

Age	Localized $n=43{,}032$	Regional $n=37{,}849$
45–54	90%	68%
55–64	90%	67%
65–74	91%	69%
75–84	90%	66%
85+	83%	60%

Source. SEER data from Yancik et al., 1989 (8).

Table 3. Age-Specific Predictive Value of Biopsies To Detect Cancer

Age at Entry	No. of Cancers Detected	No. of Biopsies Performed	Cancer Detected Per 100 Biopsies Performed
35–39	123	2,141	5.7
40–44	345	3,635	9.5
45–49	619	4,634	13.4
50–54	708	4,400	16.1
55–59	655	3,170	20.7
60–64	490	2,152	22.8
65–69	330	1,390	23.7
70–74	175	643	27.2
75–79	14	27	51.9

Source. From Baker et al., 1985 (20).

5. Accurate Prediction of Survival on the Basis of Competing Causes of Mortality Is Difficult

Given the prevalence of multiple chronic diseases among women in this age group and their influence on mortality,

Table 4. Mammography Results by Age

	<40	40–49	50–59	60–69	≥70
No. Mammograms	7,939	12,000	7,847	6,264	3,478
No. Abnormal	399	707	442	345	186
Biopsies/Abnormals (%)	24%	29%	36%	39%	44%
Cancers/Abnormals (%)	4%	7%	13%	17%	22%
Cancers/Biopsies (%)	17%	23%	36%	44%	51%
Nonpalpable CA (%)	2%	5%	9%	11%	17%
Stage 0-1 CA (%)	3%	6%	9%	13%	18%

Source. From Sickles, 1990 (22).

Table 5. Age and Life Expectancy

Present Age In Years	Average Age of Life Expectancy
65	18
75	12
85	7

Source. From Brody and Cassel, 1990 (25).

it would be useful for the clinician to have predictors that would help decide if a woman will live long enough to benefit from screening (28–30). A number of studies focusing on predictors of survival in the absence of specific diagnostic data have been conducted (31–34). In a study of selected health characteristics obtained from the Longitudinal Study of Aging, regression analysis predicting mortality based upon age, self-reported health, and function confirms the importance of all three variables in predicting mortality (35). The model did not include data on whether patients had a potentially critical medical illness because of the reliance on self-reported data. Nor did it consider whether patients had been hospitalized in the last year because this can be seen as a process indicator of care style and not merely a risk of death.

Table 6 reports the four-year mortality rates by self-reported health, function, and age. Each variable reveals similarly strong linear trends in the expected direction.

Unfortunately, the precision of this model is quite limited. To correctly predict 56% of the deaths, one must choose a cut point that incorrectly predicts nearly 25% of those who actually live. Consequently, it is unlikely that a precise, predictive tool to decide which older, or which frail woman will survive long enough to benefit from screening mammography will be developed in the near future. Nonetheless, these general factors (age, health, and function) should be considered by the physician making a decision to recommend mammography.

In the presence of good diagnostic data, the clinician should be able to make his/her own assessment as to the probability that an older woman will live long enough to benefit from screening mammography. That is, she will live at least five years before dying from a non-breast cancer cause. Where diagnostic data are indeterminate, the decision is less clear-cut. In these cases, after a thorough discussion with the patient and/or her family, a mutual decision can be made. It is important to emphasize that women who present with clinical findings, who detect a lump, or have other symptoms should receive diagnostic work-ups and treatment.

6. Quality of Life Issues Greatly Affect the Appropriateness of Breast Cancer Screening

Quality of life has at least two important and quite different dimensions when considered in the context of breast cancer screening. First, quality of life needs to be considered in calculations about the cost effectiveness of cancer screening programs. Second, poor quality of life may be a reason to forgo screening tests.

In general, cost effectiveness analysis for screening programs and, indeed, most of the research done on the efficacy of cancer screening programs use mortality as an end point. A screening program is considered effective if a substantial number of lives can be saved and if the reduction in death can be demonstrated to be a reduction in breast cancer deaths. As women get older, however, there are many competing causes of death. If a breast cancer death is prevented in an older woman, she remains at high risk to die of another disease and, thus, death will not have been averted altogether.

But because life is possibly not lengthened, does not mean that early detection of breast cancer is without value. Metastatic breast cancer is a very disabling and painful disease. Thus, it is possible that in the elderly, breast cancer screening could result in a substantial improvement in quality of life (36) without necessarily demonstrating a reduction in overall deaths. In order to detect this, research protocols would have to include measures of quality of life over the period of time of screening to demonstrate that breast cancer found at an earlier stage and effectively treated results in high quality of life in the last years of life.

The second major meaning of quality of life in screening for breast cancer relates to the use of quality of life as a criterion for forgoing many aspects of life-sustaining treatment or medical technology. There is extensive discussion in the literature of medical decision making and medical ethics about the measures of quality of life, and the use of such measures and evaluation in deciding to forgo various kinds of aggressive treatment (37,38). In general, it has been accepted that the patient should decide when the quality of life is so poor that life-sustaining measures are no longer indicated (39). In recent years, however, some major court decisions have outlined more objective criteria—for example, far-advanced dementia—in which decisions to forgo aggressive life-sustaining treatment, especially when sup-

Table 6. Four-Year Mortality Rates Among Older Women by Age, the Presence of a Medical Condition, and Selected Health and Function Factors

	70–74		75–84		85+	
	No Medical Condition	Has Medical Condition	No Medical Condition	Has Medical Condition	No Medical Condition	Has Medical Condition
Self-rated health						
Excellent, Very Good	1.1%	5.7%	11.5%	15.8%	22.2%	31.4%
Good	8.7	10.0	14.1	19.1	33.3	42.3
Fair, Poor	6.3	20.9	22.2	34.7	46.4	56.9
Activity limits						
Unable in major	—	45.2	44.4	52.5	60.9	69.8
Limited in kind/amount	5.5	14.6	20.5	30.9	42.0	38.4
Not limited	4.9	9.1	10.1	14.9	17.2	30.0
Function						
Able stamina w/o difficulty	3.2	6.9	9.2	12.6	12.5	28.1
Has difficulty in stamina	5.6	13.7	19.2	21.0	27.3	37.6
Has difficulty & unable in 1+ IADLS	8.7	31.9	25.0	43.6	52.5	57.1

Source. NHIS Longitudinal Study of Aging '84–'88 (35).

ported by family members, have been found acceptable. Clearly in the case of any kind of cancer screening, one would depend on the physician's clinical judgment in working with the patient and the family to limit unnecessary medical testing. Quality of life issues are critically relevant to good clinical judgment and to ethical decision making in this area. Special guidelines cannot be constructed for all situations.

7. A Review of Data on the Efficacy of the Screening Modalities and the Appropriate Intervals in Older Women Leaves Many Unanswered Questions

The panel reviewed nine screening studies: four intervention (experimental) studies with random assignment [HIP (40), Swedish Two County (41), Malmo (42), Edinburgh (43)], one intervention study with nonrandomized assignment (UK) (44), three case control studies [Nijmegen (45), Utrecht (46), Palli (47)], and one follow-up study (Morrison) (48). Only studies in which breast cancer mortality was compared between screened and nonscreened women, irrespective of whether or not they had a breast cancer diagnosis, were considered (49). The extent of case finding (breast cancer) is not by itself a useful measure of the value of screening since it does not necessarily result in improved health of screenees. Use of other outcomes (case fatalities or stage distribution) leads to serious difficulties in interpretation (50). Each of the nine studies reviewed showed the beneficial effects of screening among women who were at least 40, 50, or 55 years of age at entry. There is very little information available on the value of screening women more than 74 years of age (see Tables 7 and 8).

Types of screening.— We do not have direct data on whether mammography alone or in combination with clinical breast exam (CBE) is more effective in older women. The types of screening that have been shown to be effective are mammography and physical examination combined, and mammography alone. The HIP (40) study used two screening tests—mammography and professional physical examination—and there is no direct means to separate their effects on breast cancer mortality in that study. In recent studies, mammography has received more attention than has physical examination.

The effect of screening by physical examination alone has not been studied in older women. An ongoing Canadian study (51) of the efficacy of clinical breast exam versus clinical breast exam plus mammography may help clarify this issue. However, the study did not enroll women over the age of 59. There is no direct evidence that self-examination reduces mortality from breast cancer.

Intervals for screening.— The schedules of screening that have been shown to be effective have varied from approximately yearly to approximately every 33 months. In the HIP study (40), women were screened annually for a maximum of four examinations. There has been no intervention study of screening done more frequently than yearly. In the studies that followed the HIP (41-48), screening was done at intervals ranging from one year to nearly three years, but there are no randomized studies looking at the effectiveness of different screening intervals. Retrospective data from Sweden (52) suggest that an annual interval may be more important in women 40–49 than in women 50 and over.

Conclusions.— The reduction in breast cancer mortality achieved by screening has not varied systematically and substantially in relation to these screening modalities or schedules. The data are not helpful in deciding whether to screen by mammography and palpation combined or by mammography alone, nor in choosing a screening interval within the range of 12–33 months (49). These comments regarding interval do not pertain to those individual patients whose breasts are very dense or who have other physiologic

Table 7. Experimental Studies

Randomized = Mortality	Screened Women	Age at Entry	Screen M/CBE	Interval MO/MO	Frequency	Decrease in Outcome
HIP (40)	62,000	40–64	M²/CBE	12/12	4	at 14 yr
						23%
		SS: 60–64	M²/CBE	12/12		21%
1 County Swedish (41)	163,000	40–74	M¹/-	24-33/-	4	at 7 yr
						31%
		SS: 50–69	M¹/-	33/-		39%
		70–74	M¹/-	33/-		Trend
		75+	M¹/-	33/-		Poor Compliance
Malmo (42)	42,000	45–69	M²⁻¹/-	18-24/-	5	No Data
						at 9 yr
						4%
		SS: 55–69	M²⁻¹/-	18-24/-	5	20%
Edinburgh (43)	45,000	45–64	M²/CBE	24/12-24	4	at 7 yr
						17%
		SS: 50–64	M²/CBE	24/12-24	4	20%
Nonrandomized						
UK (44)	237,000	45–64	M¹⁻²/CBE	24/12	7	at 7 yr
						20%

Notes. M = mammogram; M¹ = mammogram with 1 view; M² = mammogram with 2 views; CBE = clinical breast exam; SS = subset; — = not done.

conditions and for whom an individual radiologist recommends a specific and more frequent screening interval. These comments regarding interval also do not pertain to older women who have additional risk factors for the development of breast cancer (e.g., a strong family history).

8. The Cost Effectiveness of Breast Cancer Screening Is Affected by Age in a Complex Way

Figure 1 shows the cost effectiveness of breast cancer screening for different age groups and for various prices of screening services. To provide a frame of reference, health economist Milton Weinstein has recently stated that most "generally accepted" preventive interventions have cost-effectiveness ratios below $50,000 per life year saved (53). The screening program evaluated is a long-term program of biennial screening mammography and annual clinical breast examinations. For purposes of the cost-effectiveness calculations, all costs and savings due to screening as well as life-years saved are discounted at a rate of 5%. Treatment costs (and savings) used in the computations were based on Medicare charges, which may not include all patient expenditures. Indirect costs, such as earnings lost due to workplace disability, are not included in cost-effectiveness analysis (54).

The cost effectiveness is more sensitive to the price of the screening examination than to the age group screened. The differences in cost effectiveness between age groups are not large compared to the differences in cost effectiveness caused by differences in prices currently charged for breast cancer screening services. Thus, for the 65–70-year-old group, when the price of the screening examination is $115 rather than $55, the cost per life-year saved increases by about 60%. Furthermore, at any given price, cost effectiveness becomes increasingly less favorable with advanced age for women over 70 years of age. For example, the cost per life-year saved for the 80–85-year-old group is about 50% greater than for the 65–70-year-old group.

Cost effectiveness is also dependent on interval. To the best of our knowledge, the mortality reduction resulting from doing annual instead of biennial mammography (plus annual clinical breast examination) in women 65 and older is very small (55). Balanced against this is our certain knowledge that the economic cost of doing annual instead of biennial screening is very high (about twice as much).

If breast cancer screening efforts for the older age group were more intensively targeted toward the subgroup of older women with better health status and more favorable life expectancy prospects, as our recommendations suggest, the differential in cost effectiveness by age group would be less than shown in Figure 1.

9. Low-Cost Screening Is Feasible

Currently the average cost of an examination which includes mammography and a clinical breast examination for an asymptomatic woman is about $120. The price for these services varies widely, from as low as $30 to as high as a few hundred dollars (56). The long-term experience of a number of operating facilities and a cost analysis by the Physician Pricing Review Commission demonstrates that it is feasible for a well-organized facility to offer high-quality screening mammography at a price of $50 (57). Beginning January 1, 1991, Medicare reimbursed biennial screening mammography at a rate of $55. A recent survey of mammography facilities by the General Accounting Office, however, indicated that only 7% of the surveyed facilities were charging $50 or less for a screening mammography examination (56). Organizational features that are required to achieve low-cost operation include: adequate capacity, utilization of resources so that at least 20 mammographic examinations are performed per day, batch processing and

Table 8. Nonexperimental Studies

Randomized — Mortality	Screened Women	Age at Entry	Screen M/CBE	Interval MO/MO	Frequency	Decrease In Outcome
Nijmegen (45)	30,000	35–70	M^1/-	24/-	4	at 8 yr 50%
		SS: 55–69	M^1/-	24/-	4	52%
		>70	M^1/-	24/-	4	Poor Compliance No Data
Utrecht (46)	15,000	50–64	M/CBE	12-18-24/ 12-18-24	4	at 7 yr 30%
Palli (47)	15,000	40–70	M^2-/-	30/-	4	at 7 yr 47%
BCDDP (48)	283,000	35–74	M^2/CBE	12/12	5	at 9 yr 20%
		SS: 50–59	M^2/CBE	12/12	5	24%
		60–74	M^2/CBE	12/12	5	26%

Notes. M = mammogram; M_1 = mammogram with 1 view; M^2 = mammogram with 2 views; CBE = clinical breast exam; SS = subset; — = not done.

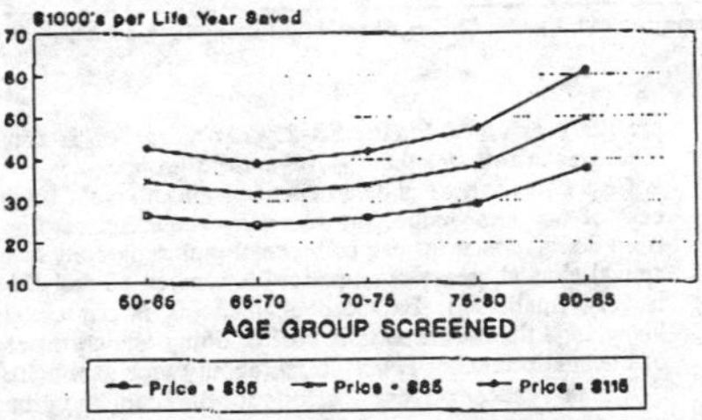

Figure 1. Cost effectiveness of breast cancer screening by age and price: Biennial screening; costs and life years discounted at 5%; price of alternating year clinical breast exams = $20. *Source*: Brown, 1991 (54), used with permission.

Table 9. Percent of Women Ever Having a Mammogram by Age

Age	% Ever
50–64	35%
65–74	29
75–84	22
85+	13

Source. Pacala and Rakowski, 1990 (61).

interpretation of films, and an interpretation fee of no more than $12 per examination. A well designed, personal computer-assisted recordkeeping and billing system may also be useful in minimizing costs (58,59).

10. The Current Extent of Breast Cancer Screening in Older Women Is Surprisingly Low

Patient and provider compliance with breast cancer screening, especially the use of mammography, is far from optimal. According to the NCI Breast Cancer Screening

Table 10. Percent of Physicians Ordering Mammography by Patient Age

Patient Age	Physicians
50–54	74%
55–59	65
60–64	60
65–69	62
70–74	48

Source. Rimer et al., 1990 (63).

Consortium, 46–74% of women between 50 and 64 years had a clinical breast examination in the previous year, and only 25–41% had a mammogram (60). Women age 65 and over are less likely ever to have had a mammogram (31) (Table 9).

Women without a usual source of care—rural, inner city, less educated, poor and minority women—are likely never to have had a mammogram. Mammography screening rates are significantly lower among Black and Hispanic women, with annual screening rates less than 10% in these minority groups aged 75 years and over (61,62).

11. Major Barriers Prevent Older Women From Mammography Screening

The two most prevalent reasons women cited for never having a mammogram are: they did not know they need one and their doctor did not recommend it (60).

Physicians do not recommend and refer older women for mammography as often as they do younger women, even though older women are at much greater risk of breast cancer (63) (Table 10). A recent survey of Massachusetts primary care physicians reported that many clinicians consciously set upper age limits and stopped ordering mammography on the basis of age alone (64).

Another barrier which may prevent women from getting regular mammograms is the discomfort and impersonal nature of the procedure. In a Canadian study, 94% of women who had undergone breast cancer screening were willing to have repeat clinical breast examination, but only 69% were willing to have repeat mammography. One-third of the women said the mammogram was moderately uncomfortable (51).

In order to improve screening rates in older women, *older women must be advised of the importance of screening.* Physicians need to recommend breast cancer screening and to explain its importance clearly.

To assure that women carry out their recommendations, physicians should be certain that their patients understand the importance of screening, and the procedures to be used (63).

A campaign of public education and outreach is essential for poor or minority women who have no personal physician or do not belong to an HMO (63). Poor and minority women may depend especially on health care in emergency rooms of local hospitals.

Special efforts must be made to overcome any language barriers. Information should be easily understood, written in large type and in the languages of the targeted populations. It should be disseminated at locations that the targeted populations are likely to frequent (65).

Women and physicians need to be educated about ways to identify qualified (certified) facilities, qualified radiologists, and how to follow up on results. Though not optimal, self-referral may be necessary, if the rate of physician referral remains low.

Mammography must be accessible. — Utilization is closely tied to easy access to screening. The lack of safe and affordable transportation is often a barrier in both rural areas and inner cities. Because older women are more likely to suffer from chronic, disabling diseases (66), or to live in unsafe areas of large cities, location of the screening may be critical.

Well publicized, mobile vans with good quality control have proven to successfully overcome this problem. Community-based screening or screening centralized in locations accessible to public transportation may be effective in reaching more older women.

Mammography must be affordable. — The cost of mammography is a formidable barrier for many older women (67). Three out of four of the elderly who are below the federal poverty level are women (68). When out-of-pocket medical expenses are considered, the poverty rate among elderly Americans grows from 12 to 17% (69). In 1990, out-of-pocket costs of essential medical care for older people averaged $1,237 annually (70).

Medicare coverage for screening mammography, which began January 1, 1991, will help to overcome the financial barriers to mammography. However, the $55 biennial cap will still leave many women unable to afford the difference between costs and Medicare coverage.

12. Factors Affecting Provider Compliance Need To Be Addressed

Physician recommendation is a key factor influencing older women's compliance with mammography screening (60). Physician-reported reasons for not recommending mammography include: the low yield of screening, concern about reliability of radiology reports, concerns that patients will not comply, lack of time, and forgetfulness (71–75). Patients at high risk because of a family history of breast cancer are more likely to be referred for mammography. However, the presence of other risk factors for breast cancer, such as increasing age, does not increase physicians' rates of mammography referral (76–78).

Cost is a frequently mentioned barrier to mammography which, ironically, is more often mentioned by physicians than patients (79–81).

Intensive efforts will be needed to improve provider compliance with breast cancer screening recommendations. Primary care physicians must be educated about the importance of continuing to perform regular clinical breast examinations on all older women. They also need to understand the benefits of regular mammography for older women whose life expectancy exceeds five years. The importance of physician recommendation and advocacy in influencing mammography compliance must be stressed. Programs that address primary care physicians' concerns as well as knowledge issues will be helpful in decreasing present barriers.

13. The Efficacy of Breast Self-Examination (BSE) in Older Women Is Uncertain

The major problem in reaching a consensus for BSE is the lack of well-designed research. In the past 10 years several studies addressing the relationship of BSE and morbidity/mortality among breast cancer patients have been published. Many (82–87) of these studies have found that, compared with nonexaminers, people who complete BSE have smaller primary tumors and less axillary node involvement. These studies may be subject to biases which cannot be adequately evaluated or controlled (88,89). The one prospective study that evaluated BSE found no mortality benefit (90). A current study (91) found no mortality benefit for BSE examiners when comparing late-stage breast cancer and case controls. They did, however, find a 35% decrease in advanced stage breast cancer when proficiency was considered, concluding that BSE might be effective if practiced correctly. Thus, there is no randomized prospective mortality-based evidence that BSE increases survival.

Information from a large ongoing population-based study sponsored by the World Health Organization (92,93), however, indicates a significantly higher number of breast cancers detected in the BSE arm as compared to the control arm. Size of tumors discovered in the BSE arm is also significantly smaller. In addition, women who have been trained in BSE are more likely to consult physicians for possible concerns related to breast cancer. Mortality data from this study are not yet available. Finally, a large prospective randomized trial for BSE is ongoing in China, but published results are not yet available.

While the scientific arguments for BSE are not compelling, the practical arguments are powerful. BSE is a simple, low cost, noninvasive procedure acceptable to older women which complements increased utilization of mammography and clinical breast examination in increasing the likelihood of early detection of breast cancer. Thus, BSE may function as an enabler, permitting women to take a more active role in their health care. The majority of tumors are still dis-

77-929 O - 94 - 2

covered by women themselves, a fact that is likely to continue in the future given the low compliance rate with mammography. In addition, the impact of not including BSE as a recommendation could be dramatic. Not including BSE as a recommendation for women 65 and over might send a powerful message to health professionals that BSE is no longer to be taught or encouraged. This message would be particularly unfortunate at a time when the reality exists that mammography may not be available to many women. To date there have been no studies to indicate that BSE results in later detection of breast cancer or has adverse psychological effects.

References

1. National Cancer Institute Statistics Review 1975-1988. Bethesda, MD: NIH publication no. 91-2789, 1991, Table II-40.
2. Miller BA, Feuer EJ, Henkey BF: The increasing incidence of breast cancer since 1982; relevance of early detection. Cancer Causes Control 1991;2:67–74.
3. Glass AG, Hoover RN. Changing incidence of breast cancer. J Natl Cancer Inst 1988;80:1076–7.
4. Glass AG, Hoover RN. Rising incidence of breast cancer: relationship to stage and receptor status. J Natl Cancer Inst 1990;82:693–6.
5. White E, Daling JR, Norstead TL, et al. Rising incidence of breast cancer among young women in Washington State. J Natl Cancer Inst 1987;79:239–43.
6. White EW, Lee CY, Kristal AR. Evaluation of the increase in breast cancer incidence in relation to mammography use. J Natl Cancer Inst 1990;82:1546–52.
7. Adami HO, Malker B, Holmberg L, et al. The relationship between survival and age at diagnosis in breast cancer. N Engl J Med 1986;314:559–63.
8. Yancik R, Reis LG, Yates JW. Breast cancer in aging women: a population-based study of contrasts in stage, surgery, and survival. Cancer 1989;163:976–81.
9. Kaesberg PR, Ershler WB. The change in tumor aggressiveness with age: lessons from experimental animals. Semin Oncol 1989;16:28–33.
10. Host H, Lund E. Age as a prognostic factor in breast cancer. Cancer 1986;57:2217–21.
11. Rose PP, Lesser ML, Kinne DW. Breast carcinoma at the extremes of age: a comparison of patients younger than 35 years and older than 75 years. J Surg Oncol 1985;28:90–6.
12. Satariano WA, Bello SH, Swanson GM. The severity of breast cancer at diagnosis: a comparison of age and extent of disease in black and white women. Am J Public Health 1986;76:779–82.
13. Clark G. The biology of breast cancer in older women. Presented at the Forum on Breast Cancer Screening in Older Women. Sturbridge, MA, August 1, 1990. J Gerontol 1992;47(Special Issue), 19–23.
14. Clark GM, Osborne CK, McGuire WL. Correlations between estrogen receptor, progesterone receptor, and patient characteristics in human breast cancer. J Clin Oncol 1984;2:1102–9.
15. Owens MA, Beardslee S, Wenger CR, et al. DNA ploidy and S-phase fraction by flow cytometry in a large breast cancer data base. Proc AACR 1990;31:184.
16. Kopans DB, Meyer JE, Sadowsky N. Breast imaging. N Engl J Med 1984;310:960–7.
17. Kopans DB. Screening mammography in women over age 65. Presented at the Forum on Breast Cancer Screening in Older Women, Sturbridge, MA, August 1, 1990. J Gerontol 1992;47(Special Issue): 59–62.
18. Tabar L, Dean PB. Mammographic parenchymal patterns: risk indicator for breast cancer? JAMA 1982;247:185–9.
19. Carlisle T, Kopecjky KJ, Hadaway EN. Breast cancer screening in the elderly. In Yancik R, et al., eds. Perspectives on prevention and treatment of cancer in the elderly. New York: Raven Press, 1983.
20. Baker LH, Chin TDY, Wagner KV. Progress in screening for early breast cancer. J Surg Oncol 1985;30:96–102.
21. Bender HG, Schnurch HG, Beck L. Breast cancer detection: Age related significance of findings on physical exam and mammography. Gynecol Oncol 1988;31:166–72.
22. Sickles E: Personal communication, 1990.
23. Cassel CK, Neugarten BL. A forecast of women's health and longevity: implications for an aging America. Western J Med 1988;149:712–17.
24. Olshansky SJ, Carnes B, Cassel CK. In search of Methuselah: Estimating the upper limits to longevity. Science 1990;250:634–40.
25. Brody J, Cassel CK. Normal human aging theory, demography and epidemiology. In Cassel CK et al., eds. Geriatric medicine: principles and practice (2nd ed.). New York: Springer-Verlag, 1990.
26. U.S. Bureau of the Census, Office of the Actuary. The centenarians. Washington, DC: U.S. Government Printing Office, 1988.
27. Verbrugge LM. Longer life but worsening health? Trends in health and mortality in middle aged and older persons. Milbank Q 1984;62:475–517.
28. Manton KG, Stallard E. Demographics (1950-1987) of breast cancer in birth cohorts of older women. Presented at the Forum on Breast Cancer Screening in Older Women, Sturbridge, MA, August 1, 1990. J Gerontol 1992;47(Special Issue): 32–42.
29. Mor V, Murphy J, Masterson-Allen S, et al. Risk of functional decline among well elders. J Clin Epidemiol 1989;42:895–904.
30. Satariano WA. Comorbidity and functional status in older women with breast cancer: implications for screening, treatment, and prognosis. Presented at the Forum on Breast Cancer Screening in Older Women, Sturbridge, MA, August 1, 1990. J Gerontol 1992;47(Special Issue):24–31.
31. Mor V, Pacala JT, Rakowski W. Mammography for older women: who uses, who benefits? Presented at the Forum on Breast Cancer Screening in Older Women, Sturbridge, MA, August 1, 1990. J Gerontol 1992;47(Special Issue): 43–49.
32. Kaplan GA, Seeman TE, Cohen RD, Knudsen LP, Guselnik S. Mortality among the elderly in the Alameda County study: behavioral and demographic risk factors. Am J Public Health 1987;77:307–12.
33. Grand A, Grunschaude P, Bogquest J, Pous J, Albarede JL. Disability, psychosocial factors and mortality among the elderly in a rural French sample. J Clin Epidemiol 1990;43:773–82.
34. Idler EL, Kasl SV, Lemke JH. Self-evaluated health and mortality among the elderly in New Haven, CT and Iowa and Washington Counties, Iowa 1982-1986. Am J Epidemiol 1990;131:91–103.
35. Office of Vital and Health Statistics Systems. The Longitudinal Study of Aging public use file: version 3. Hyattsville, MD: National Center for Health Statistics, October, 1990.
36. Cassel CK. Breast cancer screening in older women: ethical issues. Presented at the Forum on Breast Cancer Screening in Older Women, Sturbridge, MA, August 1, 1990. J Gerontol 1992;47(Special Issue): 126–130.
37. Annas GJ. Breast cancer screening in older women: law and patient rights. Presented at the Forum on Breast Cancer Screening in Older Women, Sturbridge, MA, August 1, 1990. J Gerontol 1992;47(Special Issue):121–125.
38. Zweibel NR, Cassel CK. Treatment choices at the end of life: a comparison of decisions by older patients and their physician-selected proxies. Gerontologist 1989;29:615–21.
39. U.S. Congress, Office of Technology Assessment. Life sustaining technologies and the elderly (OTA-BA-306). Washington, DC: U.S. Government Printing Office, July 1987:91–140.
40. Shapiro S, Strax P, Venet L, Rosen R. Ten-to-fourteen year effect of screening on breast cancer mortality. J Natl Cancer Inst 1982;69:349–55.
41. Tabar L, Gad A, Holmquist U, et al. Reduction in mortality from breast cancer after mass screening with mammography. Randomized trial from the Breast Cancer Working Group of the Swedish National Board of Health and Welfare. Lancet 1985;8433:829–32.
42. Andersson I, Aspergren K, Janzon L, et al. Mammographic screening and mortality from breast cancer: the Malmo screening trial. Br Med J 1988;297:943–8.
43. Roberts MM, Alexander FE, Anderson TJ, et al. Edinburgh trial of screening for breast cancer: mortality at seven years. Lancet 1990;335:242–6.
44. UK Trial of Early Detection Group. First results on mortality reduction in the UK trial of early detection of breast cancer. Lancet 1988;ii:411–6.
45. Verbeek ALM, Hendriks JHCL, Holland R, et al. Reduction of breast cancer mortality through mass screening with modern mammography: first results of the Nijmegen project, 1975-81. Lancet 1984;i:1222–4.

46. Collette HJA, Day NE, Rombach JJ, deWaard F. Evaluation of screening for breast cancer in a non-randomized study (the DOM project) by means of a case control study. Lancet 1984;1:1224–6.
47. Palli D, Rosselli del Turco M, Buiatti E, et al. A case control study of the efficacy of a non-randomized breast cancer screening program in Florence (Italy). Int J Cancer 1986;38:501–4.
48. Morrison AS, Brisson J, Khalid N. Breast cancer incidence and mortality in the Breast Cancer Demonstration Detection Project. J Natl Cancer Inst 1988;80:1540–7.
49. Morrison AS. Efficacy of screening for breast cancer in older women. Presented at the Forum on Breast Cancer Screening in Older Women, Sturbridge, MA, August 1, 1990. J Gerontol 1992;47(Special Issue):80–84.
50. Morrison AS. Review of evidence in the early detection and treatment of breast cancer. Cancer 1989;12(Suppl):2651–6.
51. Baines CJ, Miller AB, Bassett AA. Physical examination: its role as a single screening modality in the Canadian National Breast Screening Study. Cancer 1989;63:1816–22.
52. Tabar L, Faberberg G, Day NE, Homberg L. What is the optimum interval between mammographic screening examinations? An analysis based on the latest results of the Swedish two-county breast cancer screening trial. Br J Cancer 1987;55:547–51.
53. Weinstein MC. The cost-effectiveness of orphan drugs. Am J Public Health 1991;81:414–5.
54. Brown ML. Economic considerations in breast cancer screening of older women. Presented at the Forum on Breast Cancer Screening in Older Women, Bethesda, MD, January, 1991. J Gerontol 1992;47(Special Issue):51–58.
55. Office of Technology Assessment. Breast cancer screening for Medicare beneficiaries: effectiveness, cost of Medicare and medical resources required. Washington, DC: U.S. Government Printing Office, 1987.
56. General Accounting Office. Screening mammography: low-cost services do not compromise quality. Washington, DC: General Accounting Office, 1990.
57. Physician Payment Review Commission. The cost of providing screening mammography. Report to Congress. Washington, DC: 1989.
58. Bird RE. Low cost screening mammography: report on finances and review of 21,716 consecutive cases. Radiology 1989;171:87–90.
59. Sickles EA, Weber WN, Galvin HB, et al. Mammographic screening: how to operate successfully at low cost. Radiology 1986;160:95–7.
60. Breast Screening Consortium. Screening mammography—a missed clinical opportunity? Results of the NCI Breast Cancer Screening Consortium and National Health Interview Survey Series. JAMA 1990;264:54–8.
61. Pacala JT, Rakowski W. Age group differences in correlates of screening mammography. Paper presented at the Annual Meeting of The Gerontological Society of America, November 1990, Boston, MA.
62. Dawson DA, Thompson GB. Breast cancer risk factors and screening: United States, 1987. Vital Health Stat; 10(172):1989.
63. Rimer BK, Ross E, Cristinzio CS, King E. Older women's participation in breast screening. Presented at the Forum on Breast Cancer Screening in Older Women. July 31, 1990, Sturbridge, MA. J Gerontol 1992;47(Special Issue):85–91.
64. Costanza ME, Gaw VP. Cancer prevention and control practices of Massachusetts primary care physicians. Presented at the Massachusetts Division of the American Cancer Society Professional Education Meeting, Boston, MA, October 5, 1990.
65. Horm JW, Gibbs T. Breast cancer among minorities and other underserved persons: barriers to screening. Background paper prepared for the Forum on Breast Cancer Screening in Older Women, Sturbridge, MA, August 1, 1990.
66. Older Women's League. 1987 Mother's Day report: the picture of health for mid-life and older women. Washington, DC: Older Women's League, 1987.
67. Glasse L. Breast cancer screening in older women: the consumer perspective. Presented at the Forum on Breast Cancer Screening in Older Women, Sturbridge, MA, August 1, 1990. J Gerontol 1992;47(Special Issue):137–141.
68. U.S. House of Representatives, Committee on Ways and Means. Background material and data on programs within the jurisdiction of the Committee on Ways and Means, Washington, DC: U.S. Government Printing Office (Mar 3, 1986), pp 77–78.
69. Commonwealth Fund Commission on Elderly People Living Alone. Medicare's poor, filling the gaps in medical coverage for low-income elderly Americans. Baltimore, MD: Nov. 1987.
70. American Association of Retired Persons. Public Policy Institute. Report on medical expenses for older persons, 1990.
71. Frame PS. Breast cancer screening in older women: the family practice perspective. Presented at the Forum on Breast Cancer Screening in Older Women, Sturbridge, MA, August 1, 1990. J Gerontol 1992;47(Special Issue):131–133.
72. Zapka JG, Berkowitz E. A qualitative study about breast cancer screening in older women: implications for research. Presented at the Forum on Breast Cancer Screening in Older Women, Sturbridge, MA, August 1, 1990. J Gerontol 1992;47(Special Issue):93–100.
73. Cohen HJ. Breast cancer screening in older women: the geriatrician/internist perspective. Presented at the Forum on Breast Cancer Screening in Older Women, Sturbridge, MA, August 1, 1990. J Gerontol 1992;47(Special Issue):134–136.
74. Weinberger M. Physician-related barriers to breast cancer screening in older women. Presented at the Forum on Breast Cancer Screening in Older Women, Sturbridge, MA, August 1, 1990. J Gerontol 1992;47(Special Issue) 111–117.
75. Costanza ME, Stoddard AM, Zapka JG, et al. Physician compliance with mammography guidelines: barriers and enhancers. J Am Board Fam Pract 1992;5(2):1–10.
76. Selinger HA, Goldfarb NI, Perkel RL, et al. Physician compliance with mammography guidelines: a retrospective chart review. Fam Med 1989;21:56–8.
77. Lane DS, Fine HL. Compliance with mammography referrals: implications for breast cancer screening. New York State J Med 1983;2:173–6.
78. Bourguet CC, Gilchrist VJ, Kandula M. Correlates of screening mammography in a family practice setting. J Fam Pract 1988;27:49–54.
79. Rimer BK, Trock B, Balshem A, et al. Breast screening practices among primary physicians: reality and potential. J Am Board Fam Pract 1990;3:26–34.
80. Cummings MK, Funch DP, Mettlin C, Jennings E. Family physicians' beliefs about breast cancer screening by mammography. J Fam Pract 1983;17:1029–34.
81. McPhee SJ, Richard RJ, Solkowitz SN. Performance of cancer screening in a university general internal medicine practice: comparison with the 1980 American Cancer Society guidelines. J Gen Intern Med 1986;1:275–81.
82. Champion V. Breast self-examination in women 65 and older. Presented at the Forum on Breast Cancer Screening in Older Women, Sturbridge, MA, August 1, 1990. J Gerontol 1992;47(Special Issue):75–79.
83. Greenwald P, Nasca PC, Lawrence CE, Horton J, McGarrah RP, Gabriele T, Carlton K. Estimated effect of breast self-examination and routine physician examination on breast cancer mortality. N Engl J Med 1978;299:271–3.
84. Feldman TG, Carter AC, Nicastri AD, Hosat ST. Breast self examination, relationship to stage of breast cancer at diagnosis. Cancer 1981;47:2740–5.
85. Foster RS, Costanza MC. Breast self-examination practices and breast cancer survival. Cancer 1984;53:999–1005.
86. Huguley CM, Brown RL, Greenberg RS, Clark WS. Breast self-examination and survival from breast cancer. Cancer 1988;62:1389–96.
87. Hill D, White V, Jolly N, Mapperson K. Self examination of the breast: is it beneficial? Meta-analyses of studies investigating breast self-examination and extent of disease in patients with breast cancer. Br Med J 1988;297:271–5.
88. Grady KE. The efficacy of breast self-examination. Presented at the Forum on Breast Cancer Screening in Older Women, Sturbridge, MA, August 1, 1990. J Gerontol 1992;47(Special Issue):69–74.
89. O'Malley MS, Fletcher SW. Screening for breast cancer with breast self-examination. JAMA 1987;257:2197–203.
90. UK trial of early detection of breast cancer group. First results of mortality reduction in the UK Trial of early detection of breast cancer. Lancet 1988;8608:411–6.
91. Newcomb PA, Weiss NS, Storer BE, Scilps D, Young E, Voight L. Breast self-examination in relation to the occurrence of breast cancer. J Natl Cancer Inst 1991;83:260–5.
92. Semiglazov VP, Moiseenko VM. Breast self-examination for the early detection of breast cancer: A USSR/WHO controlled trial in Leningrad. Bull WHO 1987;65:3911–60.
93. Koroltchouk V, Stanley K, Stjernsward J. The control of breast cancer, a World Health Organization perspective. Cancer 1990;65:2803–10.

Secretary SHALALA. The important thing is, whatever the scientific evidence and the recommendations are, we ought to follow them to a T. For too long, this country has ignored the health care needs of women. And the President's—both in the plan as well as in our administration of the Medicare program, we intend to be absolutely up to date for coverage.

Mrs. COLLINS. Thank you very much.

Mr. WAXMAN. Thank you, Mrs. Collins.

Mr. Bliley.

Mr. BLILEY. Thank you, Mr. Chairman.

Secretary Shalala, let me welcome you to the committee to discuss the administration's health care proposal.

Dr. Shalala, last week when Mrs. Clinton testified before this committee I asked her to make available to this committee the administration's quantitative working papers concerning financing, premium caps, actuarial analysis of the benefit package and the impact of the plan on jobs and national health expenditures. Mrs. Clinton responded with the following answer, and I quote: "And we will be happy to share with you all of the data that you requested. All of our calculations, our economic models, and the like."

Dr. Shalala, much of the quantitative analytical work behind the Clinton health care plan was performed by your department. Could you give me a specific date when you can make this work available to the committee?

Secretary SHALALA. I am not sure I could give you the actual date. When the legislation is sent up to the Hill along with our backup materials on the financing, at that point we will have all of the materials ready. So you can be assured that we would be happy to sit down with your staff when we finalize the plan.

I believe Mrs. Clinton indicated in the next couple of weeks the legislation would be coming up, so we are not very far away from that date. And when the financing is finalized at that point, we would be happy to share it with you, not only the analytical materials but the individuals that worked on it, so that staffs can ask them detailed questions.

Mr. BLILEY. Thank you.

The early evaluation of the President's plan by a wide range of experts, including economists and Members of Congress, is that the plan will not cut costs nearly as much as forecast and that the Federal budget deficit will dramatically increase as a result. That is because the success of the plan depends upon unprecedented cuts in Medicare and Medicaid, as has been alluded to by the chairman of the Health Subcommittee, my friend from California. These cuts generate $285 billion in savings, which represents almost two-thirds of the plan's financing.

A cap is also placed on both private health insurance premiums and Federal entitlements. When fully phased in, the cap is equal to CPI plus the annual percentage growth in population. Your own data projects the annual growth in population at less than 1 percent, eight-tenths of 1 percent.

Dr. Shalala, to your left is a chart—and Mr. Chairman, I ask unanimous consent it be included in the record, and I will distribute copies.

Mr. WAXMAN. Without objection, that will be the order.

[The charts referred to follow:]

SUBMITTED BY CONG. THOMAS BLILEY, JR. (CHART 1)

INTERNATIONAL COMPARISON, 1985-1991

Average Annual Growth in Inflation Adjusted Health Expenditures

	Percent Change 1985-1991*
Germany	2.87
United Kingdom	4.07
Japan	4.69
Canada	4.80
Italy	5.75
United States	6.08

* Numbers are the percentage by which the increase exceeds the rate of inflation, as measured by GDP deflator.

Source: Organization for Economic Cooperation and Development

SUBMITTED BY CONG. THOMAS BLILEY, JR. (CHART 11)

INTERNATIONAL COMPARISON

Average Annual Growth in Inflation Adjusted Health Expenditures

	Percent Change*
United Kingdom	4.07
Canada	4.80
United States, under historical inflation conditions	6.08
United States, under fully phased-in Clinton proposed cap	0.80**

* Numbers are the percentage by which the increase exceeds the rate of inflation, as measured by the GDP deflator.

** Numbers are the percentage by which the increase exceeds the rate of inflation, as measured by the CPI.

Source: Organization for Economic Cooperation and Development, 1985-1991 comparison, Working Group Draft, 9/7/93

Mr. BLILEY. Chart 1 shows an international comparison of the average annual growth rate of health expenditures adjusted for inflation for the years 1985 to 1991. For example, in this period German health expenditures actually grew by 2.87 percent above the inflation rate. The Canadian single payer system grew at 4.8 percent, and the British nationalized system grew at 4.07 percent, all above inflation. All of these countries are showing significant real annual increases.

In contrast to the experience of these nationalized systems, the cap on our health care expenditures allows real growth above inflation of less than 1 percent. Dr. Shalala, this data shows that nationalized single payer systems such as Britain and Canada have not come even remotely close in limiting health expenditures to less than 1 percent above inflation. In fact, except for Germany, they have been growing at least at 4 percent per year. Even Germany has been growing at close to 3 percent. We are talking about systems that explicitly ration care.

Now, as you are probably aware, I asked Mrs. Clinton how the President's plan is going to accomplish these extraordinary reductions in health care expenditures when even nationalized systems that ration care have not remotely approached these growth limits. Mrs. Clinton said in her response that these types of reductions were feasible because Dr. Koop has estimated that we start with $200 billion of wasteful and unnecessary costs in the U.S. health care system. This $200 billion represents approximately 25 percent of all national health care expenditures.

Now, a number of physicians and hospitals have said that this $200 billion of wasteful and unnecessary care grossly exaggerates the true state of affairs. Would you give me some specific examples to justify the statement that 25 percent of U.S. health care expenditures is wasteful or unnecessary?

Secretary SHALALA. Health care—let me start by saying specifically about the charts and about how fast we intend to slow down the growth in the system, that those numbers do not include the new spending on the uninsureds. There will, in fact, be new money being put in the system because of the uninsured that aren't currently spent. So both in the new commitments from employers and from employees, the limited targeted new tax on cigarettes, there will be some new resources put into the system.

But your question really is whether we can actually get the savings in the system that we suggest we can get and how fast we can pull down the system. I would make two points about that.

The first point would be specifically on the Medicare slowdown in growth as opposed to cuts. We will be coming in with recommendations, not a cap, but specific line-by-line recommendations on where we think we can slow down the growth in Medicare spending. Our recommendations, on average, will slow down the growth of Medicare spending from three times the rate of inflation to just under two times the rate of inflation. That will still be a significant increase in the—in spending for the Medicare program.

Second, one's assumptions about the health care system and how the health care system behaves and whether it actually can squeeze enough fat and waste out of the system I think have to be done in the context of what health care is, probably the only public function we have in which technology and major scientific breakthroughs actually have an impact, sometimes upward and sometimes downward, on costs.

The New England Journal of Medicine has an article in it in the January issue which describes a significant effort by physicians in Salt Lake City to reduce the cost of—to reduce the number and, therefore, the cost of hospital stays for people who have wound infections. And what they discovered is if you start antibiotics 2 days before—2 days before the operation is actually done, the proportion of people who actually get infected is reduced significantly. In that hospital alone they talked about $500,000 in savings. The projection for just using that procedure is $1.5 billion nationally.

Whether it is finding a new vaccine or identifying scientific breakthroughs or simply doing things more efficiently, which Mrs. Clinton gave you a number of examples of, there are, in fact, numerous ways we can squeeze fat out of the system and simultaneously take advantage of new approaches to reduced costs.

Mr. WAXMAN. Thank you, Mr. Bliley.

Mr. Stearns.

Mr. STEARNS. Thank you, Mr. Chairman.

First question, Madam Secretary: When are we going to see the administration's bill?

Secretary SHALALA. I believe in about 2 weeks we expect it up here.

Mr. STEARNS. When Mr. Bliley asked you questions on the underlying assumptions, why can't we have them now, you indicate that you will give them to us after we get the bill. Since you are using those figures now——

Secretary SHALALA. I actually am going to try——

Mr. STEARNS. Are these assumption in the models and everything that you used now?

Secretary SHALALA. Congressman, I am actually not using actual numbers, and I am going to try to avoid that because the numbers which are currently being reviewed by my own department, by the Office of Management and Budget and by the Treasury will accompany the bill when it comes to the Hill and——

Mr. STEARNS. Will we get the assumptions then simultaneously with the bill?

Secretary SHALALA. Yes. We will provide any kind of background material you need at the time as well as the individuals that will go through what our assumptions were about reducing the rate of growth and about specific reimbursements and subsidies at that time.

Mr. STEARNS. Are you prepared today to say that there will be no price controls?

Secretary SHALALA. I am prepared to say that we are putting in place no price-control mechanism as anything that has been used over the last three or four decades in this country.

Mr. STEARNS. In light of the administration's plan to reinvent government and that Vice President Gore is talking about the ineptitude of the Federal bureaucracy, why are we now talking about more bureaucracy in terms of a seven-member national health board and talking about mandates from the Federal Government?

Secretary SHALALA. I do not think that we are talking about a huge bureaucracy with the national health board. Our estimates are that we are talking about as little as 100 people who would staff that board and about a seven-member board. I believe Mrs. Clinton described it as a board of directors with a limited number of functions, including reviewing the comprehensive benefit package, getting the quality assurance system up and off the ground. This is a relatively minor oversight group that would have some functions, but I don't think anyone views it as a major bureaucracy.

Mr. STEARNS. I will try to remember your words about minor oversight board.

Representative Stark has been interviewed about this, and he was quoted on NPR radio as saying: "I think there is no question that the administration's plan to eliminate Medicare as a system for the seniors will occur within 5 years. The seniors are not going to like that."

What is your response?

Secretary SHALALA. I simply don't think that is true. There are two or three things that are happening with the Medicare program. First, it is clearly—and when you see the legislation—and in our testimony we have made it clear that it is being left intact. In fact, we are adding a major new drug benefit to the Medicare program. There are currently——

Mr. STEARNS. Do you think he just doesn't understand your system? Why does he make a comment like that? He has obviously talked to you and to others and he is pretty knowledgeable.

Secretary SHALALA. Congressman Stark is a good friend and he is making some assumptions that we may not be making about the future of the Medicare program. But let me make it clear that we currently have in the Medicare program contracts with managed-care systems. We will offer opportunities to Medicare recipients. And, in fact, as people get to the end of their working life and go into retirement, they may reach 65 and decide they want to stay in their plans.

There would be opportunities for States to make proposals to the Federal Government and request permission to integrate their Medicare program, once their other program is up and running. Those reviews were required, and we will be prepared to outline what kind of criteria we will use for those reviews to protect the elderly. But I don't anticipate this is—this will be a short-time effort.

What we have done in this bill is to protect the Medicare program as it now exists, to enhance it. And to indicate that we want to see the national program up and running, we will give some people some choices.

But we do intend to protect the integrity of the program. More importantly, the integrity of the elderly. But there will be opportunities for the States to come to us and to talk to us about the eventual folding of the program.

Mr. STEARNS. Madam Secretary, I hope you will provide the committee the names of the outside private accounting firms mentioned by the President, that were used to come up with the cost of his proposal.

I want to ask you one last question. Several States have undertaken significant reforms, California and Florida, and mandatory purchasing alliances were rejected in favor of giving consumers maximum choices. Why did the administration opt out to the mandatory?

Secretary SHALALA. I think that we are not only providing choices but alliances, and we intend to give consumers maximum access.

Mr. WAXMAN. Mr. Synar?

Mr. SYNAR. Individual responsibility is one of the driving principles behind the plan. And one of the major differences between the President's proposal and some of the competing plans is the difference between employer premiums and individual mandates, which some have recommended. Could you share with the committee the reason why individual mandates were rejected?

And second, am I misunderstanding individual mandates, or would that not be one heck of a middle-class tax increase and keep up, achieving the goal of universal coverage?

Secretary SHALALA. Congressman, you are reading it exactly right. It would be, in fact, moving people in, which a vast majority of them, currently their health care is financed by their employers, moving them out of that system. Maybe their wage negotiations have been based on trade-offs between wages as well as their health care system. And for those individuals, in particular, they would be giving up—they gave up wage increases to get more health benefits, and it would be a considerable loss.

But for millions of Americans to move to an individual system, at this point, would be a broad-based tax for them because they would be mandated to pay for their own health care and that would be an added burden on them.

We did think about the individual mandate, we did review the possibilities. But fundamentally, what we were trying to do was to do a recognizable program, to build on what is good in the current program.

We currently have an employer-based system in this country. And rather than going to a very sharp turn in a new program, we—the President made the decision that we should build on what we have.

Mr. SYNAR. One of the major criticisms in the last plan was from the American Medical Association, which believed that there should be a doctor or physician on the national health care board. What was the thinking in trying to establish the board on why that would not be part of it?

Secretary SHALALA. Both on the national board—and I have deep respect for the American Medical Association and for the physicians and for their constant concern about having those who actually deliver the services to provide insight and policy advice. Both—we have—both on the national board as well as on the alliance boards, we have been careful to make sure that there are representatives of consumers as well as employers, as opposed to making sure that there were representatives of providers, as such.

I think the providers will have ample opportunity to express their views, and to—and by not locking in the national board to a specific provider group, I think that we offer the President and the Congress the widest possible choice.

Mr. SYNAR. With respect to the health alliances, we are obviously looking at a minimum of 50 or more, depending on the size of the States. Clearly, an executive director of those alliances is going to have to be one heck of a qualified person; a Wharton School of Business, M.D., hospital administrator. Is there a talent pool great enough in the United States in order to help us staff qualified health alliances throughout the country?

Secretary SHALALA. There are a lot of ex-college presidents that I think could handle it. The answer is yes.

But I also—I hope that we don't view these alliances as top-down bureaucratic structures as opposed to a structure that obviously has to fulfill the State mandates in terms of handling the financial transactions that will provide a role in terms of making sure that the certification and the quality assurance systems are in place.

But my hope is that they are lean and mean, and they contract out for certain kinds of services and that they do not become a big public-sector, nonprofit bureaucracy as such—that, in fact, we keep the resources where they belong, at the plan level, to deliver health care, and that we not substitute a Federal bureaucracy for a regional bureaucracy. And, therefore, we both limit their roles and put every emphasis on them providing guidance and fiscal responsibility as opposed to a top-down management structure.

Mr. SYNAR. Share with me, for Oklahomans in the Second District of Oklahoma who may using Kansas and Arkansas facilities because we border that, how they could use those facilities, if they choose?

Secretary SHALALA. The plans, obviously, can attract—can operate across State lines. In addition to that, the requirement that the plans contract with an academic health center will tie those academic health centers into different States. We have asked them to contract with one academic health center.

There will be a point-of-service option in which the plans could recommend or an individual could use a specialist in another place. But particularly where you cross State lines, as is true today in the Federal plans, that also operate in Virginia and Maryland, there will be opportunities for them to do that and to attract people from across State borders.

Mr. WAXMAN. Thank you, Mr. Synar.

Mr. Moorhead?

Mr. MOORHEAD. The Clinton plan proposes no change in the existing situation with the Federal Government-mandated State medical program's finance provisions of emergency medical services for immigrants who reside in the country illegally. The services are shared jointly by the Federal Government and the State.

California taxpayers will spend, roughly, $400 to $500 million this year to finance 50 percent of the cost not paid by the Federal Government. Why does the Clinton plan continue the practice of forcing certain States to pay 50 percent of the cost of providing medical services to a caseload over which they have utterly no control?

Secretary SHALALA. We will continue to help the States deal with issues of undocumented immigrants; and particularly, States like

California, New York, Florida, Texas, and Illinois. Many States have particular concerns and particular burdens.

We will do it in a couple of ways. You will see as our legislation comes up here, the beefing up of the public health service to continue to provide resources. And, in fact, energize community health centers.

There will be a larger Federal commitment for community health centers, for example. In addition to that, we have already started conversations with Chairman Waxman about the "disproportionate share" payments for hospitals, particularly for places like Southern California, that are concerned if we phase out too quickly disproportionate share or don't have a substitute for that, for hospitals and other kinds of facilities that have an overburden of particular undocumented populations.

And this is part, I think, of the kind of thoughtfulness that has to go into the design of the program so that we do not add to the States's current burdens on dealing with undocumented aliens. The issue is unevenly spread across the country, but it will require that we look at existing programs and new ways of helping the States to handle the burdens.

Mr. MOORHEAD. Well, it would appear from the information we have got that you are going to discontinue that disproportionate share program in 1996. It is still predicted that your new program will not be fully implemented at least until 1997 or later.

Who is going to pay those costs? The States, the counties, the cities? Who is going to pay those costs during that period of time?

Secretary SHALALA. Let me go back a little and point out that those institutions that currently handle a disproportionate share of a population, that will be—not be covered by the plan in terms of comprehensive benefits. Those institutions will also be getting additional revenues for the people that they currently cover using disproportionate share money, because everybody will be covered.

So a hospital in California that currently has a heavy load of those who are not covered by any kind of health plan will have that relieved by the new health plan which will cover a very high percent. So they will have more revenues coming in.

Second, for those that are left out of the system, basically, the undocumented immigrants, let me repeat again, both in what you will see in the new bill in terms of our commitments in public health—and I hope either some sensitizing of the phasing down of the disproportionate share or some other way of handling that overburden, you will see us making certain that we try to mitigate against the States having to substantially increase their revenues for this particular population.

We recognize the national role and we recognize that we may not get it perfect the first time. By the time we get through this committee, we will be a lot more sensitive to this issue.

Mr. MOORHEAD. There is tremendous concern in States, such as my own, California, because they have a burden that is much higher than they can take care of at the present time. There is some talk of increased Federal involvement to shoulder the burden of immigration policies and other things. Do you have any more detail to give us?

Secretary SHALALA. No, only that we are aware of the problem. And number two, that we have been in conversations with your colleagues on this issue, and that we certainly are available to talk about it when you see the final bill.

But it is our commitment that we need to do some things, even after the bill comes up here, that we have some careful conversations, that we absolutely do not increase the burden. Though, I would point out, that those institutions will be getting additional resources when everyone is covered. So we already are helping them significantly with the burden for those particular institutions.

Mr. MOORHEAD. I know that my time is up. I wanted to ask one more thing.

We are terribly concerned about unemployment in California right now. Are rates running——

Mr. WAXMAN. Mr. Moorhead, we really have to move on. Your time has expired.

Mr. MOORHEAD. I will submit some questions to you. Would you mind——

Secretary SHALALA. I will be happy to answer any questions that you have.

Mr. WAXMAN. Mr. Wyden?

Mr. WYDEN. The top concern that I am hearing now from consumers is about the prospect of losing choice. You have gone a long way to address this issue. But I think it is important to note that both the Democratic and the Republican plans that are on the table, in effect, encourage people to use managed care, which has contributed to this question of losing choice.

Let me ask you about an example so we can really nail down how this point-of-service idea might work. Say, we have a plan that makes the judgment that the way they want to hold down costs is simply not hire enough OB/GYN's and, in effect, women would then have to wait for an appointment. As I would understand it, it would be very helpful if plans were required to offer this service option so that a woman could choose, perhaps, to get the appointment exactly when she wants it and pay a little bit more.

Under this kind of approach, what would happen by the next year is you would have a lot of women furious at that particular plan. The plan would then have to go out and hire more OB/GYN's so that all the women in the plan the next year would be in a position to get better service; is that your understanding of how this would work?

Secretary SHALALA. Well, certainly, I would suggest to you that women that couldn't get access to OB/GYN's would send a clear message to the plan, that either you start providing those services quickly or we are going to switch to other plans. It is not just shoving them out through the point-of-service, but I think this is such a consumer-oriented approach that the pressure will be on the plan, given the characteristics of the population in the plan, to provide timely service.

As Mrs. Clinton indicated to you, we are prepared and we are reviewing the issue of point-of-service for the managed-care plans, and we, of course, are very anxious to work with you on that particular issue. But, Congressman, let me point out that most Americans don't currently have choice, that while in every poll that we see, in all of our conservations—and my own family has been on the phone to me making it—pinning me down on how much choice there is going to be in the plan.

None of them currently have any choice. What they see is an expanded opportunity in the new initiative to get more choice than they currently have.

So I believe that most Americans will have more choice under the plan that the President intends to submit in the next couple of weeks. But we can certainly fine tune it and provide more access. And you have, certainly, take the leadership on the point-of-service option that would even expand that. But I couldn't be more sympathetic.

Mr. WYDEN. Let me ask you a question on technology. Technology is responsible for about 40 percent of the rate of growth in health spending. And I think the plan needs some work in the technology area. Except for the idea possibly of a premium surcharge, it doesn't address the technology question.

I am concerned that the major thing that buyers want, HMO's, insurers, and essentially doctors and hospitals as well, is comparative data to compare one technology—a catheter, for example—to the one that they are using right now. And I doubt that the government is going to be in a position to, in effect, conduct all of these comparative trials that are needed, even with what you all are talking about.

What I would like to see us do in the plan is give drug and device companies an incentive to fund these comparative assessments themselves, so that at the beginning, before America goes off on another spending spree on technology, we could get the data up front. Is that a concept that the administration could in theory support and would be prepared to work on?

Secretary SHALALA. I certainly would be willing to work on it with you, Congressman. But I should point out that there may be a problem with the industry itself doing the analysis, and to the extent that we could mix outside analysis as well as industry-based analysis—you are one of the great experts on this, but you well know that people sometimes look with a slightly skeptical eye at this.

Mr. WYDEN. My time is up.

I want it understood that nobody is talking about letting the industry self-verify. They would bring you clinical data about promised devices in line with some government models. You all would then verify it, and then on the basis of that level of promise, it could be considered for additional regulatory fast tracking.

Secretary SHALALA. That, obviously, is both an intriguing idea and something that adds significantly to the consumer orientation of the plan. And we, obviously, would be quite enthusiastic about reviewing that with you.

Mr. WAXMAN. Mr. McMillan?

Mr. MCMILLAN. Thank you, Mr. Chairman.

Dr. Shalala, I also serve on the Budget Committee and have worked on the issue of caps on entitlement programs, and I don't disagree with your approach on that. But, overall, I am keenly interested in the analytical work that you are doing in terms of what is going to happen with total cash flows in the medical care system.

Because I think what you are proposing, if you "X" out Medicare, which you are basically excluding, which I think is a mistake, but you are going to concentrate the cash flows on the health care purchasing alliances—and it is an enormous number, if you include all the premiums that are going to be paid by the participants, which I think should be part of that analysis.

It is an enormous concentration of both power and financing. And I think therein lies a lot of our concerns and the public's concerns with what you are proposing. Because everything is going to be concentrated either in regional or corporate health care alliances, which includes virtually everyone, as I understand it, with the possible exception of the veterans who can opt in, or Medicare.

There have been a few remarks made about the Medicare savings; $124 billion over 5 years is difficult. Even the hardest-nosed, cruelest Republican budgeteers in their proposals couldn't come up but with $93 billion over 5 years.

Some of those are agonizing. We discussed a lot of them in this committee. They are going to be difficult. To move from $93 to $124 billion, it seems to me, you are going to have to deal with those things such as Congressman Wyden mentioned, excessively applied technology.

You are going to have to deal with defensive health care costs in a much stronger way than you have got in your bill, and malpractice reform. And you are probably going to have to deal with the agonizing ethical issue of terminal health care costs, which your Department puts at extremely high, as a proportion of the Medicare payout.

But taking that a step further, what concerns me is that while you have proposed $124 billion worth of cuts or moderation in the rate of growth, which I would agree with that assessment, you have also proposed $157 billion worth of increase in drugs and long-term care.

The question there arises, it is argued, and this can be debated, that right now, the rest of the system has to absorb some 30 percent of Medicare costs in cost shifting, because the reimbursement rates are inadequate. And it seems to me that we are going to have to address that excruciating issue, because that 30 percent impacts on all the rest. And if you argue, but then all the cash flow is going to then flow through the health care purchasing alliances, I would like to hear you say what your estimates are in terms of the cost for the particular groups that would be included therein. The existing Medicaid population, for example.

We are spending $124 billion on Medicaid now. Arguably, some percent of that is not in reimbursement for services performed. It is in the form of grants, such as the gentleman from California mentioned and others.

We have got to fold in the uninsured or the underinsured. I would like to know a figure on that.

How much subsidy is in here for small business? And how much subsidy is in here for not small business, but from those in the category of 50 to 5,000 employees, and not just business but any other institution?

Could you give me an estimate of roughly what the aggregate amount of subsidy is going to be for that pool that includes virtually everyone with Medicare and government?

Secretary SHALALA. Your questions are on target, Congressman. Let me say what I can and cannot say at this moment. First, your general point about how difficult it is going to be to pull down the—or to slow down the growth in the Medicare system. There is just no question about it. Everyone that has tried, it is hard to get beyond 100 million or so.

But we are coming in with a very specific list. Some of them will be familiar to you, that the committee has debated before. And some of them will be new. We bring in the list——

Mr. MCMILLAN. Will it include, possibly, means-testing on premiums and high copayments that are pretty consistent across the board?

Secretary SHALALA. I think you will find most of them are focused on providers as opposed to beneficiary, in terms of reimbursement rates. We will come in with a very specific list. There is no question that it is very difficult to do.

The only reason it will work, if we get somewhere near those numbers, is if simultaneously we are slowing down growth on the private side. You are absolutely right.

What the government of the United States has been doing for all these years, is squeezing down the government side and cost-shifting to the private side. And so in slowing down public-sector growth, we are simultaneously trying to slow down private-sector growth through the premiums, and through slowing down the growth in the premiums, to targets that we have established. And, so, we see it as a whole, in terms of slowing down the growth in the entire system.

Can we get that much savings in the system, is the fundamental issue? How much fat do you think there is in the system?

How much, in terms of just information about the effectiveness of certain kinds of equipment, of certain kinds of procedures, can we squeeze out of the system? Certainly, we think—and you cannot talk to a provider, to a patient, to anyone who is an observer or a student in the system, who doesn't think there is significant amounts of money that cannot be squeezed out of the system.

All of this, though, is not based simply on our ability to slow down growth or eliminate waste in the system, but fundamentally this approach is based on the employer-based system. Two-thirds of the financing comes from the employer and the employee. And when we come up with very specific numbers, we will give you very specific numbers, plus the assumption. In a couple of weeks, we will go through the proportions.

But we have to go back to the point that we believe that there is lots of money in the system. It may be used in the wrong ways, for emergency care over here, as opposed to prevention. But fundamentally, the financing for this new system is nothing new. It is employer-based, with the employees making a contribution, the system that we currently have. And two-thirds of the cost for the system will be borne by employers and employees. And when we come in with the numbers, you will see what pieces come from a combination of slowing down growth and phasing in Medicare into the system. We will be happy to provide those to you.

Mr. WAXMAN. Mr. Rowland?

Mr. ROWLAND. Thank you, Mr. Chairman.

Madam Secretary, some of those that I am hearing from who are concerned about our health care delivery system are those that do not feel that they have access to health care and those that are unable to pay, such as those people who are retired marginally. Those people are uninsured and underinsured, and those individuals who have to deplete all of their assets if they have a catastrophic illness.

But I am also hearing from people who are fairly well satisfied with the health care benefits that they now have. While they feel that the cost of these benefits are high, they are very uneasy about any change that may take place in the system.

They feel it may in some way jeopardize the benefits that they now have. I don't know how many families this is, but I suspect from hearing from people in my district that it is a fairly large number of people who fall into this category.

Last week a number of Members of the House on both sides of the aisle sent a letter to the President asking him if he would consider addressing those parts of our health care delivery system that need addressing immediately, in the event that we could not get in place some overall change in our delivery systems. Such things as administrative simplification, insurance reform, antifraud reform, some change in antitrust laws, many things that we feel need to be immediately done to address the problems that we have in our system.

How receptive will the administration be to looking at doing some of these things that need to be done immediately if we are not able to pass some overall comprehensive health care plan that will greatly change the way our health care delivery system will operate?

Secretary SHALALA. Dr. Rowland, the President's commitment is not to simply fix some small things in the system, but to fundamentally offer coverage to every American, to give them the security of knowing that their health care system is there. The current insecurity in the system, whether it is a Medicare recipient concerned that we are going to make some changes that affect them—even though I believe that we are going to strengthen that program with the drug benefit—or people who are currently satisfied, but many of them are worried about whether their children are going to have a health care system or whether if they leave their job or change jobs, their health care system will be there for them. We believe that on that this plan addresses the fundamental need of this country, and that is for everyone to be covered.

Simply making a few small market changes doesn't solve the problem and take steps towards increasing the quality of health care in this country, which is the central piece of the President's plan.

So, I think that the President has made it clear, as did the First Lady, that universal coverage is fundamental to our proposal, and that, with all due respect, we would like to move forward with a plan that is encompassing, that make it possible for the people that are currently happy to be more secure, but to be sure that their friends and neighbors are also covered.

Mr. ROWLAND. Certainly, you don't consider small market changes to be malpractice reform, insurance reform, antitrust reform, certainly those are not small market changes that we are talking about.

Secretary SHALALA. No, I wouldn't describe all of them as small market changes. But in combination, they don't ensure that every American has access to an adequate health care system that is affordable.

Mr. ROWLAND. If we could fix the part of the system that would assure that those people that I mentioned have access and not tinker with the system that people are already satisfied with, would you be receptive to something like that?

Secretary SHALALA. Let me step back a little and simply say that I don't believe that we are tinkering with the system that people are satisfied with. One way to look at the President's plan is to suggest that he is basically leaving in place the system that people are satisfied with; the basic employer-based system, in which employers make contributions.

For many Americans, perhaps for the majority of Americans who currently are in that system, they will not see anything significantly different. Their health insurance plan will be there. They may have more choices than they currently have.

What we are trying to do is to deal with the issues for many other Americans who don't currently, 37 million Americans and their families, who don't currently have coverage. We actually don't believe that this plan will actually either change the experience, other than more choice and improve the quality of the system for people that are satisfied with their current system. To convince them, obviously, is a big step, given your question—and I would be happy to accept an invitation to your district to try to convince them.

Mr. ROWLAND. I will be happy to extend that invitation.

Mr. WAXMAN. Mr. Upton?

Mr. UPTON. Thank you, Mr. Chairman.

Welcome. As a good football coach, I am going to try to work the clock. I have a couple of questions that I would like to ask and, hopefully, the red light will not be on before I am finished.

The first one is—I don't know if you saw today's Wall Street Journal article by Harry Schwartz, on the op-ed section where he talks about: "HMO is another roadblock for Alzheimer's drugs. The President has praised the HMO's for practicing medicine economically and avoiding the wastes he sees endemic in fee-for-service medicine, but he has never directly faced the problem that HMO economies, in part, is made possible by denying patients drugs, test procedures and operations that might help them. Americans still expect their doctors to put their patients first."

And he refers specifically to Cognex and a group health cooperative out of Puget Sound, as well as Kaiser, is denying this drug for their patients because of cost.

And the question, therefore, would be at what point would the patient's rights override the cost? Whether it be an ombudsman, as you might have suggested a little bit earlier to Mrs. Collins question.

The second question that I have pertains to pharmaceuticals. The Secretary, you, would have the ability to deny coverage of a specific drug to Medicare or Medicaid recipients, based on the price of the drug. This basically will result in price-fixing. How might these price caps stifle research and development, particularly as you look at the return on pharmaceutical manufacturer's investment? And would this have a profound impact on new drugs to treat diseases of the elderly such as Alzheimers and cancer?

And the third and last question that I hope to ask in this round of questioning pertains to early retirees. It is my understanding that the Clinton proposal provides coverage for individuals who retire early and are not yet eligible for Medicare.

I have seen a couple of cost estimates in the last week in terms of what companies might do to, quote "dump those employees from the system." And Mrs. Clinton indicated that she thought the cost might be $4.5 billion a year. And a few days ago Ira Magaziner said that he thought it would be $6 million.

What is the correct figure, and how do you estimate this figure and what are you going to do to prevent companies from "dumping" employees that decide to retire early?

Secretary SHALALA. Let me answer each of these quickly. And I would be happy to provide more detail, if you request it afterwards.

On the retirees, that is under review and it would be inappropriate for me at this moment to try to put numbers on that or to describe what our proposal will do. We, obviously, believe that picking up the employer part of retiree benefits is a good thing to do. It will help the economy. It will help many of those retirees make the transition.

And as to the "dumping" issues, I think I would rather comment on those when we have fine tuned the entire proposal.

On the issue of the behavior of HMO's, I think that it is increasingly difficult to—while we have experience with HMO's in this country, I have not read that article. I do not know of instances where those two very distinguished HMO's have refused access to a drug because of cost as opposed to an appropriate medical decision. So I would be reluctant to comment specifically on that.

But on the more general point, we see this program as a consumer-oriented program, have the consumers themselves working to influence the sensitivity and the responsiveness, working with physicians and other health professionals, as a patient-oriented system, with the patient having in their hand the power to switch, which certainly makes a difference. There is no question that decisions have to be made about the appropriateness of drugs, but we hope by insuring everyone, by putting substantial new resources into the health care system of this country and reorganizing the resources that we currently have, and by eliminating fat, and added resources for health care, that the decisions that are going to be made are medical decisions on what is appropriate for a patient.

The patients do have outs, as I discussed with Congresswoman Collins, both in using the flexibility, if they decide on going into a managed-care system; of the point-of-service, to go outside the system; in going to an ombudsman to appeal an individual decision of a physician. We will build into the systems as much—as much consumer orientation and sensitivity and quality assurance as we possibly can.

On the current drugs, I will have to provide that answer for the record. We, obviously, don't have any intention of reducing both the investment of the pharmaceuticals in research or our own investment in research. And we have to be very careful, as we negotiate prices, as the government becomes the largest purchaser of drugs, to get a fair price for the government, which ought to be below the retail price, because we are purchasing such a large amount, but simultaneously, does not interfere with the need for the companies themselves to invest in R&D.

Mr. WAXMAN. Thank you, Mr. Upton.

Mr. Dingell?

Mr. DINGELL. Thank you, Mr. Chairman.

Madam Secretary, welcome to the committee.

Secretary SHALALA. Thank you.

Mr. DINGELL. Thank you very much for your kind remarks about my dad and about my long interest in this subject of health care. And I want to express my particular commendations for the wonderful way in which you have handled the matter. And my hope is that you and I will be able to work together, as I know that we will, toward success in achieving the President's goals.

Madam Secretary, I want to deal with several questions: First, about cost; second of all, cost shifting; and third, the question of subsidies to small business, which I think could probably be handled better, because I feel it will require some statements for the record.

First of all, under this, the cost to small business is going to be about 3.5 percent of payroll.

Secretary SHALALA. Yes, though I said as I came in earlier, we are not actually locking ourselves into any of the subsidy numbers, as this moment. We are finalizing them, and we will be up here in a couple of weeks with the exact numbers.

Mr. DINGELL. At the time you do, I would like to have an indication of what the subsidy to a small business is through this device. I think the numbers are going to be substantial. And I think it is important that we have a clear understanding what those numbers might, in fact, happen to be, because I have heard small business complaints about this costing large sums of money.

There are many small businesses now providing health care to their employees who will achieve a substantial and significant benefit from having this particular plan. Not only because of the reduction in costs, the subsidy, but also because of the elimination of things like cost shifting and other problems which now inflict the small business community to a greater degree than would a large business, or a government agency, such as a State or local unit of government.

I guess I would request that at the time that you bring this plan up, that you submit something to us on that, because I think that would be an extremely important point.

Second of all, I noted that Mr. Bliley, who usually comes up with extraordinary information, and has done so again, his comments about the international comparison of inflation in medical expenditures, a two-page document here, shows that there are remarkable events afoot.

The United States shows that in terms of percent change in inflation of adjusted health expenditures, we lead the world, 6.8 percent per year. And I note that under the plan, as proposed, we will see a percentage change limited to 0.8 percent per year. That is going to require some direct cost control measures, to which I don't want to address myself at this particular minute, but I do want to observe something that I think is important and ask you to comment on it.

I note that in Britain, the share of the gross domestic product is about 6 percent for health care. And it goes up about 6 percent a year. In Canada, it's going up 8 percent and constitutes about 8 percent of the gross domestic product.

In the case of France, it goes up at 8 percent a year and constitutes 8 percent of the gross domestic product. Germany is 9 percent.

The United States constitutes 14 or 15 percent. It is going up at 15 percent a year, and will double in 6 years, and will shortly be 17 percent; and not long thereafter, will be 20 percent.

Clearly, as my old dad used to say, there is a health and humanitarian component there. But more importantly, I think there is a situation now looking us in the eye, on the basis of the figures Mr. Bliley has cited, and the figures that I have cited, that the United States is going to go broke on health care costs.

We aren't going to be able to afford the government component of the payment of Medicare and Medicaid, nor will we be able to afford the private component.

When I was rather younger, I used to point out that autos had about $800 worth of health care in them. I looked last year, or the year before, and it was $1,100. This year, it is now up to about $1,476 per car. That is more than the steel.

The biggest contractor to the auto industry is Blue Cross and Blue Shield, not the steel companies, not people who provide the paint or any of the other essential components of automobiles, but just one thing, health care.

Now, do you want to give us a comment as to how this is going to help American industry and what is going to happen to us if we don't do anything about the cost on this?

Secretary SHALALA. Thank you, Mr. Chairman.

Obviously, we believe that there is a lot of money already in the system. And while these numbers reveal that we would be coming down to almost nothing, what they don't have added to them in terms of growth is the new money that is coming into the system to cover the people that aren't currently covered. So, in fact, there will be a more substantial increase in U.S. expenditures for health care.

But unless we get our health care system costs under control, American business will be less competitive than it currently is. It is not simply beginning to slow down the growth in expenditures, but the predictability of costs in the system, which American business managers cannot handle. They simply don't know from 1 year to the next, what they ought to build in terms of their costs.

It is not only American businesses. As someone who ran one of the great American public universities, periodically my State would tell me in the middle of the year that I had to cut back on expenditures, which is not easy to do in the university when you already have the faculty in the classrooms, because the health care costs were coming in at a higher number. So it is the competitiveness of American business that is related to these cost increases.

For small businesses, it has been a disaster. The small businesses that you referred to, most small business in this country provide some health care to their employees.

They are paying 30 percent more for their premiums than if they were in a larger pool, like a large corporation. So anything that we can do to introduce stability into the system helps American business and helps the American economy, and helps everyone that has to manage any kind of an institution, in terms of their ability to plan.

And from our point of view, to have so much of health care costs in the cost of an automobile, in which we are trying to compete with the Japanese or with a Korean automobile that doesn't have those kinds of costs, is putting the American auto industry, obviously, at a disadvantage. An older industry that also has until now had to pay retirement health care costs, which are substantial.

And so, as expected, you have identified the central—one of the central issues for the American economy. And that is why I can only keep repeating, we must deal with the whole system this time. It is time that we dealt with the entire health care system, with every part of it, because of the impact on our total economy.

Mr. WAXMAN. Thank you, Mr. Dingell.

Mr. Greenwood?

Mr. GREENWOOD. Thank you, Mr. Chairman.

Dr. Shalala, I think for me and for many other Members on this side of the aisle, the most difficult part of this plan to accept is the employer mandate. I think it is difficult for a couple of reasons.

It is difficult because there is a fundamental philosophical issue about what kind of country this is and whether an individual can go out and start a small enterprise and voluntarily bring on employees, or whether every time that happens, the government will say: Well, you are required and mandated to also do this, if you want to engage in some kind of a small business.

It also is critical, because I think it is not a debatable point, that when you add to the cost of employing people, you will get a net reduction in the number of people employed. I think that is as fundamental an economic premise as there can be.

I raised this issue with the First Lady last week and suggested that even though there is a 3.5 percent floor, small employers with the lowest wages would have to pay that percentage. Some companies don't have 3.5 percent, especially in years when they are losing money. It is just not there. Even given the savings in workers' comp and auto insurance, you can't get that much blood from certain stones in the private sector.

The First Lady's response, and I will read from the transcript, quote: "And finally, I would say that the 3.5 percent is a cap. Some small businesses will be paying 1 percent, 1.5 percent. And for many small businesses that are on the margins, as you are describing, we would like to know the individual circumstances, because based on the scenarios that we have been running, we think that this would be affordable given the workman's comp decreases," et cetera.

And this came up with Chairman Dingell's question a moment ago. It is my understanding from the official-leaked document, that the 3.5 percent is not the cap, but rather it is the floor for small businesses paying lower wages, and the 7.9 percent of payroll is the ceiling.

Do I misunderstand the proposal, or did Mrs. Clinton misspeak?

Secretary SHALALA. Congressman, no. I think that since the subsidy scheme is going through review now, I am very reluctant to even talk about a 3.5 number. Certainly, we need to do that in 2 weeks from now when we come with the specific numbers. So I would like to avoid talking about the specific numbers.

In terms of the depth of the subsidies, it is our intention, the philosophy behind this is to make it possible for small businesses in this country to be able to make the transition from not paying to paying. And the subsidies will be designed based on what we know about small businesses and about their own economic health. And we will do our best to work with numbers that make it possible for them to come into the system without obviously driving them out of business.

Mr. GREENWOOD. Certainly, if you can't be that specific, in generalities, the difference between 3.5 percent as a ceiling and 3.5 percent as a floor, is a whopping difference. And the difference between 3.5 and 7.9 percent is a whopping difference. It is an order of magnitude greater than 100 percent.

Are you able to—let me finish the question, if I may—are you able to tell me whether it is conceivable that the cap is going to be closer to 3.5 percent than it is to 7.9 percent for small employers?

Secretary SHALALA. Mrs. Clinton was talking about small, low-wage firms, and identifying 3.5 percent as the possible cap for small, low-wage firms.

Mr. GREENWOOD. The smallest of the small.

Secretary SHALALA. Yes, we are talking about small, low-wage firms.

Mr. GREENWOOD. That is the ceiling. That is the least any business would pay?

Secretary SHALALA. That is the most any business would pay. When she was talking about a cap, that is the most.

Mr. GREENWOOD. I thought the 7.9 percent was the most any business would pay?

Secretary SHALALA. The 3.5 percent is focused on low-wage, small businesses, and that is what she was referring to.

But, again, I really don't want to lock myself into 3.5, or 3.4, or 3.3, when we are 2 weeks away from coming up with final numbers. But she was, in fact, talking about, at that time, about the cap on that.

Madam Chairwoman, the Congressman has raised some issues about the economic premises and our philosophy of government, fundamental issues about who ought to pay for health care, and if I could take 2 seconds and try to address those, because those are very thoughtful questions and go to the heart of what we are trying to do.

I think the first point I would make is that the current system—the current system, both tolerated and encouraged by the government of the United States, by the people of the United States, is a system based on employer mandates. That is—not mandates but an employer-employee system.

So what we are trying to do is to keep to the familiar system. To keep the good parts of health care as opposed to—and get rid of the bad parts, so we are building on the existing system as opposed to turning that system upside down. A system in which the majority of Americans who are employed are familiar, which has, we think, done us well, even though the cost containment has been a particular problem for almost every one of those businesses.

Mr. GREENWOOD. The current system is a voluntary system. What are you proposing is a forced system and that is as different as night and day.

Mrs. COLLINS [presiding]. She is trying to explain the system.

Secretary SHALALA. But the current system also relies on a system—on a set of economic decisions that are clearly made without a formal role by the government, though we have allowed it to continue, and that is that it shifts the cost of certain kinds of businesses's health care, their employee's health care on to other kinds of businesses. That those of us who have companies that pay for health care absorb the cost, and have been over the years, absorbing the cost of people who are not currently covered.

In some ways, we have been offering subsidies to a certain set of businesses in our society who, for a variety of reasons, some of them because they don't have access to proper cost-effective health care systems—one set of businesses have been absorbing the cost of another set of business.

What the President's proposal tries to do is rationalize the system—and that is introduced with a set of assumptions—a fairer system, in which all businesses and all employees share the cost, as opposed to one set of employees and employers taking on the costs of another set of employers and employees. And so, I think it is fairer to see us as trying not to radically change the system but to make the existing system that has grown up over the years fairer, and to spread out the costs among all businesses and to help those businesses that are clearly going to have trouble to be able to afford the system.

I hope that, at least in that context, you will look at the proposal as it comes down in the next couple of weeks. And I will be happy to continue the conversation with you.

Mrs. COLLINS. The time of the gentleman has expired.

Mr. Towns?

Mr. TOWNS. Thank you very much, Madam Chair.

Let me thank you, Madam Secretary, for all the work that you are doing in this area.

Let me begin by saying that I think that the boards are an excellent idea. However, I must add that when we talk about the health alliances, I have some problems in terms of how things have worked in the past, wherein African-Americans and racial minorities and, of course, women, have sort of been left out of the board room.

How can we ensure adequate representation of African-Americans and other minorities on each state management board where the decision is made as to who sits on these boards?

Secretary SHALALA. Obviously, Congressman, we would be happy to work with you. We are decentralizing and strengthening the role of the States, but also of consumers.

Those that sit on these boards would, obviously, be representative of consumers and employers. We would, obviously, like them to be representative of the communities. I am not sure, because I haven't reviewed the entire details of the final draft, of whether we put in any guidelines for the States in that regard.

But we share your concern to make sure that there is representation, a real representation of consumers of the community on these alliance boards as well as on the national board. And what I can say is we share the goal.

How we would do that, in terms of legislation and in terms of introducing sensitivity, I think, that we would have to be very thoughtful with you about how that is possible.

Mr. TOWNS. Thank you very much, I appreciate your sensitivity to that issue.

Along these lines, one other thing that I think that we must address, as well, is the cost of living, which is different in every region of the country. You know, I don't know whether there is a Brooklyn, Miss., or whatever, but there is a difference between Mississippi and New York City.

And I think that any plan that is going to work and that will be able to provide the kind of services that are needed, must be sensitive to these issues.

Also, there is another problem. And I don't know in terms of how we deal with it, but I think that is something that we cannot ignore. That is the undocumented problem in many areas of this country. Some of those are areas that are having other kinds of problems, for instance, in New York City there is an epidemic with tuberculosis, an AIDS problem, and a large undocumented problem, and a high cost of living.

And if this plan does not address that, I think it further creates problems for the region, rather than solve the problems. How can we address that?

Secretary SHALALA. I agree, Congressman. And we have made it clear that we intend to both strengthen the public health programs as part of the President's initiative to make sure that, for undocumented immigrants in particular, while we are bringing new resources into the community because everybody will be covered so the institutions will have more resources, we need to make sure that we have programs that deal with issues like TB, like immunization. It does us no good to immunize every American citizen's child while there are children of undocumented aliens that are not immunized.

On issues like AIDS, we will have to make sure that our community health centers, the emergency rooms of hospitals, the other kinds of institutions who have traditionally dealt with both low-income populations and with undocumented persons are funded appropriately to continue our commitment to them. They will, however, not participate in the comprehensive benefit package or in the alliances or in the choice of plans, but there will be other resources available to deal with those issues.

Mr. TOWNS. Thank you, Madam Chair. I yield back my time. I look forward to working with you in terms of strengthening the proposal because I think that is a giant step in the right direction. You are further along now than a lot of folks ever thought you would be.

Secretary SHALALA. Thank you very much.

Mr. WAXMAN. Thank you, Mr. Towns.

Mr. Hastert.

Mr. HASTERT. Thank the chairman.

Madam Secretary, I have some rather simple questions I think that you can probably answer rather quickly. In the past, some of the answers haven't been exactly plain, so I would appreciate it if you would bear with me in this simplicity.

If I have a plan and I work for a company of say 125 people—my company employs more than 50 workers but less than 5,000—and my plan is fully paid by my employer, will I be able to keep my present health care plan under the President's system?

Secretary SHALALA. You are talking as a consumer—as an employee?

Mr. HASTERT. I am a worker in a small factory.

Secretary SHALALA. I would need to know a little bit more about your plan. What you will have as an employee of a small factory is your employer will pay into the alliance, and you will have some choices.

If you are currently in a fee-for-service plan like Blue Cross, which is what your employer gives you an option to, I can assure you there will be a fee-for-service plan, and I would be surprised if Blue Cross isn't participating in the community.

If you are currently in an HMO, my guess is the HMO will also be competing to get qualified as a plan. So you will have a choice, but you will have choices. And the chances are pretty good that, if you are in a plan, that plan is going to qualify for the alliance, and you will be able to choose that plan.

Mr. HASTERT. But if my plan is fully paid, then I have to go to a different system or different resource?

Secretary SHALALA. Yes.

Mr. HASTERT. Thank you. Understanding that there are——

Secretary SHALALA. Excuse me. The term fully paid, let me make sure I understand it. If your employer pays 100 percent, your employer can continue to pay 100 percent and take that as a tax deduction.

Mr. HASTERT. Oh, he can?

Secretary SHALALA. Yes.

Mr. HASTERT. So there is no limitation on what an employer can deduct, even if the plan is over the $4,500 or whatever the standard plan is?

Secretary SHALALA. Your employer may save some money because you will have some choices of plans. But if your employer wants to take care of the health benefits of his or her employees and wants to pay 100 percent, you will have your choice of plans, and your employer pays 100 percent.

Mr. HASTERT. Everything is deductible?

Secretary SHALALA. Everything is deductible.

Mr. HASTERT. Even if it is above the minimum plan?

Secretary SHALALA. If it is above the minimum—well, if it is above the comprehensive benefit package, that is, if there are some additional benefits that your employer wants to purchase for you, if that is part of your—if you are in a union, we would delay the tax on that.

If your employer wanted to add some benefits to the comprehensive benefit package, those would be—and they don't currently have them—those would be taxable. But if your employer simply wants to provide the comprehensive benefit package, wants to pick one of the—you want to pick one of the plans and your employer is willing to pay for the whole thing, tax deductible, your employer gets to pay for it.

Mr. HASTERT. Thank you.

Since I will have multiple plans to choose from and one of my physicians happens to be in one plan, I choose another—let's say my pediatrician is in plan A. I happen to choose plan B because it best fits my needs. And my internist is in plan C. Can I still keep my doctors?

Secretary SHALALA. You can in a couple of different ways. The easiest thing for you to do would be to probably—your doctors would sign up for more than one plan, and they will be allowed to do that. They can sign up for the fee-for-service plan as well as if you pick a managed-care plan.

Also, we have this discussion about point of service on whether you could access a doctor through your plan that wasn't in your plan, and there will be a way to do that.

Mr. HASTERT. Third, we've talked about subsidies and caps for small businesses. There is some confusion because I have heard that small businesses could pay as little as 1½ percent of payroll or as in Florida, 3.5 percent. I understand that is not set yet. Who does set that rate, ultimately?

Secretary SHALALA. It will be set—the small business subsidy will be set by Congress as part of the legislation. The subsidy system will be set by Congress as part of the overall health plan.

Mr. HASTERT. The 7.9 percent cap of payroll would be set by Congress also?

Secretary SHALALA. Yes.

Mr. HASTERT. But that is not a tax, right? Correctly, that is not a tax. It is a——

Secretary SHALALA. No, no, no. It is a cap on the percent of your wage base.

Mr. HASTERT. Then, actuarially, if that is a part of the premium and there is not enough money to fund the health plans, could that 7.9 percent be raised eventually?

Secretary SHALALA. I think that the answer is no. When we write into legislation what the cap is for the business, the assumption is that will be the cap, that will be the maximum that the employer pays.

Mr. HASTERT. Ever?

Secretary SHALALA. Well, unless it is changed by Congress.

Mr. HASTERT. It has to be changed by Congress.

Secretary SHALALA. It has to be changed by Congress.

Mr. WAXMAN. Thank you, Mr. Hastert. Your time has expired.

Mr. HASTERT. Thank you, Mr. Chairman.

Mr. WAXMAN. I want to call on Mr. Brown.

Mr. BROWN. Thank you, Mr. Chairman.

Madam Secretary, I commend you and the President and the First Lady for your interest, particularly your interest in preventive care. I want to ask a couple of questions about that.

In many places of corporate America there are work sites, if you will. There are aggressive employer/employee nonsmoking campaigns. There are aggressive kinds of nutrition—dietary kinds of programs that help people stay well. There are stress management and fitness centers and that kind of thing.

The First Lady last week, in response to a question that I asked, said that the—I asked her about continuing or giving incentives to employers who right now have incentives of sometimes lower health care costs they negotiate, aggressive employers negotiate that with health insurance companies. I said, how are we going to continue those sort of incentives in these health alliances? She said, by and large, the responsibility will be shifted to the health alliance.

Two questions about that. Wouldn't it be better to find ways to provide incentives to the employer itself for that, number one? And, number two, how will the health alliances pick up that responsibility if what the First Lady said is the approach that is used? Or, if not, how will they do it if the employer is providing these—if the employer is doing things and the health alliance is doing things?

Secretary SHALALA. I think our thinking is that it will be in everyone's interest, as a way of keeping down the costs of health care in the community, to encourage both businesses and individuals to use the preventive care parts of the system and to encourage workplace rules about smoking, for example, but, most importantly, to encourage employees to come in and get annual physical examinations, to get their kids immunized. Because, overall, it will hold down the costs in that community of health care for that community.

The difficulty of providing discounts for individual companies is, obviously, the difficulty of having a national plan and getting everyone covered. Getting everyone oriented towards prevention is what will in the end keep all of our costs down and make us a healthier society. So what we are talking about is a fundamental change in culture and in thinking by every American, not just by individual companies.

And while we hope that individual companies will continue their wellness programs because it will make their workers more efficient and anything that they can do to cut down the number of days that their workers take off for health reasons will help them from an economic point of view so we hope those incentives will continue.

The alliances themselves will have good reason to encourage wellness because it will help hold down the costs of the premiums. So we see the incentives for the new system continuing the incentives for business because it will help them in terms of their overall economic costs and continuing—and starting the incentives for a broader program that will turn this whole country into a commitment to prevention that will help us all in the end to be both healthier both for ourselves and for our families.

Mr. BROWN. Shifting slightly but still talking, Madam Secretary, about preventive care. When you came in front of us and talked about, if I recall, joint House-Senate committee on—talking about child immunization back earlier in the year. Sometime after that, I met with a group of people in my district in northeast Ohio, people who serve, by and large, disadvantaged people. And they talked about prenatal care and immunization.

How would the President's plan ensure that coverage will—that coverage in these cases will equal the actual care provided? How is this plan going to encourage communities to reach out for prenatal care and immunization and other kinds of preventive services?

Secretary SHALALA. Under the President's plan, every American child will have available free immunizations.

The outreach programs will be twofold: One, we expect the Public Health Service to continue national outreach programs. Second, we really expect the alliances—because one of the quality assurance judgments we will make about them is the number of children that they immunize, the number of their clients that they provide prenatal care to and well-baby care.

So the prevention pieces of the program are, in fact, among those things that we expect to measure for the quality of the plans. We are going to make that report card public.

And so the alliances themselves will encourage the plans, and the plans will have every incentive, if they want a good report card, to really put some energy into making certain that each member of their alliance, where it is appropriate, uses the prevention services, particularly the children. And we have put them up front. We have made them free so that we really can make the kind of investment we need to make as a country in our kids.

Mr. WAXMAN. Thank you very much, Mr. Brown.

Mr. Kreidler.

Mr. KREIDLER. Thank you, Mr. Chairman.

Madam Secretary, I have a couple of questions that deal with unique concerns that have been brought to my attention.

Specifically, there was one that was raised earlier and has to do with the biotech companies and the issues surrounding holding the line on the cost of pharmaceuticals, and particularly as it relates to Medicare discounts and the issues surrounding the breakthrough drug committee.

Biotech companies, by and large, are very concerned about—are really working toward products that are breakthrough as opposed to "look-alike" or "me-too" drugs. Can you respond as to how that breakthrough drug committee will work?

And, second, perhaps respond to the arguments that the President's proposal would potentially inhibit investment and research for these new types of drugs.

Secretary SHALALA. Congressman, I said in another place that 30 years from now I believe that the President's plan will be judged not by whether we got the subsidies straight or whether someone remembers what our economic assumptions were at the time but whether we continue to have and extended to every American a health care system of the first quality. That requires an extraordinary commitment to research, both to basic science, whether it is in the National Institutes of Health, in our biotech companies, in our pharmaceutical companies or at the great research universities.

We have to be extremely careful. In the process of trying to get a decent price, a fair price—for, after all, Medicare is about to become the largest purchaser of drugs in the world. That gives me certain kinds of titles. But I intend to use the authority which we are requesting from Congress judiciously to get a fair price for the Medicare system because, after all, that purchase ought to give us——

And we thought about formulas and different kinds of things for current drugs, and the industry pushes very hard because they were not anxious for us to have formularies in the Medicare program, and so we worked through a proposal in which we will get about a 15 percent discount for current drugs, but we are big purchasers as part of the process.

For breakthrough drugs, the board will have a panel and we will make some pronouncements about costs, but they will not negotiate a price with the companies. And I think it is extremely important that, while the pricing for a company may deserve some public comment, because we also want to protect those that are ill, that desperately need the drug, let me assure you that we believe there has to be a very careful balance.

There is a great difference between big powerful pharmaceuticals and a much more fragile biotechnology industry. It would be, in my judgment, a terrible thing if we in any way endanger that industry in the process of designing this plan. So we enter it as great advocates for research for the need to continue research because we see the direct connection between that and the quality of health care. And I can assure you that we go in with great enthusiasm and sensitivity to discuss this with the industry.

Mr. KREIDLER. Thank you, Madam Secretary. I appreciate your recognition of the difference between those two types of firms.

Second, I would like to ask about the need that I think we all recognize for some solid, measurable cost controls in a reformed system. And as we talk about a national budget there is always the issue of how that translates for individual States and how we will control costs. Perhaps you could describe to me in some way how—kind of walk me through it, if it is possible, how that will translate from the national budget, then down through the system to individual premiums, and how that works out particularly for individual States.

Secondarily, how that would treat States that already have lower costs than—significantly lower costs in some cases than the national average.

Secretary SHALALA. Congressman, again, some of these are sort of caught up in reviews at the moment. Basically, we have avoided using the term for some time of budget, global budgets, national budgets, because what we intend to do is to give the States some ideas and some enforceable premium targets. So we are avoiding an overall budget on the entire system as opposed to trying on the average to reduce the rate of growth of the premiums.

What you are talking about, though, and what your concerns are are something that is a concern that we share, and that is, are we locking in existing costs to each State so that there is never a chance for a low-expenditure State on health care ever to raise what many people perceive as both its expenditures as well as its quality? And whether there is a way of getting some balance between the high-cost States because, clearly, the premiums are going to be set on the basis of reality on what a State is currently spending and how you bring together the differences between States.

All I can say to you at this point in time is that is a classic issue in American Federalism, one in which this Congress has struggled on almost every equalization debate that has to do with any kind of a national program, whether it has been education or health.

And what we will try to do is, while we have to base our recommendations on existing costs, we also understand the need for investment in underserved areas in the United States and to make certain that we have been sensitive to our need to invest both resources and personnel in rural areas and underserved urban areas, in places that simply have not had the opportunity. Part of that investment is getting everybody covered. We add resources to every rural area in America by simply giving everybody the health card, and in that process every rural provider suddenly has a whole new set of people that can pay.

And all I can say to you is that there is a balance there and that we will work very hard to try to achieve it.

Mr. WAXMAN. Mr. Hall.

Mr. HALL. Thank you, Mr. Chairman.

Madam Secretary, I also, of course, laud the goal, and I realize that we are in the early stages and everything sounds wonderful now—and it does sound wonderful to me and I think to the American people. And short of a governmental takeover of health care in this country or short of taxing small businesses or all businesses out of business, I support the goal, and those are things that are still to be seen.

You have been unable to answer some specific questions today, telling us that in about 2 weeks you would be able to. Is that the time you think that the bill will be introduced?

Secretary SHALALA. Yes.

Mr. HALL. We have waited since May of this year. We thought it was coming in May. Then we understood with the illness in the family and then the following death of the family it would be put off. We are 5 months later now, though, and it is going to be introduced in 2 weeks without any question, so at that time we can ask you some questions?

By the way, Dr. Rowland was inquiring about passing some less contentious but very favorable acts that would be favorable toward the goal you seek—and I know he is referring to a letter that the Doctor and many other members wrote to the President on October the 1st. And it is my understanding—I don't have this direct—that the President thought that the letter was a very good suggestion, but—well, Mr. Clinton thought it was a good suggestion, but Mrs.

Clinton didn't. And you follow Mrs. Clinton's testimony here, is that correct?

Secretary SHALALA. Yes, but representing the President.

Mr. HALL. You follow her, but you report to him?

Secretary SHALALA. Yes, sir.

Mr. HALL. I don't think that is a bad idea.

Let me ask you this. Say General Motors, for example—it is my understanding that they have about a 19 percent payroll deduction, the 19 percent of their payroll which amounts to somewhere around $24, $25 billion. Now, do they get the 7.9 percent like everyone else?

Secretary SHALALA. No.

Mr. HALL. Are they held to that figure that the unions have negotiated them to or they negotiate themselves to?

Secretary SHALALA. Yes. And they expect to be held to that number.

Mr. HALL. Is there not a provision in there, a 10-year opt-out?

Secretary SHALALA. Well, obviously, these contractual arrangements will be renegotiated, but within their numbers, of course, their retirees number. And there is a discussion within the administration about the possibility of picking up the employer share of retiree health costs so that percentage of their payroll could well come down as part of that.

We have indicated in our discussions with those that are part of collective bargaining agreements that at least for possible tax cap of any benefits beyond those offered in the comprehensive benefits package that we would wait a number of years—I think the number is 10—before we would start taxing those extra benefits. General Motors actually could make a decision to join the alliance, and, if it did that, it could use the 7.9 percent right now, the 7.9 percent tax cap——

Mr. HALL. They would probably be sued by their shareholders if they didn't, wouldn't they?

Secretary SHALALA. General Motors—those that have collective bargaining agreements intend to hold to those collective bargaining agreements. They are legally binding for them. And while General Motors and organizations that have over 5,000 have indicated they intend to stay out of the system—and I think it is important to know that everyone intends to keep their current commitments, their current collective bargaining commitments.

At some point somewhere down the road they could join the alliance and get in under the cap later, but those—that would go way beyond what current negotiations are.

Mr. HALL. Well, they could. And I am sure they are good citizens and I am not seeking out General Motors, but does your act, the one you are going to introduce in a couple of weeks, require them to?

Secretary SHALALA. No.

Mr. HALL. Are we doing it at their generosity?

Secretary SHALALA. No. My understanding of the legislation, as it is going to be drafted, is that GM is not eligible for the first 4 years for the 7.9 percent cap if they join the alliance. We do not anticipate that there will be many large corporations over 5,000 that choose to join the alliances initially.

77-929 O - 94 - 3

Mr. HALL. And the percent of their payroll could come down and who would pick that up other than very small businesses across this country?

Secretary SHALALA. I don't think it would be the—their percent of payroll may be down by that time depending on what Congress decides to do with the retirees.

Mr. HALL. These are questions that we will ask you after you introduce the package.

My time is up. Thank you, Mr. Chairman.

Mr. WAXMAN. Thank you, Mr. Hall.

I want to recognize members for a second round should they wish to ask further questions. But before I do, Secretary Shalala, I do want to indicate to you that members will certainly want to ask you questions in writing and have you respond for the record.

Secretary SHALALA. Yes.

Mr. WAXMAN. We would appreciate it if you would.

It is hard for the Chair to gauge how many members may want to ask questions for a second round, but if—well, six. If the six—seven. I know you have—the Secretary has to be out of here by 12:30. Let's go 4 minutes each, which I think is a fair allocation, and let's hope no one else comes in the room.

Mr. HALL. Maybe somebody will leave.

Mr. WAXMAN. Let's hope it is not the Secretary.

Let me start with some questions of my own. I want to ask you about the flexibility that the plan offers to States to incorporate the Medicare program under their alliances. From what I have seen so far the only conditions for giving States a Medicare waiver are that they offer the same or better benefits as regular Medicare and provide such coverage at a cost no greater than what Medicare would otherwise spend. Can you give us some additional thinking about what other assurances States would be required to give and how Medicare beneficiaries could have some involvement in such a waiver decision?

Secretary SHALALA. Well, it would be a waiver decision, Mr. Chairman. And let me start out by saying that, both in our initial decision not to integrate Medicare recipients into the program directly and in the decision to make the option available to the States, we are proceeding with great caution to reassure the senior citizens in this country that we have no intention of making their situation less secure. In fact, we want to make it more secure than it currently is.

More importantly, even with us providing the option for the States of coming in with a waiver, it will be scrutinized. We will ask for and encourage public comment by the communities itself and assume that the States themselves will carefully consult with their senior citizens before they come and talk to us about the possibility. We will be firm about making certain that there would not be lesser benefits, lesser access for our elderly and disabled citizens and will proceed with great caution.

While you have outlined the list of the specific things that we have already thought about, I am sure there are other things that we will want to take into account, and we ought to work with you and your committee very carefully to make certain that the criteria are very carefully drawn.

Mr. WAXMAN. So you would want to pin that criteria down very carefully, and the waivers would only be granted under careful scrutiny?

Secretary SHALALA. Absolutely.

Mr. WAXMAN. Since becoming Secretary earlier this year you approved broad Medicare waiver requests from Oregon and Hawaii. Other States, including Tennessee, have requests for such waivers pending and others like California are planning to submit such requests. Will the States that have received or will receive these Medicaid waivers be required to implement health care reform by January 1, 1997, like all other States or will they be able to delay implementation until their demonstrations have run their course?

Secretary SHALALA. We will expect them, Mr. Chairman, to come into the system by 1997. And we have indicated either in writing as part of the waiver that I approved or in some other way that the waiver is contingent on the President's plan coming into effect. So we expect all the States to come in by 1997.

Mr. WAXMAN. One last question. If you could, to finally put to rest the concerns of some of us have expressed about Medicare, whether the cuts are going to be too great in Medicare, which could result in a lack of access to doctors or some cutback in the quality as the Medicare budget is squeezed down, would this administration promise us that if we look at those figures carefully and see a real likelihood that there is going to be a disservice to the Medicare beneficiaries that those cuts will not be advanced by the administration?

Secretary SHALALA. Mr. Chairman, we, obviously, are looking for ways to shift resources to the new system, but we want to do it in a way that does not do any harm to current recipients of that program, and I can assure you that what we are sending up is a list of our best efforts. But we fully expect to work with this committee to make sure that in that list is not anything that would harm any of our senior citizens or disabled recipients in terms of the quality of their health care, and we will work very closely with you on that.

Mr. WAXMAN. Thank you very much.

Mrs. Collins.

Mrs. COLLINS. Thank you.

Madam Secretary, the President's proposal calls for health plans to contract for 5 years with community health centers, such as the Mile Square Health Center in my district, and other clinics which are determined to be classified as essential providers of health services for local communities.

In Chicago and other areas where there are many of these facilities, the question is twofold. Would all the health plans in the area have to contract with all of the essential providers in that area or could those health plans choose to limit the service to certain income areas is part one of the question. And part two is, why should the policy end after 5 years? Is there some assumption that after 5 years it will have less value?

Secretary SHALALA. Madam Chairwoman, we see the community health centers in this country as an important resource. They have played a strategic role in helping our low and moderate income, those undocumented aliens in accessing some health care, though not the level, obviously, that the President's plan is—the resources and the refurbishing and the invigorating of the community health centers that we plan to do is—and the requirements that the plans will have to contract with essential providers are put in place both for transition, because we understand that simply folding large numbers of low-income Americans, some of them ethnic minorities, will take some transition and some sensitivity. So we expect them to continue to play that leadership role.

They also may well become—because they suddenly will have a group of people that they have been serving that have health coverage, many of them will become integrated part of the plans themselves and will be active providers. We want to provide them with those kinds of opportunities.

The 5-year requirement was put on because we do see them going through a transition and the entire plan going through a transition. But we expect to say to you in the legislation that the Secretary will review what the experience has been with the essential providers after 5 years and come back to the Congress and have a conversation about how their roles have changed, about what our expectations ought to be for the future, what kind of funding streams we ought to provide for them in the future.

We will know more after 5 years, and in some ways it is a kind of sunset to make sure that they understand their transitional role as they are making changes, that we understand that we are trying to figure out how all these pieces fit. So it is a kind of responsible recommendation, we believe, but also reflects our commitment to the populations that they have so well served.

Mrs. COLLINS. The other part is that no health plan—am I safe in assuming that no health plan in a given area would be able to limit any kind of service that certain low-income areas receive?

Secretary SHALALA. That is correct.

Mrs. COLLINS. OK. Thank you.

I yield back the balance of my time, Mr. Chairman.

Mr. WAXMAN. Thank you, Mrs. Collins.

Mr. Stearns.

Mr. STEARNS. Thank you, Mr. Chairman.

Madam Secretary, you have said several times during this hearing that your CPI cap is not important because new money is coming into the system. I thought we would explore this.

I have a chart over there where it says 1988. It is 1998, just a little bureaucratic error here. This chart is taken from the very last page of the September 7, 1993, working draft of the health care plan and summarizes national health care expenditures. It compares the CBO current services baseline of health care expenditures without reform versus health care expenditures under the Clinton reform proposal.

This chart shows a $227 billion cumulative cut in national expenditures from the CBO baseline. It also shows these cuts from the CBO baseline rapidly accelerating in 1999 and the year 2000, and the cuts will dramatically accelerate during the next century.

Now, on the other hand, the Clinton program will be completely phased in by 1998, and this means, of course, the following:

There is entitlement one. Approximately 37 million individuals will be newly covered under the basic benefits package.

Entitlement number two, according to your analysis, two-thirds of all Americans will have a benefit package as good or better than the plans on the market today.

Entitlement three, there will be a new $72 billion Medicare drug benefit.

Entitlement four, there will be a new $80 billion long-term-care benefit.

Entitlement five, there will be a new $25 billion benefit for retirees not yet eligible for Medicare who are over the age of 55.

And last, but not least, there will be a $91 billion in budget deficit reduction.

Madam Secretary, could you tell this committee how we are going to slash national health expenditures by $227 billion while we are simultaneously creating five new Federal health care entitlements, each of which will be adding billions to national health expenditures?

Secretary SHALALA. Yes, Congressman. Without specifically referring to the specific numbers, which I would be happy to do when we get our final numbers up here, let me say that, at the beginning, the new health care plan will be financed out of employer and employee contributions extended to every employer and employee in this country who will be expected to pay something. And, therefore, there will be new resources put into the system.

The use of the word slash in terms of reducing the rate of growth in public health expenditures is exactly reducing the rate of growth. And, as I have indicated, for the Medicare numbers in particular, it will be coming in with specific recommendations. All we have done, which has been tough to do—there is no question that it is very tough to do—is to slow down the rate of growth. But the new resources being put into the system are not only our attempt to slow down the rate of growth for public expenditures but the employer and employee base which is added to the system.

Specifically, we have identified a cigarette tax as well as a tax, a payroll—a contribution by corporations who are going to stay out of the system, and we have identified and will identify that with a number somewhat over I think in the September 7th draft of $100 billion. I don't have that number pinned down at this point in time.

And so we intend to finance the system both out of savings which are produced by slowing down the growth in the public system out of new employer and employee contributions, out of two new sources of revenue, one the cigarettes and the other the alliance pieces, and by taking the public money that is currently being spent by the Medicaid system and putting it into the alliances to reimburse the alliances and to pay them for both the premium costs as well as for the other costs associated for the populations that are being phased in, the Medicaid populations.

So there are, in fact—we, in fact, go over the baseline for the first 3 years of the new system, and then it starts to come down. So we add significant new resources to the system to cover those that are now coming into the system, and we try to slow down the growth both in the private system as well as in the public system with the assumption that there are, in fact, savings in the system that we currently are—a combination of savings related to getting paperwork out of the system, getting waste out of the system.

So it is a combination of all of these things that provide the financing for the system, but there is no question that eventually we intend to slow down the growth of the system. How fast we can slow it down, what those assumptions are will be part of the debate we have when we actually get our numbers up here.

Mr. STEARNS. Thank you, Mr. Chairman.

Mr. WAXMAN. Thank you, Mr. Stearns.

Mr. Wyden.

Mr. WYDEN. Thank you, Mr. Chairman.

Madam Secretary, the great gap for senior citizens is long-term care with senior citizens getting wiped out in a matter of months as a result of these crushing bills. Earlier on, I heard some discussion from Mr. Magaziner about the possibility of setting up a voluntary part C of Medicare. Medicare has got A for hospitals, B for doctors, and the idea is that people could make voluntary contributions with the money pool to purchase long-term care.

What is the status of that? Can we expect that in the initiative in a couple of weeks?

Secretary SHALALA. I would not want to make a prediction. We certainly have had it under discussion. A number of members of the administration have been interested in that kind of an approach.

The one that we have, of course, talked about is the long-term-care reform package which includes a major expansion of home and community-based services which will help those that prefer to—would very much like to stay at home as opposed to going to institutions. And I couldn't make a prediction at this moment about whether that proposal will come out in 2 weeks.

Mr. WYDEN. I hope it will. I am one who has long supported it, since my days at the Gray Panthers, and would like to work with you more.

Let me wrap up by asking you a question on medical ethics. I think you know I feel strongly about the Oregon plan. I think, ultimately, you have to make some judgments about priorities. The administration's proposal has been very clear. We have heard some comments on the other side that it rejects government rationing of health care. The administration's proposal doesn't.

I am concerned that the private sector is going to be trying to figure out ways to ration, and we are going to have trouble seeing it. What kinds of rules and protections does the administration envisage to try to guard against private-sector rationing?

Secretary SHALALA. We believe that the quality assurance system that we are building in, which, after all, is at a completely different level of sophistication than what we currently have, will help us to encourage the plans to make medical judgments and not cost judgments that will affect the quality of care of individuals.

Let me say, though, that the current system is the worst kind of rationing. When you don't have access to health care, you are rationed out of the system. If you are poor in this country and you don't have access to—and you are working poor and you get up and you go to work in the morning and you go to a business that can't afford or doesn't want to cover your health care, that is the worst kind of rationing because you are stuck with an emergency room care or a public health clinic maybe for your kids' immunizations.

So the current system is the most terrible kind of rationing. What we need to do is to make sure that we put enough resources, obviously, into the plan, that we keep the premium increases, and I think this will be part of the debate, at a reasonable level.

So the judgments that are made are medical judgments, are thoughtful medical judgments, not judgments made on the basis of whether—on the amount of resources that are available. That would be a very delicate balance. But the quality assurance system will give us some part of the information as will, I am sure, very careful congressional and governmental oversight.

Mr. WYDEN. Let me ask also that in the days—in the last 2 weeks that we be given the opportunity with the consumer groups to try to work on the grievances and appeal procedures and the like because I think you clearly are trying to guard against this kind of private sector rationing, and they are anxious to do it. And I know your folks want to pursue it with them as well.

Secretary SHALALA. Yes. And, as you well know, we are very enthusiastic about pursuing it. We, obviously, don't want to add another layer of bureaucracy, but we must add consumer protections so that we have credibility in the system. Security also means knowing that you are going to get the kind of care that you need within the system, not simply having access to a system. So those protections need to be built in, and I appreciate your comments.

Mr. WAXMAN. Thank you, Mr. Wyden.

Mr. Upton.

Mr. UPTON. Thank you again, Mr. Chairman.

Madam Secretary, just to reflect for a moment on Mr. Wyden's question. As I understand it, the Oregon plan which a lot of us have watched with interest, would likely lose its waiver, would it not, to the President's plan?

Secretary SHALALA. Let me say that—only that the kind of impact analysis of the President's design versus the Oregon design I am sure that both the Oregon people and our people are beginning to think about, so I would not want to prejudge the level of State flexibility or how the people of Oregon, who went through a very thoughtful process, intend to fit the decisions they made into the overall structure of the President's new plan. And certainly there is State flexibility that they will be looking at.

Mr. UPTON. That leads into my question here. As we all look for innovative ways to reduce costs, one of the systems that has been set up in Michigan is a program called HealthConnect, which is a system which provides preventive health care for folks up to 125 percent of the poverty line. It is a partnership between public and private interests that provides general care, a whole host of things, and it will meet the needs of about 31,000 folks in Kalamazoo County. I would be interested to get your thoughts on how such programs will interface with the President's plan. Also as we look at innovative ways to reduce costs and order the President's proposal, particularly with self-insurance.

We have a ceiling—or a floor, rather—of 5,000 individuals for self-insurance firms to fit under. One of the plans that was offered by my colleague, Jim Cooper, which has gotten a fair amount of attention in recent days, is his plan which lowers that ceiling from 5,000 to 100 individuals, which is a real bonus, I think, to a number of communities that have watched this self-insurance system really work. And I would be interested in your comments on both those.

Secretary SHALALA. Well, the 5,000 number was set—and it is fundamental, we believe, to the focus of the plan—and that is to provide a large enough pool to make certain that we have not the current system which is a highly fragmented system, but a large enough pool so we can absorb the differences among citizens and so we can keep premium costs down. If we let too many companies opt out of the system, we get a narrower and narrower and perhaps, some people believe, a more expensive pool. And so community rating and sharing the burden of the community's health costs requires a large enough pool, and that is our concern about the pool.

On the Kalamazoo program, I do not know it, but I would be happy to look at it with you and provide some comments.

Mr. UPTON. But, in fact, as you look at these pools, the self-insurance industry thinks that they can compete quite favorably to pools in 5,000 or more. And, in fact, they would see that they have done a pretty good job at reducing costs, providing benefits to employers and employees and their families. And, in fact, they will be shutting their doors under the President's plan if the 5,000 person floor is kept versus something considerably smaller.

Secretary SHALALA. Well, I think that by exempting only those companies that are 5,000 or over, which—

After all, part of the explanation is the multistate nature of those companies. We are putting everybody else into these large enough alliance pools that provide the resources so that we can hold down premium costs and have a truly national program as opposed to allowing everybody to go their own way as they currently do or just dealing with the problems of some small businesses.

And so the 5,000 cutoff, while we are happy to have further discussions—and I am sure Congressman Cooper will be having those with us—I think there really was an intent there to leave a large enough pool.

Mr. WAXMAN. Thank you, Mr. Upton.

Mr. Hall.

Mr. HALL. Madam Secretary, let me be real brief with my questions.

It is my understanding when the First Lady was here that she indicated that the passage for this legislation is contemplated by the end of 1994. Did I hear her correctly or am I thinking of another——

Secretary SHALALA. Actually, the first time she told me we were going to pass it by the end of 1993. So I think that, in consultation with all of you, the discussion of the timing of this is that there would be hearings this fall, hearings in the spring and then passage soon after that.

Mr. HALL. And, hopefully, by the end of 1994?

Secretary SHALALA. Absolutely.

Mr. HALL. One other thing to clarify the 100 percent deductibility of insurance premiums. That is for self-employed and for large employers?

Secretary SHALALA. Large employers can deduct their portion of their contribution to the health care premiums of their employees.

Mr. HALL. Actually it would be 100 percent?

Secretary SHALALA. It could be 100 percent, yes.

Mr. HALL. Believe it or not, I have read your statement. Most of our people in our office read them and then tell us what you said. But I read it with great care, and I notice in almost every page that you refer to that we provide every American with security. Reality of American lives tomorrow, available to all of our citizens, Americans choice of health, citizens right to choose, provide every American worker and their families with a health plan, new system so that Americans can enjoy its benefits, every American an insurance card. Not exactly that, but close. Americans to be conscious not only of the cost of their care but the savings possible.

On every page, all Americans will have a coverage for an annual physical exam, capital to improve the lives of the people we represent. And, finally, it allows us to keep the promise of America. I enjoyed that. I enjoyed reading that.

I notice on page 6 you say we will strengthen our commitment to community and migrant health centers and the National Health Service Corps to guarantee that promised benefits reach all of the people whether they live in Harlem, N.Y., or Waycross, Ga. Would you add to that even if they live there illegally and in contravention of the Immigration Act?

Secretary SHALALA. Congressman, we have indicated that undocumented aliens are not eligible to participate in the comprehensive benefit package in the national health plan. But, simultaneously, we do feel a responsibility to help communities who are currently continuing to bear health costs, emergency room costs and some prevention costs and some primary care costs for people who are here illegally, and that we will continue to help those communities, though many of those health centers that you identified will now have—most of the people that they currently serve covered by the President's plan.

But there will continue to be a need in certain parts of the country to help communities to bear the costs because this country does not turn people away from emergency rooms, and we cannot turn away if we are going to keep all of our citizens healthy those that not only need emergency room care but their children that may need immunizations. But we have no intention of offering the comprehensive benefit package to non-citizens or illegal aliens.

Mr. HALL. Do you have a cost figure for undocumented aliens?

Secretary SHALALA. Well, we will have——

Mr. HALL. Or a percentage?

Secretary SHALALA. Yes. We will have a number for our commitments in public health, and we will be having a discussion with this committee about what the disproportionate share program—though maybe not as it is currently structured, what those kinds of payments will need to be for existing institutions to continue to provide support when we come in with the legislation.

While there are a variety of different numbers of undocumented aliens depending on—it is hard to count people who are here illegally. What we do know is the burden on hospitals, on community health centers, and we do know what kind of a commitment we believe it is appropriate for this country to continue that keeps us all healthier and also is, at the same time, a moral commitment.

Mr. HALL. I yield back my time. You are going to take that into consideration? That will be a part of your bill, to address the undocumented alien problem?

Secretary SHALALA. Yes, we will.

Mr. HALL. Thank you.

Mr. WAXMAN. Thank you, Mr. Hall.

Mr. Greenwood.

Mr. GREENWOOD. Thank you, Mr. Chairman. Dr. Shalala, I would like to take off where we left off last time. The President, the First Lady, and you have said that what you want to do, fundamentally, is build on the current employer-based system. You don't want to take a sharp turn in the road or turn the current system upside down.

And I appreciate that line of reasoning. But, I think there is another line of reasoning which says that the current system is a voluntary system in which employees negotiate benefits and employers provide those benefits for the most part when they can and if they can. When you go to an employee mandate you are, in fact, taking a very sharp turn in the road and turning away from the system that has brought us to a very high level of health care quality in this country.

I think this is significant because human beings behave very differently when they are acting under systems of incentives than they do when they are being coerced into doing things. You said 30 years from now you think that the President's system won't be judged on whether or not you have got your subsidy numbers straight today but by the long-term results. And I am concerned that among the long-term results could be going from a State where we have a lot of people with jobs and no health care to a State where we have a lot of people with health care and no jobs, so it is important.

Three quick questions, and these are the concerns that I have about what happens under an employee mandate.

First off, under this system, what would prevent a lot of employers, knowing that now they have to provide a stated level of benefits, from shopping for their employees? Why wouldn't they turn away the married individual with a spouse and lots of children at home, and hire the single individual because it is going to cost them less to insure that person?

Two, what do you do when the employee is required to pay 20 percent and, as we find it in every other place where people are billed and don't pay their bills, he/she doesn't pay his/her 20 percent? Does he/she get health care anyway or not? Does he/she go to jail? Does he/she get his/her wages garnished? What happens?

Finally why wouldn't employers increasingly go to a contract basis with workers rather than saying, you are going to be an employee of this firm, and I am going to be required to pay your benefits. Why would they not have a great incentive to say, I would like to take you on as a self-employed contractor. You are responsible for your health care.

Secretary SHALALA. On the married versus single person, the married person actually will be cheaper for the employer. And I think that employers——

Mr. GREENWOOD. I am assuming—I am not assuming two spouses working. I am talking about one spouse working.

Secretary SHALALA. The employer will be paying a portion of—oh, you are not assuming two people in the family?

Well, let me simply say that the employers in this country hire people on—normally do not ask people what their status is. And the difference between having a married worker and an unmarried worker, as the population changes in terms of women going to work, is not going to—is not going to be a significant factor which, in my judgment, an employer could use as a strategy if they are trying to get a product out or to run a business. So that I am not convinced that the differences will be significant.

And, in fact, assuming that more spouses are going to work, I think that will sort itself out for an employer because they will have some single people and some married people.

Second, on people that don't pay their bills—let me answer the next two very quickly—the alliances will use a collection agency, go after people to make sure that they pay their share the way any other private business or organization will do where we assume that most people will pay their portion.

And, third, there will be no advantage on a contract basis because if the majority of the individual's income is gotten from that company, they will have to pay health care benefits for that individual. So there will be no way of getting out from under the system.

Mr. GREENWOOD. OK, thank you, Dr. Shalala.

Thank you, Mr. Chairman.

Mr. WAXMAN. Thank you, Mr. Greenwood.

Secretary Shalala, you have been very helpful and patient in a marathon session this morning. We thank you very much for it. I think you have given us more information than we have had before, and when we get the legislation we will see the fine print and then we will continue our discussions with you and others working on this bill for the President. Thank you very much for being here.

That concludes our business for the day. We stand adjourned.

[Whereupon, at 12:28 p.m., the subcommittees were adjourned, to reconvene at the call of the Chair.]

HEALTH CARE REFORM
Labor and Business Views

TUESDAY, OCTOBER 12, 1993

HOUSE OF REPRESENTATIVES, COMMITTEE ON ENERGY AND COMMERCE, SUBCOMMITTEE ON HEALTH AND THE ENVIRONMENT, AND THE SUBCOMMITTEE ON COMMERCE, CONSUMER PROTECTION, AND COMPETITIVENESS,

Washington, DC.

The subcommittees met, pursuant to notice, at 10 a.m., in room 2123, Rayburn House Office Building, Hon. Henry A. Waxman, chairman, Subcommittee on Health and the Environment, and Hon. Cardiss Collins, chairwoman, Subcommittee on Commerce, Consumer Protection, and Competitiveness, presiding.

Mr. WAXMAN. The meeting of the two subcommittees will come to order.

Today, along with the Subcommittee on Commerce, Consumer Protection, and Competitiveness, we hold the third in a series of hearings on President Clinton's health reform plan, which guarantees coverage for comprehensive benefits for all Americans.

As we hold these hearings, both praise and criticism of the President's plan will be heard. In evaluating these arguments, we all need to keep in mind that we have a health care crisis in this country, and that if we persist in doing nothing—as we have for the last 12 year—things will continue to get worse, as they have for the last 12 years.

Last week, the Census Bureau reported that 37.4 million Americans had no health insurance coverage in 1992. That was an increase of 2 million from the previous year. Even more troubling, the data show that, for the fourth straight year, the percentage of the population covered through employment-based health insurance dropped. About 600,000 Americans lost employment-related coverage between 1991 and 1992. And, in four States and the District, more than one-fifth of the population had no health care coverage at all in 1992.

Obviously, we can't allow these trends to continue. We need universal coverage. The only question is, how do we get there?

There are three ways to pay for universal coverage. One is to rely on contributions from employers and workers. Another is to require every individual to purchase coverage—this would require large subsidies if it is to work. And the final way is to impose a broad based tax. The Clinton plan builds on the current system and adopts the first approach.

Today's witnesses represent workers and employers who will be asked to participate in financing coverage for all. Although none of us has the benefit of all the details of the President's plan, we have asked our witnesses to give us their initial reactions to the President's plan as they understand it, and to describe its impact on them.

Some of our witnesses will oppose the President's reliance on employer and employee financing. We will ask them to give us their ideas on alternative approaches to achieve universal coverage in this country by 1997, as the President has proposed.

I want to welcome all of our witnesses to this hearing and thank them for taking time to be with us—many of them on very short notice. I look forward to their testimony.

Before calling on our first witness, I would like to recognize my distinguished colleague and co-Chair for this hearing, Congresswoman Collins.

Mrs. COLLINS. Thank you. I want to welcome everyone to today's joint hearing of our two subcommittees on President Clinton's health care reform plan. I am pleased to co-chair with my colleague and friend, Chairman Waxman.

With today's hearing, we will begin to receive comments from the American public on the health care proposal. This Thursday, October 14, we will have another hearing to hear testimony from consumers, insurers, and providers.

Both labor and business are directly feeling the impact of shortcomings in today's health care system. The reactions of these two groups to the President's plan are fundamental to the effort for reform.

Much attention has been drawn to the employer mandates of the proposal and its impact upon employment. However, the need to get a hold of rapidly rising health care costs is more important to the creation of jobs and maintaining our competitiveness.

A hearing before our subcommittee a year ago highlighted how health care costs in our manufacturing sector were costing us thousands of jobs. We have also watched with alarm as small businesses have faced health care insurance costs that are far in excess of those of their larger competitors who were able to negotiate special deals.

I would like to thank today's witnesses for joining us to discuss these issues. I would like to conclude my opening remarks so we can maximize our time with questions for our witnesses. I yield back the balance of my time.

Mr. WAXMAN. Thank you. Mr. Greenwood?

Mr. GREENWOOD. In the interest of getting on with the hearing, I will dispense with the opening statement.

Mr. WAXMAN. Mr. Synar? Mr. Sharp?

Mr. WAXMAN. Without objection, all the opening statements Members wish to insert in the record will be made part of the record.

[The prepared statements of Mr. Manton, Mr. Stearns, and Mr. Franks follow:]

STATEMENT OF HON. THOMAS J. MANTON

Mr. Chairman, I am pleased to be here today for this joint hearing of the Subcommittee on Health and the Environment and the Subcommittee on Commerce, Consumer Protection, and Competitiveness to consider the President's Health Care Reform Proposal. I think the witnesses we will hear from today, representing organized labor and large and small business, will provide the committee with important insight into how the President's plan is being received outside the beltway. Moreover, as this committee begins consideration of this major initiative, it is imperative that we weigh the plan's effect on the commercial sector of our economy, and consider how it will affect the Nation's work force and business owners and managers.

Currently, in addition to dealing with inflationary health care costs, because our Nation lacks a comprehensive universal health care plan both of these groups are forced to pick up the tab for health care of the uninsured and the unemployed. Today we will hear if the public is willing to accept the status quo or is ready for a change.

Since the President has not yet submitted his plan in the form of legislation to the Congress, many specific areas of the plan are unclear. Instead of focussing on the unknown, I am interested today in discussing with our witnesses the bill's broad objectives and basic structure and learning their perspective on the plan. Hopefully, today we will begin to answer what I consider to be the threshold question which must be answered before the President's or any other comprehensive health care reform plan can pass: whether both workers and employers in this Nation are committed to ending the health care crisis from which our Nation currently suffers.

I thank the witnesses for being here and look forward to their testimony.

STATEMENT OF HON. CLIFF STEARNS

Thank you Madam Chairwoman: Today we meet again to discuss the issue of the President's health care reform proposal. We have had the September 7th draft of the proposal for some time now, but our progress is hampered by the fact that we have neither the completed legislation, nor the data behind the few figures that are included in the President's proposal. Last week, Secretary Shalala promised us that we would have the final legislation and data in a little over a week from today. While our witnesses today are not from the administration, I feel compelled to again emphasize the need for the President to act swiftly and decisively in delivering the bill to Congress so we can give it proper consideration.

Today's panels represent labor, large business, and small business. Prior to coming to Congress, I ran a small business, and I know firsthand how hard it is to meet a payroll week after week. Employers and employees have a very close relationship, particularly in small businesses. Employers rely on their employees to provide an honest week's work in return for an honest week's wage; employees rely on their employers to provide their continued livelihood. That means you must use good business sense to stay in business, so that you can keep meeting that payroll week after week.

We don't know whether small businesses will have to contribute 3.5 percent or 7.9 percent of their payroll to health insurance premiums under the Clinton plan because we still don't have the exact numbers. What we do know is that there are some small businesses who don't have 3 percent, 8 percent, or even 1 percent, to contribute to any new mandate. We need to think long and hard about what another employer mandate might do to these businesses.

I recently got a letter from Charles G. Brown, owner of a small trophy company in Tampa, Florida. He employs about 50 full-time employees and currently cannot afford to insure them. All of his employees earn over $12,000 per year and approximately 30 of his employees are married.

He has looked at the Clinton Plan and estimates that it will cost him at least another $130,000 per year to insure his employees. He's asked tough questions like whether providing health insurance coverage is worth closing some of his stores or laying off workers. He asked where the Federal, State, and local governments are going to make up for the lost tax base. And finally, he asked what small businesses like his are going to do when the President tells them they have to pay more when they don't have any more to pay with.

I hope our witnesses today help me find some answers to Mr. Brown's questions. Small businesses like his are the lifeblood of our economy, and the President's plan does not clearly address what we are going to do for them. Perhaps the answers lie in alternatives to the President's plan. Maybe it's time to apply some good business sense to this problem.

Thank you, Madam Chairwoman.

STATEMENT OF HON. GARY A. FRANKS

Mr. Chairman, thank you for holding these hearings today. I am very concerned about how this proposed health care package will affect America's small businesses.

I am especially concerned about how the idea of mandating employers to provide health care along with employment will affect today's economy. Employer mandates will cost jobs, reduce wages and inevitably lead to an unfair system of targeted employer subsidies.

Small business wants to have the tools to form their own privately managed, competing purchasing cooperatives, and not be required to go through the government sponsored alliances.

The Clinton plan is proposing a payroll tax, and a payroll tax has to be paid whether a company makes a profit or not. Once it is in place there is little an employer can do to keep it from going up.

We need to be concerned that we keep the American economy healthy along with the American work force. Universal health care provided by employers will not help the uninsured if there are no jobs for them to fill.

Mr. WAXMAN. Our first witness is Lane Kirkland, the president of the AFL-CIO, which speaks for over 14 million working men and women throughout this country.

Since assuming the presidency of AFL-CIO some 14 years, Mr. Kirkland has championed organized labor's long-standing commitment to universal coverage, cost containment and quality care.

Mr. Kirkland last appeared before the Subcommittee on Health and Environment exactly 2 years ago. At that time, a variety of health care proposals, including the Pepper Commission proposal, had been introduced.

Because the Bush administration was opposed to national health care reform, Mr. Kirkland called on the Congress to put together a compromise legislative package on its own.

Today, circumstances are much different than they were in October 1991. Most importantly, we have a President who is personally committed to achieving universal coverage and he wants a bill he can sign on his desk by the end of this Congress. That presents an opportunity we have not had since Mr. Kirkland took the helm of the AFL-CIO.

Mrs. COLLINS. I, too, take this opportunity to welcome Mr. Lane Kirkland, president of the AFL-CIO, to our hearing today. We are sure that he will add a great deal to the full scope of this debate that we are having here on the health care reform package.

I yield back the balance of my time.

Mr. WAXMAN. Mr. Kirkland, we are delighted to welcome you back to our subcommittee hearing. We are looking forward to your presentation. Your prepared statement will be made a part of the record in its entirety and we would like to ask you to proceed however you see fit.

STATEMENT OF LANE KIRKLAND, PRESIDENT, AFL-CIO

Mr. KIRKLAND. Thank you, Mr. Chairman. I submitted my full statement for the record and I have a few remarks.

Mr. Chairman and distinguished members of the committee, thank you for the opportunity to appear before you as Congress embarks on what working people fervently hope is the final leg of the long journey to national health care reform.

Health care for every American has long been one of labor's most cherished goals. I cut my teeth on this issue when I joined the staff of the American Federation of Labor in 1948. In that year, we campaigned along with President Truman for passage of the Wagner-Murray-Dingell bill.

If justice and common sense had prevailed, we would have carried the day. Unfortunately, we did not. For more than four decades, while the rest of the industrialized world has transformed access to health care from a privilege to a universal right, labor has been on the often lonely barricades of the fight to keep America in step.

Is it not time now after all these years for America to join the human race as far as health care is concerned?

Mr. Chairman, thanks to the vision and dedication of President Clinton and with the hard work and craftsmanship of the First Lady, we are finally ready to do it.

At our biennial convention last week in San Francisco, the AFL-CIO unanimously endorsed the President's health care reform plan which he unveiled 3 weeks ago.

The delegates did that because the plan embraces the basic goals and principles long advocated by the AFL-CIO. It would guarantee a comprehensive package of benefits to all people regardless of age, income, health or employment status.

It would contain costs by holding increases to a budget while forcing savings from a bloated and fractured purchasing system. It would maintain and improve the quality of care through evaluation procedures and steps to inform consumers so they can choose the best available health plan.

It would spread the costs of health care fairly and equitably. It would be a major step toward integrating the health care portion of workers compensation, and it would relieve industries of the staggering costs of providing coverage to early retirees.

It would finally end the link between employment and health insurance coverage, a link that has created a system that provides economic rewards to businesses that reduce or deny coverage to their workers.

The country is incapable of enduring much longer the health care system like the one we now have. Costs are skyrocketing. Insurance coverage and benefits are declining. Health care is bankrupting businesses, families and governments. If present trends continue, and they will continue in the absence of comprehensive reform, health care will consume one-fifth of our national economy by the year 2000.

By and large, labor union members now have health insurance coverage but that is a small comfort to us. Maintaining that coverage is a battle our members fight every time they go to the bargaining table. Spiraling health care costs are eating up resources that should be used to improve their wages or other benefits.

Two-thirds of our strikes are over the health care system. With the system deteriorating as it is, even those union members with the best plans cannot be sure if their coverage will be there for them if they need to use it perhaps next year or maybe a few more years down the road. Besides, they are honest and decent human beings and they are tired of seeing their friends, loved ones or neighbors or any fellow Americans have to suffer such terrible consequences simply because they do not have the good fortune to be covered by health insurance.

AFL-CIO will vigorously oppose any effort to water down the President's legislation with so-called voluntary or market-based concepts. Nothing short of full scale restructuring of the health care system, including universal coverage, cost controls, and a coordinated health delivery system will solve the current crisis.

Mr. Chairman, President Clinton and Mrs. Clinton have responded in fine fashion to the challenge of crafting a national health care reform plan that is just what the Nation so desperately needs. If you grasp this opportunity and enact the administrations's proposal, no longer will employers be seduced by the comparative economic advantages of denying health coverage to their employees or suffer because they provide it, no longer will working men or women, or anyone for that matter, live under the hanging sword of health insurance loss. And generations yet unborn will link this President and this Congress with their health and well-being.

Mr. Chairman, now is the time. This is the plan. Labor is for it. Go forth and pass it into law. Thank you, Mr. Chairman.

Mr. WAXMAN. Thank you very much, Mr. Kirkland.

[The prepared statement of Mr. Kirkland follows:]

93-27

**AFL-CIO President Lane Kirkland
before a joint hearing on
the Subcommittee on Health Care and the Environment
and the Subcommittee on Commerce, Consumer Protection
and Competitiveness of the House Energy and Commerce Committee
on
Presidents Clinton's Health Care Proposal**

October 12, 1993

Good morning, Mr. Chairman and members of the Committee, my name is Lane Kirkland, and I am President of the American Federation of Labor and Congress of Industrial Organizations (AFL-CIO). I am pleased to be testifying before the Committee this morning on President Clinton's national health care reform initiative.

While we still await the legislation itself, enough is known of the President's proposal for substantive comment and discussion and I want to share with you the AFL-CIO view for how that proposal addresses the health needs of workers and the country in general.

Delegates to the AFL-CIO convention, meeting last week in San Francisco, unanimously adopted a resolution endorsing the President's proposal and committing the Federation to a strong effort to secure comprehensive health care reform based on it in this Congress.

The convention position was predicated on the fact that the President's proposal meets the AFL-CIO principles for reform. Specifically, we find it to be a comprehensive proposal which addresses all the facets of the health problem before us. It does so in the "uniquely American way" which many have predicted would be necessary to bring our nation into line with the rest of the industrialized world, and we believe this is a strong point in favor of the President's proposal.

We also believe that, in proposing the comprehensive benefit package which the plan includes, the President has recognized the importance of assuring traditionally well-insured Americans, such as union members, that national health care reform can and will mean improved benefits, not the bare-bones approach which the health insurance industry would have us adopt. Significantly, the proposal includes a new drug benefit of immense importance to retired workers, and the kind of home and community-based long term care program which will provide seniors with much needed care in a dignified manner.

The President has wisely ignored the advice of many so-called health experts and declined to make taxation of health benefits a major part of his proposal. While union members will be asked to contribute through taxation of the kind of supplemental benefits included in the top tier of health benefit plans, the plan provides a ten year period during which wages traded off for health benefits in recent years can be built back.

One of the most important parts of the plan is that it effectively breaks the tie between employment and health coverage. While still largely employer-financed, the plan means that no longer would health coverage depend on where, or whether, an individual worked. Once enrolled as an infant, individuals would continue to enjoy the same coverage and receive care in the same way through her or his life. Whether at home, in school, in the workforce, or retired, all Americans would have the security of knowing that health care would be available to them.

The plan establishes universal health coverage in the U.S. for the first time. In this way, as in others, it represents a major step toward the kind of health program long supported by the labor movement and by the distinguished Chairman of this panel.

Another aspect of the plan central to its potential in solving America's health crisis are the tough cost control measures it contains. By controlling costs and effectively severing the link between employment and health coverage, President Clinton's health care reform would dramatically improve the budgets of workers, their families and the businesses for whom they work. By lifting the burden of early retiree health costs from the payrolls of employers, the proposal would provide much needed relief to operating budgets. And the system of global budgets and aggressive purchasing arrangements represented by regional alliances holds the promise of restoring American competitiveness in many industries.

One of the most encouraging aspects of the plan, overall, is its consumer orientation. Through consumer participation in the boards which will control the system's operation at the national and regional levels, this plan is a major step forward from our tradition of provider-dominated health care.

The plan also contains important provisions to free physicians and other care-providers to focus on their patients rather than their paperwork. It further addresses some of the long-term structural problems in the health care workforce by providing greater opportunities for frontline health care workers to learn and practice their skills.

Delegates to the AFL-CIO convention last week were enthusiastic in their support for the President's proposal. They look forward to working with you to enact legislation built on the President's proposal in this Congress.

We greet the unveiling of this plan with the hope that, at long last, America's working families will be relieved of the twin burdens of rising health care costs an diminishing coverage. No longer will they have to wonder whether they will be covered should they or a family member become sick, injured or unemployed. No longer will retirees be denied the long overdue promise that society as a whole will protect them from the discriminatory practices of our profit driven health insurance system and from the nightmare faced by the millions of elderly uninsured Americans.

For over fifty years, the U.S. labor movement has struggled to win universal health coverage as a right for everyone, as enjoyed by the citizens of other major industrial countries. Repeatedly, we have seen our efforts thwarted by powerful interest groups with a financial stake in preserving the current system.

Meanwhile, we have negotiated comprehensive health coverage for our members and their families. Thanks to the struggles waged by union members, the vast majority of workers enjoy employer-paid health coverage. The labor movement also spearheaded the effort to win health insurance for elderly and poor Americans.

Skyrocketing health-care costs have brought the patchwork U.S. system to the brink of collapse. The number of uninsured Americans has risen steadily as structural changes shifted employment towards the service sector where health benefits are less generous. Industry wrestles with the burgeoning costs of retiree health costs. The health-care industry itself has been racked by the misguided de-regulation policies of the Reagan era.

Health-care costs also threaten to bankrupt businesses, families and government budgets. If present trends are not reversed, health care will consume one-fifth of our national income by the year 2000, diverting society's scarce resources from pressing investments and social needs.

Nothing short of full-scale restructuring that achieves universal coverage and a coordinated health delivery system will solve the crisis of the health-care system. The AFL-CIO will continue to oppose proposals for change that rely on uncontrolled market forces or on incremental measures, such as insurance market reforms, because they will fail to control costs or to improve access. Such measures will only serve to delay comprehensive reforms.

For probably the first time in the history of health reform in the U.S. all the major stakeholders -- consumers, providers, and purchasers -- have joined the reform dialogue. Consumer polls show overwhelming support by the American public for fundamental reform of the health-care system. Bipartisan support for major action on health care is growing in Congress.

The AFL-CIO Executive Council met in February 1993 and adopted a set of principles to guide our discussions with the Administration on its health reform proposal. The President's health care reform plan meets the basic principles long advocated by the AFL-CIO including:

- **Universal coverage and security** -- It would guaranteed a comprehensive package of benefits to all people, regardless of age, income, health and employment status and it represents a major step towards integrating the health care portion of workers compensation.

- **Cost containment** -- The new system would hold health care cost increases to a strict budget and force savings from a bloated and fractured purchasing system. New coverage for early retirees will provide a significant economic boost for many industries.

- **Quality** -- It would include procedures to evaluate the quality of care and provide information to consumers so they can choose the best available health plan.

- **Fair financing** -- The cost of health care would be spread equitably. The plan would end the competitive advantage now enjoyed by employers that offer little or no health coverage to their workers.

President Clinton's initiative -- and his political commitment to health reform -- offers the best hope for achieving our long-sought goal of universal health coverage.

Labor is prepared to be fully mobilized every step of the way. We intend to defend President Clinton's comprehensive proposal against those who will seek to water it down and pare it back. Labor is committed to spearheading a fighting coalition of consumers, senior citizens, businesses large and small, community groups, and progressive providers.

The AFL-CIO calls on Congress to act expeditiously to enact comprehensive health reform.

Mr. WAXMAN. I will start off the questioning myself. We hear one of the criticisms of the Clinton plan that since it requires all employers to contribute to the cost of health care coverage that it will result in a loss of jobs especially in the small business sector.

As a representative or working men and women and their families, the AFL-CIO knows a thing or two about creating and preserving jobs. Since World War II, organized labor has pushed to establish employers' responsibility for health care coverage for their workers.

How do you respond to the argument made by the National Federation of Independent Business and others that requiring all employers to provide health care coverage will result in a loss of as many as 3.1 million jobs as well as reduced wages and reduced benefits?

Mr. KIRKLAND. Well, Mr. Chairman, we simply don't believe it. We believe more jobs are at risk from failure to enact a comprehensive system of health care coverage than by the enactment of it. The jobs of those whose employers provide health care coverage are at risk when there is competition with employers who would gain a competitive advantage by refusal to do so.

I don't know where those figures—not being an economist or a statistician; figures are the prisoners of assumptions. Those assumptions can be grounded in pure fantasy, as I think these are. Perhaps they got them from the back of a Cracker Jack box.

But I think they bear no relation to reality whatever.

Mr. WAXMAN. As you noted in your testimony, the Clinton plan would limit the tax deduction or exemption of the employer paid premiums only after 10 years and only for benefits not included in the basic package.

This is intended to allow wages traded off for health benefits in recent years to be built back. In contrast, the bill introduced by Mr. Cooper last week would immediately limit the amount of health care premiums that employers would be allowed to deduct to the premium for the lowest cost plan in the area.

What impact do you think the Cooper proposal will have on your ability to build back wages traded off for health benefits in recent years?

Mr. KIRKLAND. I think it would be very damaging to that prospect. I think the opportunity to readjust the relationship between health care costs and other aspects of the employment bargain ought to be preserved, as it is in the Clinton proposal.

We have seen many, many of our organizations negotiate increases in employment costs, all of which for some years have been required to be committed to the health care plan in order simply to preserve benefits.

We have organizations affiliated with us who have had no wage increases for years because every penny of the negotiation amount secured in collective bargaining has had to go to preserve existing benefits.

That situation is deeply damaging, I think, to the well-being of American workers. It accounts partly for the decline in real wages over the past few years.

We think that the Clinton proposal is a realistic and equitable approach to that.

Mr. WAXMAN. Mr. Kirkland, when Members of Congress look at this health care issue they get uncomfortable with the opposition coming from some special interest on the one hand and a lot of employers don't want the mandate that they cover their employees.

On the other hand, a lot of the medical establishment would like to see fewer cost controls, in fact they would like to see no cost controls over the system. So there is appeal to the idea that maybe what we ought to do is drop the mandate, drop the cost controls, turn to a market-based system and take away the tax deductibility for health insurance in order to drive consumers to make better choices and, as a result, to bring about more cost efficiency in the system.

How do you think your members would respond to a bill that would not cover everybody but would take away their deductibility for their employers probably leading to higher costs for health insurance?

Mr. KIRKLAND. I think, Mr. Chairman, far from being an approach toward health care reform, this would move away from it and would in some respects leave us worse off than we are now.

I find it very hard to understand the attitude of employers who wish to continue to deny their own employees decent health care. I cannot believe that most employers, small or large, as human beings, and I presume some of them are, would not welcome the opportunity to be able to cover their employees at a reasonable cost. That seems to me just simple, not only common sense, but simple humanity.

The idea that a spokesman for a small employer saying this is a God-given right that they not have to cover employees when there is available, if this legislation is enacted, a means of doing so on an equitable basis that does not create any competitive disadvantage for them but puts them on a level playing field with those employers who do acknowledge a certain human responsibility, to oppose such legislation makes no sense.

As far as the health professionals go, I believe they have made considerable progress in their attitudes and positions from what I recall back in the 1940's when the health profession, the organizations of the medical profession by and large were adamantly opposed to anything.

I would remind the chairman, as he probably recalls, there was a time when the health profession even regarded what are now called HMO's, group practice, as socialized medicine. They were bitterly opposed to any suggestion that such a thing as salaried practice might be acceptable, much less the organization of doctors into groups to provide prepaid medical care. That was regarded and treated and denounced as wholly unacceptable and totally disruptive of the American way of life.

Yet today we find those organizations, including the insurance carriers, putting forward preferred providers organizations and HMO's as the answer to the entire health care crisis, structures that they bitterly opposed at their inception.

The labor movement was among those who pioneered in the creation group practice plans and preventative medicine approaches provided through those systems. We had to fight medical societies every inch of the way. Sometimes in the initial cases here in Washington, DC., it had to go to the Supreme Court.

Mr. WAXMAN. Thank you. I want to recognize Mrs. Collins for her questions.

Mrs. COLLINS. Thank you. Mr. Kirkland, at our subcommittee hearing held 2 years ago, testimony was given that health care costs accounted for about $1,100 for each automobile produced by the big three automobile companies in the United States.

Under the President's plan, how would you expect that figure of $1,100 to change and how would the change affect your membership?

Mr. KIRKLAND. Well, of course in terms of the automobile industry, like a number of other industries, the steel industry and most of our manufacturing industries where we have been able to negotiate pretty good health care plans, the cost of sustaining those plans places those companies at a severe competitive disadvantage in the global economy where they must compete with auto, steel, and electronics producers from all over the world.

This is one good reason why the enactment of this kind of legislation is long overdue.

Mrs. COLLINS. So if the money that was saved from the health care costs would be used for R&D and capital expenditures, et cetera, it would certainly be beneficial to America as a whole?

Mr. KIRKLAND. We would regard some of those costs at least as a form of wages and we would want to negotiate the disposition.

Mrs. COLLINS. We would certainly want to put some of those in there, wouldn't we? The President's proposal allows companies with over 5,000 employees to create their own corporate alliance.

Would you want that number to stay that high or to become lower or do you have any feelings about that and how it will affect your membership?

Mr. KIRKLAND. Would you go through that once more?

Mrs. COLLINS. The President's proposal allows companies with over 5,000 employees to create their own corporate alliance. I guess my first question is would you want that number to be higher or lower?

Mr. KIRKLAND. I would prefer that it did not exist at all. I am not so keen about this option of opting out, but if that is what it takes to get the legislation through, I guess we will have to live with it.

Mrs. COLLINS. Would you think that more of your membership might get better coverage if it were lower?

Mr. KIRKLAND. I think more of our membership and I think the plan would be strengthened if there were no option.

Mrs. COLLINS. So you don't like that at all?

Mr. KIRKLAND. No, but we accept it as one of the "If that is necessary to broaden the support of the plan to the degree that is necessary to get action, we are prepared to live with it."

Mrs. COLLINS. Due to the steep escalation of health care costs, many employers have been forced to withhold wage increases in recent years. If the President's plan, complete with its cost containment mechanisms, were enacted, would you push for substantial wage increases in the first few years of the new system or would you expect an upward trend of wages to occur gradually over a number of years?

Mr. KIRKLAND. Mrs. Collins, I see the future only very dimly. The decision as to what the individual affiliates of the AFL-CIO might seek at the bargaining table is their decision depending upon the factors that weigh on that decision, the unemployment levels, the relativity of the search for assurances on contracting out, job security.

There are a host of issues at the bargaining table. I cannot say flatly what one issue would emerge as dominant.

Mrs. COLLINS. Let me ask you about Honda and Toyota. If they were, for example, to join a regional health alliance, would you expect that their average health care costs, which are now low because they have few retirees and a young work force, would actually increase under the President's plan so that their costs would be rated on the basis of a community that would have elderly and other citizens whose health expenses would be kind of high?

Mr. KIRKLAND. Mrs. Collins, that is the very essence of social insurance which I think should be the dominant consideration here, the maximum spreading of risks so as to make it equitable for all on pretty much the same basis.

If you isolate particular groups and in effect experience rate them because they may just be starting in business with a very young work force, you place a penalty on the employment of older people. You fold discrimination into the system. You give employers incentives to discriminate against older workers or other workers who might, according to insurance companies or actuarial statistics, have an experience of a high incidence of illness. I think that is part of the problem that we face today that we ought to be addressing and solving.

Mrs. COLLINS. Thank you. My time has expired.

Mr. WAXMAN. Thank you, Mrs. Collins. Mr. Greenwood.

Mr. GREENWOOD. Mr. Kirkland, my understanding is that under the Clinton health plan only employers with fewer than 5,000 full-time employees will be allowed to remain outside of the regional allowances, or employers obligated under collective bargaining agreements to jointly trusteed Taft-Hartley multiemployer plans.

Mr. KIRKLAND. That is not my understanding of the legislation, sir. I don't believe that to be the case.

Mr. GREENWOOD. As soon as I finish the question, you can straighten me out. Apparently these arrangements will be treated in the same manner as corporate alliance if they cover at least 5,000 employees in total.

The question is: Under the Clinton plan, will it be the case that a union will determine whether the employees of a particular employer will be covered under a regional alliance or a separate collectively bargained multiemployer plan?

Mr. KIRKLAND. The first premise, it is my understanding that the option election was incorporated in it at the insistence and at the urging of some large corporate employers. Given that, it is obvious that one has to, in order to have a measure of equity, include that same right for those who are in jointly trusteed plans.

As I understand it, the proposition would enable the joint trustees, not the union alone, none of these plans are administered by the union alone, the law requires them to be jointly trusteed. So it is a common decision of the employer and worker trustees of those plans to make that decision.

Mr. GREENWOOD. Let me ask you a related question. You expressed some resistance to the notion that employers with more than 5,000 employees could maintain their own self-insurance. That is part of the plan.

Mr. KIRKLAND. Yes. We argued against it. We lost that argument.

Mr. GREENWOOD. If union workers working for such a company are enjoying better health care coverage than they would if their choices were limited to those offered by the alliance, wouldn't those workers be better off in terms of the health care that they receive under a system in which the employer maintains their self-insurance?

Mr. KIRKLAND. No, sir, because if they have a contractual agreement with the employer to provide a certain level of benefits, some of which may not be included in the basic plan, those benefits would continue.

Mr. GREENWOOD. Even if they were shifted into the alliance?

Mr. KIRKLAND. Yes.

Mr. GREENWOOD. Let me shift gears and ask a more philosophical question. You referred in your opening statement to the right to health care. You also referred, I think in answering a question, to the thought that you weren't sure where employers get this notion that they have a God-given right not to offer health care.

The rights, the Bill of Rights in this county are freedoms, they are not benefits. They are opportunities to freely express ones self, to avoid self-incrimination, et cetera. We don't have rights in our Constitution that are benefits, the right to receive something from the government.

Mr. KIRKLAND. I am not addressing the Constitution, sir. I am speaking from the standpoint of justice and equity.

Mr. GREENWOOD. The question is, do you have any concerns whatsoever about rights that people feel are their entitlements when those rights don't require any particular effort by the recipient; a right to a benefit from the government whether you are working or not, whether you choose to work or not?

Mr. KIRKLAND. I don't know of any right or any privilege that you get for free in this country, sir. Certainly, people who work for a living are not getting what they earn for free and they are worthy of their hire.

Mr. GREENWOOD. I think under the Clinton proposal your benefits continue after your employment ceases?

Mr. KIRKLAND. That is right.

Mr. GREENWOOD. We are not going to see eye to eye there.

Mr. KIRKLAND. Apparently not. But I say that is an earned right just as unemployment insurance is an earned right.

Mr. GREENWOOD. You also referred to the fact that it is time for America to join the human race with regard to health care. I think you will grant that although we have not been successful at providing full access to every American to health care, that we do have the best health care in the world. Would you not concede that?

Mr. KIRKLAND. For some.

Mr. GREENWOOD. For most. Would you concede that as well? Do you have any concern that with global budgeting, which we have not had before but which we will have under this proposal, that the quality of care, particularly the quality of care that is derived from innovations in research and technology, might be threatened?

Mr. KIRKLAND. No. I think it might well be improved.

Mr. GREENWOOD. Thank you, Mr. Chairman.

Mr. WAXMAN. Thank you, Mr. Greenwood. Mr. Brown.

Mr. BROWN. Thank you, Mr. Chairman.

Mr. Kirkland, you are certainly to be applauded for the negotiations over the years that so many of your internationals and locals in your internationals have done to secure good quality health care for so many of your members.

I am a little confused about what happens to your future negotiations when the major bargaining goals are not so much health care as they have been in the last couple of rounds and you can shift back into other benefits and wages.

What will happen in the next 5 years, if you could predict, if the Clinton health care plan passes in terms of most of your internationals', most of your locals' negotiations on wages and benefits? Can you kind of flesh that out a little for us?

Mr. KIRKLAND. I find it very hard to give you an answer, sir, because we are an organization of voluntary affiliates who make their own decision as to what their agenda is at the bargaining table. They face many, many problems.

Collective bargaining is a problem solving mechanism and whatever those problems are, they are addressed at the bargaining table. Whether those problems are the prospect of plant closures, which is an affliction we have suffered for a good many years, whether it is training, health and safety, we have a terrible problem in this country of health and safety in the workplace. That reaches the bargaining table. We have been trying to address it that way. You name it. Whatever afflicts the American people, whatever is going on in our economy, in our society, eventually hits the bargaining table and has to be addressed in that way.

Fortunately, we have a system that enables workers to address it where they have collective bargaining. We are facing the problem of large scale layoffs, cutbacks of downsizing. Those issues need to be addressed in an equitable way at the bargaining table where there is collective bargaining.

The larger problem in this country is that there is not enough collective bargaining and too many workers are left subject to either employer dictates or to the minimum standards set forth by State action.

We think collective bargaining is preferable. It has proven itself. It is the only system that we believe to be compatible with a democratic society. The only alternatives are employer or State dictation. We want to see that strengthened. I think it has proved itself as to what happens when health care costs become regularized and spread equitably over the society.

Of course, most of our unions will regard that, any savings that flow from that, as opportunities to channel at least a portion of those savings into neglected areas where they have had to sacrifice over a good many years in order to preserve health care.

Our major problem in recent years in bargaining has not been to make gains in the health care field or getting broader or better benefits. It has been preserving what we have. The drive has been on by employers to cut those benefits and to escape those costs. That is where conflict has arisen at the bargaining table.

The trade unions have been in a purely defensive position trying to resist employer aggression in this area, seeking to escape those costs and to shift their burdens.

Mr. BROWN. The philosophy apparently of the Clinton administration in drafting this legislation is that health care with no out-of-pocket expenses encourages some overutilization of services evidenced by the fact that there is a copayment required in most services in this bill.

Many of your locals over the years have negotiated health care benefits with no copayments. Is that going to erode the sort of seamless support, if you will, that organized labor seems to have for this bill? And, second, is that something you are going to advocate, not having a copayment and, three, if you could kind of roll this together, is overutilization not an issue that way?

Mr. KIRKLAND. There is total copayment in all health plans negotiated across the bargaining table. Those represent foregone wages. Those are paid for by the worker, not by the employer exclusively. Benefits or wages are foregone in order to secure those benefits so the copayment is total.

As regards to the arguments for so called copayment or deductible provisions, I think they are utterly fallacious. They suggest that workers are the ones that decide when they have to go to the hospital and undergo expensive medical procedures. Those decisions are made by doctors.

The most effective ways of controlling cost increases have not been through copayments but by other approaches that are built into many of our systems that have worked well: adequate preventive care, early treatment, second opinions, and a variety of those objective devices to address costs.

Mr. WAXMAN. Thank you, Mr. Brown. Mr. Manton.

Mr. MANTON. Thank you, Mr. Chairman.

Mr. Kirkland, let start out by saying I for one am impressed by the AFL-CIO's support for the President's plan. Clearly, if we closely examine any legislative initiative of such broad scope as health care reform must necessarily be, we will all find something with which we will disagree.

It is easy to criticize the President's plan. It takes more vision and commitment to join in the process and work to make health care reform a reality. So I am pleased that the AFL-CIO has joined in the campaign to make health care reform a reality in this country.

What are your impressions of the President's plan's requirement that employees must pay 20 percent of their insurance premiums while the employer's 80 percent contribution will be capped by 7.9 percent of payroll? Do you have any suggestions about how this provision could be improved?

Mr. KIRKLAND. If the argument for copayment is to control utilization and therefore control costs, we think that is fallacious. If by copayments in those plans you arrive at a level of cost and a distribution of the burden that simply makes it more feasible to enact a comprehensive health care plan, that is another matter altogether.

I resist and regard as wrong headed and misguided the idea that this is a device to control overutilization. I simply think that is not true and is not the proper and most constructive way to do it. If it is viewed as simply a method of distributing the overall costs, that is another matter altogether as long as the opportunity to negotiate a different approach and a different method of cost treatment remains available as it is in this plan.

Mr. MANTON. Thank you. I yield back the balance of my time.

Mr. WAXMAN. Thank you, Mr. Manton. Mr. Kreidler.

Mr. KREIDLER. Thank you, Mr. Chairman.

Mr. Kirkland, I have noted that some Members of Congress, particularly some Senators, Senators Chafee and Dole, et al, have proposed a requirement that individuals purchase health insurance and that the employers would only have an obligation to present plans at group rates to their employees. This is a theory that the savings generated by operating health care in that way would come back as increased wages to the individuals.

I would like to ask two questions in relation to that. First, to what extent do you think that would happen, meaning that the savings in decreased health care expenditures would come back in increased wages?

The second would be: Do you think that building health care delivery around a budget would inevitably lead to rationing?

Mr. KIRKLAND. Well, on your first question, sir, whether any savings derive from shifting the costs of health care on to the backs of the individual as against the group through collective bargaining, whether that would result in higher wages, only if the employees are organized and are in a position to have a voice on that matter; otherwise, no.

Remind me what was your second question.

Mr. KREIDLER. It really dealt with the question Mr. Greenwood asked you earlier and perhaps to seek out a further elaboration, if you build health care around a budget, do you think doing that leads to rationing?

Mr. KIRKLAND. We have rationing now, sir. Nothing is more highly rationed in this country than health care, and it is rationed by cost and availability. It is adverse rationing. It puts the more fortunate and the richest first in line and the least fortunate and the poorest out of the line altogether.

If we enact this legislation, we substitute the inequity for that and a system of addressing what deficiencies exist in this system in terms of low quality care. There is a great deal of high quality care in this country, very expensive high quality care. There is also a great deal of low quality care, a great deal of unnecessary procedures, unnecessary operations, I think, that has been validated and proven time and time again which derived from the fact that there is inadequate peer review, peer checks, peer standards.

We believe that element of quality and availability of good quality care will be vastly improved and not diminish by such legislation.

Mr. KREIDLER. Thank you, Mr. Kirkland. I would like to commend you and the AFL-CIO for the pragmatic way in which you are approaching health care reform. I think many of us would prefer to approach health care reform in a different fashion, but realizing we have to work with what is possible, this is an important step in the right direction and I commend you for taking this position.

Mr. KIRKLAND. That is precisely the way we established it. Years ago, we established the health care committee. We had a variety of views within the trade union movement of the ideal way of providing health care.

We had strong views. We decided early on that the issue was far too important and too urgent to allow the idea to become the enemy of the necessary. We decided to approach it by setting forth certain basic criteria that were the important questions, universal access.

That is really the gut question, quality, the preservation of quality and the enhancement of quality overall, control of costs, the effective control of costs and a comprehensive schedule of benefits.

We decided, and we worked our way through it after extensive and heated debate about how ideal this approach would be against that. But on those basic principles, we had no disagreement whatever. We had unanimity. We have had an attitude that manifested itself throughout. The time was long overdue for action now. Rather than quibble and lock ourselves in an ideological position on behalf of one or the other, an approach that effectively meant those criteria ought to be acceptable.

It was also important to develop an approach that would have the broadest possible degree of acceptability with the public and other interested parties. Employers have a legitimate interest. Employers have a legitimate interest. We should not be hidebound and we should not become hidebound on it. We maintain that degree of flexibility that enabled us to, I think, address these critical issues effectively. I think it had some bearing on the plan that has evolved.

Mr. WAXMAN. Thank you, Mr. Kreidler. Mr. Hall.

Mr. HALL. Thank you, Mr. Chairman.

Mr. Kirkland, first I commend you for your many, many accomplishments and for the respect that you engender and for the time you have given in preparation and the time you have given to this committee.

I note in your opening statement you say that at your convention you all determined that we ought to make every effort to secure comprehensive health care reform in this Congress. I am sure you are aware of the fact that it has been testified here by one member of the President's cabinet, and I believe by Mrs. Clinton, that the Congress will not be able to address this until the end of 1994.

Mr. KIRKLAND. That I believe is still this Congress.

Mr. HALL. Already. But you think that is still the end of 1994.

Mr. KIRKLAND. This Congress, yes. We did not define which session. The sooner the better, but it is complicated.

Mr. HALL. No one can argue with the proposal for coverage, the ability to obtain coverage, the right not to be cancelled. The right to take it as you transfer from job to job. Certainly, I agree, and

I think most Americans agree, with the proposition that we need health reform and that everybody should be covered. I think many may have a different attitude as to how we are going to be covered, where the money will be coming from. I think that is to be expected. We cannot know that until we have seen the bill. We have not seen the bill. We were told we would see it 2 weeks from, I believe, last Tuesday and we had looked forward to it.

Let me ask you about some of the larger corporations. As you know, the fear is that small businesses are going to have to pick up the tab. That is the fear that I get in my district, and my district is probably a little more conservative than some of the other districts up and down here. Even though I have the old Rayburn district, they voted 70 to 30 percent for Goldwater against Johnson. So they are fearful that small businesses will be wiped out. I hope that doesn't happen. I pledge to work to that end.

Let me talk to you about General Motors. Are you aware of the fact that they have spent about $19 million a year or 19 percent of their payroll for their health care?

Mr. KIRKLAND. Yes, sir.

Mr. HALL. Under the Clinton proposal, it is my understanding—and once again I have not seen it, I have just listened—employers pay 80 percent or 7.9 percent of the payroll, right?

Under that, if the unions and GM have negotiated in good faith, and over hard times and good times, General Motors health costs have been negotiated to 19 percent of their payroll, under this they would only pay $7 billion rather than the $19 billion. That leaves $10 billion shortfall somewhere if General Motors opts out of it; is that your understanding?

Mr. KIRKLAND. I can't agree with those figures.

Mr. HALL. If anyone else can help you there. I can use some help, too.

Mr. KIRKLAND. I think they are roughly ball park.

Mr. HALL. My question is: If their health costs are 19 percent of their payroll and actually they are paying about 40 percent of the retirees' health care costs, you or someone has done a very good job for the people you represent that negotiated them up to a high position comparing to the 7.9 percent of the Clinton plan.

Now, I guess my question is: Will they have to negotiate themselves out of that? Will labor and those that represent labor hold them to the high degree of—and the high percentage of their payroll or are you going to allow them just to opt out and take the 7.9 percent.

Mr. WAXMAN. Will the gentleman yield to me?

Mr. HALL. Yes.

Mr. WAXMAN. Let me just clarify that the fact that my understanding of the legislation, over 5,000 would not have a 7.9 percent limit. They would not have any limit.

Mr. HALL. Since I haven't seen the bill, Mr. Chairman, I don't think either one of us can know that unless you have seen some things I haven't seen.

Mr. WAXMAN. My summary.

Mr. HALL. Your word has always been good. If that is a fact, that helps to answer the question.

I guess the next question would be, there are provisions for grandfathering for 10 years. Is that at the option of the company?

Mr. KIRKLAND. Let me address several questions involved in that. One is, one reason that the costs of employers who do provide health care coverage is so high is the degree of cost shifting that is in the system now. And I have seen estimates upwards of 25 percent or so of their costs, occasioned by the fact that they are bearing the costs of unprepaid health care for those who do not have coverage.

Those costs are shifted by the medical system that exists by the hospitals, and by the doctors that provide those services to others that do not have insurance.

Mr. HALL. So the cost would be shifted, then, to small business is what you are saying?

Mr. KIRKLAND. It would be spread back the way it should be and not loaded entirely on the backs of those who do provide care.

Mr. HALL. If there was a chance to opt out and a large company like GM or any of the other major companies didn't opt out, they would probably be sued by the shareholders, wouldn't they?

Mr. KIRKLAND. No.

Mr. HALL. If they had the opportunity to either pay $7 billion or $19 billion and they didn't opt out to pay the $7 billion, would they not be suable by the shareholders?

Mr. KIRKLAND. You will have to address a lawyer about that, sir.

Mr. HALL. I think my time has expired. I thank the Chair.

Mr. WAXMAN. Thank you, Mr. Hall.

Mr. McMillan.

Mr. MCMILLAN. I thank the chairman and I apologize for being late. You may be interested, Mr. Kirkland, to know that I arrived at the airport and the battery was dead so I had to struggle to get in here. It turned out there was a drain on the battery of 12 volts. The mechanic couldn't figure out where it was. Over the weekend, this drain killed my battery and the car wouldn't start, which is, I think, one of my concerns in that some of the features of the President's proposal would drain certain resources and load them on the backs of the others.

I think that is what I am most concerned about, the way the Health Security Act is structured. I don't think anyone here denies that problems exist in our health care system. I think we all agree on that. The question is, how we get to resolving these problems.

It is my understanding that under the Clinton plan, union workers currently receiving supplemental benefits in excess of the national benefit package would be "grandfathered" into the Health Security Act and would continue to be tax free to the employee and tax deductible to the employer. I believe the implicit assumption in the Clinton plan is that the basic package will cost somewhere around $1,800 per capita.

I am not positive what the average health care benefit is in automotive union contracts, but I have been told all things included, it may run as high as $10,000. Is that substantially correct?

Mr. KIRKLAND. It seems high to me, sir. I don't think—you would have to address that question to the actuaries in the auto industry.

Mr. MCMILLAN. Well, I think that is certainly a definable figure and one that we should focus on. The President and Mrs. Clinton justified the exception for unions——

Mr. KIRKLAND. It seems very high. The cost for providing health care under the GM plan is quite high.

Mr. MCMILLAN. The President and Mrs. Clinton justified the exception which I referred to based on wages foregone in exchange for health care benefits. However, while the health care benefits are deductible to the employer and not taxable to the employee, additional wages to the employee would have been taxable.

How do you justify union workers receiving a substantial income equivalent without paying income taxes on social security assessments while others do not receive the same benefit? Doesn't this mean that people who have no health coverage or a limited program are actually subsidizing broad coverage for others?

Mr. KIRKLAND. No, sir, I don't think you can go from there to there, logically. What we have here in terms of what needs to be done is to try and create a system under which everyone has access to the benefits that are needed to afford decent security and decent protections against the cost of health care. I do not think that the—if you want to do this through taxation, be my guest, be my guest and we will be prepared to suggest some equitable forms of taxation to do this through an entitlement system.

But if that is not to be the case, to reject the idea of an entitlement—tax-based entitlement system and to turn to the taxation of benefits that now exist is, to my mind, the most destructive way to approach the resolution of this problem. You cannot resolve the health care problems of people by taxing their health insurance benefits.

Mr. MCMILLAN. Well, while that is an interesting twist, I did not suggest that you tax employee's benefits. I am saying, though, that there may be an argument that the limitation on deductibility ought to apply to the same basic standard package which is essentially what the President is trying to extend to the uninsured or underinsured in America.

Mr. KIRKLAND. All I can say, sir, you may wish to approach this problem and raise money by taxing employee health insurance benefits.

Mr. MCMILLAN. No, I didn't say that. I have a plan to do it without taxes.

Mr. KIRKLAND. That would be a misguided approach to it.

Mr. MCMILLAN. Under the President's plan, he is going to have to find an enormous amount of additional revenue. He has already proposed sin taxes at close to $100 billion a year, which is ridiculous, but that is not going to be enough. He talked about $124 billion worth of savings from Medicare by holding down the rate of increase and yet at the same time he has turned around and offered $157 million of additional benefits to Medicare recipients.

There is no way that we are going to solve the problem of the underinsured in America unless we have some equal treatment in terms of the tax laws. We are not talking about raising taxes, we are talking about fairness and equity under the tax laws.

The Clinton proposal is loaded with extraordinary benefits for people who have health care contracts, union or otherwise, that are

77-929 O - 94 - 4

far in excess of what the proposed plan proposes to guarantee to all American citizens. I think my time has expired.

Mr. WAXMAN. Mr. McMillan, your time is up.

Mr. Kirkland wants to respond?

Mr. KIRKLAND. I disagree.

Mr. WAXMAN. Very brief response.

Mr. KIRKLAND. I would be very happy to discuss with you a system, if that is the way that you all think, that this is the quickest way to get enacted a program of comprehensive benefits with universal access to health care, a tax-based system for doing that. The worst way to do it would be to tax the—such benefits are now in existence while leaving untaxed those who don't provide those benefits.

Mr. WAXMAN. Mr. Dingell?

Mr. DINGELL. Thank you, Mr. Chairman. I ask unanimous consent to insert my opening statement into the record at the appropriate time.

Mr. WAXMAN. Without objection that will be ordered.

[The opening statement of Mr. Dingell follows:]

OPENING STATEMENT OF HON. JOHN D. DINGELL

It is a great pleasure to welcome my old friend, Lane Kirkland, to the committee. Labor has long fought for the security of working Americans; and it has led the battle for health care reform. It is most appropriate that you should be the lead witness from outside the administration on this critical issue.

At this hearing we will hear also from business large and small. I welcome those representatives to the committee, too. The interests here of business and labor are one: redesigning a system that will save our economy from the certain doom our present course assures. Competitiveness, fairly distributed financing, and security that mobility and change will not disrupt affordable coverage: these are our shared goals. Our witnesses today live the economic lessons every day. They need not theorize about these matters. I trust they have much to teach us, and I look forward to your testimony.

Mr. DINGELL. Mr. Chairman, I would like to welcome my old and valued friend Lane Kirkland to the committee. He has fought for a long time for security for working Americans and has been the leader in the battle in health care reform, and I want to commend him and welcome him to the committee.

I have several questions. I note that there are a lot of proposals now floating around to cap the deductibility of health insurance premiums.

Do you view that middle-class tax?

Mr. KIRKLAND. Absolutely.

Mr. DINGELL. I find myself curious about this because I hear members talking about this as the mechanism under which they are going to finance health care. It strikes me what this kind of tax proposal does in fact is to tax those few who are having a modicum of success in providing health care for themselves to take that away from them to provide a health care benefit for those who have none or have vastly less.

Is that a fair analysis?

Mr. KIRKLAND. Very fair, sir.

Mr. DINGELL. Is that a fair way——

Mr. KIRKLAND. Very accurate.

Mr. DINGELL. Is that a fair way to do it?

Mr. KIRKLAND. No.

Mr. DINGELL. I don't think so, either.

Mr. KIRKLAND. I would add——

Mr. DINGELL. Now, I understand that opponents of the President's plan claim that it will cost jobs. You have a long history of concern for work and workers and there are few Americans who are concerned more with keeping and creating good jobs than you.

What is your view of this criticism, Mr. Kirkland?

Mr. KIRKLAND. I think I addressed that a little earlier. I think the best way to cost jobs is to do nothing to preserve the so-called system which I think is destructive of jobs. That places the American farm producers at a competitive disadvantage in the world, involves rapid and mounting and unpredictable costs, and that is what is lethal to job opportunities in this country.

I think the solution solving this problem, if you—you are very fortunate as a country if you can find one major—a major area of critical, deep-seated problem that can be solved at a cost figure for the solution if it can be attached to it and then solved. There are so many problems where that is not true. This is what social insurance is all about. It is a way of defining the effective costs of a solution.

Mr. DINGELL. Now, I have heard a lot of discussion about how this proposal that has been brought forward by the President is going to benefit the auto industry. I would note—and I want you to tell me if you agree—that any industry which has large numbers of retirees who are now covered would be benefited.

Is that not so?

Mr. KIRKLAND. Yes.

Mr. DINGELL. So the auto industries would benefit?

Mr. KIRKLAND. Certainly.

Mr. DINGELL. Steel companies? Instruction industries?

Mr. KIRKLAND. Yes.

Mr. DINGELL. Building trades would benefit?

Mr. KIRKLAND. Yes.

Mr. DINGELL. Oil and gas companies? Life line companies would benefit? Railroads would benefit? Tankers would benefit——

Mr. KIRKLAND. I think everyone would benefit.

Mr. DINGELL. Barge lines would benefit? Agribusiness would benefit, would they not?

Mr. KIRKLAND. Yes.

Mr. DINGELL. So it is not something directed only at the Midwest or, let's say, the peculiar manufacturing endeavors that we have in the Middle West; is that right?

Mr. KIRKLAND. That is correct.

Mr. DINGELL. Now, I observed that labor has argued strenuously for a single-payer approach for reform. That happens to be the view that I think will best do that.

How comfortable are you with the middle course that the President has struck?

Mr. KIRKLAND. As I indicated earlier, we had long debates about this. We considered all the possible alternative approaches. We elected to base our opposition and other conclusions upon the degree to which a plan addressed certain critical basic principles: Universality, comprehensiveness of benefits, the preservation of quality and effective cost controls.

We elected not to get hung up on a contest between abstract ideals or models existing elsewhere and a pragmatic, passable, enactable solution that would attract the breadth of support that was necessary to secure enactment.

If I had my way, I wouldn't depart too much from the plan that your father developed, the Wagner-Dingell bill. I started out plugging that and I still think it is possibly the best. I also am convinced that it couldn't attract enough votes, and if you all would kindly tell me that there are the votes there to pass a system with a tax-based entitlement fund, I would gladly embrace it.

Mr. DINGELL. Now——

Mr. KIRKLAND. But I do not believe that to be the case.

Mr. WAXMAN. Mr. Dingell, do you wish additional time?

Mr. DINGELL. No, Mr. Chairman, I will await my turn. Thank you.

Mr. WAXMAN. Thank you. We have with us a distinguished member of our full committee, Mr. Sharp, and I wanted to recognize him at this time without objection.

Mr. SHARP. Thank you, Mr. Chairman. I appreciate you letting me sit in. I defer questions at this point.

Mr. WAXMAN. Thank you. Mr. Kirkland, we are honored that this is your first appearance on the Hill on this issue of national health insurance and we very much appreciate your being with us.

I want to just see if any other members want to ask additional questions before we move on to other witnesses. But I want to commend you for being here and not only leading the fight at this stage of the debate but for over the years, which I have said in the past and want to repeat today, will mean that when we do get to the point where we do have national health insurance, I think you and the labor movement will deserve an enormous amount of credit.

Do any members wish to have a second round for questions?

Mr. Greenwood.

Mr. GREENWOOD. Very briefly, a number of Members of Congress and others have listed as their number one concern about this proposal the credibility of the numbers, the calculations that have been utilized to make this thing pay for itself. Senator Moynihan has been among those who expressed that concern.

Has the AFL-CIO done any kind of independent cost and benefit analysis of the President's plan to come up with your own independent conclusion about this? Or, are you relying on the administration's calculations?

Mr. KIRKLAND. I think, sir, we have not, no. The answer to your question is we have not. We do not have the—anything approaching the technical capacity for running computer models and developing the numbers that exist in the executive branch.

And I want to say clearly that, over the years, it has been impossible, proven impossible to advance any complex social insurance legislation involving calculations of that kind, technical work of that kind without a strong executive branch initiative. That has been the history of Social Security.

It has been the history of every piece of social insurance legislation ever enacted. It can't be done through the Congress in the face of executive branch noncooperation or resistance or the absence of leadership from that branch. That has been abundantly demonstrated and proven, too.

So we have now an executive branch that is deeply committed to health insurance that I am convinced is making a thoroughly honest effort to come up with the most accurate figures that they can ascertain and presenting them to us and to you candidly and accurately, and I have no grounds for believing that those figures will not be reliable insofar as it is possible to see the future.

The problem, sir, is not the availability of resources. We are spending in this country, enormous, enormous amounts on health care, more than any other country in the world per capita. And much of that is involved with unnecessary processes, redundant processes, wasteful processes.

If we could—it seems inconceivable to me that we cannot take the money that is being spent now and fashion out of that a system and a program that would provide universal coverage and universal access to all. I believe that money is now being spent within the system and if more effectively used and effectively directed, it could accomplish the objectives that we have. I would say something further, if you will permit me to wander off that question.

It is not just a question of humanity in terms of providing for those who don't have access to care who face the chance of catastrophe every day and experience it too often. We conducted extensive hearings. Every member of our Executive Council served on a panel that went out to different locations within this country over the course of a year to various cities, and we invited every element of society that had a concern or an interest in this subject to appear before that committee.

We had before those committees—and there were a number of them—nurses, hospital administrators, doctors, patients who had faced these problems and faced the quality—the problem of effective access to care in this country.

We had—and this to me is very, very important—we had representatives of city governments, mayors, health administrators. We had representatives of State governments who had the problem of addressing these, and one thing emerged very, very clearly in those hearings and from any candid examination of the facts, the cities and States of this country are under a suffocating burden of costs that they are grappling with inadequately.

The solution of the health care problem through an orderly system, through a credible system—which I did think the President's plan is—would do more to ease that burden—that virtually intolerable burden that cities and States are grappling rather poorly. They are drowning in it—than anything else we could do.

If you lift those burdens, those costs from those cities and those States and those budgets, you would free up resources and man- and womanpower to address many other critical problems that the States and the cities are unable to grapple with effectively today. And I think it would give us the opportunity to take a leap forward in the improvement of quality of life in this country in many, many areas in addition to the direct medical care issue.

Mr. GREENWOOD. Thank you, Mr. Kirkland. I also would note that while it may be true that most social insurance programs that have moved forward in the country have been initiated by the executive branch with leadership such as you have described, it also has been the case that the cost of most of those programs has been severely underestimated by those administrations by several orders of magnitude. That is what concerns some of us.

Thank you.

Mr. KIRKLAND. Well, I would also say, sir, that those burdens of costs that this country faced do not emerge from those social insurance programs that have been put in properly. If you eliminated Medicare, if you wiped it out, if you wiped out the old agents survivor insurance system, the budget—the deficit of this country would not go down, it would go up. It would go up very sharply.

Mr. WAXMAN. Thank you, Mr. Greenwood.

Mr. KIRKLAND. The idea that the problems of this country faces stems from these social insurance entitlements is, to my way of thinking, pure idiocy if you look at the facts.

Mr. WAXMAN. Thank you, Mr. Kirkland.

Any other member wish to ask an additional question? We are going to this side, if anybody on the Democratic side——

Mr. DINGELL. Mr. Chairman, I have just a few questions.

I have observed with interest that there are three basic alternatives to the President's plan. Mr. Cooper's plan, the Senate Republican plan, and the House Republican plan.

Now, I note Mr. Cooper requires managed competition. Is that right?

Mr. KIRKLAND. As I understand it.

Mr. DINGELL. Does it require anything else that would contribute to cost containment or to application towards universal coverage for the people who would be concerned?

Mr. KIRKLAND. Not that I am aware of, Senator—Congressman.

Mr. DINGELL. I note that the maximum that could be covered under the Cooper plan would be approximately one-third of the persons who do not now have coverage.

I note that the Senate Republican plan requires individual to—individuals to obtain their own coverage. I am curious how would that work in practice? How many people would be able to get coverage? How many would get coverage and what would be the increase in the number of people who would have coverage?

Mr. KIRKLAND. I am totally unable to answer that question.

Mr. DINGELL. Do you think anybody else could?

Mr. KIRKLAND. No.

Mr. DINGELL. Now, I note that my good friends on this side, the House Republican plan offers a plan which requires employers to develop a package, but I note that no one is required to offer that package to employers—to their employees and there are no standards which are fixed for the plan itself. How would that work in practice?

Mr. KIRKLAND. Beats me.

Mr. DINGELL. Now, I note on cost containment my good friend, Mr. Cooper, has a tax cap which we have already discussed and he would apply essentially managed competition.

What would that do in terms of containing costs?

Mr. KIRKLAND. I suspect very little, sir.

Mr. DINGELL. Now, I note that my House Republican colleagues would require administrative supervision—or rather, administration simplification and malpractice reform. What would the practical effects of that be in terms of containing costs?

Mr. KIRKLAND. Modest if at all.

Mr. DINGELL. Now, I noticed that the Senate Republican plan has only one mechanism which would control cost increases and that is the tax cap. How would that standing in splendid isolation work?

Mr. KIRKLAND. I really can't say, sir.

Mr. DINGELL. Well as a matter of fact, I can't either. Now, I would just note for the record that Mr. Clinton's package includes budget constraints and controls, managed competition, and real penalties for exceeding the budget. It strikes me that is probably a prescription for actually achieving some measure of containment of costs, does it not?

Mr. KIRKLAND. Yes. And I think that is the only approach, of those being put forward, that has the promise of being effective. It is not a novel, unprecedented approach. We have—I recall some years ago we had a long discussion of this issue within the group called the Labor Management Group which consists of the heads of some major companies and group of trade union officers that meets from time to time and undertakes to see if there are areas of agreement that we can reach, and recognizing that the health care costs issue was one that pressed both labor and management and was not amenable to being resolved across the bargaining table.

Individual negotiation, what was a broad national social program, we tried to work our way out to agreement on some cooperative approaches that we might undertake. And we did reach such agreement with these companies and developed some guidelines for dealing as consumers of health services jointly together as labor and management with the providers of health services on a regional and local basis, and those guidelines were widely distributed to employers and to unions involved in health plans, and a number of undertakings were engaged in along those lines in various places that resulted in the development of a negotiated budget. This was all on a private basis.

Mr. DINGELL. That is why you chose to control costs?

Mr. KIRKLAND. Yes.

Mr. DINGELL. I would note one very interesting thought. In 1870, a well-known, creeping socialist by the name of Otto Bismarck began to move forward to a program of national health insurance. In the early 1900's, a well-known, creeping socialist, King Edward of Britain, began to move forward to a system of national health insurance to cover the British people.

In the 1970's, another well-known, creeping socialist by the name of Richard Milhous Nixon came forward with a similar plan which required employers to offer plans which met standards which provided real coverage. I wonder where these three creeping socialists are now when we so desperately need them.

Mr. KIRKLAND. I take it that is a rhetorical question.

Mr. WAXMAN. The gentleman's time has expired with that rhetorical question. Further second round.

Mr. McMillan.

Mr. MCMILLAN. I would like a brief answer to a couple of the questions that the chairman raised. The Cooper plan would extend benefits up to 200 percent of the level of poverty through to the individual. I think that would be to family income of $4,000, $5,000, or $6,000, which may not be quite high enough in my judgment, at least in terms of partial benefits, but it does do that.

The Republican plan would mandate that business provide access to health insurance, but not pay for it. Furthermore, the Republican group plan has reform in it to make it very easy for the individual to get into a group, avoiding adverse risk selection, and it has full portability. I think this is a free market alternative to what the President proposes. In the President's plan, the only thing that really controls cost is fixing the price by a central board that would then dictate to the health care purchasing alliance what they would pay.

I would point out that, unlike the President's bill, both the Cooper bill and the Republican plan have very effective malpractice reform features in them. You mentioned yourself, Mr. Kirkland, that what we need to do is to get at the cost drivers underlying our spiralling health care costs.

Former Surgeon General Coop has testified that unnecessary costs may account for as much as 25 percent of health care diagnostic and treatment costs, a major portion of which is defensive medical procedures which are driven by fear of malpractice lawsuits.

When we are spending 14 percent of Gross Domestic Product on medical care in contrast to Canada, which spends 8 percent, which I think is the next highest, we can stay within our current expenditures to provide high quality health care to all of our citizens if we can wring our excess cost and make the right kinds of trade-offs.

I think you appropriately mentioned the fact that small municipalities and towns are finding that they can't afford to provide health care. I would suggest that is one of those trade-offs and wanted to direct a question to you that is somewhat in line with the previous question I asked, namely why unions should be provided special benefits not available to the rest of the population.

I understand that the Clinton plan would pick up 80 percent of the costs of early retirees prior to the time they come under Medicare at the age of 65, which could be an enormous cost to the system. This is essentially inequitable with what is provided to everybody else. Do you think this is a fair statement?

Wouldn't there be a rather extraordinary benefit for those who have early retirement contractual medical care benefits that would be picked up by the Federal government at 80 percent of their costs, which may in some cases range as high as, say, $5,000, $6,000 a year?

Mr. KIRKLAND. I think it is quite warranted, sir, that this problem of early retirees be addressed in this plan the way it has been addressed. We have a problem in this country, a major problem of which forced early retirement has become a leading manifestation. Company after company after company are downsizing by forcing people into early retirement or offering them Hobson's choices of early retirement or the highway. And any program that failed to address that issue and address that problem would be terribly deficient.

The impact of that problem on companies has been drastically increased by the decisions of the Federal Accounting Standards Board which requires them to be accounted for in advance of their actual occurrence, which has had a tremendous impact on company balance sheets. And I think that there is a problem that has to be addressed. I don't think there can be any effective system that doesn't deal with it.

Mr. MCMILLAN. In other words, the cost should be picked up by the taxpayer for contracts and agreements entered into by private companies and union negotiators. I thank the chairman.

Mr. WAXMAN. Thank you, Mr. McMillan.

Mr. Hall?

Mr. HALL. Thank you, Mr. Chairman.

Mr. Kirkland, on—back in February of this year at an Executive Council meeting you advocated universal coverage and security, cost containment, quality and fair financing. I don't quarrel with any of those, but I do need to know to whom you allude under the fair financing where you say the plan would end the competitive advantage now enjoyed by employers that offer little or no health coverage to their workers.

Now, I am not trying to be smart or clever, but you are not referring to the Fortune 500 people there, are you?

Mr. KIRKLAND. I am referring to those employers who do not provide health care coverage.

Mr. HALL. Basically the big ones provide it, don't they?

Mr. KIRKLAND. By an large, I would guess so, yes.

Mr. HALL. Would you be alluding——

Mr. KIRKLAND. I think the big ones provide it both because of the fact that the establishment of health care plans was pioneered through collective negotiations with major companies and also because through the instrument of collective bargaining small companies have been able to become part of larger groups and thereby economize.

It is not just the Fortune 500, sir. It is also many, many small employers that are included in health care plans that are made economical by the fact that the group as a whole is broader through these jointly administered Taft-Hartley funds which typically cover a great many small employers.

The average construction employer covered by these plans is very, very small and they are in competition with other small employers who do not provide them. They are in direct competition.

Mr. HALL. Yes, sir.

Mr. KIRKLAND. And they are paying the costs of the benefits of the employer who does not provide it, the medical costs.

Mr. HALL. The employer who does provide it is usually the small employer with 3 to 5 to 10 to 30 employees?

Mr. KIRKLAND. In competition with small employers who do provide it.

Mr. HALL. And I guess my question is: That is the small business people across this country to whom you allude that they offer little or no health courage? I am not asking you to comment on why they don't or why they should. It would be wonderful if everyone could, but those are the people to whom you refer, are they not?

Mr. KIRKLAND. I don't know what you define as a small company, sir. There are many—the largest—I think the second largest company in the country—according to the last figures that I saw not too long ago—was an employer engaged in the provision of temporary contract employers who are not covered by health insurance. That is the second—in terms of employment, the number of people working through that company, it is the second largest in this country.

Mr. HALL. I totally——

Mr. KIRKLAND. And it does not provide health care.

Mr. HALL. I totally agree with you that they ought to be pulled into the realm of fairness. I am not talking about them——

Mr. KIRKLAND. If I may answer your question.

Mr. HALL. Please do.

Mr. KIRKLAND. If you lump together employees of McDonald's franchises, that is a hell of a big company. Even the ones that—the employees that are—the United States ones that are directly operated by that company, that is a large employer. If you add the junk food—the fast food places all together in this country that do not provide health insurance for their employees, they are larger than the auto and steel industry combined.

Mr. HALL. Do you have an opinion or figure on their numbers?

Mr. KIRKLAND. I can provide that to you, sir. It is several hundred thousand.

Mr. HALL. OK. That is my question.

Mr. HALL. And I think—do we agree that the people to whom you refer are basically small business people?

Mr. KIRKLAND. They are not small business people.

Mr. HALL. Whether they are combined or others or not?

Mr. KIRKLAND. McDonald's is not a small business. The providers of Manpower, Inc. is not a small business. The Taco Bell is not a small business. Pizza Hut is not a small business. None of them provide health insurance.

Mr. HALL. Well, they must know it because I get more complaints from small businesses across my district—and perhaps these other gentlemen or ladies have a different count than what I do—but they are very fearful that they are the ones that are going to be targeted to pick up the pay for the large companies being allowed to drop under the opt-out provision in the Clinton plan.

Mr. KIRKLAND. Perhaps I have a more hopeful view of humanity of the people who run small or large businesses than what you indicate your finding from their communications, but I should think——

Mr. HALL. Perhaps you do.

Mr. KIRKLAND. I should think together with all of those whom you cite who don't want to do, there are many, and many who would like to do it but are not able to do it because of the enormous costs of doing it under the present system, and because those are with whom they are in competition may not do it.

I have heard small businessmen say that if the guy across the street or the other end of the town in the same business that he is in has to provide it and their terms of competition are equal, he would welcome it because he doesn't like seeing his employees with whom he works at close quarters suffer the risks and the catastrophic results of ill health and accidents and other problems that could wipe them out, simply as a human being.

Mr. WAXMAN. Thank you very much, Mr. Hall.

Mr. HALL. Thank you, Mr. Chairman.

Mr. WAXMAN. We are going to have to move on.

Mrs. Collins.

Mr. KIRKLAND. I would like to believe that those are in the majority.

Mrs. COLLINS. Mr. Kirkland, I want to thank you for appearing before us this morning. One of the things that I noticed during your long and lengthy testimony here is that you have given, as you have said, a great deal of long-term thought to this question.

I was encouraged by the fact that you said that you had met with a number of people who are interested in this—doctors, nurses, and so forth—which led me to believe that you have done a great deal in exploring the facts and that you know something about or have learned about the real life impacts of what this legislation, when we get it, is likely to do and how good it is going to be for our people.

Instead of being surveyed by public opinion or public sound bites and generalized pronouncements, that in fact you have studied the issue and we are grateful for your expertise.

Thank you for coming.

Mr. KIRKLAND. Thank you.

Mr. WAXMAN. Thank you very much, Mr. Kirkland. We appreciate your being with us.

Mr. KIRKLAND. Thank you, sir.

Mr. WAXMAN. We look forward to working with you.

Our second panel consists of representatives of large employers: Curtis H. Barnette is the chairman and chief executive officer of Bethlehem Steel Corporation. Margaret H. Jordan is vice president of Southern Cal Edison Company. Luther M. Ragin, Jr. is the vice president and chief financial officer of Earl G. Graves Limited. Edwin J. Wingate is the senior vice president of personnel for the Dayton Hudson Corporation. And Anthony Palizzi is the executive vice president and general counsel of K Mart.

I want to thank each of you for being here today for this hearing. We appreciate your willingness to testify on the record without the benefit of the statutory language of the administration's bill. I am informed that the administration's legislation should be introduced by the end of this month.

Without objection, your prepared statements are going to be in the record in their entirety. What we would like to ask each of you is to limit your oral presentation to no more than 5 minutes.

Mr. Barnette. There is a button on the base of the mike. Be sure to push it forward.

STATEMENTS OF CURTIS H. BARNETTE, CHAIRMAN, BETHLEHEM STEEL CORP.; MARGARET H. JORDAN, VICE PRESIDENT, SOUTHERN CALIFORNIA EDISON CO.; LUTHER M. RAGIN, JR., VICE PRESIDENT, EARL G. GRAVES LTD; EDWIN H. WINGATE, SENIOR VICE PRESIDENT, DAYTON HUDSON CORP.; AND ANTHONY PALIZZI, EXECUTIVE VICE PRESIDENT, KMART CORP.

Mr. BARNETTE. Good morning, Chairman Waxman and Chairman Collins, and members of the subcommittees. I do want to thank you for this opportunity to appear before you and discuss the concerns of Bethlehem Steel and the steel industry about this health care issue.

We believe that there is no area of public policy that will have a greater impact upon the Nation's future economic growth than health care policy. At stake is the well-being of our citizens and the competitiveness of the American industrial base.

We are very pleased to support the objectives of the Clinton health care proposal for health care reform. It is comprehensive. It sets forth necessary standards at the Federal level, and it provides a role for the States and implementation.

We believe that the plan will impose better discipline on private and public health care, increased competition among health care plans and reduce administration expenses. But this a national issue. This is not a Democratic issue. It is not a Republican issue. It is a national issue. And we are encouraged by the signs that Republican and Democratic leaders are willing to work with the President to achieve reform.

Health care expenditures total more than $820 billion in 1992. It exceeded our investments in education and research, investment in new plants and equipment, a major source of our Nation's future economic growth. Health care expenditures in the steel industry for active and retired employees and dependents now exceed $1 billion a year, a cost of $5.50 per hour worked.

Our industry's health care costs are two to three times higher than those of the rest of the world steel industries. Most other foreign steel industries have health care and pension costs paid for by their government and not by private companies. In our industry, health care bills for employees, retirees, and dependents amount to about $8,600 per active employee compared to $3,600 in Canada. We compete with Canada and our benefit packages are very much the same.

In our company, we have today 21,000 employees. We have 170,000 health care beneficiaries, active employees, their dependents and beneficiaries. We believe that fundamental health care reform must be followed by certain basic principles. We think many are set forth in the Clinton plan and, with your permission, I would like to suggest seven.

First aggregate growth in health care must be controlled through the use of global budgets or spending targets. Second cost shifting must be controlled by having all payers pay the same. We need a standard benefit package as the third point. The quality of health care must be maintained through practice protocols.

Fifth, administrative waste simply must be eliminated through standard identification cards, claim forms, and electronic processing. Malpractice reform is needed, sixth. And seventh, Medicare must remain the primary payer for the elderly.

I know that the subject of this hearing is health care. We view health care as one interrelated key public policy issue with many others to make this country competitive. And the other certainly include the economic plan, the international trade agreements we are trying to negotiate as well as infrastructure rebuilding.

We certainly look forward to working with the Congress and the administration in efforts to bring about prompt and comprehensive health care reform.

Thank you.

[The prepared statement of Mr. Barnette follows:]

CURTIS H. BARNETTE
CHAIRMAN AND CHIEF EXECUTIVE OFFICER
BETHLEHEM STEEL CORPORATION
REMARKS BEFORE THE HOUSE SUBCOMMITTEE ON HEALTH AND THE ENVIRONMENT AND THE HOUSE SUBCOMMITTEE ON COMMERCE, CONSUMER PROTECTION AND COMPETITIVENESS
OCTOBER 12, 1993

Good morning Chairman Waxman and Chairwoman Collins, and members of the Subcommittees.

Thank you for the opportunity to appear before your Subcommittees to share Bethlehem Steel's views and concerns about the Health Care crisis facing our Nation and the opportunities we have to deal with this challenge. This issue affects the public and private sector. It affects everyone in our country.

Bethlehem has 21,000 active employees and 170,000 Health Care beneficiaries -- active employees, retirees and their dependents -- we had Health Care costs of $237 M in 1992 or $9,518 for each active employee.

Bethlehem supports the basic principles of Health Care Reform outlined by President Clinton in his presentation before the Joint Session of the Congress on September 23, 1993. We also commend the First Lady for her leadership on this issue, and we agree with President Clinton that Health Care Reform must be comprehensive in scope and address the six key principles he set forth -- security, simplicity, savings, choice, quality, and responsibility.

President Clinton is right --- our Nation's fragmented Health Care System simply is not working. It is not meeting the needs of the American people by providing affordable, quality, and efficient care to all of our citizens.

There is no area of public policy that will impact our Nation's future economic growth more than our policy on Health Care. Our Nation's Health Care System is the most expensive in the world, and without change, it will cripple our ability to compete in the global economy.

Addressing the problems of our Health Care System is an urgent public policy issue which can only be addressed by fundamental changes legislated at the National level. The piecemeal changes of recent years have not given us equitable access, controlled costs, assured quality, or provided public satisfaction. The result is a system that fails to provide care for many and is far too costly for everyone.

As you know, expenditures for Health Care currently consume over 14% of GNP -- more than $820 billion in 1992.

In spite of all this spending, we still have over 37 million of our citizens who are uninsured. Expenditures for Health Care far exceed our investments in education and research and development. They also exceed our investment in new plants and equipment, a major source of our nation's future economic growth.

At stake is the competitiveness of the American industry in the international marketplace.

While I recognize that the subject of the hearing is Health Care, most respectfully, I would submit that Health Care Reform is only one of the major issues that must be resolved, since it is closely interrelated to other pending key public policy issues. If you believe, as we do, that the national interest requires a modernized and profitable steel industry in this country, then Health Care, fair trade of steel imports, infrastructure rebuilding, and the responsible application of our environmental laws, are all of great importance.

Our steel industry today is the low cost, high quality producer of steel products for the U. S. market. This has happened through significant restructuring and capital spending. The steel industry today has approximately 169,000 employees, down by almost 58%, from 399,000 in 1980. Private companies, not foreign governments, pay the expenses of this restructuring including pension and Health Care costs for deserving retirees and their dependents, and a decreased active workforce has to pay these expenses. We are still the open market for steel trade, and a net importer of steel products. Foreign subsidies and dumping continue to seriously injure the domestic industry, so that enforcing our trade laws and keeping them strong and effective is essential.

Bethlehem and other steel companies have provided Health Insurance for their employees for more than four decades. Runaway health costs are threatening the continued viability of employer provided Health Care Programs. Since the end of 1980, the United States steel industry has made significant progress in improving its competitive position. Productivity has doubled and quality has improved to world class levels. Employment costs have been carefully controlled so that our wage costs -- exclusive of health insurance -- have increased only 38% since 1980. In stark contrast, Bethlehem and other steel companies have experienced a 285% rise in the cost of Health Care benefits.

Annual Health Care expenditures for the steel industry for active and retired employees and their *dependents exceed $1 billion, with a cost of $5.44 per hour worked. This represents a Health Care cost of over 17% of total employment costs.*

Our industry's Health Care costs are two to three times higher than those of the rest of the world's steel industries, and most of them have their Health Care and pension and benefit costs paid for by their government -- not by private companies.

Health Care costs show no sign of moderating, despite the increased use of deductibles, copayments, preadmission certification, and aggressive managed care and HMO/PPO arrangements. Consequently, this cost is becoming an increasingly important factor limiting the United States' ability to compete in the global market. For example, Bethlehem's shipments total about 10 M tons of steel. Health Care accounts for six percent of its total cost, or $25 per ton that is not available for necessary investments in plant and equipment, research and development, benefits and employee training.

Among our major foreign steel competitors the United States has the highest per capita Health Care cost. In the United States, this cost is borne principally by the larger employers. Whereas in Canada, Europe, and Japan, the cost of Health Care is spread more equitably among all employers and/or the public. For example, on an annual basis, the United States steel industry's Health Care bill for employees, retirees and their dependents totalled approximately $8,680 per active employee in 1991. In Canada, the next highest cost nation, that figure was approximately $3,600.

This is a significant cost difference, particularly when you consider that steelworkers in the United States and Canada have basically the same benefit package. The difference is even more dramatic in comparison to our major European competitors. Because steel is an international commodity and U.S. companies must compete in the global market, this cost differential is simply not sustainable in the long run.

Health Care cost problems in the steel industry are compounded because we provide medical coverage for active employees as well as retirees. Our current work-force is approximately 21,000 and we support Health Care costs for 170,000 Health Care beneficiaries including 70,000 retirees. These pension and Health Care legacy costs place American industry at a competitive disadvantage because such costs are not born by our international competitors, but by their governments.

Bethlehem and other steel companies have recognized the problem. We took steps beginning in the early 1980's by implementing various managed care programs to control rising Health Care costs and increasing employee cost sharing and implementing various managed care programs to control rising Health Care costs. These efforts, unfortunately, represent "Band-Aids" which only momentarily slowed down the escalation in costs. They do not -- and cannot -- attack the underlying inflation which is driven by uncontrolled increases in utilization charges by medical providers.

Even though Bethlehem's Health Care plans include the full range of managed care programs, we saw our costs rise by 43% in the last three years, from $165 million in 1989 to $237 million in 1992.

The steel companies and the United Steelworkers of America recognized that our nation's Health Care system was in crisis and that fundamental reforms were necessary. Accordingly, in 1989, seven major steel companies and the steelworkers union agreed to work together for a national policy on health.

In August of 1992, the seven steel companies -- Armco, Acme, Bethlehem, Inland, LTV Steel, National Steel, Wheeling-Pitt -- and the Steelworkers Union -- agreed to a plan for Universal Health Insurance Coverage.

The keystones of that joint Labor/Management plan are universal access and meaningful cost control through the use of expenditure targets and an all payer payment system.

Bethlehem, other steel companies, and the steelworkers union have also been actively supporting the efforts of the National Leadership Coalition for Health Care Reform, a diverse group of business, labor, consumer and provider organizations that have been working together since 1989 to develop a plan for comprehensive Health Care Reform.

We're encouraged that a number of the principles supported by the steel industry and the National Leadership Coalition have been incorporated in President Clinton's proposal and in proposals by members of Congress.

If we are to expand access and control costs, we must accept the need for a stronger governmental role in Health Care. Currently, the private sector does not play on a level playing field in Health Care.

Cost shifting has devastated the private sector, both small and large employers. Cost shifting is probably the most important factor in the destabilization of our Health Care System. In the absence of fundamental reforms that benefit our Health Care payers, cost shifting can only grow worse.

We believe that fundamental reform at the National level should be consistent with the following principals addressing cost, access, and quality:

1. *Aggregate growth in our Nation's Health Care System must be controlled. We support the use of global budgets or spending targets to bring the annual escalation in Health Care costs down to an acceptable level (the CPI inflation rate).*

2. *Cost shifting must be eliminated. Legislation is needed to ensure that public and private payers pay the same for Health Care. All payer regional reimbursement schedules for provider fees should be established.*

3. *All Americans should have the security of health insurance with a standard benefit package. We support the principal that working Americans should be covered for health insurance through the workplace -- with appropriate subsidies for small business -- and that non-working Americans, regardless of their circumstances, should be covered through broad community programs, like the Regional Alliances proposed by President Clinton.*

4. *We must ensure that we maintain the quality of Health Care with the use of appropriate tools such as practice protocols, technology assessment, quality measurement systems, and National Quality Data Bases.*

5. *Administrative waste must be eliminated through the use of standard identification cards and claim forms and electronic processing.*

6. *Malpractice reform is needed to reduce costs associated with medical malpractice suits and defensive medicine.*

7. *Medicare must remain as the primary payer for the elderly.*

I am pleased with the broad scope of President Clinton's proposal for Health Care Reform. The Clinton Plan is comprehensive in nature, sets forth necessary standards at the Federal level and provides a role for the States in implementation. We believe that the Plan will impose better discipline on private and public Health Care spending, increase competition among Health Care plans, and reduce administrative expenses.

We are also encouraged by the clear signs that Republican and Democratic leaders in the Congress are intent on achieving reform.

The growing seriousness of our Health Care crisis and increasing public concerns have combined to create a new opportunity and need for major change in our Health Care System. As a Nation, we can no longer ignore the Health Care crisis before us. Health Care must be placed at the top of the public policy agenda.

President Clinton has presented us with the challenge for Health Care Reform. We must successfully meet the challenge, and we must do so immediately. We look forward to the details of the President's Plan when it is presented to Congress. Bethlehem is anxious to work with your Subcommittee, the members of Congress and the Administration as we seek to achieve comprehensive reform of our Health Care System.

I thank you for the opportunity to meet with you today.

Mrs. COLLINS [presiding]. Ms. Jordan.

STATEMENT OF MARGARET H. JORDAN

Ms. JORDAN. Good morning Madam Chairwoman and members of the subcommittees. I am Margaret Jordan, vice president of health care and employee services for Southern California Edison, the Nation's second largest electric utility providing service to 11 million people in a 50,000 square mile area in central and southern California. I appreciate the opportunity to testify on the critical need to reform our Nation's health care system.

Edison provides health care for more than 55,000 employees, retirees and their family members. We offer our employees and our retirees a choice of six HMO's as well as company administered indemnity with a network of providers.

President Clinton and the First Lady deserve a lot of credit for their efforts to get comprehensive reform off the ground. From our perspective at Southern Cal Edison, it is a big step in the right discretion. Today, growth and health expenditures prevents Edison from investing in improvements in our operations. We face several factors, some unique to us, which exacerbate our situation.

Health care costs in Southern Cal are much higher than the rest of the Nation. This contributes to our weak economy, an erosion of our customer base, and to the migration of companies to other States with more favorable business conditions.

As a regulated utility, we have to justify the reasonableness of our rates before the California Public Utilities Commission. Because we haven't been able to fully recover increases in health care costs, we have had to forego spending in this area. And if this situation continues, it will affect our long-term ability to compete in an increasingly deregulated utility industry.

We need comprehensive reform to eliminate soft shifting. Edison bears the cost shifted from uncompensated care under reimbursement of public programs and from company spouses and dependents of employees who work for other companies with no or limited health care coverage.

Some elements of the President's plan that we applaud are we support universal coverage. We support the requirement that all businesses must contribute their fair share to the cost of their employees' care. Without an employer mandate, universal coverage will be almost impossible to achieve.

We welcome the proposed comprehensive standard benefit package. We agree with the President's proposal that successful reform must address the entire health care system. This comprehensive approach is necessary because health care is related to the interactions and the interdependencies of many subsystems.

We support restructuring of the health care market. And we specifically favor those features of managed competition embodied in the administration's proposal that can spur health care providers to compete more on cost and quality rather than on health coverage based on least risks.

We believe Americans should continue to have the ability to choose health plan providers and treatment. Along with safeguarding choice, we also strongly believe consumers must become more informed about the trade-offs involving costs and quality and accept individual responsibility in efficiently using the health care system.

And finally, we support the administration's efforts to improve overall quality in our health care system. But let me mention a few reservations that we do have.

First, we don't think corporate alliances should be required to offer a fee-for-service option but rather should have the flexibility to decide the most appropriate options. Managed care plans can significantly cut costs and improve quality care and reliance on fee-for-service medicine, means less efficiency and less reliability of health care providers.

Second, we don't believe the proposal, as it stands, encourages the creation of corporate alliances because it places administrative and financial burdens on large companies. We need corporate alliances competing with regional ones to encourage more competition in cutting costs and improving service in the delivery system.

And finally, we are concerned about the potential for open-ended assessments on corporate alliances. Large companies are prepared to pay their fair share, but they should not be forced to make up for shortfalls in publicly sponsored programs through special assessments or cost shifting.

In closing, we again applaud President Clinton and the First Lady for their initiative on this tough issue. We need to keep the momentum going. We need a bipartisan effort that builds on the strengths of this proposal. And in that spirit, Southern Cal Edison has joined with other concerned organizations to form the Health Care Reform Project, a member of AFL-CIO, a nonpartisan coalition of consumers, business, labor and health care providers.

The changes for enacting are now better than ever and it is a tremendous opportunity for all of us to help secure the ills of our present system.

Thank you.

Mr. WAXMAN. Thank you very much for your testimony.

[The prepared statement of Ms. Jordan follows:]

STATEMENT OF MARGARET H. JORDAN, VICE PRESIDENT, SOUTHERN CALIFORNIA EDISON COMPANY

Mr. Chairman, Madame Chairwoman and Members of the Subcommittees:

My name is Margaret H. Jordan. I am Vice President of Health Care and Employee Services for Southern California Edison (SCE). I appreciate the opportunity to testify today regarding President Clinton's health care reform proposal. Southern California Edison is the nation's second-largest electric utility serving four million customers in Central and Southern California. SCE provides health care coverage for more than 55,000 employees, retirees and their family members. Currently, we offer our employees and retirees a choice of six health maintenance organizations and a company-administered managed indemnity plan that includes a preferred provider organization (PPO) option.

Today, I would like to briefly discuss SCE's interest in health care reform and emphasize what we consider to be the many positive aspects of President Clinton's proposal.

SCE's Concerns About Health Care

The health care system is not working for all Americans and especially not for American business, the major payer. The federal government is also adversely impacted, with health care spending as a major contributor to growth in the federal budget deficit. The rapid escalation of health care expenditures places a substantial burden on the economy. This diverts funds from other important initiatives, such as education and improvements in the nation's infrastructure, which are key to enhancing our worldwide competitive position.

The issues are well known: cost, access and quality. Health care costs are rising two-to-three times faster than the rate of general inflation, making health insurance increasingly unaffordable. This has resulted in 37 million uninsured Americans and many more who have inadequate coverage. While we spend more per capita on health care than any other nation, this is not reflected in the health status of our population. Our spending emphasizes acute care rather than prevention -- we treat symptoms of disease rather than causes. In addition, the current system has excess capacity, costly duplication of technology and lacks uniform quality.

As in the public sector, growth in health expenditures prevents SCE from investing in improvements in its operations. In addition, we are faced with several factors -- some unique to us -- which exacerbate the situation. Health care costs in Southern California are much higher than those in the rest of the nation. This has contributed to unfavorable economic conditions in Southern California which, in turn, have led to erosion of our customer base, as many companies have migrated to states with a more favorable business climate. As a regulated utility, we have to justify the reasonableness of our rates before the California Public Utilities Commission. Because we have been unable to fully recover increases in health care costs, we have had to forego spending in other areas. If this situation continues it will impact our long-term ability to compete in an increasingly deregulated utility industry.

In addition to these compelling economic reasons for comprehensive health care reform, the private sector bears the additional burden of cost shifting. Cost shifting occurs when providers increase charges for patients who have insurance to make up for treating patients without coverage, as well as reimbursement shortfalls from public programs. This phenomenon increases costs for businesses that offer coverage (which tend to be larger employers). Cost shifting also occurs among private payers and is related to dual-income households selecting the best benefits at the least cost, which often means that larger companies are left to pay a disproportionate share of the bills.

In 1989, to moderate the growth in our health care expenditures, we embarked on a three part strategy to restructure our health care benefits. The components included incentives for more efficient use of services through the introduction of cost sharing; encouraging the reduction of health risks by rewarding healthy lifestyles; implementing a PPO with negotiated pre-set rates, thereby reducing the impact of cost shifting; and the adoption of a focused utilization management program. These efforts helped to significantly moderate our medical cost trend from year-to-year, but not to the level of general inflation.

SCE is well aware of the need for health care reform. Our position is not based on our inability to control our own costs, but rather on the understanding that even though we have been successful in moderating our expenditure growth, the action of individual companies alone is insufficient in addressing the underlying forces driving health care inflation.

Positive Elements of Clinton's Health Care Proposal

We commend the President and Mrs. Clinton for recognizing the need for health care reform and the commitment and leadership they have demonstrated to seeking a long-term solution to this crisis. The proposal is both comprehensive and complex. It contains elements SCE finds constructive and some we believe should be revised. I will briefly outline some of these.

Universal Coverage: SCE has long supported universal coverage -- not just because we believe it represents good public policy, but because without it, cost shifting will continue. The security provided by universal coverage will allow people to change jobs without having to worry about coverage. The comprehensive and standard nature of the benefit package is also welcomed, as it will provide people access to the services they need and create the necessary foundation for health plans to compete on an equal basis.

System-wide Reform: The proposal recognizes that successful reform must address the entire health care system, not just certain parts. A comprehensive approach is prescribed because many of the problems with health care are related to the interaction and interdependencies of the many subsystems. Currently, for example, when Medicare spending is reduced, the private sector often ends up paying for the shortfalls that providers experience. Incremental reforms will not provide the necessary long-term results, and will serve only to delay the implementation of more comprehensive reforms. This proposal also attempts to combine pieces of the current fragmented system by integrating health-related services such as mental health, long-term care, the public health system and the medical component of workers' compensation. This integration will enhance the ability for care to be managed along the entire spectrum of services, resulting in improvements in quality while reducing costs.

Restructuring of the Health Care Market: The implementation of Corporate and Regional Health Alliances, a guaranteed benefit package and insurance reforms, including the removal of pre-existing exclusions, has the potential to create a level playing field on which health plans will compete on the basis of cost and quality, rather than on the selection of better risks. This will change the incentives in the system and encourage the restructuring of health care delivery. Restructuring will assist in eliminating waste, enhancing the efficiency of delivery and encouraging the more rational allocation of resources. We believe as health plans recognize that revenues are limited, they will put their primary emphasis on improving their operating efficiencies and the quality of their clinical outcomes.

Choice: We agree that health care is a personal matter and consumers should continue to have discretion in choosing their health plans, providers and course of treatment. Reforms should safeguard choice and provide enhanced information for consumers to base their decisions. Individual responsibility regarding healthy lifestyles and appropriate use of the health care system should also be encouraged. Informed consumers will play a pivotal role in the success of reform.

Quality: Perhaps most significantly, the proposal recognizes and addresses the lack of uniformity in quality throughout the system. We believe the proposed quality management program will play a key role in both enhancing clinical quality and containing costs by reducing inappropriate care which currently occurs due to variations in clinical practice. Developing interactive information systems to measure and track clinical outcomes will be essential to this endeavor. Better information will improve accountability in the health care delivery system. We also support the effort to research, develop and disseminate practice guidelines, especially for new technologies.

Areas of Concern Regarding Clinton's Health Care Proposal

We believe certain aspects of the proposal could be improved and should be subject to debate. Specifically, the following three areas should be reconsidered: 1) the elimination of the requirement to offer a fee-for-service health plan option, 2) making Corporate Alliances a realistic alternative, and 3) equitable financing.

Fee-for-Service Option: We find the requirement for alliances to offer a fee-for-service option a step backwards. In recent years we have tried to encourage our employees to join managed care plans, which we believe not only reduce costs, but also improve quality.

Fee-for-service medicine contains the wrong incentives and this type of payment system does not promote efficiency or accountability. While we recognize that in some parts of the country fee-for-service plans make sense, we do not believe that Corporate Alliances should be required to offer them wherever they are available. In addition, it is our view that choice can be maintained without moving back to fee-for-service medicine.

Corporate Alliances: Currently, the proposal does not encourage creation of Corporate Alliances. We believe that this is poor public policy for a number of reasons:

- Large companies, such as SCE, have been a major factor in the evolution of managed care; without them, an important innovative force will be lost.
- Corporate Alliances, as one of several purchasers making decisions, will generate competition among health plans.
- By encouraging the development of both Regional and Corporate Alliances, multiple sources of purchaser expertise will be created and alliances will become operational more quickly and with less effort.
- Administrative costs and complexity may increase for multistate companies if they are required to join multiple Regional Health Alliances, all of which will have their own rules and procedures.
- Finally, large employers acting on behalf of their employees will have more leverage with health plans than individual consumers operating through Regional Health Alliances.

As the proposal currently stands, we believe that few companies will opt to form Corporate Alliances due to the additional administrative and financial burdens placed on them. This is unfortunate, because these alliances could make an essential contribution to the success of the reforms and the evolution of the health care delivery system. We are not asking for the continued pre-emptions currently afforded by ERISA, because we understand how they impede state-level reforms, instead, we are requesting that Corporate Alliances be made a realistic option. By joining Regional Alliances, employers are reduced to mere payers. We believe that the continued involvement of willing employers in purchasing health care for their employees will have a significant beneficial effect on the health care system and should be encouraged.

Equitable Financing: We are concerned that the funding may not be commensurate with universal coverage. We are willing to pay our "fair share," but we do not believe large companies should continue to be called upon to make up for funding shortfalls particularly from publicly financed programs, i.e. Medicare and Medicaid, through either special assessments or costs shifting.

Conclusion

Finally, in support of this proposal and in recognition of the critical need for health care reform in America, SCE urges a bipartisan effort to build upon the strengths of this proposal and enact legislation to increase access to quality health care for all Americans. SCE has joined with other concerned organizations to form the Health Care Reform Project which advocates the passage of comprehensive reform legislation. The Project is a nonpartisan coalition of consumers, business, labor and providers.

We applaud the President and Mrs. Clinton for seizing the initiative on health care reform and developing a comprehensive proposal that addresses the many complex issues involved. We agree with the vast majority of the proposal and especially support universal coverage and the newly created incentives for restructuring of the health care delivery system. We look forward to working closely with you and your colleagues over the coming months to jointly develop the best possible health care reform legislation for America.

Mr. WAXMAN. Mr. Ragin.

STATEMENT OF LUTHER M. RAGIN

Mr. RAGIN. Good morning Madam Chairwoman, Mr. Chairman. My name is Luther Ragin, and I am vice president and chief financial officer of Earl G. Graves Limited, a New York holding company which owns two of the Nation's largest minority business enterprises, Black Enterprise magazine and the Pepsi Cola of Washington, DC.

Black Enterprise, our flagship, is a monthly periodical read by more than 2 million people which has chronicled the achievements and challenge of African-American entrepreneurs, managers, and professionals for nearly a quarter of a century.

Pepsi Cola of Washington, D.C., the Nation's largest minority Pepsi franchise, is a recent joint venture of our president and CEO, Earl G. Graves, basketball legend Magic Johnson and the Pepsi Cola Company. With 65 employees in New York, Chicago, and Los Angeles, and 150 in the Washington area, our company is steeped in entrepreneurial values and is an exemplar of the strides African-Americans have made in entering the economic mainstream of our country.

As a representative of that company and of that tradition, I am pleased today to have the opportunity to address these joint hearings on the Clinton health care proposals as we understand them and to discuss their impact on our business. The focus of my testimony will be Black Enterprise, since our Pepsi franchise purchases health benefits for its employees from the Pepsi Cola Company.

Those benefits currently include a choice of self-insured health plans including fee-for-service in the context of a comprehensive cafeteria plan. The impact on Pepsi of the President's proposals, therefore, are best addressed by a representative of that company.

As the Chairs are aware, in the absence of specific legislation, our comments here are based on the broad goals and general direction of the President's proposals. Let me say clearly that the President's proposals are bold, they are balanced, and they address a major piece of unfinished business in American social policy.

The debate ought not to be whether our health care system requires fundamental change but how to accomplish that change. In this connection, our own experience at Black Enterprise shows a high cost of the status quo. Health insurance premiums for our employees have nearly doubled in the past 5 years. Indeed, last year we paid as much in employee health insurance premium as we did in Federal, State, and local corporate income taxes.

Over the past years, Black Enterprise has covered comprehensive health care benefits to its full-time employees with a choice of traditional indemnity plans and one or more HMO's. We have embraced the concepts of individual responsibilities. Benefits are not free.

Employee contributions are approximately 40 percent of premium costs, although the effective contribution rate is much lower since employees may make their contribution with pre-tax dollars from a section 125 or so-called "Cafeteria Plan."

In addition, we have voluntarily capped employee contributions at 7 percent of an employee's base pay. Our employees value the opportunity to choose a health care plan. Given a choice of plans and, importantly, asked to commit their own dollars to the plan which best meets their needs, we have found that nearly two-thirds opt for lower cost managed care networks and HMO's.

We understand and accept the pragmatic basis for employer provided health insurance. We could not imagine attracting or retaining quality staff without health insurance as the centerpiece of our benefit program. While so-called "employer mandates" rarely elicit much enthusiasm from the business community, particularly smaller entrepreneurial companies such as ours, we believe that this is a case where sound social policy and sound business policy are closely aligned.

We clearly do not support placing undue financial burden on the business community and therefore would welcome the President's proposals to provide subsidies to businesses with fewer than 50 employees whose health care costs exceed a certain percentage of payroll. While our own company would not benefit from this proposal, the subsidy is an important safety net for small employers and new ventures.

We trust that as Congress wrestles with the details of health care reform, it does not sacrifice the principle of universal access. Universal access is a prerequisite to achieving an equal opportunity society where individuals are limited only by their talent and effort.

The preservation and maintenance of one's health and the access to the means to do so is inextricably linked to the ability to compete and succeed. Persons without access to preventive medicine and primary care whose health care is relegated to acute medicine in a hospital emergency room are less likely to achieve their full potential as productive employees, citizens, or taxpayers.

Mr. WAXMAN. Thank you very much Mr. Ragin. That whole statement is going to be in the record. We appreciate your presentation.

[The prepared statement of Mr. Ragin follows:]

TESTIMONY OF LUTHER M. RAGIN, JR.
VICE PRESIDENT AND CHIEF FINANCIAL OFFICER
EARL G. GRAVES, LTD./BLACK ENTERPRISE MAGAZINE

Good Morning. My name is Luther M. Ragin, Jr. and I am Vice President and Chief Financial Officer of Earl G. Graves Ltd., a New York holding company which owns two of America's largest minority business enterprises: Black Enterprise Magazine and Pepsi Cola of Washington, D.C., L.P. Black Enterprise, our flagship, is a monthly periodical read by more than two million people that has chronicled the achievements and challenges of African-American entrepreneurs, managers and professionals for nearly a quarter of a century. Pepsi Cola of Washington, D.C., L.P., the nation's largest minority Pepsi franchise, is a recent joint venture of our President & CEO, Earl G. Graves, basketball legend Earvin ("Magic") Johnson and the Pepsi Cola Company. With 65 employees in New York Chicago and Los Angeles and 150 in the Washington area, our company is an exemplar of American entrepreneurial values and, in particular, of the strides African Americans have made in entering the economic mainstream of our country.

As a representative of that company and of that tradition, I am pleased today to have the opportunity to address these joint hearings on the Clinton Health Reform Proposals, as we understand them, and to discuss their impact on our business. The focus of my testimony will be Black Enterprise since our Pepsi franchise purchases health benefits for its employees from the Pepsi Cola Company and consequently is able to take advantage of economies of scale and market power commensurate with a workforce of more than 30,000 persons. The impact on Pepsi of the President's proposals, therefore, are best addressed by a representative of that company.

In the absence of specific legislation, my comments are based on the broad goals and general direction of the President's proposals, as articulated by the President in his Message to the Congress and as amplified in subsequent remarks. Let me say clearly: the President's proposals are bold, balanced and address a major piece of unfinished business in American social policy. The debate ought not to be whether our health care system requires fundamental change, but how to accomplish that change. In this connection, our own experience at Black Enterprise shows the high cost of the status quo: health insurance premiums for our employees have nearly doubled in the past five years. Last year, we paid as much in employee health insurance premiums as we did in federal, state and local corporate income taxes.

Over the years, Black Enterprise has offered comprehensive health care benefits to its full-time employees with a choice of a traditional indemnity (or fee for service) plan and one or more HMOs. We have also embraced the concept of individual responsibility. Benefits are not free. Employee contributions are approximately 40% of premium cost, although the effective contribution rate is much lower since employees may make their contributions with pre-tax dollars from a Section 125 or so-called "Cafeteria Plan". Our employees value the opportunity to choose their health plan. Given a choice of plans and, importantly, asked to commit their own dollars to the plan which best meets their needs, we have found that nearly two-thirds opt for lower cost, managed care networks and HMOs.

We understand and accept the pragmatic basis for employer-provided health insurance. We could not imagine attracting or retaining quality staff without health insurance as a centerpiece of our benefit program. While so-called "employer mandates" rarely elicit much enthusiasm from the business community, particularly smaller entrepreneurial companies such as ours, we believe this is a case where sound social policy and sound business policy are closely aligned. We clearly do not support placing undue financial burden on the business community and therefore welcome the President's proposal to provide subsidies to businesses with fewer than fifty employees whose health care costs exceed a certain percentage of payroll. While our own company would not benefit from this proposal, the subsidy is an important safety net for small employers and new ventures.

We trust that as Congress wrestles with the details of health care reform, it does not sacrifice the principle of universal access. Universal access is a prerequisite to achieving an equal opportunity society where individuals are limited only by their talent and effort. The preservation and maintenance of one's health and the access to the means to do so is inextricably linked to the ability to succeed. Persons without access to preventive medicine and primary care, whose health care is relegated to acute medicine in hospital emergency rooms, are less likely to achieve their full potential as productive employees, citizens or taxpayers.

I would remind the members of these committees that the staggering social cost of tens of millions of uninsured and underinsured Americans, is borne in substantial part by the private sector and particularly by those employers who provide insurance for their workforce. The cost of "emergency room medicine" for the uninsured is reflected in the premiums that our company and others pay for their own employees. This cost-shifting phenomenon is a major contributor to the explosion of health care costs for all employers, but particularly for small businesses which do not have the market power to negotiate preferential rates with hospitals or other health care providers.

Our company believes that President Clinton's proposals signal movement in the right direction. Our company believes that universal access to quality, cost-effective health care, combined with individual responsibility, are critical elements of any reform package. We also believe that any plan must include credible and effective measures to control costs. While these

measures should be market-based, flexible regulatory approaches must also be considered. We accept that provision of health insurance to employees should be an obligation of employers, although we would argue strongly that the individual employer be given wide latitude to determine what level of employer contribution (whether 80%, 50% or 100%) is appropriate.

Today there is a unique opportunity to forge the broad national consensus for health care reform into concrete action. And to get it right. The goal of quality and cost-effective health care for all Americans will require an extraordinary partnership between the public and private sectors. Such pragmatism is the genius of America. Clearly the magnitude of the challenge requires nothing less.

Mr. WAXMAN. Mr. Wingate.

STATEMENT OF EDWIN H. WINGATE

Mr. WINGATE. Chairman Waxman.

Mr. WAXMAN. There is a button on the base of the mike.

Mr. WINGATE. Chairman Waxman, Cochairman Collins, thank you very much for allowing me to be here. My written testimony contains background on the Dayton Hudson Corporation, outlines our support for health care reform. I would use my limited time to raise a few of our many concerns with the administration's proposal.

I would like to also correct an error that was made in our testimony on page five, line five. The figure $100 million should read $110 million.

First, the President's plan provides for payroll premiums as low as 3.5 percent going up to a maximum of 7.9 percent.

It is a fact that, in general, merchandise retail establishments with fewer than 50 employees account for 58.3 percent of U.S. retail sales and account for 60.6 percent of employees in that sector of retailing. As large and small retailers sell the same products purchased from the same vendors to the same customers, we see no justification for a major difference in medical care payroll premiums.

We oppose a two part system; 3.5 for small and 7.9 for large is not an appropriate balance. More properly, it would be based on the ability and start-up position.

We do believe that companies that encourage employees to pay a portion of their health care costs contribute to keeping costs low. We have 180,000 employees, 65,000 enrolled and 45,000 eligible are insured elsewhere; 75,000 are part-time employees and are not currently covered.

Our costs will increase from $110 million to $175 million per year. What will this cause? First of all, perhaps an 11 percent reduction in earnings and perhaps a $600 million reduction in market value of our stock. Many of our shares are held by pension funds and individuals who rely on those incomes for future retirement.

We can go another route, a reduction of 15,000 part-time employees, or we can approach a substantial reduction in wages to offset the $65 million increase in costs. We don't care for any of these. Retailing has been a major creator of jobs and we fully expect some rethinking in terms of this load.

Third, nontaxed excess benefits have been and are a contributor to excessive demands for medical treatment. Its presence represents cost-shifting to those without benefits. The level playing field argument should prevail on this issue as it does on others.

The annual value of such excess benefits tax has been estimated as high as $25 billion per year, a 10 year value, present value of that amount has a current value of about, using a 6 percent discount factor, nearly $200 billion.

Four, we oppose the administration's plan to pick up 85 percent of the cost of early retirement plans and care benefits some companies have standing. These programs were put into effect voluntarily for business leaders by the companies that did so. The New York

Times recently referred to this as a "big wet kiss" for those companies so favored.

Ira Magaziner's cost estimate for the administration per year for a single adult is $1,800. In contrast, Hewitt Associates, a highly regarded national benefits firm, estimates such a plan will cost $2,270 per year, or 26 percent more than the $1,800 or $4.5 billion. Present value at a 6 percent discount for that benefit is $90 billion to $180 billion, depending on which numbers you choose. All things being equal, this would translate into a 9.9 percent payroll tax or a large deficit.

Six, we have introduced long-term term at this time. Let's focus on fixing acute care first. Neither is fully understood nor predictable in its cost implications.

Seven, the administration proposes we have only one purchaser of care in each region. There is an allowance for large firms. We believe there should be multiple purchasing alliances as well as multiple employer groups in each area.

In summary, as we will work toward universal coverage, quality improvements and cost control of medical delivery, we must avoid unaffordable levels of premiums and taxes on the one hand, and deficit spending on the other. Phase-in of coverages and costs, deny expensive and excessive concessions to interest groups, design perhaps a less generous plan and higher participation on the part of individuals may be all that may be necessary.

I am reminded of the story of the guy who went into a pizza shop and ordered a pizza. Its owner said, do you want it cut into six or eight pieces? And the man said, make it six, I don't think I can eat eight pieces.

Mr. WAXMAN. Thank you.

[Testimony resumes on p. 140.]

[The prepared statement of Mr. Wingate follows:]

Testimony on Health Care Reform
by Edwin H. Wingate
Senior Vice President, Personnel
Dayton Hudson Corporation
Minneapolis, Minnesota

October 12, 1993

Dayton Hudson Corporation is America's fourth largest general merchandise retailer. We operate nearly 900 discount and department stores in 33 states under the names of Target, Mervyn's, Dayton's, Hudson's and Marshall Field's.

We are the nation's 16th largest employer in the private sector with about 180,000 employees and sales of $20 billion per year.

For the past four years, Dayton Hudson has been an active supporter of nationwide health care reform. I am pleased to have this opportunity to present to your subcommittees our views on President Clinton's proposal for reform.

Briefly, we favor:

- Medical coverage for all Americans.
- Elimination of cost-shifting, including cost-shifting from Medicare to the private sector.
- A nationwide basic health care package for medically necessary care with emphasis on primary care.

- Formation of competing organized and vertically integrated medical delivery systems which emphasize Continuous Quality Improvement and outcomes-based practice of medicine.
- Cost-containment which will achieve Consumer Price Index levels of health care cost increases.
- A five- or six-year phase-in of increased costs for businesses that experience large cost increases due to plan design and plan requirements.
- Incentives for increasing the supply of primary medicine physicians and for providing for medical services to under-provided geographic areas.
- Consolidation of the various forms of medical coverages (Workers Compensation, Medicaid, Medicare, auto insurance medical, etc.) into a single, nationwide offering.
- Administrative, tort, insurance and malpractice reform.
- Financing through sin taxes (alcohol and tobacco), taxes on excess benefits to individuals and non-deductibility for tax purposes for corporations for excess benefits, payroll premiums (individual and corporate), and through quantified savings from various forms of reform.
- Government, business community and individual focus on improvement in lifestyle as it relates to mental and physical well-being.

While we support national reform, we have great concern over many of the elements of the Administration's announced reform proposal. Several of those concerns are as follows:

A. CONCERNS OF DAYTON HUDSON CORPORATION AS A LARGE RETAILER

1. "LEVEL PLAYING FIELD"

Most large manufacturing firms have provided richer, more heavily subsidized medical plans to employees than have been provided by food and non-food businesses and by small employers. As a consequence, when two-income families with wage earners in two different enterprises have a choice of where they are covered, they naturally choose the richer, less expensive plan. Large manufacturing companies are arguing for a "level playing field" -- that is, a requirement that will result in each employer paying "its share." As an aside, we believe that the higher employee contribution to coverage, common in retailing, has made our employees more committed to cost containment.

This "level playing field" argument should apply equally within an industry. However, the Clinton plan would result in Dayton Hudson's (and other retailers with more than 50 employers) paying a 7.9% payroll premium, but would allow retailers with fewer than 50 employers to pay as little as 3.5%. We see this as unfair.

According to the 1987 Census of Re tailing (the most recent such report), published by the U.S. Department of Commerce Bureau of Census, establishments with fewer than 50 employees account for 58.3% of U.S. retail sales (excluding autos and eating and drinking) and account for 60.6% of employees in that sector of retailing. As large and small companies sell the same products purchased from the same vendors to the same customers, we see no justification for a major difference in medical care payroll premiums.

As a means of encouraging entrepreneurial efforts, it might be sensible to subsidize premiums for the first three or four years a new business is in existence, but a blanket subsidy, particularly in the case of retailing, is not consistent with the "level playing field" concept.

2. PHASE-IN OF INCREASED COSTS

As a general rule, large industrial companies with skilled and semi-skilled full-time workforces have offered richer, more heavily subsidized medical plans (often providing 100% of medical care premiums for employees and dependents) than have low-margin retail and service industries. Additionally, and for competitive reasons, most service and retail companies have provided limited or no medical coverage for part-time employees.

Dayton Hudson's situation is representative of what food and non-food retailers would experience if the President's plan were implemented today.

Dayton Hudson employs about 180,000 people, and has an annual payroll of $2.2 billion.

- 105,000 of our employees are eligible for medical coverage. Only 65,000 have elected coverage.
- 40,000 of our employees who are eligible for coverage have declined coverage. (Either they are covered elsewhere or they have elected to be self-insured.)
- The company pays 65% of the premiums; employees pay 35%.

- 75,000 of our employees (most of our part-timers) are not offered medical insurance.
- Our company's 1993 medical costs are expected to be $110 million.

If we suddenly had to pay 80% of premiums (7.9% of payroll), rather than the current 65%, insure the 40,000 eligibles who have chosen not to be covered at work, and also insure the 75,000 part-time employees, our annual cost would increase by 60%, from $100 million to $175 million, -- a $65 million increase.

How could we absorb this expense? Here are the obvious alternatives:

a) Reduced Profits

With 75 million shares of common stock outstanding, we could simply reduce earnings per share by 54¢. At this level, 1992 earnings would have been reduced from $4.82 per share to $4.28 per share. That earnings reduction would have reduced our stock price by at least $8 per share (using a 15 multiple price earnings ratio) and reduced the total market value of our companies' shares by $600 million. High percentages of our shares are held by pension funds and other funds that underpin retirement income of large numbers of individuals. Such events would also have adverse effects on our financial ratings which would increase the cost of our borrowing money, further reducing earnings and market value.

b) Reduced employment

Like most retailers, we have "downsized" our employment to the point that we are not able to give our customers the services they would like to receive. However, in an effort to tolerate a $65 million increase in costs, we would have to reduce our payroll costs by that amount. In terms of part-time employees, we would have to reduce that count from 75,000 to 60,000 -- 20% of that population, or 15,000 jobs.

Among the 33 states we serve, our employment in California would be most heavily affected, as nearly 30% of our workforce is in that state.

c) Reduced wages

d) A combination of the alternatives listed above

Phase-in of cost increases and reduction of costs are clearly necessary. A phase-in could be managed, based on the promised and achieved containment of health care cost inflation. Total reduction in costs could be achieved by a lower total company contribution (65% to 70% of plan costs versus 80% proposed by the Administration).

As a practical matter, we simply cannot support reform which would have the initial impact of a 60% increase in costs.

Remarks by Edwin H. Wingate
page 7

B. CONCERNS RELATED TO FINANCING

1. 10-year moratorium on taxing excess benefits

The Administration has indicated it will not tax excess benefits (benefits above the national plan level) for ten years.

Dayton Hudson strongly endorses immediate taxation on such excess benefits and supports non-deductibility of the cost of such excess benefits for corporate income tax purposes.

Excess benefits on a subsidized basis (absence of taxation) have been and remain a significant contributor to increased demand for medical treatment. Its presence represents cost-shifting to those without such benefits. The "level playing field" argument should prevail on this issue as it does on others. The annual value of such excess benefits tax has been estimated as high as $25 billion per year (company and individual tax). At most, such exemption should continue only through the term of existing labor contracts for unionized workers and unionized companies, and for one or two years for non-contractual arrangements.

The present value (10 year stream of $25 billion per year taxes discounted at 6%) of this ten year moratorium (with individual tax rates assumed to be 20% and corporate tax rates assumed to be 38%) is about $200 billion.

2. Relieving corporate obligations for early retiree medical premiums

As part of their employment offer and for reasons they alone know, many corporations (particularly those with high seniority, high pay, hourly employees) have willingly offered rich early-retirement arrangements to induce pre-age 65 retirements. Such arrangements have often included 100% company-paid medical coverage. These arrangements were not made for altruistic reasons but were rather in return for a benefit or bargaining value to the granting company.

The Administration's plan contemplates relieving these obligations, and has now estimated the cost of this concession to be $6 billion per year, which at a 6% discount rate has a present value cost of $86 billion. The General Accounting Office estimates the annual cost to be closer to $9 million per year, or a present value cost of $129 billion. A recent Hewitt Associates study indicates a $12.5 billion annual cost or present value of $179 billion.

There also is a probability that employees and employers will have a further incentive to effect retirement before age 65 (which incidentally opposes public policy of encouraging the retention in the workforce of that group of employees).

In view of the reasons for the existence of these early-retirement arrangements and the amounts involved, does it make sense to shift these costs to the general population? We think it does not. A recent NEW YORK TIMES article referred to this concession as a "big wet kiss" for those companies that would be favored by this approach.

3. Cost estimate for the Administration's standard set of medical plan provisions

Under the proposed standard plan, the Administration's per year cost estimate for a single adult is $1,800. In contrast, Hewitt Associates, a highly-regarded compensation and actuarial firm, has estimated such a plan will cost $2,270 per year, or 26% more than the $1,800.

A 26% difference could result in payroll premiums of 9.9% of payroll, all other things being equal.

At the least, this difference in projections requires an exhaustive analysis of the facts. Deficit spending or 26% increases or cost increases of magnitude are not acceptable answers.

4. Long-Term Care

Our position on this issue is simply that we should first reform and assure that we can manage cost inflation in the acute care system before we take on an additional burden which is neither fully understood nor predictable in its cost implications.

C. CONCLUSIONS

The case for universal health care coverage, quality improvement, and cost control has been made. We believe an employer-based system is the appropriate approach to coverage. The question is how far and how fast can we go in meeting the need, without damaging our economy or given segments of it -- and without increasing the national debt.

As we work toward universal coverage, quality improvements and cost control of medical delivery, we must avoid unaffordable levels of premiums and taxes on the one hand, and deficit spending on the other. Phase-in of coverages and costs, as well as less costly, less generous standard plan provisions and higher participation in costs of coverage by employees, may be necessary.

Dayton Hudson representatives look forward to participating in the development of nationwide reform. We welcome the opportunity to discuss further our concerns and ideas with members of Congress and with their staffs as the debate continues.

# # #

Mr. WAXMAN. Mr. Palizzi.

STATEMENT OF ANTHONY PALIZZI

Mr. PALIZZI. Thank you, Mr. Chairman.

Madam Chairwoman and distinguished members of both subcommittees, my name is Tony Palizzi.

I am executive vice president and general counsel of Kmart Corporation. Thank you for the opportunity to testify today on the President's plans for overhauling our Nation's health care system. It is my privilege to be here today to offer Kmart's view on this vital issue.

As the health care reform debate continues, you will hear many statistics, but one of the most important statistics is about jobs. Kmart is part of an industry that employs 20 million Americans—1 in 5 U.S. Workers. Kmart and its subsidiary companies (which includes Waldenbooks, Borders Books, Builders Square, The Sports Authority, OfficeMax and PACE) alone provide jobs for over 350,000 employees. We operate over 4,000 retail outlets in all 50 States, including more than 2,400 Kmart stores.

As a large employer, and as a member of the retail industry, Kmart is deeply concerned that while President Clinton's proposal will expand benefits for our workers, it will, at the same time, place jobs of those workers at risk. The proposal's mandate that employers bear the majority of health care costs, and the extremely complex implementation procedures threaten the continued employment of low wage and part-time workers—the very workers the President's plan aims to help. I am here today on behalf of Kmart, and retail companies across the Nation, to tell you that, as much as we might like to, retail employers simply cannot absorb the massive costs of this heath care reform plan under the Clinton plan.

Under the Clinton plan, Kmart's costs would increase dramatically. We presently pay over $250 million a year for health care benefits for our employees. To provide the benefits which the administration proposes and to include part-time employees, we estimate that our uncapped costs could approach $700 million, an increase of over $400 million. Even if we accept the administration's most optimistic projections and believe that costs can be capped and that the hoped-for financing and promised subsidies will materialize, we still estimate that our costs will go up almost $150 million. We simply will be unable to absorb the increased costs that such a plan would create.

We all know the face of retailing in the United States, familiar national chains like Kmart and thousands of small retail businesses on Main Street America. In many areas, retail establishments are the core of a community or neighborhood.

Companies like Kmart, and other large and small retailers, provide the jobs that make ends meet for millions of American families, and give important work opportunities to millions more part-timers who are single parents needing flexible schedules, older workers who want to keep active, teenagers getting a first job after school and their first taste of the working world, and college students working to contribute to their educational expenses.

What unites these varied retail workers is that they are typically low wage, and often part-time, temporary or seasonal employees. That is because our industry differs from the traditional manufacturing model—our doors are open 7 days a week, some of us 24 hours a day, and peak buying periods define much of the business. As a result, we depend on a flexible work force and create jobs to meet our unique needs.

The retail industry is an engine that drives new job creation in the United States. Retailing provides one-fourth of all jobs going to previously unemployed workers, and has contributed to our Nation's economic vitality by generating over 300,000 new jobs each year for the past 2 decades. From January of 1992 through January 1993, Kmart, alone, created 9,000 new jobs. Every time we open a new Kmart store, we create approximately 125 jobs; Super Kmart Centers hire 375 to 600 employees in each market. In 1993, 53 new Kmart stores and 17 new Super Ks will open. Approximately 50 new Kmart stores and 63 new Super Ks are scheduled to open in 1994. These statistics translate into a lot of new paychecks.

The continued ability of Kmart and other U.S. retailers to create jobs and to contribute to national economic prosperity would be threatened by the massive new costs the President's health care proposals will place on employers. While we applaud President Clinton and his advisors for pushing the debate on health care reform forward. Kmart believes that health care reform must be achieved without sacrificing hundreds of thousands of retail jobs.

A mandate requiring employers to pay their employees' health insurance expenses directly translates into increased labor costs for business. The reality is that the hardest hit sectors of the economy will be small firms and labor-intensive industries with high concentrations of low wage and part-time workers, such as the retail industry.

We ask for a reality check on the savings estimates and revenue sources which the administration claims will fund not only subsidies for small and low wage firms, but also the generous benefits package. Can we pay for this approach?

The plan assumes that $238 billion can be squeezed out of Medicaid and Medicare over 5 years, and that the annual growth rate of these programs can be limited to 4 to 5 percent annually. Achievement of these cuts is questionable, as evidenced by the struggle during recent budget negotiations to cut $56 billion from the deficit in 5 years. As all of you know, these proposed cuts in expected growth in Medicare and Medicaid will be painful.

Kmart fully supports health care reform. We pay ever-increasing costs for health care for many of our workers, and endorse a wide range of reform measures, including health insurance purchasing cooperatives to offer health coverage more efficiently and at lower costs, the promotion of managed care utilization to control health care costs, insurance reforms, guaranteed access, renewability and portability of coverage, medical malpractice reforms to reduce the practice of defensive medicine, and administrative and paperwork reforms to simplify insurance claims processing.

Kmart supports the concept of universal access and believes that it is an important component of health care reform. Reform, however, cannot come at the expense of bankrupting or forcing small companies out of business, nor must it place the enormous cost on larger, labor-intensive companies, who simply cannot financially accept such a burden without resorting to the unpleasant solution of massive cuts in employment.

We are in favor of health care reform. Changes in our system can be a very positive step for our country and for all Americans, and in turn positive for business. But reform should be in steps that can make sense. It is not our intent to take a position which is solely in Kmart's or retailing's interests. Rather, it is our intent to argue for an approach that, in the long run, is best for most Americans.

Everyone, including Kmart, wants health care to be available to everyone. But most people do not want a plan full of promises that cannot be kept. Like most Americans, we only ask for a plan that is affordable and that does not result in significant job losses. We do not have all the answers, but we believe that any plan that is adopted should first require real and measurable results that health care costs can be reduced or contained. Then and only then will true universal health care for all Americans be a realistically achievable objective.

It would be a mistake to create more large governmental bureaucracies to provide something for which we have no evidence we can pay for, and when we have no evidence that government can make it work. Once the giant is out of the cage, there will be no way to get him back in.

Please, as each of us must do every day with our personal affairs or our businesses, let's not buy something until we know and can show that we will be able to pay for it.

Mr. WAXMAN. Thank you, Mr. Palizzi.

[Testimony resumes on p. 153.]

[The prepared statement of Mr. Palizzi follows:]

STATEMENT OF
KMART CORPORATION
BEFORE A
JOINT SESSION OF
THE SUBCOMMITTEE ON COMMERCE,
CONSUMER PROTECTION AND COMPETITIVENESS AND
THE SUBCOMMITTEE ON HEALTH AND THE ENVIRONMENT
COMMITTEE ON ENERGY & COMMERCE
UNITED STATES HOUSE OF REPRESENTATIVES
OCTOBER 12, 1993

Madam Chairwoman/Mister Chairman, Mr. Stearns, Mr. Bliley and distinguished members of both Subcommittees, my name is Anthony Palizzi. I am Executive Vice President and General Counsel of Kmart Corporation. Thank you for the opportunity to testify today on the President's plans for overhauling our nation's health care system. It is my privilege to be here today to offer Kmart's view on this vital debate.

As the health care reform debate continues you will hear many statistics but one of the most important statistics is about jobs. Our company is part of an industry which employs 20 million Americans -- one in five U.S. workers. Kmart and its subsidiary companies (including Waldenbooks, Borders Books, Builders Square, The Sports Authority, OfficeMax and PACE) alone provide jobs for over 350,000 employees. We operate over 4,000 retail outlets in all 50 states (including more than 2,400 Kmart Stores).

As a large employer, and as a member of the retail industry, Kmart is deeply concerned that, while President Clinton's proposal will at once expand benefits for our workers, it will, at the same time, place the jobs that are key to those benefits at risk. The mandate for employers to bear the majority of health care costs and its extremely complex implementation threaten the continued employment of lowerwage and part-time workers -- the very workers the President's plan aims to help. I am here today on behalf of Kmart and retail companies around this nation to tell you that, as much as we might like to, retail employers simply cannot absorb the massive costs of this health care reform plan

We all know the face of retailing in the United States -- familiar national chains, such as Kmart, and small retail businesses on every Main Street in America. In many areas retail establishments are at the core of a community or neighborhood.

Companies like Kmart, and other large and small retailers, provide the jobs which make ends meet for millions of American families, and give important work opportunities to millions more part-timers who are single parents who need flexible schedules, older workers who want to keep active, teenagers getting a first job after school and their first taste of the working world, and college students working to contribute to their educational expenses.

What unites these varied retail workers is that they are typically lower-wage, and often part-time, temporary or seasonal employees. That's because our industry differs from the traditional manufacturing model -- our doors are open seven days a week (some of us 24 hour a day) and peak buying periods define much of the business. As a result, we depend on a flexible work force and create jobs to meet our unique needs.

The retail industry is an engine which drives new job creation in the United States. Retailing provides one fourth of all jobs going to previously unemployed workers and contributes to our nation's economic vitality by generating over 300,000 new jobs each year for the past two decades. From January of 1992 through January of 1993, Kmart alone create 9,000 new jobs. Every time we open a new Kmart store, we create approximately 125 new jobs; Super Kmart Centers hire 375-600 employees in each market. In 1993, 53 new Kmart stores and 17 new Super Ks will open. Approximately 50 new Kmart stores and 63 new Super Ks are scheduled to open in 1994. These statistics translate into a lot of new paychecks!

The continued ability of Kmart and other U.S. retailers to create jobs and to contribute to national economic prosperity would be threatened by the massive new costs the President's health care proposals would place on employers. While we laud President Clinton and his advisors for pushing the debate on health care reform forward, Kmart believes that health care reform must be achieved without sacrificing hundreds of thousands of retail jobs.

A mandate requiring employers to pay their employees' health insurance expenses translates directly into increased labor costs for business. The reality is that the hardest hit sectors of the economy will be small firms and labor-intensive industries with high concentrations of lower-wage workers -- such as the retail industry.

Unlike higher-wage industries which may be able to shift forms of compensation to reflect greater health care costs, the retail industry cannot shift the increased labor costs imposed by a mandate. The fundamental economic truth is that in lower-wage jobs the only way to reduce labor costs is to reduce labor -- in business where labor costs are a large portion of overall costs the effect will inevitably be massive job losses. Enactment of the Clinton plan would result in the loss of thousands of jobs within Kmart Corporation.

The President's plan promises "discounts" or subsidies for small and lower-wage businesses and affordable health care costs. Despite these provisions, , for many retailers costs could double or possibly triple. Kmart fears that the costs and administrative burdens -- particularly of covering part-time, temporary and seasonal workers -- will force our company and many other retail employers to realign our workforces, to eliminate part-time jobs, to rethink temporary jobs and to cut-back severely on new positions and wage increases. Studies show that over 70 percent of part-time employees are individuals who prefer part-time employment or have to work part-time because of family needs or schedules. In today's very diverse society this particular type of job opportunity is crucial.

The Administration has been downplaying the fact that the health care reform plan could cause serious problems in the labor market and has been highlighting the safeguards allegedly in place for small and lower-wage firms. Kmart believes that these so-called safeguards, and the financing to fund reform, must receive careful scrutiny.

If the financing proposed by President Clinton to fund health care reforms cannot be achieved, how will the President be able to deliver the subsidies promised to businesses and individuals? Just last week the Administration increased its estimate of the cost for these subsidies by $16 billion -- for an overall cost of $405 billion over five years.

Under the Clinton plan, Kmart's costs would increase dramatically. We presently pay over $250 million each year for health care benefits for our employees. To provide the benefits which the Administration proposes and to include part-time employees, we estimate that our uncapped costs could approach $700 million, an increase of over $400 million. Even if we accept the Administration's most optimistic projections and believe that costs can be capped and that the hoped-for financing and promised subsidies will materialize , we still estimate that our costs will go up $150 million. We simply will not be able to absorb the increased costs that such a plan would create. The cost of a mandate poses a threat not only to jobs of our employees but also to Kmart's continued viability as a business.

We ask for a reality check on the Administration's savings estimates, and the revenue sources which they claim will fund not only subsidies for small and lower-wage firms, but also the generous benefits package. Can we pay for this approach?

The plan assumes that $238 billion can be squeezed out of Medicaid and Medicare over five years and that the annual growth rate of these programs can be limited to 4 to 5 percent annually. Achievement of these cuts is questionable, as evidenced by the struggle which marked the recent budget deal to cut $56 billion from these programs over five years. As all the members of the Energy and Commerce Committee know, these cuts in expected growth in Medicare and Medicaid will be painful.

Economists say that the Clinton Plan will cost much more than the Administration officials have estimated. Recently Martin Feldstein, chairman of President Reagan's Council of Economic Advisers, predicted that the price tag for Clinton's reforms could be up to $120 billion more in the first year alone.

These added costs will be shouldered by businesses around this country; in effect the President's plan imposes what is essentially an employment tax.

The President's plan also places other administrative burdens and costs on retail employers which will have a disproportionately negative impact on our industry. Because of the large percentage of part-time workers we employ, the requirement that employers pay pro-rated premiums for part-time would mean that retailers would have to perform complex calculations to determine the correct premium payment for each part-time worker. These burdens and costs could outweigh the economic benefit derived from part-time workers and force retailers to eliminate these positions. This is bad for retailers, and bad for the many workers who chose part-time work. Retail employers could lose scheduling flexibility and workers could lose job opportunities.

The Clinton Plan's 30-hour definition of full-time employment will also hurt part-time jobs in retailing. Employers would be required to pay 40% of health care coverage for employees who work 15 hours per week -- less than half a full-time work week. Retailers would no longer hire two, 15-hour part-time workers when they would be better off with one 40-hour worker. These added costs, coupled with the administrative burdens cited earlier, could have the disastrous effect of eliminating many part-time jobs in the retail industry.

Madam Chairwoman/Mister Chairman, Kmart fully supports health care reform. We pay ever-increasing costs for health care for many of our workers and endorse a wide range of reform measures, including health insurance purchasing cooperatives to offer health coverage more efficiently and at lower costs, the promotion of managed care utilization to control health care costs, insurance reforms, including guaranteed access, renewability and portability of coverage, medical malpractice reforms to reduce the practice of defensive medicine, and administrative and paperwork reforms to simplify insurance claims processing.

Kmart supports the concept of universal access and believes that it is an important component of health care reform. Reform, however, cannot come at the expense of bankrupting or forcing small companies out of business, nor must it place the enormous costs on larger, labor-intensive companies, which simply cannot financially accept such a burden without resorting to the unpleasant solution of massive cuts in employment.

We are in favor of health care reform. Changes to our present system can be a very positive step for our country and for all Americans, and in turn positive for business . But reform should be insteps that can make sense. It is not our intent to take a position which is solely in Kmart's or retailing's interests. Rather, it is our intent to argue for an approach, that, in the long run, is best for most Americans.

Everyone, including Kmart, wants health care to be available to everyone. But most people do not want a plan full of promises that cannot be kept. Like most Americans, we only ask for a plan that is affordable and that does not result in significant job losses.

We do not have all the answers, but we believe that any plan that is adopted should first require real and measurable results that health care costs can be reduced or contained. Then and only then will true universal health care for all Americans be a realistically achievable objective.

It would be a mistake to create more large governmental bureaucracies to provide something for which we have no evidence we can pay for, and when we have no evidence that government can make it work. Once the giant is out of the cage, there will be no way to get him back in.

Please, as each of us must do every day in our personal affairs or our business, let's not buy something until we know and can show that we will be able to pay for it.

Mr. WAXMAN. We are going to call on members for questions. I will yield first to Mr. Greenwood.

Mr. GREENWOOD. Thank you, Mr. Chairman. I appreciate your consideration of my schedule.

I would like to address a question to Mr. Wingate, and preface it by saying that those of us who are more skeptical than others about this plan are compelled to ask the most difficult questions that we can.

We are worrying that Americans might go from a set of circumstances in which they are employed without health care to another set of circumstances in which they are unemployed with health care? Certainly, to the extent that companies feel compelled to lay off employees, those employees will get government-provided health care; but they will not have a job.

In your testimony you state that if you have to pay 7.9 percent of payroll and insure the thousands who choose not to be covered, Dayton Hudson's costs for health care would increase 60 percent, from $110 million to $175 million, which would be a $65 million increase.

You also say that to meet these increased costs you may have to cut up to 15,000 jobs. Could you talk in detail about the potential for such devastating job loss in your company?

Mr. WINGATE. First of all, we hope we avoid it by redesign of the plan. Second, I mentioned there are other alternatives such as lower earnings which affects stock price and the value of shareholders' equity or we can do a combination or decrease wages.

I am not saying that is the only resource. We hope we don't have to face that. But if we were to use the device of controlling that increased cost by the size of our work force, it would result in that kind of a reduction.

Mr. GREENWOOD. Let me follow up on your comment that you hope you can avoid such devastating job loss by altering this proposal. Can you give us a suggestion or two as to how you would like to see us alter this proposal so that it would be conducive to avoiding layoffs?

Mr. WINGATE. I think on a national basis we have to be dead certain of the kinds of costs we are imposing on this economy. Once that is behind us, we have to look at what we can afford without deficit spending. Once that is done, it might be necessary to phase in and step up as we attain savings. Also perhaps we have to have a different kind of a plan.

I am not addressing that as a sole conclusion as well as requiring that employees pay a larger slice because we have found, contrary to the previous testimony, that we do encourage more propitious use of health care if there is more involvement by the employee.

Mr. GREENWOOD. One of the concerns frequently raised by all of us is that for someone who is without any health insurance, a catastrophic illness or injury can be devastating economically. I remember, when I first graduated from college, that my father said, "you will now purchase a major medical policy with a very large deductible. I don't care how big the deductible is, but I don't want your illness to cost me my home."

I wonder how you would feel about a less drastic step. What if we required all employers to at least provide a similar major medical backup so that all employees would be covered. The employee would have a deductible that, at least, he or she would find manageable should a member of their family be stricken with a catastrophic illness.

Mr. WINGATE. That is an approach. I am so overwhelmed by the immensity of the problem we have, trying to solve that one issue is not within my realm of ability.

Mr. GREENWOOD. You testified that Hewitt Associates, one of the Nation's actuarial firms, said that the Clinton administration has underestimated the cost of the plan by 26 percent. The administration estimates the cost for a single adult at $1,800 annually, while Hewitt estimates the cost to be $2,270 annually, an increase of 26 percent.

You then correctly state that a 26 percent difference could result in payroll premiums of 9.9 percent rather than the 7.9 percent that the administration is estimating.

Would you comment further on how the administration's proposal is built on what appears to be smoke and mirror numbers rather than reality?

Mr. WINGATE. I think any proponent is likely to be optimistic. I think that has happened in this case.

Mr. WAXMAN. Thank you, Mr. Greenwood. Mrs. Collins.

Mrs. COLLINS. Ms. Jordan, it is my understanding that a subsidiary of Southern California Edison called Mission Energy operates electric utility plants in other countries and that you are presently negotiating to buy a major share of a Mexican utility called Carbon Two.

My questions are twofold: One, how your average health care costs of workers in the United States compare to workers in other countries; and, second, what health care costs will you be paying in Mexico if your acquisition comes about.

Ms. JORDAN. We don't have an isolated amount for employees in Mission Two. That is a separate company.

Mrs. COLLINS. So they are only contained in the subsidiary?

Ms. JORDAN. In the subsidiary company. I don't have those costs.

Mrs. COLLINS. Would you provide them to us?

Ms. JORDAN. We can get them.

Mrs. COLLINS. Will you send them to me?

Ms. JORDAN. Yes, I will be happy to.

Mrs. COLLINS. Are health care costs a factor in your company's decision to invest abroad?

Ms. JORDAN. I don't know.

Mrs. COLLINS. Why do you have Mission? Is it just to invest abroad?

Ms. JORDAN. I am not representing the corporation. I am here only for the utility. I am not in a position to answer the questions you are asking me.

Mrs. COLLINS. Mr. Barnette, for older United States industries retirement costs are an expensive factor. Nationally, firms that are new entrants into such industries have young work forces.

How much does your company expect to save on retiree health plans under the Clinton plan and what will you do with these savings in order to improve your company's competitiveness vis-a-vis foreign producers?

Mr. BARNETTE. Our current retired health care costs amounts to $241 million. We have 21,000 active employees. Each of our active employees are accounting for nearly $10,000 for medical costs to support that population.

With respect to the Clinton plan, we have some general estimates, but that plan is still evolving. One thing is certain, we know where our health care costs will be in the year 2000 at the rate we are going now. They will approach $450 million under current revenues and with our current work force. We cannot permit that to happen.

If the Clinton health care plan causes health care spending to be held to the consumer price levels, assuming that as a working hypothesis, that trend rate is so substantially less than our current health care trend rate that provision alone to restrain the level of spending would have a significant effect on Bethlehem Steel and I think similarly situated companies.

As to international competitiveness, a ton of steel coming into this country, largely unfairly traded because of foreign subsidies and dumping, simply does not bring as a burden of that ton of steel the expenses of health care and pension benefits. That is true in this country.

Mrs. COLLINS. Mr. Ragin, would you expect major companies would purchase health coverage through regional health alliances and will they also want to purchase supplemental health care benefits such that the companies might do it for their employees?

Mr. RAGIN. I would anticipate that larger companies that have the option of purchasing through an alliance or going it alone would make that decision primarily based on what taxes or other situations may affect or govern that choice.

Mr. WAXMAN. Thank you, Mrs. Collins. Mr. McMillan.

Mr. MCMILLAN. I want to thank all of the panel for your contributions. I think we have heard some excellent testimony. I wish we had time to really dig into the effects of this because I think as it affects each of your businesses and the small businesses who will testify later once you have had a chance to really analyze it.

This is where the water really hits the wheel in terms of the reality of this plan. I have a few questions I would like to ask pursuant to this.

Mr. Barnette, I think your written testimony indicates that your health care costs per employee were $9,518.

Mr. BARNETTE. That is correct.

Mr. MCMILLAN. And your overall costs have increased 285 percent since 1980. Does this include some additional benefits or does it include shrinking benefits because of increasing costs?

Mr. BARNETTE. I think it is the latter, Congressman. Certainly there have been modest benefit increases in the health care benefits provided to our employees. We have just completed a negotiation, a somewhat precedent breaking 6-year contract with the union workers and the health care benefits are relatively stable.

Mr. MCMILLAN. It is common for small businesses that don't have the buying power of large corporations to see their premium costs jump up 50 percent from one year to the next, causing them to reduce benefits or discontinue plans.

77-929 O - 94 - 6

That was something I was trying to get at with Mr. Kirkland, albeit very unsuccessfully. This has to do with what I think is a glaring disparity between what the President is proposing in his guaranteed benefits package which, if we can nail him down, is roughly $1,800 for an individual with assumed copayments, deductibles, et cetera.

But for the person, say, on or about the poverty level or with about $12,000 or $13,000 a year income, that figure would be the level of subsidy.

Yet, under the Clinton proposal, you would be able to maintain the tax deductibility of your costs which are at $9,518 per capita. How can the Federal government justify that because it seems in one case the cost to the Federal Government is $1,800, and the cost in your case is, after tax value of the revenue forgone by reason deductibility, assuming a 36 percent corporate tax rate of $2,800 to $2,900. Is that an accurate analysis?

Mr. BARNETTE. It is a complex question, Congressman.

Mr. MCMILLAN. I am trying to reduce it to a comprehensible level.

Mr. BARNETTE. My answer is that given the magnitude of the health care beneficiary population that we are providing health care benefits for, surely at the corporate level the dollars we are spending to provide those benefits should be tax deductible.

What happens to the benefits screen as provided to individuals, that will be one of the most difficult questions Congress will address and it will also be part of the collective bargaining process in years to come.

I think that we are in a very early step in the micro development of this whole process. It is going to take us some time to work many of these issues out.

Mr. MCMILLAN. My concern is that implicit, if not explicit, in the Clinton plan is a high concentration of bureaucratic decision-making and purchasing. The Federal Government is going to be doing it for 88 percent of the population. Only 12 percent of the population is represented by companies of your size, many of whom will most certainly choose to opt out of their corporate alliances and into health care purchasing alliances.

Maybe your corporation is not in a position to do that by reason of contracts and so forth, so it is understandable that the administration would include in their plan features that really ease that transition.

But this places an enormous burden on the U.S. taxpayer when in fact we don't have the resources to transfer to unmet needs. I am really concerned about that.

What would happen to your corporation if you decided to self-insure, and then had an additional 1 percent surtax imposed for presumably funding academic medical centers, which, in fact, we already fund under Medicaid and other special grants in the Federal budget?

What would happen to your business if you had another 1 percent of your payroll that had to go directly to transfer into the Federal treasury?

Mr. BARNETTE. It would be of far less consequence, Congressman, than the exorbitant increases we are getting now with no national system in place. Each of our companies must know what the plans are, whether we will be in an alliance or attempt to continue our own health care systems and make cost evaluations based upon that.

I regret that at this point we are simply not in a position to make that decision. Whether we would attempt to have our own plan and the costs attendant to that or whether we would elect to join an alliance, I would hope to have the opportunity to appear again when we know what the specific alternatives are, and we will be pleased to present you with as much of an individual analysis on an individual company as we can.

We are working closely with the United Steelworkers and the National Health Care Coalition group and have data developed there. We would be pleased to submit that to the subcommittee.

Mr. MCMILLAN. I am sure you have given that a lot of thought. I hope you will join with those of us in Congress who are concerned about this, whether it is the Clinton plan, the Senate plan, or the Cooper plan, that if we don't get ahold of the cost problems, not only in pricing but the underlying cost drivers in health care, and we can go through a whole litany of what they are, then that 1 percent will not remain 1 percent over time. It can change drastically.

I think it is important that we get at the cost drivers early in this, otherwise we are kidding ourselves.

Mr. BARNETTE. I agree. We certainly need to get ahead of the cost issue early. Our recommendation is to do it through budgeting and single payer systems and going in some respect even further than the Clinton plan.

There are examples of those concepts working. Next door in Maryland in the hospital system there is a system working quite effectively. We have a large employer in merchandise and it stands behind a very advanced plan they have tried there.

Mr. WAXMAN. Thank you. Mr. Brown.

Mr. BROWN. One of the most attractive features of the Clinton plan is their interest and encouragement of preventive care, everything from prenatal or immunization, sort of highlighting those companies that aggressively run antismoking campaigns and encourage their employees to be tested preventatively more frequently and fitness centers and that kind of thing.

Would you comment briefly in the interest of time and then I would follow up with a series of written questions. What do you do in preventative care from encouraging pregnant women to get care to fitness centers and to antismoking campaigns. Mr. Barnette?

Mr. BARNETTE. We have a wellness program within Bethlehem. We just opened in our community a Bethlehem health care clinic. Not being sure of the results of that, the opening weekend we had 5,000 individuals show up to examine the opportunities of this clinic.

We have extensive programs within the company to promote preventative medicine and preventative care.

Mr. BROWN. Another question for all of you at the same time. Are all these services open to all employees?

Mr. BARNETTE. Yes, they are Congressman. I think one of the great costs in our national health care system is the inability of so many uncovered beneficiaries to have the opportunities to have access. We pay the price for their eventually getting medical care often at emergency rooms and hospitals because they don't have access to the kinds of preventative programs that some of us are able to provide.

Ms. JORDAN. Congressman, at Edison we have multiple programs of prevention to encourage early treatment. We offer preventive benefits in our basic benefit package. We have a program for good prenatal outcomes. We have a preventative health account in which people are encouraged to join fitness centers and other types of things.

We are not sure what the actual cost savings are for that particular one, but we believe in the long-term it really does help. We have a good health rebate program for early screening around cholesterol and high blood pressure.

We have an active smoking cessation that is working well, and I could show you those statistics. So we have a number of programs in that area.

Mr. RAGIN. We have a smoke-free environment in all of our offices in all locations around the country. We have in our New York location a fitness room and aerobics program for employees which they may engage in during work hours. We have substance abuse counseling for those employees, fortunately few in number, who have been afflicted by that.

We require our employees to have health insurance, either with us or demonstrate they have it through a spouse or through other arrangements that they have insurance to meet their health needs.

Mr. WINGATE. We have established smoke-free environments. In our distribution areas where there is lifting and carrying, we have put in work out programs. We encouraged employees through our design to be paying 35 percent of the coverage, so they are deeply involved in prevention as well.

We are the initiator of the Business Health Care Action Group in Minneapolis to deliver care on an organized basis where the provider is involved with us, too, in terms of managing health care costs, and the provider is involved in carrying some of the risk of a population that does not take care of itself.

Mr. PALIZZI. At Kmart, we have a number of programs in place. We have well baby care. We have HMO's across the country that specialize in preventative care, we have preventative medical, dental. We have active nonsmoking programs. We have substance abuse counseling and active safety programs in all stores and distribution centers.

Mr. BROWN. Have any of you made any calculations on the costs of these programs and on determining if you will continue these after the Clinton plan is in effect? What kinds of benefits you are getting as employers?

Mr. WINGATE. One thing we have done is charge a premium for those who smoke. We have determined that we have about 40 percent greater costs for smokers than we have for nonsmokers. It is a big deal. So that pays dividends.

Mr. BROWN. Has it affected smoking habits?

Mr. WINGATE. Yes, it has.

Mr. BROWN. Better than a cigarette tax?

Mr. WINGATE. That is right.

Mr. PALIZZI. It is hard to quantify the savings, but I would add that in the last couple of years our health care costs have come down. The increase is less. Two or three years ago we were witnessing increases of 10 to 12 percent. The last couple of years we have been able to get that down to a 4 to 5 percent per year increase. How much of that is due to these programs is difficult to quantify, however.

Mr. WAXMAN. Thank you. Mr. Moorhead.

Mr. MOORHEAD. Thank you, Mr. Chairman.

Under the Clinton health plan, companies that provide a richer package than the administration is proposing will be allowed to continue that 10 percent without the employees suffering tax consequences. Meanwhile, all employees will be subject to tax consequences if their employers want to offer a richer package. With costs of $9,518 per employee, Bethlehem Steel will surely receive the advantage of a 10-year grandfather provision.

Mr. Barnette, could you explain what you believe to be the justification for this?

Mr. BARNETTE. I think that you are perhaps asking two questions, Congressman. One is the tax ability of the corporation and the other is the tax implications to the individuals.

With respect to the corporation, I think surely whatever our health care costs are should continue to be corporate deductible expenses. As to the employee, however, I think that is a matter of transition.

My understanding of the tax implications of the proposals under consideration is that in existing plans that the benefits being provided to employees in excess of the standard package would not be imputed as income to the employees during the transitional period.

To my understanding, it is a matter of collective bargaining as to the benefit we are required to pay for the next 6 years, as a matter of our long-term contracts. The tax implications of that to the individual—and I am confident that Congress will be addressing that—my understanding is that there will be no tax implications.

Mr. MOORHEAD. What do you do when the 10 years runs out or the current contract that you have runs out? The employees may have to take a considerably reduced quality of insurance policy from what you are now giving them or else if you provide for them in collective bargaining you won't be able to take a deduction for cost of living from that. Won't that create a problem for you?

Mr. BARNETTE. It is my understanding that the standard package benefits in the Clinton plan to many, not just to Bethlehem Steel, but to the benefits we are offering now, this process is going to take some time to be implemented. We at Bethlehem are not awaiting the enactment of the Clinton or any other plans to attempt to increase efforts for reduced health care costs. We have every action we know today under way to try to achieve that.

When we come up in 6 years, which will be the next point of negotiation for us, if the plan is in place at the national level I think it will greatly affect the dynamics of collective bargaining.

Mr. MOORHEAD. What you say the Clinton plan would offer and what you are now paying for—what the present plan says you can pay for there is $2,200 and you are paying $9,500.

Mr. BARNETTE. That is the current cost for our active employees supporting the entire 170,000 beneficiaries that we have. That is the number you are referring to.

Mr. MOORHEAD. If you are paying $9,500 for what is $2,200, you are getting a poor deal. There ought to be some renegotiation someplace along the line. It doesn't make any sense.

Mr. BARNETTE. The $10,000 number, using that as a general term, is the cost to our company per active employees to supply all the benefits of the health care population of 170,000. The individual expenses of an individual active employee could be substantially less than $10,000. It is closer to $4,000 to you or $4,200.

For a retiree, it would be less than that. But I think we are perhaps talking about two different things. To me, the relevant issue is how much does it cost per active employee.

Mr. MOORHEAD. You said on page seven that the aggregate growth health care system must be controlled. I think all of us understand that. It depends upon how it is controlled. Do you support the use of global budgets to bring costs down to an acceptable level, the CPI inflation rate? Is the CPI cap good enough for an industry that has 17 percent of our national product? Would you like to have that applied to your industry, the steel industry?

Mr. BARNETTE. How would you apply that?

Mr. MOORHEAD. By setting price controls which is what we are going to have to have in the health care industry.

Mr. BARNETTE. If we had 3 percent CPI price increases in the basic steel industry, those would be very substantial. Today, a ton of steel is selling at less than it was in the 1980's, yet the quality is much better. Our prices have not kept pace with inflation.

Mr. MOORHEAD. What I am concerned with as we go into the area of rigid price controls, it may end up applying to a lot of people whose costs are greater for one reason or another.

Mr. BARNETTE. I wish it was 3 percent. It is much more than that. It is closer to 10 percent on an annualized basis.

Mr. WAXMAN. The gentlemen's time has expired. Mr. Manton.

Mr. MANTON. I will ask one question and hopefully the entire panel can answer within my 5-minute time period.

Assuming arguendo that the President's plan as now formulated would pass, what one change would you like to see if you had your druthers? I will start with Mr. Barnette.

Mr. BARNETTE. That is a very difficult question. I want to return to it as I think about it a little more. But I think it would be earlier controls on costs, moving promptly to all payer rates, moving promptly to budgets and marketing, to get costs under control sooner than might be provided for in the currently drafted plan.

Mr. MANTON. Ms. Jordan.

Ms. JORDAN. I would say there needs to be more in favor of the current proposal, as I read it. We need to have more purchasers out there so that there is a multiple competition in terms of purchasers as well as competition among plans.

The way that I see it structured is really a lot of disincentives for large corporations to remain in the mixture as a large purchaser. We need to be there so we can pressure the delivery system to change because that is where the cost savings are. You can only put that leverage on it by having large purchasers who can leverage it.

Mr. MANTON. Mr. Ragin?

Mr. RAGIN. We believe employees should be given wide latitude to determine the level of employer contribution, be that 80 percent, 50 percent or 100 percent.

Mr. WINGATE. I would say pay for what we are taking aboard.

Mr. PALIZZI. Primary emphasis on cost containment and until that is achieved stress on the employer mandate.

Mr. WAXMAN. Mr. Dingell.

Mr. DINGELL. I would like to commend the panel for a very helpful presentation. You have done that in terms of the time that you have. I am curious. I have heard about the coverage of retirees. As I understand the Clinton plan, it would require all retirees to be covered the same way under the Federal plan; is that correct? All retirees would be covered the same way under the Clinton plan, isn't that a fact?

Ms. JORDAN. Yes, sir.

Mr. DINGELL. So I gather, then, that Bethlehem Steel, Earl G. Graves, Limited, Southern California Edison, Dayton Hudson and Kmart would all cover their employees the same way; is that right?

Mr. WINGATE. The same way but not in the same amount. As I understand it, the government would not be supporting existing requirement plans. We have not given away the shop and others have.

Mr. DINGELL. You have raised an interesting question. There seems to be some difference between Dayton Hudson and Kmart and Bethlehem Steel or Southern California Edison. I am trying to understand what that difference is. They have a more generous plan for their retirees; is that right?

Mr. WINGATE. Which they traded away for bargaining or business reasons.

Mr. DINGELL. They gave away the shop when they took care of retirees?

Mr. WINGATE. That is my view.

Mr. DINGELL. Is it also your view, Mr. Palizzi?

Mr. PALIZZI. Kmart provides for the ability of that retiree to stay in our health care program, but at his or her cost. We do not provide payment for retirees.

Mr. DINGELL. So you have no plan for retirees?

Mr. PALIZZI. We allow them to stay in our plan but we make no contribution to early retirees' health care benefits.

Mr. DINGELL. Then perhaps Mr. Wingate, do you pay any?

Mr. WINGATE. We pay about $30 per month for each employee for early retirees.

Mr. DINGELL. How much does the retiree pay?

Mr. WINGATE. About 80 percent of the cost.

Mr. DINGELL. So you pay $20 and he pays $80?

Mr. WINGATE. It is $30 and about $120.

Mr. DINGELL. I am beginning to understand your objection. You would be compelled to treat your retirees the same way that Mr. Barnette and Mr. Ragin and Ms. Jordan's employees would be compelled to be treated; is that right?

Mr. PALIZZI. That is not my understanding.

Mr. DINGELL. That would raise your cost. I think that is a proper position for you to take. You are looking at the interests of your shareholders, and I commend you for that.

Have you overlooked the fact that the government would pay 80 percent for all your retirees, that 80 percent of the cost of your retirees would be covered? Then they would pay only 20 percent. You say you pay 20 percent and the government pays 80, is that right? I am not sure your describing the situation is all that much different.

I have another interest here that you kind of tweaked. What percentage of your employees now have health care coverage? Do you cover all your employees full-time and part-time or just full-time?

Mr. WINGATE. I think I covered that in my testimony. We do not offer insurance to part-time employees.

Mr. DINGELL. So your part-time employee has no coverage whatsoever?

Mr. WINGATE. By employment.

Mr. DINGELL. What about you, Mr. Palizzi?

Mr. PALIZZI. We provide health care coverage for full-time employees, which is 30 hours a week or more. We pay for 70 percent. The employee pays for 30 percent.

Mr. DINGELL. What about the part-time?

Mr. PALIZZI. Persons who work under 30 hours a week are not provided health care coverage by our company.

Mr. DINGELL. What percentage, if you please, gentlemen, are your full-time and part-time employees?

Mr. PALIZZI. In our case, full-time represents about 76 percent of the work force of over 200,000 employees.

Mr. WINGATE. We are about the same.

Mr. DINGELL. What percentage of your employees stay with you until retirement time?

Mr. WINGATE. It is hard for us to say because we have been a growing company, as most of retailing has been. It is a moving target. I would say a very small percentage of the part-time employees do.

Mr. DINGELL. A small percentage of the part-time.

Mr. WAXMAN. Mr. Dingell, your time has expired. Do you wish a couple additional minutes?

Mr. DINGELL. It would help, yes.

Mr. WAXMAN. The gentlemen will be yielded 2 additional minutes.

Mr. DINGELL. What percentage of your employees stay until retirement?

Mr. WINGATE. I cannot say. We are growing very rapidly.

Mr. DINGELL. It would be a very small percent.

Mr. WINGATE. I don't know.

Mr. DINGELL. Would it be a large percent?

Mr. WINGATE. It might be, yes, for full-time employees. How about you, Mr. Palizzi?

Mr. PALIZZI. I don't know the percentage. We are a company that has been around for almost 100 years. We have a company-paid pension plan for almost 50 years and many people receive benefits from that plan. The percentage of full-time employees who stay until retirement, I don't know.

Mr. DINGELL. But you say your retirees can continue under the plan but they don't get any company contribution for health care?

Mr. PALIZZI. Yes, that is correct. By staying under the plan, they purchase it at a better rate than if they had to purchase it on a plan outside.

Mr. DINGELL. Is that the case for you, Mr. Wingate?

Mr. WINGATE. No. We pay about 20 percent of the premium and they enroll if they wish.

Mr. DINGELL. When you gave away the store, what did you give your retirees?

Mr. BARNETTE. Most respectfully, Mr. Chairman, we think we provided a well-earned benefit and health care to our employees and retirees. Most of our employees remain with our company and retire from our company. The cost difference between retirees and active employees and the retirees, both labor and management, the percentage is slightly different, but in general we pay a substantial amount of health care expense.

Mr. DINGELL. I don't want you to get the idea that those are my views. Those happen to be Mr. Wingate's. I am sure you appreciate being quoted, Mr. Wingate.

Mr. WINGATE. I do.

Mr. WAXMAN. Thank you, Mr. Chairman.

Let me pursue a few questions. You have given us your views on whether there ought to be a mandate. One of the major elements of the President's proposal would be to set limits on health care plan premiums to reduce the growth of inflation.

Several of you testified your companies have been engaged in aggressive efforts to increase employees' cost sharing. Yet, as Mr. Barnette testified, for some of you these efforts have only momentarily slowed down escalation costs.

The President's plan calls for the establishment of a national health board to impose limits on annual increases in public and private sector spending for the standard benefit package. Do you, members of this panel, support that part of the President's proposal, and if not, do you have an alternative approach to protect workers from health care costs?

Mr. BARNETTE. We support the principle and would even strengthen it.

Ms. JORDAN. We support the program but would like to see the details.

Mr. RAGIN. I would agree with Ms. Jordan's comments.

Mr. WINGATE. We are in the same position.

Mr. PALIZZI. We would support anything that would help control the costs of health care.

Mr. WAXMAN. Mr. Barnette, you mentioned earlier that you will have to decide early whether your company would participate in regional alliances or form your own corporate alliance. On what basis would you make that decision?

Mr. BARNETTE. I would review the plan in its final form and then apply the demographics of our work force to that plan. Having done that, we would of course need to know the premiums charged and the costs to us of continuing along the same lines as we are today.

I have some intuitive feelings about what we are likely to do, but I must apologize they are nothing more than that. We have tried to do some costing with our actuaries at this point in time but there are still so many provisions of the plan that are not yet that specific, and, then again, costs in the regional alliance, and we operate in different parts of the country where there could be different costs.

I am sorry I cannot give you a better answer than that right now.

Mr. WAXMAN. Mr. Wingate, you indicated that your company pays what percent of the employees' coverage?

Mr. WINGATE. Sixty-five percent.

Mr. WAXMAN. So the employee would pay the 35 percent. Do all your employees choose to pay that 35 percent?

Mr. WINGATE. Sixty-five thousand of our 105,000 eligibles have taken coverage and 45,000 have not. Many are insured elsewhere and many are uninsured.

Mr. WAXMAN. Mr. Palizzi, what percentage do your employees pay?

Mr. PALIZZI. We pay 70 percent.

Mr. WAXMAN. More of the cost is absorbed by the employee. How many take the coverage?

Mr. PALIZZI. I don't know the exact number but probably 80 to 85 percent.

Mr. WAXMAN. I think that all of you have been very helpful. I commend you for your testimony. You have differences that are very obviously due to the business you are in. All of you do cover your employees to one extent or another. From the point of view as employers who provide insurance, you want to make sure the costs are controlled so you can continue to cover those costs. I think that is an important part of the challenge before us.

We will break now and return at 1:40 to hear the last panel.

Mr. MCMILLAN. Mr. Chairman, there are several questions I would like to ask. Would it be possible to direct written questions to the witnesses?

Mr. WAXMAN. Yes, let me ask members of this last panel, Mr. Wingate and others, I would like to ask that members having additional questions or members who have other questions they want to ask, we would appreciate it if you would send them for the record.

[The following letters were submitted:]

ALEX McMILLAN
9TH DISTRICT
NORTH CAROLINA

COMMITTEE ASSIGNMENT
ENERGY AND COMMERCE COMMITTEE
BUDGET COMMITTEE
REPUBLICAN LEADER'S TASK FORCE ON HEALTH
REPUBLICAN LEADER'S TASK FORCE ON THE ECONOMY

Congress of the United States
House of Representatives
Washington, DC 20515-3309

October 18, 1993

Mr. Curtis H. Barnette
Chairman and Chief Executive Officer
Bethlehem Steel Corporation
1170 Eighth Avenue
Bethlehem, Pennsylvania 18016

Dear Mr. Barnette:

Thank you for your appearance before the subcommittees on Health and the Environment and Commerce, Consumer Protection, and Competitiveness. I appreciate your willingness to answer some of my questions in written form, especially in light of the number of questions that you have already answered verbally.

As I mentioned to you after the hearing, it would be very helpful to me and the rest of my committee if you could provide a written explanation of your standard benefits package. This should cover the major medical portion of the policy (both inpatient and outpatient), along with any preventive care, mental health, dental, prescription, or eyeglass benefits. Furthermore, I believe that it would also interest the committee if you could give us, in detail, information on any and all supplemental packages that you either provide or offer to your employees, whether or not matching funds from your company are involved. Financial estimates of the standard benefits package and any supplemental package would also be appreciated.

In your statement, you pointed out that Bethlehem Steel had health care costs of "$9,518 per active employee" in FY92. You explained later in your testimony that this figure was in reality lower in that your statement included the costs of retiree benefits. It would be very helpful to me and the Members of my committee if you would provide us with the actual cost per active employee and the aggregate actual cost for the standard and additional benefit packages, excluding any retiree costs. Furthermore, if you could give me some detail as to the cost per retiree, the total cost to your company, and the benefit package that retirees receive, I would be most appreciative.

I would also like to ask you whether or not, as proposed under the Clinton plan, your corporation would choose to self-insure as a corporate alliance or instead place all of your employees into the regional health alliances. My understanding of the President's proposal is that self-insured corporation would not be eligible for the 7.9% cap as would those who join the regional alliances. Furthermore, Hillary Rodham Clinton testified before my committees that self-insured corporate alliances would also be required to pay 1% of their payroll to the federal government to help fund "academic health centers," even though those types of pursuits are already funded under Medicare, Medicaid, GME provisions, and others. If you would not choose to self-insure as a corporate alliance, is there any scenario you can imagine where a large corporation such as yours, functioning under the same rules as proposed by President Clinton, would in fact decide to self-insure?

Finally, I would like to follow up on my question concerning the gap in real actuarial costs for coverage between your plan and the proposed Clinton plan. President Clinton is using roughly $1,800 per person as the actuarial cost of his plan, where your real world experience indicates that the true cost is much higher. I think that it is fair to assume that if you take the numbers that you have generated from my first question, specifically the true cost per employee Bethlehem Steel pays for health care benefits, and subtract President Clinton's figure, both you and I will see a substantial "gap" in the cost, possibly as much as $2400. In the Clinton proposal, there is no concrete way to pay for this difference, either in money or reduced benefits. How do you propose that this gap be filled? Do you believe that major corporations such as your should cover this shortfall, or will the costs be shifted to the federal government, and through it the U.S. taxpayer?

Again, I appreciate your willingness to answer these questions, and I look forward to hearing from you soon on these issues.

Sincerely,

Alex McMillan
Member of Congress

AM:jmm

Southern California Edison Company
P. O. BOX 800
8631 RUSH STREET
ROSEMEAD, CALIFORNIA 91770

MARGARET H. JORDAN
VICE PRESIDENT

TELEPHONE
818-302-5519

October 19, 1993

Honorable Cardiss Collins
Chairman
Subcommittee on Commerce and Consumer Protection
Committee on Energy and Commerce
U.S. House of Representatives
H2-151, Ford Office Building
Washington, D.C. 20515

Dear Ms. Collins:

I appreciated the opportunity to testify at the October 12, 1993 hearings you and Congressman Henry Waxman held on the Administration's proposal for health care reform. You asked me two questions regarding Mission Energy. In my introduction I indicated that I am the Vice President of Southern California Edison, the utility company, responsible for health care and employee services. In this capacity I am not responsible for the Mission Companies.

Therefore, I forwarded your questions to Edward R. Muller, President and CEO of Mission Energy. You can expect his response to your questions in the very near future.

Thank you again for receiving my testimony on the critical issue of health care reform.

Sincerely,

Margaret H. Jordan

Margaret H. Jordan

cc: Ed Muller

[Brief recess.]

Mr. WAXMAN. The meeting of the subcommittees will please come to order.

On our third panel we will be hearing from small businesses. I am particularly looking forward to hearing from these witnesses because we all know that the small business people have concerns about this legislation.

Our witnesses reflect the diversity of small business in America. Fred Marks, the chairman, and Spencer Putnam, the vice president, will speak on behalf of the Vermont Teddy Bear Company in Shelburne, Vt.; Judy Wicks, president of the White Dog Cafe in Philadelphia; Elizabeth Hebson is owner of Hackney's on Lake, Inc., a family restaurant chain in suburban Chicago; and Ann Blakeley is president of Earth Resources Corporation, a consultant firm specializing in hazardous waste management located in Ocoee, Fla.

I want to thank you all for joining us today. Your prepared statements will be part of the record in their entirety. I would like to ask each of you to limit your presentation to no more than 5 minutes.

I know, Mr. Putnam, you have a plane to catch, so let's begin with you.

STATEMENTS OF SPENCER PUTNAM, VICE PRESIDENT, AND FRED MARKS, CHAIRMAN, VERMONT TEDDY BEAR CO.; LIZ HEBSON, OWNER, HACKNEY'S RESTAURANT; JUDITH A. WICKS, PRESIDENT, WHITE DOG ENTERPRISES, INC.; AND ANN BLAKELEY ON BEHALF OF NATIONAL FEDERATION OF INDEPENDENT BUSINESS

Mr. PUTNAM. Thank you, Mr. Chairman. My name is Spencer Putnam, and I am the vice president and chief operating officer of the Vermont Teddy Bear Company. My father, William F. Putnam, M.D. had a general medical practice in Vermont and New Hampshire from 1936 until 1978. I remember during the 1950's that some of his patients paid him for his medical services with chicken eggs, carpentry, domestic work, and other forms of barter. I know that many of his patients paid him nothing at all.

This did not trouble my father. What troubled him deeply was that he knew that there were thousands of citizens of Vermont and New Hampshire who did not come to him for medical care because they were ashamed of their inability to pay for it.

They delayed their medical care until their conditions got worse and that brought on them greater health problems and increased their financial exposure as well.

In the 1940's, my father was calling for a nationalized health care system because he believed that health care access should be a birthright of all Americans regardless of their ability to pay. In the 1950's, he resigned from the American Medical Association because of that organization's intractable opposition to such a system.

I share the deep satisfaction I know he would have felt to see this issue placed at the forefront of our national agenda.

We have moved long beyond the era when barter for medical services is practical. Now that I am the chief operating officer of a small American manufacturing firm, I have the front row seat on how the health care crisis affects Americans on a daily basis.

As a dynamic small employer of 200 individuals, the Vermont Teddy Bear Company is dependent for continued growth on a healthy and secure work force. Over the past 7 years, we have been engaged in a grim game of hopscotch, jumping from one health insurer to another in an effort to mitigate increasing costs and to avoid loss of coverage for some of our so-called "high-risk employees." We are convinced that only a nationally coordinated effort can solve the health care crisis that America faces today.

The Vermont Teddy Bear Company accepts the responsibility of providing a health care benefit for several reasons. Obviously, healthy workers are more productive; equally important, workers freed from the stress of worrying about the health of relatives and the costs of medical care will be better able to perform their work-related duties.

We also believe that providing a health care benefit is part of our corporate responsibility.

Many employers are concerned that the cost of this health care will threaten their competitiveness or very existence. The program as proposed by the administration already includes some protection for small employers. It should also be accompanied by aggressive governmental measures to encourage entrepreneurism and small business viability in various ways.

Currently, we split the costs of health care coverage about equally with our employees and spend in the aggregate an amount equivalent to about 8 percent of our payroll for health care premiums. However, less than 60 percent of our employees are enrolled. These costs will only go up if we do nothing. Even if our company's share of health care costs rises as a result of the new national health security act, we welcome the fact that it brings health security to all of our employees, and believe that in the long run it will save us money and increase employee productivity.

Mr. WAXMAN. Thank you.

Mr. WAXMAN. Mr. Marks.

STATEMENT OF FRED MARKS

Mr. MARKS. Thank you. Spencer has probably used 4 of our 5 minutes so I will make my statement brief.

I don't know that this gives us a greater claim to wisdom, but we were chosen as the best little company in America by the National Federation of Independent Business People, who seem to be in a little contrary position to where we stand.

It is my strong belief that we have a moral obligation to all our citizens, and particularly to our employees, to provide them with benefits and a wage which makes it possible for them to live. The continual hassle over things like the minimum wage where the world was coming to an end every time we raised the minimum wage a nickel has proven to be nothing but a straw man. I think the same thing applies here.

I think the benefit is essential, and we as business people will find a way to deal with it. Thank you.

Mr. WAXMAN. Thank you very much. Sounds like you are deserving of that award.

[The prepared statement of Messrs. Putnam and Marks follows:]

STATEMENT OF SPENCER PUTNAM AND FRED MARKS, VERMONT TEDDY BEAR COMPANY

The Vermont Teddy Bear Company is a manufacturer of 100% American made teddy bears producing over 300,000 stuffed animals per year and based in Shelburne, Vermont. It employs 200 workers (of whom 170 are full time) in production, sales and marketing, administrative, and management positions. In addition, the company utilizes a pool of over 150 homeworkers who function as independent contractors, some of whom work primarily for The Vermont Teddy Bear Company. The company pays between 50% and 60% of the cost of a basic medical/health insurance plan which is available to all full time employees. However, only 58% of its employees subscribe. No health care benefit is extended to homeworkers.

Financially the company has gone through two distinct phases, a struggling phase and a commercially successful phase.

Through good times and bad times the company has been committed to providing a health care benefit to its employees. Management has been frustrated at its inability to provide more comprehensive coverage or to absorb more of the cost to provide wider access to the plan. It is our belief that good health among employees is essential for their productivity. Furthermore, health care security, reducing stress both at work and at home, also enhances productivity. But beyond this, we consider providing a health care benefit part of our corporate responsibility to our employees and to our community.

Like other Americans employers and citizens in general, a major concern in regard to the health care crisis is the cost, both to the employer and to the employees. Jumping from one insurance carrier to another in order to contain the cost of insurance coverage has become an almost annual event for our company. Despite these efforts, some 42% of our full time employees are not covered by our health plan, a significant number of them because they are unable to afford even our subsidized health insurance premium.

Another major concern has been our difficulty in providing insurance for people with pre-existing conditions. On two occasions our switch in health insurance provider was caused by the need to preserve the coverage which we had been offering to such people.

It has been a constant struggle for the company to provide the range and scope of coverage which our employees desire. Most frequently mentioned in this regard are coverage for vision care, dental and orthodontic work, and various preventive procedures. Employees have also been bedeviled by the burden of complicated paperwork involved in dealing with certain private insurance companies. This burden is increased by the refusal of certain providers to handle insurance claims directly for our employees.

Most employees wish to retain flexibility and freedom in the selection of their doctors and other medical providers.

Finally, the company management is concerned about medical coverage for its independent contractors (homeworkers). Although for a variety of reasons the independent contractor arrangement is beneficial for the homeworkers and company alike, the company recognizes that the same health care worries and illness that it wishes to provide its on-site employees is equally important for the productivity and well being of its independent contractors.

A national commitment to solving the health care crisis in America is essential. That 37 million citizens of the most advanced industrialized nation of the world should not have medical coverage is scandalous. That 14% (and rising) of our gross domestic product is currently being devoted to health care expenses is reckless. This is one leadership position that the United States should abdicate immediately.

These factors undermine the economic strength and international competitiveness of our nation. Beyond that they tear at our social fabric and run counter to our ideals of a society which offer equal protection and equal opportunity to all of its citizens.

Only a nationally coordinated commitment to solving these problems has any chance of success. The Vermont Teddy Bear Company endorses the pursuit of the six principles set forth by President Clinton in connection with the health security act: security, savings, quality, choice, simplicity, and responsibility. We particularly applaud the inclusion of mental health services and the emphasis on the practice of preventive medical care.

Many small business are threatened by this added cost and feel that layoffs may be required to take on this burden. The government must address this issue by aiding and stimulating the economy with SBA loans, etc. The Vermont Teddy Bear Company and its employees jointly now spend nearly 8% of payroll on medical coverage which provides inadequate protection to only 58% of its employees.Although as employers we realize that our share of these expenses will rise from just under 4% to just under 8% of our payroll, we gladly accept this added burden in exchange for the health, security, added productivity, and sense of well being that it will offer to our employees and all American citizens.

Mr. WAXMAN. Ms. Hebson.

STATEMENT OF LIZ HEBSON

Ms. HEBSON. Thank you, Mr. Chairman. My name is Liz Hebson. I am in the restaurant business. I appreciate the opportunity——

Mr. WAXMAN. Pull the microphone a little closer to you.

Ms. HEBSON [continuing]. To present my views today because I, too, have been alarmed by the skyrocketing costs of health care. I am hopeful that some solution can be reached in the search for health care that is both affordable and available. But like most restaurateurs, I am greatly alarmed about the aspects of President Clinton's proposal to reform health care.

My family owns a small chain of five casual dining restaurants in the suburban Chicago area called Hackney's. My father started the business in 1939. Ours is a family restaurant chain in every sense. I am the oldest of seven children. Each of us works there, as do all but one of our spouses. Three of our four grown children, along with my niece and her husband, have chosen to work in our business. Our business family extends to more than 300 employees and a payroll of $3.3 million.

Hackney's is a successful business. Over the years we have survived the many economic ups and downs of the restaurant industry—like in 1992, when a remarkably high number of claims drove the cost of our employee health care coverage to more than twice what we had budgeted. It ended up costing more than $300,000, but we were able to absorb it because we are relatively secure financially.

We own our own properties. We have no debt. And we keep liquid enough to withstand occasional financial emergencies. So we took a loss for that year, the first time in my memory that our company ever had to do so. And we hoped it would be the last.

It may not be. To absorb the 7.9 percent payroll tax of the Clinton proposal would cost us about $260,000 annually, roughly the same amount we once considered an unfortunate and outrageous one-time cost. We can't afford another loss like that. And this assumes that tip income is not part of the formula, which I believe has not yet been addressed.

Once, I believed that nothing short of a catastrophic fire threatened my business and my industry. But many restaurateurs won't survive a new payroll tax or premium—I am not so good at this. Well, you have it in front of you. I will finish in 1 second.

Mr. WAXMAN. We have got the testimony. So just don't worry about the time, but go right ahead.

Ms. HEBSON. All right.

Maybe if I drank this. I am not much of a politician, I don't think.

All right. I am just going to plain read it.

But many restaurateurs won't survive a new payroll tax or premium, especially when they have already absorbed a reduction in the deductibility of meals and when—I don't know why that sentence seems to get me—and may soon face an increase in the minimum wage. Hackney's will survive, but not without a serious change in the way we do business.

I don't pretend to be an economist or an expert on health care, but I do know my industry. I know that we operate on some of the thinnest profit margins in American business. I know that competition for restaurant business is intense and largely driven by price. When you raise prices, it means you lose customers.

I know that restaurants are extremely labor intensive and that we rely heavily on part-time and entry-level workers. And I know that in this context, employer mandates make for misguided policy. When you add to our costs with something like this mandated payroll tax for health care, we can't take it merely from profits. Where are we going to get the money? Inevitably, this means cutting jobs.

Part-timers just won't be worth the hassle, which is too unfortunate for students and mothers and moonlighters, who need to work, but who just can't work full-time. The constraints of employer mandates would build in a bias against them.

I have no idea why I can't read this. I have read it a hundred times.

At the same time, the responsibility of overseeing health care compliance will, ironically, force us to add employees—bookkeepers. We already have one full-time employee who devotes very nearly all of her efforts to handling the administration of our current health care program—shoot.

Mr. WAXMAN. Well, we do have that statement.

Ms. HEBSON. Maybe that would be best. We will just skip the rest.

Mr. WAXMAN. We will have that in the record, and we very much appreciate it, but maybe you can respond to some questions when everybody else is finished. Thank you very much.

[The prepared statement of Ms. Hebson follows:]

Statement of Liz Hebson
Hackney's Restaurant
Chicago, Illinois

Thank you, Mr. Chairman.

My name is Liz Hebson. I'm a restaurant owner. I appreciate the opportunity to present my views today because I, too, have been alarmed by the skyrocketing costs of health-care and I'm hopeful that some solution can be reached in the search for health-care that is both affordable and available.

But, like most restaurateurs, I am greatly alarmed about some aspects of President Clinton's proposal to reform health-care.

My family owns a small chain of five casual dining restaurants in the suburban-Chicago area, called Hackney's. My father started the business in 1939.

Ours is a family restaurant chain in every sense. My six brothers and sisters and I each work there, as do all but one of our spouses. Three of my four grown children have chosen to work in our business. Our business family extends to more than 300 employees and a payroll of $3.3 million.

Hackney's is a successful business. Over the years we've survived the many economic ups and downs of the restaurant industry.

Like in 1992, when a remarkably high number of claims drove the cost of our employee health-care coverage to more than twice what we had budgeted. It ended up costing more than $300,000, but we were able to absorb it because we're relatively secure financially. We own our own properties. We have no debt. And we keep liquid enough to withstand occasional financial emergencies. So we took a loss for that year -- the first time in my memory that our company ever had to do so. And we hoped it would be the last.

It may not be. To absorb the 7.9 percent payroll tax of the Clinton proposal would cost us about $260,000 annually, roughly the same amount we once considered an unfortunate and outrageous one-time cost. We can't afford another loss like that! And this assumes that tip income is not part of the formula, which I believe has not yet been addressed.

Once I believed that nothing short of catastrophic fire threatened my business and my industry. But, many restaurateurs won't survive a new payroll tax or premium, especially when they've already absorbed a reduction in the deductibility of meals and when they may soon face an increase in the minimum wage. Hackney's will survive, but not without a serious change in the way we do business.

I don't pretend to be an economist or an expert on health-care. But I do know my industry.

I know that we operate on some of the thinnest profit margins in American business.

I know that competition for restaurant business is intense and largely driven by price.

I know that restaurants are extremely labor intensive, and that we rely heavily on part-time and entry-level workers.

And I know that, in this context, employer-mandates make for wrong-headed policy.

When you add to our costs, with something like this mandated payroll tax for healthcare, we can't merely take it from profits. Either we raise menu prices, which is extremely anti-competitive, or we cut costs in other parts of the business.

This inevitably means cutting jobs. All of us will look to consolidate responsibilities as much as possible.

On top of this, the additional bureaucratic and financial costs related to employees will force us to rely solely on full-time employees. Part-timers just won't be worth the hassle. Which is too bad for students and mothers and moonlighters, who need to work, but who just can't devote full-time hours. The constraints of employer mandates would build in a bias against them.

At the same time, the responsibility of overseeing health-care compliance will, ironically, force me to add employees -- bookkeepers. I already have one full-time employee who devotes very nearly all of her efforts to handling the administration of our current health-care program, which we offer to all 58 of our salaried employees.

If we extend that program to all 300 employees, I'll probably have to add at least two more full-time bookkeepers. That will mean at least $75,000 just to cover the administrative aspects of this program -- and that cost was not reflected in the $260,000 I mentioned earlier.

I see no other alternative. For one thing, it is prudent business to track and recompute all transactions, just as I do vendor invoices. For another, how else do we keep track of an employee, who is partly covered by another employer or by a father who has to pay for the kids, and who lives in another state?

Intuition tells me that no number of employees will be adequate to help us through that bureaucratic maze.

And finally, I'd like to add my skepticism about the cost projections of this proposal. It doesn't compute. Let's say it costs $150,000 - 200,000 to insure 58 employees, as it does at my restaurants. How do we insure 300 people for $260,000, as this program proposes to do?

It doesn't compute.

For it to work, either the quality of health care will drop to unacceptably low levels, or the government -- which has no profit margin whatsoever -- is going to absorb costs that we cannot even imagine. And when I say the government will absorb these costs, I mean you and me and every U.S. taxpayer.

Which brings me to a frustration that I have felt in trying to assess the impact of this health-care system on my business. I haven't seen any details. Therefore, I can speak only in general terms. One of the reasons our business has been successful is that we never make any major decision without knowing the details. To do otherwise would be irresponsible. I'm hopeful that soon we'll see the details of this proposal. To do otherwise would be more than irresponsible.

The bottom line of my testimony, Mr. Chairman, is that this health care proposal is fraught with problems that scare the daylights out of business people like me.

At the very least this approach to reforming America's health-care system will force some of us to ponder why we're in this in the first place. It will breath new meaning into an old saying: We're not in business for our health. We're in this to make a profit. We want to provide a living for our families and to provide a living for our employees and their families.

This proposal, as well-meaning as I'm sure it is, will constrain us from doing either.

Mr. WAXMAN. Ms. Wicks.

STATEMENT OF JUDITH A. WICKS

Ms. WICKS. Thank you, Mr. Chairperson. My name is Judy Wicks. I am founder and president of White Dog Enterprises, trading as White Dog Cafe. We are a 10-year-old business located in central Philadelphia. We are a successful single-location restaurant with a regional market, and we have been recognized in national publications for our quality, creativity, and work environment.

Including our adjacent gift shop, we employee 96 people total, or the equivalent of 75 full-time employees. Our estimated 1993 sales are $3,600,000 with a payroll of $1,086,000.

Like most restaurants I know of, we provide insurance for some but not all of our employees. Under the Clinton health reform plan, we would be required to pay an increase in health insurance expense of $56,000 to $81,000 per year, depending on whether tip income is included in payroll, in order to provide health insurance coverage for all employees. Despite the increase in cost to my company, I am in favor of the Clinton health care reform plan for the following reasons:

Looking at the big picture, the Clinton plan will cost society less than the current system because it will emphasize preventive care and include a number of important cost containment measures. In providing health insurance for all, everyone will end up paying for it in one way or the other. If government provides it, taxes will go up. If employers provide it, consumer prices will go up.

Under the employer-based system, health insurance will become a cost of doing business that will be incorporated into all our budgets.

The financing of health insurance coverage should be employer based, since most people are currently covered by their employers and, therefore, extending this system is the most practical solution.

Government subsidy of small businesses under a cap system will make comprehensive health insurance affordable to small business, which will, in turn, make us more competitive with big business in the labor market. We are gaining the value of health care coverage for all of our staff without paying for the total cost.

The restaurant business has traditionally been undervalued with lower profits and lower wages than most other industries. Health care reform will give us the opportunity to raise our prices as a group to reflect the true cost of preparing and serving meals for people, which should include health insurance for all workers.

This is not a substantial raise in prices. We estimate an increase of less than 3 percent to cover our increased expenses under the health care reform plan.

Our economy should support the same benefits for small business employees as for large business and government employees. Working for a small company, such as a restaurant, should not mean that you do not have access to affordable health care.

Under the new plan, our administrative staff will no longer be burdened with researching insurance plans and collecting employee contributions, since regional alliances will be responsible for negotiating insurance and collecting from both employer and employee.

Because the reform plan provides that everyone contribute to health cost with no free rides, consumer consciousness of cost controls will be increased and a broad-based constituency will develop to help combat the greed of excessive profits and system abusers.

In our State, Workers' Compensation insurance is out of hand. We pay $46,000 a year for Workers' Compensation, while making almost no claims. Automobile insurance is also skyrocketing. Our policy for two vehicles is currently $8,000 per year.

Under the health care reform plan a commission is being set up to study the feasibility of transferring the financial responsibility for all medical benefits, including those under workers' compensation and auto insurance to the new health system.

Along with my general support of the health care reform plan, I would like to express several concerns with suggestions, which are as follows.

Including the tipped income of servers as part of payroll is an unfair burden to a fragile industry. This precedence was set several years ago when restaurants were required to start matching social security withholdings from declared tips. This tax on tip income, which is not a part of our payroll, cost us $22,600 last year. If declared tips are also added to payroll to calculate health insurance rates, we would pay an additional $23,300 for health care insurance, using 1992 figures again, based on wages we never paid.

A fair compromise would be to base both FICA and health insurance rates on the portion of tips that make up the equivalent of minimum wage. We should be responsible for including this as part of our wages. Lowering the FICA contribution will help alleviate the financial hardships of restaurants who are, as an industry, going through difficult economic times.

Setting the number of employees at 50 to determine small employers' eligibility for lower caps based on average wages penalizes labor-intensive businesses such as high-quality restaurants. For instance, in the restaurant business, those of us who buy fresh produce and humanely raised meat directly from family farms are more labor intensive than those who buy frozen foods originating from factory farms. We should not end up being penalized because we care enough to hand-prepare organic herbs and vegetables and make breads from scratch.

Restaurants should be encouraged to provide as many jobs as possible and not take shortcuts when it comes to providing high-quality, nutritious food. I suggest increasing the number from 50 to 100 employees or using a gross receipts figure of $5 million in categorizing restaurants as small employers.

The importance of cost containment cannot be emphasized enough. No business can afford to write a blank check for health insurance coverage. While small businesses and average people pay more for health care, waste and greed must be eliminated from the system.

In looking at the big picture, it is crucial that we address the astronomical cost of violence to our society. President Clinton has said, "One of the reasons American health care is so expensive is that our hospitals and emergency rooms are full of people who are cut up and shot."

The Director of the Centers for Disease Control and Prevention, Dr. David Satcher, says, "Violence is the leading cause of lost life in this country today. If it is not a public health problem, why are all those people dying from it?"

I ask our Congress and our President to examine the cause of violence in our society. As long as our government demonstrates to our children and the international community that we resolve conflicts and disagreements with military might, we cannot expect anything different in our homes, in our schools, and in our streets.

As a small business person, I do not resent paying for health insurance coverage for my staff under an affordable, quality health plan. In fact, I look forward to that opportunity. What I do object to is the 40 to 50 percent of my Federal income taxes that go to the military. As long as we spend more money on killing than we do on healing, then we will continue to suffer from an illness that no health care plan will ever cure.

Mr. WAXMAN. Thank you very much, Ms. Wicks.

Ms. Blakeley.

STATEMENT OF ANN BLAKELEY

Ms. BLAKELEY. Thank you. Thank you for this opportunity to testify before this joint subcommittee on the important subject of health care reform. I appreciate the opportunity to share my views with the committee and the views of the National Federation of Independent Business, whom I am representing today.

NFIB has accumulated much information over the course of a decade on the health insurance needs of the small business community and what they would like to see in a reform package. NFIB is the Nation's largest small business advocacy organization representing more than 600,000 small and independent businesses.

My company, Earth Resources Corporation, specializes in the management of particularly hazardous materials. We have developed unique technologies for the handling of waste compressed gases and other hazardous materials, such as shock sensitives and pyrophorics. I currently employ 30 people.

Health insurance was first cited as the number one problem for small business owners in the 1986 NFIB Foundation survey. Since that time, the cost of health insurance has been rated the number one small business problem. In recent years, it has become twice as critical as the number two problem, which is Federal taxes on business income. For this reason, reforming the Nation's health care system has become NFIB's number one priority.

Everyone agrees that health care reform is necessary, and I applaud this administration's initiatives in tackling such a complex problem. While we wait for the details of the President's health care reform plan to be submitted to Congress, we have identified some preliminary areas of concern and positive opinions as to the proposed plan.

NFIB believes the following are positive aspects of the plan: Self-employed individuals will be allowed to take a permanent 100 percent deduction for health insurance premiums; insurance reforms are proposed in the President's package that would make insurance easier and less expensive to purchase; purchasing groups are created to enable small businesses and individuals to band together to purchase insurance more affordably; paperwork and administration is simplified; antitrust restrictions are loosened; and finally, medical liability reform, while it needs to be strengthened, will create an alternative dispute resolution mechanism and limit attorneys' fees.

There are, however, parts of the plan we find troubling. The first and foremost is the employer mandate. Under the President's plan, employers are required to pay at least 80 percent of premiums for all employees and their dependents, including part-time and seasonal employees. Small businesses survive on cash not profitability. While profitability is critical to long-term survival, a profitable small business can go out of business if it does not have enough cash to make payroll and pay bills on a weekly basis.

A mandate will critically impact the cash flow of a small business, particularly start-ups or those firms that have not reached a mature enough level to have cash reserves.

There have been statements made that the proposed plan will not affect those businesses currently providing health insurance. Unfortunately, this is not the case. I currently provide health insurance for my employees. Total health care costs for my company are approximately 6 percent of our total payroll. Our employees pay a percentage of that cost.

Under the proposed mandates and caps, our costs for providing health insurance to our employees will almost double, increasing approximately $37,000 per year. This represents two nonprofessional positions we will have to eliminate in order to comply with the mandates in the proposed plan, which is almost 7 percent of my work force. This increase assumes that the cap will not exceed 7.9 percent of payroll.

Given the fact that the administration admits that its financing mechanism for this plan does not balance, I and others in the small business community are extremely concerned that the caps will not hold.

At the same time, we have to eliminate positions to comply with the mandate; due to increased costs, we will have to increase the amount of administrative time to comply with the new paperwork requirements. Small businesses currently have to maintain payroll records and do tax returns for FICA, Medicare and Federal unemployment, State unemployment separate records with different requirements for Workers' Comp; and if, as in our case, our employer provides a retirement plan such as 401K, separate records with different requirements to administrate the plan and comply with ERISA. This does not include other personnel recordkeeping requirements such as those required for COBRA and documentation for defense and hire and fire decisions.

Another area of concern is the standard benefit plan that is consistent with the Fortune 500 plan. This is not what most small firms offer and may be too highly priced for many small employers.

When my firm was smaller and younger, we offered a basic benefit package that we could afford. As my business has matured, we have increased the benefits we offer. Today, our health insurance plan provides most of the features proposed in the President's plan, with notable exceptions such as children's dental and vision. For firms such as mine who already offer a very good package, the cost will definitely increase. In cases of firms who cannot currently afford health care insurance, a package such as this will have a devastating effect, resulting in even more loss of jobs and small business failures.

Even administration officials acknowledge the potential loss of 200,000 to 700,000 low-income jobs if some type of subsidy doesn't accompany mandated employer-provided health benefits.

The White House attempts to address the job loss problem by including subsidies. However, the subsidies are temporary and if the savings do not materialize, the subsidies will be cut back. Small businesses do not want subsidies; they want affordable health insurance coverage.

The small business community is extremely concerned about the potential burden this proposal may place on the economy and believes that better alternatives do exist. Many have already been introduced in the Congress. Proposals that do not increase payroll costs on employers, particularly new businesses, would avoid the inevitable job loss associated with expensive mandates.

[Testimony resumes on p. 200.]

[The prepared tatement of Ms. Blakeley follows:]

STATEMENT OF

ANN BLAKELEY
Earth Resources Corporation

Thank you for this opportunity to testify before this joint subcommittee hearing on the important subject of health care reform. I appreciate the opportunity to share my views with the subcommittees and the views of the National Federation of Independent Business, whom I am representing today. NFIB has accumulated much information over the course of a decade of research and communications on the health insurance needs of the small business community and what they would like to see in a reform package.

NFIB is the nation's largest small business advocacy organization, representing more than 615,000 small and independent business owners nationwide.

Health insurance was first cited as the number one problem for small business owners in a 1986 NFIB Foundation survey, Problems and Priorities. Since that time, the cost of health insurance has been rated the number one small business problem. In recent years, it has become twice as critical as the number two problem, "federal taxes on business income." For this reason, reform of the nation's health care system has become NFIB's top issue priority.

SMALL BUSINESS AND HEALTH INSURANCE COVERAGE

NFIB Foundation surveys found that small business owners view health insurance as the top fringe benefit they make available to their employees, both out of a sense of familial obligation and competitive necessity. According to NFIB studies, firms that provide insurance tend to be the more stable, mature, more profitable firms, and have more full time employees than their counterparts that do not offer insurance. NFIB's members tend to be more stable and mature than the general small business community. A larger percentage of them (nearly two-thirds) provide health insurance as a fringe benefit. Of the firms that do not offer health insurance, two-thirds say they would do so if they could afford it.

The question of how many employers are currently providing health insurance should be important to all those who are committed to reforming the system because the President's proposal will require all employers who do not currently provide insurance to spend at least 3.5% of payroll to pay for coverage. And many other employers who have not been able to cover all of their employees or who have not provided coverage that is as rich as that envisioned in the President's plan will be paying more than they have in the past.

Because the small business community is extremely concerned about the potential burden this proposal may place on the economy, we believe that understanding how many employers are and are not providing health benefits for their employees is a vital component in the health care debate. While the White House has indicated that the "vast majority of employers currently provide health insurance for their employees", all the data we have seen paint a very different picture.

Based on data from the Health Insurance Association of America (HIAA), the Census Bureau, the Congressional Budget Office, the U.S. Small Business Association and others, we find that between 40 and 45 percent of employers provide health insurance. This percentage is driven by the huge number of employers with fewer than five employees (about 3,000,000 firms), of which only 26% provide coverage.

Percent of Firms that Do and Do Not Offer Health Insurance (HIAA, 1989)

Firm Size	Offer	Do Not Offer
fewer than 5 employees	26%	74%
5-9 employees	54%	46%
10-24 employees	72%	28%
25-49 employees	90%	10%
50-99 employees	97%	3%
100 or more employees	99%	1%
Total	42% *	58%

* A 1992 HIAA study adjusted this figure to 40%.

Even the U.S. Small Business Administration's estimate on this matter states that 53.7% of employers provide health insurance for their employees. NFIB believes this figure is inflated because of the method used to extrapolate the data to the population as a whole. But even if you accept the SBA figure at face value, it still contradicts the White House claim.

The smaller the firm the less likely it is to provide health insurance. Not only do these firms pay higher administrative costs, but health insurance premiums represent a larger percent of their payroll because they tend to employ more marginal, lower wage workers. The lower the pay of the employee, the heavier the burden of health insurance premiums.

In general, we have found that cost is the primary determinant of small business owners' purchase of health insurance coverage. Health insurance is often the largest payroll item in a small firm, more than the cost of workers' compensation and liability insurance combined. Recent polls by Foster and Higgins showed a 79% increase in the cost of employee coverage over a four year period to $3,968. For many small firms, this figure can be considerably higher. Small businesses find the health insurance market extremely volatile and unpredictable, experiencing sudden cancellations and 20-300% annual premium increases. They pay 30-40% more in administrative costs than their larger counterparts, and struggle to find and retain their coverage. In order to keep their coverage, many have been forced to increase employee cost-sharing.

Employers of all sizes have been trying to find ways to control and slow rapid and unpredictable premium increases. Larger firms have been able to contain costs by self-insuring and moving into managed care arrangements. Smaller firms, however, have limited access to managed care options and are usually unable to self-insure. As a result, they are faced with expensive state mandates, state premium taxes, medical underwriting and higher administrative expenses.

EMPLOYER MANDATES AND JOB LOSS

The ever increasing burden of federal mandates on employers continues to raise the cost of starting or expanding a business and hiring employees. According to numerous studies, the result of these higher costs will be jobs lost or not created. A July 1993 survey of 2400 small businesses in seven cities, conducted by University of Michigan professor Catherine McLaughlin, indicated that one third would decrease their numbers of full time employees if they faced a mandate.

A 1000 member survey of the American Economics Association in June 1993 indicated that 80% of the economists interviewed projected a decrease in employment among all employees as the result of requiring employers to provide health benefits to low wage employees.

77–929 O - 94 - 7

Another empirical study, conducted by the Employment Policies Institute in September 1993, concluded that requiring employers to pay for worker's health insurance expenses would increase labor costs, leading to the loss of 3.1 million jobs. These job losses would be concentrated in just a few industries. 75% or more would be in restaurants (828,000 lost jobs), other retail trade (726,000 lost jobs) and agriculture (194,000 lost jobs). Other industries that will see disproportionate job loss are construction, repair services, personal services and private household services.

A CONSAD Research Corporation study conducted in May 1993 found that three leading health care reform plans requiring employer mandates could impact 7.5 million to 18 million jobs in terms of reduced wages, reduction of other benefits and potential cuts in hours worked. Job loss estimates ranged from 400,000 to over 1 million.

Even Administration officials acknowledge the potential loss of 200,000 to 700,000 low income jobs if some type of subsidy does not accompany mandated employer provided benefits, as was reported in The New York Times on August 30, 1993.

The White House attempts to address the job loss problem by including subsidies. However, the subsidies are temporary -- the mandates are permanent. If the White House's predicted savings do not materialize, the subsidies may be doomed.

Small businesses do not want subsidies, they want affordable health insurance coverage. This was proved by a recent Gallup poll of small business owners that showed nearly half (46%) of business owners who opposed the mandate in the President's plan said the idea of a subsidy would strengthen their opposition to an employer requirement.

THE ADMINISTRATION HEALTH CARE REFORM PLAN

Everyone agrees that health care reform is necessary and we applaud this Administration's initiative in tackling such a complex problem. While we wait for the details of the President's health care reform plan to be submitted to the Congress, there has been enough information to formulate some preliminary opinions on the plan as we know it. ***We believe the following are positive aspects of the plan:***

- **Self employed individuals will be allowed to take a permanent 100% deduction for health insurance premiums, rather than the current 25% temporary deduction.**

- **Insurance reforms are proposed in the President's package that would make insurance easier and less expensive to purchase.** These include guaranteed coverage for all regardless of health status, elimination of the pre-existing condition limitation, adjusted community rating, and guaranteed portability of coverage. We identified these as primary areas in health insurance reform in Florida and they were passed in Florida during the 1992 legislative session.

- **Purchasing groups are created to enable small businesses and individuals to band together to purchase insurance more affordably.** Members of the purchasing groups will receive detailed comparative information on health plans to help them make more effective choices for their money.

- **Paperwork and administrative simplification, including standard forms for claims, reimbursement, enrollment and plan visits, and electronic networks for data transmission and record keeping, will keep down costs and ease compliance.**

- **Antitrust restrictions are loosened to make it easier for hospitals to jointly purchase medical equipment and allow doctors to share information and form networks of providers.**

- **Medical liability reform, while it needs to be strengthened, will create alternative dispute resolution mechanisms for each health plan, limit attorneys' fees and include a collateral source rule.**

There are, however, parts of the plan we find troubling:

- **Under the President's plan, all employers are required to pay at least 80% of premiums for all employees and dependents, including part time and seasonal employees.**

Small businesses survive on cash, not profitability. While profitability is critical to long term survival, a profitable small firm can go out of business if it does not have enough cash to make payroll and pay bills. A mandate will critically impact the cash flow of small business, particularly start-ups or those firms that have not reached a mature enough level to have cash reserves.

There have been statements made that the proposed plan will not affect those businesses currently providing health insurance. Unfortunately, this is not the case. The proposed plan will adversely impact my business and my employees.

I currently employee 30 people and provide health insurance for my employees. Total health care cost for my company is approximately 6% of our payroll. We pay approximately 70% of the employees' cost and 25% of the additional amount required for dependent coverage. In 1992 we implemented a Section 125 plan (cafeteria type plan) which allows our employees to pay for their portion of benefit with pre-tax money. Prior to implementing Section 125, we paid 80% of the employees' cost and one third of the additional premium for dependent coverage. We were able to lower our cost after implementing Section 125 without impacting our employees' take home pay.

The elimination of the Section 125 option will decrease many employees' take home pay who currently pay for their portion of health insurance with pre-tax dollars.

Under the proposed mandates and caps, our cost for providing health insurance to our employees will almost double, increasing by approximately $37,000 per year (based on annualized, 1993 year to date payroll). This represents two non-professional positions we will have to eliminate in order to comply with the mandates in the proposed plan. This increase assumes that the cap will not exceed 7.9% of payroll. Given the fact that the administration admits that its financing mechanism for this plan may not balance, I (and others in the small business community) are extremely concerned that these caps will not hold.

- **Under the proposed plan, payment calculations are complicated and cumbersome.** Employers must calculate payments based on four categories of "family status" (single individual, couple without children, single parent family, two parent family) and specific wage categories. If there is more than one worker in the family, employers must determine the per employee cost by the following formula: 80% of family premium divided by the average number of workers per family for that region.

- **In addition to the complexity of calculating the payments, recordkeeping and paperwork requirements involved in this proposal are far reaching.** Employers must track the changing "family status" of each employee, furnish employees' names and other relevant information to the regional alliance, notify the alliance of new enrollees and forward new registration material within

30 days. At year end employer must reconcile total premium payments and report to the alliance. Complete (and separate) records must be kept for alliance audits.

This means that, while we have to eliminate positions to comply with the mandate due to increased costs, we will also have to increase the amount of administrative time to comply with the new paperwork requirements. Small businesses currently have to maintain payroll records and tax returns for FICA, Medicare, federal unemployment, state unemployment, separate records with different requirements for Workers' Compensation, and if, as in our case, an employer provides a retirement plan such as 401k, separate records with different requirements to administer the plan and comply with ERISA. These records do not include other personnel record keeping requirements such as those required for COBRA and documentation requirements for defense in hire/fire decisions.

- **A standard benefit plan that is "consistent with a Fortune 500 plan" is not what most small firms offer, and may be too highly priced for many small employers.**

When my firm was smaller, we offered a basic benefit package that we could afford. As my business has matured, we have increased the benefits we offer. Today, our health insurance plan provides most of the features proposed in the President's plan with notable exceptions such as childrens' dental and vision. For firms such as mine who already offer a very good package, the cost will definitely increase. In cases of firms who cannot currently afford health insurance, a package such as this will have a devastating effect, resulting in even more loss of jobs and small business failures.

- **While we are heartened that purchasing groups are included in the proposal, they appear to have turned into quasi-governmental monopolies with broad regulatory powers.**

- **Approved health plans are allowed to contract exclusively with single source suppliers, which could mean many small independent service providers such as pharmacies will lose significant amounts of business to larger chains.**

- **The national board envisioned by the President is charged with establishing and enforcing health care spending limits.** How these spending limits are calculated by the board is unclear. In addition, the board appears to add a new layer of federal bureaucracy to the program and gives inordinate power to the federal government to regulate the system.

- **States that are not in compliance with their budget may be able to levy an additional payroll tax on employers in order to meet the state budget.**

- **States are allowed to opt out of the new system and may choose a single payer system for all or part of the state.** In addition, states are allowed to restrict the number of purchasing alliances in the state, thus reducing competition and increasing the possibility of quasi-governmental alliances.

- **States are <u>allowed to add benefits to the standard package</u>, although they must be separately funded.** What is to keep a state, many of which have added state mandated benefits prodigiously in the past, from adding to the size and cost of the benefit package?

- **The definition of what makes up <u>payroll</u>, not yet determined, will be critical in the determination of total cost.** Our payroll fluctuates as much as 20% per month depending on the amount of overtime we have to pay our field crews to meet deadlines. Will <u>overtime</u> be considered as compensation in the calculation and will you penalize those companies that pay overtime? Other issues include how <u>bonuses</u> will be treated and company vehicles that are currently taxed as income.

- **Companies that have developed, trained and educated their work force will be penalized for developing a work force that merits greater compensation per employee.**

- **Mandating that employers pay for dependents of employees will result in <u>discrimination</u> against these employees.** Insurance companies now want health single people in their plans. The mandate, as proposed, will result in many small businesses being forced into looking for the same type of employee.

The small business community is extremely concerned about the potential burden this proposal may place on the economy and believes that better alternatives do exist. Many have already been introduced in the Congress. Proposals that do not increase payroll costs on employers, particularly new businesses, would avoid the inevitable job loss associated with expensive mandates.

<u>FLORIDA'S HEALTH CARE REFORM LAW</u>

In 1993 Florida passed one of the most far reaching and ambitious health care reform packages in the country. Governor Chiles was extremely committed to this effort and brought many varied groups together in order to enact this landmark legislation. The law combines aspects of the managed competition concept with strong cost containment mechanisms to bring the costs of insurance down and provide incentives for employers and individuals to purchase coverage. Specifically, our law does the following:

- establishes eleven regional Community Health Purchasing Alliances (CHPAs) run predominantly by business owners;
- provides access to lower cost policies for firms with 50 employees or fewer;
- informs consumers on price, quality and outcomes data;
- allows a larger number of businesses to take advantage of the insurance reforms enacted by the legislature in 1992;
- enacts modified community rating (adjusted for tobacco use, age, region); and
- imposes no mandate on employers.

Governor Chiles brought together the affected parties in developing our health care reform package. Working together the small business community (represented by NFIB and others), large employers, health care providers, health insurance providers and consumers developed a health care reform package without employer mandates. In this way, we are solving the problems associated with the current health care system in Florida without the effects of job loss and business failure a mandate would cause.

As someone who has been involved in the reform effort, I am extremely concerned that the programs we have worked so hard to develop will not have a chance to succeed before the federal government imposes their mandates and requirements. This Administration has acknowledged that states should have more autonomy in determining their own destiny, however, the proposed plan defeats Florida's efforts before they have a chance to get started.

A SMALL BUSINESS HEALTH CARE REFORM PLAN

Following is a list of guiding principles which we believe any comprehensive reform plan should follow. Taken together, we believe these measures will increase access to affordable health coverage and help to contain cost increases. While the list is not all-inclusive, it does represent the results of numerous surveys of small business owners over the last several years.

- **Formation of health insurance purchasing groups should be encouraged.** By joining together to purchase health insurance, small businesses and individuals can reduce costs through administrative savings and risk-sharing. Referred to as "health alliances" by the Administration, these purchasing groups should operate under the following guidelines:

  -- The alliance should act as a health insurance broker, negotiating annual agreements with insurers and approved health plans, enrolling members, collecting premiums and disseminating cost and quality information to help consumers make educated health care choices;

  -- enrollment in the alliance should be completely open, with purchasers free to choose the plan that best suits them;

  -- states should allow multiple purchasing groups in each area and operation across state lines;

  -- the size of the purchasing group should be large enough to be effective, but not so large as to essentially create a "single-payer" entity within a state (i.e., membership in a single alliance should probably be restricted to firms with 100 employees or fewer, certainly not more than 500. We are currently collecting data to determine where the optimum number for small business lies); and

  -- the alliance should be run by a local purchaser-controlled board.

- **Self-employed business owners should be allowed a permanent 100% tax deduction for health insurance premiums purchased for their employees and themselves.** Self-employed business owners such as sole proprietors, partnerships and S-corporations are allowed only a 25% deduction; that deduction is temporary and has currently expired. Expanding and making permanent the tax deductibility of premiums would enable many of the nearly five million uninsured self-employed to buy coverage for themselves and the millions they employ.

- **Insurance company practices should be reformed to make health insurance coverage easier and less expensive to buy.** Being able to count on obtaining insurance with fairly stable premiums would enable more small business owners to purchase coverage for themselves and their employees. Specifically, any reforms in this arena should include:

-- elimination of the preexisting condition limitation;

-- guaranteed access to policies, regardless of medical condition, and guaranteed renewal of policies;

-- the elimination of experience rating and the institution of a faire rating system such as rating bands or a system in which individuals are community rated, with considerations made for age and sex; and

-- portable insurance coverage for all, regardless of employment status.

- **Financing of the new system should be spread as equitably as possible, without overburdening our primary job creating sector -- the small business community.** Historically, small business has had a difficult time obtaining affordable health insurance coverage for its employees. For the millions of employers who find coverage prohibitively expensive, proposals that increase payroll taxes and force <u>all</u> businesses to cover <u>all</u> employees will be particularly devastating and should be rejected.

The small business community strongly opposes broad employer mandates to pay for health care reform. Recent surveys show that 88 percent of small business owners oppose a federal mandate requiring employers to purchase health insurance for all employees.

A September 1993 Gallup poll put the number at 85%. Although the majority of small firms provide health insurance, most fear a broad government mandate for two reasons: the business owner's flexibility would be gone, and an expensive, government-dictated benefits package could mean that their already high costs would escalate further. The bottom line is that mandated coverage may force many new and marginally-profitable businesses to lay off employees or shut down altogether. It would also significantly reduce the profitability of more established companies and inhibit their ability to expand and create jobs.

Similarly, those who wish to fund the new system by imposing a payroll-based premium are ignoring certain realities of the small business market place. Because small firms are so labor intensive, this would in fact be the worst possible choice. Payroll taxes have no real link to profitability and will only stifle new business start ups and inhibit job creation because they are indirectly a tax on jobs. Rather, reforming the system to make affordable coverage more widely available will encourage more small business owners to purchase coverage for their employees.

In addition, NFIB believes that the tax code should be amended to help control health costs and make purchasers of health coverage, whether employers or individuals, more cost-conscious in their choices:

-- the employer deduction for health insurance should be capped, with the savings used only to broaden access to basic standard health coverage;

-- the employee's current tax exclusion for health benefits should be capped;

-- the deduction/exclusion for both employers and employees should be tied to the average cost of the lower-priced health plans;

-- the deduction for the self-employed (currently 25% and expired) should be permanently increased to 100% of the cost of the average plan; and

-- the above mentioned tax deduction should be tied to participation in a purchasing group, in order to encourage small business owners to join.

■ **Costly state benefit mandates and anti-managed care laws should be preempted.** Enactment of certain state laws have significantly limited the availability of affordable health plans and discouraged the growth of managed care systems. State mandates alone can raise the cost of insurance 30 percent. Pre-empting these mandates and repealing restrictive state anti-managed care laws would allow small business owners easier access to affordable plans and greater access to cost-saving managed care arrangements.

However, NFIB does not oppose state laws that require free and open competition for the business of managed care patients. NFIB members oppose exclusive contract arrangements with certain providers, such as pharmacies, within managed care systems. Small business owners believe that managed care systems can hold down costs effectively with open competition among many providers who are able to sell the same product at the same competitive price. Several states are currently considering laws that require managed care systems to allow all providers to compete.

■ **A uniform, affordable standard benefits package should be developed in consultation with business, consumers, and state and local governments.** However, regardless of who determines what is in a "basic standard benefits package," care must be taken to ensure that the plan is at a level necessary to assure adequate coverage and care but remains affordable. As such, we should consider the packages developed by the most efficient and cost-effective health maintenance organizations. Developing Fortune 500 type "benchmark" packages that are too generous will price them out of the reach of individuals and small business owners. It is imperative that the package be affordable to both employers and individuals.

■ **Accountable health plans (AHPs) should compete to provide high quality, low cost coverage to purchasers of health care.** In order to be successful, it is crucial that there always be multiple, truly competitive AHPs. AHPs should operate as follows:

-- AHPs should be registered;

-- enrollment should be open in all AHPs;

-- plans must be subject to all reforms imposed on the insurance industry, including restrictions on the preexisting condition limitation, modified community rating, guaranteed availability, guaranteed renewability, portability, etc.;

- -- AHPs must offer the uniform benchmark benefit package;
- -- cost outcomes reports should be developed by all AHPs;
- -- plans may charge different prices, but not based on health status;
- -- plans should compete on the basis of price, quality and any additional services they can offer;
- -- plans should not impose waiting periods or deny access to any enrollee, except in the case of capacity limits;
- -- if higher premium plans are offered, the difference should not be covered (must be paid by individual or employer); and
- -- consumers should be offered a choice among "actuarially equivalent" delivery options: HMO, PPO, or traditional fee for service. However, employers who are contributing to the cost of the premium should be allowed to encourage employee enrollment in a particular plan.

■ **Attempts to control costs by imposing spending restraints or "global budgets" fail to address the root causes of the problem and should be avoided.** Many have suggested the imposition of "global budgets" -- caps on overall health care spending -- in order to bring health expenditures under control. However, NFIB believes that global budgets are fundamentally unworkable (especially within a managed competition framework) and will lead to increased rationing of health care. Currently, most experts agree that we do not possess the relevant data on which to base such allocations. Further, global budgets do not address the root causes of health care inflation, nor do they provide any incentives to increase efficiency in delivery of care.

■ **Changing our medical malpractice laws.** The current malpractice crisis only adds to the already astronomical cost of treatments, services, medical devices and pharmaceuticals, and inhibits research and development of new products. We believe that serious reform of the medical liability system can reduce the overuse of excessive and costly defensive medicine and save about $30 billion a year. Medical liability reform should consider the following:

- -- limits on awards for noneconomic damages;
- -- caps on attorneys fees;
- -- encouragement of alternative dispute resolution;
- -- allowing use of treatment guidelines and protocols as a defense in a malpractice case; and
- -- enterprise liability, which will create "deeper pockets" and encourage lawsuits, should be rejected.

- **Implementing administrative and paperwork reforms.** As much as one quarter of every health care dollar in the U.S. goes to paperwork and administrative costs. Economies of scale for small firms mean that more of their health care dollar -- up to twice as much as large businesses -- goes to cover paperwork and administrative costs. As such, simplifying paperwork requirements and reducing administrative costs must be a part of any health care reform:

  -- uniform claims forms should be developed; and

  -- electronic claims filing, billing, and enrollment should be more widely utilized.

- **If an independent board or national entity is set up to oversee the new health care system, it should be guided by the following principles:**

  -- its functions should be limited to establishing standards for information collection and data reporting, outcomes and consumer information, setting the general parameters of an affordable standard benefits package, and general oversight;

  -- such a board should not become simply another bureaucratic government entity that inhibits innovation and effective reform;

  -- the board must include purchasers, be insulated from political pressures, and not staff driven; and

  -- the board's functions should not include setting price controls and/or spending caps.

- **Consumer information and education is essential.** NFIB strongly believes that informed consumers make more cost-conscious decisions relating to their health care. Currently, part of the reason that health care costs are going up so rapidly is due to the fact that consumers have lost their buying power in the health care market. Most Americans are shielded from the true cost of their insurance coverage and the cost of medical care, largely because the premiums are borne by employers. As a result, there is little or no incentive to search out the highest quality health product at the lowest cost, a theory fundamental in the purchasing of most other goods.

- **Miscellaneous...**

  In addition, NFIB strongly supports the following:

  -- improved access in rural and underserved areas;

  -- increased emphasis on preventative health;

-- removal of most antitrust restrictions on the medical community to allow providers to collaborate and pool resources;

-- increased cost-sharing among employers and employees to encourage cost-conscious decision making;

-- low income assistance to the poor and near poor;

-- substantial phase-in to allow smaller firms to adjust to the new system; and

-- an exemption for start up firms for a period of time.

CONCLUSION

As you can see from the list of principles above, there are numerous items on which all parties agree (formation of purchasing groups, insurance reform, malpractice reform, administrative reform, etc.). The controversial items, while critical, are few. We urge the Committee to seek passage of these consensus items as soon as possible.

We look forward to working with the committee to craft a reform measure that will control costs and encourage more small firms to purchase coverage for their employees. We hope to work with you to pass a reform measure in the 103rd Congress.

Thank you.

Mr. WAXMAN. If you don't mind, the rest of that will be part of this statement in the record.

And I would like to ask you, Ms. Blakeley, if you are providing coverage for your employees now at 6 percent of the payroll and the Government will take all those administrative burdens off you, because you won't have to run the insurance program, it will be part of this alliance, and you will have a cap of only 7.9 percent that would be placed on you, how could you say that your cost would double?

Ms. BLAKELEY. The—we currently provide—we have, first of all, a cafeteria-type plan which pays 70 percent of the employee's portion which ends up being a 20 percent net impact to their net pay because of tax benefits. We pick up an additional 25 percent of the family coverage for people who have dependents. If I am mandated to pay 80 percent, including the family portion, that is where the bulk of the increase comes in.

Second, from what I understand of the proposed plan, I am not only going to have to track my employees, but I have to maintain records as to what their family does. If their spouse works, the computation for the amount that you have to pay for individuals is extraordinarily complicated and, actually, the recordkeeping requirements, from what I understand, will increase.

Mr. WAXMAN. Right now, with your employees, you have to keep the records of when they use the health insurance, how much their premiums will be. A lot of that will be taken off of you to be run by the alliance, wouldn't it?

Ms. BLAKELEY. No. We once a year choose a health plan, and individuals—I don't track when they use the health care plan.

Mr. WAXMAN. OK. Now, what you are suggesting—because this is a real problem in this country, we have so many people uninsured. What you are suggesting is that we take some steps in insurance market reforms and some of our points; but you know, I indicated in my opening statement there are 2 million Americans, many of them employees of small firms, that lost health coverage between 1991 and 1992, so we have got to reform this system.

You are against the President's proposal to require all employers to contribute to health care coverage to their employees and dependents with substantial subsidies. You want us to adopt insurance market reforms, including guaranteed issue, regardless of health status, elimination of waiting periods, adjusted community rating and portability of coverage.

Now, if we have those insurance reforms, that seems to me that would make matters worse by making health insurance even more unaffordable. Shouldn't we expect that most people who buy health insurance in such a market would have poor health status leading to large increases in premiums?

And remember that, unlike the President, you are not proposing to protect small firms with a cap on their financial obligation for health care, and you are not proposing to limit the annual increases in the premiums that insurers can impose. So shouldn't we expect even more small employers, faced with ever-escalating premiums, to simply drop their coverage?

Ms. BLAKELEY. We addressed this issue in Florida, and we were able to pass health insurance reform in the State of Florida without an employer mandate; and we did this by implementing a managed competition system where—which is current—it is not quite implemented yet. That is one of the issues that I had hoped to address was that we are very concerned that we won't be allowed to make it work, that the Federal Government will impose the mandates.

Mr. WAXMAN. Let me interrupt you. I am sorry to, but I was given a note that Mr. Putnam and Mr. Marks have to leave.

I don't have any particular questions for you. I thought you gave us excellent testimony, and I commend you for the fact that you are covering your employees and you want to do something about the problem, and Mr. Putnam, that you realize that when employees don't have coverage that they go without care.

Let me ask any of my colleagues if they have any specific questions for the two of you, and then otherwise we will let you go.

Mrs. COLLINS. I just had a very short question.

Mr. Marks, has your company's decision to provide health insurance for employees ever jeopardized your ability to turn a profit, especially in the earlier years when you had only 20 or 30 employees?

Mr. MARKS. We have grown to 200 employees. It has got to be a pretty dramatic statement, I think I will make now, and that is if a company can't afford to supply a living wage and appropriate benefits to employees, it shouldn't be in business. Part of doing business is paying salaries and paying benefits, and if you can't price your product accordingly, then somebody is pricing their product better than you and you shouldn't be in business. That is a way to deal with these things.

Mrs. COLLINS. Thank you very much.

Thank you, Mr. Chairman.

Mr. WAXMAN. Mr. Brown?

Mr. BROWN. Mr. Chairman, thank you for your comments and your open-minded attitudes.

Your company, does your company do any kind of preventive sort of care, wellness programs for employees, any kinds of—whether it is no-smoking campaigns or encouraging pregnant women to get prenatal care or doing any kind of systematic—do you have any sorts of fitness centers on the premises, things like that?

Mr. PUTNAM. We heard the listing by the larger corporations that were represented here, and I wish that we could spin out a list like that. We do have a nonsmoking environment. We do subsidize fitness programs or activities of one kind or another and our health care plan is one—we are currently on is a partially self-insured one, which provides feedback to the employees, if they use it wisely, and can lower their premiums, if they use it judiciously.

Mr. BROWN. If I could follow up with that, Mr. Chairman.

Does that—what does that mean if you are—when and if this bill passes, you are part of the health alliance, your rates are not so much affected by the kinds of wellness, preventive programs you do since you are thrown into the larger pool, will you have the economic incentives and will you plan to continue to do those sorts of programs anyway?

Mr. PUTNAM. It is a high priority of ours to increase those programs. It is really a sign of immaturity as a company that we don't do more of that now. We have grown extremely rapidly and have only recently begun to be able to implement those, so we will certainly strive to improve those programs.

Mr. BROWN. Regardless of whether you see the sort of more certain payback, because of more healthy employees, in terms of your own costs, of your own insurance?

Mr. PUTNAM. But that is the reason for doing it. We see a direct relationship between encouraging healthy habits in our employees and the cost of health care. So it is in our best interests to encourage that kind of program.

Mr. BROWN. Thank you, Mr. Putnam.

Thank you, Mr. Chairman.

Mr. WAXMAN. I want to thank both of you. I know you have to run and catch your plane. I want to recognize Mr. McMillan to pursue questions of others if he wants to at this point.

Mr. MCMILLAN. I thank the chairman. I guess my question should be directed to Ms. Hebson and Ms. Blakeley, since I think both of you expressed opposition generally to the President's proposed plan.

Do you see need from your perspective for health care reform in any fashion?

Ms. HEBSON. Yes, definitely, yes.

Mr. MCMILLAN. Would you highlight a few things that you think need to be addressed.

Mr. WAXMAN. Would you turn on the mike and come a little closer.

Ms. HEBSON. Does it go off by itself because I don't remember turning it off.

I think that the cost—I am so sorry that I couldn't finish my speech. I am like that at times.

Mr. MCMILLAN. It will be in the record, and we will all make a point of reading it.

Ms. HEBSON. That is good.

I think the biggest problem with health care is that it costs so much. I don't think there is anything wrong with the quality of it. I think it is wonderful. But it costs a fortune, and so all you have to do to get health care fixed is to get the costs in line and if you could get the costs in line, more people could get into it; that would solve some of the access problems, too.

So that, to me, is the biggest problem; and there is only one way that I have ever seen since I have been alive and since I have ever read any economics and that is to use the free enterprise system, competition. Those kinds of things are the only things that keep prices in line. That goes for the restaurant business and that goes probably for health care, too; but I am not a doctor, and I wouldn't guess.

Mr. MCMILLAN. Would you agree that even given good competition, which I agree with, we probably would continue to have the problem of an element of the population who cannot afford medical care? Furthermore, that many of them work for smaller businesses that may tend to have little wage rates?

Ms. HEBSON. Like ours.

Mr. McMILLAN. Do you think there is some need to expand the level of government subsidy for those who can't pay because we all end up paying for it anyway?

Ms. HEBSON. I think if the government could afford it—if they weren't completely broke, I think it would be great. But in our business, if we can't afford something, we don't buy it. And that is why we are still in business.

Mr. McMILLAN. Some of the Clinton proposal is based on the assumption, which I share, that when we spend more than 25 percent more per capita than any other Nation in the world on health care, then if we do get a hold of the things that are driving costs out of control, then we would have the resources to provide adequate health care to everyone. I believe it is a question then of getting our priorities straight.

Ms. HEBSON. That sounds that way.

Mr. McMILLAN. Suppose we had a system that, instead of mandating payment by small businesses, or anyone else for that matter, basically it was an expanded subsidy that went to the individual based on their income?

Ms. HEBSON. I am sorry. What?

Mr. McMILLAN. There would be a subsidy to the individual, based on their income, so that they could then buy into, with that subsidy, a plan that you might offer.

Ms. HEBSON. Exactly.

Mr. McMILLAN. For instance, if you had an employee that had $12,000, they might get 100 percent subsidy.

Ms. HEBSON. Maybe that would work, too. I mean, I have only this one little chance to say what I think would work, and I think it would be if small businesses like mine, who do not insure all their workers—we do insure some, like our core workers, but we don't insure all our part-time workers at all; that is, definitely we insure only about a sixth of our employees.

But if—when we all work together, whether it is the government, the employees, big business, little business, everyone together—if there is enough money in the system, as you say, there must be an answer that everyone could get their health insurance; but the only way or—or their health care.

However, if you build it on the employer paying, maybe, because the employer has been paying for 80 percent of or 85 percent of the United States people, maybe that is why it is so expensive right now, you know. Why build on a system that might have been wrong in the first place?

Mr. McMILLAN. Can I continue?

I didn't give Ms. Blakeley a chance to answer those questions.

Mr. WAXMAN. The gentleman will be given 2 extra minutes.

Mr. McMILLAN. Are we going to have a second round?

Mr. WAXMAN. I would just as soon we have one round. How much time do you want?

Mr. McMILLAN. About 5 minutes.

Mr. WAXMAN. Let's do second rounds.

Mr. McMILLAN. Since I am the only one here, give me 15 then.

Mr. WAXMAN. How about taking a couple of minutes more now, and then you will have a chance?

Mr. McMILLAN. OK, fine.

If I could shift, then I will come back to you, Ms. Blakeley.

Mr. WAXMAN. Without objection. Two additional minutes.

Mr. MCMILLAN. I did ask Ms. Wicks one because she is an advocate of the plan as I take it. Do you have a health care plan for your employees now?

Ms. WICKS. Yes.

Mr. MCMILLAN. Would you mind telling me what it costs, a percentage of your payroll?

Ms. WICKS. It costs $30,000 a year. And our payroll is a million so what does that come to?

Mr. MCMILLAN. Three percent?

Ms. WICKS. Right.

Mr. MCMILLAN. So you are going to have an increase.

Ms. WICKS. A dramatic increase.

Mr. MCMILLAN. Of about half a percent.

Ms. WICKS. It will go to 7.9.

Mr. MCMILLAN. How many employees do you have?

Ms. WICKS. Ninety-six employees, total.

Mr. MCMILLAN. So you wouldn't come under the small business exemption?

Ms. WICKS. Unfortunately not.

Mr. MCMILLAN. You would be capped at 7.9 percent, so you would have an increase.

Ms. WICKS. Of more than double.

Mr. MCMILLAN. Right, and your argument is that you should be able to pass that on to your customers.

Ms. WICKS. Right, and I don't think it is a big deal to do that if—for any of us, to tell you the truth, because we figure it is going to cost us about—we will have to raise our prices about 3 percent to cover the increased expense in health care. That is not a whole lot.

If you pay $10 per meal, it is, you know, $10.30; I think it is well worth it to do that. I feel that the market will bear it.

Mr. MCMILLAN. It will probably have an exponential effect because probably your suppliers would have the same thing and be passing price increases on to you.

In retail—I used to be in the retail grocery business—you are at the tail end of the pricing chain, so these things expand exponentially on down the system. So in—particularly with industries that have a lot of part-time employees, which include retailers and restaurants, probably the magnitude of the cost in price increases that you would have to pass on are going to be rather enormous.

Ms. WICKS. I feel we would pay the same thing in order to cover everybody in this country for health insurance. It has to come from somewhere; if we didn't pay it through raising prices, we would have to pay it through taxes. Because I believe that everybody should be covered.

Mr. WAXMAN. Thank you, Mr. McMillan.

Mrs. Collins.

Mrs. COLLINS. Ms. Blakeley, you testified that currently your company provides health insurance through just one health insurance plan. Under the President's proposal, your employees would be able to select a health plan from among many, perhaps dozens, through their regional health care alliances.

Under which system do you think your employees would have a greater choice of providers and plans and be more able to change if they are not satisfied with the care they were receiving?

Ms. BLAKELEY. This is another thing that we did in Florida in our health care reform efforts that we have done over the last couple of years. You will have a choice between plans, and I do like the idea of having a choice with a regional alliance. What I don't like is the mandate. The mandate is definitely going to impact jobs; it has to.

Mrs. COLLINS. Well, the question is which—what do you think your employees will be better off with, with the greater choice of both providers and health care plans?

Ms. BLAKELEY. Absolutely. The one thing I like about the reform on all the different plans is to have individuals have a greater choice in the number of plans that they can choose from.

Right now, the way it is done is, I analyze the different plans, given the cost, and I have a certain number of parameters when I make a decision as to which health care plan to offer my employees. So I think it is going to be a very positive thing in all the plans that they will have a greater choice.

Mrs. COLLINS. Ms. Hebson, do some of your employees for whom you provide health insurance get coverage for dependents, or have spouses who are employed elsewhere?

Ms. HEBSON. Yes. We—out of the—there are 56, and 2 COBRA's that we do insure; but if you don't count the COBRA's, it is 28 have single coverage because they don't have any family and 28 dependent coverage because they do.

Mrs. COLLINS. Do you think it is fair that the other spouses' employers don't have to contribute at all to their family health insurance premium, and that they let the full burden fall on your shoulders?

Ms. HEBSON. I think the employees are doing the best they can. I don't think they are trying to hurt me in any way.

Mrs. COLLINS. Does it hurt you in any way?

Ms. HEBSON. I never thought of that, you know. It is just—there is a lot——

Mrs. COLLINS. Do the spouses and dependents work for you?

Ms. HEBSON. Do the spouses and dependents work for us? Sometimes they may.

Mrs. COLLINS. But as a rule, do they?

Ms. HEBSON. As a rule, they probably do not.

Mrs. COLLINS. So it does not bother you that their insurance coverage is by people who work for you?

Ms. HEBSON. To tell you the truth——

Mrs. COLLINS. If they work. If they are working someplace else, and you are paying their insurance coverage.

Ms. HEBSON. And we are paying their insurance?

Mrs. COLLINS. Does that bother you?

Ms. HEBSON. Because they don't have any coverage at their other spot?

Mrs. COLLINS. Yes.

Ms. HEBSON. That doesn't bother me, no.

Mrs. COLLINS. That doesn't bother you. So you think it is OK.

Ms. Blakeley, if the reform proposal that you set forth at the end of your written testimony were to become law, how would employees of businesses who choose not to participate be covered? That is one question.

And also if these and other groups of people will still be uninsured, continuing this cycle of cost-shifting to those who don't have any health insurance, wouldn't health care costs continue to spiral upward?

Two questions in one.

Ms. BLAKELEY. First question—let me make sure I understood what you asked—was the implementation of the principles of a plan, is that correct, that was at the end of my written statement?

Mrs. COLLINS. Let me read the question. That is it, yes.

Ms. BLAKELEY. And how would that affect the individuals whose—OK, if an employer did not chose to offer health insurance? The way I understand the regional purchasing alliance, individuals could buy health insurance through those alliances.

One of the problems that you have right now is you can have access to health care if you are unemployed—and I keep going back to this—the problem is especially for the very small businesses and the start-ups and the very immature businesses. I can absorb the additional premium because my business is 10 years old, and I have the cash reserves to do that. I could not have absorbed it when I was 1 year old.

So all those people would not be employed today. That is my concern level with the mandate. So what happens, from what I understand, the individuals can go into the alliances to buy their own health care coverage.

Mrs. COLLINS. Let me ask you the second part because you didn't give the answer to that. If these and other groups of people would still be uninsured, continuing the cycle of cost shifting that exists today, wouldn't health care costs continue to rise?

Ms. BLAKELEY. If—from what I understand—and I don't have the numbers in front of me, I apologize—the majority of small businesses want to provide health insurance for their employees. I am not saying 100 percent.

Mrs. COLLINS. How would these people get some insurance?

Ms. BLAKELEY. Wait a minute. Excuse me.

Mrs. COLLINS. How would these people be insured?

Ms. BLAKELEY. The majority of the businesses, if you get down to an affordable plan, will provide that for their employees. OK. And what you are doing is, you are bringing more people into this system.

The health care system wants all young, healthy, single people in the system, just like employers and health insurance providers want young, healthy people in the system.

Mrs. COLLINS. May I ask you something? What about those who are not as young and as healthy, how would they be provided for?

Ms. BLAKELEY. The same thing, which—you go to community rating, which is part of the proposal that does away with the discrimination between age and health status.

Mrs. COLLINS. Would you say these people have to get their own insurance or be eligible for Medicare or something of that kind?

Ms. BLAKELEY. What I am saying is, there would be options in the plan that would allow people to purchase their own insurance without an employer mandate.

Mrs. COLLINS. OK.

Mr. WAXMAN. Thank you, Mrs. Collins.

Mr. Brown.

Mr. BROWN. Thank you, Mr. Chairman.

Ms. Blakeley, the Vermont Teddy Bear Company who just unfortunately left, suppose there was another teddy bear company called the Blakeley Teddy Bear Company that located right across the street.

Now, Vermont covers all its workers with apparently pretty good health insurance. Your company, the Blakeley Teddy Bear Company, decides not to provide any health care insurance. That means that they aren't as competitive as you, because their costs are higher presumably, because you aren't paying health care. It means when their employees—when your employees go to the hospital and they are uncovered, that hospital costs—the hospital takes care of them at no cost to employees because they don't have health insurance; and it means that the Vermont Teddy Bear Company employees' health plan gets so expensive.

So basically you have a competitive advantage over them because you aren't paying for insurance at this new company you are forming in Vermont; and second, you have an advantage because their costs are going up because your employees aren't paying.

What is fair about a system like that?

Ms. BLAKELEY. Well, first of all, my company would provide health insurance, OK, because I believe it is good business. You get better——

Mr. BROWN. I understand that. I appreciate that.

Ms. BLAKELEY. I want to make my position very clear. I do provide health insurance, and I will continue to do that with any company I start.

As far as the fairness issue on that, I have no—there are a number of proposals floating around that address that issue without an employer mandate. My problem is this: I have no problem with mandating individuals to have coverage. I have no problem with requiring companies to provide a plan without mandating that they pay for it, OK, so that individuals can make those decisions.

There are a number of proposals out there that hit a little more of a middle road.

My concern is this: When my company had three to five people, this kind of mandate would have put us out of business. We did not have the cash to survive this.

Now, I have heard a lot of people talk about raising prices. I want to go back to something I said in my testimony, or in my statement: Small business survives on cash. If you have to pay today for a health insurance plan and you raise your prices today, you have got a severe cash flow problem. That is another issue that hasn't been raised.

So the problem that you have there is, you increase the number of small business—very small business failures, and you will definitely increase the number of people out of work. And going back to, does that help the system? No, it doesn't because you are burdening the welfare system or the unemployment system while you are solving your health care issue. That doesn't make any sense. It is not good business.

Mr. BROWN. If everyone, if one restaurant—you know, take both restaurants—here covers some of their employees, not all; but if Ms. Wicks' restaurant covers everybody and Ms. Hebson's restaurant doesn't and, say—put them both that they both cover some of their employees now, under this plan they obviously are not—they join the alliance under this plan. Their costs will go up roughly, comparably—roughly the same amount, why is that so anti-competitive? Why is that going to put one of them out of business?

Ms. BLAKELEY. OK. That is a very good question.

Here is one of the problems: If I am a restaurant and I am 1 year old and I am a restaurant and 10 years old—if I am 10 years old, I am going to survive; if I am 1 year old, I am probably not.

Mr. BROWN. If you are 1 year old—neither of these two restaurateurs that testified has under 50 employees, right? I know Ms. Hebson——

Ms. BLAKELEY. I believe everybody is over 50.

Mr. BROWN. So that the plan, the plan, the Clinton plan as more or less written—although we haven't, as you know, seen it yet precisely doesn't account for—it accounts for people.

The smaller businesses are getting a subsidy because they are under 50; these larger, if they have been in business 6 or 10 years or whatever it sounds like, they have both done very well without that subsidy of under 50 employees, so much of your problem is taken care of that way because they get—they get that assistance because they are smaller businesses. And the government in a sense is recognizing, yes, they have got these problems because they are less mature, newer start-ups.

Ms. BLAKELEY. Are you talking about the subsidies?

Mr. BROWN. Yes. The under-50-employee subsidy and the lower cap on all of that.

Ms. BLAKELEY. My concern on the caps and the subsidy is, I have already heard rumors saying they aren't going to hold because the numbers aren't working, it is going to be more expensive than what you have got now.

My concern is—don't anybody take this personally, but I don't trust the government to keep their word on caps. We have been told too many times that certain things will be leveled at a certain level. It is like, right now my health care cost is 6 percent of my payroll, while I am doing my numbers on 7.9; I know better. I cannot make a business decision based on today; I have to make a business decision based on what might impact me or most likely will impact me. So that is one of the problems with the subsidies.

Most small business people are extraordinarily skeptical of that argument.

Mr. BROWN. Keep in mind, as the chairman—one more comment real quick, Mr. Chairman, if I could.

Keep in mind, as the chairman said, that your administrative costs absolutely will be less.

Ms. BLAKELEY. Absolutely not. They will not, not the way I understand the plan. My administrative costs will significantly go up, the way I understand the proposed plan.

Mr. BROWN. Why?

Ms. BLAKELEY. You have to track so many more things. Right now, all I track is who elects to come into the health insurance program. I offer an insurance program. If people opt into it, that is fine. And that is all I track, and I do a payroll deduction for their portion of that.

Under the new program, you not only have to track your employee, you have to know if their spouse works, you have some really complicated formula to come up with the amount that you have to pay, including 80 percent of the amount of the people in the area. It is very complicated.

So I have to know if my employee's wife works or if their children work.

Mr. WAXMAN. If the gentleman would yield. Don't you do that now, or do you not provide coverage for the rest of the family?

Ms. BLAKELEY. It is a one-sheet piece of paper that the employees themselves fill out and send to the insurance company. I don't track that.

Mr. WAXMAN. That is all they are going to have under this proposal.

Mr. BROWN. It goes to the alliances now, right. I am sorry, would the chairman yield? I am sorry.

Go ahead, I am sorry.

Mr. WAXMAN. OK. I think we had better move on.

Mr. Manton.

Mr. MANTON. Thank you, Mr. Chairman. Most of the questions that could be asked probably already have been asked. I and, I believe, some of the members who are still here had an opportunity earlier this year to visit in Europe and look at the United Kingdom and France and Germany; and I think the numbers are right, if I remember them correctly: The United Kingdom runs about 6 percent of their gross national product on health care; France is about—was about 9 percent, I believe; Germany, 10 percent, and we are—they provide universal health care. You may or may not like what they provide. They are all a little different; most of the health plans are based on historical backgrounds or cultural backgrounds.

But here we are spending about 14 percent of our GNP, and yet we still have this pool of people—13, 14 percent—who are not covered. But it seems to me we have enough money in the system to bring everybody in, and everybody really is in the system.

If someone who has no coverage goes out and gets shot or stabbed, as was mentioned in some of the testimony, or gets run over by a car, and they have no insurance and they go down to the emergency room, well, we don't toss them out into the street. We cover them. We operate. We put them in the hospital for whatever number of days it takes, and then we build the cost of that into the system, so that we are all paying now anyhow and not really getting our money's worth because of the lack of preventive care and so forth.

In looking at some of the prepared questions, most of you either in your testimony or in your written statement have indicated that you believe in universal health care as an ideal. Most of you are covering your employees in whole or in part and are willing, I think, to go the distance if we structure this plan right so it doesn't make you anticompetitive or put you in the red trying to keep records and so forth.

I guess my question, as a wrap-up for me—and I asked this of the large business panel as well—if this plan were to become law, or about to become law, what is the one thing that troubles you the most and how would you change that, if you could, starting with Ms. Hebson?

Ms. HEBSON. The thing that worries me the most is that I have no idea how they could pay for it with the figures because they don't add up at all. In Europe, they have a big VAT tax. Didn't you have a VAT tax when you went out to eat in Europe?

Mr. MANTON. Yes, and at one time there was a proposal floating around here to finance health care with a VAT tax. I think that is somewhat alien to Americans.

Ms. HEBSON. When you saw big business here and they were in favor of it, like Mr. Kirkland said, if you use common sense and justice you can do best in this, but you have to put the figures down and use your common sense.

Do you think Ford Motor Company with 19 percent health care costs would have that 19 percent if it didn't really cost that much? They are as big as an alliance would be and it costs them 19 percent.

Mr. MANTON. Maybe they are giving away the store, too.

Ms. HEBSON. I don't know. I don't work for them, but it kind of looks like it costs 19 percent for them to do it, otherwise why would they pay it? You cannot say it would cost 7.9 percent; 7.9 percent would not give our 300 employees decent health care.

When I looked at the figures and pushed them out, it would take about $600,000 to give our employees, all of them, what, we give 50. The government would say we could do that for $260,000. Even if the government knew how to do really good economies, you cannot get that far. It is impossible. If I had one thing to say, I would say go back to the drawing board because this doesn't compute.

Ms. WICKS. My biggest fear is cost containment. I am willing to pay more and I think the average person is willing to pay more, but sometimes I feel that the drug companies, insurance companies, et cetera, are going to continue to reap excessive profits.

I would like to have a stronger statement about drug companies. The health care plan is going to ask drug care companies to try to be reasonable. I am not sure whether that is strong enough.

I am also concerned about malpractice. I think there should be tighter controls on that. I think the system will continue as it is now, have the average person be paying for things where those in powerful positions will continue to make more and more. The money is going somewhere. There should be enough money to cover all this with what we spend on health care.

We should try to figure out where is it wasted and where are the excessive profits and deal with those rather than raising the amount that the average person will pay.

Mr. MANTON. So you would change the cost containment part?

Ms. WICKS. Yes.

Mr. MANTON. My time is up, but could I have permission to have Mrs. Blakeley answer?

Mr. WAXMAN. Go ahead.

Ms. BLAKELEY. My biggest concern is definitely the employer mandate on an unaffordable plan. When I say an unaffordable plan, the proposed plan has been set up to be an extremely expensive one and most small employers would not be able to provide that kind of coverage given the current cash situation.

Mr. MANTON. Thank you. Thank you, Mr. Chairman.

Mr. WAXMAN. Let me ask you, Ms. Hebson, you have 300 employees; is that right?

Ms. HEBSON. Yes.

Mr. WAXMAN. You insure 56 out of 58. Are the others part-time employees or full-time?

Ms. HEBSON. They would be a mixture of both.

Mr. WAXMAN. What happens to them, do they have insurance?

Ms. HEBSON. You know, some do and some don't.

Mr. WAXMAN. Those who don't, when they get sick they will go to the hospital and they will get care and the cost of that care will be passed on to those who are insured. So for the insurance that you now pay, that cost will increase.

For Ms. Wicks, if her cafe was in your neighborhood and she covers all employees her costs will go up because all your employees are not covered. Shouldn't all of your employees be covered?

Ms. HEBSON. I don't think that is my expertise. My expertise is as a small business person.

Mr. WAXMAN. You know what it is like in this country, if you don't have insurance, you don't go to a doctor until you get real sick.

Ms. HEBSON. It can be very hard for people. I would love for the world to be perfect.

Mr. WAXMAN. How many of the employees are relatives?

Ms. HEBSON. I would say about one-fifth.

Mr. WAXMAN. How do you draw the line on some full-time employees not getting coverage?

Ms. HEBSON. Well, because we are a small business it is very personal. Sometimes they are covered just for no other reason but that they need the insurance.

Mr. WAXMAN. I guess the point I am trying to make to you is we think all Americans ought to have coverage. You are saying you don't think you can afford it.

As Mrs. Wicks pointed out, the government should pay for those people by raising taxes. Don't you think we have to ask you to pay for most of your people?

Ms. HEBSON. Yes, I do. You always do.

Mr. WAXMAN. We are trying to make this system fair for everyone. Mrs. Wicks wonders if it is affordable. She has a serious question in her mind whether the government can hold down the costs. That is a good point. Cost containment won't work unless everybody is covered. It is like a dog chasing its tail. The reason why it won't work is that when Ms. Hebson's employees who are not covered get sick and they get care somebody will have to pay for that.

Do you think the hospitals are in a business to give away services? They cannot afford it any more than you can. Somebody has to pay for it and it is passed forward to those who are insured.

Ms. Wicks points out that she would like to see cost controls. But to say you should not have the obligation at all means for most small businesses they are going to find a reason not to cover their employees. You point out that sometimes it is because they are new. But Ms. Hebson's outfit is not new. It has been around for several generations.

I don't understand your point being one I should take seriously if we have a restaurant that has been around for a number of years. They have a cash problem but they have not seen fit to cover their employees obviously because they cannot afford it. We are running in circles. Bring the system into place and cover everybody. If we are going to cover everybody, we have to raise taxes or ask business to do it and then subsidize it.

Ms. BLAKELEY. There is another way to do that, though. If you get the costs down and you have employers who choose to provide, then, that is good. If you wanted to mandate that everybody has coverage then do that, but don't mandate that the small business person, who may not have the money, do it.

Mr. WAXMAN. Do you think an employee at her restaurant will have enough money to go out and buy it?

Ms. BLAKELEY. The same argument, how is that small business person going to go out and find the money for health insurance when they cannot afford it now? You compound a problem. You have somebody without health insurance and also somebody without a job.

Mr. WAXMAN. We will have to balance that out. It is not an easy problem. Everybody would say we ought to cover all Americans at an affordable price and we would all like to pay only what we feel is affordable. Ms. Hebson?

Ms. HEBSON. I don't think the only way you can do it is to make employers pay it.

Mr. WAXMAN. Give us alternatives.

Ms. HEBSON. Make individuals pay it.

Mr. WAXMAN. What is the highest priced employee that you have who is not covered with insurance? How much does that person make?

Ms. HEBSON. I want to answer honestly but you want me to guess. I would only be able to guess. Here is the tough part: We need to address this problem so that insurance can be affordable.

Mr. WAXMAN. Do you have people at the minimum wage?

Ms. HEBSON. Yes, of course.

Mr. WAXMAN. Could they afford to buy a policy?

Ms. HEBSON. If the system were fixed they could, yes.

Mr. WAXMAN. Mrs. Collins.

Mrs. COLLINS. Mr. Chairman, when we began on this panel I was on the telephone and I did not have an opportunity to welcome this panel. I thought it incumbent on me being from Illinois to recognize the fact that Mrs. Hebson is from my great State of Illinois and I want to welcome her.

Mr. WAXMAN. You have been very helpful. We are struggling with this issue. We are trying to balance a lot of concerns. If we were designing health care from the start none of us would do it this way where employees have anything to do with it. Most people have their insurance on their jobs and that is the way the President suggested we build on the subject.

Thank you for being with us. We look forward to struggling on these issues with you. We stand adjourned.

[Whereupon, at 2:50 p.m., the subcommittees were adjourned, to reconvene at the call of the Chair.]

HEALTH CARE REFORM
Consumer, Insurer, and Provider Advocates

THURSDAY, OCTOBER 14, 1993

HOUSE OF REPRESENTATIVES, COMMITTEE ON ENERGY AND COMMERCE, SUBCOMMITTEE ON HEALTH AND THE ENVIRONMENT, AND THE SUBCOMMITTEE ON COMMERCE, CONSUMER PROTECTION, AND COMPETITIVENESS,

Washington, DC.

The subcommittee met, pursuant to notice, at 10:05 a.m., in room 2123, Rayburn House Office Building, Hon. Henry A. Waxman, chairman, Subcommittee on Health and the Environment, and Hon. Cardiss Collins, chairwoman, Subcommittee on Commerce, Consumer Protection, and Competitiveness, presiding.

Mr. WAXMAN. The meeting of the subcommittees will come to order. Today we are continuing our joint hearings.

With the Subcommittee on Commerce, Consumer Protection, and Competitiveness on President Clinton's health reform plan. While the details of this plan are not yet available, the President's address last month to Congress left no doubt about his commitment to guaranteed coverage of comprehensive benefits for all Americans.

On Tuesday, we heard from workers and employers, on whom the President proposes to place much of the responsibility for paying for universal coverage. Spencer Putnam of the Vermont Teddy Bear Company reminded us that failure to reform the health system "tears at our social fabric, and runs counter to our ideals of a society which offers equal protection and equal opportunity to all of its citizens."

President Clinton's leadership has given us a real opportunity to build a just system that offers all Americans the benefits of our unparalleled medical progress. But we can only realize these goals if we are willing to distribute the costs of health care fairly and impose effective constraints on the growth of these costs over time. Although our witnesses on Tuesday disagreed among themselves on the issue of financing, they were unanimous in their support for effective cost controls.

Our witnesses today represent advocates on behalf of consumers, insurers, and providers. We recognize that it is difficult to prepare testimony without the benefit of a detailed legislative proposal, and we appreciate the willingness of our witnesses this morning to give us their initial reactions to the plan as they understand it. We expect to consult with them again once the President's bill is introduced.

Before I call on our first panel, I would like to call on my distinguished colleague and cochair of this hearing, Congresswoman Collins.

Mrs. COLLINS. I would like to welcome everyone to today's joint hearing of our two subcommittees on President Clinton's health care reform plan and I am pleased to once again cochair this hearing with my colleague and friend Chairman Waxman.

This is another of what will be an extensive series of hearings at which we will receive comments from the American public on the President's health care proposal. This past Tuesday, October 12, we held a hearing at which we received testimony from labor, large businesses, and small businesses.

As we embark on this landmark legislation which for the first time will guarantee every American the right to health care, we intend to hear from as many witnesses as possible on a wide variety of topics.

Today's witnesses represent some of the principal stakeholders in the health care reform debate. The providers, as the medical professionals who will continue to deliver the health care under the reformed system, will be very directly affected by any changes in the way they are asked to provide those services.

Insurers, who would continue to operate under the proposal would see their roles significantly altered; and consumers, as the common denominator among all Americans in the health reform debate, must ultimately decide how we should proceed to ensure that all Americans receive the quality health care and health security they deserve.

I would like to thank our witnesses for joining us today to shed light on these very important issues. At this point, I would like to conclude my opening remarks in order to take full advantage of the time we have with our witnesses.

Mr. WAXMAN. Thank you, Mrs. Collins.

Mr. Bliley?

Mr. BLILEY. Thank you, Mr. Chairman.

I would like to join you in welcoming our witnesses to today's hearing. This is a particularly important hearing because today for the first time our committee will be hearing from three very important groups that will be greatly affected by health care reform: the elderly, the provider community, and the insurance industry.

First let me say that it is very unfortunate that this is our fourth hearing on the administration's health care proposal and we still do not have an introduced bill so that both members and the public could work off actual legislation and not just the unofficial September 7th "working draft."

Because we are working from a "moving vehicle," both Congress and the public are given different and frequently contradictory explanations about the plan by administration witnesses. Last week when the Secretary of HHS testified before this committee, she could not in many instances answer specific questions about the administration plan because she stated that the plan is "a work in progress" and elements of the plan were literally changing as she was testifying.

Interestingly the American public has not been fooled. In an October 12 Washington Post poll 8 out of 10 Americans said they do not think Clinton has a complete plan, and 7 out of 10 said that the President has not told the public everything it needs to know to judge its effect.

We have also not seen any of the administration's "working papers" concerning the assumptions and quantitative analysis of the plan's financing, cost containment, and economic impact of jobs.

Since I am not aware of one independent health care expert or economist who has found the administration's financing and cost containment proposal credible, it is critical that this documentation be made public so that Congress and the public can determine the validity of the analysis. I would like to remind my colleagues that the first question I asked Mrs. Clinton at our September 28 hearing was her willingness to make available to the committee the task force quantitative work product.

Let me quote Mrs. Clinton's response: "We will be happy to share with you all of the data that you requested, all of our calculations, our economic models, et cetera."

Well, it is 16 days later, and we are still waiting. The committee has not received even one page of analysis from the administration.

I hope we can get commitments from both the full committee and subcommittee chairpersons that every witness that appears before this committee before the legislation is introduced will get a second chance to comment in open commitment hearings on the actual bill. This is the only fair and equitable course of action when facing this unprecedented circumstance, where we are holding hearings on a "draft conceptual proposal."

Let me make some brief comments concerning our witnesses today. No group has more at stake in this proposal than consumers. The impact on Medicare beneficiaries is a good example. The cap on Medicare cuts $124 billion from the Medicare program in 5 years. Then beginning in the year 2001, the annual growth in the Medicare program will be limited to approximately 3.5 percent. This rate of growth is significantly less than the current rate of growth, which is 11.6 percent, and in inflation-adjusted terms, represents zero growth. Also, the administration-proposed growth rate has never been remotely approached by any western country, including Britain and Canada, which explicitly ration health care to the elderly. I strongly believe that the elderly must ask themselves if they will suffer from health care rationing under the Clinton plan.

Now, let's turn to the providers. Under the Clinton plan, physicians and hospitals will face a new bewildering combination of global budgets and price controls; and a new level of intrusive control and micromanagement by a national board, dozens of advisory councils, alliances, and State boards which will make health care the most regulated sector of the entire economy.

Plus, there is a real question concerning the survival of fee-for-service under the Clinton plan. If health care has to be rationed under the Draconian Clinton price controls, it will be physicians who have to make these terrible decisions.

Finally, what is the future of the health insurance industry and the thousands of people they employ? Can any health insurer survive with mandatory community rating of a guaranteed benefits package and a premium cap set at CPI? More importantly, will any insurer even want to participate in such a "managed market" where they are almost guaranteed to lose money.

I hope we can get some answers to these questions today. Thank you.

Mr. Chairman, I apologize for the length of the statement.

Mr. WAXMAN. Mr. Stearns?

Mr. STEARNS. Good morning and thank you, Mr. Chairman.

Today's witnesses represent the spectrum of individuals involved in a modern health care system: insurers, providers, and consumers. Each of these groups has a specific and important role to play in the delivery of health care in America today.

The Clinton health care plan proposes to substantially change how these groups relate to one another and we must examine these changes closely. Chairman Dingell and subcommittee Chairwoman Collins and others have led the way in examining the regulation of our Nation's insurance companies, particularly regulation for solvency.

The one thing we have learned from our hearings is that solvency regulation cannot be ignored for any kind of insurance, whether they are a property casualty firm or a life health firm. Unfortunately in the rush to develop health care plans that provide universal coverage and a host of other benefits for everyone, we are ignoring the impact on insurance companies' solvency.

For instance, the Clinton plan separates rate-making from solvency. In addition, insurers are required to provide a host of new benefits in a basic package to everyone while at the same time being required to cap their premium increases. The premium caps placed on insurers eliminates the flexibility needed when taking on a new benefits program and the additional 37 million uninsured to the system.

When insurers can't adjust premiums properly to reflect these new additions and changing risks, they can't make sound underwriting decisions and when they don't make sound underwriting decisions, they become insolvent. And when they become insolvent, the guarantee funds have to pay off the policyholders and eventually we are all forced to pay through higher premiums and fees.

The Clinton plan raises many more insurance and solvency questions. How are insurers supposed to price their plans without the appropriate body of experience? What happens if they price their products incorrectly? What happens if all the adverse risks gravitate to a particular insurance plan? These are all questions that aren't adequately answered by the document that we have received from the White House to date.

Mr. Chairman, I welcome this opportunity to discuss the implications of the Clinton plan and other plans on the solvency of insurers. We need to ask ourselves the basic question of what kind of choice will be left if we put most of the programs out of business.

Several years ago, Chairman Dingell illustrated the problems of insurance company insolvencies in the Oversight and Investigation Subcommittee in the report entitled "Failed Promises." I only hope that we consider the lessons of that document in designing a health care insurance plan unless we want to find ourselves many years down the road writing a sequel.

Thank you, Mr. Chairman.

Mr. WAXMAN. Thank you, Mr. Stearns.

Mr. Cooper?

Mr. COOPER. Thank you, Mr. Chairman. I have no opening statement.

Mr. WAXMAN. Our first panel this morning includes organizations that represent consumers of health care services including low-income families and the elderly. Becky Cain is president of the League of Women Voters of the United States. The league is a nonpartisan citizen organization that works to encourage informed and active participation in government. Gail Shearer is the manager for policy analysis for the Consumers Union, the publisher of the Consumer Reports and other consumer education materials.

Judith Brown is the chairman of the board of directors of the American Association of Retired Persons, AARP, which represents 33 million older Americans. Ron Pollack is executive director of Families USA, a national consumer advocacy organization working for health care reform.

I want to welcome you to our hearing today. We are pleased to have you with us. Your prepared statements will be entered in the record in their entirety. We would like to ask you to limit the oral presentation to no more than 5 minutes.

Ms. Cain, we will start with you. Let me spell out for everybody the terms of the 5-minute rule. We will have a timer. At the end of 5 minutes, we would appreciate a concluding sentence. We will have to be strict about the 5-minute rule so we can hear all the testimony.

When we get to the point of questions, if the bell rings and members are in the middle of a sentence, we will let that question be asked and a response to the question, but we would hope it would be a brief one at that point.

STATEMENTS OF BECKY CAIN, PRESIDENT, LEAGUE OF WOMEN VOTERS OF THE UNITED STATES; GAIL SHEARER, MANAGER, POLICY ANALYSIS, CONSUMERS UNION; JUDITH BROWN, CHAIRMAN, BOARD OF DIRECTORS, AMERICAN ASSOCIATION OF RETIRED PERSONS; AND RONALD F. POLLACK, EXECUTIVE DIRECTOR, FAMILIES USA FOUNDATION

Ms. CAIN. Thank you.

Madam Chairwoman, Mr. Chairman, members of the subcommittees, I am Becky Cain, president of the League of Women Voters of the United States. I am very happy to be here today to comment on President Clinton's proposed health care reform plan.

The League of Women Voters is a nonpartisan citizen organization with approximately 200,000 members and supporters nationwide. The health care system has concerned league members for several years. In 1990, we began a 3-year intensive study on the delivery and financing of health care in the United States.

Leagues and league members across the country carefully examined the problems and considered solutions to the health care crisis. After thousands of hours of grass roots debate, league members

77-929 O - 94 - 8

reached consensus on health care reform. That consensus is the basis for my testimony today.

The League of Women Voters believes that fundamental health care reform must provide universal access to quality health care to all U.S. residents regardless of ability to pay and must include stringent cost control measures for health care outlays. It is clear that our current health care system is failing. It is failing our Nation's families and it is failing our Nation's economy.

Americans feel uncertain about their ability to afford adequate care. An extended hospital stay or long-term care for aging parents can deplete any family's budget. Our Nation's businesses cannot compete in a world economy and we cannot assure good paying jobs when health care costs are spiraling out of control. Something is fundamentally wrong when mothers can't afford prenatal care, when children don't receive routine vaccinations, when working families can't afford health insurance, and when older parents are left destitute without long-term care.

In a recent national public opinion poll, Americans ranked health care as the most important issue for citizens to get involved in, more important than the economy and the environment. Health care is on the mind of every citizen in America today and the League of Women Voters wants to ensure that the concerns of citizens are on the mind of every legislator involved in shaping tomorrow's health care system.

As citizens, we say to you our elected representatives as clearly and as forcefully as we can, fix these problems. Pass comprehensive health care reform.

The League of Women Voters believes that President Clinton's health care reform proposal marks a critical step forward. It will fix some of the fundamental flaws in our Nation's health care system and it does represent reform.

Under the plan, Americans will be covered no matter where they live, where they work, or how much they earn. The plan's basic benefits package will be a boon to people's health. For the first time, all Americans will be guaranteed coverage for preventive, primary, and acute care and reproductive health services, including abortions, are in the plan. Mental health services and long-term care are also included but are limited to keep costs down.

Among the plan's most critical features are its built-in cost control mechanisms. By standardizing forms, introducing new competitive structures, and limiting spending, the plan has effective ways of cutting waste and reducing costs.

The President's plan is not perfect, but it is fair. It will need some fine tuning in the legislative process. For example, citizen and consumer participation must be included in all aspects of the plan's implementation to ensure that government-sponsored programs are responsive to people's needs.

The administration of the health care system must be a process in which citizens can express their views and participate. We believe that State and Federal programs and especially the health alliances that will be created as a result of reform should follow the Federal policy of open government, including open meetings, full access to information, an open regulatory process, adequate comment periods, and other protections to make sure that citizens are involved and aware.

The health care system must also be responsive to the needs and perspectives of people as consumers. We believe that health alliances should as stated in the plan disseminate information to consumers regarding quality and access, prepare comparative reports on the quality of health plans, providers and practitioners; and conduct education program to assist consumers in choosing health plans.

We ask that you take the initiative and give us reform please.

Thank you, Mr. Chairman.

Mr. WAXMAN. Thank you, Ms. Cain.

[Testimony resumes on p. 234.]

[The prepared statement of Ms. Cain follows:]

THE LEAGUE OF WOMEN VOTERS

President
Becky Cain
St. Albans, West Virginia

Vice-Presidents
Diane B. Sheridan
Taylor Lake Village, Texas

Peggy Lucas
Minneapolis, Minnesota

Secretary-Treasurer
Robin Seaborn
St. Petersburg, Florida

Directors
Pat Brady
Springfield, Virginia

Marilyn F. Brill
Danville, Pennsylvania

Jane S. Garbacz
Wilton, Connecticut

Bobbie E. Hill
Camden, Arkansas

Debbie Macon
West Bloomfield, Michigan

Beverly K. McKinnell
St. Paul, Minnesota

Linda Moscarella
Taos, New Mexico

Nancy Pearson
Tacoma, Washington

Carole Wagner Vallianos
Manhattan Beach, California

Kathleen Weisenberg
Atherton, California

Executive Director
Gracia M. Hillman

TESTIMONY BEFORE THE

SUBCOMMITTEE ON COMMERCE, CONSUMER PROTECTION AND COMPETITIVENESS

AND THE

SUBCOMMITTEE ON HEALTH AND THE ENVIRONMENT

OF THE HOUSE COMMITTEE ON ENERGY AND COMMERCE

ON

PRESIDENT CLINTON'S HEALTH CARE REFORM PLAN

BY BECKY CAIN, PRESIDENT

THE LEAGUE OF WOMEN VOTERS OF THE UNITED STATES

October 14, 1993

Madame Chairwoman, Mr. Chairman, members of the subcommittees, I am Becky Cain, president of the League of Women Voters of the United States. I am very happy to be here today to comment on President Clinton's proposed health care reform plan. I would also like to discuss the critical need for comprehensive health care reform and to outline the League's views on what should be included in any effective reform plan.

The League of Women Voters is a non-partisan citizen organization with approximately 200,000 members and supporters in all fifty states, the District of Columbia, Puerto Rico and the Virgin Islands. For almost 75 years, Leagues across the country have worked to encourage the informed and active participation of

1730 M STREET, N.W., WASHINGTON, D.C. 20036
202 429-1965 FAX: 202 429-0854

Printed on recycled paper

citizens in government. The League is expert at giving citizens the tools necessary to make important decisions on critical public policy issues.

The health care system has concerned League members for many years. In 1990, we began a three-year intensive study on the delivery and financing of health care in the United States. Leagues and League members across the country carefully examined the problems and considered solutions to the health care crisis. After thousands of hours of grassroots debate, League members reached consensus on health care reform. That consensus is the basis for my testimony today.

The League of Women Voters believes that fundamental health care reform must provide universal access to quality health care for all U.S. residents regardless of ability to pay and must include stringent cost control measures for health care outlays.

It is clear that our current health care system is failing. It is failing our nation's families and it is failing our nation's economy. Millions of Americans are losing the battle to keep up with rising health care costs. As a nation, we spend $1 out of every $7 we earn on health care. Families feel uncertain about their ability to afford adequate care. An extended hospital stay or long-term care for aging parents can deplete any family's budget. Our nation's businesses cannot compete in a world economy, and we cannot assure good-paying jobs, when health care costs are spiralling out of control.

For those who cannot afford health insurance -- and 37 million people have no health insurance -- the picture is even more grim: no doctor when one is needed, no medicine when illness strikes. Something is fundamentally wrong when mothers can't afford prenatal care, when children don't receive routine vaccinations, when working families can't afford health insurance, and when older parents are left destitute without adequate long-term care.

In a recent national public opinion poll, Americans ranked health care as the most important issue for citizens to get involved in -- more important even than the economy and the environment. Health care is on the mind of every citizen in America today. And the League of Women Voters wants to ensure that the concerns of citizens are on the mind of every legislator involved in shaping tomorrow's health care system.

As citizens, we say to you, our elected representatives, as clearly and as forcefully as we can: Fix these problems; pass comprehensive health care reform.

The League of Women Voters believes that President Clinton's health care reform package marks a critical step forward. It will fix fundamental flaws in our nation's health care system. It is real reform.

Under the plan, Americans will be covered no matter where they live, where they work or how much they earn. The plan's basic benefits package will be a boon to people's health. For the first time, all Americans will be guaranteed coverage for preventive, primary and acute care; and reproductive health services, including abortion, are in the plan. Mental health services and long-term care are also included, but are limited to keep costs down.

Among the plan's most critical features are its built-in cost control mechanisms. By standardizing forms, introducing new competitive structures and limiting spending, the plan has effective ways of cutting waste and reducing costs.

The President's health care plan is not perfect but it is fair. It will need some fine-tuning in the legislative process. For example, citizen and consumer participation must be included in all aspects of the plan's implementation to ensure that government-sponsored programs are responsive to people's needs.

The administration of the health care system must be a process in which citizens can express their views and participate. We believe that state and federal programs, and especially the health alliances, that will be created as the result of health care reform should follow the federal policy of open government, including open meetings, full access to information, open regulatory processes, adequate comment periods, and other protections to make sure that citizens are involved and aware.

The health system must also be responsive to the needs and perspectives of people as consumers. We believe that health alliances should, as stated in the President's plan, disseminate information to consumers regarding quality and access; prepare comparative reports on the quality of health plans, providers and practitioners; and conduct education programs to assist consumers in choosing health plans.

The President included consumer representatives at many levels of the plan. As the panel that deals with consumer protection issues, you know that it is critical for the consumer's perspective to be included at every level.

In short, we believe the President's plan is an effective blueprint for health care reform and we urge its speedy consideration.

I would like to take a few minutes to outline the League's views on several key points that we believe should be included in any health care reform plan.

First, a reform plan must achieve universal coverage for all U.S. residents. Reform must establish a basic level of quality health care regardless of ability to pay.

Universal access is the basic test of the humanity of our health care system. The most advanced nation on earth must be able to assure adequate health care for all.

Universal access is also important as a cost control measure. Under the present system, cost shifting occurs when uncompensated care for the uninsured is passed along to the rest of us in the form of higher prices. In addition, illnesses left untreated because people don't have insurance are much more expensive to cure when someone finally goes to the emergency room.

How can universal coverage be achieved? The League favors a national health insurance plan financed through general taxes -- a so-called "single-payer" plan. We also believe that an "employer-mandate" system is acceptable.

Under an employer-mandate system, employers would be required to pay most of the costs of purchasing health care coverage for their employees and their families, who would pay the balance. The government would pay for those who are not in the work force, while small businesses would receive subsidies to assist them in providing coverage.

Because it builds on the existing system, under which most people get health insurance coverage through their family's employment, an employer-mandate system can achieve universal access without large disruption of the health care delivery system. In addition, because health care is a traditional form of compensation, and because it assures a healthy and productive workforce, it is appropriate for employers to continue to pay for health care.

Some have proposed that universal access be accomplished by requiring individuals to purchase health insurance. Often these proposals also provide tax incentives to encourage participation. Because such a system is very difficult to enforce, and because the type of coverage in such proposals is usually very spartan, this method can fall short of providing universal access to quality care. The League does not support such proposals.

Another important access issue is the problem of underserved areas. Too often, quality health services are not available in rural areas or inner cities. It is critical that the United States allocate resources to underserved areas and train health care professionals in needed fields.

The second crucial issue for any health care reform plan is the type of coverage that is included. The coverage must be broad and inclusive enough to protect people's health. But coverage must be limited to ensure that costs are not excessive. Striking the proper balance is one of the most difficult issues in the health reform debate.

The League of Women Voters believes that a basic package of quality services should include the prevention of disease, health promotion and education, primary care (including prenatal and reproductive health services), acute care, long-term care and mental health care. Dental, vision and hearing care are also important but lower in priority.

Primary care, the general "wellness" care received by a patient, is critical. Currently, the lack of primary and preventive care often results in serious illness and expensive medical intervention. By providing care such as prenatal care to all pregnant women and routine vaccinations to all children, we can save lives and money.

Acute care, the treatment of illnesses or injuries, is also critical. Providing this care to all U.S. residents would reduce cost shifting and help control costs, in addition to ensuring better health for all.

As Americans live longer, the need for long-term care is a reality for almost every family. Long-term care for persons who are chronically ill or mentally or physically disabled is also essential. Our current infrastructure for long-term care, however, is lacking. We need to look for new ways to deal with these problems, such as care in the home, that are not exceedingly expensive. In any case, a start must be made on long-term care.

A start must also be made on mental health care. It is abundantly clear that mental health care pays real dividends in lives saved, in pain relieved, in families assisted and in workers helped to remain productive.

I would like to say a few words about abortion services. We believe that abortion services must be included in the standard benefits package, just like any other safe, effective and legal medical procedure. A woman and her doctor must make the difficult decisions about reproductive health care -- Congress has no business making those decisions. Generations of women and men have fought to ensure access to safe abortion services. Such services are now included in many women's existing health plans. Make no mistake, removing abortion services from the benefits package would take away something fundamental from women across the country.

The third key issue in health care reform is cost control. A simple look at the numbers illustrates the problem. Between 1980 and 1991, the total amount spent on health care per family more than doubled. Without strong action, it will more than double again by the year 2000. America's families can't afford this and neither can America's businesses.

The League believes it is absolutely essential to achieve a reasonable total national expenditure level for health care. In order to control costs, legislation to reform the health care system should include specific cost-cutting measures such as:

- o the reduction of administrative costs;
- o regional planning for the allocation of personnel, facilities and equipment;
- o the establishment of maximum levels of reimbursement to providers;
- o malpractice reform;
- o the use of managed care;
- o utilization review of treatment;
- o mandatory second opinions before surgery or extensive treatment; and
- o consumer accountability through deductibles and copayments.

Such techniques hold real promise for controlling costs. According to some estimates, at least $130 billion a year is spent on unnecessary care. Managed care, which is designed to limit inappropriate or excessive utilization of health care services, can provide more efficient and econ mical delivery of care. Increased consumer accountability through deductibles and copayments can also help cut overutilization.

With 24 cents of every health care dollar going to administrative costs, it is apparent that administrative procedures must be streamlined, resulting in substantial savings. In Canada, which uses a single-payer system, the cost is 11 cents of every dollar. It is also vitally important to reduce duplication of services, facilities and equipment, such as costly, high-tech diagnostic machines.

In addition to specific cost control techniques, however, health care reform must include an overall mechanism to ensure that savings add up. There must be a back-up mechanism to oversee and coordinate cost-cutting efforts. We think that global budgeting can provide that needed mechanism. National and regional boards comprised of policy makers, medical professionals, and consumers could set goals or limits for spending at the national, state and local levels. Governments and health providers would then operate within those limits. Careful consideration needs to be given to how global budgeting will operate. We need to make sure that cost controls are consistent with quality and are not arbitrarily imposed. But the need for such global budgeting is clear. We believe it should be included in health care reform legislation.

The fourth and final key issue in health care reform is how to pay for it. Substantial savings can be achieved over the current health care system, and these savings should be applied to ensuring that all U.S. residents have a basic level of quality health care. No doubt a large part of the debate over the next several months will be over the size of those savings. Whatever the outcome, however, we believe that the goal of universal access is worth paying for.

That is why we support increased taxes to finance a basic level of health care for all, provided effective cost control strategies are employed. Although it is outside the jurisdiction of this committee, I would like to make a few additional points about taxes.

The League looks at a variety of factors when evaluating the acceptability of taxes, but we are particularly concerned that the overall health care reform package is fair, equitable and progressive. The League would support a general income tax increase to finance national health care reform and could support restrictions on the deductibility of health care benefits. We strongly oppose a value added tax (VAT) or national sales tax. This is a highly regressive tax and would unfairly burden low and middle-income Americans.

The League does support increases in so-called "sin taxes" on such products as cigarettes and alcohol as part of a reform package that encourages Americans to lead healthy lifestyles. Such taxes discourage the excessive use of these harmful products and will actually serve as "preventive medicine."

In summary, the League of Women Voters calls on Congress to enact national health care reform that provides for universal access to quality health care and for stringent cost control measures.

Health care reform will need bipartisan support. The League is encouraged that many of the goals for reform are now shared by key members of both political parties on Capitol Hill. Congress must not lose sight of the costs of inaction on this critical issue. Americans cannot afford a protracted political battle on national health care reform. There will be no perfect solution to this crisis. Not everyone will get everything they want. But, for once, everyone has the possibility of getting what they need. This, in itself, will be a giant step forward.

We need a viable plan that gives all Americans a more humane health care system. The President's plan is an effective blueprint for reform.

Congress must now seize the momentum. There can be no turning back. It is time to forge ahead and enact comprehensive health care reform.

Mr. WAXMAN. Ms. Shearer?

STATEMENT OF GAIL SHEARER

Ms. SHEARER. Thank you.

Consumers Union appreciates the opportunity to present our views on the Clinton Administration's proposal for health care reform. Consumers Union's efforts in support of health care reform, like those of Chairman Waxman and Chairwoman Collins and many committee members, go back many years.

I brought with me today one of the first issues of Consumer Reports from February 1939, over 50 years ago. Our article on health care concludes "It has become obvious that the people of the country intend to see to it that the whole population shall benefit from discoveries of modern medical science. The only question before the country now is how soon."

It is time for us to finally end the Nation's health care nightmare and answer this question now. Consumers cannot and should not have to wait longer for a solution to the health care crisis. Consumers Union is eager to help you analyze the elements of health care reform from the consumer perspective.

As your subcommittees help lead the Congress' consideration of the reform plan, we also urge you to keep in touch with the average American consumer, the people whose lives are either improved by a health care system that works well or whose lives are destroyed by a health care system that fails them. Only by keeping in touch with these consumers will the Congress be able to stand up to the many special interests that will seek to make their case in order to develop a health care program that meets consumer expectations and needs for health care reform.

To meet the needs of consumers, any health care reform must offer five key things. First, universal quality health care with comprehensive benefits, cost containment, fair share financing, public accountability and consumer choice of health care providers. While we continue to believe that a single-payer health care system would best meet the health care needs of American consumers, we are pleased that the Clinton Administration has embraced many of our principles.

We believe that the Clinton proposal would move the Nation's consumers closer to health care security. Still it leaves room for significant improvements. The strongest part of the health care plan is its commitment to universal health care protection. The Nation can no longer rely on the free market and wishful thinking when it comes to health care security. Health care is not a commodity like detergent and VCR's that can be bought and sold in the marketplace and rated in Consumer Reports. While the free market works well for things we buy at Kmart, it utterly fails when it comes to surgery, checkups, and other health care services.

The proposal, if enacted, would offer relief to the million of Americans who are now denied protection due to their financial status or preexisting conditions. The plan offers security to everybody against unforeseen events such as development of serious illness or loss of jobs.

I plan to briefly summarize Consumers Union's plan, five ways to improve the Clinton proposal and five elements that must be protected in the face of strong special interest opposition. The Clinton health care proposal makes a good start at providing consumers with health care security. The following five changes would help make it even better at meeting consumers' needs and expectations for health care reform.

First, protect low- and middle-income consumers from paying a disproportionately high share of health care costs. Here we suggest that we limit the percent of income to 2 percent of income that should go toward the family's share of premiums.

Second, we believe that the State single-payer option should be encouraged. The Clinton proposal allows States to establish a single-payer health care system, but includes a provision that seems to discourage States from doing so. We think that the State single-payer option should not be merely tolerated, but that it should be encouraged.

Third, make freedom of choice of provider a real option for people of all income levels by requiring all health alliances to offer a fee-for-service plan that costs little more than the average plan.

Fourth, include in the proposal a blueprint for phasing in nursing home benefits and expanded community care benefits. We recognize, as should Congress, that these benefits will require a substantial new funding base and we recommend that you consider increasing taxes to pay for expanded long-term care benefits.

Fifth, give the National Health Board the authority to regulate prescription drug prices that apply to all Americans, not just the Medicare and Medicaid eligible. The administration's draft plan has several provisions that will help keep prescription drug prices in check, but we believe that the plan needs to go further. We strongly recommend that the National Health Board's responsibility include the authority to regulate prescription drug prices. If drug prices were a river, they would already be well above flood stage. It is meaningless to talk about voluntary price controls since prices are already so out of line.

Every element of the Clinton health care proposal will be subject to attacks from a variety of special interests. We have identified five areas where we believe the consumer interest lies in keeping the provisions that are in the draft plan.

Briefly universal in 1997, cost containment for both the public and private sectors, limit the corporate alliances to 5,000 employees and more, keep out medical malpractice caps and keep the benefit package comprehensive.

Thank you.

Mr. WAXMAN. Thank you very much for your statement.

[Testimony resumes on p. 247.]

[The prepared statement of Ms. Shearer follows:]

Testimony of

GAIL SHEARER

MANAGER, POLICY ANALYSIS

CONSUMERS UNION

Consumers Union[1] appreciates the opportunity to present our views on the Clinton Administration's proposal for health care reform. Consumers Union's efforts in support of health care reform -- like those of Chairman Waxman, Chairwoman Collins, and many Committee members-- go back many years. In 1939, Consumer Reports noted that forty million Americans received inadequate medical care and called for enactment of the Wagner National Health Bill, which would have been a "cornerstone for a national health program."[2] In 1946, Consumer Reports supported the Wagner-Murray-Dingell Bill, which would have established federal compulsory health insurance.[3] In 1975, Consumer Reports published a comprehensive comparison of five proposals for national health insurance and established five goals that a national health insurance plan must meet to serve the consumer interest. Consumer Reports published a two-part series, "The Crisis in Health Insurance" in 1990, and a three-part series in 1993 that reviewed wasted medical care dollars, consumer

[1]Consumers Union is a nonprofit membership organization chartered in 1936 under the laws of the State of New York to provide consumers with information, education and counsel about goods, services, health, and personal finance; and to initiate and cooperate with individual and group efforts to maintain and enhance the quality of life for consumers. Consumers Union's income is solely derived from the sale of Consumer Reports, its other publications and from noncommercial contributions, grants and fees. In addition to reports on Consumers Union's own product testing, Consumer Reports with approximately 5 million paid circulation, regularly, carries articles on health, product safety, marketplace economics and legislative, judicial and regulatory actions which affect consumer welfare. Consumers Union's publications carry no advertising and receive no commercial support.

[2]"The Wagner Bill and mr. Gannett," Consumer Reports, April 1939, p. 20 and "By Popular Demand," Consumer Reports, February 1939, p. 32.

[3]"Bureaucracy in Medicine?," Consumer Reports, April 1946, pp. 110-111.

satisfaction with Health Maintenance Organizations, and solutions to the health care crisis.

In 1939 -- over fifty years ago -- our article concluded: "It has become obvious that the people of the country intend to see to it that the whole population shall benefit from the discoveries of modern medical science. The only question before the country now is 'how soon?'" It is time for us to finally end the nation's health care nightmare and answer this question "now!" Consumers can not and should not have to wait longer for a solution to the health care crisis.

Consumers Union is eager to help you to analyze elements of reform **from the consumer perspective.** As your Subcommittees help lead the Congress's consideration of the reform plan, we urge you to also keep in touch with average American consumers -- the people whose lives are either improved by a health care system that works well, or whose lives are destroyed by a health care system that fails them. In developing its health reform proposal, the Clinton Administration was successful in reaching out to the consumers who are on the receiving -- or non-receiving -- end of health care in America.

Only by keeping in touch with these consumers will the Congress be able to stand up to the many special interests that will seek to make their case, in order to develop a health care program that meets consumers' expectations and needs for health care reform.

CONSUMER PRINCIPLES FOR HEALTH CARE REFORM

To meet the needs of consumers, any health care reform plan must offer:

universal, quality health care (with comprehensive benefits) for all U.S. residents -- regardless of age, income, employment status or health status;

cost containment with a national health care budget and control over wasteful paperwork and procedures;

fair-share financing with savings from cost containment as a central funding source and additional funding obtained on a fair and equitable basis;

public accountability with consumers well represented on all boards overseeing health care; and

consumer choice giving consumers the freedom to choose where they will go for health care and who will provide it.

While we continue to believe that a single-payer health care system could best meet the health care needs of American consumers, we are pleased that the Clinton Administration has embraced many of these principles. We believe that the Clinton proposal would move the nation's consumers closer to health care security. Still, it leaves room for significant improvements.

THE CLINTON HEALTH CARE REFORM PLAN
A CONSUMER PERSPECTIVE

We have evaluated the Administration's draft health care reform plan (dated September 7, 1993) against the five consumer principles listed above. Attached to this testimony is our analysis (including a summary). The strongest part of the health plan is its commitment to **universal health care protection.** The nation can no longer rely on the "free market" and wishful thinking when it comes to health care security. The proposal -- if enacted -- would offer relief to the millions of Americans who are now denied protection due to their financial status or to pre-existing conditions. The plan offers security to everybody against unforeseen events such as development of serious illness or loss of jobs.

The Clinton health care proposal incorporates elements that we have long supported, including (1) a standard, comprehensive benefit package for all Americans; (2) control over health care premiums set by the National Health Board, rather than the free market; (3) a prohibition of balance billing, and (4) rejection of caps on damages for victims of medical malpractice. The attached analysis explores in more detail both the strengths and the weaknesses of the Clinton proposal.

In the remainder of my written testimony, I will summarize our comments by presenting five areas where we believe the plan needs to be strengthened, as well as five components that must be defended against attack and erosion from special interests.

FIVE WAYS TO STRENGTHEN THE CLINTON HEALTH CARE PROPOSAL

The Clinton health care proposal makes a good start at providing consumers with health care security. The following five changes would make it even better at meeting consumers' needs and expectations for health care reform.

1. Protect low- and middle- income consumers from paying a disproportionately high share of health care costs.

While all employers are assured of not having to pay more than 7.9 percent of their payroll cost for health insurance premiums, individuals and families are offered no such protection by the draft proposal. We believe that the employee's share of the premium (which is proposed to be 20 percent of the weighted average plus any amount of premium exceeding the average) should be capped at about 2 percent of income for plans that cost less than (or equal to) the average. Without such a cap, low wage workers who are not eligible for a subsidy could face a very steep burden, especially if they want the freedom to choose their own doctor. In addition to limiting premiums as a percent of income, we recommend that you consider reducing the cost-sharing requirements in the low cost-sharing plan to ensure that deductibles and coinsurance requirements do not serve as a barrier to health care for anybody in this country.

2. Encourage the state single payer option.

The Clinton Administration health care proposal allows states to establish a **single-payer** health care system, but includes a provision that seems to discourage states from doing so. It would require that states appropriate revenue from "sources other than those established by this Act" to pay for the program. It is not clear to us what this means, but its direction is wrong.

Does it preclude a state from imposing a payroll tax, one of the provisions of most single-payer legislation? In light of the ability of a single-payer system to achieve the principles of universality, cost containment, accountability to consumers, freedom to choose providers, and fair financing, the federal government should affirmatively provide the necessary funding to states to encourage them to adopt a single payer health care system.

3. **Make freedom-of-choice of provider a real option for people of all income levels by requiring all health alliances to offer a fee-for-service plan that costs little more than the average cost plan.**

Freedom to choose their health care provider is one of the most highly valued features that consumers seek in their health care system. Consumers want to be able to continue long-standing relationships with their family doctors, specialists, pediatricians, and other health care providers. Often, one family will have an array of doctors, making it impossible to follow them all to one HMO. Consumers want to be assured that if serious illness strikes, they will have access to the highest-quality specialist and specialized treatment centers.

All consumers -- even those that can afford the fee-for-service option -- face considerable uncertainty about whether their current doctors will be available to them. We are concerned about the possibility that freedom of choice of provider could be a luxury only the rich can afford. We recommend that in negotiating for a fee-for-service health plan, health alliances should be required to make this option available to all, by limiting the premium differentials (above the average cost plan) that can be charged by fee-for-service plans.

4. Include the blueprint for phasing-in nursing home benefits and expanded community care benefits.

The United States faces a growing long-term care crisis that will only get more severe as the population ages. Consumers Union has concluded that the private insurance market is incapable of solving the nation's long-term care problem -- it will never cover people who can not afford the high premiums, nor will it protect people whose pre-existing conditions make them uninsurable. The draft health plan includes an important community based care benefit. But the requirement that potential beneficiaries must be unable to perform three "activities of daily living" limits the benefit to a small portion of people in need of long-term care. For example, a person incapable of moving around (e.g., from bed to a chair) and unable to go to the bathroom by herself can not be left home alone all day long, but may not qualify for the new community-based benefit.

Consumers Union supports including in the health plan a blueprint for future expansion of public long-term care benefits, including both expanded community based care and nursing home care. We recognize -- as should the Congress -- that these benefits will require a substantial new funding base, and we recommend that you consider increasing estate taxes (possibly by taxing capital gains at death), charging premiums for persons with incomes above a certain level, and increasing income taxes, and/or payroll taxes.

5. Give the National Health Board the authority to regulate prescription drug prices that apply to all Americans, not just the Medicare- and Medicaid-eligible.

The Administration's draft plan has several provisions that will help to keep prescription drug prices in check. The National Health Board, for example, can make public declarations regarding the reasonableness of launch prices for new drugs and can study and report on the reasonableness of drug prices. In addition, rebates of at least 15 percent of the average manufacturer price are required for drugs issued through Medicare and Medicaid. We believe the plan needs to go further. The United States is the only industrialized country that makes no effort to regulate drug prices, forcing U.S. consumers to pay higher prices to help pay for research that benefits citizens of other countries, who pay much lower prices. The Office of Technology Assessment recently reported that during the 1980's, pharmaceutical companies on average earned about 15 to 30 percent more profit than was needed to attract adequate investment capital. We strongly recommend that the National Health Board's responsibilities include the authority to regulate prescription drug prices.

FIVE PROVISIONS TO FIGHT TO KEEP

Every element of the Clinton health care provision will be subject to attack from a variety of special interests. We have identified five areas where we believe the consumer interest lies in keeping the provisions that are in the draft plan. We urge you to carefully consider the interests of the average American consumer in preserving these important elements of health care reform.

1. Universal health care must be a reality by 1997.

Extending universality to all Americans must NOT be dependent on achieving cost savings and must not be phased-in with a vague timetable. Universality must be a reality by 1997. The plan must resist attempts to make the employer responsibility **voluntary** or participation in health alliances **voluntary**. The level playing field for all employers and the end to cream-skimming by health insurers are critically needed elements in the plan.

2. Cost containment through limits on public and private spending must be kept.

Global budgets and premium caps to curb cost growth in both the public and private sector health spending are essential. The plan appropriately includes curbs on health care spending, and this backstop protection should not be sacrificed to give the failed "free market" cost containment efforts yet another chance to drive up health care costs. Also, Congress must guard against health care provider pressure to abandon the ban on balance billing and physician self-referral. These are two culprits that have contributed to today's high costs. You also must resist all efforts to grant antitrust exemptions (beyond the guidelines in the draft plan) for doctors, hospitals, and pharmaceutical companies.

3. Keep most large employers in the system.

The draft plan would allow employers with more than 5000 workers to operate in a separate "corporate alliance" system, presumably with a tax of one percent or so to help pay for research that benefits everyone in the country. The "corporate alliance" system should NOT be expanded by reducing the minimum 5000 worker level, because to do so would undercut the goal of achieving a universal system that treats all Americans the same and would contribute to a multi-tier system. The tax on corporate alliances should be preserved and set at a fair level: not only does it help pay some of the costs and subsidies of the system, but it helps decrease the incentive for large employers to opt-out of the system, reducing the "tiering" of health care. It is crucial that corporate alliances be required to offer the standard benefits package and be subject to the same set of rules that apply to health plans in regional alliances.

4. Protect the victims of medical malpractice.

It is vital that consumers most severely injured by doctor negligence be fairly compensated; there should NOT be any caps on malpractice awards for pain and suffering.

Contrary to the mythology that has evolved around the medical malpractice problem, malpractice premiums account for a very small portion of health care costs -- only about one percent. The Congressional Budget Office recently concluded that changes in the medical malpractice liability system would have a small impact on national health expenditures, and they therefore declined to "score" any savings. Goals of medical malpractice reform should be to identify and discipline doctors guilty of repeated medical malpractice, and to increase the ability of the system to fairly compensate malpractice victims.

5. Keep the benefits package comprehensive.

One of the strengths of the Clinton Administration health care reform package is the comprehensiveness of the benefits package, including a range of benefits such as prescription drugs, some long-term care benefits, and mental health benefits. The benefits package must not be whittled away, or else the concept of universal protection and security will be compromised, and a burgeoning supplemental market will develop and help perpetuate a multi-tiered health care system.

Thank you very much for the opportunity to testify today. We look forward to working with your Subcommittees as this important debate continues

Mr. WAXMAN. Ms. Brown?

STATEMENT OF JUDITH BROWN

Ms. BROWN. My name is Judy Brown and I am chair of the board of AARP. We thank you for the opportunity to testify today.

As a member organization of over 33 million members, AARP has a long-standing and profound interest in comprehensive reform of our health care system. We commend President and Mrs. Clinton for the bold and constructive plan for accomplishing reform. We also commend the congressional leaders in both parties and this committee for commitment to addressing this issue now.

Enactment of health care reform will require not just bipartisan cooperation, but bipartisan leadership. AARP will not support or oppose the President's plan or any plan blindly. The day after the President's speech, we began the latest round of our forum field hearings across the country to ask our members what they think.

We have already held thousands of hearings and forums over the past 3 years. We will carefully analyze the President's plan in terms of its effect on our members, their families, and the Nation.

Our written testimony identifies many promising features of the plan as well as some significant concerns. I would like to focus my oral remarks on a few major areas.

First financing and cost containment. We commend the President for establishing at the outset of the debate explicit financing for comprehensive reform and look forward to an open discussion of the cost and financing estimates as congressional committees and the public demand proof that health care security can be financed as proposed. This scrutiny is critical because if the proposed savings and revenues do not materialize, then important benefits such as prescription drugs and long-term care, benefits that are at the core of the older population support for health care reform, will be reduced and/or the entire reform effort may be jeopardized.

Experience has shown that cost estimates only grow as the legislative process advances. We agree with the two critical aspects of the President's proposal to curb health care costs. First, there must be universal coverage. Second, cost containment must be systemwide.

In the absence of system-wide cost containment and universal coverage, AARP will strongly oppose further Medicare cuts. The association will continue its assessment of the proposed cuts, and I must admit they are very alarming on their face, as we examine the effectiveness and feasibility of proposed savings in the private sector.

AARP generally supports the President's proposal to limit the growth in health plan premiums in the private sector. The CBO recently found that between 1985 and 1991, per capita spending in Medicare, which has been subject to cost cutting, grew at a much slower rate than the per capita spending in the rest of the health care system.

The association supports the President's call for sin taxes on tobacco and the efforts to build upon existing financing mechanisms particularly the requirement that employers pay 80 percent of health care premiums. Nevertheless, AARP believes that broader, more progressive and more stable sources of revenue are needed to accomplish truly comprehensive health care reform.

Long-term care—AARP is particularly pleased that the President's proposal includes a modest start for home- and community-based care for persons of all ages and all incomes. The inclusion of long-term care is essential to our members and critical to AARP's support for any health care reform proposal.

However, we have several concerns about the proposed long-term care. They include the issues of whether funds are subject to appropriation and sequestration. What happens if States run out of money and will the States be at risk and therefore less willing to participate in the program?

While AARP generally supports State flexibility and experimentation, we are concerned that the tremendous variation and fragmentation that exists, especially under Medicaid, might persist. We are concerned about Medicare's integration into health care alliances.

In closing may I say, gentlemen and Madam Chairwoman, we commend the President and the many Members on both sides of the aisle who have brought the issue of health care to this stage. We recognize that reform may be needed to be phased in over a number of years and that adjustments will be needed along the way, but we must have health care reform, it must be comprehensive, and we must have it now.

Thank you.

Mr. WAXMAN. Thank you, Ms. Brown.

[Testimony resumes on p. 272.]

[The prepared statement of Ms. Brown follows:]

STATEMENT

of the

AMERICAN ASSOCIATION OF RETIRED PERSONS

Good morning. My name is Judith Brown. I am Chair of the Board of Directors of the American Association of Retired Persons (AARP). Thank you for the opportunity to testify today as the Committee probes the public commitment to health care reform and reviews the President's plan.

As a membership organization of 33 million older Americans, AARP has a longstanding and profound interest in this debate. Roughly half of our members are between the ages of 50 and 64; the other half are over 65. Approximately one-third of our members are still in the workforce.

Over the past few years, we have listened closely to what our diverse membership and their families want in a health care system. Despite their differing circumstances, the vast majority of Americans, old <u>and</u> young, have stressed a need for broader protections against the high costs of health and long-term care.

Three weeks ago the President stood before Congress and the American people and pledged his leadership in fixing our broken health care system. He called on members of both political parties to seize the "magic moment" of opportunity by enacting universal and comprehensive health care. AARP commends President Clinton for his bold and constructive plan for accomplishing reform. We also commend the First Lady, Congressional leaders in both parties, and this Committee for a commitment to addressing this issue <u>now</u>. We believe that true reform must cover everyone, maintain high quality, make health care costs affordable, and include vital prescription drugs and long-term care.

Lessons From The Past

A great national debate has begun, a debate that will affect <u>every</u> family and that cuts across socioeconomic, cultural, and racial lines. Older Americans welcome the opportunity for

Congress and the President to demonstrate not only that they are listening to the American people, but also that both parties can work together constructively toward much-needed change in our health care system. Before outlining the Association's views on the President's plan, and in light of the long memories of most AARP members, we find it useful to offer an historical perspective on today's health care debate.

Almost sixty years ago, President Roosevelt signed into law the landmark Social Security program. Social Security was a bold response to the growing crisis of insecurity among American families. Thirty years later the Medicare and Medicaid programs were enacted. Like Social Security, Medicare's protections are universal and its financing is broad based. Consequently, Medicare and Social Security are popular among all age groups. Medicaid, on the other hand, is means tested and state administered. Both of these factors have led to flaws that must be avoided in a reformed health care system.

Just five years ago, the Medicare Catastrophic Coverage Act was enacted and then repealed by Congress and the President. AARP learned some valuable lessons from that episode, lessons that we hope will serve us and policymakers well.

First, we learned that incremental gap-filling in the current health care system simply won't work with the American people. Older Americans viewed the new Catastrophic benefits as too meager to warrant widespread support, particularly because long-term care was not included.

Second, we learned that financing for health benefits cannot be narrowly imposed on a small segment of the population. Medicare beneficiaries were required to pay 100% of the cost of the Catastrophic program, increasing the flat and income-related premiums to extraordinary levels.

Third, we discovered that estimates for financing the new benefits proved inadequate at many points along the way, requiring cutbacks in benefits before the bill was enacted.

<u>Fourth</u>, we found it unrealistic to front-load the "pain" of additional beneficiary payments without a corresponding "gain" in benefits. While most older Americans have shown great patience in their lives, asking them for a full downpayment well in advance proved unacceptable.

<u>Finally</u>, we learned that the American people must clearly understand the benefits and costs of change in the health care system and that all of us need to listen and be prepared to respond knowledgeably to their concerns. After the Catastrophic bill was enacted, misinformation abounded and clear-cut answers to legitimate questions were in short supply. Since then, AARP has made a major effort to educate our members about the problems in the current health care system and to listen more attentively to our members' concerns and preferences. This time around, the challenge is much greater, and we simply must get it right.

AARP is deeply committed to comprehensive health care reform <u>now</u>. If reform must be phased in over a number of years because the financing is not adequate in the short term, then so be it. If mid-course adjustments are needed along the way -- and they will be -- then build in the means to determine them and carry them out. But it is imperative that Congress enact a comprehensive approach at the outset -- establish in legislation a "blueprint" for a reformed health care system -- not simply patch up spots pell-mell from year to year.

<u>Key Elements of Health Care Reform</u>

What does AARP mean by comprehensive reform? At a minimum comprehensive reform must provide:

- o A federal guarantee that all Americans have access to affordable, high-quality health and long-term care;

77-929 0 - 94 - 9

- o System-wide cost containment that eliminates cost-shifting and slows the explosive growth in health spending;

- o Comprehensive benefits that include prevention, physical and mental health care, prescription drugs, home and community-based care, and nursing home care;

- o Health delivery system reforms that increase access to care in underserved areas and reward efficient, high-quality care; and

- o Broad-based, fair and affordable financing, so that government, businesses, and individuals all pay their share and everyone is protected against the high costs of care.

AARP's proposal for comprehensive health care reform, "Health Care America," was developed with the extensive involvement of AARP members across the country. Its centerpiece is a strengthened and expanded Medicare program through which everyone would be eligible for a comprehensive, nationally mandated package of medical and long-term care benefits. Employers would be required to pay for at least 80 percent of their workers' benefits, either through the public program or through the same or better private coverage. In addition to ensuring access, the system would continue to foster choice, diversity, and innovation in the delivery of health services. The system would be accountable to consumers through a new Federal Health Care Commission that would set spending targets and establish other rules.

<u>AARP Views on the President's Plan</u>

Now that the President's plan is before Congress and the American people, we have shifted our attention to reviewing its many details while using "Health Care America" as a guide. AARP will not support or oppose the President's plan blindly. The day after the President's speech, we began a series of field hearings across the country to ask our members what they think. We will carefully analyze the plan in terms of its effect on our members, their families, and the nation. We will assess its status at each step of the legislative process, and work to improve it. As a start, we have already identified many promising features of the plan as well as some significant concerns.

System-Wide Cost Containment

Rapidly growing health care costs now rob our nation's economy, businesses, and families of the financial security which we all need to prosper in the future. And many families, including millions of families of older Americans, find it increasingly difficult to even see the future around the mounting health care bills on the kitchen table.

There is much in the President's proposals to curb health care costs with which we agree:

First, universal coverage must accompany cost controls if they are to be successful. A reform proposal that fails to assure that everyone has coverage will only lead to another vicious round of cost-shifting between payers and between providers. With universal coverage, providers will know that they will receive adequate payment for their services. And families will be reassured that they can seek necessary care at the appropriate time without being turned away. Only with the security of universal coverage can we all focus on a more efficient use of health care resources.

Second, cost containment must be system-wide. We just witnessed the latest round of Medicare cuts -- $56 billion in the 1993 budget reconciliation act. Those cuts will do little to either slow the overall rate of health care cost growth in the economy or provide a better long-term solution to the budget deficit. Just like the proverbial squeezing of one end of a balloon, cuts in Medicare-only payments to providers inevitably pop up in higher costs to employers and individuals. And even more troublesome for Medicare beneficiaries, Medicare-only cuts increase the chance that physicians and other providers will not treat them.

In order to contain health care costs in the economy, the President's plan establishes separate mechanisms for limiting public and private health care costs. Limits on public programs such as Medicare and Medicaid would come in the form of aggregate spending caps, enforceable through the congressional budget process. The new National Health Board and regional alliances would enforce premium limits in the private sector, which would be backed up with a penalty tax if a limit is breached. AARP believes that these mechanisms -- if made to work in concert as part of a system-wide approach -- hold significant promise for containing costs. It will be important for Congress to establish the level and phase-in schedule for health spending limits based on the health care needs of Americans, and not based on arbitrary savings-driven targets. It will also be important to achieve an equitable balance between public and private savings.

The Medicare cap is estimated to achieve $124 billion in savings between 1996 and the year 2000. Medicare cuts in the past ten years have already created large gaps between what Medicare and private insurance pay for the same service. Right now, Medicare pays an average of only 65 cents for every dollar that private insurance pays physicians. AARP strongly supports reducing and eventually eliminating this payment gap.

In the absence of system-wide cost containment and universal coverage, AARP would strongly oppose further Medicare cuts -- especially large-scale cuts such as $124 billion. Even with comprehensive reform, we are doubtful that the Medicare program could sustain such enormous reductions without creating quality and access problems for beneficiaries. The Association will continue its assessment of these cuts -- which are alarming on their face -- as we examine the effectiveness and feasibility of proposed savings in the private sector.

Premium limits in the private sector would finally begin to address cost growth where heretofore there has been no constraint on spending. The Congressional Budget Office recently found that while Medicare spending grew at an annual per-capita rate of 3.1 percent between 1985 and 1991, total U.S. health spending grew at an annual per-capita rate of 4.8 percent. The reason for this difference is that Medicare is controlled through the federal budget process but private health care spending is not. The fact that Medicare pays for care of a generally higher cost population makes this even more striking.

AARP generally supports the President's proposal to limit the growth in health plan premiums. If done right, premium limits could protect individuals and families from high costs in a way that is easily understood and broadly effective. And, it is premiums that are most visible today to the average family. We do not believe that premium limits necessarily will lead to lower-quality care or rationing of care as some provider and insurance interests suggest. The Association recognizes that Congress may need to revisit spending limits in both the private and public sectors after reform is in place, but it is critical to legislate system-wide and enforceable controls at the outset to guide insurer, provider, and consumer behavior.

The Association is concerned, however, that the lack of short-term cost controls in the President's proposal could lead to immediate "profiteering" by health providers and insurers at the expense of patients and consumers. Moreover, since the proposed Medicare cap would require substantial cuts in 1996 before the premium limits take effect, cost-shifting between Medicare and private payments could reach unprecedented levels.

AARP further believes that effective cost containment throughout the health care system will prove to be the linchpin for making reform work. If reform fails to control private-sector costs, then federal subsidies to individuals and businesses will be higher, gaps between Medicare and private payments will grow, and Congress will be faced with the choice of scaling back guaranteed benefits or generating additional revenues to pay for reform.

Financing

Just one year ago, many of the health care reform proposals floating around Capitol Hill and within the Administration lacked at least one fundamental element -- financing. While no one pretended that paying for health care reform would be easy, only a few proposals contained explicit funding sources. AARP commends the President for establishing at the outset of the debate explicit financing for comprehensive reform. We look forward to an open discussion of the cost and financing estimates as congressional committees and the public demand proof that health care security can be financed as proposed by the Administration. This scrutiny is critical because if the proposed savings and revenues do not materialize, then important benefits will be reduced and/or the entire reform effort may be jeopardized. Experience has shown that cost estimates only grow as the legislative process advances.

The Association supports the President's call for "sin" taxes on tobacco as both a much-needed source of revenues and a barrier to smoking. Of concern, however, is the estimate of revenue generated as a higher tax reduces utilization. Congress should consider expanding this policy to include alcohol, which also contributes to health care costs.

We also support the President's effort to build upon existing financing mechanisms, particularly the requirement that employers pay 80 percent of health plan premiums. Nevertheless, AARP believes that broader, more progressive, and more stable sources of revenue are needed to accomplish comprehensive health care reform. In our own plan, "Health Care America," we proposed an option of a 3 percent income tax or 5 percent VAT dedicated entirely to health care. Both tax options proved acceptable to our members when linked to a full benefit package, including comprehensive long-term care.

More serious concerns are raised by the Administration's heavy reliance on planned reductions in Medicare and Medicaid spending to free up the federal funds necessary to provide universal coverage, to protect low-wage businesses and low-income individuals, and to provide additional benefits such as a Medicare drug benefit and long-term care. The Administration's plan projects $238 billion in savings over six years from the cap on Medicare and Medicaid. Less attention has been given to an additional $259 billion that would be transferred from Medicare and Medicaid to alliances to pay for current beneficiaries who are shifted into the alliances.

There is good reason to be skeptical about whether savings of this magnitude can or should be obtained from Medicare and Medicaid. During the 1980s, Medicare spending was cut by over $80 billion cumulatively. Another $43 billion was cut in OBRA 1990 over five years, and OBRA 1993 reduced spending an additional $56 billion over five years. One of the serious risks of cuts of this magnitude is that they will institutionalize the disparity in reimbursement between private insurance and the Medicare program, making it more difficult for Medicare beneficiaries to gain access to physicians. These savings, even if they can be achieved quickly, are not a permanent financing source. Once the system is made more efficient, we will need to identify more lasting sources for the public cost of health care delivery.

While we understand that the Administration's Medicare savings proposals are only an "illustrative" list and are comprised mostly of deeper cuts in provider payments, one proposal stands out as a significant departure from the current program -- income-relating the Part B premium.

AARP has strongly opposed this proposal outside the context of health care reform, arguing that it would constitute nothing more than a cost-shift to beneficiaries without adequate control over system-wide spending. We have also maintained that if Part B premiums were income-related, then premiums throughout the health care system should be income-related as well. It does not seem fair that taxpayers would continue to subsidize the health care premiums of a Wall Street executive with a salary of more than $1,000,000 dollars a year while subsidies to Medicare beneficiaries with much lower incomes are substantially reduced. If Congress and the President believe that "income relating" premiums is a good idea for the elderly and disabled, then it is at least as good an idea for the rest of the country.

Universal Coverage and Comprehensive Benefits

AARP is very pleased that the President's plan recognizes the importance of universal, comprehensive coverage. Just last week, the U.S. Census Bureau announced that 2 million more Americans were without health insurance at the end of 1992 than at the end of 1991.

This erosion of coverage cannot continue. As the President stated in his address to Congress: All Americans must have "health security; health care that can never be taken away; health care that is always there."

AARP strongly supports the requirement in the President's plan that premiums be community-rated so that individuals under age 65 are neither rewarded nor penalized on the basis of characteristics such as age, gender, or health status. Community rating is the most equitable way to share responsibility and risk across the American population. It is the way insurance should operate, and largely once did in this country. Community rating has important labor market benefits as well, since it substantially reduces disincentives for employers to hire and retain older workers.

Health coverage must not only be available; it must be affordable as well. Individuals alone cannot afford to pay the high cost of premiums, rather it must be a shared responsibility among businesses, individuals, and the government. The President's plan asks all employers -- as well as employees -- to contribute to the cost of care. AARP strongly supports this approach. This mandate would help to level the currently uneven playing field where some businesses -- including many small businesses -- pay more than their fair share, while others pay nothing. More importantly, employer contributions are critical to achieving universal coverage without substantial increases in federal income taxes. By requiring individuals to pay something toward their care, the President's plan can reinforce the principle of personal responsibility -- a principle already put into practice in the Medicare program through its premiums, copays, and deductibles.

Legitimate concerns have been raised about the loss of jobs in the small business sector as a result of the employer mandate. In an economy as complex as ours, the net effect on jobs is difficult at best to estimate. However, estimates of the net effect on employment of AARP's "Health Care America" proposal, which includes universal coverage and an employer mandate, indicate that employment is reduced at most by only .3 percent in the first two years after implementation. By the third year, job growth resumes, and by the fifth year, employment is higher than it would otherwise have been without reform. In other words, health care reform, even with an employer mandate, can be an investment in the nation's long-term economic growth.

Many working and non-working families will also need assistance in paying their share of premiums, deductibles, and coinsurance. While the plan notes that subsidies would be available to the under-65 population with incomes up to 150% of poverty, far more information is needed on the amount of the subsidies at each income level. We are also concerned that low-income Medicare beneficiaries might not receive the same protections. Currently, over 3.5 million Medicare beneficiaries are dually eligible for Medicaid benefits. Many of these are eligible to receive full or partial subsidies for out-of-pocket health costs through the QMB program. It is unclear whether such protections continue under the plan. It will be important to assure that these subsidies are maintained and strengthened in a reformed health care system, so that there can be a consistent policy across the age span regarding low-income persons.

What is and is not included in the benefits package is one of the most fundamental questions for consumers. The package proposed by the President takes a major step in covering a number of benefits that are typically omitted from or severely restricted in most private plans, such as immunizations, regular check-ups, mammograms, and other preventive services. We are also pleased that mental health and substance abuse services will be covered. We are concerned, however, that the limits on, and required cost-sharing for, both inpatient and outpatient care will prevent some individuals with mental illnesses from receiving needed services. The Administration's promise to place mental health care on a par with physical health care by the year 2001 simply must be fulfilled.

AARP strongly supports a guaranteed comprehensive benefit package for all Americans. In that light, we are deeply disappointed that the President's plan would not provide the same preventive benefits or out-of-pocket protections (i.e., a limit on out-of-pocket spending and full elimination of balance billing) for Medicare beneficiaries as it would for younger populations. We are hopeful that these gaps can be filled as the proposal works its way through Congress. The need for health care does not decline when one celebrates his or her 65th birthday.

Long-Term Care

AARP is particularly pleased that the President's proposal includes some coverage for home and community-based care for persons of all ages and incomes. The new program represents a serious though modest start towards addressing the unmet needs of millions of American families. The inclusion of long-term care is vital to our members and critical to AARP's support for any health care reform proposal.

Clearly, Americans of all ages strongly support such inclusion. A survey conducted for AARP this past April found that 90 percent of the respondents felt that including long-term care in a health reform proposal was important. Support for health care reform increased from 46 percent to 82 percent when long-term care was included. More recently, in a poll conducted for AARP less than two weeks ago, 86 percent of adults of all ages stated that they would be less in favor of the President's health care proposal if long-term care coverage were not included. And, in a study conducted last year for AARP by DYG, Inc., the amount that individuals were willing to pay for coverage increased substantially when both home care and nursing home care were included.

Long-term care is an issue that touches all of our lives at some point in time through family and friends. In our view, it would make no sense to provide protection against an acute illness but leave people vulnerable if they suffer from a chronic problem, especially since the need for these services is so interrelated. The disabled of all ages are much higher than average users of medical services and require both kinds of care to meet their complex service needs.

Unfortunately, while approximately 37 million people lack basic medical insurance, virtually all Americans lack protection against long-term care expenses. Moreover, to a family sitting around the kitchen table, there is no difference between spending $20,000 on hospital care and spending $20,000 on home care. It is still $20,000 they probably do not have. To achieve true security, savings and quality in our health care system, care must not be limited only to the provision of services by a hospital or doctor; long-term care must also be included.

Since AARP is committed to advocacy for a health care program that will serve persons of all ages with disabilities, we are pleased that approximately one-third of the 3 million Americans who would receive help under this new program are under age 65. In addition, the proposal could finally provide much needed support and respite to caregivers--primarily mothers, wives and daughters--who are shouldering enormous burdens taking care of their loved ones. Many caregivers are jeopardizing their own health and, in some cases, are forced to leave the labor market, thereby suffering not only short-term loss of income, but also long-term reduction in Social Security and private pension benefits. Concern about the cost of long-term care -- financial as well as emotional -- is in fact greatest among those in the 50-64 year old group.

The Association is supportive of giving families choices and options they currently do not have, as the proposal would do. Our current system suffers from an institutional bias, which tears families apart and forces too many people to slowly deteriorate or go into nursing homes prematurely because they cannot receive care where they want it most--in their own homes.

Although AARP is pleased with the proposed expansion of home and community-based services, several questions and concerns remain. For example, the reliability of the funding for the program is a concern. Would funding be subject to annual appropriation or sequestration? Because a capped federal contribution is contemplated, we wonder what would happen if a state runs out of money before the end of its fiscal year. Could services simply be cut off? Will states be at risk and, therefore, less willing to participate in the program? The experience to date with the Section 4711 Frail Elderly program, which is an optional capped entitlement to the states, does not inspire confidence.

Questions also remain regarding the basic structure of the new program. Although AARP generally supports state flexibility and experimentation, we are concerned that the tremendous variation and fragmentation that exists, especially under Medicaid, might persist. State flexibility needs to be balanced by clear federal standards to require the provision of basic services, to promote efficiency, and to assure that consumers are fully protected. In addition, it appears that states have the option not to participate in the program at all. Such an approach could pose serious problems if poorer states, for example, elected not to establish this program for its most vulnerable citizens.

In addition, although AARP supports the modest Medicaid improvements and private insurance standards proposed for nursing home care, millions would remain vulnerable to impoverishment due to lack of protection against these enormous costs. The single greatest fear which families confront in long-term care is the devastating costs of a nursing home stay which now average $30,000 a year and reach $60,000 a year in some parts of the country.

AARP looks forward to working with members of this Committee and with other members of the Congress to help ensure that long-term care remains an integral part of the health care reform package and that all Americans who suffer from serious chronic and disabling conditions receive the help they need.

Prescription Drugs

We are pleased that the President's health care reform proposal includes a comprehensive outpatient prescription drug benefit for all Americans, including Medicare beneficiaries. AARP is extremely concerned about the lack of access to prescription drugs (an estimated 72 million people do not have coverage), particularly among older Americans. The combined effects of high prices, heavy utilization, and the absence of affordable insurance coverage for prescription drugs have significantly reduced access to needed drug therapies for older Americans. A recent national survey sponsored by AARP showed that:

- o older Americans use significantly more prescription drugs than other age groups to maintain their health;

- o prescription drug insurance coverage declines rapidly as age increases; and

- o out-of-pocket costs for prescription drugs are significantly higher for older Americans than for their younger counterparts.

As a result, many older Americans cannot afford high prescription drug prices and are too frequently denied access to essential, often life-saving, medications -- compromising their health status and making them more likely to receive unnecessary <u>and</u> more expensive acute care. About 10 percent of those surveyed said they have had to cut back on necessary items, such as food and heating fuel, to afford their medications.

The incorporation of a prescription drug benefit in health care reform will ensure access to important, often life-sustaining, drug therapies to all Americans, especially those who are most vulnerable to losing access today. Lack of a prescription drug benefit today contributes substantially to unnecessary hospital admissions and other conditions that can be prevented or controlled through pharmaceuticals. With more breakthroughs in drug development, medical care in the future will increasingly rely upon drugs and biotechnological products.

We are also pleased that the President's proposal includes effective cost containment mechanisms as an essential part of the Medicare drug benefit. We are concerned, however, that pharmaceutical manufacturers are already engaged in a major lobbying effort to eliminate any meaningful cost containment provisions from the proposed plan. In fact, we understand that the industry's leading association is attempting to scare Medicare beneficiaries into falsely believing that the President's cost containment efforts will result in the absence of Medicare coverage for important breakthrough drug therapies. We do not believe this is true.

<u>In this regard, we strongly encourage the President and the Congress to remain firm in their commitment to contain prescription drug costs under the Medicare drug benefit</u>. If effective cost containment is eliminated from the proposal, the Medicare drug benefit will quickly become unaffordable to both taxpayers and beneficiaries. This was clearly the case during the development of the Medicare Catastrophic Coverage Act (MCCA). Due to the lack of effective cost containment, the projected cost of the MCCA drug benefit (and the resulting estimates of premiums to be paid by beneficiaries) skyrocketed even before the bill made its way through Congress. Recent comments by Administration spokespersons about re-estimated costs and beneficiary premiums are disquieting on this front.

The pharmaceutical industry argues that every dollar sought by policymakers to contain drug prices will come directly out of research and development of important breakthrough medications. We believe this is simply false. Much more than legitimate research and development activities go into the manufacturer's price of a drug. Thus, drug manufacturers have many choices as to where they can be more efficient and cut costs.

In fact, according to a recent study by the Senate Special Committee on Aging, only 16 percent of the manufacturer's price of a drug goes toward research and development compared to the 36 percent that goes toward profits, marketing, and advertising. In addition, drug manufacturers' revenue will increase substantially under the President's plan as millions of Americans who currently lack coverage for prescription drugs will gain that coverage. Much of this revenue could be used for legitimate research and development endeavors.

<u>Vulnerable 50-64 Year Olds</u>

About half of AARP's 33 million members are under the age of 65. In listening to these members, we have discovered some disturbing trends. A 1992 study of public attitudes toward health care reform conducted by DYG, Inc. for AARP revealed that the 50-64 year-old population is much more critical of the health system than are other age groups. Not yet eligible for Medicare, this age group is the most concerned about the cost of health care and the security of their coverage. Only about half of 55-64 year olds are in the workforce, and a disproportionate share of those who are employed earn low wages, work in smaller firms and industries least likely to offer coverage, or are self-employed. Gaps in coverage for this age group may also result from retirement or Medicare enrollment of an older spouse, divorce from or death of a working spouse, early retirement for medical reasons, or insurance industry underwriting practices that are increasingly squeezing less healthy individuals out of the group market.

AARP is pleased that the President's plan would provide health security for a segment of this vulnerable population -- so-called "early retirees." Such a system for retiree coverage would also help to restore the competitiveness of industries that have previously borne a disproportionate share of retiree health costs. According to the draft proposal, retired workers age 55 to 64 who meet the 40-quarter work requirement would receive a government subsidy for 80 percent of the premium for the nationally guaranteed benefit package. Former employers who now pay retiree health benefits would continue to contribute toward retiree coverage by paying the retiree's 20-percent share of the premium.

While this feature represents a significant improvement, the plan does not offer comparable protections for non-working, vulnerable 50-64 year olds who do not meet the Social Security requirement of 40 quarters of work. It is our understanding that retirees age 55 to 64 who do not meet this requirement would potentially be liable for the entire cost of their health premium in the alliance. This is of particular concern for women in this age group, who may not have the necessary work history but are now widowed or divorced.

A related concern is the plan's restriction of Medicaid coverage for supplemental services to recipients of cash assistance only (i.e., SSI and AFDC recipients). One out of every three current Medicaid recipients age 50 to 64 is eligible on a basis other than cash assistance. Over 20 percent of these near-elderly Medicaid recipients do not work and have incomes over 150 percent of poverty, leaving them without either employer contributions or federal subsidies to help ensure their access to health coverage under the alliances.

Some have suggested that a more straightforward, efficient, and fair way to assuring coverage for the 55-64 year old group is to lower the age of Medicare eligibility to 55. AARP believes that Congress and the President should consider this approach as a possible alternative to the more limited "early retiree" proposal.

Governance, Quality, and the Consumer

The President's plan proposes a new system for governing and organizing health care financing and delivery. For most consumers it will mean getting coverage, receiving information about health plans, evaluating quality, and lodging grievances through a new entity called a regional alliance, rather than going through an employer or an insurance company. The plan also proposes to establish a National Health Board at the federal level that would be responsible for setting national standards, enforcing the national health budget, and overseeing state administration of the new health system. Finally, the proposal gives states important new roles and flexibility in managing a reformed health care system.

We strongly agree with the President that our system for providing coverage and delivering care must be more responsive to consumers. Consumers need to have a say not only in their selection of health plans, but also in governance and assuring quality throughout the health care system.

According to a draft of the President's plan, states will play critical roles in health care reform. They will be responsible for establishing health alliances and qualifying and regulating accountable health plans. States will be given a great deal of flexibility to manage health care financing and delivery within their borders. While we recognize the innovations in health care financing and delivery developed in some states, we have serious questions about whether overly broad state flexibility will benefit consumers.

Under the President's proposal, for example, states could establish regional alliances as either nonprofit corporations or a state agency. If the alliance is a nonprofit corporation there must be a board of directors comprised of equal representation by consumers and employers. If the regional health alliance is a state agency, however, there is no requirement for a board of directors. This poses serious questions about adequate consumer participation. We would suggest that the governance structure of any type of regional health alliance be controlled by consumers since they are both the recipients of care and the ultimate source of financing. While a few states have been pioneers in their effort to reform health care, most of our experience with states -- who are faced with far more limited fiscal bases -- has been less than encouraging. Whether from the vantage point of nursing home quality standards or the manipulation of funds under disproportionate share hospital payments, the record of states does not recommend greater responsibility. Much more needs to be done in this area as legislation advances to assure good stewardship.

<u>The Association welcomes many of the President's initiatives to improve the quality of care</u>. Because accurate and useful consumer information will be critical to public accountability and choice, we are particularly pleased to see that an extensive consumer information program has been proposed. Among the elements of the new quality program that we applaud are: (l) the use of consumer surveys to measure access to and satisfaction with care, as well as its outcomes; (2) the development of uniform encounter and claims forms, key to a nationally standardized database, and (3) the development of a core set of quality and performance measures.

We must recognize, however, that it will take a long time to develop and implement the data systems which are envisioned, and that many critical performance and quality measures -- particularly those which measure the quality of care for persons with chronic physical and mental illnesses -- are not yet available. We believe that there must be sufficient resources to develop the necessary information and data infrastructures, and that these funding sources should be specified in the proposal.

While consumer information is a critical component in the overall quality assurance strategy, by itself it will not adequately address consumer concerns about the potential for poor quality care. As proposed, the plan does not clearly identify what entities are to be responsible for protecting consumers from incompetent providers. Especially in light of the time it will take to develop an effective consumer information system, the apparent lack of external quality review, independent from payer (alliance) and provider (plan) responsibilities, seems to be an important "missing piece" in the proposed quality system.

In addressing these matters, the roles of state medical licensure boards and insurance regulators need to be carefully articulated. The proposal to eliminate the Medicare Peer Review Organization (PRO) program without a clear successor entity also raises a number of concerns. On the basis of what criteria would the decision that Medicare beneficiaries are adequately protected in the new system be made, and what entity or entities would pick up current PRO functions?

Another important consumer protection is access to independent and timely appeal mechanisms in the event of quality problems or denials of care. While the proposal does note that plans must provide "due process" for patients to appeal denials or reductions in coverage, these protections are not specified, and it appears that it would be left up to the plans to decide how much process is due. AARP believes that there should be nationally uniform due process protections for all consumers.

Medicare Integration Into Health Alliances

AARP concurs with the decision to retain Medicare as a separate program. Indeed, in the President's plan, Medicare can be thought of as its own national health alliance. While we believe that ultimately the entire health care system should be seamless, we also believe that for the time being, it is preferable to permit Medicare beneficiaries to remain in a system that is tested and popular. Medicare beneficiaries simply do not have adequate experience with the alternative delivery systems that the President's proposal envisions would predominate in the reformed system. The current Medicare coordinated care strategies have not attracted sufficient numbers of beneficiaries or participating health plans to adequately test the viability of alternative delivery systems for older populations. HCFA reports that as of September 1, there were 1.7 million Medicare beneficiaries enrolled in risk HMOs--or only about 5 percent of the 34 million Medicare beneficiaries. Furthermore, there are sections of the country where beneficiaries do not even have the opportunity to select a Medicare HMO. Mathematica Policy Research reported that in January 1992, participating plans served 40 different metropolitan areas across 28 states, which left half of the Medicare population without the opportunity to enroll in an HMO.

The limited experience that beneficiaries have had with alternative systems and their hesitation to deviate from the traditional Medicare program suggest that decisions concerning the integration of Medicare into the new environment should be made with great care. Currently, there is a system in place that is generally responsive to the special vulnerability of the Medicare population. Inevitably, as we begin to reform the nation's health care system there will be a period of volatility and instability in the system as new infrastructure is built and systems changed. For those who are most physically dependent on the system, we believe that it is prudent to preserve a program with a good track record, at least until the new system has proven successful.

If and when a decision is made to integrate the Medicare program with the remaining system, it is the Association's expectation that there would be a genuine integration, that is, Medicare beneficiaries would have access to the same benefits, the same cost sharing, the same premium contribution ratios, and the same low-income protections as all other population groups.

We are concerned that, in the interim, Medicare beneficiaries could face a serious dilemma. If they decide to remain in the Medicare program because they are wary of changing to an unfamiliar, competitive environment, they could be seriously disadvantaged because it appears that significant disparities between the alliance programs and traditional Medicare will be permitted. For example, under traditional Medicare, there will be higher cost sharing, no cap on out-of-pocket costs, and less generous low income protections. Once a beneficiary has foregone the opportunity to enroll in an alliance, (s)he could face these differences permanently. Other serious questions arise:

- o How much in premiums will those over 65 be charged if they purchase coverage through a regional alliance? The president's proposal clearly indicates that health plans will negotiate separate rates for those over and under age 65. It further indicates that Medicare will make a fixed contribution to the alliances "equal to the costs that Medicare would be projected to bear," but it is unclear how this calculation would be made.

- o Will beneficiaries who decide to "experiment" with coverage through the alliance have an opportunity to return to the traditional Medicare program each year through an open enrollment process?

- o Will beneficiaries who return to traditional Medicare be able to purchase needed medigap coverage that is not medically underwritten?

In the absence of greater detail, it is difficult to assess what the impact of obtaining coverage through an alliance would be on Medicare beneficiaries.

In addition, we have concerns about how current Medicare beneficiaries who are working will be treated in the new system. For what benefits package will they be eligible? How much will employers, the Medicare trust fund, and beneficiaries each contribute?
While many individuals over 65 are likely to elect to receive health care through regional alliances, there will be a group of beneficiaries who continue to receive coverage under traditional Medicare. To adequately cover the costs of this group it will be necessary to build-in an adjustment to the cap on federal spending for Medicare to take into account the higher expenditures that may be generated as this population ages.

A further issue concerning integration of Medicare beneficiaries into broader systems relates to the authority that would enable the states to integrate Medicare beneficiaries into health alliances. The Association urges that such authority be conditioned on clear requirements and procedures that include ongoing federal oversight. Interested states must demonstrate and the federal government must assure appropriate access, high quality of care, appeals rights, etc. <u>We are not convinced that states would be able to develop and maintain consistent, high standards with respect to oversight and enforcement that would be necessary to support a takeover of the Medicare program</u>. Moreover, unless the Medicare funds were earmarked for use by beneficiaries, we would have concerns that states might divert such funds for other purposes. Before entering into this type of arrangement with the states, the federal government must be able to justify with confidence and certainty how state integration will *improve* the current system.

<u>Conclusion</u>

In conclusion, Mr. Chairman, AARP commends the President, as well as the many members on both sides of the aisle who have brought the issue of health care reform to this stage. The President's plan incorporates many of the features that AARP has supported in its own proposal. At the same time, both the scope of the President's plan and the need for greater clarity on certain key provisions, not least of them financing and the ability to deliver the coverage promised, require careful consideration. We hope and trust that the next several weeks of hearings in the Congress as well as the Administration's continuing refinement of its proposal will contribute to a greater public understanding of all the plans before Congress and ultimately move the debate toward bipartisan legislation in the second session of the 103rd Congress.

If there's one thing we should all agree on, it's that the status quo is not an acceptable option.

Mr. WAXMAN. Mr. Pollack.

STATEMENT OF RONALD F. POLLACK

Mr. POLLACK. Thank you.

Distinguished members of the panel, I am delighted to be here this morning. In my written testimony, I have expressed our support and admiration for the administration bill, but rather than repeating the testimony that you have in our written presentation, let me focus on three or four matters, depending on how quickly the 5 minutes runs.

The first thing I would like to focus on is the question of how we achieve comprehensive coverage for everybody. I hope that irrespective of the various differences that will exist among the various interest groups and among this panel on both sides of the aisle, I hope that the bedrock principle that we all can agree on is that we need to achieve serious and meaningful security for all Americans.

Now, to achieve security for all Americans, it means that we have to make sure that everybody is covered and the coverage that they receive is comprehensive coverage. Now we hear a great deal about 378 million people who don't have insurance, but there are a good number of people who have insurance who are in deep fear that they are going to lose insurance.

Each and every month, of the people who have insurance today, 2.25 million Americans lose health insurance coverage. They may not lose it for a terribly long period of time. Many of them lose it for 3, 5 or 7 months or maybe 1 year, but whoever loses health insurance coverage is part I think of the growing number of Americans who are saying the bedrock principle of health care reform has got to be the achievement of real security for everybody.

How are we going to achieve that security for everybody? I suggest that we have four alternatives in terms of what you will be considering. One approach would be to say let's try to make some changes with respect to the insurance system and hope that those changes are going to reach everybody. I suggest to you that approach is not going to be satisfactory to the American public that feels terribly insecure about the health care system today.

A second choice is we can say the government is going to do it. The government should provide health insurance coverage for everybody. That can work, but I suspect that some of you may have some problems with respect to that because of the tax implications of that particular approach.

The third approach would be to say we are going to say to the workers of America that it is your responsibility to get coverage on your own. I suggest to you that while that certainly is something that is feasible, you certainly can go at it through this approach. In order to make this work, there are going to have to be significant subsidies and well and above the kind of subsidies that are necessary under an employer mandate in order to make that work and the real test as to whether an employee mandate or an individual mandate is going to work will depend upon the kinds of subsidies that need to be provided to individuals in order to make sure that they can fulfill that responsibility.

I suggest to you that the tax implications of an employee mandate are going to be considerably greater than they are for an employer mandate.

The fourth choice is the choice that the President has opted for, and that is to essentially extend what we have today, essentially an employer-based system, and make sure that everybody who is employed receives their coverage through their employment and that we deal with the problems that small businesses have with respect to fulfilling that responsibility.

Now I think all of us in this room share a deep concern about the well-being of small businesses. Small businesses truly are the backbone of America's economy and I think we all should be sensitive to it. But my hope is that the debate with respect to small businesses focuses on the nuts and bolts of what they need to make this kind of responsibility work, and that includes such things as is the subsidy that is provided to employers, is that adequate, how can that be modified, a pooling arrangement that will make health care cheaper for them, and eliminating the cost shifts that too many small businesses bear today.

Thank you.

Mr. WAXMAN. Thank you very much.

[Testimony resumes on p. 287.]

[The prepared statement of Mr. Pollack follows:]

Testimony by

Ronald F. Pollack
Executive Director

Families USA Foundation

Chairman Waxman, Chairwoman Collins and Members of both subcommittees:

Thank you for inviting me to testify today about the impact of the Clinton health plan on American families. Families USA is enthusiastically supporting the Health Security Act of 1993.

Our current health system has deprived American families of the peace of mind of knowing that they will always be able to take care of their families' health care needs. Families USA has looked at a wide variety of problems American families are experiencing with our current health care system and analyzed how President Clinton's Health Security Act will address these problems. As the following analysis shows, the Clinton health reforms, if enacted, will provide the security and peace of mind that American families so profoundly lack today.

PEOPLE WHO WILL LOSE THEIR INSURANCE

Jerry and Donna Weldon live in Fenton, Missouri with their two young children. Jerry is a plumber and the family is covered through Jerry's union. Every three months, Jerry must work a certain number of hours to qualify for health insurance coverage. Lately, work has been slow, so Jerry is working fewer hours and the number of work hours required by the union for health insurance will be increasing. The Weldons' eight-year old son has leukemia and he is scheduled for a bone marrow transplant this fall. After this procedure, he will need ongoing medical care and prescription drugs. The Weldons are worried that they will lose their insurance in the future because of Jerry's lack of work and the increasing number of required work hours for coverage.

Over two million Americans lose their health insurance each month. Over 57 million Americans will be without insurance for some time in 1993.[1] Most of these people will lack insurance for less than five months, yet a significant portion will lack insurance for six months or more.[2] During this time, families are at grave financial risk if they become sick or injured.

As of 1997, under the Health Security Act, Americans can no loner lose their health insurance. A health security card will guarantee all Americans nationally—defined, comprehensive health benefits that continue without interruption regardless of any changes in health, employment or economic status. Workers and their families will receive insurance coverage through their employment. Self-employed or unemployed people and their families will purchase coverage directly. Self-employed families' insurance premiums will be fully tax deductible, instead of only 25 percent deductible as they are now. Businesses and families having the greatest difficulty paying for premiums will receive discounts to make their premiums affordable.

Families will choose from a variety of health plans offered by regional health alliances where they live. Employees of firms with more than 5,000 employees may choose from at least three plans offered by their firm. Americans over age 65 will continue to enroll in the Medicare program, as they do now, and will also have the option of choosing a plan through their health alliance.

Under the Health Security Act, the Weldons would always have the same comprehensive insurance, regardless of how much work Jerry can get.

INADEQUATE INSURANCE

Susan and David Mast live in Wheaton, Maryland, with their two young children on an income of $20,000. David Mast is a self-employed contractor and purchased health insurance coverage on his own. He paid $4,000 for his family's health insurance in 1992, but couldn't afford the extra $4,000 a year maternity coverage would have cost. Even then, the coverage wouldn't have been effective for one year. Their youngest child was born in February 1992. Susan Mast worked two jobs as a proofreader and typesetter, and took in babysitting and accounting work, to pay off the $3,300 bill from that birth.

Millions of Americans currently have inadequate insurance that can leave them with thousands of dollars in medical bills. Such inadequate coverage is most common for families who buy non-group coverage and can only afford or qualify for very limited coverage with high deductibles, high copayments or limitations in benefits. Some families can only purchase policies with low lifetime payment levels, thereby leaving them vulnerable to high debts if a serious illness strikes.

Families USA estimates that 18 million Americans who have insurance are currently spending ten percent or more of their pretax income on out-of-pocket health expenses, *excluding* expenses for nursing home care, health insurance premiums, Medicare payroll taxes, federal, state and local taxes, and wages lost because of their employers' costs for health insurance.[3] Economists generally consider individuals to be underinsured if they are *at risk of* spending ten percent or more of their income on out-of-pocket health costs.[4]

The Health Security Act will guarantee all Americans comprehensive health coverage. The comprehensive benefit package guarantees access to a full range of services. The benefits include a variety of preventive services available at no cost. In addition, prescription drug, dental and mental health services are more generous than many plans today. No individual will have to spend more than $1,500 annually for covered services and no family will have to spend more than $3,000 annually.

The guaranteed national benefits have no lifetime limitations on coverage and include: hospital services; emergency services; services of physicians and other health professionals; a variety of preventive services; mental health and substance abuse services; family planning services; pregnancy-related services; hospice; home health care; extended-care services; ambulance services; outpatient laboratory and diagnostic services; outpatient prescription drugs and biologicals; outpatient rehabilitation services; durable medical equipment, prosthetic and orthotic devices; vision and hearing care; preventive dental services for children; and health education classes.

Under the Health Security Act, the Mast family would always have comprehensive health benefits, including full maternity coverage.

HIGH PRESCRIPTION DRUG COSTS

Iona O'Neill is an 83 year old resident of Spring Hill, Florida. Iona's income from Social Security is less than $700 per month. She has no insurance covering prescription drug costs. Iona suffered bladder cancer and now spends $300 per month on medicine. Her income is too high, however, to qualify for any public assistance with prescription drug costs.

Paying for prescription drugs is an onerous burden for many Americans. An estimated 72 million Americans currently lack health insurance for prescription drugs.[5] Medicare does not cover outpatient prescription drug costs. Elderly persons take more prescriptions, on average, than younger people and have higher drug costs, but less than half (49%) of all elderly Americans have prescription drug coverage.[6] As a result, elderly persons pay almost two-thirds (64%) of their prescription drug costs out of pocket.[7]

Prescription drug costs have increased much faster than inflation. From 1985 to 1991, inflation was 21 percent. Yet the cost of prescription drugs increased 66 percent over the same period and the cost of the 20 brand-name drugs most commonly purchased increased 79 percent.[8] Americans, therefore, not only pay significant amounts out of pocket for prescription drugs, but these costs are consuming a larger and larger portion of their incomes.

As of January 1, 1996, under the Health Security Act, Medicare beneficiaries will no longer see prescription drug costs eating up their incomes if the Health Security Act is enacted. They will be eligible for a new outpatient prescription drug benefit. After an annual deductible of $250 per person, Medicare beneficiaries will pay only 20 percent of prescription drug costs up to an annual maximum of $1,000. The benefit will be part of Medicare Part B. Ninety-seven percent of Medicare beneficiaries elect Part B coverage and pay Part B premiums that cover 25 percent of Part B costs. After 1996, the deductible and out-of-pocket maximum will increase only for inflation.

All Americans under age 65 also will have coverage for prescription drug costs as of 1997. After a maximum annual deductible of $250 for individuals or $400 for families, individuals will pay either $5 per prescription or 20 percent, depending on the health plan. If an individual's health costs exceed $1,500 or a family's costs exceed $3,000 in a year, they will no longer have to make any additional payments for prescription drugs.

Under the Health Security Act, Iona O'Neill would pay only the first $250 each year of her prescription drug costs and 20 percent of her prescription drug costs up to $1,000. If she spent $1,000 on prescription drugs in a year, Medicare would cover the remainder of her prescription drug costs. For this new benefit she will pay a small increase in her premium for Medicare Part B.

EARLY RETIREES LOSING THEIR HEALTH BENEFITS

Kazimer "Casey" Patelski and his wife Bonnie live in Costa Mesa, California. Casey was a design engineer for McDonnell Douglas for 28 years. He helped design various aircraft, missiles, satellites and the Skylab Space Station. Casey, who suffered from polio as a young man, turned down numerous job offers from other companies over the years because of the generous retirement benefits, including health insurance, promised by McDonnell Douglas. When Casey retired at age 63, he was assured that he and Bonnie would have health insurance coverage for the rest of their lives. A year later, McDonnell Douglas announced that it was eliminating health insurance benefits for all retirees. The Patelskis were able to purchase health insurance from the company to cover them for four years. After that, the Patelskis will have to try to find individual coverage for Bonnie, who will be 58 and not yet qualify for Medicare.

Companies across the country are reducing their work forces by encouraging employees to take early retirement. Former employers are the primary source of health insurance for retirees who are not yet eligible for Medicare. One-third (32%) of the retirees covered by their former employers are under age 65.[9] In light of skyrocketing health care costs and new accounting rules requiring employers to report this liability, companies are cutting health benefits for current and future retirees.

In the last few months, both McDonnell Douglas and Unisys corporations eliminated all health benefits to their current retirees, leaving some 45,000 retirees and their families without health insurance protection.[10] These corporations are not alone. A recent major survey of larger corporations found that 12 percent of companies responding have eliminated or plan to eliminate all retiree health benefits. Another 56 percent have reduced or plan to reduce health benefits covered.[11]

The Health Security Act will provide early retirees with guaranteed health coverage. Under the Act, the federal government will pay 80 percent of premiums for retirees between the ages of 55 and 65. For retirees whose previous employers currently pay retiree health costs, their employers will now be required to pay the retirees' share of premiums (20 percent).

Under the Health Security Act, the federal government would pay 80 percent of Mrs. Patelski's health insurance premiums until she is eligible for Medicare.

JOB LOCK

When Melanie Wood was pregnant with her third child, she intended to leave her job with the Harris County juvenile probation department to become a full-time mother. At the time, the family had health insurance coverage through Melanie's job. Jordan, now ten, was born with Sturge-Weber syndrome, a congenital neurological disorder that left him blind in his left eye and caused a large port-wine stain over most of his body that requires laser treatments. Jordan also has hydrocephalitis and needs a shunt to drain excess fluid from his brain. Melanie started calling insurance companies from her hospital bed immediately after Jordan's birth and she found that Jordan was uninsurable. Since her husband, Randy, is self-employed, Melanie was forced to return to work in order to keep health insurance protection for her family. Melanie wants to be at home with her children, but if she leaves her job, her family will no longer qualify for insurance.

American families with a member who has a chronic health condition can easily find themselves in the position of being unable to change jobs because the family is dependent on the health insurance obtained through one family member's job. One in five (19%) workers report that they or a family member are locked in their jobs because new work offers limited or no health insurance.[12] The worker, or the worker's spouse or children, may have existing health problems that will prevent them from being able to get new insurance after a job switch. Small businesses and individuals experience great difficulty obtaining comprehensive health coverage for people with preexisting health conditions. A worker seeking to change jobs may find a potential job that does not offer health benefits at all.

The Health Security Act, immediately upon enactment, will prohibit insurers from excluding preexisting conditions for individuals and their families who were insured within the previous 90-day period. For individuals and their families who were not previously insured, insurers can limit coverage for preexisting conditions for no more than six months. The Act also immediately requires insurers to accept all newly-hired, full-time employees and their families added to groups currently insured. By 1997, the Act prohibits exclusions for preexisting conditions under any circumstances.

As of 1997, under the Health Security Act, all employers will contribute 80 percent of average premium costs for health insurance for workers and their families, or more if they choose. Workers will no longer have to choose between jobs that offer health benefits and those that do not.

Under the Health Security Act, if Melanie Wood became a full-time mother, the Wood family would be able to get health insurance through the regional health alliance for the same premium as everyone else in the region. The family would be able to fully deduct the cost of the premium since Randy Wood is self-employed.

SMALL BUSINESS OWNERS AND THEIR FAMILIES

Ann and Hubert Maddux live in Corpus Christi, Texas with their four-year-old daughter and infant son. Hubert runs a tackle shop and makes approximately $25,000 a year. As a small business owner, the best insurance Hubert could get for himself and his family was through his alma mater in 1986. At that time his premiums were $1,000 a year. After their daughter was born with Downs Syndrome and serious heart defects, the Maddux family's premiums increased to $17,000 annually. Recently they were able to reduce the premium to $14,400, but they have to pay a $1,000 deductible per person and half of the first $2,500 in covered expenses per person. Both children need prescription drugs which the family's insurance does not cover. Medicine for the children costs the family between $100 and $200 a month.

Small business owners, employees and their families encounter great difficulties obtaining affordable health insurance. Small groups generally must pay ten to 40 percent more for health insurance than large groups. Business owners experiencing problems like those of the Maddux family often face much higher premiums.[13] Small groups are at a disadvantage because they lack the bargaining power that enables larger groups to negotiate reduced provider payments and premium rates.

Likewise, small groups bear much of the burden of paying for uncompensated care to the uninsured, since they do not have the clout to negotiate reduced provider and premium rates. Small groups pay higher administrative costs for insurance than larger groups. Administrative costs can account for up to 40 percent of premium costs for very small groups, as compared with six percent of premium costs for very large groups.[14]

Small group premiums are often experience-rated, which means that they are based on the actual claims experience of the group.

Since small groups cannot spread the claims costs across many persons, experience-rated premiums are often high and can escalate rapidly if one member of the group has a serious health problem.[15] According to a survey by the National Federation of Independent Business, the high cost of health insurance is the most pressing problem confronting small business.[16]

Those who would purchase health insurance as individuals or as part of a small business group face another formidable barrier to health coverage--medical underwriting practices. Medical underwriting is the process by which an insurer evaluates the health history and the potential for poor health status, and high claims, for an individual or group. In addition, insurance companies often deny coverage to small employer groups based on the nature of the industry, such as agriculture, retail or construction, or offer them only limited coverage because of employees' health status or claims experience. Based on current underwriting practices, approximately 15 percent of all small businesses are ineligible for insurance or eligible only for restricted coverage.[17]

The Health Security Act will end the discrimination small groups and individuals have experienced in the insurance marketplace. Most Americans will obtain their insurance through consumer-controlled regional health alliances where they live. This pooling of individuals and businesses will result in lower premiums for those who previously purchased insurance as small businesses or individuals. By purchasing insurance through regional pools, small businesses and individuals will benefit from the negotiating power of large groups with insurance companies.

Under the Act, small businesses and individuals will no longer see their premiums skyrocket from year to year. The Health Security Act will limit the amount by which insurance companies can raise their premiums each year. Since everyone will have health coverage, small businesses and individuals will no longer bear the disproportionate burden of paying a large hidden surcharge for care to the uninsured.

Under the Health Security Act, all employers in the region will pay 80 percent of the average premium cost to the purchasing alliances, or more if they choose, and employees and business owners will select their families' coverage from among the various plans in that area. Insurers will no longer be able to set the premiums for small businesses on the basis of that group alone. Instead, premiums will be based on health costs for the entire region. Everyone under 65 who obtains insurance through their regional health alliance will pay the same premium regardless of age or health status. Insurers will no longer be able to reject businesses or individuals for any reason.

Small businesses and families will be eligible for significant federal assistance with premium costs. No business with under 5,000 employees will have to spend more than 7.9 percent of its payroll for health insurance costs. Businesses with 50 or fewer employees will pay less if their average wages are $24,000 or less. The lowest wage small businesses will pay only 3.5 percent of payroll. Families and individuals with incomes below 150 percent of poverty (about $22,000 for a family of four) will be eligible for assistance with paying their share (20 percent of average premiums) of the premium.

Under the Health Security Act, the Maddux family would have comprehensive health benefits for the same premium as all other neighboring Texas residents. After paying a $250 annual deductible for each family member, they would be responsible for 20 percent of their prescription drug costs or $5 for each prescription, depending on their plan, until they had annual medical costs of $3,000. Once they spent that much, they would no longer have any out-of-pocket costs for a comprehensive range of services.

LONG TERM CARE AT HOME

Roz and Harold Barkowitz live in North Miami Beach, Florida. Harold is a 72-year-old retired shoemaker who had to give up his business six years ago to care for Roz, age 67, who has multiple sclerosis. They had to sell their house and move into an apartment because Roz could no longer climb the stairs. They get no outside assistance caring for Roz, only someone who comes to clean once a week. Harold's greatest fear is that something will happen to him and he will no longer be able to care for Roz. He currently spends 24 hours a day taking care of her.

Virtually every American family eventually confronts a long term care crisis. At any given time, there are an estimated three and one-half million Americans who have great difficulty taking care of themselves. These persons require assistance with three or more of the five most basic activities of daily living--eating, bathing, toileting, dressing and getting out of a bed or chair. The services that they need are largely non-medical in nature and, as a result, options for financial assistance or insurance coverage are very limited.

Approximately half of these Americans currently do not receive any paid home care services.[18] They want to continue to live in their homes and communities rather than go to a nursing home. But they and their family caregivers need help. Based on one study, families devote an average of 57 hours per week to caregiving for their frail elders.[19] Over one-third of informal caregivers are elderly and one-third report being in poor health themselves.[20] Currently American families that use paid home care must spend thousands of dollars out of pocket for that care.[21]

The Health Security Act establishes a major new program to provide services to individuals with severe disabilities without regard to age. Beginning in 1996, under the Act, the federal government will provide significant new funds to states to enable the development of individualized plans of care for persons with severe disabilities. These persons will be eligible for services that include personal assistance and other services that help these persons continue to live in their homes and community. This new program will be fully phased in by the year 2000. Individuals will be responsible for copayments based on income.

Under the Health Security Act, Mr. and Mrs. Barkowitz would be eligible for the services of someone to assist Mr. Barkowitz with caring for his wife. The new program will make such care affordable. With a major federal program supporting home and community-based services, it would be easier to find appropriate assistance for Mrs. Barkowitz.

EMPLOYEES VULNERABLE TO ARBITRARY BENEFIT LIMITS

John and Joan Cleveland of St. Louis, Missouri had health insurance through Joan's employer, a company that is self-insured. John was diagnosed with leukemia in September 1990, and he needed a bone marrow transplant. Even though his insurance had a $500,000 lifetime maximum, the policy capped coverage of organ and tissue transplants at $75,000. John's transplant cost about $250,000. John died of complications from his transplant in June 1993.

Approximately 40 percent of all employees and their families are covered by employer health plans that are self-insured.[22] Self-insured companies do not purchase health insurance from a private insurance company. Instead, they pay the cost of their employees' medical care directly.

The federal Employee Retirement Income Security Act of 1974 (ERISA) protects the financial solvency of employee benefit plans, like retirement and insurance plans. This law exempts self-insured employers from state mandates, regulations and premium taxes. As a result, the U.S. Supreme Court recently ruled that self-insured employers may limit or eliminate health insurance benefits at any time, even after an employee or a family member contracts a serious illness. As a result, employees of self-insured companies have found themselves in the tragic position of developing very serious illnesses and watching employers respond by limiting benefits for that illness—with employees having no recourse.

Self-insurance was once common among only the largest firms. However, smaller and smaller companies are now choosing to self-insure in an effort to save money. Self-insurance is now common with companies with as few as 100 employees. In 1986, only 46 percent of all employers that offered health insurance were self-insured. By 1992, 69 percent were self-insured.[23]

Upon enactment, the Health Security Act will prohibit all employers and insurers from imposing caps or exclusions on coverage for specific medical conditions or any lifetime limit on benefits. The Act will require all businesses, whether they pay for their employees through a regional health alliance or through their own health alliance, to provide the comprehensive benefits specified by federal law or to offer even more extensive coverage.

Under the Health Security Act, John and Joan Cleveland would have had to pay no more than $3,000 out-of-pocket for John's medical expenses in the year that he had his bone marrow transplant.

EMPLOYERS WITH SKYROCKETING PREMIUMS

Roger Flaherty owns a small company, Floor Covering Resources, in Kensington, Maryland. He has two employees, and they are covered by a small group health insurance plan. Both employees have ongoing health problems. In 1987 Roger paid $285 a month to cover these employees. He now pays $786 a month. In November 1993 his premiums will increase to $946 a month. The business pays the full cost of the insurance. Roger is committed to providing health insurance for his employees, but doesn't know if he can continue to afford it.

The amount American families and businesses are charged for health care has far outpaced increases in family income and business profits. Average family income increased 88 percent from 1980 to 1991, while average family spending for health care increased 147 percent. In 1992 alone, health care inflation caused the equivalent of a five percent cut in American families' take-home pay.[24]

Today, business spending for health care nearly equals the amount corporations make in after-tax profits.[25] By contrast, in 1980, business health care spending amounted to 41 percent of corporations' after-tax profits.[26] If health care inflation had been held to the same rate of inflation as in the rest of the economy from 1980 to 1992, health care costs for businesses today would be one-third less than they are. This difference averages about $1,000 per worker.[27]

By 1997, the Health Security Act will limit the amount by which insurance companies can raise premiums. By 1999, American families will no longer have to swallow health insurance premium increases that are larger than general inflation. American families will see larger wage increases and more disposable income and businesses will see less of their profits eaten up by health cost increases.

77-929 O - 94 - 10

Under the Health Security Act, Mr. Flaherty would see his health insurance premiums for his employees go up no faster than inflation.

CARE UNAVAILABLE FOR MEDICAID BENEFICIARIES

In late 1990, Sherri Wilburn of Blount County, Tennessee learned she was pregnant. Although she qualified for Medicaid coverage, neither Sherri nor a social worker at the local health department could find a doctor willing to provide Sherri with prenatal care. Sherri was finally able to schedule her first doctor visit for a date in her seventh month of pregnancy. Three days before her scheduled appointment to begin prenatal care, Sherri went into labor. Her daughter, Cassandra, was born with brain damage and was hospitalized for months. Cassandra will need special education and ongoing physical therapy. According to one of Cassandra's doctors, Sherri's pregnancy was "complicated by a lack of prenatal care."

Low-income Americans face numerous barriers to medical care, even when they are covered by Medicaid, the government's health insurance program for low-income persons. Approximately one of every five adults who receives Medicaid experiences problems getting health care. Last year, almost one out of five adults receiving Medicaid were turned away by a hospital or a doctor. Another 20 percent had to go to an emergency room for care because they did not have a regular doctor.[28]

Doctors are often reluctant to see Medicaid beneficiaries because Medicaid pays far less than private insurance for medical care. One-quarter of all physicians will not accept any Medicaid patients. Another one-third limit the number of Medicaid recipients they see. Over half of all pediatricians report that they will not accept any Medicaid recipients, or limit the number they will accept.[29]

Under the Health Security Act, all Medicaid beneficiaries will have access to the same plans offered by the regional health alliances as everyone else. For individuals eligible for Supplemental Security Income (SSI) or Aid to Families with Dependent Children (AFDC), the Medicaid program will make payments to the health alliances that allow the beneficiaries to choose among all health plans with premiums equal to or below the average. Persons currently receiving Medicaid, but not eligible for cash assistance, will obtain their health insurance through their regional health alliance in the same manner as all other persons.

Under the Health Security Act, Sherri Wilburn would have her choice of any insurance plan offered in her Tennessee region with an average premium or lower. All such insurance plans would have to provide easily accessible prenatal care. Her regional health alliance would provide her with information on the quality of

prenatal care provided by each plan offered in her region.

CONCLUSION:

As our examples indicate, enactment of the Health Security Act of 1993 would go a long way to ensuring Americans that health care coverage will be there when they need it. We want to work with you to achieve passage of this comprehensive bill and to improve the aspects that we believe need strengthening.

The lowest income Americans must be assured that their premiums and cost-sharing requirements do not create financial barriers that prevent them from getting the care they need. All consumers must be assured that the consumer members of the National Health Board and regional Health Alliances are truly representative and accountable to the public.

We look forward to working with you to achieve health security for all Americans.

Endnotes

1. Families USA Foundation, *Losing Health Insurance* (Washington, DC: Families USA Foundation, 1993); and Families USA Foundation, *Half of Us: Families Priced Out of Health Protection* (Washington, DC: Families USA Foundation, 1993).

2. Katharine Swartz, John Marcotte and Timothy McBride, "Spells Without Health Insurance: The Distribution of Durations When Left-Censored Spells are Included," *Inquiry* vol. 30, (Spring 1993), pp. 77-83.

3. Families USA Foundation, *Half of Us*.

4. Pamela J. Farley, "Who Are the Underinsured?" *Milbank Memorial Fund Quarterly/Health and Society* vol. 63, no. 63, (1985), pp. 477-501.

5. John Rother, "Statement of the American Association of Retired Persons on the Health Care Crisis in America: A Growing Threat to Economic Security," Testimony before the Joint Economic Committee, U.S. Congress (Washington, DC: AARP, September 15, 1993).

6. American Association of Retired Persons Public Policy Institute, "Older Americans and Prescription Drugs: Utilization, Expenditures and Coverage," *Issue Brief Number Nine* (Washington, DC: AARP, September 1991).

7. Families USA Foundation, *Prescription Costs: America's Other Drug Crisis* (Washington, DC: Families USA Foundation, 1992).

8. Families USA Foundation, *Prescription Costs*.

9. Steven DiCarlo, Jon Gabel, Gregory de Lissovoy and Judith Kasper, *Research Bulletin: Facing Up to Postretirement Health Benefits* (Washington, DC: Heath Insurance Association of America, 1989).

10. Michael Clements, "DuPont Resists Trend to Cut Retiree Benefits," *USA Today*, March 12, 1993, p. 2B.

11. Hewitt Associates, *FASB Retiree Health Accounting* (Lincolnshire, IL: Hewitt Associates, October 1993).

12. Henry J. Kaiser Family Foundation and Louis Harris and Associates. "News Release: One in Five American Families Victim of 'Job Lock.' High Cost and Lack of Insurance Top Reasons." (Menlo Park, CA: Kaiser Family Foundation, October 15, 1993).

13. Government Accounting Office, *Employer-Based Health Insurance: High Costs, Wide Variation Threaten System* (Washington, DC: Government Printing Office, September 1992).

14. Congressional Research Service, *Private Health Insurance: Options for Reform,* Report for the Subcommittee on Health, the Committee on Ways and Means, U.S. House of Representatives (Washington, DC: Government Printing Office, 1990).

15. General Accounting Office, *Health Insurance: Cost Increases Lead to Coverage Limitations and Cost Shifting* (Washington, DC: Government Printing Office, 1990).

16. William J. Dennis, Jr., *Small Business Problems and Priorities* (Washington, DC: The NFIB Foundation, 1992), p. 8.

17. Wendy Zellers, Catherine McLaughlin, and Kevin Frick, "Small Business Health Insurance: Only The Healthy Need Apply," *Health Affairs* vol. 11, no. 1, (Spring 1992), pp. 174-180.

18. Data provided by Lewin-VHI, Inc. This estimate includes persons with physical disabilities only. It does not include persons with cognitive impairments due to limitations in the data.

19. Alzheimer's Association, *Time Out! A Case for a National Family Caregiver Support Policy* (Washington, DC: Alzheimer's Association, 1991), p. 2.

20. The Pepper Commission, *A Call For Action* (Washington, DC: Government Printing Office, 1990), pp. 94-95.

21. Families USA Foundation, *The Heavy Burden of Home Care* (Washington, DC: Families USA Foundation, 1993).

22. Cynthia B. Sullivan, Marianne Miller, Roger Feldman, and Bryan Dowd, "Employer-Sponsored Health Insurance in 1991," *Health Affairs* (Winter 1992), pp. 172-185.

23. Edward Felsenthal, "Health Plans Are Self-Insured By More Firms," *Wall Street Journal*, November 11, 1992; and Foster Higgins, *1992 Health Care Benefits Survey* (Princeton, NJ: Foster Higgins, 1993).

24. Families USA Foundation, *Health Spending: The Growing Threat to the Family Budget* (Washington, DC: Families USA Foundation, December 1991) and Service Employees International Union, *Out of Control, Into Decline: The Devastating 12-Year Impact of Healthcare Costs on Worker Wages, Corporate Profits and Government Budgets* (Washington, DC: SEIU, October 1992).

25. Cathy A. Cowan and Patricia A. McDonnell, "Business, Households and Governments -- Health Spending 1991," *Health Care Financing Review*, Vol. 14, no. 3 (Spring 1993).

26. Cowan and McDonnell, "Business, Households and Governments."

27. Service Employees International Union, *Out of Control, Into Decline.*

28. Kaiser Family Foundation. "News Release: New Survey Shows Significant Gaps in Medicaid Safety Net" (Menlo Park, CA: Kaiser Family Foundation, March 17, 1993).

29. John K. Iglehart, "The American Health Care System: Medicaid," *The New England Journal of Medicine* vol. 328, no. 12. (March 25, 1993), pp. 896-900.

Mr. WAXMAN. Let me start off the questioning by asking whoever wants to respond, if we don't enact legislation that provides for universal coverage and cost controls, what do you see as the consequences for consumers over the next 5 or 10 years?

Ms. SHEARER. That is our fear, that the nightmare will continue and just after the year 2000, we can expect health care costs to be going up to about 20 percent of GDP level, which has catastrophic implications for consumers, because it will mean that expenditures on other things—education, food and housing—will be crowded out. I think that the situation is alarming now and it makes action now really critical.

Mr. POLLACK. Mr. Chairman, let me take the numbers that Gail just offered with respect to the gross figures nationally and translate that to a family basis. In 1980, we in America were spending on average $2,600 per family for health care. Today we are spending almost $8,000 per family on average for health care. If we don't do anything about the current projections, we are going to wind up spending $14,000 per family for health care at the end of this decade.

Clearly that burden is too staggering for a good number of Americans to shoulder. It means more and more families are going to drop the kind of coverage that they need to protect themselves and businesses are going to find this burden so staggering that they are going to drop coverage and shift more of the costs on to families.

Ms. CAIN. Mr. Chairman, I would think that any kind of legislation without those two ingredients really would not be reform in terms of consumers.

Ms. BROWN. And I would say that the American public would not accept that.

Mr. WAXMAN. Our colleague Mr. Cooper has introduced legislation that would limit the deductibility of health insurance premiums for employers to the level of the lowest cost plan in an area. Unlike the President's plan the Cooper bill would not require employers to contribute to health care coverage for their employees and it would not limit the rate of growth in health insurance premiums. What are the implications of a scheme like that for consumers?

Ms. SHEARER. Could I start with the macro-picture once again? Over the summer, the CBO did a study that showed that because last year's bill did not call for universality by the year 2000, about 25 million consumers would continue to be left out of the health care system. It also concluded that by the year 2000, health care costs would continue to increase about $20 billion above the baseline. I think unfortunately, the proposal does not meet consumers' needs with regard to universality or cost containment.

Mr. POLLACK. I have a great deal of admiration for Congressman Cooper's efforts with respect to the debate on health care. With respect to the bill itself, I must say that I think it falls short of the bedrock necessity of achieving security for all Americans.

I wish that Mr. Cooper, who I think used very heavily the work of the Jackson Hole group, would have used the Jackson Hole Group's recommendation with respect to coverage for everybody including the employer mandate. My hope is that we can work with

Representative Cooper to ensure that everyone does get the coverage.

Mr. WAXMAN. We want to assure that everyone gets coverage, although that bill doesn't lead to that guaranteed result. But what will it mean for consumers who now have health insurance if the deductibility is lost to their employers? Are they going to pay more for health insurance, are they going to pay the same, are they going to pay less or are they going to go into the lowest-priced HMO?

Ms. SHEARER. In real terms it makes health insurance more expensive. It is likely to lead to employers ratcheting down their coverage closer to the low-cost plan. It is likely to basically lead to more out-of-pocket costs for premiums for consumers. On the positive side, it is likely to make consumers somewhat more cost sensitive in shopping for insurance and theory has it that this will put downward pressure on costs.

Mr. WAXMAN. The President purports to do that as well. One last question—we are hearing from later witnesses today that the President's plan doesn't give consumer choice. Do your organizations feel—certainly you have a lot of strong feelings about the fact that consumers ought to have some choice—do you believe the President's plan will impair the ability of consumers to choose their own doctors?

Ms. BROWN. I am not sure that we know enough of the details on that to be able to give you the kind of answer you would like to have.

Mr. POLLACK. If you look at the surveys of businesses, you will find that increasingly businesses are limiting the choice that employees have. From 1990 to 1993, three times as many businesses said to their workers, "Here is the plan that you have to opt into. Here is the list of doctors and you have no choice about that."

If we don't get reform, there will be very limited choice. Already there is too limited a choice for too many Americans. I think the Clinton plan improves choice inasmuch as it says to the employer, "You pay into the health alliance, but worker, you are the one who is going to choose which plan you are going to get into."

On the question with respect to Congressman Cooper's plan on the question of tax limitations, that question I think is inextricably linked to what will be in the benefit package, and I am very concerned in terms of any limitations on tax benefits until we see what is in the comprehensive or not-so-comprehensive benefit package. If it is not a comprehensive benefit package, then I am very troubled to see a limitation on tax treatment.

If on the other hand it is a very comprehensive benefit package, then my response would be different. Unfortunately, as I understand, I believe that the determination as to what would be in that benefit package is left for a later time by a board and we don't yet know exactly what the benefits would be at this juncture.

Mr. WAXMAN. Mrs. Collins?

Mr. COOPER. Mr. Chairman, would I be permitted to respond?

Mr. WAXMAN. When we get to you.

Mrs. Collins?

Mrs. COLLINS. It is anticipated that many of today's health insurers will exit the market through the transition years, leaving their policyholders without any insurance at all. There are a number of suggestions that have been floating around of some kind of high-risk pool or assignment of various policyholders or even guaranteed issue at average rates for each block of businesses.

I wonder what kind of system you think should be established for the protection and coverage of consumers in those kinds of circumstances?

Ms. SHEARER. The interim period? Well, there are some provisions, and here again we are anxious to see the details of the proposal. There are some suggestions that insurers will not be allowed to drop blocks of business in the interim. I think that high-risk pools do not have a good record in terms of keeping costs low and providing the access that we need. I think that is a tough question and we can provide you more information as we work through this.

Mrs. COLLINS. Do any of the others have any suggestions?

Ms. BROWN. I think there are some States that are doing a good job of using a pool approach and perhaps using a pool approach and marrying it to the insurance pools. The insurance private providers would enable you to have a transition, but everyone must have that opportunity in a cost-efficient way.

Mrs. COLLINS. Numerous insurers are opposed to premium caps, expressing concern that the caps are going to result in decreases in quality, services and access to sophisticated medical technology. I would like to know if this is likely to occur and if so, do you think that the value of having premium caps would outweigh such drawbacks?

Ms. BROWN. We think that this is something that is going to have to be watched very carefully. We are concerned that if we don't have premium caps that once again we are going to have escalating costs and health care will not be able to be afforded. The whole plan is going to have to work its way through some of those difficulties. We are going to have to keep our eye on it as we go through it.

Mrs. COLLINS. Do you think that premium caps might be akin to the limits on Medicare and Medicaid expenditures in the plan and, if so, do you think that those caps would be necessary to create a level playing field where the burdens of cost containment are borne equally by the public and the private sectors?

Ms. BROWN. There are many issues with that, but that the whole American public must be treated equally and fairly and if we work through the process we should be able to do it so that there is good research and development.

Mr. POLLACK. I think this issue is extremely important. I think the question about what Medicare and Medicaid cuts are like is not as important alone as they are in terms of what is done in tandem with the private sector. Today Medicare pays about two-thirds of what private insurance pays doctors and hospitals. Medicaid pays about half. That means that we have private insurance paying here, Medicare over here on Medicaid down here. That means that there is a clear disincentive for a doctor or a hospital to treat a Medicare patient or a Medicaid patient because they receive considerably less in payment for the service to those individuals.

If we exacerbate that differential by putting pressure on Medicare and Medicaid to the exclusion of similar pressure in the private sector, it means that differential is going to increase. That is going to mean two very specific problems will get worse. Number one, Medicaid and Medicare patients are increasingly going to find the doors closed to them when they go to doctors and hospitals. Medicaid patients already experience that and some Medicare patients are beginning to experience that.

Second, for those doctors and hospitals that do treat Medicare or Medicaid patients, the way they make up for it is by cost shifts and by increasing costs for everybody else. I think whatever we do with respect to Medicare and Medicaid it is important that it be done in tandem with what we do in the private sector.

Mrs. COLLINS. Ms. Cain, I have been questioning previous witnesses, including Mrs. Clinton and Secretary Shalala, on the need to keep health insurers from attempting to redline areas to avoid low-income and minority consumers. Do you think the provisions in the plan are adequate and how can we keep this practice from occurring?

Ms. CAIN. We share your concern about the need to address that issue. I don't know that there are enough specifics in the plan to guarantee that. We look forward to working with you to guarantee that in the plan.

Mrs. COLLINS. Thank you.

Mr. WAXMAN. Mr. Bliley?

Mr. BLILEY. Thank you, Mr. Chairman. Early evaluation of the administration's plan is that it will not cut costs as much as forecasted and that the Federal budget deficit will dramatically increase as a result. That is because the plan depends upon unprecedented cuts of $238 billion in the Medicare and Medicaid programs. These cuts generate almost two-thirds of the plan's financing. They are generated by a cap that is placed on the Federal entitlements and private health insurance premiums.

When fully phased in, the cap is equal to CPI plus the annual percentage growth in population. This means that when the U.S. health expenditures are adjusted for inflation and population, there will be no real growth in the health care system under the administration's premium cap. Let's put this in perspective by looking at this chart of average annual growth rates in health care expenditures of our western neighbors.

Mr. Chairman, I ask unanimous consent under the committee's rules to distribute this chart to all members.

Mr. WAXMAN. Without objection.

[The chart referred to follows:]

Average Annual Growth in Per Capita Health Expenditures

(Adjusted for Inflation, 1985 -1991)

Country	% Increase (1985-1991*)
Turkey	9.61
Spain	6.69
Italy	5.55
Finland	4.97
Iceland	4.48
Luxembourg	4.41
Norway	4.30
Japan	4.24
Belgium	3.95
United Kingdom	3.84
Canada	3.58
Portugal	3.41
France	3.26
Austria	3.05
Netherlands	2.94
Ireland	2.67
Greece	2.26
Australia	2.08
New Zealand	2.06
Germany	2.05
Denmark	2.03
Switzerland	1.82
Sweden	0.48
United States	**0****

*** Numbers are the percentage by which the increase exceeds the rate of inflation, as measured by the GDP inflator.**

**** Number as presented in 9/7/93 Administration Proposal.**

Sources: Organization for Economic Cooperation and Development, 1985-1991 comparison; Working Draft - Clinton Health Care Plan, 9/7/93.

Mr. BLILEY. This chart shows the average annual growth rate in health expenditures adjusted for inflation and population growth for the years 1985 and 1991. Let's look at Italy, the third country from the top of the list. In this period Italian health expenditures adjusted for population growth grew annually at 5.5 percent above the inflation rate. The equivalent annual growth rate under the Clinton premium and entitlement caps adjusted for inflation and population would be zero.

Let me repeat—under the administration's caps, there would be no real growth in health expenditures. This table shows that no country except for Sweden has come even remotely close in limiting health care expenditures to zero real growth.

The socialized medical system of the United Kingdom grew at 3.84 percent per capita above inflation while the Canadian single-payer system grew at 3.58 percent per capita above inflation. In the case of these two countries we are talking about systems that explicitly ration care to the elderly and possess medical technology vastly inferior to the United States. Under the administration's cap, we would have the slowest growing health system in the western world. We would be growing significantly slower than our economic competitors like Japan, Germany and France.

But our future growth rates would also lag significantly behind countries like Turkey, Spain, Portugal, Ireland and Greece. Now I have asked Mrs. Clinton and the Secretary of HHS how the administration's plan is going to accomplish these extraordinary reductions in health care expenditures when even systems that ration care and possess vastly inferior medical technology and treatments have not remotely approached these growth rates. And we have not received satisfactory responses to this critical question.

On the other hand, these caps are the linchpin to the entire financing of the Clinton plan because only with these Draconian caps can the President finance this $400 billion expansion with less than $150 billion of new revenue. If you remove these caps from the proposal, it falls apart like a house of cards.

Ms. Brown, I would like to ask you, do you believe that we could grow this slowly?

Ms. BROWN. Obviously, sir, we are as concerned as you are with the cuts in Medicare and Medicaid. We are not sure that they can be realized. We are very concerned that those cuts impact on the pieces of the proposal that directly affect older people. We think we—what we are doing is we are giving you the task of, as our leaders in Congress, of determining how we are going to work through this and create a health care bill which we must have, craft something that appears to be fair to all parts of our society.

AARP obviously is going to watch very carefully where the funding is and what kinds of cuts.

Mr. BLILEY. I would like to follow up with that. If we somehow were able to do this, how severe would health care rationing be in this country? Obviously we would have to ration care if we are going achieve this, and would this have a particular effect on the elderly?

Ms. BROWN. We are uncomfortable, obviously, with using the word "rationing." We are not sure that the logic follows automatically. We think that there are ways in which we could craft a program which would be fair to all parties and we need to try to do that.

Mr. BLILEY. I would like any suggestions you have on how to do it.

Ms. BROWN. We would be happy to share that with you.

Mr. WAXMAN. Thank you, Mr. Bliley.

Mr. Stearns?

Mr. STEARNS. Thank you, Mr. Chairman.

Ms. Brown, I think you are taking the bulk of the questions because many Members on my side are concerned about the administration proposing increasing two entitlement programs under Medicare with pharmaceutical drugs and also long-term care, yet cutting back the 5-year period revenues for Medicare.

So what my staff and I were talking about is why don't we look to the AARP Public Policy Agenda which is this book—this is a very good book, an impressive book—and looking at how you would do this. We went to page 119, called Financing Health Care Reform. There were two quotes there I would like to read to you and maybe you could explain them to me.

Most of the people I deal with in Florida are on Medicare and they are very concerned about the President's proposal in this respect. Page 120 it says, "It is difficult, however, to detect fraud and abuse under the current system and there have been problems associated with efforts to recover losses. Others suggest that reductions in Federal spending and entitlement programs such as Medicare and Medicaid could finance health care reforms. While there is an opportunity for Medicare savings in the context of systemwide measures that have real potential to contain and not merely shift costs, these savings are not adequate."

So from your book, it is indicating that the savings that the administration is projecting are not going to be adequate to do this. It goes on and says "AARP believes that significant reforms of the health care system will require additional public revenues."

I presume you mean by that taxes. So at the same time they have two new entitlement programs plus they are reducing it. You are saying, without the two new entitlement programs, we are going to need additional revenues as revenues from other sources, additional public revenues, as revenues from other sources will not be adequate to pay for the desired changes.

My question is based upon what is in your book and my concern and yours, perhaps you can help me through this.

Ms. BROWN. As you know, AARP developed what is called Health Care America, which is our health care proposal prior to Mr. Clinton becoming President. In that we wrestled also with the issue of how do you finance it and how do you keep fraud and abuse and all the other things that we think might be occurring at a limit? We had two proposals in our bill for financing.

One was a 3 percent income tax. The other was a value-added tax. We recognize that health care cannot be done if it is to be done well, unless it is done completely and we shore up the pieces, because what we have now is cost shifting. We have older people paying more out of pocket. We have many people who are uninsured and underinsured.

If we are going to do it, we have to do it right. Older people have stepped up to the table. We have done our part before, sir. We will do it again.

The issue is making it as fair as possible to all people and we do not want older people to be singled out and asked to do more than their portion.

Mr. STEARNS. Would I be correct in saying that AARP is recommending added value-added tax or 34 percent across the board or a combination of both to solve the problem and you are saying that the Clinton Administration proposal would not solve the problem based upon what you say in this book?

Ms. BROWN. No, I am not saying that, sir. There is always more than one way to solve a problem. We are concerned about what we have seen as to whether or not it is adequate to do the job. We think that there are many ways in which we can contain costs. That is an absolute, but we think we will be kidding ourselves and you will be kidding the American public if we attempt to pass a bill where the numbers aren't real.

Mr. POLLACK. Mr. Stearns, if I may on this particular question—certainly the task with respect to government financing is much greater if you are saying the government has a responsibility of providing coverage for everybody. Then the costs would be considerably higher. But the Clinton plan offers three different additional financing vehicles to achieve that goal.

One, it says to employers that don't provide coverage today that you need to fulfill the same responsibility that other employers already have achieved. That is a significant way in which achieving coverage for everybody is financed.

Second, it does include sin taxes with respect to tobacco; and third it includes a 1 percent tax on those larger corporations that do not opt into the health alliances. So the problem that you are raising about a very substantial amount of money that needs to be financed becomes a whole lot more acute if you are putting that whole burden on the government.

This plan does not do that and therefore you don't need the same kind of financing that would be necessary if the government was relied upon to do that job.

Mr. WAXMAN. Thank you, Mr. Stearns.

Mr. Cooper?

Mr. COOPER. Thank you, Mr. Chairman. I appreciate your kindness in giving my bill almost equal time in your remarks. I hope that means when markup comes, we will also have equal time.

There seems to be a great deal of concern that our approach—that our bill may be too popular. I would urge my colleagues to get a copy of H.R. 3222 and find out for themselves what other people are so afraid of that might catch on. We think that we have the only bipartisan approach; everybody pays lip service to that goal. We think we have already achieved it. We think it is essential that you have the collective wisdom of both parties coming up with the best medicine and things that will work back home.

Other than ask questions, I would like to clear up misconceptions about our approach. On universal coverage, we agree with President Clinton that you need to cover the poor and near-poor up to about double the poverty level. If you look at the 37.4 million uninsured today, that is about 60 percent of the uninsured problem there and we agree that needs to be achieved now.

We also agree with the Clinton administration that the insurance system needs to be user friendly. There should be a community-rated system, no more denial of coverage of preexisting conditions, no more experience rating. You should be able to get and keep coverage no matter how sick your family or you have been, where you work, when you work. Benefits have got to be portable.

CBO indicated about half the remaining uninsured will sign up voluntarily once you clean up today's rotten system. No subsidy, no coercion is required to get those folks to enroll. They will be overjoyed to have affordable coverage available to them.

Finally, they will feel the insurance system is working for them, not against them. That is about 70, 80 percent of the uninsured problem right there.

Then you get to the question of the employer mandate. CBO tells us they have never scored legislation proposing an employer mandate or an individual mandate, for that matter. Well, I think we should get CBO and other guidance before we automatically assume this is good medicine for the economy.

The employer mandate has some positive features; but 30 percent of the uninsured have no contact with employers whatsoever. So how will the employer mandate reach those folks? There are lots of legitimate questions we need to be asking over the next 12 months to make sure we are prescribing good medicine.

By the way, Dr. Alain Enthoven, the lead economist of the Jackson Hole Group, paid me the high compliment of concluding that we were right, our group was all along, in not having an employer mandate in our bill.

Another issue is tax deductibility. I appreciate AARP's testimony pointing out on page 9, "It does not seem fair that taxpayers would continue to finance the health care premiums of a Wall Street executive with a salary of more than $1 million a year while subsidies to Medicare beneficiaries with much lower incomes are substantially reduced."

There is a terrific equity and efficiency question. The Federal Government's third largest health program, the program with no name, that people are afraid to discuss: Medicare, Medicaid, and then this program that the Pepper Commission omitted mention of. We spend about $70 billion a year trying to help people buy health coverage, but it is a very unfair and inefficient program.

We can make it better through a corporate tax change. The corporations understand the need to do without affecting individual tax status except to grant people, workers and the self-employed a new tax break. The average American has only been able to deduct the second medical catastrophe of the year; the first today is never deductible. We have to clean that up.

That is a serious omission in the Clinton plan. They help the self-employed but do not reach out to the employee in this fashion. We want everybody who pays the bills for low-cost basic coverage to be able to deduct, whether their title is employer or employee or self-employed.

Finally, on the basic benefits package, our package is $300 richer per individual than the Clinton package according to the CBO estimates. The actuarial value of it is that much greater. We think we can have a better basic package.

Thank you.

Mr. WAXMAN. Thank you, Mr. Cooper.

Mr. Franks?

Mr. FRANKS. Thank you, Mr. Chairman.

The President's plan will be delivered to Congress now I believe within the next 2 weeks. However, we do have three House bills on health care reform that have already been presented. Two bills have well over a hundred sponsors. As was mentioned, the Cooper-Grandy bill would have bipartisan support.

Have you had a chance to review the House Republican bill which has more cosponsors than any other health care reform bill? In particular, do you have any comments about the Medi-save component of the House Republican bill?

Ms. SHEARER. I do not have—been having a little bit of difficulty getting copies of some of these bills. One of our concerns about Congressman Michel's approach is that it does not provide for universality. There is a lot of talk of——

Mr. FRANKS. I beg to differ. It does.

Ms. SHEARER. Universal access perhaps. There is a problem here in terminology. A lot of people talk about universal access to health care. We feel that a mandatory nature of the health care program is very important. As long as you give people who think they are healthy, think they are not at risk, as long as you give them the option of not having health insurance, you do not have the benefit of premium dollars or tax dollars they would contribute to make the system work.

Mr. FRANKS. Do you have any feelings about—any comments about the Medi-save component of the plan?

Ms. SHEARER. There are several different Medi-save proposals. We are concerned about the experience you have with IRA accounts in general in terms of them serving the needs of higher-income people as opposed to lower-income people.

We are concerned about linking it to catastrophic coverage when what this could mean is people do not get the early care that people need because they may not use their Medi-save account because perhaps the proposal allows them to get the money back at the end of the year.

We have a number of concerns. We can provide you more comments as we get copies of the bill.

Mr. FRANKS. We will be sure to get you a copy of the bill that has the most co-sponsors at this point. I would also like to get that to the other members of the panel and hopefully you can send back a written response as to your feelings about the plan because you do not have any remarks at this time.

Ms. BROWN. If I may, sir, we are uncomfortable with that being a stand-alone. As a stand-alone it will not, for some of the reasons stated already, we are not comfortable that it could be workable and be what we need to do for all America.

Mr. FRANKS. Are you referring to the Medi-save component of the plan?

Ms. BROWN. Yes.

Mr. FRANKS. Thank you, Mr. Chairman.

Mr. WAXMAN. Thank you, Mr. Franks.

Mr. Kreidler?

Mr. KREIDLER. Thank you, Mr. Chairman.

First, I would like to point out I am always pleased to see this particular chart that Mr. Bliley brings. I see additional numbers are added to it today.

First, I would find it more interesting to point out the percentage of the gross domestic product—national earnings, so to speak—that is spent on health care in each of those countries that is listed there. I think we would find, on average, they spend about one-third less on health care than does the United States.

Mr. POLLACK. At least.

Mr. KREIDLER. When you see that, probably every single country there or almost every country there also has universal coverage, save the United States, of course.

I have enough respect for the American free enterprise system to believe that if we build on the system we have today with private insurance companies delivering the care, that we should be able to get the waste, abuse, and fraud out of the American system; and thereby see some substantial savings that will enable us to do the kind of health care reform all of America needs.

Mr. POLLACK. I would say, Mr. Kreidler, if Muggsy Bogues rose by 5 percent that probably you would have one reaction to it. If Manute Bol rose by 5 percent, you might have a different reaction. Clearly we are looking at entirely different bases when we are talking about these kinds of figures.

Mr. KREIDLER. That is true.

Ms. Brown, I have a question here on an issue that I am sure you are familiar with. You expressed some valid concerns about the proposals to save $238 billion from Medicare and Medicaid payments. Hospitals and other provider groups have also expressed concerns. Some of them want to shift Medicare to some kind of managed competition model. The President's plan would apply that model to the rest of the system. My own State of Washington is an active health care reformer that would use managed competition in Medicare if Congress approves.

How willing are senior citizens to accept the kind of choices the President is asking other citizens to accept, choices among health care plans rather than choices among individual doctors?

Ms. BROWN. I think for older Americans, the opportunity to have choice is really essential for them; and we appreciate the part of the plan which leaves Medicare as it is and does give older people an opportunity to opt out of Medicare and into a managed care plan if they so choose. And we think there might be some of that which would occur, but we want to be sure that if older people decide to opt out that they are not going to be penalized for that.

The issue of health care for all Americans, we all know there are a lot of people out there that are really hurting and have had a lot of—we all here hear the horror stories of what is going on. So although we do believe that Medicare needs to stay as it is and that—I have done forums now in Wichita, Kans., out in Culver City, Calif. AARP members want to continue to be able to have choice and stay with Medicare if they can.

Mr. KREIDLER. Thank you.

I don't know who to ask this quick question of but I think most of us agree on the goal of universal coverage. We all know someone will have to pay for it. One of the main differences between the President's plan and the major Senate Republican proposal is who has to pay for health care coverage. The President would require employers to pay 80 percent of the costs. Senators Chafee and Dole would require individuals to pay the full costs.

Assuming any plan we enact would include subsidies for those lower-income people to help with costs, what is your view on the pros and cons of employer mandates versus individual mandates?

Mr. POLLACK. I would say that the conundrum Mr. Cooper, for example, didn't respond to and that I think your question raises is, if you go to an individual mandate, the subsidies that must be provided to individuals in order to make that affordable need to be considerably higher.

So you really have a very tough balancing choice with respect to an individual mandate. That is one, do you provide sufficient subsidies to make it possible for people to afford to purchase insurance? And if you do, then the fiscal implications are rather significant.

If, on the other hand, you are focused on the fiscal implications, then I suggest that it is going to be very difficult to provide the subsidies that are needed to make it affordable.

I think a good number of people are very afraid as well who currently receive their coverage through their employer that if we say in legislation that this is an individual responsibility rather than an employer responsibility, we will see an erosion of our employer-based system that we have today.

I think very few workers believe that if an employer no longer fulfills that responsibility of providing care, that they are going to get an equal increase in their salaries. Most people do not believe that. They may get some increase in their salaries. There may be some increase in profits. There may be some other ways that those savings will be spread.

So I think it is going to cause a great deal of apprehension on the part of workers in America if we say it is an individual responsibility rather than just expand modestly what already our system is, namely an employer-based system.

Mr. WAXMAN. Thank you, Mr. Kreidler.

Mr. Greenwood?

Mr. GREENWOOD. My light is not working. My microphone is. Thank you, Mr. Chairman.

I would like to direct a question to Ms. Shearer, if I may. The primary cost containment tool used is global budgeting in the administration's bill. It sets a limit on the total amount spent in regions, areas, States, or nations so that essentially you squeeze out the waste and the inefficiencies. That is a good idea if your estimates as to the cost of the system are accurate. You can get rid of the fat and have a more efficient system. If your estimates of the fat are too high, however, then you run your scalpel into the bone. That is what a lot of us are a little worried about.

In the July 1992 Consumer Reports that your organization published, there is an article called "Waste in Health Care Dollars." The article begins with this quote, "Of the $817 billion we will spend this year on health care, we will throw away at least $200 billion on overpriced, useless, even harmful treatments and on a bloated bureaucracy."

The article states that several leading but unidentified—at least unidentified in this article—researchers argue that 20 percent of medical procedures are unnecessary and wasteful. It appears that this 20 percent figure is from the 1980's Rand study. Since the July 1992 article, the Rand Corporation has published two additional studies in the February 10, 1993 issue of the Journal of the American Medical Association.

Mr. Chairman, with unanimous consent, I would like to place these two articles in the hearing record.

Mr. WAXMAN. Without objection.

[Testimony resumes on p. 317.]

[The articles follow:]

Original Contributions

The Appropriateness of Use of Coronary Artery Bypass Graft Surgery in New York State

Lucian L. Leape, MD; Lee H. Hilborne, MD, MPH; Rolla Edward Park, PhD; Steven J. Bernstein, MD, MPH; Caren J. Kamberg, MSPH; Marjorie Sherwood, MD; Robert H. Brook, MD, ScD

Objective.—To determine the appropriateness of use of coronary artery bypass graft surgery in New York State.

Design.—Retrospective randomized medical record review.

Setting.—Fifteen randomly selected hospitals in New York State that provide coronary artery bypass graft surgery.

Patients.—Random sample of 1338 patients undergoing isolated coronary artery bypass graft surgery in New York State in 1990.

Main Outcome Measures.—Percentage of patients who had bypass surgery for appropriate, inappropriate, or uncertain indications; operative (30-day) mortality; and complications.

Results.—Nearly 91% of the bypass operations were rated appropriate; 7%, uncertain; and 2.4%, inappropriate. This low inappropriate rate differs substantially from the 14% rate found in a previous study of patients operated on in 1979, 1980, and 1982. The difference in rates was not due to more lenient criteria but to changes in practice, the most important being that the fraction of patients receiving coronary artery bypass grafts for one- and two-vessel disease fell from 51% to 24%. Individual hospital rates of inappropriateness (0% to 5%) did not vary significantly. Rates of appropriateness also did not vary by hospital location, volume, or teaching status. Operative mortality was 2.0%; 17% of patients suffered a complication. Complication rates varied significantly among hospitals ($P<.01$) and were higher in downstate hospitals.

Conclusions.—The rates of inappropriate and uncertain use of coronary artery bypass graft surgery in New York State were very low. Rates of inappropriate use did not vary significantly among hospitals, or according to region, volume of bypass operations performed, or teaching status.

(*JAMA*. 1993;269:753-760)

AT THE REQUEST of the Cardiac Advisory Committee of the state of New York, we conducted a study of the appropriateness of use of coronary artery bypass graft (CABG) surgery, percutaneous transluminal coronary angioplasty (PTCA), and coronary angiography in New York State in 1990. New York differs from most other states in that the Department of Health has limited the number of centers where cardiac procedures are performed. Before expanding the number of centers that perform these procedures, the state wished to know how appropriately they were being used. In this article, we present a detailed description of our methods and the results for CABG. In subsequent articles in this series we present results for PTCA[1] and coronary angiography.[2]

See also pp 761, 766, and 794.

Coronary artery bypass graft surgery is one of the most commonly performed operations. For some patients with coronary atherosclerosis, it has been shown to be lifesaving,[3,4] and in many others it relieves angina.[5] However, a previous study[6] of patients operated on in three randomly selected hospitals in a western state in 1979, 1980, and 1982 showed a significant fraction (14%) of inappropriate use. Inappropriate use was defined as performing the procedure under circumstances where the medical risks exceeded the medical benefits.

Since that time, the practice of coronary revascularization has changed remarkably. Bypass surgery has become safer and medical therapy has improved. Most importantly, PTCA has emerged as an alternative method of revascularization. For all of these reasons it is appropriate to reassess whether there is still substantial overuse of coronary artery bypass surgery.

From RAND (Drs Leape, Hilborne, Park, Bernstein, and Brook, and Ms Kamberg) and Value Health Sciences Inc (Dr Sherwood), Santa Monica, Calif; Harvard School of Public Health, Boston, Mass (Dr Leape); the Departments of Medicine (Drs Hilborne and Brook) and Pathology and Laboratory Medicine (Dr Hilborne), the School of Medicine, and the School of Public Health (Dr Brook), UCLA, Los Angeles, Calif; and the Schools of Medicine and Public Health, University of Michigan, Ann Arbor (Dr Bernstein).

Reprint requests to RAND, 1700 Main St, Santa Monica, CA 90406-2398 (Dr Brook).

Assessing the appropriateness of use of any procedure for a particular clinical indication (scenario) depends on evaluating at a point in time what is known about the probabilities and values (utilities) of the possible outcomes that will occur if the procedure is or is not used. If the value of the benefits (prolonged life, relief of pain, and cure of disease) outweigh the value of the risks (operative mortality, complications, pain, and anxiety), then performing the procedure is appropriate. There are two sources of information for assessing appropriateness: outcome data and judgments of experts. Each has its strengths and weaknesses.

Assessing appropriateness by analysis of outcomes is the ideal. If complete, consistent, and generalizable evidence about the risks and benefits of applying a procedure were available for each of its possible indications, the assessment of appropriateness could be made solely on the basis of those data. There are several reasons why this is virtually never possible.

First, for any procedure, there are literally hundreds of substantially different clinical scenarios for which it might be beneficial. Outcome information is never available for all of these uses or, for that matter, for more than a small fraction of the most common indications. Second, outcome studies are often outdated by the time the results are available. The pace of technologic change is such that by the time information from even well-designed and well-executed randomized trials is available the nature of the treatment may have changed so significantly that the conclusions are not sufficient for making a decision in a specific patient. Thus, while more and better outcome data are desperately needed, it is likely that the data will always lag clinical advance and be incomplete.

Third, even current outcome data can seldom be used *as is*. Data from similar studies may conflict, the conditions under which studies are carried out and the selection of patients vary, and findings in one population may not be generalizable to another. Like all scientific data, outcome data must be evaluated and interpreted before it can be applied.

Even though outcome data are often inadequate, decisions must nevertheless be made every day by myriads of patients and physicians about whether procedures should or should not be used. The RAND/UCLA appropriateness method deals with the deficiencies of outcome data by asking experts to provide an assessment of appropriateness after they have reviewed the available information. It recognizes that physicians have a wealth of knowledge from their education and experience that enables them to make sound judgments about the validity of the outcome data as well as for situations where data are absent. It also recognizes that for a great many clinical situations a consensus does, in fact, exist.

The strengths of the appropriateness method are that it evaluates all available outcome information, it is efficient and comprehensive, and the recommendations are applicable at the time they are rendered. The weaknesses of the method are that it is limited by the available outcome data and group judgments are subjective. Because of the latter, rigorous methods must be used to structure the way in which the decisions are framed and the manner in which the judgments are rendered.

Studies of appropriateness are therefore not a substitute for outcome studies but a way to define at a point in time, using the best available data and expert methods, which services are and which are not appropriate for individual patients.

METHODS

Development of Indications and Appropriateness Criteria

Criteria for measuring appropriateness were developed by a previously described method.[7,8] First, the relevant literature published from 1971 to 1990 concerning effectiveness and risks of CABG was reviewed. A total of 670 articles were abstracted. The results of these studies were synthesized into an annotated summary of the evidence for effectiveness and risks for each of the indications for CABG. Next, based on the literature review and consultation with experts in cardiology and cardiac surgery, a set of clinical scenarios, which we call indications, was derived that encompassed all possible reasons (both appropriate and inappropriate) for performing CABG that might arise in clinical practice.

Each indication consisted of a unique combination of clinical information and other factors that are considered in recommending surgery. Each indication is specified in sufficient detail that patients within a given indication would be reasonably homogeneous, and performing bypass surgery for the indication would be equally appropriate or inappropriate for all patients with that indication. An example of a typical indication is CABG indicated within 21 days of an acute myocardial infarction in a patient who has continuing pain, a low operative risk, an ejection fraction of 15% to 35%, and in whom coronary angiography has demonstrated significant triple-vessel disease. Each term in the indication is defined in a glossary that accompanies the indications.

There were a total of 996 indications for CABG, organized into eight groups, called "chapters," according to presenting symptoms: chronic stable angina, unstable angina, during an acute myocardial infarction, within 21 days following a myocardial infarction, asymptomatic, near sudden death, complication of coronary angioplasty or angiography, and CABG performed with valve surgery. Indications were arranged within each chapter according to the extent of significant anatomic disease as revealed by coronary angiography (eg, left main, three vessel), level of operative risk, the results of an exercise stress test or thallium scan, ejection fraction, anginal class, adequacy of medical therapy, and the patient's comorbidity as assessed by our modified Parsonnet score.[9,10]

The definitions for the specific factors were developed and agreed on by the expert panel that later rated the indications for appropriateness. For example, significant arterial disease was defined by the panel as (1) a reduction in the luminal diameter of 50% or more, and (2) for all but the left main coronary artery, a reduction of at least 70% in the lumen of at least one vessel.

Panel Selection and Appropriateness Ratings

Nine expert clinicians were selected from nominations provided by the relevant specialty societies: the American College of Cardiology, American Heart Association, Society of Thoracic Surgeons, American Association for Thoracic Surgery, American College of Physicians, and American College of Surgeons. Panelists were all highly respected specialists chosen for their expertise and national influence. They represented all geographic regions of the country and both academic and private practice. They were asked to provide their personal judgments, not positions of the societies that nominated them. The panel included three cardiac surgeons, three cardiologists who performed angioplasty, one noninterventional cardiologist, and two internists. The panel was convened in November 1990.

Panelists were provided with the literature review and, after reading it, were asked to rate each indication for the appropriateness of performing CABG using their best clinical judgment and considering an average patient presenting to an average surgeon performing CABG surgery in 1990. Appropriateness was defined to mean that the expected health benefit (quality of life and/or longevity) exceeded the expected negative consequences (pain, disability, and risk of death) by a sufficient margin that the procedure was worth performing. Cost of the procedure was not considered in the appropriateness rating. Extremely appropriate indications were rated as 9, extremely inappropriate indications as 1, and those neither appropriate nor inappropriate as 5.

The ratings were confidential and took place in two rounds, using a modified Delphi process. The first round of ratings was performed at home. These results were then collated and presented to the panelists at a second round during a 2-day meeting attended by all panelists. Each panelist received the anonymous ratings of all the other panelists as well as a reminder of his own ratings. The panel reconsidered and refined the definitions of some of the factors. In addition, the panel provided ratings for additional chapters: ventricular arrhythmias, congestive heart failure, and postmyocardial infarction after 21 days. Because CABG and PTCA are often alternative treatments, each indication was rated three ways: appropriateness of CABG in a patient who is not also a candidate for PTCA, appropriateness of CABG in a patient who is a candidate for both PTCA and CABG, and appropriateness of PTCA compared with medical therapy. This required each panelist to provide nearly 3000 appropriateness ratings.

Appropriateness Scores

The final appropriateness rating was the median of the nine panelists' ratings after the second round of ratings. An indication was considered appropriate if the median rating was 7 to 9, inappropriate if the median rating was 1 to 3, and uncertain if the median rating was 4 to 6. In addition, an indication was considered uncertain if there was disagreement, regardless of the median rating. Disagreement was defined as more than two panelists' assigning a rating in both the inappropriate range (1 to 3) and the appropriate range (7 to 9). Four percent of ratings were with disagreement.

After computation of the appropriateness scores, ratings that were appropriate for either bypass or angioplasty were returned to the panelists who in a third round rated these appropriate indications for necessity, ie, was the procedure of crucial importance. An indication was defined as crucial or necessary if a panelist believed that a physician has an obligation to recommend CABG or PTCA because it is clearly the best option available to the patient. A procedure was considered crucial to the extent that all four of the following criteria were met: (1) the procedure was appropriate without disagreement, (2) it would be improper care not to provide this service for most patients, (3) the likelihood of benefit was significant, and (4) the extent of the benefit was not small. An indication was most likely to be rated as crucial when there were outcome data confirming the effectiveness of bypass surgery (such as in the treatment of left main coronary artery disease). An indication could be appropriate, ie, of benefit and preferable to the alternatives, without being crucial.

The literature review, listing of all 2990 appropriateness ratings, definitions of terms, and the final panel ratings of appropriateness and necessity have been published as a monograph[10] available from RAND, Santa Monica, Calif.

Data Collection and Sample

Using the indications, definitions, and ratings provided by the expert panel, a medical record abstraction form was created to capture the data needed to determine the appropriateness of performing CABG in the sample patients. Under the supervision of the Island Peer Review Organization, medical records were abstracted by experienced nurses trained in the use of the form. All abstracted records were reviewed by an Island Peer Review Organization nurse supervisor for completeness, accuracy, and consistency. Photocopies of the admission note, the discharge summary, and reports of stress tests, echocardiograms and other noninvasive tests, coronary angiograms, and operative notes were provided for interpretation by the physician overreader. Each abstract was then reviewed by a RAND physician who coded the results of the key tests and the angiogram. Each patient was then assigned to a specific clinical chapter (eg, chronic stable angina or unstable angina). To ensure confidentiality of information, we assigned coded identifiers to patients, hospitals, and physicians. Once the data collection process was completed, the files linking these identifiers were destroyed.

We obtained a sample of patients who had CABG surgery in 1990 in nonfederal hospitals in New York State by means of a two-step sampling process. First, we randomly selected a sample of hospitals stratified according to two characteristics, upstate or downstate location and volume of CABG operations performed in 1989. Downstate location included New York City, Long Island, and Westchester County, and upstate was the remainder. Low-volume hospitals were those that performed fewer than 325 operations. (Twenty percent of patients receiving CABGs in 1989 in New York were operated on in hospitals performing fewer than 325 CABG operations that year.) Four hospitals were excluded from the sample because the programs were new (one), temporarily suspended (one), or the volume of cases was insufficient to provide 90 cases for study (two). In each of the four strata we randomly sampled approximately equal numbers of hospitals performing CABGs. Fifteen of 30 hospitals performing CABGs were selected.

To obtain our desired sample of 90 patients per hospital, we reviewed a random selection of 1426 medical records. Fifty-five records were excluded because another major procedure was performed in conjunction with CABG or because the procedure was miscoded as CABG. Twenty records (1.4%) were not located. Of 1351 records in the final sample, 13 records (1.0%) were excluded because critical data were missing and could not be obtained from the referring physician. A total of 1338 records were abstracted for analysis. The results of the exercise stress test were frequently not in the record. For patients in whom the results of the test would affect the rating of appropriateness (predominantly patients undergoing elective CABG for single- and two-vessel disease) we requested a report from the referring physician. We obtained all but 10 of these missing reports; for these 10 patients, we assumed that the stress test had not been done or that it was not strongly positive.

Analysis

We assigned an indication to each patient based on the information abstracted from the record. In cases where more than one indication applied to a patient, we assigned the one that had the higher appropriateness score. Patients who were candidates for both CABG and PTCA and for whom the panel rated PTCA more appropriate (ie, the rating of CABG for a patient who is a PTCA candidate equals 1 to 3 without disagreement) constituted a special group. In accordance with the panel's decision, these patients were given a rating one category lower than the rating that would have applied for CABG if they had not been PTCA candidates (eg, rating of "uncertain" if the CABG rating is "appropriate" when the patient is not a candidate for PTCA).

In addition to appropriateness, we analyzed surgical mortality, which we defined as in-hospital death occurring within 30 days following operation, and major complications by hospital.

All results were population weighted according to the number of cases performed in each institution. All SEs were inflated as necessary to compensate for the design effects of the two-stage sample.[11,12] Most results are presented as a mean rate and a 95% confidence interval (CI). The CIs for rates were calculated using the normal approximation, and truncated at zero if the approximation extended below zero. Comparisons between two categories are presented as relative risks (RRs) with 95% CIs: these were calculated from bivariate logistic regression results. Differences in distribution across multiple categories were tested using the χ^2 statistic for the unweighted contingency table.

For comparisons across hospitals or between groups of hospitals, complication rates were standardized for case mix. We used indirect standardization, with the predicted hospital complication rates calculated from logistic regressions with age category, risk category (modified Parsonnet score), angiographic disease category, indications chapter, and emergency status category as independent variables.

Differences in standardized complication rates across hospitals were tested by comparing two logistic regressions, one with hospital indicator variables, one without; both regressions included the standardizing variables. Under the hypothesis of no difference among hospitals, twice the difference in log likelihood between the two equations was distributed as χ^2. Differences in standardized complication rates between groups of hospitals are presented as RRs with 95% CIs; these were calculated from the estimated coefficients of the group indicator variable in logistic regressions that also included the standardizing variables.

RESULTS

Seventy-six percent of the patients were men and 69% were less than 70 years of age. Fourteen percent of patients were 75 years of age or older, and 3% were 80 years of age or older. Three quarters of the bypass operations were performed for either left main (21%) or three-vessel (55%) disease. Four percent of patients had single-vessel disease (Table 1).

Ninety-three percent of operations were for one of three clinical chapter categories: chronic stable angina (43%), post–myocardial infarction (28%), or unstable angina (22%) (Table 2). Of the 2990 scenarios rated by the panel, 315 were actually used in this sample of 1338 patients. One patient (0.02%) failed to meet the criteria for significant disease (70% stenosis for at least one vessel [except for left main disease] and 50% stenosis for all other affected arteries). Overall, 59% of patients were in the low-risk group as judged by our modified Parsonnet score, 31% were in the moderate-risk group, and 10% were in the high-risk group. For the most common categories (chronic stable angina, unstable angina, post–myocardial infarction, and asymptomatic), the percentage of high-risk patients did not vary substantially. Six percent of CABG operations were performed as emergencies.

Nearly 91% of the bypass operations performed in these patients were rated appropriate, 7% uncertain, and 2.4% inappropriate (Table 3). Most of the appropriate cases (82% of all procedures) were also rated as crucial. The major reason for an inappropriate rating was use of CABG when, in the panel's judgment, PTCA would have been preferable. More than half of the 28 inappropriate bypass operations (61%) would have been rated as uncertain or appro-

Table 1.—Appropriateness of Coronary Artery Bypass Graft According to Anatomical Disease in 1338 Patients in New York State in 1990

			Appropriateness, %			
Location of Disease by Angiography*	No.	%	Appropriate and Crucial	Appropriate	Uncertain	Inappropriate
Left main	280	21	95	3	2	0
Three vessels	735	55	94	3	3	0
Two vessels, with PLAD†	144	11	58	25	16	1
Two vessels, other	125	9	36	24	29	11
Single vessel, with PLAD	23	2	22	39	30	9
Single vessel, other	30	2	17	21	31	31
Insignificant disease‡	1	0.02	0	0	0	100

*Minimum of 50% narrowing in all affected vessels, with 70% narrowing in at least one artery (except for left main).
†PLAD indicates proximal left anterior descending artery.
‡Angiographic findings did not meet the minimum criteria.

Table 2.—Selected Data on the Use of Coronary Artery Bypass Graft in 1338 Patients in New York State in 1990 by Clinical Indications Chapter*

	Patients			Appropriateness, %				
Indications	No.	%†	High Risk, %‡	Appropriate and Crucial	Appropriate	Uncertain	Inappropriate	Mortality, %§
Chronic stable angina	545	43 (39-48)	6 (4-9)	86 (82-89)	7 (5-9)	5 (3-7)	3 (1-4)	0.5 (0-1)
Unstable angina	309	22 (19-25)	12 (8-16)	88 (84-91)	6 (3-8)	6 (3-8)	1 (0-2)	4 (2-6)
Post–myocardial infarction								
6 h-21 d	254	18 (15-21)	10 (6-15)	81 (75-88)	5 (2-9)	11 (5-16)	2 (0-5)	1 (0-3)
22-91 d‖	141	10 (8-12)	12 (7-17)	77 (70-84)	9 (5-14)	10 (5-15)	4 (1-7)	1 (0-3)
Asymptomatic	39	3 (2-5)	16 (4-27)	31 (17-46)	48 (30-65)	16 (4-28)	5 (0-15)	0
Congestive heart failure	28	2 (2-3)	24 (4-44)	88 (74-100)	2 (0-7)	10 (0-22)	0	11 (0-23)
Complication of PTCA or coronary angiography¶	10	0.9 (0.4-1.5)	72 (42-100)	100	0	0	0	15 (0-38)
Cardiogenic shock/ acute myocardial infarction	9	0.5 (0.1-1.0)	44 (9-78)	0	100	0	0	30 (0-62)
Near sudden death	2	0.1 (0.0-0.3)	0	100	0	0	0	0
Insignificant disease	1	0.02 (0.00-0.09)	0	0	0	0	100	0
Totals	**1338**	**100**	10 (8-13)	82 (80-85)	8 (7-10)	7 (5-9)	2 (2-3)	2 (1-3)

*Numbers in parentheses are 95% confidence intervals.
†Weighted percentages do not add up to 100 due to rounding.
‡On admission as assessed by modified Parsonnet score.[7]
§30-d in-hospital mortality.
‖Patients for whom the reason for evaluation and subsequent bypass surgery was a myocardial infarction within the 22- to 91-d period. The expert panel rated these patients according to symptom (eg, chronic stable angina, unstable angina, or asymptomatic).
¶PTCA indicates percutaneous transluminal coronary angioplasty.

Table 3.—Appropriateness of Coronary Artery Bypass Graft in 1338 Patients in New York State in 1990

Category	No. (%)	95% Confidence Interval
Appropriate and crucial	1096 (82.3)	79.6-85.1
Appropriate	114 (8.3)	5.6-9.9
Uncertain	100 (7.0)	5.4-8.6
Inappropriate	28 (2.4)	1.5-3.2

Table 4.—The Most Frequently Used Indications by Appropriateness Category*

Indications	No. of Cases	Appropriateness Rating
Appropriate†		
Chronic stable angina, class I/II, treated with maximal medical therapy, three-vessel disease, ejection fraction >35%, candidate for PTCA, low risk	61	9
Post–myocardial infarction angina, 6 h-21 d, three-vessel disease, ejection fraction >35%, candidate for PTCA, low risk	60	9
Uncertain‡		
Post–myocardial infarction, 43-91 d, asymptomatic, with less than strongly positive exercise ECG, three-vessel disease, ejection fraction ≥50%, not candidate for PTCA, low risk	7	6
Post–myocardial infarction, non–Q-wave, asymptomatic, with less than strongly positive exercise ECG, three-vessel disease, ejection fraction >35%, not candidate for PTCA, moderately high risk	5	6
Inappropriate§		
Chronic stable angina, class I/II, treated with maximal medical therapy, with less than strongly positive exercise ECG, two-vessel disease without proximal left anterior descending involvement, ejection fraction >35%, candidate for PTCA, low risk	4	3
Asymptomatic, with less than strongly positive exercise ECG, two-vessel disease without proximal left anterior descending involvement, ejection fraction <50%, not candidate for PTCA, low risk	2	3

*PTCA indicates percutaneous transluminal coronary angioplasty; and ECG, electrocardiogram.
†1210 cases were rated appropriate, of which 1096 were also rated crucial.
‡100 cases.
§28 cases.

priate if PTCA had not been an available option for these patients. However, candidacy for PTCA was not a major cause of uncertain ratings. Only 3% of uncertain cases were so rated because PTCA was preferred to CABG. Uncertain ratings also seldom (4%) resulted from polar disagreement of panelists. Instead, uncertain ratings almost always (93%) reflected panel consensus that the benefits and risks were about equal. Crucial ratings also reflected a high degree of panel consensus. Of crucial cases, all nine panelists' ratings were in the 7 to 9 range for 80%, and eight of nine ratings were in the 7 to 9 range for an additional 10%. In no crucial case was there more than a single dissenting inappropriate rating.

The distribution of appropriateness did not vary substantially among the major clinical categories (Table 2) but did vary according to extent of anatomic disease (Table 1). Only 2% of operations in patients with left main disease and 3% of those in patients with three-vessel disease were rated less than appropriate, but 28% of operations in patients with two-vessel disease and 52% of operations in patients with one-vessel disease were rated less than appropriate. Patients with left main and three-vessel disease represented 76% of cases but accounted for 82% of all appropriate cases and 87% of appropriate cases that were also rated crucial. Patients with single-vessel disease comprised 4% of the sample but accounted for 39% of the inappropriate cases and 16% of the uncertain cases. The majority of uncertain cases (59%) were patients with two-vessel disease.

Inappropriate cases had several important characteristics. First, they had less severe disease. One patient did not meet the requirement of 70% stenosis in at least one vessel, and all of the remainder had either one- or two-vessel disease. None of the inappropriate cases had a stress test classified as very positive, and 11 of 28 were asymptomatic at the time of surgery. On the basis of the modified Parsonnet score, inappropriate cases were more likely to be in the high-risk category (19% vs 10% for all patients). Finally, the majority of inappropriate cases were also potential candidates for PTCA. Examples of appropriate, uncertain, and inappropriate cases are presented in Table 4.

Appropriateness did not differ significantly across age categories (P=.09), but appropriateness did vary by presenting symptoms (P=.0001), eg, operations in asymptomatic patients were more likely to be rated as uncertain or inappropriate (21%) than were those in all patients (9%) (RR, 2.8; 95% CI, 1.7 to 4.3) (Table 2).

Mortality and Complications

Operative mortality, defined as in-hospital death within 30 days of surgery, was 2.0% overall (Table 2). Operative mortality was significantly higher for patients 75 years of age and older (5.7%) compared with 1.4% in patients less than 75 years of age (RR, 4.2; 95% CI, 1.1 to 13.6). Mortality was significantly higher in patients with cardiogenic shock (30%), PTCA complications (15%), and congestive heart failure (11%) (RR for all three, 10.1; 95% CI, 3.8 to 22.9, compared with all other patients). Mortality was significantly lower for patients with chronic stable angina (0.5%) or those who were asymptomatic (0.0%) (RR for both, 0.1; 95% CI, 0.0 to 0.5).

Complications occurred in approximately 17% of patients (Table 5). Many patients with complications suffered more than one. Nearly 8% required reoperation in the immediate postoperative period, 3% because of continued bleeding or tamponade. Seven percent of patients had at least one major cardiac complication (perioperative myocardial infarction [2.3%], cardiac arrest [2.9%], arrhythmia requiring defibrillation [1.7%], or insertion of a permanent pacemaker [1.0%]). Nearly 6% of patients required prolonged ventilatory assistance, and 2% of patients suffered a cerebrovascular accident. The use of blood transfusions varied substantially among patients and among hospitals. While 33% of patients received no transfusion, 24% required transfusion of more than 3 U.

Mortality rates and the incidence of all types of complications were closely related to the operative risk as predicted by the modified Parsonnet score. Patients in the high-risk category were much more likely to die (4.5% vs 0.2%) (RR, 21; 95% CI, 5 to 74) or to have complications (32% vs 11%) (OR, 3.0; 95% CI, 2.6 to 3.5) as were patients in the low-risk category.

Interhospital Comparisons

Among hospitals the inappropriateness rate varied from 0% to 5%, and the uncertain rate varied from 3% to 15%, but neither these differences nor their combination were significant (Table 6). However, the variation in the fraction of patients rated appropriate and crucial (71% to 89%) was significant (P=.02). After adjustment for Parsonnet score, severity, age, clinical indication chapter, and emergency operation, differences in operative mortality also were not significant (P=.43) (Table 7). However, risk-adjusted complication rates varied significantly from 9% to 26% (P=.009). The number of patients requiring more than 3 U of blood also varied markedly among hospitals: 5% to 57% (P=.008). The correlations of hospital inappropriateness rates with mortality and with complication rates were small and nonsignificant (r=.01 and −.03, respectively).

Table 5.—Complications Following Bypass Surgery in 1338 Patients in 1990

Complication	No. of Patients (%)	95% Confidence Interval
Any*	249 (17.1)	13.8-20.3
Reoperation	111 (7.7)	5.7-9.7
Ventilatory assistance for >3 d	101 (5.9)	3.6-8.2
Bleeding requiring reoperation	43 (3.0)	2.1-3.9
Cardiac arrest	42 (2.9)	1.7-4.2
Acute myocardial infarction	32 (2.3)	1.5-3.1
Sternal wound infection	29 (2.1)	1.1-3.2
Cerebrovascular accident	27 (1.8)	1.0-2.5
Groin-wound infection	25 (1.7)	1.0-2.4
Arrhythmia requiring defibrillation	22 (1.7)	1.0-2.4
Insertion of permanent pacemaker	16 (1.0)	0.4-1.6
Acute renal failure	15 (1.0)	0.2-1.8

*Some patients had more than one complication.

Table 6.—Appropriateness of Performing Coronary Artery Bypass Graft Surgery by Hospital

	Appropriateness, %*			
Hospital	Appropriate and Crucial†	Appropriate	Uncertain‡	Inappropriate§
A	86	9	4	1
B	77	12	10	1
C	81	8	9	2
D	88	6	4	2
E	71	12	15	2
F	85	9	3	2
G	89	2	6	3
H	79	12	7	2
I	73	10	12	5
J	79	13	6	2
K	86	7	8	0
L	78	6	11	5
M	88	4	7	1
N	81	11	8	0
O	88	7	3	2

*Percentages may not add up to 100 due to rounding.
†P=.02.
‡P=.09 for uncertain and inappropriate combined.
§P=.67.

Table 7.—Adjusted Mortality and Complication Rates of Bypass Surgery by Hospital*

			Complications, %		
Hospital	High Risk, %†	Mortality, %‡	Any§	Cardiac‖	Transfusion >3 U, %¶
A	7	2	9	4	5
B	9	5	26	13	39
C	6	2	13	2	15
D	19	1	20	8	22
E	13	1	22	9	45
F	4	4	16	5	2
G	10	3	19	7	19
H	7	2	26	7	25
I	14	2	21	5	30
J	7	3	16	10	10
K	18	2	25	8	57
L	16	2	18	6	39
M	16	0	21	13	29
N	12	2	12	6	17
O	4	0	9	4	15

*Indirectly standardized for Parsonnet score, disease severity, age, indication chapter, and emergency status.
†As judged by modified Parsonnet score on admission. P=.004.
‡P=.77.
§P=.009.
‖P=.19.
¶P=.008.

Appropriateness did not vary significantly according to hospital CABG volume, location, or teaching status (Table 8). While the fraction of patients with high operative risk did not vary significantly between high- and low-volume hospitals, or between teaching and nonteaching hospitals, patients in upstate hospitals were less likely to be in the high-risk category than those in downstate hospitals (7% vs 12%) (RR, 0.6; 95% CI, 0.4 to 1.0). Complications were also less common in upstate hospitals (13% vs 19%) (RR, 0.7; 95% CI, 0.5 to 0.9), and patients in upstate hospitals were less likely to receive transfusion of more than 3 U of blood (14% vs 29%) (RR, 0.4; 95% CI, 0.2 to 0.6). There were no significant differences in complication rates according to volume or teaching status (Table 8).

COMMENT

This study found that in New York State in 1990 fewer than 3% of CABG operations were performed for inappropriate reasons and 7% for uncertain reasons. These results differ considerably from those reported earlier in which the inappropriate rate was 14% and the uncertain rate was 30%. There are at least four possible explanations for these differences: First, the previous study may not have been representative, ie, the 14% inappropriateness rate might have been higher than the overall rate in the United States as a whole. Second, the appropriateness ratings of the 1990 panel may have changed so that cases previously rated inappropriate would now be rated as appropriate or uncertain. Third, overall practice patterns may have changed so that fewer patients are now being operated on for inappropriate reasons. Fourth, New York State may be atypical; rates of inappropriate and uncertain use may be significantly higher in other regions of the country. All four reasons probably contributed to the differences.

It is possible that the earlier study was not representative of bypass surgery in 1979, 1980, and 1982. It was an analysis of patients treated in three hospitals in one geographic region and may not, therefore, have been generalizable to the entire country. However, it was a randomized sample of both hospitals and patients, and the fraction of inappropriate use was similar in magnitude to those found for other major procedures.[13]

Could the differences we found in rates of inappropriate and uncertain care merely reflect differences in panel ratings, not differences in practice? There are least three reasons that panel ratings might differ: First, ratings would (and should) change in response to new information from outcome studies that alter the benefit-risk ratio for certain clinical scenarios. Second, scenarios could be defined differently. Third, the 1990 expert panel might have been more lenient. The first of these did occur: outcome data published between the studies demonstrated increased benefit of CABG for a wider range of indications, such as patients with three-vessel disease without reduced left ventric. function and patients with two-vessel disease with a strongly positive stress test. The mortality of elective CABG

Table 8.—Appropriateness, Percentage of High-Risk Patients, and Adjusted Complication Rates by Selected Hospital Characteristics*

Characteristics	Volume† Low, %	High, %	Location‡ Upstate, %	Downstate, %	Teaching Hospital§ Yes, %	No, %
Appropriateness						
Appropriate and crucial	81 (76-86)	83 (79-86)	82 (79-83)	83 (78-87)	81 (77-84)	83 (79-87)
Appropriate	9 (6-11)	8 (6-10)	10 (7-13)	7 (5-9)	9 (6-11)	8 (6-10)
Uncertain	8 (6-11)	7 (3-10)	6 (4-8)	7 (5-10)	8 (6-10)	7 (4-9)
Inappropriate	2 (1-3)	2 (1-4)	2 (1-3)	3 (2-4)	3 (1-4)	2 (1-3)
High-risk patients	13 (9-16)	10 (7-13)	7‖ (5-10)	12‖ (9-15)	13 (9-18)	9 (6-11)
Complications¶	22 (17-28)	16 (13-20)	13 (9-18)	19 (16-22)	20 (16-24)	15 (11-19)

*Numbers in parentheses are 95% confidence intervals.
†Low-volume hospitals performed fewer than 325 coronary artery artery bypass grafts in 1989.
‡Downstate hospitals include those from New York City, Long Island, and Westchester County. Upstate hospitals are in the remaining regions of the state.
§Teaching hospitals are the primary university hospitals.
‖$P<.05$.
¶Indirectly standardized for Parsonnet score, disease severity, age, indication chapter, and emergency status.

also decreased during this period, overall and for patients with poor ventricular function, shifting the benefit-risk ratio for some patients.

Definitions also changed, in part to reflect changes in practice. Clinical scenarios were defined for the 1990 panel in more detail than for the previous panel, most significantly to take account of the great importance of surgical risk. The effect of these changes was to make the 1990 panel ratings more stringent: the definition of significant disease for one- and two-vessel disease required at least one vessel to be narrowed by 70% instead of 50% as in the earlier ratings; all clinical scenarios were rated at three levels of risk instead of one; the results of the stress test were more frequently included in the definition of the scenarios. Finally, the panel explicitly considered the appropriateness of CABG in the context of the availability of PTCA, which resulted in CABG being rated uncertain or inappropriate for some clinical scenarios that were previously rated appropriate. All of these changes should have made it more likely that a given case would be rated inappropriate, not less.

To test the hypothesis that the difference in results was due to changes in the panel ratings, we examined the inappropriate cases from the earlier study using the 1990 panel ratings. For the 55 inappropriate cases from the earlier study, changes in the definition of the clinical scenarios made rerating impossible for nine cases. Of the remaining 46 cases, 45 (98%) were still inappropriate when rated with 1990 ratings (modified to accept 50% narrowing as the definition of significant disease and to consider all cases as low risk). One case was rated uncertain.

A third possible explanation for the differences we found could be changes in practice. Indeed, how bypass surgery is performed has changed markedly in the decade between these two studies. But it is the development of PTCA that has had the greatest effect on patient referrals for surgery. While 7442 patients underwent CABG in our study hospitals in 1990, 6391 patients underwent PTCA in those same hospitals that year. Whereas in 1979, 1980, and 1982 we found 51% of study patients underwent CABG for one- or two-vessel disease, in New York State in 1990, it was 24%. Because virtually all of the inappropriate use in both studies was in operations performed for one- or two-vessel disease, the decrease in the number of these patients coming to surgery alone could account for half of the reduction in the rate of inappropriate CABG.

Practice patterns could also have been affected by precertification requirements of the peer review organizations. In New York State in 1990, the Island Peer Review Organization required all candidates for CABG to meet one of the following screening criteria prior to admission or undergo physician review: left main or three-vessel disease, prior myocardial infarction, an abnormal electrocardiogram, an abnormal stress test, or angina that is not well controlled by medication. Not surprisingly, all of the 28 patients in our sample who received an inappropriate rating easily met these broad and inclusive screening criteria. In fact, 91% of the patients with inappropriate ratings from the prior study also met them. It is unlikely that precertification requirements have had much effect on practice.

A fourth explanation for the difference between the two studies could be that the selection of patients for CABG in New York State is different from that in other states. There are important reasons why this could be so. For nearly 40 years the New York Cardiac Advisory Committee has exercised an oversight function that includes reviews of institutional performance of cardiac surgery, investigation of centers with suboptimal results, and periodic site visits of all centers. Under a certificate of need statute, the state Department of Health has strictly limited the number of cardiac surgical centers and has set high standards for credentialing surgeons, training of staff, necessary equipment, and minimum annual volume of open heart operations per hospital. Angioplasty is only authorized in hospitals with CABG capability.

Finally, surgeons are required to file detailed reports of all cardiac surgical procedures with the department, which annually reports risk-adjusted mortality data by hospital and, recently, also by surgeon. In addition to providing comparative information for statewide assessment, the detailed reporting procedures afford a strong incentive for each hospital to monitor its own performance. Perhaps as a result of these restrictions, the total number of CABG procedures performed (alone and with other procedures) in New York State in 1989 was 13 715,[14] or 74 per 100 000 patients, half the national rate for CABG of 148 per 100 000.[15]

Our examination of surgical complications confirms the work of others that the rate of complications varies remarkably by hospital. We did not evaluate the appropriateness of blood transfusions, but the extreme variation that we found among institutions in the use of blood transfusions mirrors the findings reported by Goodnough et al.[16] The correlation of appropriateness with the complication rate at the individual hospital level was −.03 and with operative mortality was .01, confirming earlier observations that hospitals and physicians who have the ability to achieve excellent technical results do not necessarily select their patients more appropriately. Similarly, we found no significant correlations of rates of appropriateness with location, volume, or teaching status of hospitals.

While the overall 2.4% rate of inappropriateness encompasses hospitals with individual rates that vary from 0% to 5%, these differences are not statistically significant and may well represent annual variations. The high level of appropriate and crucial use, 82% of the bypass operations performed, while exemplary, raises a concern that some patients might have been denied needed surgery. It is time to look for underuse, especially among the uninsured and in the minority communities.

The low rate of inappropriate use of CABG in New York State reflects high standards of performance by cardiac surgeons and cardiologists. These findings should reassure both patients and payers that there is very little inappropriate use of bypass operations in New York State. While these exemplary outcomes result from multiple factors, including changes in the practice of surgery that have made bypass surgery safer and more successful and the diversion of patients with less severe disease to medical treatment or to PTCA, it seems inescapable that the oversight and feedback provided by the Cardiac Advisory Committee and the Department of Health in New York State have played a major role. For this reason, our findings may not be generalizable to the country as a whole. However, they do provide evidence that physicians and regulators can work together to achieve high standards of care.

This work was supported by grants from the Commonwealth Fund, the John A. Hartford Foundation, the Morgan Guaranty Trust, the New York Community Trust, and the New York State Health Department.

The development of the appropriateness ratings was carried out as part of the Appropriateness Initiative, a joint effort with the Academic Medical Center Consortium and the American Medical Association, Chicago, Ill. We are grateful to the member institutions of the Academic Medical Center Consortium for their participation and assistance in the project.

The high level of data collection was achieved in large measure because because of the support and assistance of Frederick Parker, MD, who chaired the subcommittee of the New York State Cardiac Advisory Committee under whose auspices the study was performed. We thank John Kirklin, MD, and the members of the New York Cardiac Advisory Committee, Barbara Genovese, and Joan Keesey at RAND, Santa Monica, Calif, and Harry Feder, MPA, and Dorothy Knowlton, RN, at Island Peer Review Organization for their support and assistance during this project; and Carol Roth, RN, MPH, at Value Health Sciences Inc, Santa Monica, Calif, for invaluable assistance in abstractor training, data collection, and analysis.

We are also indebted to the members of the Coronary Artery Bypass Graft and Percutaneous Transluminal Coronary Angioplasty Panel who gave generously of their time, their knowledge, and their wisdom: Robert S. Dittus, MD, MPH; David P. Faxon, MD; Mark A. Hlatky, MD; J. Ward Kennedy, MD; Nicholas T. Kouchoukos, MD; Floyd D. Loop, MD; Alvin I. Mushlin, MD, ScM; Richard O. Russell, Jr, MD; and William S. Stoney, Jr, MD.

References

1. Hilborne LH, Leape LL, Bernstein SJ, et al. The appropriateness of use of percutaneous transluminal coronary angioplasty in New York State. *JAMA*. 1993;269:761-765.
2. Bernstein SJ, Hilborne LH, Leape LL, et al. The appropriateness of use of coronary angiography in New York State. *JAMA*. 1993;269:766-769.
3. Alderman E, Bourassa M, Cohen L, et al. Ten-year follow-up of survival and myocardial infarction in the randomized Coronary Artery Surgery Study. *Circulation*. 1990;82:1-18.
4. European Coronary Surgery Study Group. Prospective randomized study of coronary artery bypass surgery in stable angina pectoris: a progress report on survival. *Circulation*. 1982;23:67-71.
5. European Coronary Surgery Study Group. Long-term results of prospective randomized study of coronary artery bypass surgery in stable angina pectoris: European Coronary Surgery Study Group. *Lancet*. 1982;2:1173-1180.
6. Winslow CM, Kosecoff JB, Chassin M, Kanouse DE, Brook RH. The appropriateness of performing coronary artery bypass surgery. *JAMA*. 1988;260:505-509.
7. Park RE, Fink A, Brook RH, et al. Physician ratings of appropriate indications for six medical and surgical procedures. *Am J Public Health*. 1986;76:766-772.
8. Chassin MR, Park RE, Fink A, Rauchman S, Keesey J, Brook RH. *Indications for Selected Medical and Surgical Procedures: A Literature Review and Ratings of Appropriateness: Coronary Artery Bypass Surgery*. Santa Monica, Calif: RAND; 1986. Publication R-3204/2-CWF-HF-HCFA-PMT-RWJ.
9. Parsonnet V, Dean D, Bernstein AD. A method of uniform stratification of risk for evaluating the results of surgery in acquired adult heart disease. *Circulation*. 1989;79(suppl I):3-12.
10. Leape LL, Hilborne LH, Kahan JP, et al. *Coronary Artery Bypass Graft: A Literature Review and Ratings of Appropriateness and Necessity*. Santa Monica, Calif: RAND; 1991. Publication JRA-02.
11. Kish L. *Survey Sampling*. New York, NY: John Wiley & Sons Inc; 1965.
12. Cochran WG. *Sampling Techniques*. 3rd ed. New York, NY: John Wiley & Sons Inc; 1977.
13. Chassin MR, Kosecoff J, Park RE. Does inappropriate use explain geographic variations in the use of health care services? a study of three procedures. *JAMA*. 1987;258:2533-2537.
14. Office of Health Systems Management New York State Dept of Health. *Annual Report of Cardiac Diagnostic and Cardiac Surgical Centers: 1990 Summary Report*. Albany: New York State Dept of Health; 1991.
15. National Center for Health Statistics. Detailed diagnoses and procedures: National Hospital Discharge Survey, 1989. *Vital Health Stat 13*. 199_. No. 108.
16. Goodnough LT, Johnston MFM, Toy PTCY, Transfusion Medicine Academic Award Group. The variability of transfusion practice in coronary artery bypass surgery. *JAMA*. 1991;265:86-90.

The Appropriateness of Use of Percutaneous Transluminal Coronary Angioplasty in New York State

Lee H. Hilborne, MD, MPH; Lucian L. Leape, MD; Steven J. Bernstein, MD, MPH; Rolla Edward Park, PhD; Mary E. Fiske, MD; Caren J. Kamberg, MSPH; Carol Pindar Roth, RN, MPH; Robert H. Brook, MD, ScD

Objective.—To determine the appropriateness of use of percutaneous transluminal coronary angioplasty (PTCA) in New York State.

Design.—Retrospective randomized medical record.

Setting.—Fifteen randomly selected hospitals in New York State that provide PTCA.

Patients.—Random sample of 1306 patients undergoing PTCA in New York State in 1990.

Main Outcome Measures.—Percentage of patients who underwent PTCA for indications rated appropriate, uncertain, and inappropriate.

Results.—The majority of patients received PTCA for chronic stable angina, unstable angina, and in the post–myocardial infarction period (up to 3 weeks). Fifty-eight percent of PTCAs were rated appropriate; 38%, uncertain; and 4%, inappropriate. The inappropriate rate varied by hospital from 1% to 9% (P=.12); the uncertain rate, from 26% to 50% (P=.02); and the combined inappropriate and uncertain rate, from 29% to 57% (P<.001). There was no difference in appropriateness when the institutions were grouped by volume (fewer than 300 procedures annually or at least 300 procedures annually), location (upstate vs downstate), or by teaching status.

Conclusions.—Few PTCAs were performed for inappropriate indications in New York State. However, the large number of procedures performed for indications that were rated uncertain as to their net benefit requires further study and justification at both clinical and policy levels.

(*JAMA*. 1993;269:761-765)

FOLLOWING the performance of the first percutaneous transluminal coronary angioplasty (PTCA) in 1977, its use has become increasingly more common, and it is now advocated as the procedure of choice for many patients with symptomatic single- and two-vessel coronary artery disease.[1] However, the use of PTCA has been subject to less evaluation than the procedure it can replace, coronary artery bypass graft (CABG) surgery.

See also pp 753, 766, and 794.

No formal assessment of the appropriateness of use of PTCA has been performed, and randomized controlled trials comparing the efficacy of PTCA with CABG and medical therapy are still under way.[2] Nevertheless, the extent of use of PTCA in the United States approximates that of CABG.[3] Paralleling the increase in PTCA use nationally, the number of PTCA cases performed in New York State increased 105% from 1986 to 1990.[4] At the request of the New York Cardiac Advisory Committee, we performed a study that assessed the appropriateness of PTCA in New York State in 1990.

From RAND (Drs Hilborne, Leape, Bernstein, Park, Fiske, and Brook, and Ms Kamberg), Santa Monica, Calif; the Departments of Medicine (Drs Hilborne and Brook) and Pathology and Laboratory Medicine (Dr Hilborne), School of Medicine, and the School of Public Health (Dr Brook), UCLA, Los Angeles, Calif; Harvard School of Public Health, Boston, Mass (Dr Leape); the Schools of Medicine and Public Health, University of Michigan, Ann Arbor (Dr Bernstein); and Value Health Sciences Inc, Santa Monica, Calif (Ms Roth).

Reprint requests to RAND, 1700 Main St, Mail Stop 3F, Santa Monica, CA 90406-2398 (Dr Hilborne).

METHODS

The development of appropriateness and necessity ratings is detailed in the article on CABG surgery by Leape et al[5] in this issue of *JAMA*. The literature review for PTCA, including the panel ratings of appropriateness and necessity, is available from RAND, Santa Monica, Calif.[6]

Sample

We obtained a random sample of patients who underwent PTCA in 1990 from non–federal hospitals in New York State by means of a two-step sampling process. First, we selected a sample of hospitals stratified according to two characteristics: volume and geographic location (ie, upstate or downstate). The volume stratification was performed based on the annual number of CABG surgeries performed at each location; this resulted in two groups of PTCA patients, those undergoing PTCA in hospitals in which either fewer than 300 PTCAs or at least 300 PTCAs were performed per year. We randomly sampled approximately equal numbers of hospitals performing PTCA in each stratum, for a total of 15 hospitals. Second, within each hospital, we requested an average of 98 medical records (total, 1467) from a random sample of patients who

Table 1.—Demographic and Clinical Characteristics of Patients Undergoing Percutaneous Transluminal Coronary Angioplasty (PTCA) in New York State in 1990

Characteristics	% (95% Confidence Interval)
Age, y	
19-49	17 (14-20)
50-59	26 (23-29)
60-64	18 (16-19)
65-69	16 (14-17)
70-74	13 (11-16)
75-79	7 (5-9)
≥80	3 (2-5)
Female	31 (27-35)
Race	
White	91 (86-96)
Black	3 (1-5)
Hispanic	4 (1-6)
Other	2 (1-4)
Coronary artery disease risk factors	
Hypertension	51 (49-52)
Family history	50 (46-54)
Hypercholesterolemia	45 (39-50)
Smoking	28 (22-33)
Diabetes mellitus	23 (21-25)
Anatomic disease	
Left main	0.4* (0-0.9)
Three vessels	16 (12-20)
Two vessels	
With PLAD artery†	8 (6-11)
No PLAD artery	29 (25-32)
One vessel	
With PLAD artery	12 (8-17)
Not PLAD artery	34 (30-38)
Insignificant disease‡	0.2 (0-0.4)
Cardiac history§	
No myocardial infarction	
No previous revascularization	32 (28-35)
Previous PTCA	12 (8-15)
Previous CABG	4 (3-5)
Myocardial infarction	
No previous revascularization	38 (33-43)
Previous PTCA	10 (9-12)
Previous CABG	6 (4-7)

*All patients had protected left main disease (a patent bypass graft around the left main obstruction).

†PLAD (proximal left anterior descending) artery is defined as an obstruction before the first septal perforator.

‡Angiographic findings did not meet the minimum criteria established by an expert panel: a minimum of 50% narrowing in all affected vessels, with 70% narrowing in at least one artery (except for left main disease).

§CABG indicates coronary artery bypass graft; 2% (23 patients) had both a previous PTCA and a previous CABG. These categories, therefore, are not mutually exclusive.

Table 2.—Appropriateness of PTCA in 1306 Patients in New York State in 1990 by Clinical Indications Chacter*

Indication	Total No. of Patients	Appropriateness, % Crucial	Appropriate	Uncertain	Inapprop
Chronic stable angina	519	34 (30-37)	23 (18-28)	42 (37-48)	1 (0-2)
Unstable angina†	356	52 (47-56)	13 (10-16)	34 (30-38)	2 (0-3)
Acute myocardial infarction‡	32	6 (0-10)	93 (83-100)	0	1 (0-4)
Post–myocardial infarction§	308	32 (23-40)	30 (25-34)	35 (27-44)	3 (1-6)
Asymptomatic	76	0	3 (0-7)	53 (46-70)	39 (26-52)
Flash pulmonary edema	6	0	33	53	17
Near sudden death	1	100	0	0	0
Ventricular arrhythmias	2	0	0	100	0
Insignificant disease‖	5	0	0	0	100
Palliative procedure	1	0	0	0	100
Total	1306	35 (31-39)	23 (20-25)	38 (35-41)	4 (2-6)

*PTCA indicates percutaneous transluminal coronary angioplasty. Numbers in parentheses are 95% confidence intervals. Percentage totals may not add up to 100 due to rounding.

†Chest pain thought to be due to myocardial ischemia requiring hospitalization (and infarction is ruled out).

‡Within 6 h of an acute myocardial infarction with or without shock.

§From 6 h to 21 days following an acute myocardial infarction.

‖Angiographic findings did not meet the minimum criteria established by an expert panel: a minimum of 50% narrowing in all affected vessels with 70% narrowing in at least one artery (except for left main disease).

received PTCA in 1990. Seventy-five records could not be located and 60 were excluded because the procedure did not meet inclusion criteria (eg, the study was not performed during 1990 or the patient did not receive PTCA). In addition, we excluded 26 patients for whom we were unable to locate an exercise stress-test report. The final sample compromised 1306 PTCA cases.

Analysis

We assigned each patient to a unique indication (clinical scenario) based on the methods described by Leape et al.[5] We also analyzed the special situation of a "culprit" lesion for a subset of PTCA patients. In the setting of an urgent or emergent admission (eg, unstable angina or acute myocardial infarction), some patients with multivessel disease may undergo PTCA only of the culprit lesion, ie, the lesion thought to be responsible for the acute change.[7] Because, in the absence of an emergency, CABG is often preferred for patients with multivessel disease and because the panel did not address this issue, we performed a sensitivity analysis to investigate the possible effects of culprit-lesion PTCA. First, results were calculated without consideration of the culprit lesion. Second, appropriateness was assessed by considering patients who underwent urgent PTCA of the culprit lesion as if they had only single-vessel disease. For example, a post–myocardial infarction patient with triple-vessel coronary artery disease who received a single-vessel PTCA was analyzed after first placing the patient into the single-vessel–disease category (other clinical factors, such as ejection fraction and risk, were left unchanged).

Appropriateness and complication results were weighted to reflect the population of patients who underwent coronary angioplasty in New York State during 1990 and SEs were adjusted to correct for the design effects of the two-stage sampling process.[8,9]

RESULTS

Table 1 shows the demographic and clinical characteristics of the study patients. Sixty-nine percent of patients were men. Ninety-one percent were white, 3% were black, and 4% were Hispanic. The median age was 50 years, and 77% were less than 70 years old. Using our modified Parsonnet score,[5] 70% of patients were in the low-risk category, 22% were in the moderately high-risk category, and 8% were in the very high-risk category.

The majority (91%) of procedures were performed for indications falling into three clinical chapters: chronic stable angina (40%), unstable angina (27 and post–myocardial infarction (2 An additional 6% of procedures were performed on asymptomatic patients (Table 2). Eighty-three percent of PTCA procedures were performed on patients with either single-vessel or two-vessel disease. Regardless of the extent of disease, the vast majority of patients (84%) received only single-vessel PTCA. Of these, 49% were performed on the left anterior descending artery, 22% on the left circumflex artery, and 29% on the right coronary artery. Most patients (67%) had a single-lesion angioplasty. Twenty-five percent had double-lesion angioplasty and 8% received angioplasty of three or more lesions. There were 284 patients (22%) who met our criteria for culprit-lesion angioplasty (Table 3).

Angioplasty was completely successful in 88% of procedures. In accordance with conventional criteria, we defined complete success as residual luminal stenosis less than 50% for all lesions attempted. An additional 5% of patients had procedures that were partially successful (ie, less than 50% luminal stenosis for at least some of the lesions attempted). Patients with diffuse disease, long lesions, total occlusions lasting for more than 3 months, and lesions at jor bifurcations (ie, type C lesions) h been shown to have a lower success rate.[10] In our study the complete success rate for patients with any of these low success rate characteristics was 5% lower than for patients with lesions lacking any of them (83% vs 88%, $P<.01$).

Appropriateness

Thirty-five percent of procedures were performed for indications rated appropriate and crucial by our expert panel. An additional 23% of procedures were performed for appropriate indications; 38% were uncertain and 4% were performed for inappropriate indications (Table 2). Among the 496 cases rated uncertain, 58% received a median rating of uncertain, 27% received a median rating of appropriate yet CABG was preferred, and 15% were uncertain because of panelist disagreement. Similarly, for the 61 cases rated inappropriate, 92% were explicitly rated as such and 8% were rated uncertain yet CABG was preferred. There were no clinically important differences in the appropriateness rates for patients in the three major clinical chapters: chronic stable angina (57%), unstable angina (65%), and post-myocardial infarction (62%).

For patients with a culprit lesion, the sensitivity analysis shows that when a culprit lesion is considered, the percentage of these cases that are rated uncertain declines significantly (from 43% to 22%) (Table 3). Almost all of these cases became either crucial or appropriate. The percentage of PTCAs rated inappropriate did not change. The effect of this analysis on the entire sample, however, was much less: 38% of angioplasties were rated crucial; 24%, appropriate; and 34%, uncertain. The percentage of inappropriate angioplasties remained unchanged at 4%.

Examples of the most frequently occurring appropriate, uncertain, and inappropriate indications are shown in Table 4.

Table 3.—Effect of Adjusting for Culprit Lesion for the 282 Unstable Angina, Acute Myocardial Infarction, or Post–Myocardial Infarction Patients With a Culprit Lesion*

	Appropriateness, %			
	Crucial	Appropriate	Uncertain	Inappropriate
Culprit Lesion Cases				
Unstable angina† (n=145)				
Before adjustment	47 (46-53)	7 (1-13)	45 (40-50)	1 (0-3)
After adjustment	44 (35-53)	27 (21-33)	27 (21-33)	2 (0-4)
Acute myocardial infarction‡ (n=12)				
Before adjustment	16 (0-43)	84 (57-100)	0	0
After adjustment	0	100	0	0
Post–myocardial infarction§ (n=125)				
Before adjustment	16 (3-28)	40 (29-57)	44 (34-54)	0
After adjustment	54 (47-61)	27 (23-31)	18 (12-24)	1 (0-3)
All three categories (n=282)				
Before adjustment	31 (22-41)	24 (16-33)	43 (38-48)	0.6 (0-2)
After adjustment	46 (40-52)	30 (26-34)	22 (17-26)	2 (0-3)
All Cases in Each Clinical Category (Culprit and Nonculprit Lesions)				
Unstable angina, acute myocardial infarction, and post–myocardial infarction (n=696)				
Before adjustment	40 (34-47)	24 (20-28)	33 (29-37)	2 (0-5)
After adjustment	46 (40-43)	27 (23-30)	24 (19-28)	3 (0-5)
Entire sample (n=1306)				
Before adjustment	35 (31-39)	23 (20-25)	38 (35-41)	4 (2-6)
After adjustment	38 (35-42)	24 (21-27)	34 (30-37)	4 (3-6)

*Culprit lesion is defined in the "Analysis" section of the text. One patient with flash pulmonary edema and one patient with near sudden death with culprit lesions are not listed. Numbers in parentheses are 95% confidence intervals.

†Chest pain thought to be due to myocardial ischemia requiring hospitalization (and infarction is ruled out).

‡Within 6 h of an acute myocardial infarction with or without shock.

§From 6 h to 21 d following an acute myocardial infarction.

Table 4.—The Most Frequently Used Indications by Appropriateness Category

Indications	No. of Cases	Appropriateness Rating
Appropriate		
Severe chronic stable angina (class III/IV) treated with maximum medical therapy, single-vessel nonproximal left anterior descending obstruction in a patient with low risk and an ejection fraction >35%	59	8
Post–myocardial infarction, within 21 d of an acute myocardial infarction, with continuing chest pain (postinfarction angina), single-vessel nonproximal left anterior descending obstruction in a patient with low risk and an ejection fraction >35%	56	8
Uncertain		
Severe chronic stable angina (class III/IV) with pain on using maximum medical therapy, three-vessel disease in a patient with low risk and an ejection fraction >35%	32	7*
Mild to moderate chronic stable angina (class I/II) for a patient treated with less than maximal medical therapy, with single-vessel nonproximal left anterior descending obstruction, low risk, and an ejection fraction >35%	30	7†
Inappropriate		
Asymptomatic patient without a very positive exercise stress test, single-vessel nonproximal left anterior descending obstruction in a patient with low risk and an ejection fraction of ≥50%‡	14	3

*Uncertain because coronary artery bypass graft was preferred.

†Uncertain because of panel disagreement.

‡All other inappropriate indications had less than 10 occurrences each.

Mortality and Complications

The PTCA procedural mortality of 1.4% was directly related to risk as determined by the modified Parsonnet score. Among low-risk patients, 0.2% died compared with 2.3% of high-risk patients and 9.5% of those who were at very high risk ($P<.001$). Mortality was also related to patient age. Patients less than 60 years of age had a mortality rate of 0.2%; corresponding rates in older groups were 1.2% of patients aged 60 to 74 years, 4.4% of patients aged 75 to 79 years, and 14.3% of patients aged 80 years and older ($P<.001$).

Forty-six patients (3.5%) required emergency CABG surgery because of a PTCA complication. Repeat PTCA during the hospitalization secondary to vessel closure was required in an additional 2.5% of patients, and 1.9% sustained an acute myocardial infarction following PTCA but before discharge. Fifty-five patients (4.2%) required transfusion, including 20 (43%) of the 46 emergency CABG patients and 35 (2.8%) of the 1260 patients who did not require CABG. Among the non-CABG patients receiving transfusion, 26% received 1 U, 43% received 2 U, and 31% received more than 2U of blood. One patient had a cerebrovascular accident and 22 had periprocedural cardiac arrest. Three patients were returned to the catheterization laboratory because of bleeding. The PTCA complication rate was independent of whether the patient had a prior CABG. More women (13%) than men (8%) experienced a complication ($P=.004$).

Interhospital Differences

Individual hospital inappropriateness rates for PTCA ranged from 1% to 9% ($P=.12$). Institutional appropriate and crucial rates varied from 24% to 43%, appropriateness rates from 13% to 36%, and uncertain rates from 26% to 50% (Table 5). When crucial and appropriate cases were grouped and compared with the group of cases rated either uncertain or inappropriate, combined uncertain and inappropriate rates by hospital varied from 43% to 71% ($P<.001$). Severity-adjusted hospital-specific mortality varied from 0% to 5% and overall complication rates (complications include a coronary vascular event requiring CABG or repeat PTCA, acute myocardial infarction, blood loss sufficient to warrant transfusion or a return to the catheterization laboratory, cardiac arrest, wound infection, or death) ranged from 4% to 17%. These differences in mortality and complication rates were not statistically significant.

There were no significant appropriateness differences among hospitals when grouped by volume of procedures performed, location (upstate or downstate), or teaching status (Table 6).

Table 5.—Appropriateness of Performing PTCA* by Hospital (Not Adjusted for the Performance Culprit-Lesion PTCA)

	Appropriateness, %			
Hospital	Appropriate and Crucial	Appropriate	Uncertain	Inapproor
A	36	35	26	3
B	33	23	38	6
C	33	20	44	2
D	42	20	34	3
E	31	36	29	3
F	40	22	36	2
G	24	24	43	9
H	30	13	48	9
I	31	23	37	9
J	45	18	33	3
K	37	28	31	3
L	28	16	50	6
M	43	22	34	1
N	34	20	39	7
O	33	20	46	1

*PTCA indicates percutaneous transluminal coronary angioplasty. Percentages may not add up to 100 due rounding. $P=.12$ for inappropriate vs crucial/appropriate/uncertain. $P<.001$ for inappropriate/uncertain vs cruc appropriate.

Table 6.—Appropriateness, Percentage of Very High-Risk Patients, and Adjusted Complication Rates Hospital Characteristics*

	Volume, %†		Location, %‡		Teaching Hospital, §	
	Low	High	Upstate	Downstate	Yes	No
Appropriateness						
Appropriate and crucial	35 (31-39)	35 (31-40)	37 (31-42)	34 (29-40)	39 (33-45)	[illegible] (29-3
Appropriate	23 (18-28)	22 (20-25)	20 (18-23)	24 (21-27)	20 (17-23)	[illegible]-2
Uncertain	38 (31-44)	38 (35-42)	40 (35-46)	37 (34-40)	37 (32-42)	39 (35-[illegible]
Inappropriate	4 (3-6)	4 (2-6)	3 (2-4)	5 (2-7)	4 (3-5)	4 (2-6)
Very high-risk patients	8 (6-11)	7 (5-10)	7 (4-10)	8 (5-11)	9 (7-11)	7 (5-9)
Complications‖	11 (8-14)	10 (8-12)	10 (8-13)	11 (8-14)	11 (9-14)	10 (8-12)
Mortality	2 (1-2)	1 (1-3)	1 (0-2)	3 (1-4)	1 (1-2)	1 (1-2)

*Numbers in parentheses are 95% confidence intervals.
†Each low-volume hospital performed fewer than 300 percutaneous transluminal coronary angioplasties in 199
‡Downstate hospitals include those from New York City, Long Island, and Westchester County.
§Teaching hospitals are the primary acute care facility associated with a medical school.
‖Complications are indirectly standardized for the modified Parsonnet score, ejection fraction, disease sever age, indication chapter, and emergency status. Complications include a coronary vascular event requiring corona artery bypass graft or repeat percutaneous transluminal coronary angioplasty, acute myocardial infarction, blood los sufficient to warrant transfusion or a return to the catheterization laboratory, cardiac arrest, wound infection, or dea

COMMENT

This study found the rate of inappropriate use of PTCA in New York State in 1990 to be 4%. This inappropriateness rate is very close to that of inappropriate use of CABG surgery in New York State and is considerably lower than rates of inappropriate use reported in previous studies of other procedures.[11,12] However, the fraction of patients in whom the procedure was performed for uncertain indications was 38%. Most of these indications were rated uncertain because the median panel rating was within the uncertain range (ie, between 4 and 6), reflecting the panel's judgment that the benefits and risks of the procedures for these indications were about equal. The uncertain rating rarely was assigned because the expert panel was widely divided with respect to its final appropriateness ratings. Adjusting the patient classification for the presence of a culprit lesion decreased the uncertain rate slightly (from 38% to 34%).

There are a number of explanations for the high uncertain rate. The most important is the shortage of outcomes data. Because appropriateness determinations are outcomes-driven, our expert panelists frequently did not have sufficient information to make a definitive appropriateness assessment. Second, even when PTCA is successful, long-term results, particularly the high restenosis rate, have led some to question the long-term benefit of PTCA.

Third, the coronary revascularization field is rapidly changing. New catheter designs and the introduction of alternatives such as coronary atherectomy and coronary stenting alter the feasibility and outcomes of nonsurgical coronary revascularization,[13-16] continually changing the benefits and risks. Our findings of a high success rate in patients receiving PTCA for lesions that were previously considered to have a low success rate illustrates this point.[10] While the immediate success rate in these patients was lower than those without these lesion characteristics, it is much higher than in previous reports. The increased success rate probably results from both increased experience and advancin technology. This demonstrates how im portant it is for appropriateness rating to represent current, state-of-the-ar practice, particularly for an evolving technology. Because the ratings used ir this study are evidence-based, result from randomized controlled trials currently under way might change the appropriateness ratings of some of the clinical scenarios (indications). It is essential that these results be incorporated into updated ratings promptly.

This study had three limitations. First, our findings suggest that PTCA, like coronary angiography[17] and CA[illegible] is rarely used inappropriately in Ne[illegible] ork State. These findings, however, may not be generalizable to other states or to the United States as a whole because New York State limits the number of facilities and physicians performing PTCA to 31 centers. Second, we have no information concerning the validity of coronary angiogram interpretations. Because the angiographic extent of disease is essential for determining appropriateness, if there is systematic overreading of angiograms, the extent of inappropriate use could be substantially higher. We have no evidence that overinterpretation is prevalent or reason to suspect that it occurs; however, we are investigating the validity of angiographic interpretation. Finally, our panel did not expressly address use of culprit-lesion angioplasty. Considering culprit-lesion PTCA as if it were performed for single-vessel disease reduces the uncertainty rate and increases the appropriateness rate. If the panel had considered culprit-lesion angioplasty explicitly, their ratings may have been different. Our sensitivity analysis, however, suggests that separate culprit-lesion ratings would have had a minimal effect on our conclusions.

How should these ratings of appropriateness by applied? One logical application is as a source document for the development of clinical practice guidelines to assist clinicians and patients with difficult clinical decisions. These appropriateness criteria are developed by an expert panel considering the average patient presenting to the average physician performing PTCA in the average hospital. In individual patients, extenuating clinical circumstances may necessitate special interpretations of appropriateness ratings. Nevertheless, these ratings can be used as a place to begin a discussion with a patient. Quality assurance and utilization review programs should only use these ratings as a screen to identify cases for individualized professional review. Irrespective of their use, to be of value these ratings must be regularly updated as new information becomes available. Updating should occur at least every 2 years and whenever data from randomized trials are released.

The high rate of use of this procedure for uncertain indications (38%) and the variation by hospital also should be addressed. At the very least, patients considering undergoing PTCA for clinical scenarios rated uncertain should be fully informed that with the current state of scientific knowledge the benefits of the procedure when used for these indications are about equal to its risks. For uncertain scenarios it would be reasonable to require practitioners to report outcomes data as a condition of reimbursement so that ultimately the value of the procedure for these clinical scenarios could be established. Health policy analysts and the public as a whole may also wish to consider whether it is in the interest of society to use limited public funds to pay for procedures rated uncertain before making procedures that are crucial and/or appropriate more available to patients who are uninsured or underinsured.

This work was supported by grants from the Commonwealth Fund, Morgan Guaranty Trust, and the New York Community Trust.

We thank Frederick Parker, MD, and the members of the New York Cardiac Advisory Committee for their support and advice during this project. We are indebted to Joan Keesey, Barbara Genovese, Marjorie Sherwood, MD, Amar Iqbal, MD, and Jacqueline Kosecoff, PhD, for their assistance in abstractor training, data analysis, and project coordination. We also thank Harry Feder, MPA, and Dorothy Knowlton, RN, of Island Peer Review Organization, without whom this work could not have been completed.

We also express our deepest appreciation to the members of the Coronary Revasculiarization Appropriateness Panel for the time they devoted to reviewing the literature and providing the appropriateness and necessity ratings used in this project. Members of the panel included the following: Robert S. Dittus, MD, MPH; David P. Faxon, MD; Mark A. Hlatky, MD; J. Ward Kennedy, MD; Nicholas T. Kouchoukos, MD; Floyd D. Loop, MD; Alvin I. Mushlin, MD, ScM; Richard O. Russell, Jr, MD; and William S. Stoney, Jr, MD.

References

1. King S III. Percutaneous transluminal coronary angioplasty: the second decade. *Am J Cardiol.* 1988; 62(suppl K):2K-6K.
2. BARI, CABRI, EAST, BABRI, and RITA: coronary angioplasty on trial. *Lancet.* 1990;335:1315-1316.
3. National Center for Health Statistics. Detailed diagnoses and procedures, National Hospital Discharge Survey, 1989. *Vital Health Stat 13.* 1991;13; No. 109.
4. Office of Health Systems Management, New York State Dept of Health. *Annual Report of Cardiac Diagnostic and Cardiac Surgical Centers: 1990 Summary Report.* Albany: New York Dept of Health; 1991.
5. Leape LL, Hilborne LH, Park RE, et al. The appropriateness of use of coronary artery bypass graft surgery in New York State. *JAMA.* 1993; 269:753-760.
6. Hilborne LH, Leape LL, Kahan JP, Park RE, Kamberg CJ, Brook RH. *Percutaneous Transluminal Coronary Angioplasty: A Literature Review and Ratings of Appropriateness and Necessity.* Santa Monica, Calif: RAND; 1991. Publication JRA-01.
7. Vacek JL, Rosamond TL, Robuck W, Kramer PH, Beauchamp GD. Prognosis of culprit lesion PTCA in acute myocardial infarction for multi versus single vessel disease. *Cathet Cardiovasc Diagn.* 1991;24:161-165.
8. Kish L. *Survey Sampling.* New York, NY: John Wiley & Sons Inc; 1965.
9. Cochran WG. *Sampling Techniques.* 3rd ed. New York, NY: John Wiley & Sons Inc; 1977.
10. Ryan TJ, Faxon DP, Gunnar RM, et al. Guidelines for percutaneous transluminal coronary angioplasty: a report of the American College of Cardiology/American Heart Association Task Force on Assessment of Diagnostic and Therapeutic Cardiovascular Procedures (Subcommittee on Percutaneous Transluminal Angioplasty). *Circulation.* 1988; 78:486-502.
11. Chassin MR, Kosecoff J, Solomon DH, Brook RH. How coronary angiography is used: clinical determinants of appropriateness. *JAMA.* 1987;258: 2543-2547.
12. Winslow CM, Kosecoff JB, Chassin M, Kanouse DE, Brook RH. The appropriateness of performing coronary artery bypass surgery. *JAMA.* 1988;260: 505-509.
13. Shapiro TA, Herrmann HC. Coronary angiography and interventional cardiology. *Curr Opin Radiol.* 1992;4:55-64.
14. Vlietstra RE. Advances in coronary interventional techniques. *Int J Cardiol.* 1991;32:175-181.
15. Anderson HV, Roubin GS, Leimbruber PP, Douglas JS Jr, King SB Jr, Gruentzig AR. Primary angiographic success rates of precutaneous transluminal coronary angioplasty. *Am J Cardiol.* 1985; 56:712-717.
16. Tuzcu EM, Simpfendorfer C, Dorosti K, et al. Changing patterns in percutaneous transluminal coronary angioplasty. *Am Heart J.* 1989;117:1374-1377.
17. Bernstein SJ, Hilborne LH, Leape LL, et al. The appropriateness of use of coronary angiography in New York State. *JAMA.* 1993;269:766-769.

The Appropriateness of Use of Coronary Angiography in New York State

Steven J. Bernstein, MD, MPH; Lee H. Hilborne, MD, MPH; Lucian L. Leape, MD; Mary E. Fiske, MD; Rolla Edward Park, PhD; Caren J. Kamberg, MSPH; Robert H. Brook, MD, ScD

Objective.—To determine the appropriateness of use of coronary angiography in New York State.

Design.—Retrospective randomized medical record review.

Setting.—Fifteen randomly selected hospitals in New York State that provide coronary angiography.

Patients.—Random sample of 1335 patients undergoing coronary angiography in New York State in 1990.

Main Outcome Measures.—Percentage of patients who underwent coronary angiography for appropriate, uncertain, or inappropriate indications.

Results.—Approximately 76% of coronary angiographies were rated appropriate; 20%, uncertain; and 4%, inappropriate. Inappropriate use did not vary significantly between the elderly (ie, patients aged 65 years and older) and nonelderly, 4.7% and 3.9%, respectively. Although the rate of inappropriate use varied from 0% to 9% among hospitals, the difference was not significant. Rates of appropriateness did not vary by hospital location (upstate vs downstate), volume (fewer than 750 procedures annually or at least 750 procedures annually), teaching status, or whether revascularization was available at the hospital where angiography was performed.

Conclusions.—Although coronary angiography was used for few inappropriate indications in New York State, many procedures were performed for uncertain indications in which the benefit and risk were approximately equal or unknown.

(*JAMA*. 1993;269:766-769)

IN 1989, more than 1 million Americans underwent coronary angiography, a sevenfold increase from a decade earlier.[1,2] Wide variations in the population-based use rate of this procedure within the United States[3] and between the United States and other countries[4] have led some to question how appropriately it is being used. In two previous studies, inappropriate-use rates of 17% in the elderly in the United States[5] and 17% in adults in the United Kingdom[6] have been reported. The current study evaluated the appropriateness with which coronary angiography was performed in New York State in 1990. In the two related articles in this series,[7,8] we have reported on the appropriateness of coronary artery revascularization.

From RAND, Santa Monica, Calif (Drs Bernstein, Hilborne, Leape, Fiske, Park, and Brook, and Ms Kamberg); the Schools of Medicine and Public Health, University of Michigan, Ann Arbor (Dr Bernstein); the Departments of Medicine (Drs Hilborne and Brook) and Pathology and Laboratory Medicine (Dr Hilborne), the School of Medicine (Drs Hilborne and Brook) and the School of Public Health (Dr Brook), UCLA, Los Angeles, Calif; and Harvard School of Public Health, Boston, Mass (Dr Leape).

Reprint requests to RAND, 1700 Main St, Santa Monica, CA 90406-2398 (Dr Bernstein).

METHODS

Overview

We have previously described the methods by which we developed appropriateness ratings of possible indications (clinical scenarios) for the use of coronary angiography.[5,6] Based on a review of the medical literature, we developed a mutually exclusive and comprehensive set of 2111 possible indications for which coronary angiography might be used in 1990. The indications were grouped into 10 clinical categories corresponding to the patient's primary symptom or reason for having the procedure, such as chronic stable angina, unstable angina, or acute myocardial infarction. Using a modified Delphi technique, a nine-member expert physician panel composed of three interventional cardiologists, two noninterventional cardiologists, two cardiothoracic surgeons, one internist, and one family physician rated all possible indications.[9] The definitions and methods that the panel used are previously described.[5] The literature review and final ratings have been published as a monograph available from RAND, Santa Monica, Calif.[10]

See also pp 753, 761, and 794.

Sample

We obtained a random sample of patients who underwent coronary angiography in 1990 from nonfederal hospitals in New York State by means of a two-step sampling process. The hospitals were stratified based on three characteristics: (1) geographic location (upstate vs downstate); (2) number of coronary angiographies performed in 1989 (fewer than 750 procedures or at least 750 procedures), and (3) whether the hospital in which coronary angiography was performed was authorized to perform coronary artery bypass graft (CABG) surgery. We selected approximately equal numbers of hospitals from each stratum to yield a final sample consisting of 15 of the 56 hospitals in which coronary angiography was performed. Within each hospital, we randomly selected the medical records of 99 patients who underwent coronary angiography in 1990. Of the 1479 records selected, we located 94% (n=1387) and excluded 52 because 49 did not contain a coronary angiography (coding error), and three were incomplete.

Analytic Approach

We assigned each patient to a specific indication based on the abstracted information.[5] All results were weighted to reflect the population of patients who underwent coronary angiography in New York State during 1990.[11-13] Most results are presented as a mean rate and a 95% confidence interval (CI). Confidence intervals for rates were calculated using the normal approximation and truncated at zero if the approximation extended below zero. Logistic regression was used to compare between two categories (eg, elderly and nonelderly). Differences in distribution across multiple categories were tested using the χ^2 statistic for unweighted contingency tables.

Table 1.—Demographic and Clinical Characteristics of 1335 Patients Undergoing Coronary Angiography in New York State in 1990

Characteristics	% (95% Confidence Interval)
Age, y	
19-49	17 (16-19)
50-59	25 (22-27)
60-64	19 (17-21)
65-74	27 (25-30)
≥75	12 (10-13)
Median	61
Women	35 (31-40)
Race	
White	78 (67-89)
Black	10 (4-15)
Hispanic	9 (2-15)
Other	4 (2-6)
Cardiac risk factors	
Hypertension	53 (50-57)
Family history	12 (8-15)
Hypercholesterolemia	41 (34-48)
Smoking	28 (25-31)
Diabetes mellitus	25 (22-27)
Cardiac history*	
Myocardial infarction	48 (43-54)
PTCA	7 (5-10)
CABG	8 (7-11)
Anatomic disease†	
Left main	8 (6-10)
Three vessels	25 (22-29)
Two vessels, with PLAD‡	6 (4-7)
Two vessels, other	13 (9-17)
Single vessel, with PLAD‡	3 (2-3)
Single vessel, other	12 (9-15)
Insignificant disease	33 (31-35)

*PTCA indicates percutaneous transluminal coronary angioplasty; and CABG, coronary artery bypass graft.

†Minimum of 50% narrowing in all affected vessels, with 70% narrowing in at least one artery for non–left main disease; for left main disease a minimum of 50% narrowing. Data are from the coronary angiogram.

‡PLAD (proximal left anterior descending) artery stenosis is defined as an obstruction before the first septal perforator.

Table 2.—Appropriateness of Use of Coronary Angiography in New York State in 1990 by C… Indications Chapter*

Indication	Patients, %	Appropriateness, % (95% Confidence Inte… Appropriate and Crucial	Appropriate	Uncertain	Inappropr…
Unstable angina†	28	88 (85-92)	0	12 (8-15)	0
Chronic stable angina	22	45 (36-54)	28 (20-36)	24 (15-33)	3 (0-5…
During an acute MI‡	18	51 (34-68)	7 (3-11)	40 (28-52)	3 (0-5…
Following unstable angina§	7	91 (85-98)	8 (1-15)	1 (0-2)	0
Following MI‖	7	64 (43-85)	13 (5-21)	10 (0-21)	13 (1-25…
Asymptomatic	4	44 (19-70)	1 (0-3)	28 (9-47)	27 (14-…
Chest pain of unknown origin	3	42 (31-52)	10 (0-25)	8 (0-16)	40 (24-5…
Following CABG	3	65 (40-90)	24 (6-42)	11 (0-28)	0
Miscellaneous¶	9	55 (45-64)	21 (15-28)	24 (17-31)	0
Total	...	64.1 (59-69)	11.5 (8-15)	20.2 (19-22)	4.2 (3-5)

*MI indicates myocardial infarction; and CABG, coronary artery bypass graft surgery. Percentages may not … up to 100 due to rounding.

†Coronary angiography performed during an admission for unstable angina.

‡This is defined as within 10 d of the onset of MI.

§This is defined as within 3 mo of hospital discharge following an episode of unstable angina.

‖This is defined as within 3 mo of an MI (but more than 10 d after its onset).

¶This category includes patients with a variety of conditions including congestive heart failure, ventricular … rhythmias, near sudden death, and valvular heart disease.

RESULTS

Demographic and Clinical Characteristics

The median age was 61 years and 12% were aged 75 years and older. Sixty-three percent were men and 71% were white. Almost half of the patients had a previous myocardial infarction while fewer than 10% had a prior percutaneous transluminal coronary angioplasty (PTCA) or CABG (Table 1). Left main coronary artery disease was found in 8% of the patients at angiography while three-vessel disease was discovered in 25%. In one third of patients, no significant coronary artery disease was found (Table 1). Almost half of all angiographies were performed in patients either with unstable angina or during an acute myocardial infarction (Table 2).

Appropriateness

Approximately 76% of coronary angiographies were considered either crucial or appropriate, 20% uncertain, and 4% inappropriate (Table 2). The rate of inappropriate use of coronary angiography was similar for elderly (ie, aged 65 years and older) and nonelderly patients, 4.7% and 3.9%, respectively. There was a significantly greater chance of patients' undergoing coronary angiography for inappropriate indications if they were asymptomatic (27% vs 1.2%; RR, 22; 95% CI, 9 to 42), if their presenting symptom was chest pain of uncertain origin (40% vs 1.2%; RR, 32; 95% CI, 19 to 47), or following a recent myocardial infarction (not performed during the myocardial infarction admission; 13% vs 1.2%; RR, 10; 95% CI, 4 to 23) compared with the overall inappropriate rate excluding these three clinical indications groups, called "chapters."

Forty percent of coronary angiographies performed in patients experiencing an acute myocardial infarction, 28% in asymptomatic patients, and 24% in patients with chronic stable angina were rated as uncertain. Twenty percent of the coronary angiographies (n=55) that were rated uncertain were so rated because of disagreement among the panelists; the other 213 angiographies had a median appropriateness rating ranging from 4 to 6 without disagreement. The most common appropriate, uncertain, and inappropriate cases are displayed in Table 3.

Interhospital Comparisons

Although the rate of inappropriate use varied from 0% to 9%, uncertain use from 13% to 31%, and crucial use from 49% to 71% among hospitals, the differences among hospitals were only significant (P=.04) between crucial and less than crucial (Table 4). We also examined whether differences in inappropriate use might exist between upstate and downstate hospitals, high- and low-volume hospitals, teaching and nonteaching institutions, and by whether PTCA and CABG were performed at the hospital where the coronary angiography was performed. There was more uncertain use in teaching hospitals, those located downstate, and those performing fewer than 750 coronary angiograph… per year, but all other differences we… not significant (Table 5).

COMMENT

This study evaluated the apropria… ness of use of coronary angiography… the state of New York. The 4.2% in… propriate rate of coronary angiograp… that we found in this study is sign… cantly less than the 17% rate … r… for 1981 for a national sample of patier… aged 65 years and older[14] (P<.0001). T… difference was also present for Ne… York State patients aged 65 years a… older. However, the proportion of el… erly patients who received angiograph… for uncertain indications was 21%, mo… than twice the 9% uncertain use ra… previously reported for 1981 (P<.000… The proportion of patients who unde… went angiography for appropriate in… cations remained unchanged at 74%.

This change in the distribution of … appropriate and uncertain use of angio… raphies in patients aged 65 years a… older from 1981 to 1990 may be due … any or all of the following: First, t… reasons patients undergo coronary a… giography have changed substantial… during the past decade. In 1990, almo… half of the coronary angiographies we… performed for two conditions: unstab… angina (28%) and acute myocardial i… farction (18%). In 1981, the figures we… 20% and 2%, respectively. Second, so… panel ratings changed over time. F… example, the use of coronary angiogr… phy in 33 patients with unexplained ca… diomegaly or congestive heart failu… (2.5%) was rated as uncertain in …0. … 1981, based on the available li… …ur… performing coronary angiography w… considered inappropriate for patien… with congestive heart failure who d…

Table 3.—The Most Frequently Used Indications by Appropriateness Category*

Indications	No. of Angiographies (%)	Appropriateness Rating
Appropriate†		
Unstable angina (not following an MI), in patients aged <75 y, during the admission for unstable angina but after the first 24 h, and pain resolves or is controlled by inpatient medical treatment	180 (13.5)	7
Unstable angina (not following an MI), in patients aged <75 y, during the admission for unstable angina but after the first 24 h, and pain persists or recurs after admission	109 (8.2)	9
Uncertain‡		
Acute MI in patients aged <75 y, between 12 h after symptom onset and discharge, if they have no strong contraindications to either thrombolytic therapy or CABG/PTCA, did not receive thrombolytic therapy, and MI is uncomplicated non–Q-wave infarction with no submaximal exercise stress test	65 (4.9)	6
Unstable angina (not following an MI) in patients aged <75 y, within 24 h of admission for unstable angina and pain resolves or is controlled by inpatient medical treatment	27 (2.02)	4
Inappropriate§		
Within 12 wk of an acute MI, in patients aged <75 y, with non–Q-wave infarction who have been discharged from initial hospitalization, have experienced no chest pain, did not undergo an exercise stress test or a stress imaging study, and either did not undergo ambulatory electrocardiographic monitoring or showed no evidence of silent ischemia on such monitoring	10 (0.75)	3
Acute uncomplicated non–Q-wave MI in patients aged >75 y, between 12 h after symptom onset and discharge, if they have no strong contraindications to either thrombolytic therapy or CABG/PTCA, did not receive thrombolytic therapy, and did not undergo a submaximal exercise stress test	6 (0.45)	3

*The total number of angiographies was 1335. MI indicates myocardial infarction; CABG, coronary artery bypass graft; and PTCA, percutaneous transluminal coronary angioplasty.
†1017 cases were rated appropriate.
‡268 cases were rated uncertain.
§50 cases were rated inappropriate.

Table 4.—Appropriateness of Use of Coronary Angiography in New York State in 1990 by Hospital*

		Appropriateness, % (95% Confidence Interval)			
Hospital	No. of Patients	Appropriate and Crucial	Appropriate	Uncertain	Inappropriate
A	90	59 (49-69)	18 (10-26)	20 (12-28)	3 (0-7)
B	90	69 (59-79)	13 (6-20)	16 (8-23)	2 (0-5)
C	89	71 (61-80)	6 (1-10)	19 (11-27)	4 (0-9)
D	90	67 (57-76)	16 (8-23)	16 (8-23)	2 (0-5)
E	88	66 (56-76)	10 (4-17)	23 (14-32)	1 (0-3)
F	89	66 (44-65)	10 (4-16)	19 (11-27)	4 (0-9)
G	90	54 (44-65)	19 (11-27)	18 (10-26)	9 (3-15)
H	88	49 (38-59)	18 (10-26)	27 (18-37)	6 (1-11)
I	90	71 (62-81)	8 (2-13)	17 (9-24)	4 (0-9)
J	90	70 (60-80)	12 (5-19)	13 (6-20)	4 (0-9)
K	89	57 (47-68)	16 (8-23)	26 (17-35)	1 (0-3)
L	88	58 (48-68)	17 (9-25)	19 (11-28)	6 (1-11)
M	86	58 (48-69)	8 (2-14)	31 (22-41)	2 (0-6)
N	89	66 (56-76)	13 (6-21)	20 (12-29)	0
O	89	66 (56-76)	10 (4-16)	18 (10-26)	6 (1-10)

*There is a significant difference among hospitals for those procedures judged crucial vs less than crucial (ie, appropriate, uncertain, or inappropriate) (P=.04). There was no significant difference for inappropriate vs other categories (P=.19) or inappropriate and uncertain vs appropriate and crucial (P=.31).

not also meet criteria based on angina.[5] Third, the regulatory environment in New York State may contribute to the lower rate of inappropriate use.

The inappropriate rate of use of coronary angiography described in this study also differs significantly from the results recently reported by Graboys et al,[15] who concluded that 50% of coronary angiographies are not indicated. Their conclusion was based on the evaluation of 168 self-selected patients who sought second opinions during a 7-year period beginning in 1981. The two studies are not comparable. First, ours was a population-based study, which used a randomized sample that was representative of all patients who underwent coronary angiography in New York State in 1990. Second, patients in the study by Graboys et al were healthier and were referred for elective angiography; 89% were either asymptomatic or had mild angina (class I or II). Fewer than one third of patients in our study were in these categories; 53% of our patients underwent coronary angiography for an acute myocardial infarction or unstable angina.

It is likely that some of the patients in the study by Graboys et al would have been classified as inappropriate by our criteria. In particular, 27% of our asymptomatic patients were judged inappropriate, but they represented only 4% of patients undergoing coronary angiography. However, since the clinical reasons used to judge a case as inappropriate are not described in sufficient detail in the article by Graboys et al, it is impossible to tell whether patients with similar clinical characteristics would be judged the same with regard to appropriateness. In contrast, our criteria, as previously mentioned,[10] are explicit and in the public domain so that clinicians can assess their face and content validity.

It is also important to consider the results of this article in relationship to the results reported in the other two articles[7,8] in this series. The appropriateness of use of these diagnostic and therapeutic cardiovascular procedures within a single state varied significantly by procedure (Table 6). For example, the crucial rate was 82% for CABG, 64% for coronary angiography, and 35% for PTCA. Conversely, the uncertain rate was 7% for CABG, 20% for coronary angiography, and 38% for PTCA. This variation was not explained by hospital location, volume of cardiovascular procedures, teaching status, or whether PTCA and CABG were performed at the hospital where the coronary angiography was performed. Thus, even within a single specialty, appropriate use of one procedure does not necessarily lead to appropriate use of another. Identifying inappropriate use requires directly assessing the appropriate use of each procedure independently since extrapolation of data from one procedure to another may lead to erroneous conclusions. This process may be justified for all expensive, frequently used, or high-risk procedures.

How might this information on the appropriateness of these three procedures be used? The answer will vary depending on who is viewing the data. Government officials under strong political pressure to reduce health care costs might authorize public funds to pay for only those procedures rated crucial, because these services must be made available to everyone enrolled in the public programs. Cardiologists, on the other hand, would feel obligated to offer their patients every possible chance to improve their health. While cardiologists might agree that none of these procedures should be offered for inappropriate indications (ie, 4% of angiographies and PTCAs and 2%

77-929 O - 94 - 11

Table 5.—Appropriateness of Use of Coronary Angiography by Hospital Characteristics*

	Volume†		Location‡		Teaching§		Attached‖	
Appropriateness	Low, %	High, %	Upstate, %	Downstate, %	Yes, %	No, %	Yes, %	[illegible]
Appropriate and crucial	58 (50-66)	65 (61-70)	64 (59-69)	64 (57-61)	64 (57-71)	64 (59-69)	65 (60-70)	[illegible]
Appropriate	14 (9-18)	11 (7-15)	13 (9-16)	11 (6-15)	10 (6-15)	13 (10-17)	11 (6-15)	14
Uncertain	25 (22-28)	19¶ (18-21)	18 (17-20)	21# (19-24)	22 (19-24)	18¶ (17-20)	20 (18-22)	20
Inappropriate	3 (1-5)	4 (3-5)	5 (4-6)	4 (3-5)	4 (3-5)	4 (4-5)	4 (3-5)	4

*Numbers in parentheses are 95% confidence intervals.
†Low-volume hospitals performed fewer than 750 coronary angiographies in 1989.
‡Downstate hospitals include those from New York City, Long Island, and Westchester County.
§Teaching hospitals are the primary acute care facility associated with a medical school.
‖Attached hospitals have the ability to perform revascularization procedures (eg, percutaneous transluminal coronary angioplasty or coronary artery bypass graft
¶$P \leq .01$.
#$P \leq .05$.

Table 6.—Appropriateness of Use of Coronary Angiography, Percutaneous Transluminal Coronary Angioplasty (PTCA), and Coronary Artery Bypass Graft ;C in New York State in 1990

		Appropriateness, % (95% Confidence Interval)			
Procedure	No. of Patients	Appropriate and Crucial	Appropriate	Uncertain	Inapproc
Coronary angiography	1335	64 (59-69)	12 (8-15)	20 (19-22)	4 (3-5
PTCA	1306	35 (31-39)	23 (20-25)	38 (35-41)	4 (2-6
CABG*	1338	82 (80-85)	8 (7-10)	7 (5-9)	2 (2-3)

*Percentages may not add up to 100 due to rounding.

of CABGs), they might feel strongly that these procedures should be made available for all other indications, if desired by the patient, and that the procedures should be paid for by the government or insurance companies.

The most important player in making this decision is, of course, the patient. Unfortunately, the patient's attitudes toward this decision are unknown. The patient may trust the physician's recommendations and want the physician to have the freedom to recommend the best treatment and have the government or insurance company pay for it. Then only inappropriate care would not be available. However, regardless of their individual preferences, patients (ie, the public) may agree that only the procedures judged appropriate (ie, 90% of CABGs, 58% of PTCAs, and 76% of coronary angiographies) would be paid for as part of a basic benefits package or subsidized by public money.

In summary, the current study described in this series of three articles was designed to examine overuse of three cardiovascular procedures. We found little evidence of inappropriate use of any of these procedures in New York State; however, a significant proportion of two of the three procedures are being performed for uncertain indications for which benefit and risk are thought to be about equal. Additional clinical research will help to define more precisely how much benefit or risk is associated with use for these indications.

What remains unanswered is whether patients who could benefit from coronary angiography, PTCA, and CABG are not receiving the procedure. Are the procedures being underused especially in underserved or minority populations? The same ratings developed in this study should be applied to patients who could benefit from these procedures but who may not be receiving them. This study of underuse will take on added importance as cost-containment pressures increase and reimbursement for physicians cha Increasing the health of the Amer public will require simultaneous elim tion of both underuse and overuse.

This work was supported by grants from Commonwealth Fund, Morgan Guaranty Trust New York Community Trust, and the […] State Department of Health.

We thank Frederick Parker, MD, and the members of the New York Cardiac Advisory Comm for their support and advice during this project also wish to thank Laurie McDonald for comp programming; Barbara Genovese, David Hac MD, Carol Roth, RN, MPH, Margorie Sherw MD, Amar Iqbal, MD, and Jacqueline Kosec PhD, for their assistance in abstractor training, analysis, and project coordination. We are grateful to Harry Feder, MPA, and Dorothy K ton, RN, of the Island Peer Review Organizatio their tireless efforts in data collection.

Finally, we express our deepest appreciatic the members of the Coronary Angiography propriateness Panel—Gottlieb Friesinger, Sidney Goldstein, MD; David Hickam, MD; Ro Jones, MD; George Kaiser, MD; Spencer King, Patrick Scanlon, MD; Joseph Scherger, MD, M and William Sheldon, MD—who contributed time, scholarship, and insight.

References

1. Gillum RF. Coronary artery bypass surgery and angiography in the United States, 1979-1983. *Am Heart J.* 1987;113:1255-1260.
2. National Center for Health Statistics. Detailed diagnoses and procedures: National Hospital Discharge Survey, 1989. *Vital Health Stat 13.* 1991;108:110.
3. Wenneker MB, Epstein AM. Racial inequalities in the use of procedures for patients with ischemic heart disease in Massachusetts. *JAMA.* 1989;261:253-257.
4. Gray D, Hampton JR, Bernstein SJ, Kosecoff JB, Brook RH. Audit of coronary angiography and bypass surgery. *Lancet.* 1990;335:1317-1320.
5. Chassin MR, Kosecoff J, Solomon DH, Brook RH. How coronary angiography is used: clinical determinants of appropriateness. *JAMA.* 1987;258:18:2543-2547.
6. Bernstein SJ, Kosecoff J, Gray D, Hampton JR, Brook RH. The appropriateness of the use of cardiovascular procedures: British versus US perspectives. *Int J Technol Assess Health Care.* In press.
7. Hilborne LH, Leape LL, Bernstein SJ, et al. The appropriateness of use of percutaneous transluminal coronary angioplasty in New York State. *JAMA.* 1993;269:761-765.
8. Leape LL, Hilborne LH, Bernstein SJ, et al. The appropriateness of use of coronary artery bypass graft surgery in New York State. *JAMA.* 1993;269:753-760.
9. Park RE, Fink A, Brook RH, et al. Physicians ratings of appropriate indications for six medical and surgical procedures. *Am J Public Health.* 1986;76:766-772.
10. Bernstein SJ, Laouri M, Hilborne LH, et al. *Coronary Angiography: A Literature Review and Ratings of Appropriateness and Necessity.* Santa Monica, Calif: RAND; 1992. Publication JRA-
11. Kish L. *Survey Sampling.* New York, NY: J Wiley & Sons Inc; 1965.
12. Cochran WG. *Sampling Techniques.* 3rd New York, NY: John Wiley & Sons Inc; 1977.
13. Huber PJ. The behavior of maximum likeli estimates under non-standard conditions. In: P *ceedings of the Fifth Berkeley Symposium on Ma ematical Statistics and Probability.* Berkeley: U versity of California Press; 1967;1:221-233.
14. Chassin MR, Kosecoff J, Park RE, et al. Do inappropriate use explain geographic variations the use of health care services? a study of thr procedures. *JAMA.* 1987;258:2533-2537.
15. Graboys TB, Biegelsen B, Lamper […] CM, Lown B. Results of a second-opinion […] patients recommended for coronary angiograp *JAMA.* 1992;268:2537-2540.

Mr. GREENWOOD. The first is entitled "The Appropriateness of the Use of Coronary Artery Bypass Surgery in New York State." This study found that only 2.4 percent of the bypass operations were inappropriate. The study's conclusion is: "The rate of inappropriate, uncertain use of coronary artery bypass graft in New York State were very low. Rates of inappropriate use did not vary significantly among hospitals or according to region, volume of bypass operations performed, or teaching status."

The second article is entitled "The Appropriate Use of Percutaneous Transluminal Angioblasty in New York State." In this study 4 percent were found inappropriate. The authors concluded: "Few percutaneous transluminal angioblasties were performed for inappropriate indications in New York State."

So for these two procedures, at least, leading medical researchers have determined the rate of inappropriateness is between 2 percent and 4 percent, not 20 percent the figure that seems to be tossed around.

If I were to generalize the 2 percent level of inappropriateness to all of the thousands of medical procedures performed by physicians, I would be committing the same error that I fear your publication did. That is, to take the figure of 20 percent inappropriateness gathered from the study and multiply it by the entire U.S. health care budget to get the $2 billion figure.

This is more than an academic debate. In Mrs. Clinton's testimony before this committee, she stated that one of the primary reasons she believed we could slow the growth of health care expenditures more than any other country in the world is that Dr. Koop told her that there are $200 billion of inappropriate services performed annually.

Would you like to comment on that?

Ms. SHEARER. I would be interested in seeing the two articles you mentioned. First of all, the 20 percent figure did not take into account the fact that GAO estimates that 10 percent of health care costs are basically fraud and abuse. So it may actually be an underestimate.

There is a recent study in California by the Medicare Advocacy Project that shows the break in coronary bypass alone at six Asian HMO's in the Los Angeles area vary by a factor of six from one HMO to another. So there are questions about whether some health programs are actually doing too many and some too few.

The study that you cite dealt with New York State. It may well be that New York State has come up with some procedures to monitor unnecessary procedures better than other States. In any case, what I would like to do is review the articles and get back to you.

Mr. GREENWOOD. I think my point in framing the question is that I would not assume the 2 percent from New York nor the 4 percent but I would caution all of us not to take any of these studies on the high end either and to assume that the rate is applicable across the country. If the doctor told you that on average people have X amount of fat between here and their bone, and therefore we are going to cut you to that point, I think you might want a little bit more detailed information.

Thank you, Mr. Chairman.

Mr. WAXMAN. Thank you, Mr. Greenwood.

Mr. Brown?

Mr. BROWN. Thank you, Mr. Chairman.

A couple of questions for Ms. Cain and Ms. Shearer. You talked in your testimony about preventive care. I think one of the best features of the President's program is he wants to finally get the country in line with really providing the kind of preventive care we should have been providing all along.

Is the proposed plan expensive enough in providing preventive care?

Ms. CAIN. We find the provisions of the basic package are very good.

Ms. SHEARER. I agree. Look at the health insurance many of us have today. Prevention is not in there. It costs me about $300 to take my kids to the doctor for a check-up. I think the Clinton proposal is a major step forward when it comes to prevention.

Mr. BROWN. The plan—I am not sure the plan reaches far enough in terms of health alliances and encouraging employer-based kinds of preventive care. How do we encourage and help the alliances, help the businesses, the number of smaller businesses that are in the health alliance, encourage them to do preventive care? How do we do better outreach?

Certainly the plan covers mammograms, covers prenatal care, immunization, all of that. How do we provide better outreach to get people to take advantage of the preventive care finally available to them?

Mr. POLLACK. Mr. Brown, one thing that I think is very important to note is that in the Clinton plan, there are financial incentives that are very different from other things that are covered in the plan for preventive care. Unlike some of the other services that are provided that are part of a deductible and have a copayment, preventive care does not require any copayments.

So one of the very important features in the Clinton bill that hopefully will be preserved is that for preventive care, there will not be a requirement of cost sharing with respect to preventive care. That in and of itself I think will be some inducement for people to seek preventive care, because they will not have the same kind of payment responsibilities they have for other kind of care.

Ms. CAIN. I think we also need an education component as well for many of the people who have unfortunately not had an opportunity to seek services until there was a crisis or emergency and went to the emergency room. There will be education needed to let people know that now they can get preventive care and it will not be, as he mentioned, a requirement of payment in full up-front.

That we can also speak to the business people in understanding, and I think they do and will, that a healthy work force is a productive work force.

Ms. BROWN. I just think also if we make it readily available and easy to obtain and if we can continue to figure out ways to incentivize our medical system to keep people well instead of treating people well once they become sick, we will have done a great thing.

Mr. BROWN. Even when we have seen prenatal care covered, not nearly enough pregnant women take advantage of it. What do we do about that?

Ms. CAIN. I think that is where the education has to be a major component, to let people know the service is available and let them know the benefits of it. It definitely has to be coupled with education.

Mr. BROWN. How do we do that?

Ms. CAIN. We can outreach. Since it will be employer mandated, we can reach those who will be employed. Through the health alliances, it is my understanding people not covered that way would be covered through the health alliances.

A major component of what they do would need to stress reaching these people and letting them know the services available, the benefits to them.

Mr. POLLACK. The health alliances, their boards, would be composed of consumers as well as employers. Hopefully, among the various functions of the health alliances would be the kind of outreach we are talking about here. Certainly the employers could try to make sure there is a program that effectively does this through the workplace and consumers can help make sure that happens through the various consumer organizations in the community.

Mr. BROWN. Thank you, Mr. Chairman.

Mr. WAXMAN. Thank you, Mr. Brown.

Mr. Slattery?

Mr. SLATTERY. I have two questions. First, I would like to hear the panel's response to this whole idea of premium caps as a way of controlling costs; from your perspective, is it workable or not?

One of the reasons I have been so skeptical to embrace the idea of global budgets is simply because I am of the opinion when the global budget is reached and if Congress has to vote on it, it will vote to raise the budget in a heartbeat. I don't see global budgets as really being an effective way of controlling costs.

Is there anybody who thinks this Congress will say no to the American public when it comes to health care expenditures by refusing to raise the cap?

We are in a different world. It is not going to happen. The Congress, the President will raise the cap if you have a global budget, when that cap is achieved. I don't think there is any question about that.

I have sort of dismissed that whole idea as a way of dealing with cost containment. Now the question I have is whether the premium cap approach is workable. I am not convinced it is workable, because my reservation has been that if the private insurance companies are out in the real world and told that they must provide a basic package of benefits at a certain price, and if they cannot make money providing that basic package of benefits at that price, then what are they going to do? They are going to hand you their keys and say, "I am out of business, we are out of here." How do we deal with that?

I am curious from your perspective how this premium cap approach is going to work to contain costs?

Mr. POLLACK. I want to first reiterate a point I made before. I think many of us on this panel are very concerned about the fast rising costs of Medicare and Medicaid and its impact on the deficit.

Mr. SLATTERY. Yes.

Mr. POLLACK. My concern—and here is where I think the premium caps have a significant relationship with what we do in Medicare and Medicaid—all too often we hear proposals that would place arbitrary limitations on the growth of Medicare and Medicaid, whatever the arbitrary limitation is.

Mr. SLATTERY. Those will not work because of the cost shifting. We know that. That is the experience we have seen.

My question, though, goes to the question of these premium caps. If we tell—put yourself in the position of being president of an insurance company, fast forward here 2 years. You are president of XYZ insurance company. The government says you have to provide these benefits to everybody that works through your front door. You say, Yes, sir. You go out and try to provide this insurance coverage to everybody at the price the government says you must offer it at.

My question to you is, when it becomes obvious to you can no longer provide all the benefits that the government tells you you must provide at the price you must provide it at, what are you going to do?

Mr. POLLACK. I guess first of all, I have more confidence that this is not in any way a draconian cap whatsoever. We are spending next to the closest country 40 percent more, or at least 35 percent more than any other country with respect to health care.

Now, a cap on premiums in and of themselves is not going to do a whole lot; but if you combine it with a variety of other measures that are included in the Clinton proposal, including efforts to change the system towards administrative simplicity, to achieve some savings there, to try to make sure we squeeze out fraud and abuse that exists today, we are moving to a system that is going to have a different set of incentives.

Today under our fee-for-service system, every incentive exists for overmedicalization. Now, it is true that we may move too far in the opposite direction. I am concerned about that.

But I think that as we move away, as we inevitably will, apparently under each of the proposals that are pending, I think that some of the tremendous amount of spending that we spend today and that would increase significantly in the future under a fee-for-service system would change rather considerably.

Now, would I say that an insurance cap premium cap has got to be sacrosanct and can't be revisited? No, I would not say that. I think it is useful to impose some kind of discipline in the system as long as it is not mindless discipline.

Mr. SLATTERY. One of the things that is troubling that I have been in this institution for 10 years now—this is my 11th year—I observed the way this place works. This place is not good at saying no to organized interest groups. People that vote, the organization struggles to say no to. I am not convinced we will have the steel to say no to a budget cap nor raising the cap on insurance premiums in the event the cap is reached, and what we have done is forced rationing of some kind through this process.

I guess my question to you all is, do you share my concern about this or do you really think these things are going to work?

Ms. CAIN. In response to your question, we do support the global budgeting concept. If nothing else, it does put light on the subject.

Currently these kinds of things take place behind closed doors. At least the process will be out in the open. Citizens will understand what is happening to them and will have an opportunity to participate with you in a dialogue as to what does and does not happen.

I believe there are other kinds of businesses like utilities that operate under a similar, if not exact same regulatory process, where certain limits are set on the amount to charge and their ability to provide the service and they still continue to do business. So there are other examples that might be comparable.

Mr. WAXMAN. Thank you, Mr. Slattery.

Mr. Hastert?

Mr. HASTERT. I want to thank the chairman.

Ms. Brown, you've talked about supporting a value-added tax or a 3 percent income tax. Did I read that correctly?

Ms. BROWN. What I said was that AARP, as part of its Health Care America, which was our health care proposal which we put out in 1992, 1991, we had two different cost funding proposals. One was a 2 percent income tax and the other was a value-added tax.

Mr. HASTERT. Is that something you polled your members, something they supported as well?

Ms. BROWN. We polled our members. They indicated if the proposal was fair to all Americans and if it contained the pieces that we felt were important, which are contained in our testimony, that Americans would be willing to pay for such a plan.

Mr. HASTERT. Do you feel the Clinton proposal, as it stands today—of course, I understand we don't know all the funding details, it has been quarantined until this plan comes to the Hill, whenever it does—do you think it is a fair plan?

Ms. BROWN. There are parts of the Clinton proposal we are comfortable with and other parts we are not comfortable with. We are obviously very uncomfortable with the numbers of dollars that are supposed to come from Medicare and Medicaid and there are other parts of it that we have indicated we are not comfortable with.

Mr. HASTERT. In other words, Medicare is basically held harmless in the proposal as far as restructuring. But on the other hand, taking the $128 billion out of Medicare, with adding two huge entitlements, a pharmaceutical benefit, and picking up retirees from business at age 55 certainly adds to that cost.

What do you think might happen if we cut Medicare funding by $128 billion on top of the $50 some billion that we have already cut in the President's tax bill, while increasing benefits? What happens to the services?

Ms. BROWN. I don't think we are saying there is no way that Medicare could be—the spending could be reduced. I think what we are saying is, we are not sure the proposal as it stands is realistic.

AARP stands ready to help in any way that we can and older Americans stand ready to participate in a plan where we do not want older Americans singled out. Right now, Medicare is a plan and a process which has the ability where it is easier to go and say we are going to reduce services there. The private sector, we cannot do that yet.

I think what we are saying is not that older Americans are unwilling to have Medicare expenses lowered; but we want to be sure that expenses are controlled for all Americans and that what occurs is fair.

Mr. HASTERT. I want to be able to clear my own mind on your position. You do not advocate then folding Medicare into the whole system; is that correct?

Ms. BROWN. We have some concerns about that.

Mr. HASTERT. What are they?

Ms. BROWN. We are concerned that it be done in such a way that it is not unfair to older Americans, as I said before. Right now, first we understood older Americans could opt into a private plan, into an alliance if they so desired and then come back. We now understand that is not true.

I think we have to wait and see what the plan really proposes. Then we will be ready to state that.

Mr. HASTERT. Mrs. Cain, Mrs. Clinton stated the President's health care plan will provide Americans with more choice than they have today. Do your members tend to agree with that, that there would be more choices than people have today when you take a whole system and vertically integrate it instead of having all the individual entrepreneurs out there?

Ms. CAIN. We believe there has to be some comprehensive reform. We are basically supportive of the ways that this plan seems to approach it. Choice was not a major issue for our members when we did our study. They felt managed care was a viable option for cost containment.

I would also like to tell you we, too, are willing to pay for reform if it included universal coverage and cost containment. We would be willing to pay through sin taxes or increased taxes, but our members were opposed to an increased value-added tax.

Mr. WAXMAN. Mr. Pallone?

Mr. PALLONE. Thank you, Mr. Chairman.

I wanted to say I was listening to what Ms. Brown said, particularly about Medicare, and that is of great concern to me, this whole idea of, you know, whether or not the cuts are disproportionate for seniors. I am very concerned about that; that, you know, we do not go after Medicare and make those cuts, and in effect seniors disproportionately pay in this whole process.

The other serious concern I have is whether or not the effect of those cuts is going to have such a negative impact that they may not be worth the trade-off of having the prescription drug coverage or the expanded home health care.

One of the concerns I really have is with regard to the long-term care element. I am just a little concerned that the seniors out there think they are getting more than they are going to get. Clearly we are not talking about custodial care. The First Lady made that clear. But at the same time, it seems very vague in terms of what kind of community-based services are really going to be available in the proposal.

When I had my town meetings, the seniors said to me, Are we going to get extra weeks of skilled nursing care? Is a personal attendant going to be paid for? For how many weeks? You cannot go in and say, We are going to give you more long-term care. They want to know specifically what.

I guess we do not have the specifics of this trade-off in terms of expanded care services versus the cuts in Medicare, as well as what does the expanded care mean.

As far as home health care, what do you see happening here? What would you like to see happen? I think that is a very important point.

Ms. BROWN. We are very concerned that the home health care element is not specific enough. We are not sure what will happen if the States run out of money. What is the risk the States run?

We see older Americans trying desperately to stay in their homes. They would like to do that. If there were a valid mechanism to enable them to do that in the plan, it would be helpful.

As far as our members are concerned, if long-term care and drugs—the drug support is not in there, the support of our members goes down dramatically. And last week we did a poll in California, and for all ages, all ages, the support of health care in America goes down dramatically if you do anything to long-term care and the drug piece of it.

Americans feel that is an important part. They want it for all of their—for everyone.

Mr. PALLONE. You also mentioned a very important point about State funding. With regard to most of these home care elements that exist now, a lot of that money is paid for by the States. I am not sure that I understand—in other words, you could have huge variations theoretically.

Ms. BROWN. Absolutely.

Mr. PALLONE. Between what one State does and another State does.

Ms. BROWN. Absolutely. This morning I was taking a walk with some of my fellow board members. One of them is from Florida. She told me there are 20,000 requests for home health care and other kinds of assistance through the area agency on aging that are absolutely unable to be tended to; and that does not include the people who walk in the door. She went because she needed something for her mother. It was unavailable. She said they are not even keeping track of people who come in the door.

Mr. PALLONE. That is the heart of the matter. Granted, I certainly believe money spent on the home health care will save us money in the long run, because we will avoid custodial care, hospital care. But these programs now are very unfunded on the State level.

I am really concerned about the level of funding that would be necessary to make these expanded programs available.

Ms. BROWN. It has to be done in a way where we can be sure that it is going to last.

Mr. POLLACK. This should not function, Mr. Pallone, like the Medicaid program functionings. What we ought to have when this is fully phased in, an understanding of the number of people in each State who have these deficiencies as activities of daily living, that the eligibility, as I understand it, in the Clinton plan is anybody who needs help with three activities of daily living would get assisted. That is the basis by which funds would be allocated to the States. Once fully implemented, all of those people should receive assistance. That is what the legislation guarantees.

Mr. PALLONE. Thank you.

Mr. WAXMAN. Thank you, Mr. Pallone.

I want to thank each of you for your testimony today. It has been an excellent job and has given us a lot to think about.

Let me announce we have a vote on the House Floor. We will take a short break to respond to that vote. We will continue on with this hearing without a break and will just keep on moving in order to complete the agenda for today. I hope we will not be interrupted too frequently with votes, but while some Members are responding to votes, others will come back and continue the hearing, and hopefully without interruption.

So we will take a very short break and then start with our next panel.

[Brief recess.]

Mr. WAXMAN. The meeting will please come to order.

Our second panel consists of representatives of health insurance organizations: Mr. Lawrence P. English is president of CIGNA Health Care and represents the Alliance for Managed Competition, a coalition of five companies that provide health insurance to more than 60 million Americans.

G. David Hurd is chairman and chief executive officer of The Principal Financial Group, testifying on behalf of the Health Insurance Association of America. Mr. Steven Tringale is senior vice president for external affairs of Blue Cross/Blue Shield of Massachusetts. He represents the National Blue Cross/Blue Shield Association.

Jack Maurer is senior vice president and chief actuary for PFL Insurance Company, testifying on behalf of the Council for Affordable Health Insurance.

We are pleased that you are with us. We would like to ask each of you to limit the oral presentation to no more than 5 minutes.

Mr. English, why don't we start with you.

STATEMENTS OF LAWRENCE P. ENGLISH, PRESIDENT, CIGNA HEALTHCARE, ON BEHALF OF ALLIANCE FOR MANAGED COMPETITION; G. DAVID HURD, CHAIRMAN, HEALTH INSURANCE ASSOCIATION OF AMERICA; STEVEN TRINGALE, SENIOR VICE PRESIDENT OF EXTERNAL AFFAIRS, BLUE CROSS AND BLUE SHIELD ASSOCIATION; AND JACK MAURER, CHIEF ACTUARY, PLF INSURANCE CO., ON BEHALF OF COUNCIL FOR AFFORDABLE HEALTH INSURANCE

Mr. ENGLISH. Thank you, Mr. Chairman.

I am Lawrence English and I am president of CIGNA Health Care representing CIGNA and the Alliance for Managed Competition, which is an internal coalition made up of Aetna, CIGNA, Met Life, Prudential and Travelers. Together these companies provide health care and insurance to more than 60 million Americans.

I wish to emphasize at the outset the fact that the alliance companies strongly support the broad goals of health care reform described by President Clinton. We are encouraged by his call for a bipartisan approach. We believe that will undoubtedly be necessary to produce a practical and beneficial change in our system.

Moreover, there are many specifics of the President's plan we believe should be supported enthusiastically. Among them are the concept of universal coverage, portability, the elimination of preexisting condition clauses, the elimination of cherry-picking underwriting practices, the use of community rating, the concept of a standard benefit plan, and malpractice reform.

These concepts are not new. We have been advocating these and other reforms for some time.

We do have some concerns regarding several of the tools the administration plans to use to achieve its goal. We are concerned about the almost exclusive reliance on central planning and regulatory control rather than a reformed marketplace. We are concerned about the proposed use of premium caps as a cost containment measure.

They will stifle competition. They will drive away the private capital that is needed to continue restructuring of the health care delivery system that is already under way and will lead to rationing.

We are also concerned with the size and the power of the health alliances. Alliances were originally conceived to be cooperatives in which individuals and small employers could freely select from a wide array of competing health plans. In the current proposal, these cooperatives have emerged as giant regulatory bodies whose staff could limit the number of health plans to be offered and would dictate the prices they could charge.

We strongly urge your consideration of the Managed Competition Act of 1993 introduced last week with broad bipartisan cosponsorship by Congressman Cooper of this committee. We believe the Managed Competition Act holds great promise to control costs and to assure universal access without the imposition of price controls, global budgets or regulatory alliances.

The market has already begun the process of transforming health care in this country in the cottage industry. It is now truly a efficient system focused on both quality and cost. Large- and medium-size employers are driving this transformation. They know full well that health care cost has impaired their competitiveness and they are getting their costs under control and maintaining quality by moving their employees into managed care programs at record rates.

Government might best proceed to encourage more market-based change by first not squaring off capital with the specter of price controls, by not creating unnecessary bureaucracy that will surely add to administrative costs and by not relying on huge health alliances to pick two or three private programs.

Second, the government should focus on those having the most trouble with our current system, small employers and individuals. Everyone would benefit from the improved security that will surely result from comprehensive insurance reform.

In addition, the creation of purchasing cooperatives designed to assist small employers and individuals gain access to the market would make the promise of security a reality. These reforms would transform today's inefficient market for small employers into one that would have intensive competitive.

We are convinced that these reforms can be achieved, but would have broad support. As a result, the President and the Congress could achieve their goal for major reform of the health care system and capital containment would be available for the restructuring of the market and the private market would continue the vital and effective process it has already begun in making managed health care cost work.

But most important of all, the American people would enjoy universal access to the best medical system in the world delivered through free, efficient, and competitive markets.

Thank you.

[The prepared statement of Mr. English follows:]

Lawrence P. English
President, CIGNA HealthCare

Representing The Alliance for Managed Competition

Madam Chairwoman and Mr. Chairman, my name is Lawrence P. English, and I am president of CIGNA HealthCare. Today, I represent both CIGNA and the *Alliance for Managed Competition, which is an informal coalition of five companies that provide health care and insurance to more than 60 million Americans.

My company, CIGNA HealthCare, is one of the nation's largest providers of managed medical and dental care services and group life and health insurance. It operates a nationwide network of 77 health and dental maintenance organizations in the United States and 109 preferred provider organizations that serve nearly 5 million members across the country. CIGNA HealthCare also is one of the largest providers of managed mental health and substance abuse programs and a leading provider of employee disability management and medical cost control services. Currently, we provide insurance coverage to more than 14 million people.

At the outset of my testimony, I would like to emphasize the fact that the Alliance companies strongly support the broad goals of health reform described by President Clinton. We welcome the bipartisan cooperation that undoubtedly will be necessary to produce practical, beneficial changes.

With that position clearly noted, I would first like to comment on how the Alliance companies view the administration's plan. Second, I would like to put in perspective the type of fundamental questions the business community is asking about health care reform. Then I would like to offer some observations on the substantial changes that already are taking place throughout the industry and on practical efforts to initiate immediate additional reform.

First, some general thoughts about the administration's proposal. We are encouraged by the President's call for a bipartisan approach. Health care represents almost 15 percent of the U.S. economy. Reforming it will be an extraordinarily complex task that will require the intellect, diligence and good will of both political parties and of the numerous private sector "for-profit" and "non-profit" institutions that engage in health care delivery. No one has all of the answers, and it would be a tragedy to see the debate surrounding this important issue dominated by partisan or ideological arguments.

There are many specifics in the President's plan we believe should be supported enthusiastically. For example, such principles as:

- universal coverage;
- portability;
- the elimination of pre-existing condition limitations and "cream skimming" and "cherry-picking" underwriting practices;
- administrative efficiency through the elimination of paperwork and claim forms,
- a standard benefit plan;
- community rating;
- the implicit emphasis on network-based delivery systems;
- the idea of purchasing cooperatives or, if you prefer, health alliances, to make markets more efficient;
- malpractice reform; and
- the objective, consistent measurement of quality and outcomes.

*AETNA, CIGNA, MET LIFE, THE PRUDENTIAL, and THE TRAVELERS

These concepts are not new to us. We have been advocating them for some time, and they form the essence of the administration's plan.

So, as I said, there is much that is encouraging. But, at the same time, we have some concerns, particularly regarding several of the tools this plan would use to achieve its goals. Our concern is that certain approaches will adversely affect our ability to achieve long term improvements while producing unintended consequences. This may be a once-in-a-lifetime opportunity for reform. Therefore, it's important to do the very best we can.

Specifically, we are concerned about the administration's almost exclusive reliance on central planning and regulatory control, rather than confidence in a reformed market place in which consumers and providers can respond to positive incentives to make wiser and more efficient health care choices.

If this proposal were to become law, we believe the new regulatory bureaucracies at both the state and federal level that would be created are excessive. New regulatory or oversight responsibility would be given to numerous existing federal agencies, while a new agency -- a National Health Board, with very broad powers -- also would be created. In addition, each of the 50 states would have at least one health alliance with powers to regulate all aspects of health care, which we believe would likely increase administrative costs. (without improving care for consumers.)

We also are concerned about the proposed use of premium caps as a cost containment measure. The proposal, as we know it, would impose rigid, centrally planned budgets that would result in sweeping price controls for a major sector of the U.S. economy. Our opinion is that such controls would have highly undesirable consequences on the delivery system of health services without delivering their goals.

From my own personal experience, I know that price controls don't work. Many knowledgeable individuals from virtually every field and persuasion have spoken to their ineffectiveness of price controls. I do not believe the government can stop clever people from evading them. Who will rule on the exceptions? Who will decide how to price a new treatment, a new technology, a new drug?

Further, it is my opinion that price controls will stifle competition. And they will drive away the private capital that is needed to continue the restructuring of the health care delivery system already underway.

Most important perhaps, it is impossible to conceive that national budgets can be met through the savings the administration envisions as a result of proposed Medicare and Medicaid cuts. Are there inefficiencies in the system? Yes, of course, there are, and they need to be eliminated. However, wringing them out will not provide sufficient funds to pay for all of the uninsured, expanded coverage for most, and add new benefits, such as pharmaceutical and long-term care for the elderly. The numbers simply aren't realistic, and they don't take into account other costly implications of the proposed changes. For example, the economic costs associated with increased coverage for retirees are immense and very difficult to forecast, as are the cost implications of the graying of America, which will generate increased use of the health care system.

Also difficult to quantify is the deterioration in quality, the delays and the outright unavailability of technology and medical procedures that are readily available today. In short, the arbitrary rationing that is sure to result from this kind of plan.

We also are very concerned with what the plan has done to the concept of purchasing cooperatives. Health Insurance Purchasing Cooperatives, HIPCs, or Alliances as they have become to be known, were originally conceived to be cooperatives in which individuals and small employers could freely select from a wide array of competing health plans at reasonable prices.

In the current proposal, these cooperatives have emerged as giant regulatory bodies -- covering more than 99 percent of all businesses and more than 80 percent of employees -- whose staff could limit the number of health plans to be offered and would dictate the prices they can charge. I am convinced that the size of these cooperatives will diminish competition, not increase it, and it will likely eliminate the incentive private employers currently have to continue to improve the health of their employees. They also are likely first steps in what eventually would become a single-payer, government-run system similar to that in Canada.

So, in summary, our view of the administration's plan is mixed. We unabashedly agree with its goals, but we have concerns about the some of the means it would employ to achieve them Resolution of these issues is not insurmountable. There are practical solutions which will not do harm to the 80-90% of our health care system that serves the vast majority of Americans well. We are committed to working with you to find those solutions.

Beyond our own perspective on reform, I've spoken with many of CIGNA HealthCare's clients and potential clients. I've heard many of the questions they have voiced about the administration's proposal. It is clear to me that, over the next several months, each company's management will be deciding which proposal works best for its respective business. The conclusions undoubtedly will vary, depending on a firm's size, employee mix and number of retirees. But the questions all are certain to ask are the following:

- o Do we want the state or federal governments or both to establish the level of health care tax -- disguised as mandated premiums -- our company and our employees will pay in the future?
- o Do we want to have a direct role in determining the health benefits available to our employees and the cost of those benefits?
- o Do we want rules and benefits to vary from state to state?
- o Do we want to transfer the management of fifteen percent of the economy to the government?
- o And finally, what will the real cost of change be to our company going forward?

Answers to these questions are essential in judging whether the proposed changes will benefit or restrict economic growth in our country.

Now, let me offer some comments on the reform efforts already occurring within the health care industry.

Large and medium-sized employers already are driving reform. They know full well that escalating health care costs have impaired their competitiveness. They wield a very big economic stick, and they are using it to get their medical costs under control and maintain the quality of care. They are moving their employees into managed care plans at a record rate. As a result, more than 41 million Americans are now enrolled in HMOs and many more are in Preferred Provider Plans, Point of Service Plans as well as other plans involving some aspects of managed care.

The record shows that this spread of managed care techniques is rapidly reducing the rate of growth in health care expenditures. In other words, responding to consumer demand. It is changing the very infrastructure of the industry: doctors are joining networks or organizing themselves, hospitals are merging, new health plans are forming and new capital is being invested -- all of which has increased competition exponentially.

Further, increased competition for this business places enormous pressure on us to enhance the quality of what we do for employers and their employees. Quality programs are proliferating. Every insurer I know of that wants to be a part of the health care system is focusing on system improvements that will strengthen service and lower administrative costs. They're moving ahead with "new world" technologies that use electronic data interchange and electronic funds transfer that will soon lead to a paperless health care system.

Even more exciting is the fact that competition is leading to innovations in medical care --innovations that improve treatment while lowering costs. For example, CIGNA HealthCare has developed more effective medical management procedures for pediatric asthma patients, improved existing biopsy procedures that aid in the diagnosis of breast cancer and initiated programs to identify and treat potential high-risk pregnancies.

All of these innovations improve the quality of treatment, from the patient's point of view, and at the same time, save millions of dollars. And, we are not alone in our innovations. Other managed care providers can cite similar innovations.

Moreover, not all of the improvement is coming from managed care providers. Employers, recognizing that lower health care cost is a competitive advantage, have initiated wellness programs aimed at keeping their employees healthy. Nutritional counseling, smoking cessation, fitness centers and well-baby programs are becoming common in the modern workplace.

The market has begun the process to transform the delivery of health care from the cottage industry it is now, with lots of inefficiencies, into a truly efficient system focused on quality and controlling costs.

Without being too presumptuous, I would like to suggest how the government might best proceed to encourage and move to a more market based system. From my perspective, government must level the playing field so that health plans compete on quality and efficiency not risk selection. We should put in place incentives so that consumer and employers will fulfill the public interest through the pursuit of their self interests. Government should not scare off capital -- as it surely will -- with the specter of price controls. Should not create unnecessary bureaucracy that will add to administrative costs. Should not limit competition by having huge bureaucratically laden alliances pick two or three favored plans. Encourage competition. Let it flourish.

I, also, very much support and urge the government to play a part in enhancing competition and reforming those portions of the market that are not working well. I believe the federal government should create a Standard Benefits Plan, which would enhance competition and simplify administration. I think it should put in place an apolitical National Health Board to define the standard benefits plan, accredit accountable health plans (AHPs) and collect outcomes data.

Perhaps most important of all, I suggest that the government should focus on those having the most trouble with our current system. The problem, simply stated, is that small employers find all too frequently that group health insurance is difficult to get or too expensive to provide for their employees. Under current practices their premium rating can be distorted by a single claim, pre-existing condition limitations can make changing carriers difficult or impossible, and administrative and marketing costs can consume a disproportionate amount of their premium relative to large employers. Individuals face the same problem and, to make matters worse, they do not get the same tax preference employers get.

Everyone would benefit from the improved security that will result from comprehensive insurance reform. Surveys clearly show that, while the overwhelming majority is happy with its health care, people are frightened by the thought that they could lose their job or that their employer will cancel their plan, and that they will be unable to find affordable health insurance.

To correct these inefficiencies, I think the President and Congress would do well to focus on insurance reforms that eliminate pre-existing condition limitations, individual risk selection, and assure portability. I suggest they also should consider the creation of, or encourage the states to create, purchasing cooperatives designed to assist small employers and individuals gain access to the market at competitive rates.

These reforms would transform today's inefficient market into one that would be intensely competitive. All -- not just a few -- health plans would have to compete in the purchasing cooperative. The benefits would be standard. Employees and individuals would have free choice, and there would be no risk selection -- competition would be based only on price and quality -- and it would be fierce.

Competition, based on consumer choice, would decide who would offer service and who would not. These cooperatives would increase access, bring down cost and improve quality. The number of uninsureds would decrease. Americans would have the security of knowing that, if they lose their jobs or change jobs, they could find affordable health insurance -- a virtual guarantee of portability. And, ultimately, the remaining uninsured could be given government vouchers or tax credits which would enable them to participate in the purchasing cooperative on an equal footing with other individuals. Eventually, Medicaid and even Medicare beneficiaries also could be brought into the cooperative, and universal coverage could be achieved without massive government intrusion.

I am convinced that these reforms could be achieved. They would have broad support, including ours. As a result, the President and Congress would achieve their goal for major reforms of the health system, capital would continue to be available for the restructuring of the market and employers would be able to continue the vital and effective progress they have already begun to make in managing health care costs and maintaining quality. But most important, the American people would enjoy greatly expanded access to quality care and the best medical system in the world, delivered through free, efficient and competitive markets.

Madam Chairwoman, Mr. Chairman, President Clinton and Mrs. Clinton have taken a brave step forward. Their goals are noble, and we heartily endorse and support them. Let us hope that in the spirit of building a bipartisan program, we can reconcile the many issues that undoubtedly will be raised in the coming discussions and bring about reform of the health care market place which will enhance competition, rationalize incentives, and promote wise decision making by providers and consumers alike. The American health care system will continue to have the best trained doctors, the most modern facilities and the best technology, equally available to all Americans.

Thank you very much.

Mrs. COLLINS [presiding]. Mr. Hurd?

STATEMENT OF G. DAVID HURD

Mr. HURD. I am Dave Hurd, CEO and chairman of The Principal Financial Group headquartered in Des Moines, Iowa. We are the fourth largest life and health insurer in the United States measured by the amount of money that customers send to us.

I am also chairman of the Health Insurance Association of America with 270 members and some 65 million people insured. The Health Insurance Association has been actively working on reform beginning in 1990. We constructed a set of initiatives to be enacted at the State level and those have progressed so that now 40 States have enacted them in whole or in part aiming at making more certain that small employers could obtain and keep coverage for their employees.

In 1992, our association constructed a vision of what we saw in the—as a possible health care future for America and I would like a copy of that vision to be part of our written statement for the record.

Mrs. COLLINS. Without objection, so ordered.

Mr. HURD. My comments are relative to the proposal that President Clinton offered, based on the working draft. We have no inside information. When the actual bill comes out, we would appreciate the opportunity to testify again.

We are very pleased that the Congress and the President are focused on health care reform and believe that focus is going to cause us to actually accomplish it. We think the President set the goals that he mentioned in his speech are important and relevant and we subscribe to them.

Within our own vision for health care reform, we see these as the fundamental point. First that we have cradle-to-grave coverage for all Americans. We believe that point is key to many of the other reforms.

Second, coverage where there is no exclusions for existing or previous illness, coverage that can't be cancelled if you get sick, coverage that goes with you if you change jobs or lose your job, coverage towards which both the employer and the employee pay. Just mandating that the employer pay is not sufficient.

We also have to mandate that the individual participate. Coverage that is subsidized for those who can't afford the premiums, coverage that provides incentives for healthy lifestyles, strong emphasis on wellness and prevention.

As Larry emphasized, coverage that very much uses managed care techniques and moves us on to further levels of sophistication in those mechanisms for controlling costs. In addition, we are for tort reform and the dissemination of price and quality data and a single claim form, an end to the cost shifts from Medicare and Medicaid to private insurers. But three things in the proposal especially we have great difficulty with and I want to comment in the brief time left.

The mandatory health alliances, we think the health alliances or purchasing groups are probably a good idea and should be tried. We would like to see them done on a voluntary basis. The States are busy creating similar alliances now and all those so far are on a voluntary basis.

As to premium caps and price controls, the insurance business over the last decade has earned less profits of less than 2 percent of premium over that time period. My mental vision of a price control environment is the claims piling up and the premiums trickling in inadequate amounts and what does the insurer do at that point.

My impression is similar to that Congressman Bliley talked through this morning, that other nations have had, not been able to hold cost increases down to the level proposed in the Clinton plan and a recent CBO report pointed out that effective limits on premium increases would affect both quantity and quality of health coverage to Americans and access to new medical technology.

Last, I would say that we are very much in favor of individual responsibility and prevention and we have a number of ideas in this area.

Thank you.

Mrs. COLLINS. Thank you.

[Testimony resumes on p. 371.]

[The prepared statement and attachment of Mr. Hurd follow:]

STATEMENT OF

G. DAVID HURD

CHAIRMAN AND CHIEF EXECUTIVE OFFICER

THE PRINCIPAL FINANCIAL GROUP

and

CHAIRMAN. HEALTH INSURANCE ASSOCIATION OF AMERICA

Good morning, Mr. Chairman, Madame Chairwoman, and Members of the Committee. My name is David Hurd and I am the Chairman and Chief Executive Officer of the Principal Financial Group, the fourth largest U.S. life insurance company ranked in premium income. I also serve as Chairman of the Health Insurance Association of America which represents approximately 270 commercial insurers covering approximately 65 million Americans, and am here on their behalf.

Chairman Waxman and Chairwoman Collins, we commend the President for coming forward with an ambitious blueprint for reform of the nation's health care delivery and financing system. With approximately 37 million Americans currently without health insurance coverage, and health care costs consuming an ever greater share of the Gross Domestic Product, there can be no question regarding the imperative for comprehensive reform.

In his speech to a Joint Session of Congress on September 22, President Clinton identified six fundamental principles on which any reform plan must be based: security, simplicity, quality, savings, choice, and responsibility. These are the same principles on which HIAA's own Vision for Reform was constructed last year. I would like to submit a copy of our Vision Statement for the record.

In communications with the Administration, Members of Congress, and the general public, HIAA has repeatedly stressed its wholehearted support for these principles, and has proposed specific means by which they can be implemented. Let me emphasize what we're for:

- "Cradle to grave" coverage for all Americans.
- No exclusions for existing or previous illness.
- Coverage cannot be canceled if you get sick.
- If you change jobs or lose your job, coverage goes with you.
- Employers and employees both pay toward coverage.
- Subsidies for those who cannot afford premiums.
- Control malpractice lawsuits and unnecessary tests.

- **Publish price and quality data.**

- **Single claim form to control paperwork.**

- **Incentives for healthy lifestyles. Emphasis on wellness and prevention.**

- **Stop shifting costs of Medicaid and Medicare to those with private insurance.**

- **Using managed care to control costs.**

While we have only reviewed the September 7, 1993 "Working Group Draft" and not actual legislative language, there are elements on which we and the Administration would seem to agree. There are, however, three particular points of disagreement with the President's plan:

- reliance on exclusive health alliances;

- use of premium caps and other price controls.

- the use of flat community rating.

HEALTH ALLIANCES

The President's plan calls for the creation of large, government-mandated purchasing pools through which everyone, except persons employed by an employer with more than 5,000 employees, must purchase insurance. The theory underlying this concept is that a large pool of purchasers will have significant market clout to bargain for low-cost health care – market clout which small employers lack today. These mandatory government alliances will be responsible for selecting which health plans will be offered and will have the power to limit the number of plans offered even if there is consumer interest in purchasing an excluded plan. This does not seem consistent with the goal of consumer choice or the goal of competition. This approach removes the employer from the equation except as a contributor toward the insurance costs of employees and their dependents. The employer becomes simply a "checkwriter" in the new system. This lessens substantially employers incentives to offer wellness programs to lower health benefit costs. The employer loses the "bargaining power" promised by the alliance because the alliance, not the employer, selects the limited number of plans to be offered.

All individuals and employers with less than 5,000 employees will be denied a key choice in the new system – they may not be allowed to retain their current insurance coverage or plan. Not all plans will be allowed to compete in the new system. What happens to those consumers who want to retain their current plan? Or purchase their coverage from an agent, who is, in essence, a benefits advisor to the employer? Below are a number of ways that the Administration's plan, according to their September 7, 1993 "Working Group Draft", will actually deny choice for millions;

- In a state which elects to establish a single-payer health care system, there will be no choices of health plan at all (page 54).

- If a plan's premium exceeds the average by 20%, it need not be offered by the health alliance even if some families want to buy it (page 60).

- An alliance may exclude a plan if the proposed premium would cause the alliance to exceed its budget target even if some families want to buy it and even if the premium difference is insignificant in amount (page 61).

- An alliance may offer no fee-for-service plan if in its judgment the plan is not viable (page 62). (How can they know it's not viable if they don't offer the plan to find out if there is sufficient interest in it? What standard is used for viability?)

- An alliance may offer only one fee-for-service plan (page 62). (There are differences in fee-for-service plans even if every physician and hospital in the community is included. These include differences in promptness of paying bills, and differences in levels of customer service and satisfaction.)

Proponents of these alliances also suggest that significant administrative savings can be realized. HIAA believes such savings have been overestimated. Certain administrative functions must be performed by the alliance. These include plan enrollment, premium collection, claims payments, and fraud detection. Under the President's plan, enrollment is handled through the alliance. Today, employers handle employee and dependent enrollment. That cost is not reflected in their insurance premiums. Most employers send premium payments directly to the insurer or health plan. Under the President's plan, the alliance will handle the enrollment of individuals, collect the employer and employee share of the premium, and forward premium payments to the plan selected by the employee. This can result in significant administrative expense for the alliance when one considers that everyone, except employees of the very largest employers in the region, must purchase coverage through the alliance.

Health alliances are untested. The states that have authorized purchasing alliances have made them voluntary. The Administration's plan forces anyone who works for a company with less than 5,000 employees, and all people with individual health insurance coverage, into the new alliance structure. In essence, that means that 80% of all Americans, roughly 200 million people [these numbers include everyone except 30 million Medicare recipients and 20 million workers and dependents whose employers would be eligible to establish Corporate Alliances. Source: "Congressional Health Care Workshops" materials dated September, 1993], will be receiving health coverage through an untested alliance system. There is no precedent for such massive change to a process so essential to the welfare of all Americans. After all, according to a June 1993 "Harvard School of Public Health" survey, 77% of Americans surveyed are pleased with their health care coverage.

The health alliance structure effectively bars the entry of new plans after the initial years. Plans not selected in the first year will be unable to compete in the region, and will not be around to bid the following year. Within a few years, only a handful of competitors will remain in each alliance area. The plans that survive may not be the most efficient and effective. Success in the early years of the alliance may depend more on a plan's ability to "sell" itself to individual consumers through media advertising, than on the quality or efficiency of the care it delivers. The plan creates a disincentive for competition that would lead to market constriction. If consumers do not like the plans offered by the alliance and are on the receiving end of poor customer service (for example, they can't get their calls to the 800 number answered) they do not have any alternative – it is the "only game in town."

One alternative to monopoly health alliances are voluntary health alliances. HIAA would favor having the government establish purchasing cooperatives or alliances on a voluntary basis. Under this system, employers and individuals would not be forced to purchase their coverage through the alliance, they would have the option of purchasing through the alliance, or maintaining their current coverage. All health plans, whether or not they participate in the health alliance, would have to play by the same rules so that neither the alliance nor plans operating outside the alliance would receive an inequitable share of risk. Insurance reforms, such as the elimination of pre-existing condition limitations, and guarantee issue of insurance, along with a risk adjustment mechanism, would be applied to plans offered both inside and outside the alliance.

If health alliances are truly more administratively efficient and better at pooling risks, then the carriers operating through the alliance will have lower premiums and will naturally gain market share. If, on the other hand, employers and individuals prefer to deal directly with an insurance company rather than a large government bureaucracy, they would have that choice. The market, not the government, should determine which is the more efficient way to insure all Americans. For instance, the State of California has set up a voluntary purchasing plan called the "Health Insurance Plan of California." This plan is administered and marketed by Employers Health Insurance Company, a subsidiary of Lincoln National, an HIAA member company. The plan was up and running on July 1, 1993, and has grown substantially. In just three months the plan has covered a total of 14,500 enrollees. Eighteen plans are offered for participants to choose from, 15 HMOs and 3 PPOs. A total of 900 employer groups, varying in size, from 5 and 50 employees each, participate. The State of California is split into 9 geographic regions. Today, two-thirds of the new groups are sold by agents. The plan receives over 2,000 calls per day for information. Other states are in various stages of setting up voluntary purchasing alliances – Florida, Washington and Minnesota, to name a few. All alliances that have been developed on a state level have voluntary, not mandatory participation.

PREMIUM CAPS AND PRICE CONTROLS

The U.S. experimented unsuccessfully with price controls in the early 1970's; we should not repeat the mistakes of the past. Price controls would entail extensive government rationing because in order to control costs you must control volume as well as prices. The Administration's proposal, after a transition period, would constrain national health care spending to increase no faster than the rate of increase in the Consumer Price Index, plus population growth. To achieve this, the plan would cap premiums charged to a weighted average premium. Limiting health insurance premiums doesn't affect rising provider charges, the increasing volume and sophistication of services provided, or continuing medical progress. In a study released last month, the Congressional Budget Office questioned the efficacy of premium controls, commenting that they would have undesirable consequences – "Effective limits on premium increases would affect both the quantity and quality of health insurance coverage available to consumers and their future access to new medical technologies."

Implementing the President's plan will require significant new capital investment, but there will be no incentive for private investment. In a price controlled/premium capped market, companies will be severely impaired in their efforts to attract capital. Capital will be needed to organize the networks of hospitals, doctors, and other providers that are the core of the new system. Capital is needed to assure that health plans have adequate reserves to cover unexpected losses and guarantee solvency. The new system will require more capital than the current system, both to cover the 37 million uninsured, and to cover the many millions of employees who will have to shift from self-insured employer plans to fully insured plans offered through the health alliance system. Most self-insured plans are not likely to have any significant reserves to offset the capital requirements. These capital requirements raise great concern about the solvency of health insurers. Over the last decade, the profit margin of the health insurance industry has averaged 1.75% (see attached chart). With that narrow margin, if the premium cap is set too low and carriers are unable to cover submitted claims, insolvencies will occur.

Premiums will be limited at the same time new and unpredictable demands are being made on health plans and insurers. Insurers will have trouble predicting their expected costs because the following factors will not be known ahead of time:

- How much care will the formerly uninsured use once they are insured?
- Whether the risk adjustment mechanism will adequately protect the plan against a greater-than-average proportion of high-cost enrollees?
- What assessments will be imposed by the various guarantee funds that will be set up to protect consumers from insolvencies?

COMMUNITY RATING

The administration's plan envisions the use of pure community rating to determine premiums, establishing separate rates to reflect family status. Community rating will increase premiums for younger, healthy workers and low-risk people who make healthy lifestyle choices, for example, non-smokers. Why should those who exercise regularly and don't smoke pay more for their coverage to subsidize those who smoke two packs per day? The young, who are least able to afford coverage and tend to use the system less end up paying more in the new system.
Regional alliance members will have to pay higher premiums to subsidize the additional costs of:

- underpayment by the government for Medicaid eligible;
- bad debts of people who don't pay their premiums (health plans cannot drop people for non-payment of premiums under the Administration's proposal);
- people who are currently enrolled in state-operated high-risk pools;
- early retirees no longer covered by their employers' plan.

As these Subcommittees are well aware, privately-insured patients pay higher prices in order to make up both for uncompensated care (the uninsured) and undercompensated care (Medicare and Medicaid). Universal coverage will all but eliminate uncompensated care, but the Administration's proposed method of financing its proposal will make Medicare underpayment much worse than it is today. We see no evidence that this effect has been taken into account in the Administration's estimates of likely premiums under its plan.

RISK ADJUSTERS

Congress, in reforming the health care system of today, will most likely need to include some method of risk adjustment, i.e., some way of matching premium revenues received by health insurers with the underlying risk of the population they are enrolling. The American Academy of Actuaries' has said that "under most reform proposals, some form of health risk adjustment will be required to allow reform strategies to work effectively." We agree. This is because all reform proposals, including HIAA's own Vision for Reform, call for open enrollment and rating restrictions of one degree or another and thereby disassociate the premium the carrier is allowed to charge from the costs the carrier expects to incur in serving a particular individual or group.

If we want insurers to compete on their ability to manage the cost of providing needed care, rather than on their ability to select the healthiest risks – and we do – then we have to make sure that the premiums insurers charge reflect only their administrative efficiency and their effectiveness in managing care; not variations in the underlying risk of the people they have enrolled.

This is what a risk adjustment mechanism is supposed to do. Whether a successful risk adjustment mechanism can be developed remains to be seen. Various methods have been proposed, but none has yet been tested for this purpose on an employed population. We have a group of actuaries looking at the problem, and they tell us that much depends on whether insurers are enrolling groups or individuals.

The difference in health care costs from individual to individual in a given year is extremely large. The variation among employer groups, even relatively small ones, is much less.

If individuals get to pick, as individuals, which health plan they want, their knowledge of their underlying health situation is likely to influence their choice of plan. Somebody with 2 or 3 chronic conditions, for example, is more likely to choose a conventional fee-for-service plan, to guarantee that they will be able to see all the specialists they have already established relationships with. Somebody with few health problems is more likely to choose a plan with a limited network of providers, especially if it's less expensive. This leads to a situation in which plans that offer greater choice of provider tend to get sicker enrollees than the average.

Theoretically, an effective risk adjustment mechanism would adjust for this biased selection. As a practical matter, however, our actuaries tell us that no system capable of adjusting for this kind of systematic biased selection has yet been developed and tested. Significant further research will be needed. HIAA research staff is working with member company actuaries to conduct the initial research and test models that would be applicable on an interim basis.

On the other hand, the risk characteristics of employer groups are better known and can be estimated with readily available demographic data. Until a better risk adjuster can be developed and demonstrated, our actuaries believe an interim mechanism can be implemented based on information that is currently available to carriers. The mechanism would adjust for differences in geography, family type, age, gender and industry to the extent these characteristics are reflected in their premium rates. The mechanism would also include a mandatory reinsurance pool for spreading the cost of a limited number of high-cost, nondiscretionary conditions among all carriers and insureds. A critical point is that this interim mechanism will work adequately only if insurers are enrolling employment-based groups of individuals. The mechanism is not sufficient to adjust for the biased selection that is likely to occur if individuals choose their own health plans. This is one reason why we think mandatory health alliances with individual choice of health plan are not viable.

COST CONTAINMENT

Fraud and Abuse

Each year we lose 10% of our total health care expenditures to fraud and abuse. That translates into an annual loss of nearly $80 billion. If we stopped payment on $80 billion in fraud, we could provide more than $2,000 in health insurance to every American who currently has no coverage. Health care fraud does not just waste precious resources, in many cases it subjects patients to unnecessary treatments or therapies.

Health care fraud involves a variety of activities. Most commonly, fraud involves billing for services that were never provided. Another frequent type of fraud is falsification of diagnoses or dates of services. Health care fraud is difficult to detect and prosecute. The current environment within which the health care industry must operate contributes to difficulty in detection. Payers are expected to pay claims quickly – fast claims payment is counter to the time-consuming nature of fraud investigations. Information sharing among payers is problematic. If insurers share information, they are vulnerable to the risk posed by provider lawsuits for defamation of character (state tort liability).

In July, the HIAA released a survey of 79 of its member companies, representing 65% of the commercial market, on anti-fraud programs. The total tracked savings in 1992 was $112 million, an increase of more than 150% in the last two years.

HIAA is very pleased with President Clinton's plan to combat fraud and abuse in health care. The parts of the plan that we especially like are: the new statutes which help combat fraud; the strengthening of federal penalties for wrongdoers; the anti-fraud standards for electronic media claims; and the increases in funding for government enforcement against fraud.

Administrative Simplification

Electronic data interchange (EDI), most commonly called a "paperless claims system" can directly improve information exchange in the health care industry. The benefits include efficient communication, improved patient care, and lower administrative costs. As the insurance industry has evolved and become more responsive to competition and the need to reduce costs, EDI usage has increased. Health care providers are at various stages of automation. Approximately one-third of U.S. physicians have the capability to submit claims electronically. Practice management systems are the most common type of automated systems within physician practices. There are approximately 3,000 different types of practice management systems nationwide.

We recognize that all parts of the health care industry must streamline administrative processes. HIAA is committed to working with others in the industry to increase standardization. We participated in, and wholeheartedly support, the recommendations of the Workgroup for Electronic Data Interchange (WEDI). The key recommendations include:

- recognition of specific standards for transactions
- a specific time schedule for implementation of a "paperless claims system"
- standardized billing and claims submission

HIAA commends the President for his plans pertaining to administrative simplification. The implementation of such plans will go a long way toward reducing administrative costs and the "hassle factor" in the health care industry. The notable parts of the President's plans are: standardized reimbursement forms; automation of insurance transactions; and the streamlining of Medicare.

Medical Liability Reform

Each year, medical liability, or medical malpractice, adds significantly to the nation's health care costs. The threat of lawsuits and the ease with which they may be brought are important driving factors in the increase in the practice of "defensive medicine," which adds billions of dollars to the cost of health care. Doctors pay over $5 billion in medical liability insurance premiums. These costs are passed on to consumers. A recent study found that the system could save $36 billion over 5 years by eliminating defensive medicine practices. Liability costs also increase the cost of pharmaceuticals and medical devices. HIAA supports federal medical malpractice reforms that will: reduce the incidence of medical malpractice by improving risk management, using practice protocols as a valid defense against malpractice claims, and better policing of health care delivery. We are pleased that the "Working Group Draft" includes the notion of an alternative dispute resolution mechanism. The HIAA is concerned that the "Draft" does not contain any limits on extra contractual damages and allows states to set up enterprise liability demonstration projects.

Individual Responsibility and Prevention

An issue that is not spoken of often in the context of health reform is individual responsibility. Smoking is one of the single most preventable causes of death in the U.S. today. It is estimated that lifetime excess expenditures on current or previous smokers is about $6,239 per smoker, with a cumulative burden of $500 billion on the U.S. economy. Violent crime, substance abuse, poor nutrition, unsafe living conditions, and family breakdown all contribute to health care costs. No degree of access to medical services, no advances in medical technology, can substitute for healthful lifestyles as a means for maintaining good health. HIAA actively supports wellness promotion and illness prevention, as well as proposals to educate consumers about how best to use the medical care system. Individuals should have financial incentives to be economical in choosing providers and in using preventive and well care services.

LONG-TERM CARE

HIAA is pleased to see that the Administration supports several provisions which would clarify the tax treatment of private long-term care insurance. These changes would greatly increase the affordability of these products and help millions of Americans protect themselves against catastrophic long-term care expenses.

If the Administration continues to promote the tax changes we seek, HIAA would also support the creation of federal standards for long-term care insurance products. However, such standards must not be so onerous that they prohibit all but "cadillac" policies from being sold. Equally important, consumers should be allowed to purchase federally-approved policies in all states; separate state approval should not be necessary.

We have two concerns with the newly proposed national home care program. First, a far better use of limited tax dollars would be to target care to those unable to protect themselves, and encourage those who can afford to do so, to purchase private protection. Secondly, we are concerned that the Administration will "sell" the public on this program as a down-payment toward a national solution to long-term care when even this modest home care benefit is estimated to cost $80 billion over five years. Costs alone dictate that the ultimate solution must be a public-private partnership.

TRANSITIONAL INSURANCE REGULATIONS

The transition to a new health insurance market could take several years, especially if the new market structure is as unnecessarily complex and unwieldy as the President proposes to make it. The Administration has proposed, according to their "Working Group Draft", a set of regulations to govern insurers' behavior during the transition. While the Administration's intent is not clear in the drafts we have seen, we would oppose any attempt to prohibit insurers from withdrawing entirely from the health insurance business or any significant part of it, such as the individual market or the small group market. In a free country, government should not coerce any corporation or person to continue in any particular line of business.

Some of the proposed transition rules we would support. In fact, they closely parallel insurance reforms we have been promoting at the state level for several years. I refer here to such requirements as guaranteed renewal of coverage, automatic acceptance of new entrants in currently covered groups, and portability improvements which prohibit exclusion of coverage for pre-existing conditions when previously insured people change jobs or their employers change carriers. These reforms can be implemented very quickly, and do not require a new bureaucratic structure the President proposes.

Other proposed transition rules present severe difficulties for insurers. The rules establish de facto premium caps by giving states the right to approve or disapprove rate increases in excess of a yet-to-be-prescribed percentage. For reasons explained earlier in greater detail, we oppose limiting insurers' ability to charge rates sufficient to cover the real costs of serving their enrollees. Also, there are administrative problems with the proposed interim rating structure. It differs significantly from the rating reforms that have been enacted in more than half the states in the past three years and will therefore require significant time and administrative effort on the part of both states and carriers to implement, all for a scheme that would remain in place for a year or two.

CONCLUSION

In conclusion, I want to again emphasize that we support more of the President's plan than we oppose. We want to be a responsible participant in the national health care debate and want to work with the Administration and Congress to develop national reform which achieves universal coverage, promotes individual responsibility and cost containment, preserves choice and maintains the quality of our health care system.

During this discussion, we must remember that our health care system has many excellent features and we should build on them.

Attachment A

HIAA

Health Insurance Association of America

VISION STATEMENT

Our vision is a society of healthy individuals and communities. Our nation, through systemic change, will build upon our employer-based system to create a consumer-responsive, prevention-focused, affordable and cost-effective health system which fosters individual responsibility, human dignity, improved health status, and enhanced quality of life for all.

VISION GOALS

- *Promote a healthy and productive existence for all Americans, maximizing the dignity and quality of life for each individual.*
- *Encourage Americans to take personal responsibility for maintaining good health regarding lifestyle factors within their ability to control.*
- *Recognize, as a society, that heroic efforts to extend life are not always appropriate or desirable. Dignity, quality of life, and the potential of returning to a healthy existence must be considered in treatment decisions and in the allocation of resources.*
- *Provide compassionate care to all people, especially to those who are chronically or terminally ill and cannot recover from their illnesses.*
- *Stabilize health care costs as a percentage of individual financial capacity--earned income and other sources.*
- *Harmonize health care spending with other essential national requirements--the environment, education, the economy and security.*

March 24, 1993

1025 Connecticut Avenue, NW Washington, DC 20036-3998 202/223-7780 Telecopier 202/828-4511

GUIDING PRINCIPLES

Reform of our health care system requires comprehensive change. Change must include a shift in emphasis away from sickness and repair and toward health and wellness. The principles below comprise a unified whole, not a cafeteria menu. All elements integral to universal coverage and cost containment must be implemented together, not piece-meal nor staged over time one state at a time. HIAA believes that reform of our system must be guided by the following principles:

1. **Reform must rely on competitive, pluralistic, and flexible delivery and financing systems in which all players--public and private alike--abide by the same rules. Government should not anoint winners; winners should be determined by the marketplace--a marketplace free to abandon failures and embrace promising new ideas.**

2. Universal, "cradle to grave" coverage must be achieved by requiring all employers and individuals to pay for an essential package of benefits which should include primary, preventive and catastrophic coverage. Government cannot shirk its role; it must help subsidize those employers and individuals who cannot afford to purchase an essential package.

3. Insurers and other private payors must issue and renew coverage for all. To protect insurer solvency and maintain employer incentives to control costs and promote employee wellness, insurers can, within limits, establish premium rates which reflect risk. Coverage must be portable; there must be no pre-existing condition limits once in the system; and the problem of "job lock" must be eliminated.

4. Reform must build on our employment-based system. Employers' active participation in financing, selecting, and administering an essential package of coverage is critical to maintaining an open, flexible, and innovative health care system. Given their significant financial commitment, employers must retain control over their employees' health care coverage. Therefore, requiring employers to participate solely through group purchasing pools would invalidate the cornerstone of our employer-based system.

5. Changing the delivery system is fundamental. Managed care should be the primary vehicle for achieving sustained systemwide cost savings; we must allow it to evolve and develop into its next generation, including full participation of Medicare and Medicaid beneficiaries in managed care systems. A defining element of managed care systems will be their ability to collect and publish data which allow purchasers to compare outcome and price information. Employers and managed care systems will also provide incentives that promote healthy lifestyles and

77-929 O - 94 - 12

personal responsibility. Managed care alone may not sufficiently control systemic health care costs. Therefore, alternative approaches (such as expenditure targets and all-payor systems) should be explored as an additional means of controlling health care costs.

6. Government's role must be one of an enabler, not of a "doer". A primary and essential function must be to eliminate cost-shifting to private payors. Self-regulatory bodies will develop, implement and enforce rules of conduct for all players. These include rules of market behavior for all private and public payors, rules for providers to follow to ensure consistent payment levels which eliminate cost-shifting, and standards for electronic data interchange and for reporting outcome and cost information. Government-sanctioned self-regulatory bodies will also define essential package(s) of care, evaluate technologies for their cost-effectiveness, and establish a mechanism for pooling certain cost and utilization data. In addition, government must enact legislation reforming the malpractice adjudication system.

7. Tax preferences should be limited to the essential package of care, thereby motivating the public to seek the best value and providing additional revenue to finance expanded health care coverage.

CREATING A WORKING HEALTH CARE SYSTEM

We Americans have shorter life spans, higher infant mortality rates, and higher rates of violent death than do the citizens of other industrialized countries. Yet we pay more for health care per capita and more in total health costs--close to $900 billion a year--than does any other country in the world. Furthermore, an estimated 37 million people in the United States do not have health care coverage; if we as a society continue "business as usual," that number is expected to reach 40 million by the year 2000.

To make matters worse, the private sector has had to shoulder more than its fair share of the costs. The Prospective Payment Assessment Commission estimates that, in 1990, private payors paid $22.5 billion more than the costs incurred by their hospital patients to make up for losses hospitals experienced from the uninsured as well as Medicaid and Medicare patients. Put another way, private payors paid an average of 128 percent of actual provider costs; this amounts to almost a 30 percent "tax" on hospital costs paid by the nation's employers.

Clearly, these trends must be reversed. Over the last year, the Vision Committee of the Board of Directors of the Health Insurance Association of America (HIAA) met to discuss health care reform. The Committee members approached their task as

Americans who happen to know about health insurance rather than as health insurance executives who happen to be Americans.

HIAA's vision is a framework for comprehensive reform. Its underlying premise is that everyone with a stake in the success of American health care, including insurers, will have to do what it takes to create a working health care system. It reflects the conviction that the nation's health care needs can best be met by a competitive and pluralistic system, not a monolithic one, and that the private sector will continue to play a dominant role in financing health care. It calls for universal coverage for all and changes in the behavior of providers, payors, including insurers, and the public. It advocates that government be an "enabler," not a "doer," that it eliminate cost-shifting, and that it establish guidelines for everyone to follow. Our vision is premised on comprehensive reform; all initiatives central to its goal of universal coverage and cost containment must be implemented together, and in coordination with one another, to ensure maximum success.

Taken together, these reforms will lead to a sustainable reduction in the growth of health care costs and improve the health of the American people. We recognize, however, that these reforms will require significant new government spending. We have identified one possible revenue source--a limit to the tax preference employer-sponsored health insurance currently enjoys--but we recognize that other sources will be needed as well. It is critical that these newly generated tax dollars be applied only to building a health care system that will produce long-term sustainable savings; new revenues should not be wasted perpetuating the status quo.

The health insurance industry anticipates further discussion on many aspects of the system it proposes. Some areas need more thought, and some gaps need to be filled. As areas of uncertainty are clarified, this paper, which is not final, will be modified to reflect these changes. Some lack of specificity will have to be tolerated while we struggle to find solutions to difficult issues. (For purposes of this discussion, "health care" refers to services to prevent, diagnose or treat medical conditions. The reforms proposed here do not apply to coverage outside of the essential package, such as disability income, supplemental hospital indemnity, specified disease, Medicare supplement or long-term care insurance.)

COMPONENTS OF THE NEW SYSTEM

1. *Based on Pluralistic Financing and Delivery Systems*

Reform must rely on market-based pluralistic and competitive financing and delivery systems. Pluralism and choice are what engender competition--competition among ideas, among companies, among plans, and among values such as cost, quality and convenience. Only true competition can assure that our health care system remains flexible and open to innovation, so that it will continue to evolve to better meet consumers' needs in the future. A system with many buyers and sellers will assure breadth and depth of services and responsiveness to consumers. Market forces must be allowed to determine which systems shall succeed.

Comprehensive health care reform will require an expanded federal role to eliminate costly variations in state regulation and assure uniform standards--a level playing field--for all public and private payors. It will also require that government remove barriers to the growth of pluralistic, competitive systems.

2. *Builds on an Employer-Based Foundation*

Employers have a unique interest in maintaining employee health--as it affects productivity. Therefore, employers must provide coverage for all their employees and dependents. Employers will pay for at least part of this coverage. Some employers will receive government assistance to help cover their employees.

All employers, regardless of their size, will select plans based on the performance of competing managed care systems. A system built on an employer base is categorically inconsistent with the concept of exclusive group purchasing that bypasses employers altogether, thus relieving them of their responsibilities. Purchasing pools, such as group association and multiple employer plans, are common methods of obtaining coverage. We have no objection to a variety of demonstrations and experimentation with other forms of purchasing pools provided employer participation is voluntary. In no case should employers be required to buy health insurance solely through group purchasing arrangements.

A competitive and pluralistic system should allow purchasing pools to exist side by side with other methods of arranging coverage. Insurance reform measures will prevent any one entity from bearing an inequitable share of risk because all payors will follow the same market rules to guarantee coverage.

In addition, employers should:

- be free to experiment with and invest in a variety of approaches in providing an essential package of coverage;

- provide incentives to promote healthy behavior; and

- have incentives to help restrain costs because some element of their experience is considered.

3. *Achieves Universal Coverage for an Essential Package*

All Americans will have continuous coverage for an essential package of primary, preventive, and catastrophic care. Achieving universal coverage will require a series of mandates--on government, employers, insurers and individuals. How to divide these responsibilities will probably be the most difficult and controversial aspect of health care reform. Ultimately, it will be a political decision, not a health care decision. Clearly governments--federal and possibly state--will bear the cost of covering low-income people. Employers, in our view, should at the very least be required to incur the costs of offering health insurance to their employees.

HIAA supports a requirement that employers help pay for coverage for their employees and dependents. Even a modest employer payment would heighten employer cost consciousness and help restrain health care inflation. So-called employer mandates, however, are in effect a mandate on employees as well as employers, since employee premium contributions are envisioned in virtually all employer mandate plans. We are reserving judgment on how the costs should be shared between employer and employee, recognizing that there are practical limits on the ability of both employers and employees to shoulder the financial costs of a health care mandate. It may be necessary--however the cost is divided--to phase in the mandates over a period of years, taking account of any other employer mandates--such as increases in the minimum wage--that may be imposed at the same time. If an employer mandate is phased in, it will be necessary to coordinate it with other aspects of health care reform. For example, certain aspects of insurance market reform are not feasible absent a mandate; the two reform measures must be synchronized.

To achieve universal coverage, the following steps must be taken:

- Government must require all employers to arrange and help pay for an essential package of coverage for their employees and dependents. All individuals--those employed and those not connected to the work force--are required to obtain such coverage.

- Government must help employers and individuals who cannot afford to purchase an essential package. (Certain employers receive financial help, but they cannot "opt out" by paying a tax instead.)

- All individuals--those employed and those not connected to the work force--must receive the same tax incentives to purchase an essential package.

- The essential package covers primary, preventive, and catastrophic care. Government will authorize an independent body of providers, payors, employers and consumers to define the essential package of coverage. The design of this package must be flexible to encourage cost-conscious behavior; it must have inherent limits to prevent continuous expansion, recognizing that people's wants and desires may exceed society's resources; and it must not overlap or duplicate medical care coverage available elsewhere such as under workers' compensation and automobile insurance.

- There should be no difference in the essential package of coverage received by the poor and the non-poor. Government will finance coverage for low income individuals, but there will no longer be the need for a separate Medicaid program.

4. *Ensures Universal Coverage Through Market Reform*

Market reform must be premised on a government requirement that all individuals and employers purchase coverage. In this environment, all health plans will be subject to national rules of market behavior to guarantee universal and continuous coverage. The same rules will apply to all health plans, whether offered by commercial insurers, Blue Cross/Blue Shield plans, HMOs, self-insured employers, government, or any other entity. Problems such as "job lock" and lack of coverage for pre-existing conditions will be resolved. The rules of market behavior will:

- require that coverage be made available to every employee in an employment-based group;
- assure that every individual will be able to purchase the essential package, regardless of their health, financial or employment status;
- guarantee that coverage will not be cancelled, terminated or not renewed based on the health status or claims experience of any individual or group;
- prohibit insurer rating practices that create large rate differentials for groups of similar age, sex and geographic composition;
- maintain, at the same time, insurers' ability to calibrate rates to risk--pure community rating results in market disruption and works against cost containment in a variety of ways; and
- establish a form of reinsurance or risk-sharing to compensate for inequitable distribution of risk.

5. *Creates Sustained Cost Containment By Systemic Change in Financing and Delivery Systems*

Changing the health care delivery system is fundamental. The actual delivery of care must be substantially better organized than it is today to meet the needs of patients, purchasers, and providers. Therefore, managed care should be the primary vehicle for achieving sustained systemwide cost savings, and must be allowed to evolve and develop to its next generation. Managed care systems will serve the health care needs of communities by offering essential packages of care; they may also offer supplemental coverage.

Different forms of managed care coverage will compete on a level playing field. These competing forms of coverage include plans employing managed care techniques such as utilization review as well as managed care structures such as HMOs, PPOs, other network-based health plans, and evolving models. However, a defining element of all managed care systems will be their ability to collect and publish data which allow purchasers to compare outcome and price information across managed care systems.

Managed care systems will be permitted to pay providers in a variety of ways that encourage cost-effectiveness and quality care, including physician risk-sharing incentives, so that providers are rewarded for the cost-effective use of medical resources. New payment systems should encourage greater provider autonomy in decision-making and reduce the "hassle factor" that now results from micromanaging by payors.

Managed care systems will be user-friendly, efficient, and paperless. Administrative costs, and waste and fraud, will be significantly reduced. Improved alliances between providers and insurers will promote enhanced financial and managerial control of managed care systems, timely and responsive customer service, quality assurance programs, and fraud prevention.

Both managed care systems and employers will provide incentives that promote healthy behavior including discounts, promotions, and education. These incentives will reduce health care costs related to unhealthy lifestyle choices and will promote personal responsibility for one's health.

Given government's enormous buying power and its ability to influence provider costs, there should be strong incentives, perhaps requirements phased in over time, that Medicaid and Medicare beneficiaries fully participate in managed care systems to eliminate cost-shifting and control costs and utilization.

As managed care continues to develop, it will result in significant cost containment. However, managed care alone may not sufficiently control systemic health care costs. Therefore, alternative approaches (such as expenditure targets and all-payor systems) should be explored as an additional means of controlling health care costs.

6. *Controls Systemwide Costs Via New Government Role*

Government will establish an entity that oversees and relies on one or more self-regulatory bodies to develop, implement and enforce rules of conduct for all players in the health care system. The regulatory framework will include all interested parties in the health care system--providers, insurers, employers, government, and the public. One, or possibly several, self-regulatory bodies will perform the following functions:

- establish consistent rules of market behavior for all health plans--those provided by insurers, self-insured employers, HMOs, government, or any other entity (see point 4);

- define essential package(s) of coverage that is made available to all, regardless of their income, age or employment status (see point 3);

- establish rules for providers to follow which ensure that they set consistent payment levels for all public and private payors for the same service. These rules should:

  - recognize that different payors may use different payment methods; and

  - assure that payments reflect real economic costs and value to providers and payors (such as convenience, service, adherence to quality standards, cost-effective practice patterns, or meeting additional contractual obligations).

  (In no case, however, should the rules allow providers to grant discounts to one payor simply by increasing the cost to another payor. The most important outcome of these new rules is to eliminate government's chronic failure to pay the true costs of care for poor and elderly Americans. In other words, Medicaid and Medicare should no longer receive special deals with providers at the expense of the rest of the population.)

- develop standardized guidelines for electronic data processing and a nationally uniform claim form to achieve an efficient and paperless system;

- evaluate technologies (i.e., drugs, procedures, and equipment) for their cost-effectiveness; sanction clinical guidelines (developed by appropriate professions) that can be used as legal defense against malpractice claims; determine valid experimental treatments eligible for reimbursement through participation in clinical trials;

- establish standards for the reporting of outcome and cost information published by managed care systems;

- establish a mechanism for pooling certain cost and utilization data on a regional, state and/or national basis to assist all payors in controlling costs and utilization, to help managed care systems produce outcome and cost data, and to help the government-authorized entity to develop guidelines that ensure that providers set consistent payment levels;

- enact legislative reforms of the malpractice adjudication system;

- enact legislation that allows insurers to exchange information for the purpose of identifying fraudulent providers; and

- consider actions needed to change the mix and supply of physicians and to increase the supply of physicians in inner cities and rural areas.

7. *Establishes Equitable Rules for All*

Government will require all public and private payors to play by the same rules. To achieve this level playing field, the regulatory framework must:

- avoid duplicative or overlapping regulation among the states or between the state and federal levels;

- remove all state regulatory control over anti-managed care laws, mandated benefits laws, and provider contracting laws;

- prohibit states from mandating additions to the essential benefit package; and

- amend ERISA to allow this regulatory structure to successfully implement the above responsibilities.

8. *Promotes Equitable Tax Policy*

Government must implement tax policies that eliminate perverse incentives for health care spending.[1] An unlimited tax preference for employer-sponsored health benefits does not promote cost-consciousness among employees. Instead, tax preferences for the essential package of coverage should be:

---

[1]As noted earlier, this vision addresses reform of the acute care medical system; it does not address long-term care financing reform. HIAA continues to support several recommendations in the latter area, including favorable tax treatment of long-term care insurance, on the grounds that the increased availability of affordable private insurance will have a significant impact on reducing future public (Medicaid) spending on long-term care.

- capped at a level equal to the essential benefit package;
- extended to the self-employed and to those who purchase the coverage outside of an employment setting;
- inapplicable to any premiums for health benefits in excess of the essential package; and
- inapplicable to cost-sharing requirements, such as deductibles and copayments, for the essential package.

Employers would continue to be allowed to deduct 100 percent of their contributions to employees' health coverage, even if their contributions are for coverage in excess of the essential package. (But employees are taxed on the excess.) In addition, the inequitable taxation of various payors must also be addressed to help level the playing field in the new system.

The revenues from these tax changes should be used only to help pay for health care reform. HIAA could not support these tax changes if cost-shifting is not adequately addressed or if the revenues generated from these changes are not specifically applied to health care reform.

SYSTEMIC FACTORS DRIVING COSTS ARE SLOWED

We have proposed many ways to create a sustained reduction in the growth of health care spending. Everyone will have continuous coverage so people will not wait until they are ill before seeking care. Managed care systems will discourage excess doctor visits, unnecessary hospital and specialist care, and technology use that is not cost-effective. Physicians will be empowered to practice effective, not defensive, medicine. Managed care systems will offer essential packages of care that will compete on price and value.

Providers will not be able to shift costs among payors, so true market competition will compel providers to become more efficient. A government-authorized entity will evaluate, and slow the use of, expensive technologies that are not cost-effective. Administrative simplicity, a paperless system, and standardized claim forms will save money and help control fraud and waste. Coverage of preventive care and incentives for healthy lifestyles will pay off over the long-run. Tax advantages will be limited to the value of the essential package of care, thereby motivating everyone to seek the best value.

Successful reform will yield measurable results and trends that will compare favorably to those of other nations on costs and on a variety of quality measures (such as mortality, percent who smoke, and height/weight standards).

HIAA will continue to refine its vision of health care reform. However, we are committed to achieving the objectives outlined.

Fixing the health care system will lift a sizable burden from our collective shoulders, yielding resources and liberating energies for other critical issues on the nation's social agenda.

SEPARATE ISSUE PAPERS

Additional issue papers are being developed on selected subjects. In some instances, these are descriptive papers discussing the pros and cons of the issue. In other cases, these are supplemental papers providing more detail than what is proposed herein. Topic areas include:

1. Problems in using premiums caps to control costs
2. Centrality of employers in providing coverage
3. Problems in using group purchasing pools as the only means of gaining coverage
4. Extent of tax-favored treatment for health insurance
5. Nature of federal ~~and~~ state responsibilities
6. Implementation and enforcement of employer and individual mandates
7. Insurance in the new market
8. Determining the essential package of coverage
9. Medicare and Medicaid in health care reform
10. Technology assessment
11. Tort reform
12. Individual responsibility, wellness and prevention
13. Medical care coverage under Workers' compensation and auto insurance
14. Eliminating fraud and waste
15. Long-term care
16. Electronic data interchange

Attachment B

PROFITABILITY OF SELECTED SECTORS IN THE HEALTH CARE AND HEALTH INSURANCE INDUSTRIES 1980-1991

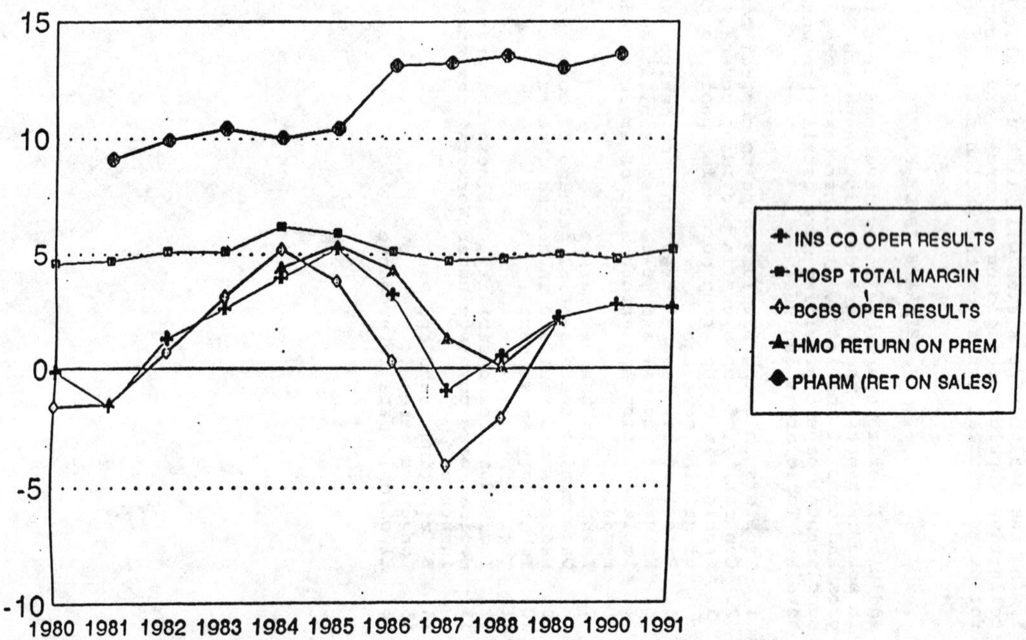

TRENDS IN PROFITABILITY FOR SELECTED SECTORS IN THE HEALTH CARE AND HEALTH INSURANCE INDUSTRIES, 1980–1991

Year	(1) Insurance Company Operating Results (% of Prem)	(2) Hospital Total Revenue Margin (% of Tot Rev)	(3) Blue Cross Blue Shield Operating Results (% of NSR)	(4) HMO Return on Premium (Net Gain as % of Earned Prem)	(5) Pharmaceutical Manufacturers Return on Sales (Median %)
1980	(0.2)	4.6	(1.6)		
1981	(1.6)	4.7	(1.5)		9.1
1982	1.3	5.1	0.7		9.9
1983	2.6	5.1	3.1		10.4
1984	4.0	6.2	5.2	4.4	10.0
1985	5.3	5.9	3.8	5.4	10.4
1986	3.2	5.1	0.3	4.3	13.1
1987	(0.9)	4.7	(4.1)	1.3	13.2
1988	0.5	4.8	(2.1)	0.1	13.5
1989	2.2	5.0	2.1	2.1	13.0
1990	2.8	4.8			13.6
1991	2.6	5.2			

(1) HIAA survey of its top 20 members.
(2) AHA Hospital Panel Survey.
(3) Blue Cross Blue Shield net subscription revenue.
(4) McKinsey & Company, Health Care Payor Annual.
(5) Fortune Magazine, various issues.

Attachment C

Fact Sheet
Health Care Coverage, Costs And Potential Savings

Table of Contents

I. National Health Expenditures

- National health expenditures were $751.8 billion in 1991. :

Table 1
National Health Expenditures by Source of Funds
[Billions of Dollars]

	1991	1993e	1995e	2000e
Total, all sources	752	903	1,102	1,740
All private funds	422	482	573	860
Out-of-Pocket	144	170	203	303
Private Insurance	244	274	325	492
Other	33	39	45	65
Government	330	421	529	880
Federal	223	290	366	618
State and Local	107	131	163	262
Medicare	*123*	*153*	*191*	*328*
Medicaid	*98*	*151*	*202*	*360*
Percent of GDP	13.2	14.4	15.6	18.1
Per capita[a] expenditures ($)	2,868	3,380	4,050	6,148

a. HCFA uses Social Security area population estimates for counts of persons in calculating per capita cost estimates.

Source(s): Health Care Financing Review, Fall 1992, Vol. 14, No. 1, Health Care Financing Administration.

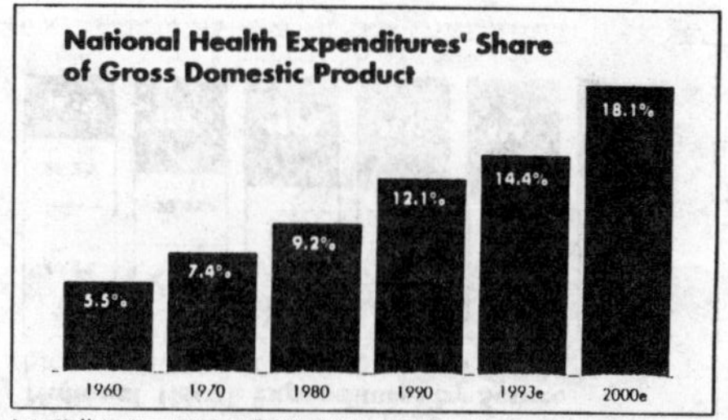

Source: Health Care Financing Review, Fall 1992, Vol. 14, No. 1, Health Care Financing Administration.

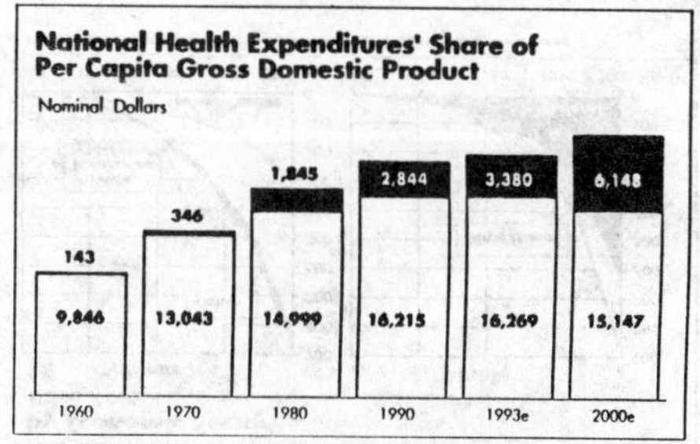

Source: Health Care Financing Review, Fall 1992, Vol. 14, No. 1, Health Care Financing Administration

- Of the $752 billion spent on health care in 1991
  - 33 percent was paid by private insurance;
  - 19 percent was paid out-of-pocket;
  - 30 percent was paid by the federal government;
  - 14 percent was paid by state and local government.

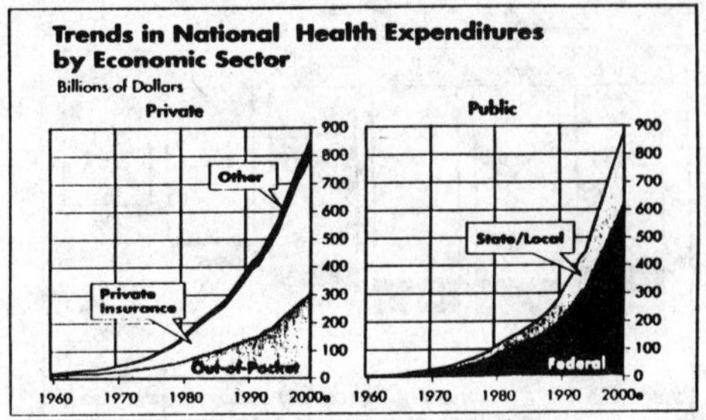

Source Health Care Financing Review, Fall 1992, Vol. 14, No. 1, Health Care Financing Administration.

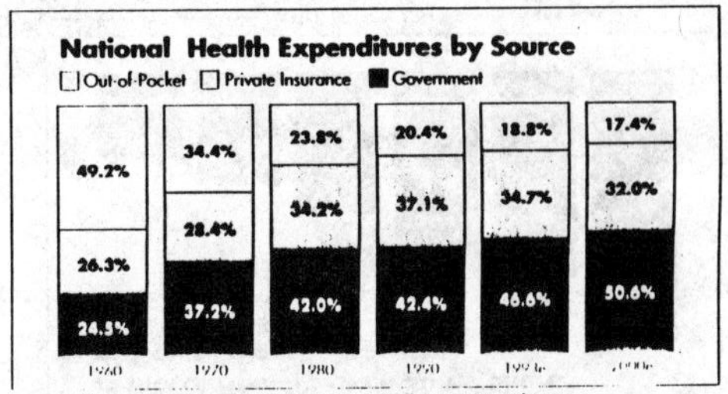

Source Health Care Financing Review, Fall 1992, Vol. 14, No. 1, Health Care Financing Administration

- Employers contributed $188 billion toward private group health care coverage in 1991, 25 percent of the total expenditure for that year.
- Workers compensation programs paid $18 billion in 1991.
- Personal health care expenses are projected to rise by 9.5 percent per year between 1993 and 2000. Factors contributing to this rise are:
  - Population increase: 8 percent
  - Demographic composition: 5 percent
  - Use per person: 8 percent
  - General inflation: 34 percent
  - Intensity and price increase: 45 percent

Source: Projections of National Health Expenditures, October 1992, Congressional Budget Office, U.S. Congress.

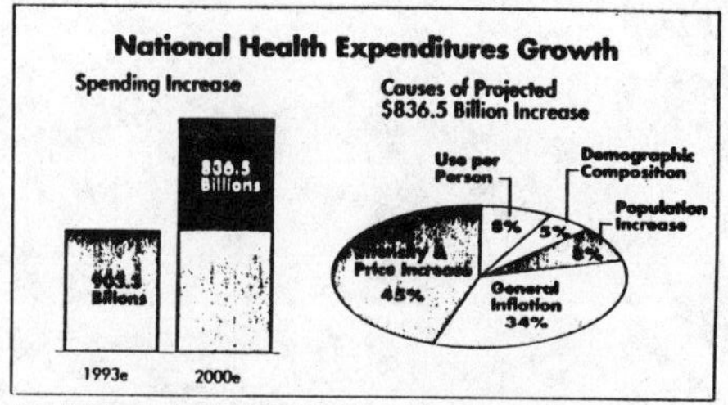

Source: Health Care Financing Review, Fall 1992, Vol. 14, No. 1, Health Care Financing Administration.

II. Cost Shifting to Private Payers

- Government underpayment of costs and uncompensated care continue to cause hospitals to shift costs to private payers at an increasing rate. Estimates indicate that the shortfall in government payments doubled in just three years from 1989 to 1992.

Table 2
Hospital Undercompensated and Unsponsored Care
[Billions of Dollars]

Source	1989	1990	1992
Medicare	6.9	8.2	14.4
Medicaid	4.2	4.6	8.1
Unsponsored care	8.9	9.6	11.9

Source(s) Lewin ICF, April, 1992; ProPAC, Report to Congress, June 1992

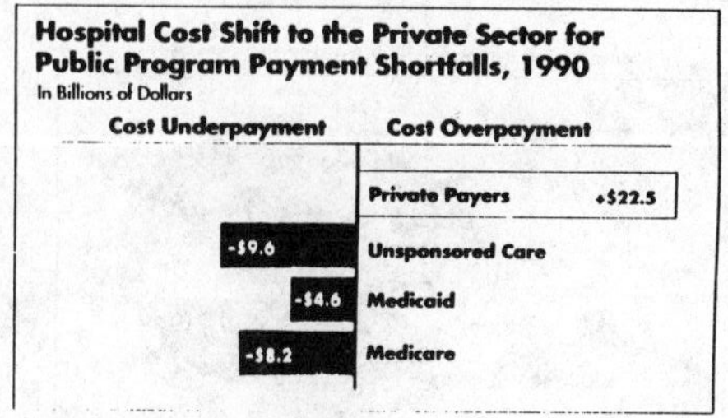

SOURCE ProPac, Report to Congress

- Private payers paid 128 percent of hospital costs in 1990 to compensate for government underpayment of costs and uncompensated care.

- Estimates for 1992 indicate that the cost shift increased to almost $35 billion: $23 billion from government program shortfalls and $12 billion from uncompensated care. This figure represents almost 30 percent of the estimated $119 billion total paid by consumers (private insurance or out-of-pocket) for hospital care expenses in 1992.

III. Health Insurance Coverage

- Employers are the primary source of health expense coverage for almost 6 out of 10 Americans:

Table 3
Primary Source of Health Insurance Coverage
[Millions of Persons [a]]

	Persons	Percent
Total Population	248.7	100.0
Employer-Based Private	142.3	57.2
Other Private	17.6	7.1
Medicare	30.4	12.2
Medicaid	19.3	7.8
CHAMPUS	2.5	1.0
No Health Coverage	36.6	14.7

[a] Uses only primary source of coverage, not coverage from all sources, e.g., persons over 65 still employed are covered by employer plans

Source(s): Sources of Health Insurance and Characteristics of the Uninsured, EBRI, January, 1993 [Based on 3/92 Current Population Survey]

Primary Source of Health Insurance Coverage

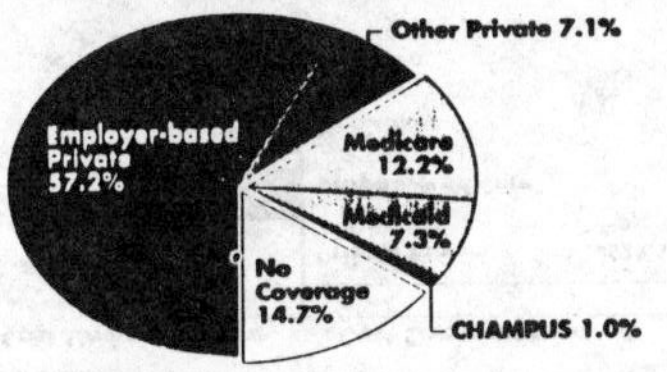

SOURCE: Sources of Health Insurance and Characteristics of the Uninsured, EBRI, January, 1993

Who Are The Uninsured?

- Low income people are more likely to be uninsured:

Table 4
Uninsured Nonelderly Population
by Family Income

Family income as a percentage of poverty level	Persons without health insurance coverage: Millions	Persons without health insurance coverage: Percent of class
0-99%	10.5	32.6
100%-124%	3.3	35.9
125%-149%	3.3	33.5
150%-199%	5.0	25.2
200%-399%	10.1	13.6
400% or more	4.1	5.7

Source(s): Sources of Health Insurance and Characteristics of the Uninsured, EBRI, January, 1993

Insurance Coverage of Nonelderly Population by Family income as a Percentage of Poverty

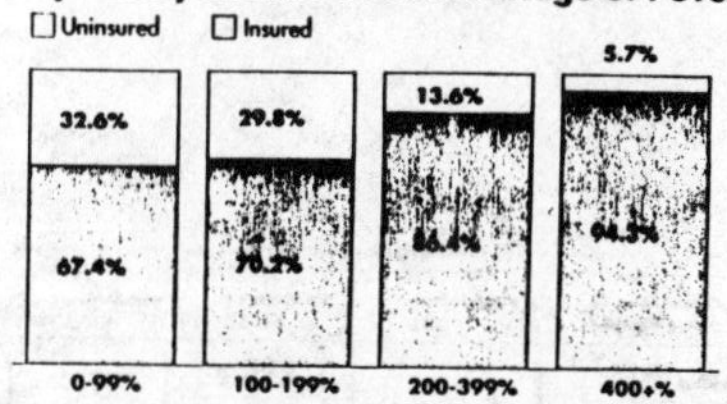

SOURCE: Sources of Health Insurance and Characteristics of the Uninsured, EBRI, January, 1993

Insurance Coverage of Nonelderly Population by Family income as a Percentage of Poverty
Millions of Persons

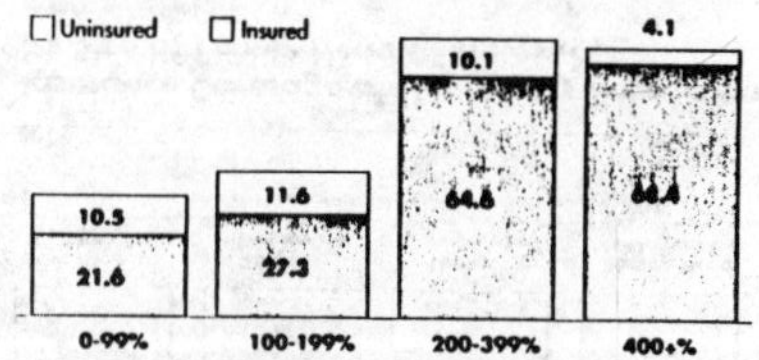

SOURCE: Sources of Health Insurance and Characteristics of the Uninsured, EBRI, January, 1993

- People who work for small firms are more likely to be uninsured:

Table 5
Uninsured Nonelderly Population
by Size of Family Head's Employer

Size of firm	Persons without Health Insurance Coverage	
	Millions	Percent of class
Fewer than 25 Employees	13.3	27.4
25-99 Employees.............	5.2	20.7
100 or More Employees. ...	12.2	10.2
Family Head is Nonworker	5.6	22.6

Source(s): Sources of Health Insurance and Characteristics of the Uninsured, EBRI, January, 1993

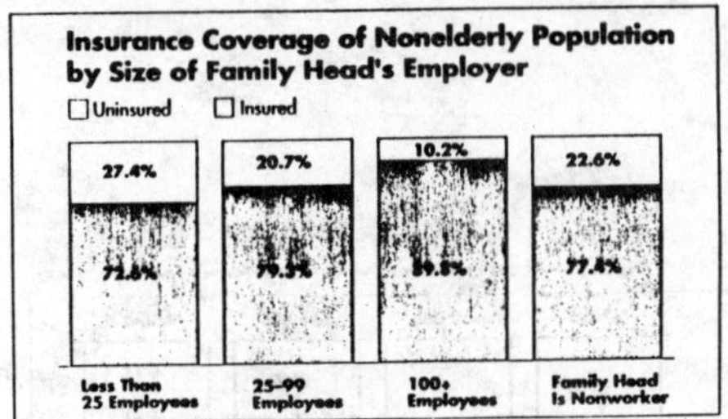

Insurance Coverage of Nonelderly Population by Size of Family Head's Employer

SOURCE: Sources of Health Insurance and Characteristics of the Uninsured, EBRI, January, 1993

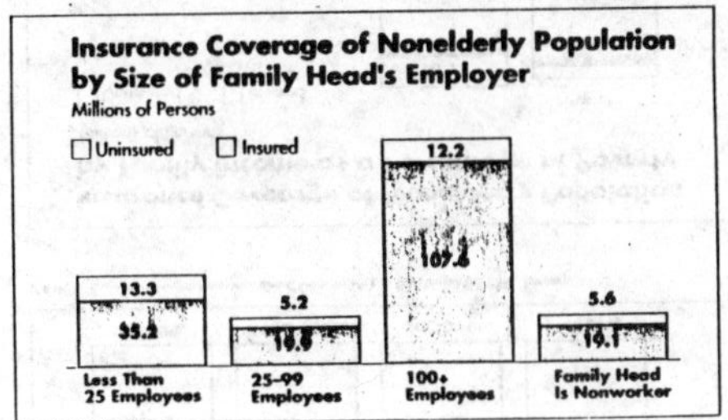

Insurance Coverage of Nonelderly Population by Size of Family Head's Employer

SOURCE: Sources of Health Insurance and Characteristics of the Uninsured, EBRI, January, 1993

IV. Managed Care

- Managed care plans covered over half (54 percent) of the workers provided employer-sponsored health insurance in 1991. This compares to slightly more than one fourth just four years ago (27 percent in 1987).
  - 25 percent of workers are enrolled in HMOs;
  - 22 percent are enrolled in PPOs;
  - 7 percent are in POS plans;
  - 38 percent are in conventional plans with utilization management provisions;
  - 8 percent are in conventional plans with no utilization management provisions.

Source: HIAA Survey of Employer-Sponsored Group Health Plans, 1987, 1991

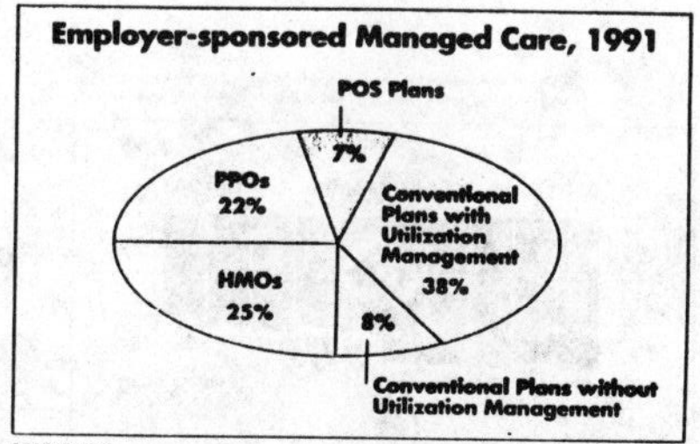

SOURCE: HIAA

- Blue Cross/Blue Shield and commercial insurers owned over 40 percent of all HMOs and accounted for over one quarter of all enrolles in 1992.

Table 6
HMO Ownership
[Percent]

	By Number of HMO Plans	By HMO Enrollment
Insurers	28.9	15.4
Blue Cross/Blue Shield......	13.5	12.3
Others	57.6	72.3

Source(s): GHAA, National Directory of HMOs, 1992

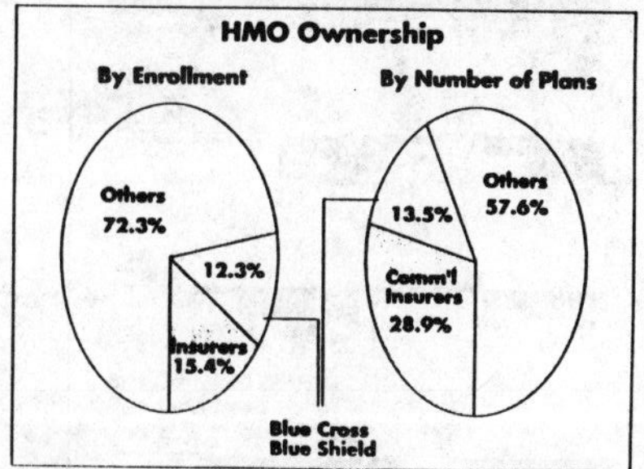

SOURCE: GHAA

- Six percent of Medicare beneficiaries and 12 percent of Medicaid eligibles are enrolled in network-based managed care plans.

V. Health Insurance and Health Care Provider Profitability

- Health insurance profits have lagged considerably behind health care provider profits:

Table 7
Measures of Profitability
[Operating Results as a Percent of Premiums/Revenues]

Year	Commercial Insurance	Blue Cross/ Blue Shield	HMOs	Hospitals	Drug Firms
1980	(0.2)	(1.6)	N.A.	4.6	N.A.
1981	(1.6)	(1.5)	N.A.	4.7	9.1
1982	1.3	0.7	N.A.	5.1	9.9
1983	2.6	3.1	N.A.	5.1	10.4
1984	4.0	5.2	4.9	6.2	10.0
1985	5.3	3.8	5.5	5.9	10.4
1986	3.2	0.3	4.1	5.1	13.1
1987	(0.9)	(4.1)	1.0	4.7	13.2
1988	0.5	(2.1)	-0.1	4.8	13.5
1989	2.2	2.1	2.1	5.0	13.0
1990	2.8	3.0	4.4	4.8	13.6
1991	2.6	2.4	4.6	5.2	N.A.

Source(s): HIAA Survey of Operating Results, AHA Panel Survey, Blue Cross Blue Shield, McKinsey & Co. Health care Payor Annual, Fortune Magazine.

- Commercial insurers net gain averaged only 1.9 percent of premiums over the period 1980 to 1991;
- Hospitals have maintained profits at about 5 percent of revenue;
- Pharmaceutical companies' profits have risen from 9 percent in 1981 to over 13 percent in 1990.

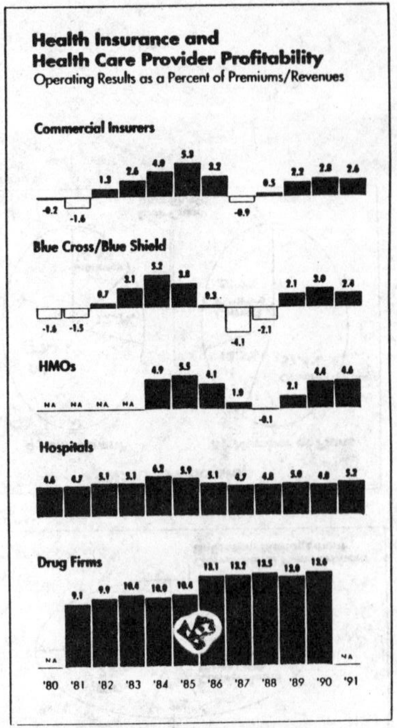

Sources: HIAA Survey of Operating Results, AHA Panel Survey, Blue Cross Blue Shield, McKinsey & Co. Health care Payor Annual, Fortune Magazine

- Between 1982 and 1990, average physicians' net income rose from 7 times the average earnings of non-farm workers to over 9 times the non-farm workers' average.

VI. Potential Health Care Savings

- Considerable savings can be achieved over the long term by focusing attention on such areas as the elimination of fraudulent and abusive practices, unnecessary health care services, administrative simplification, and improving personal health status.

Fraud and Waste:

- One quarter of all health care spending ($230 billion of an estimated $903 billion in 1993) could be eliminated by reducing fraud and unnecessary services.
  - Health care fraud comprises 10 percent ($90 billion) of all spending;
  - Unnecessary services comprise 13 percent ($115 billion) of all spending:
    - 7 percent ($65 billion) from hospitals,
    - 3 percent ($25 billion) from physicians,
    - 3 percent ($25 billion) from drugs.
  - Defensive medicine accounts for 3 percent ($25 billion) of all spending.

Source: Vulnerable Payers Lose Billions to Fraud and Abuse, GAO, May, 1992; HIAA calculations based on estimates from Robert Brook article for PPRC: Practice Guidelines and Practicing Medicine: Are they Compatible?, October, 1988; Estimating the Costs of Defensive Medicine, Lewin-VHI, January, 1993

Administrative Simplification:

- Standardized claim formats and transmission systems utilized by electronic data interchange can reduce administrative costs by 18 percent. Estimates of government program administration and net cost of private health insurance in 1995 are placed at $56 billion. The

Potential Health Care Cost Savings by Elimination of Fraud and Waste
Billions of Dollars

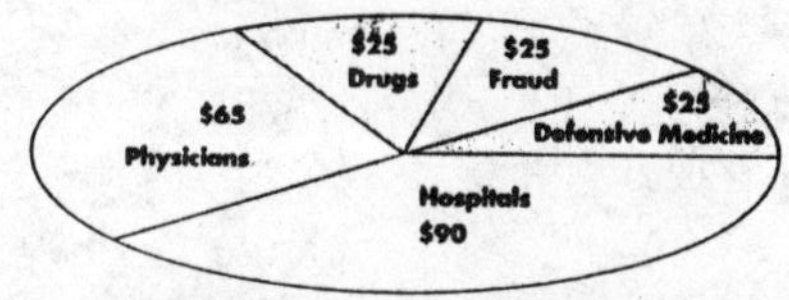

Source: Vulnerable Payers Lose Billions to Fraud and Abuse, GAO, May, 1992; HIAA calculations based on estimates from Robert Brook article for PPRC: Practice Guidelines and Practicing Medicine: Are they Compatible?, October, 1988; Estimating the Costs of Defensive Medicine, Lewin-VHI, January, 1993

Potential Health Care Cost Savings by Changing Lifestyle Patterns
Billions of Dollars

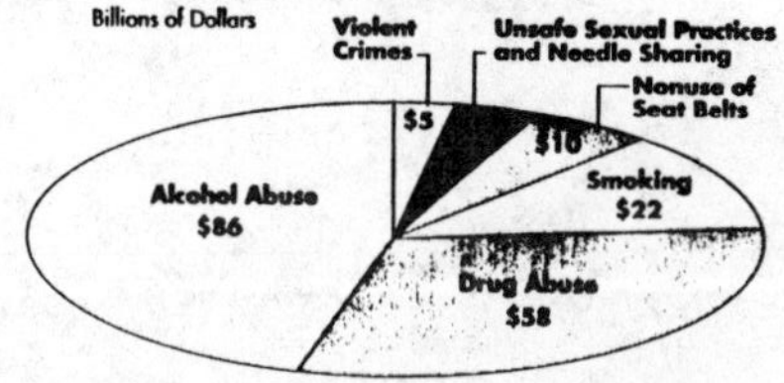

Source Workgroup for Electronic Data Interchange, Report to Secretary of U.S. Department of Health and Human Services, July 1992

Workgroup on Electronic Data Interchange has estimated the potential savings from these standards at $10 billion a year.

Source: Workgroup for Electronic Data Interchange, Report to Secretary of U.S. Department of Health and Human Services, July 1992

Consumer Behavior:

- Changing life-style patterns could greatly reduce health care costs and the number of unnecessary deaths each year. An estimated $188 billion was spent in 1990 on health care needs that could be eliminated by societal change or change in personal behavior.

Table 8
Consumer Behavior

Condition	Estimated annual cost in 1990 [Billions of Dollars]	Estimated number of deaths [Persons]
Alcohol abuse	86	105,000[a]
Drug abuse	58	10,000
Smoking	22	390,000
Nonuse of seat belts	10	45,000
Unsafe sexual practices & needle sharing (AIDS)	7	25,000
Violent crimes	5	50,000

a Deaths include those from motor vehicle

Source(s): Cost: American Medical Association, Centers for Disease Control, National Safety Council. Deaths: Healthy People 2000, U.S. Department of HHS, PHS

Mrs. COLLINS. Mr. Tringale?

STATEMENT OF STEVEN TRINGALE

Mr. TRINGALE. Thank you.

My name is Steven Tringale and I am senior vice president from Blue Cross/Blue Shield of Massachusetts. I am pleased to be here today and to have the opportunity to testify not only for the Massachusetts plan, but on behalf of the Blue Cross/Blue Shield Association.

Let me take a moment to tell you about Blue Cross/Blue Shield of Massachusetts. We have been providing coverage to citizens of Massachusetts for almost 60 years, and we currently provide health benefits for over 2.4 million people.

Many people still think of Blue Cross/Blue Shield as indemnity coverage. That is no longer true. In Massachusetts, nearly half our enrollment is in managed care networks and we have the largest number of HMO subscribers in the State, a State that is near the top of the list in terms of HMO enrollment nationally.

We also provide guaranteed medigap and individual coverage to everyone in Massachusetts through community-rated products. First and foremost, we believe that comprehensive health care reform is urgently needed in this Nation. In Massachusetts, Blue Cross has filed small group, medigap and individual market reform legislation which includes many of the provisions in the President's proposal. We applaud the President's leadership in putting the issue on the top of the legislative agenda and his call for a bipartisan effort to achieve rapid reform.

We agree with the President in many key areas. First, insurance reform is desperately needed to assure that every American can get coverage and to stop practices that penalize persons who are old or sick or are at risk of becoming ill. In addition to important consumer protections, insurance reform will mean that insurers will have to stop competing based upon risk selection and start managing costs through managing care if they want to compete in the new marketplace.

Elimination of preexisting conditions, guaranteeing portability, guaranteeing issue and renewability of coverage as well as administrative simplification and modified community rating should be the cornerstone of any insurance reform proposal.

Second, we support the President's incentives that would encourage managed care networks. Our experience has shown that is the most effective way of controlling health care costs and still delivering the highest quality of health care available. As a former regulator of hospital prices, I know that strict rate-setting formulas do not work. Far too much time and energy is spent interpreting the regulations then devising mechanisms to maximize reimbursement within those regulations.

State-imposed rate-setting and price control strategies inevitably inhibit the kind of innovation and rapid health system reconfiguration that we are now witnessing in Massachusetts. Networks built off the foundation of quality primary care providers also provide us the best opportunity to bring quality preventive and health promotion services to our subscribers.

Finally, we believe that if we ever have successful reform we must guarantee the coverage of every American. A strategy to achieve universal coverage should be included in any proposal passed by Congress and be based on a fair and equitable sharing of cost among all the players in the system.

However, there are two elements of the President's proposal that cause us concern, large regulatory and mandatory alliances and premium caps. Neither are necessary to achieve the goals of universal coverage and cost containment. The administration's plan relies on alliances being in place in every State before universal coverage and cost containment strategy begins.

I don't believe it is necessary to hinge enactment of these reforms on entities which don't even exist today. We think premising reform on this will risk the overall success of health reform and ultimately will delay it. Also these alliances oversee huge budgets.

For example, in Massachusetts, the alliance would be responsible for a budget of about $18 billion in public and private health care expenditures, a number which is larger than the current total State budget at this time. These alliances will increase and not decrease administrative cost by duplicating many functions now performed by employers in health plans.

In fact, passage of meaningful insurance market reform will bring about the purported benefits of health alliances through guaranteeing access to quality health coverage in an environment where all the incentives are to manage care, reduce cost and differentiate your product to the consumer through superior customer service.

Also we believe that arbitrary premium caps will not work and are susceptible to being driven by short-term budget priorities and politics that have little to do with the efficient operation of a health care system in any jurisdiction. As the individual in charge of two rate-regulated insurers of last resort in Massachusetts, I have unfortunately witnessed this phenomena and have seen its impact on our business and consequently on our subscribers.

Finally, I would like to emphasize that we want to work with you in crafting a practical, workable and comprehensive health reform solution.

Thank you very much.

[Testimony resumes on p. 383.]

[The prepared statement of Mr. Tringale follows:]

STEVEN TRINGALE
SENIOR VICE PRESIDENT OF EXTERNAL AFFAIRS,
BLUE CROSS AND BLUE SHIELD ASSOCIATION

Madame Chairman, Mr. Chairman, and members of the committee, I am Steve Tringale, Senior Vice President of External Affairs of Blue Cross and Blue Shield of Massachusetts. Blue Cross and Blue Shield of Massachusetts is a member of the Blue Cross and Blue Shield Association, the coordinating organization for the 69 independent Blue Cross and Blue Shield Plans throughout the nation. Collectively, the Plans provide health benefits protection for about 68 million people. I appreciate the opportunity to testify regarding the draft White House health care reform proposal's insurance reform component.

Insurance Reform: The Foundation of Health Reform

There is a consensus across this nation and in Congress that insurance reform is one of the central elements in comprehensive health care reform. Fundamental changes in the basic rules within which insurers operate is a key element of **the Administration's draft health care reform proposal.**

As Congress begins the debate on health care reform legislation, I cannot overemphasize the significant impact of insurance reform on carrier practices. The types of insurance reforms that I will discuss would move the market away from competition based on risk selection. Risk selection is the reason we do not have true price competition in health care. It is easier for many insurers and HMOs to hold down costs by screening out high risks than by managing overall health care costs. A clear illustration of this point is that 4 percent of any population will generate about 50 percent of all the claims costs. Many insurers, if they have the choice, will invest in techniques to avoid those high risks rather than invest in techniques to manage cost.

Insurance reform eliminates risk selection as a tool for maintaining competitive prices. Instead, insurers would have to compete on the basis of their ability to manage costs.

We believe that strict federal standards for the market conduct of insurers is the first and most important step toward reshaping the health care market -- and assuring fairness to consumers. **We are pleased the Administration's proposal contains the following standards:**

1. Require insurers to accept everyone regardless of their health status or employment;

2. Strictly limit the length and use of waiting periods for pre-existing conditions and prohibit them entirely for people who have been continuously covered;

3. Prohibit insurers from dropping people or groups when someone gets sick, and require insurers to offer continued coverage when a person loses his or her job;

4. Require insurers to set premiums fairly and not penalize people who are sick or older; and,

5. Require insurers to comply with requirements for administrative simplification, including increased reliance on electronic data interchange and conformity to standards.

These same strict standards must apply to more than insurers and Health Maintenance Organizations. Self-funded plans must play by the same rules and be held to the same standards as health plans. **We are glad that the Administration's plan requires self-funded plans to comply with these new standards.**

Insurance Reform By Itself Is Not Enough

While new rules for insurers are an essential part of health care reform, by themselves they will not be sufficient to contain costs and achieve universal coverage.

Cost controls: New standards for the way insurers do business can be an underpinning of a successful cost containment strategy. In addition, insurance reform will allow individuals, employers and employees to weigh both price and quality when purchasing coverage by requiring:

1. Standardization of health benefit designs. **While we do not believe** a single standardized benefit design, **as required in the Clinton plan, will be workable, a limited number of standardized benefit designs will allow consumers to easily compare products.**

2. **Health plans to report standardized data on quality of care and subscriber satisfaction.**

3. A limit on the tax deductibility of employer contributions for health benefits to an amount consistent with cost-efficient health plans.

The Administration's plan contains each of these important incentives. These features will encourage the expansion of organized delivery systems that have a proven ability to change inefficient and ineffective utilization patterns and cause providers to become more efficient providers of health care.

Universal coverage: Making more affordable insurance available would reduce the number of people without insurance benefits, but it would not lead to universal coverage. A requirement for employers to offer and contribute to the cost of health benefits, and for individuals to accept and pay for the balance of the premium, would be necessary to achieve universal coverage.

Such a requirement, however, would impose a severe burden on many small employers. To make it possible for small employers to comply with the mandate, subsidies would be needed. These subsidies should be targeted to companies that rely heavily on low-wage workers.

<u>Need to Increase Competition and Maintain Stability</u>

Two elements of the Clinton Administration's recent proposal cause us concern. These include the proposal's reliance on large regulatory Health Alliances to perform an extraordinarily broad and complex range of functions, including compliance with the new standards of market conduct, and the proposal's reliance on global budgets and premium caps to control costs. We do not believe either large alliances or premium caps are necessary to achieve the goals of universal coverage and cost containment. Instead, we are concerned that both may lessen the effectiveness of the new rules governing the insurance market.

Large regulatory alliances: The Health Alliances would be called on to perform an extraordinary range of functions. Large regulatory Health Alliances would result in an immediate conversion of the vast majority of insurance from group coverage to individual coverage. While individual choice may be a long term goal for reform, dismantling the system of group coverage poses grave risks for market stability. For example, fewer than 6,000 private business establishments have 1,000 or more employees. However, these establishments have more than 12 million employees -- more than 13 percent of total private sector employment. Abruptly requiring these millions of employees to individually select their health plan would have two destabilizing effects.

First, the administrative complexity of processing enrollment -- on an individual basis -- for 12 million individuals and families would add substantially to administrative costs. In addition, it would be almost impossible to avoid major confusion and disruption.

Second, as millions of individuals changed health plans -- both initially and annually -- the mix of risks -- and resulting costs -- insured by each health plan would change substantially and unpredictably. Such changes in enrollment are particularly likely because of several other elements of health reform, including standardization of benefits and community rating. Both provisions would change premiums significantly for many employers and individuals. Insurers cannot predict how consumers would react to such increases, making it very difficult for insurers to set premiums. They would literally have to set premiums in advance of knowing the characteristics of their enrollment.

The Administration has emphasized that a risk adjuster would address these problems of risk selection. We support risk adjustment, but do not believe that risk-adjustment methods would be sufficiently advanced to solve the problem. Our studies have consistently found that all health plans are not equally likely to cover higher-risk subscribers. In part, these differences reflect the extent to which some insurers can avoid enrolling people that are likely to need medical care. And in part, these differences reflect the preference of younger and healthier individuals and families for health care products such as Health Maintenance Organizations. Whatever the cause, it is not uncommon to find differences in risk of 20 percent or more across insurers and HMOs.

These differences in risk become important if community rating is adopted without a proven, reliable method of adjusting for differences in risk. Coverage from a plan that has suffered adverse selection could cost consumers considerably more -- for the same set of benefits -- than coverage from a health plan that has avoided high-risk subscribers. It has been established that many individuals and families will change health plans in response to differences in premiums of as little as $20 per month. Those who are most likely to change carriers are younger and healthier subscribers.

Risk adjustment is still in its infancy. The impact of age and sex on costs has long been recognized. For example, a person age 55 will, on average, incur costs that are four times higher than a person age 25. However, these simple demographic adjustments account for only a small part of the difference in premiums that can be attributed to risk selection. For example, in a comparison of products that are virtually identical in terms of benefits and provider networks, demographic factors accounted for only a small fraction of the difference in costs. When additional information is considered, including measures of self-reported health status and use of health services in prior years, we can account for more of the difference in costs. But, even our best methods account for less than half of the difference. States are currently experimenting with a number of solutions to the problem of risk adjustment, but none have yet proven themselves.

Unless an effective method of risk adjustment is developed, plans serving higher-risk groups and communities could be forced from the market. In practical terms, this means that we should proceed cautiously with reforms that may make it impossible for health plans with higher-risk subscribers to compete on a level playing field.

77-929 O - 94 - 13

We recommend that options for individual choice be expanded gradually. Voluntary purchasing cooperatives could be formed to allow small employers to offer their employees choice of health plans on an individual basis.

With respect to rating reform, community rating with demographic adjustments should be enacted for small employers, with between 2 and 49 employees. Such a requirement would eliminate those rating practices that have made health coverage unaffordable for many small employers and have had the most destabilizing effect on the small group markets. Insurance premiums would no longer vary widely for a small employer with older employees or an employee with a serious health problem. And rate increases from year-to-year would become more predictable for small groups. It would also be possible to develop, test, and refine more effective methods of risk adjustment while maintaining stability in the larger group market.

Premium Caps and Global Budgets: Global or alliance budgets administered through premium caps promise less spending, but we believe they would prove to be ineffective and would preclude a smooth transition into a more competitive and efficient system.

1. Premium caps would be driven by federal budget priorities and politics that have little or nothing to do with health care. One decision in Washington would determine the amount of money available to provide needed health care in each Health Alliance area.

2. By relying on a process that is not a reliable predictor of how fast communities should be expected to eliminate inefficiencies, premium caps would force the rapid downsizing of provider networks, reduced availability of sophisticated diagnostic and treatment technology, increased waiting times for consumers, and a decline in customer service. Plans that cannot comply with the limits would either be forced from the market -- or forced into insolvency. The end result would be fewer choices for consumers.

3. Premium caps would limit the innovation needed to truly change behavior, by limiting the ability of health plans to invest in ways of better managing practice patterns and achieving better outcomes for their members.

4. In the absence of proven methods of risk adjustment, health plans could exceed their premium cap because they have enrolled higher-risk subscribers not because they do not effectively manage costs.

Although some argue that premium caps are needed to enforce limits on spending, we believe that the new rules for health insurers will lead to vigorous price competition that will be more effective in controlling costs over the long run and support a more orderly transition into a reformed health care system.

Conclusion

I would like to reiterate our strong belief that insurance reform is the key to containing costs and assuring access to coverage. Reforms are needed to make coverage available for employers that have an employee who has a serious medical condition, reduce the wide variation in premiums charged to groups based on their health status, limit increases in premiums for small employers that result when an employee develops a serious medical problem, and assure coverage for individuals with existing medical conditions.

Federal policies to give employers and individuals a greater incentive to select cost-efficient health plans that delivery high quality care, and to enable them to compare the options that are available in a reformed market will complement insurance market reform. The benefits of reform can be realized without resorting to either premium caps or large Health Alliances that could actually work against the objectives of reform.

Mrs. COLLINS. Mr. Maurer?

STATEMENT OF JACK MAURER

Mr. MAURER. Thank you very much, Congresswoman Collins for inviting me. I represent the Council for Affordable Health Insurance. This is a group of about 30 small- to medium-sized companies. It is about 30 because membership seems to be growing each day, so by the end of the day, it may be more. We are working on other memberships.

My name is Jack Maurer. I am an actuary. I have been in the field of health insurance financing for approximately 30 years. Our organization represents companies that probably have about 3 million policyholders, so in the whole scheme of things, we are probably kind of small. We kind of look at ourselves as maybe the company that doesn't have the blimp. But we do feel we are the organization whose members are where the rubber meets the road.

We are on Main Street. We are dealing with self-employed people. And we know their concerns and we try to serve them as best we can.

That being said, the Clinton program has addressed a fundamental problem and there are a few aspects of it which surprisingly we can support. The 100 percent deductibility of health insurance premiums is probably something that our clientele should have had a long time ago so that they could be treated the same way as employees of large corporations.

We feel that a lot of the problems that have arisen in the small group market probably could be addressed to a great extent if they had tax equity with the large employers. The small group reform ideas include portability, renewability, guaranteed continuation of coverage, is something that we wholeheartedly support. We support the notion of guaranteed access to health coverage for all citizens.

We also support the idea of purchase groups negotiating for their memberships. In fact we deal with them today. We have a number of purchase groups that negotiate for our particular products. The key here in our opinion is that these associations or purchase groups, whatever you want to call them, be voluntary, and that we don't develop a system where the choices come down to one or two alliances or plans or what have you that Federal or State bureaucracies have determined is proper for every American.

Some of the problems we have with the Clinton plan—it appears to me from what I can glean from reading the 430-page report, it leans very, very heavily on bureaucratic control over 14 percent of our economy, and I personally find that kind of scary. For example, the National Board, if I could just jot down some of the powers they have: Draft model enabling legislation and regulations for the States to adopt; review and approve State implementation plans; distribute start-up funds to the States; approve and monitor the alliances proposed by the States; set and enforce an annual health budget for the Nation; allocate the budgeted amount between the various alliances; issue an identification number to every person in the United States; define standard benefit plans that everyone has to have; regulate premiums plans charge; establish risk adjustment mechanisms and on and on. I think you get the idea.

Thank you.

[The prepared statement of Mr. Maurer follows:]

Testimony of
Jack Maurer, Chief Actuary
PFL Life Insurance Company

on behalf of the
Council for Affordable Health Insurance

I would like to thank Chairwoman Collins and Chairman Waxman and the Members of the Subcommittees for the opportunity to come before you and share with you the concerns of the Council for Affordable Health Insurance about health care reform generally and the President's proposal specifically.

Let me say first that the Council for Affordable Health Insurance is an association of approximately 30 health insurance companies and related organizations which collectively provide insurance coverage to some 3,000,000 people in the United States. These companies specialize in the very small group, individual, and supplemental coverage markets. The average sized group covered by these companies is four persons and their dependents.

These companies came together to organize this association in March of 1992, because of our experience in these difficult markets and our fundamental concern that the direction health care reform was taking would be bad for our customers, bad for the health care system, and bad for our country.

We do not dispute the idea that fundamental changes are sorely needed in the way health care is financed in this country. But we are gravely concerned that many of the proposed changes would take away the things that are best about our system and encourage the very practices that have created the problems.

Our first task as an association was to set down on paper a set of reforms that we believe will improve our health care system by providing security and affordable coverage to all Americans. I have provided copies of this position ~~paper~~ to the subcommittee.

Since that initial work, we have continued to do original research to elaborate on the ideas we support. For instance, just this week we are releasing a comprehensive study on the impact that Medical Savings Accounts would have on our health care system. As part of this research we have constructed a computerized model of the entire health care system, using a ground-up, actuarial approach that accounts for variations in the behavior of the entire under age 65 population based on such factors as age, income, health status, and category of employment.

This study indicates that by the end of five years, Medical Savings Accounts would be chosen by 65% of those given that option. Furthermore, over this five year period, the health care system would enjoy considerable savings: $391 billion in constant dollars, or $588 billion when inflation in medical costs is taken into account.

These savings would result from dramatic reductions in administrative costs, patient-induced moderated utilization of the health care system, and system-wide cost effects due to greater price consciousness on the part of patients.

With this one reform alone, the numbers of uninsured would be halved in just five years, and the effect on the federal budget would be negligible.

This would be accomplished without new taxes; without deficit spending; without more bureaucracy; without lost jobs; without arbitrary price controls; and without the rationing of health care services.

Copies of this study have been made available to the Members of the Subcommittees.

Now, I would like to share with you some of our concerns about the President's proposal as we understand it. We realize that the proposal is being revised even as we sit here today, so my comments are based on the 239 page outline that was distributed some weeks ago.

There are a number of things in Mr. Clinton's proposal that we can support enthusiastically:

- Full deductibility for the self-employed and individuals who purchase their own coverage is one of our fundamental positions, and we applaud the President for correcting this basic inequity in the present system.

- Insurance reforms that make sure coverage is fully portable when people change jobs or employers change insurers, including continuation of coverage for terminated employees; that prohibit the singling out of individuals for cancellation or rate increases; and that limit rate variations attributable to health status. These are all part of our program, and we support efforts to enact them into law.

- Joint purchasing arrangements for economies of scale and greater clout in the market place is a wonderful idea. In fact, this is how most of our members currently market their products -- through local Chambers of Commerce, associations of small businesses like the National Association of the Self Employed, or affinity groups such as the Soybean Growers Association. We would suggest taking this further to encourage non -employment based purchasing as well, through mechanisms such as church groups, schools, housing projects and the like.

However, there are many elements of the President's proposal that rely on centralization of power, oppressive regulation, and economic projections that are wishful thinking. Please allow me to share just a few of these problems with you:

Level of Benefits. The benefits proposed by the President are extremely generous. Virtually the only things not covered are adult dental and vision, and 100% coverage of mental health and substance abuse. I expect these benefits are more generous than most of the people in this room have ever received in their working lives. It certainly covers a lot more than any plan I have ever had. This is a very expensive package.

The Cost of Coverage. Under the Clinton plan, the *maximum* anyone would have to pay for coverage is 9.7% of their wages (7.9% employer's share, and 1.8% employees share). This is simply not enough money to pay for the benefits proposed. The Department of Health and Human Services released figures just last week that showed the *average* percent of income spent by Americans on hospitals, physicians and prescription drugs alone is 11.5%. Obviously if you add in dentists and nurses and home health care and mental health care the cost goes up even more. Another point of comparison is a study done recently by the Wyatt Company of 900 large employers. This study showed the cost of a benefit package at the 50th percentile of generosity ranged anywhere from 9.7% to 18.9% as a percent of wages. The lowest average cost for a very modest set of benefits was 9.7% -- the same as the President's maximum for a much richer set of benefits.

Disparate Impact on Special Circumstance. Some people will be greatly advantaged, while others will be equally disadvantaged under the proposed system. For example:

- The self-employed will have to pay both the employer's share and the employee's share of the assessment, and will be eligible for a subsidy only if their income is below $24,000. That means anyone who is contemplating becoming self-employed will have to pay nearly 10% of their income for health insurance alone, on top of all the other taxes they have to pay.

- Owners of Subchapter S Corporations can choose whether to take compensation in the form of wages or profits. By limiting their wages to $12,000 and taking the rest in profits, they would be able to obtain the maximum subsidy available.

- Small, high wage firms such as law firms, will only have to pay whatever the premium amount would be, while low wage firms would have their costs determined as a percentage of payroll. The low wage firm will very likely be paying well below the actuarial value of the coverage, while the high wage firm pays only the actuarial value of the coverage, and a much lower percent of wages. If the average premium is $5,000, a ten-person law firm with an average wage of $125,000 would pay 4% of wages, while a ten-person dry cleaner with average wage of $25,000 pays a total of only $2,425 per person (9.7% of wages), or less than half of the $5,000 premium. This arrangement results in an enormous system-wide shortfall, even ignoring the additional specific subsidies that would kick in for lower-wage firms.

Draconian Centralized Power. The President would appoint a 7 member National Health Board to serve staggered four year terms and have the following powers:

- Draft model enabling legislation and regulations for the states to adopt.
- Review and approve state implementation plans.
- Distribute start-up funds to the states.
- Approve and monitor the alliances proposed by the states.
- Set and enforce an annual health budget for the nation.
- Allocate the budgeted amount between the various alliances.
- Issue an identification number to every person in the United States.
- Define the standard benefit plans
- Regulate the premiums health plans may charge.
- Establish a risk adjustment mechanism for health plans
- Set capitalization and solvency standards for health plans
- Set standards for guaranty funds.
- Establish and manage a quality management system.
- Monitor and make comment on prescription drug prices.

This Board is accountable to no one and may be removed from office only for malfeasance.

The Health Alliance is also very powerful. It is created by the state, with a board appointed, presumably by the Governor. It may not include anyone with a professional interest in health care. It has the following powers:

- Picks and chooses which health plans may participate.
- Negotiates with these health plans a level of premium to stay within the level of expenses set by the National Health Board.
- Sets the fee schedule that fee-for-service plans must follow.
- Enrolls every person in its region, and keeps track of what health plan they have chosen.
- Requires every person moving into its area to register with the Alliance within 30 days.
- Collects all the premium payments and forwards them on to the health plans.
- Approves all marketing materials the health plans are allowed to use.
- Holds an annual open enrollment period.
- Negotiates "inter-alliance" arrangements.
- Prepares and distributes "report cards" evaluating the merits of each health plan.

Between the power of the National Health Board and the Health Alliance, there is very little remaining for the consumers to have power over. If we really believe in the campaign slogan of "Putting People First" this is exactly the wrong way to do it.

Cost Controls. Finally, the President's plan does nothing to change the central dynamics of the health care system that have been driving up costs for the past fifty years in this country -- that is the notion that if someone else is paying for it, I might as well grab all I can.

While it is true that this plan would have consumers choose which plan they will enroll in each year, and that may get them to think about costs once a year, it is also true that once that decision has been made, there are no disincentives to patients to consume all the health care services they can. Instead, the plan relies on external constraints to monitor consumer (and physician) behavior and restrict their access to "unneeded" services.

There are many problems with this approach, including these:

- Although HMOs have been widely available for the past twenty years, only 40 million people are currently enrolled in them. We don't know how many people have tried an HMO and gone back to traditional plans, but there is ample anecdotal evidence that people like HMOs until they get sick and really need services, then they want the full range of providers and services available to them. People in America do not like having outsiders second guessing what is appropriate medical treatment for them and their families.

- We don't dispute the idea that there are many unnecessary services delivered each year. However, it is much easier to determine what was unnecessary in retrospect than it is prospectively. The prospect of denying someone a service because an outside reviewer has said it is unnecessary remains daunting.

- It is by no means clear that HMOs and other managed care programs are necessarily less expensive than traditional plans. We do know that

HMOs attract a younger and healthier population, and much of the average lower cost is due to that selection. Even with that population advantage, HMOs are often more expensive than traditional plans. The employer survey conducted each year by Foster Higgins discovered this year that 52% of employers said their HMO plans were less expensive than their traditional plans, but 30% said they were more expensive and 18% said there was no difference.

- Managed care certainly incurs additional administrative costs, which may or may not result in overall savings.

None of this is to imply that managed care is not worthwhile. It may well be, especially for high-cost, complex procedures. But to impose institutional control on who you may see for a check-up or where youi can take your kids for immunizations is government-induced oppression for no good reason. The idea that these programs are somehow a panacea for the cost problems in this country represents a fundamental misunderstanding of what is driving cost increases in health care. The notion also underestimates the American preference for self-determination and the fierce resentment of external controls. Governmentally mandated behavioral controls in health care will most assuredly lead to popular resistance like we have never seen before in this country.

If it is possible to create a system that enables people to regulate their own behavior and control their own use of resources, it is certainly worth pursuing. Such a system is available through the use of Medical Savings Accounts, in combination with meaningful insurance reforms, and voluntary use of managed care programs.

This system would meet all the criteria the President laid out in his speech to Congress, without imposing a top-down system of central controls on the behavior of the American people. The Council for Affordable Health Insurance urges the Congress to take a very serious look at this approach before rushing to embrace the dangerous system proposed by the Administration.

Mrs. COLLINS. Mr. Tringale, it is possible that many of today's health insurers are going to exit the market during the transition years, leaving their current policyholders without any kind of health insurance. If this were to occur, how would your companies be affected? Are you likely to offer insurance to all of those who would lose their coverage due to market exits, and if so, would you do so at average premium rates for each class of policy?

Mr. TRINGALE. We would certainly stay in the market and try and extend coverage to as many individuals as possible. We believe that we will see continued consolidation in the Massachusetts marketplace. In many ways, we have already seen the consolidation that a lot of people envision under the Clinton bill.

In terms of would we be able to offer that at an average price, it is too early to determine that especially given the lack of specificity in terms of benefit design and other provisions of the bill.

Mrs. COLLINS. Mr. Hurd?

Mr. HURD. For some years now there has been a steady exiting from the business of a number of health insurers and I think it is reasonable to expect that would continue in the future. However, you have got many willing participants in the marketplace to pick up those customers who would lose their coverage, and if this framework is designed correctly, mandating that everyone participate, you can simultaneously have the rules that the insurers must guarantee issue and that the range of price that could be charged would be compressed. So I think that the market can deal with this transition period if it is carefully designed.

Mrs. COLLINS. Thank you.

Mr. English, I believe you may have voiced your opposition to mandatory premium caps being included in the President's plan. So, my question is, even so, would you support efforts to voluntarily keep premium increases to a minimum and if that is the case, roughly what percentage do you think would be a reasonable annual increase if there were no caps? What percentage do you think would be unreasonable?

Mr. ENGLISH. Madam Chairwoman, I support a free market system. In a free market system, it is competition that sets the level of price. Our experience as a managed care operator has been as we have moved employees from pure indemnity plans, plans where people have a totally unmanaged approach to medical care, where they can have whatever they want, wherever they want into managed care programs, the rate of increase has been cut at least in half.

In many of our managed care programs this year, we are seeing low single-digit rates of increase. In some managed care programs, we have seen zero or even negative rates of increase. For me, however, to be able to guarantee an across-the-board level of increase or rate of percentage is impossible. I can't do that. I don't believe it can be done in a free market environment.

Mrs. COLLINS. Do you agree with that, Mr. Tringale?

Mr. TRINGALE. Essentially on all the points Mr. English raised. We too have a full product portfolio which goes from traditional indemnity coverage down to staff model HMO's and very tightly-managed models and we are seeing very, very low rates of increases right now.

I think one of the toughest things of guaranteeing a specific rate of increase would be the ability to move consumers, to educate consumers, the acceptance of consumers to move as fast as might be necessary to get them into those models which would allow us to have any comfort level at all about trying to guarantee that we could hold overall rate increases to a certain amount. We still have a significant indemnity population in our State.

Mr. HURD. Over the last few years, our company has invested $300 million in the creation of HMO networks. We are planning on doing another half billion dollars in the next few years and that is what the expectation is. You will be able to earn a profit or rate of return on that investment.

If we get an environment where there is going to be price controls or price caps, this is a thin margin business. I think it will pose excruciating decisions for the business community as to trying to put the additional capital in versus the fear that the losses will be very large in a price controlled environment.

Mrs. COLLINS. Thank you.

Mr. Bliley?

Mr. BLILEY. Thank you.

First let me ask unanimous consent to distribute to the members of the committee this chart.

Mrs. COLLINS. Without objection, so ordered.

[The chart referred to follows:]

Restrictions on Fee-For-Service: Can You Really Choose Your Doctor?

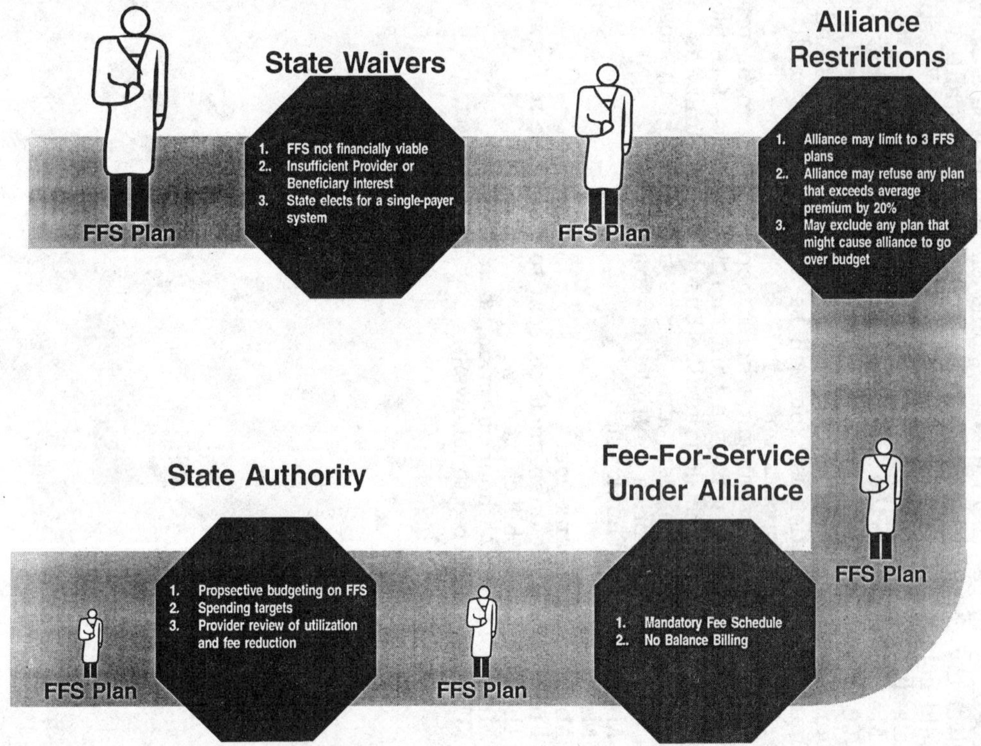

Mr. BLILEY. Initially I was going to use this line of questioning on restrictions on fee-for-service with our next panel which is comprised of our physician representatives and I will give them a chance to comment. But first because of Mr. Hurd's testimony and the fact that it will be your companies that will have to create the accountable health plans, I would like your input.

The administration states over and over that fee-for-service is an option that all alliances must offer and the American public places free choice on their personal doctor as one of their primary concerns. But when you work through the fine print of the September 7 draft, the fee-for-service option appears to shrink and then disappear just like our doctor friend on the chart to your left, for in the Clinton plan, the proposed fee-for-service eliminates many of the elements of fee-for-service.

Let's walk with our fee-for-service doctor through the stop signs or, as Ira Magaziner would say, the tollgates and see if we can still find our fee-for-service doctor after this long and tortuous journey. First, there are a number of ways that States can waive a fee-for-service option. These include, one, a fee-for-service plan is not viable, page 62 of the September 7 draft.

Two, there is insufficient provider of beneficiary interest, page 62; or three, the State elects a single-payer system, page 54.

Second, the fee-for-service makes it past the State waivers. It then faces a number of alliance restrictions. First, even if many fee-for-service plans want to contract with an alliance, the alliance can limit fee-for-service plans to three, page 61.

Second, an alliance may refuse to contract with a plan that exceeds the average premium by 20 percent, page 60. This will almost exclusively affect higher cost fee-for-service plans. Finally, the alliance may exclude any plan that might cause an alliance to go over budget, page 61. This would primarily affect higher-priced fee-for-service plans.

Three, now there are two more alliance restrictions on fee-for-service plans. First there must be a mandatory fee schedule; and second, no balanced billing is allowed.

Four, but we are not finished. The State has the following additional authority: States have the authority to impose prospective budgeting on FFS plans, page 62. It can establish spending targets, page 63. And it can periodically review utilization and reduce payments to physicians for services to comply with this budget, page 63.

I think it is safe to say that no physician or insurer has ever been or ever seen or participated in an FFS plan with these types of restrictions. At this point in our journey, there is very little fee-for-service option left. After passing through these four stop signs, FFS has been whittled away to nothing. It is like telling the American public you can choose an FFS plan as long as it walks and talks like a HMO.

Second, The Washington Post October 12 poll shows that the American people have not been fooled. The lack of freedom of choice is identified as the public's number one complaint with the Clinton plan. I would like Mr. Hurd from Principal Insurance Company, Mr. English from CIGNA, and Mr. Tringale from Blue Cross to comment on this chart since you represent the large insurers who will have to put these plans together.

Mr. HURD. I think your description is graphic and accurate. I think there are additional hurdles for the fee-for-service plan to the degree that individuals choose plans rather than groups such as employers. The selection can become even more intense and cause the prices to rise for fee-for-service plans.

I would add the observation that just as managed care is changing, fee-for-service plans are changing and they are moving to new levels of sophistication that will help control costs, and we believe there should be efforts to keep them viable in the marketplace.

Mr. BLILEY. Do you agree with Mr. Hurd's statement, Mr. English?

Mr. ENGLISH. Yes. I think your analysis is quite accurate. Under the proposal with global budgets, I think as Mr. Hurd said, there are even more hurdles. I believe there could be assessments against plans that overspend what was budgeted as well. It is hard to imagine the fee-for-service concept existing in the kind of environment that is imagined in this plan.

Mr. BLILEY. Mr. Tringale, Mr. Maurer, do either of you disagree with what Mr. Hurd and Mr. English have said?

Mr. TRINGALE. Essentially I agree. In fact, that dynamic is already occurring in the mass marketplace.

Mr. MAURER. I agree. You are seeing a movement towards more managed care and negotiated fee-type arrangements as part of just a free market response to the finances that exist today. I think it will continue to do so as long as it is free to do so in a free open market.

If these are good ideas, and I won't say they are or they aren't, get out there and compete with everybody else and they will blow everybody else out of the water.

Mr. BLILEY. Thank you. I thank the Chair and apologize for trespassing on my time.

Mrs. COLLINS. Mr. Brown?

Mr. BROWN. Mr. Hurd, you said you were interested in prevention and had some ideas. Would you specify some of them, what we should be doing?

Mr. HURD. Three or four thoughts. One, I think employers are a driving force towards prevention and wellness and we ought to design this system to keep that incentive there for them to behave in that fashion. I think there are ways of doing that.

One example might be the Wellness Councils of America have a rating system for employer wellness plans at bronze, silver and gold level. If this could be a regulatory arrangement, perhaps employers that qualified at those levels could be given cost discounts in relation thereto. I think many things can be done with individuals.

In our own company's plan, we have discounts to employees for not smoking, for seat belt fastening, for height and weight within certain broad limits, et cetera. I think over the years we could develop and make those much more sophisticated. Those are a few ideas.

Mr. BROWN. Mr. Maurer, you note in your testimony that the benefits package might be too generous, but many describe the traditional design of our health insurance as a sickness system which oftentimes negates the importance of prevention. Tell us what part of the President's package that you would like to delete, the part of the preventive package that you would like to delete?

Mr. MAURER. Where to begin? I would say that the real fundamental difference we have here is that where we come in we are talking about a maximum freedom of choice for the consumer, for the individual. We want to devise a system whereby everybody has a guaranteed access to our health care system. That does not mean that everybody is forced into a particular benefit plan, be it rich, be it meager, or what have you. We feel that the individual is the best person to determine what his needs are.

As far as the particular question with the primary care, one of the main parts of our program, probably the centerpiece, is the support of the medical savings accounts. This is a mechanism whereby actual dollars will be put into an account for the individual with the idea that this money is available to support his primary care, to get his checkups, get his kids immunized, all of these things that are not high-cost items.

Coupled with that, we support catastrophic coverage for individuals to buy. These would be low cost, high deductible, I would say a wide range of deductible depending upon what each individual determines is his best mix of what he wants to take care of himself and where he feels he needs institutional help when the costs get too great. So I would say that the fundamental difference we have with the Clinton plan is one of forcing people into a particular type of benefit program versus our program, which is to give people the empowerment so they can pick and choose the type program they want that best suits their circumstances.

Mr. SHERROD BROWN. But are including several of the preventive elements of the Clinton plan a bad idea or a good idea in your mind?

Mr. MAURER. I think it is an outstanding idea that people have the ability to get preventive care. I think in our particular system right now we probably have the best health care available if people have the ability to get it, but I don't think it is the government's position to tell people they have to go to this doctor or that doctor or that HMO or that PPO or EPO or IPA to get your kids immunized.

I think they can figure out where to go and they will go to the guy who charges $25 rather than $50 if it is coming from an account they have control over.

Mr. BROWN. Thank you.

Mrs. COLLINS. Mr. Greenwood?

Mr. GREENWOOD. During the hearing today and throughout this debate, there has been a lot of discussion about the amount of fat in the system. I am sure you heard the earlier discussions that some estimate it to be 20 percent. Apparently Dr. Koop thinks it is 20 percent.

A two-part question: What are your estimates on the percentage of fat in the system?

And second, under the market-driven system, the incentives are really with the companies that you represent, the health insurers, to root out excessive administrative costs, overutilization, fraud, duplication of medical technology, excess profit taking, and undeserved fees. The incentives are there for you, the insurance companies, to squeeze that out, and I assume that constitutes most of the 20 percent or whatever the figure is.

The second part of my question is what tools do you need in order to squeeze this waste and inefficiency and fraud and abuse out of this system that either you find in the administration's proposal or that you don't find in the administration proposal?

Mr. Hurd?

Mr. HURD. I have no estimate on how much——

Mr. GREENWOOD. Comment on the 20 percent.

Mr. HURD. I guess at the common-sense level, it feels a little high. However, if you include in that the concept of real change in the practice of medical care, maybe this is something that is achievable. You gave some examples earlier this morning about coronary bypasses and angioplasties and how there was a very low percentage of those that were not needed.

However, if our medical establishment developed other means of dealing with the blockage of arteries through the use of diet and counseling, et cetera, perhaps that would be a much lower-cost alternative and as it came into place, you would see an abrupt decrease in cost. The definition of what is waste in the current system is probably a slippery thing.

The only point that comes to my mind on the second question, and we probably need to go back and think about it and get back to you in writing, is wondering whether or not aspects of the antitrust laws that prevent useful collaborations which are aimed at either decreasing waste or rooting out fraud.

Mr. GREENWOOD. Thank you.

Mr. English?

Mr. ENGLISH. Congressman, it is impossible to put a figure on the thing of waste and fraud. All my life I have heard arguments coming from all political parties that we are going to solve all kinds of problems eliminating waste and fraud. It is hard to define. I can assure you there is not 20 percent pure waste and fraud in our system.

If there were, free market competition would have rooted it out long ago. There are questions around practices. Do we do replacement for an 80-year-old person? Do we keep people alive for long periods of time? If you throw some of those societal issues into the equation and say we shouldn't do them and count those as part of the number, it may be higher than the 2 or 3 percent, but it is very difficult to measure.

The important thing as to what we need to get whatever inefficiencies there are in the system, whether they are unnecessary test and procedures or waste and fraud out, I believe is competition. I see this happening every day. Large employers are moving their employees into managed care programs. They have realized that a process of managed care, which I would define as a partnership among the payer, the employer, if you will, patients and the provider aimed at keeping people well in the first place and getting them well once they get sick is the most effective way of getting excess cost out of the system, and I see it work every day.

I do not see competition working effectively however for small employers or for individuals. Here you have a very inefficient market. Marketing administrative cost eats up a disproportionate amount of their premium. Preexisting condition clauses make it impossible to move from one carrier to another, so there isn't really choice.

I believe we need in that segment of the market—say firms with fewer than a hundred employees and individuals—a free market purchasing cooperative in which preexisting condition limitations are excluded where community rating is used, and where companies would compete purely on the basis of price and quality.

Everyone would have to report their quality the same way. I believe that kind of efficiency will reform the small case markets. I think things would continue to gravitate toward managed care and we would get whatever the excess cost in the system is out of it very quickly.

Mr. WAXMAN. Mr. Cooper?

Mr. COOPER. No questions.

Mr. WAXMAN. Mr. Hastert?

Mr. HASTERT. Thank you, Mr. Chairman.

Mr. Hurd, you talked about incentives with regard to your company and others setting up wellness programs. In your opinion, do you take away the incentives for companies to do a good job and to get people in preventive medicine and wellness programs when you put everybody in the same risk pool, which happens when you create huge health alliances?

Say for instance in my area, the metropolitan statistical area that covers my area in northern Illinois would be 4 or 5 million people. You have smokers in with non-smokers. You have people who take huge health risks in with people who don't have health risks.

On the other side of the insurance industry, wouldn't that be like putting people with 10 tickets on the same premium level with people with a perfect driving record?

Mr. HURD. I think pure community rating would be a detriment because it would not allow incentives for employers and for individuals to do things that would produce healthier lifestyles.

Mr. HASTERT. But in a sense, while we haven't seen all the details of the bill coming from the administration, it appears that their proposal would eliminate such incentives?

Mr. HURD. Some of the talk is that we, in grouping people together in large pools, that the rates that relate to them are pure community rating and that certainly is destructive of any effort to——

Mr. HASTERT. So the cost efficiencies that you and other companies have been able to develop in health care over the last 10 years are basically out the window?

Mr. HURD. You can say any employer is going to continue to have an interest in having a healthy work force, but when you take away incentives that will impact on this element of cost, you decrease incentives. I think it would be possible to usefully design in some reflection back to employers of their own costs and so they could get the benefit of whatever activities they did that would help hold down cost.

Mr. HASTERT. Mr. Maurer, you kind of represent the small guys in this equation. A lot of the innovation and entrepreneurial savings is coming from the smaller industries. You have created incentives for people to do a better job at a lower cost.

Could you compete in a statistical area health plan service area that may include most small insurance companies? Can you take on responsibility of a 5 million statistical area?

Mr. MAURER. Well, I think we would find a way to compete. It would be up to me to convince our board of directors we won't go broke doing it.

Mr. HASTERT. Can we keep you people on board or do we lose you?

Mr. MAURER. It kinds of depends, but don't worry too much about us. Worry about our clients. Worry about the people we serve. I am kind of bringing you their message as much as ours. They feel that the Clinton plan, what they know of it, they feel the Clinton plan is asking them to buy something they don't need, they don't want, they can't afford, and they shouldn't have to pay for it.

These are very responsible people. They are very willing to pay for the first $500, $1,000 or whatever of normal first dollar care that they or their family needs. They want protection if they get some catastrophic illness. Then they need the protection. They don't want to go broke if somebody comes down with cancer or has a bad accident.

These are the types of things that we insure against. Now, if you are going to impose the Clinton plan on everybody, many of these people are not going to be able to afford it. You will find a number of them will just say "I am going out of business. I will be an early retiree and get it free," that type of an approach.

Mr. HASTERT. If you look at what would happen, the plan requiring a 7.9 percent premium payment for employers and a tax on employees or premium payment by employees. It seems to me—and we haven't been able to get the numbers out of the administration, so as numbers appear, a lot of the economic experts on health care say there is not enough money. There is a $100 billion shortfall in cash flow.

We don't know because we haven't seen it yet, but if that's the process, and if you don't charge enough premium, what happens in your system?

Mr. ENGLISH. If I am operating in a managed care plan where I have control over the providers, I suppose I have the option of reducing the level of service.

Mr. HASTERT. Is that rationing?

Mr. ENGLISH. Yes. If I am in an indemnity environment where I am simply paying the bills as they come in and those bills are rising more rapidly than I am allowed to raise premiums, I go out of business.

Mr. HASTERT. So either we ration health care under this system if that economic cash flow is not enough or we start to raise that 7.9 percent premium cost, is that correct?

Mr. ENGLISH. I don't think there is any question.

Mr. HASTERT. So a 7.9 percent payment by employers and a 2 percent payment by employees is probably just the tip of the iceberg?

Mr. ENGLISH. Unless we are willing to live with rather Draconian rationing and a very different health care system than the American people have come to expect.

Mr. HASTERT. Thank you.

Thank you, Mr. Chairman.

Mr. WAXMAN. Mr. English, following up on your last points, do you think that there is no savings to be realized in our health care system—that we can't wring out some of the expenditures that now go into that system and direct it for services and eliminate some of the waste that we can't afford?

Mr. MAURER. I think there are all kinds of savings available. I wouldn't say there is 20 percent, but if it were proved to be 20 percent, I would not be overly amazed. We have a situation that has grown up over the past 50 years where there has been a blank-check mentality where there is no incentive for the patient in a doctor's office setting to have any interest on what the services are costing him.

Mr. WAXMAN. What about the incentive for insurance companies, for the doctors that decide what services are needed so often? Have they had the right incentives?

Mr. MAURER. Probably not.

Mr. WAXMAN. It seems to me the concept of managed competition is based on the premise that the consumer is not paying enough money and if the consumer paid some more money, then the consumer would want to make sure that health care is more affordable.

Mr. MAURER. It is not that the consumer is not paying enough money. The consumer is not paying enough attention. You are relying upon institutions to police the system, but you are putting the person who is getting the service in a position where he has no interest in the cost of that service. That is why we support things like medical savings accounts. That is why we support things like tax equity.

We have 50 years of building up an employer-based system where institutions have been making these decisions and I think that is a lot of reason why we have gotten to where we are now.

Mr. TRINGALE. There are clearly opportunities for savings in the system, some from administrative simplification, but the vast majority on the medical claims side. There are probably three kinds of utilization savings that I can think of off the top of my head, all of which don't obviate the need to be concerned about cash flow because they don't return immediate savings. One is inappropriate utilization. That is one we are doing a much better job in our managed care plans than we were in the past where we need to expand primary physicians, incentives for training for more primary care physicians, some of the components that are in the plan. That will continue to improve and should improve over time.

The second is avoidable utilization, which I characterize as different from inappropriate. Avoidable utilization has to deal with everything, including education, issues related to alcohol, tobacco, accident and violence prevention, which is a huge issue for places like Boston with urban inner-city hospitals and immunization protection which will cost money in terms of the short-term cash flow issues, but will engender savings in the system in the long term.

The third, and I think it gets back to Congressman Greenwood's question, where there aren't sufficient tools right now relate to what I would call societal savings in terms of what we do with last-year-of-life issues, we need a national health policy for that more than we need a regulatory board now so we have a forum to discuss those issues.

All three of those areas I think hold promise for sayings. I am not sure that you can bring a whole lot of money out of the system real quickly on those issues now.

Mr. HURD. We fear that price controls would cause gridlock and interrupt these many efforts that are already in place and could be increased by the legislation.

Mr. ENGLISH. Mr. Chairman, I too believe there are savings to be had in the system. I would like to explain my comment about rationing. I am concerned that if we simultaneously promise the American people a benefit package which is on a par with the plan available to Fortune 500 plans, a richer plan for most people, at the same time cut Medicare and Medicaid spending by almost a quarter of a trillion dollars, creating tremendous pressure for those physicians and other providers to shift that cost to the private sector, clamp controls on the private sector at that time, that the combination of those things will in very short order result in either people going out of business or in some form of rationing of health care in this country.

Mr. WAXMAN. I want to thank you all for your presentation. I am sorry I wasn't able to be here for all of it, but I think you have been very helpful to us.

Our third panel includes Dr. Clifton Cleaveland, president-elect of the American College of Physicians. He also practices internal medicine in Chattanooga, Tenn. Linda Shinn is serving as the interim executive director of the American Nurses Association. She is also testifying today on behalf of a number of nursing specialty and educational organizations.

Dr. Lonnie Bristow is chairman of the Board of Trustees of the American Medical Association. Dr. Paul Ebert is the director of the American College of Surgeons.

Thank you for being here today. We look forward to your testimony. Each of your full written statements will be in the hearing record so I would like to ask you to limit your statements to 5 minutes.

STATEMENTS OF CLIFTON R. CLEAVELAND, PRESIDENT-ELECT, AMERICAN COLLEGE OF PHYSICIANS; LINDA SHINN, EXECUTIVE DIRECTOR, AMERICAN NURSES ASSOCIATION; LONNIE R. BRISTOW, CHAIRMAN, AMERICAN MEDICAL ASSOCIATION; AND PAUL A. EBERT, DIRECTOR, AMERICAN COLLEGE OF SURGEONS

Mr. CLEAVELAND. Thank you, Mr. Chairman. I am Cliff Cleaveland, president-elect of the American College of Physicians. We as an organization are committed to fundamental reform of our Nation's health care system and therefore support President Clinton's blueprint for change. As a practicing physician, this is a time of great excitement. It is a time of great frustration and times of heartbreak.

The excitement is the technology, the interventions, the drugs, the wondrous things that we can bring to the care of sick patients, the new strategies that we can use in preventive medicine. The frustration occurs from the numerous hours and the enormous amount of money that go into dealing with a bureaucracy which seems at times to feed on itself which deprives my patients of the precious dollars that could be better directed to their care.

It is a time of heartbreak, and the heartbreak relates to those individuals that I see who have no access to health care, who have no insurance or who are trapped in a job because they have developed an illness that keeps them from moving jobs for fear of losing their health care coverage. Each day at work I spend 1 to 3 hours coping with the paperwork and the red tape.

I would rather do what I do best with those hours, look after my patients. Each day I deal with anonymous reviewers at the other end of phone lines which micromanage me to death. Their time and my time is wasted, the patients are not served, the system is not served.

The American College of Physicians looks to the President's plan with great hope for fixing a health care system that frankly has become unglued. First and foremost, the plan will provide peace of mind for every single American that they will have lifelong guaranteed access to good health care, not cabin class or tourist class, but first-class care. Patients will be allowed to choose their physician and their health plan. Thus when they lose jobs or change jobs, the health care coverage will not be broken.

These provisions will enable patients to do the most cost-effective thing they can do, and that is to forge and maintain a long-term relationship with a physician whom they trust. The President's plan will allow me to be a professional. It will take away a mountain of paperwork.

The President's plan argues as the College long has argued that health care reform must restore primary care physicians to a central role in the delivery of health care. Our training allows us to manage the care of the total person in a cost-effective manner.

The President's plan recognizes this key role of primary care physicians by addressing issues of reimbursement and incentives for young physicians to consider careers in primary care. The American College of Physicians believes that serious cost containment is essential to real health reform.

We support the Clinton plan in its use of competitive mechanisms within a national health care budgetary framework to control costs that at the present are frankly runaway. While we support many elements of the President's plan, let me mention some concerns we have. First and foremost, we are concerned with the malpractice reform component. The need to practice defensive medicine is one of the significant causes of skyrocketing health care costs.

Lawsuits are time consuming and expensive for all concerned. We would urge that non-economic damage awards to plaintiffs be capped. We recommend adding provisions which would eliminate joint and several liability, and we urge that mechanisms be studied and developed for alternatives to resolve very complex biomedical disputes outside of a courtroom environment.

We are concerned that the Clinton plan does not guarantee physician representation on the very important National Health Board which will have a vital part in overseeing our Nation's health planning and decision-making. We look forward to a joint endeavor with Members of the Congress and members of the administration.

These are not commodity issues. This is a sacred trust we share in looking after our fellow citizens at a very vulnerable time in their lives, when they are sick, when they are afraid, when they are alone. I look forward very much to what I think will be a vital partnership.

Thank you, Mr. Chairman.

Mr. WAXMAN. Thank you.

[The prepared statement of Dr. Cleaveland follows:]

Statement

of the

American College of Physicians

Good morning. Mr. Chairman, Members of Congress, and distinguished guests, my name is Dr. Clifton R. Cleaveland. I am President-elect of the American College of Physicians, the nation's largest medical specialty society, representing 80,000 physicians practicing internal medicine and its subspecialties. I practice internal medicine in Chattanooga, Tennessee.

The College is committed to fundamental reform of our nation's health system, and supports President Clinton's blueprint for change. The President has developed a comprehensive proposal, and we pledge to work with him and the Congress to get legislation passed as soon as possible. If all of us are committed to reform -- and keep that central goal in sight -- it will be possible to find agreements on the specific elements of the package.

Mr. Chairman, when physicians look at our nation's health system, they see a system in critical condition. They see that many of their patients do not have insurance. Those that are covered are not secure, because they know that at almost any moment, they can lose their insurance. They see a dissolution of the doctor-patient relationship due to the system's fragmentation and insurance rules. They see more paperwork and bureaucracy, and less ability to make the clinical decisions for patients they are trained to make. In sum, they see a system that doesn't work.

The College believes the President has put forward a workable plan that can fix the health care system for physicians and their patients. Specifically, it promises to:

- guarantee health security which will protect the doctor-patient relationship;
- restore professionalism to medical practice;
- support primary care; and
- provide meaningful cost containment.

Universal coverage and health security protect the doctor-patient relationship

The President's plan guarantees health care coverage for all Americans. It makes clear that health care is a fundamental right -- not an economic privilege.

The ACP has long endorsed universal coverage as an essential piece of any health reform plan. Mr. Chairman, you know the facts. Those without insurance total in the tens of millions. Moreover, those lucky enough to have insurance are at risk of losing their coverage if they change jobs, become unemployed, or get sick.

The consequences are enormous. Because they lack insurance, many of these Americans fail to get the care they need. Uncompensated care means that those with insurance end up paying for those without it. In addition, millions of Americans are trapped in their jobs because if they change jobs they lose their insurance.

By providing Americans with health security, the President's plan gives piece of mind to millions of American families who will know they can always get the care they need. Moreover, this guarantee will protect, and even improve, the doctor-patient relationship.

Right now, many of our patients have little choice over which doctor they can see. Often, their employer chooses their health plan, and that particular plan may restrict their choice of doctor. If the employer changes coverage, patients often have to see a new doctor. Furthermore, when they change jobs or lose their job, the patient's insurance coverage changes -- again, jeopardizing the continuity of care.

Under the Clinton plan, though, things will be different. Consumers, not their employers, will be allowed to choose their own health coverage, including the health plan their physician belongs to. Through the mechanism of the health alliance, when they change jobs or lose their job, their health coverage will follow them. In addition, the Clinton plan requires that consumers have the option of either joining a fee-for-service plan or being able to go outside a managed care plan. These provisions will enable patients to forge and continue long-standing relationships with their doctors. This is essential to the well-being of patients and the professional satisfaction of physicians.

The plan restores professionalism to medical practice

In addition, the President's health proposal promises to restore professionalism to the practice of medicine. Physicians today are increasingly frustrated by the health care system. They are being overwhelmed by paperwork, red tape, and excessive government regulation. While many of these regulations are well-intentioned, and our health system must contain methods of quality assurance and accountability, physicians must be given more responsibility and autonomy to make clinical decisions.

Insurance practices are also burdensome for physicians. With some 1500 insurance companies nationwide, each with their own claims forms, coverage determinations, and utilization review requirements, physicians often feel as if they are in the insurance business.

Mr. Chairman, it is time to permit physicians to spend our time doing what we are trained to do -- what we want to do. Physicians want to spend their time taking care of patients, not taking care of paperwork.

The President's plan recognizes this. We applaud the initiative to reduce the mountain of paperwork to one insurance claim form, and the creation of a "health security card". We are also pleased that he has proposed regulatory relief. Freeing physicians from unnecessary and burdensome regulations will allow physicians to spend more time caring for their patients, and less time worrying about bureaucrats. For example, in areas such as clinical laboratory requirements (CLIA), it is critical that we strike the appropriate balance between accountability and quality of care, and costly and burdensome intrusions into a physician's practice.

Support for primary care

The College has long argued that health care reform must restore primary care physicians to a central role in the health delivery system. In many communities across the country, primary care physicians are working hand-in-hand with other health professionals to provide Americans with high quality and cost effective health services. Nonetheless, far too many Americans still do not get the primary care services they need. Therefore, it is essential that the new health system expand these collaborative efforts. At the same time, it is critical that we increase the supply of primary care physicians by reforming our nation's medical education system to change the current severe imbalance between primary care physicians and subspecialists.

We applaud President Clinton for his recognition of the key role played by primary care physicians through increased reimbursement and delivery system changes. Moreover, the plan's call for changes in graduate medical education will help ensure that we can eventually achieve an appropriate balance between generalists and specialists. We hope to work with this Subcommittee to refine these proposals.

Meaningful cost containment

The ACP believes that serious cost containment is essential to real health reform. This country cannot afford, and will not achieve, universal health coverage without controlling costs. Mr. Chairman, we must limit the growth rate of health care spending.

We support the Clinton plan because it is the only plan that directly tackles the rising cost of health care. It does this through a combination of competitive mechanisms and a national health care budget. First, the plan changes incentives in the system, forcing health plans to compete on the basis of price and quality, careful use of resources, administration simplification, and other devices. Second, the national health care budget will act as a backstop. The budget does not call for either price controls or caps on physician fees. Rather, it challenges health plans to work cooperatively with providers and patients to hold down spending.

Limiting health spending will not mean the end of fee-for-service medicine, as some have charged. Indeed, the Clinton plan requires that fee-for-service plans be available to all Americans. In addition, other countries have shown that through negotiated fees, fee for service arrangements can operate within a budget. A fee-for-service plan in which providers practice conservatively should be able to deliver high quality care and compete successfully within premium constraints.

Mr. Chairman, the ACP is supportive of the goals, and many of the elements of the President's plan. But, like all pieces of complex legislation, the Clinton plan contains provisions that we feel need improvement.

Malpractice Reform

A primary concern is that the malpractice reform components of the plan are weak. Mr. Chairman, our medical liability system needs fundamental reform. Instead of our current adversarial system, we should strive to develop a system that focuses on ways to improve the quality of medical care.

Unfortunately, all too often discussions about malpractice reform have turned into shouting matches between doctors and lawyers. That obfuscates the real issue. Our nation's malpractice system does not work -- for injured persons or physicians. Lawsuits are time-consuming and expensive for both sides. Many victims of malpractice don't receive timely and adequate awards. In fact, only six out of every 100 patients who experience adverse outcomes as a result of negligent care receive compensation.

In addition, physicians feel threatened and often believe they must perform procedures merely to protect themselves from liability. A recent poll showed that 78% of America's physicians reported that the threat of medical liability suits causes them to order tests they might otherwise consider unnecessary. This causes the physician-patient relationship to suffer, and in some instances, patients lose access to certain types of health care.

The Clinton plan's malpractice reform provisions do not go far enough. We urge that non-economic damage awards to plaintiffs be capped. We believe a cap will act similarly to the global budget -- putting boundaries on the system. In addition, we would add provisions eliminating joint and several liability and strengthening alternate dispute resolution mechanisms. We look forward to working with you and other committees to strengthen these provisions.

Physician Role

Another concern is the physician's role in the new system. Physicians are on the front lines of health care delivery, and are responsible for their patient's health. Consequently, they must be an integral part of the management of the new system.

Toward that end, we were disappointed that the Clinton plan does not guarantee physician representation on the new National Health Board, that will be such a vital part of our nation's health planning and decision-making. In addition, although each health alliance will have an advisory provider panel, we are concerned that decisions about clinical practice will be made without sufficient physician input.

It is also critical that physicians perform quality assurance activities in the new system. Currently, our system of utilization review and quality assurance is overly burdensome. Utilization review is performed on a case-by-case basis by many different entities that use different, secret, and often inconsistent criteria. Moreover, these criteria often do not focus on quality of care.

As we reform our health system, it is essential that we develop a quality assurance mechanism that uses explicit public criteria and balances internal mechanisms of quality improvement with external accountability. While profiles of practice patterns can be used to identify possible problems, physicians and other providers should perform detailed monitoring of quality and problem solving.

Moreover, we believe that as outlined, the plan will not achieve the Administration's stated goal of the development of provider-controlled, community-based health plans throughout the country. Physicians must have the necessary tools to compete with traditional insurers and other entities seeking to become health plans.

For example, the proposal should not require that all health plans be "insurance companies" as defined by many state statutes. Moreover, a physician-governed plan should not be subject to the same capital and solvency requirements of a traditional insurer. In addition, technical assistance, including the opportunity to receive timely advisory legal opinions, should be made available to doctors seeking to form health plans.

No New Bureaucracies

An additional concern that we want to highlight today is the issue of creating unintended bureaucracy. We must remember that health alliances are "purchasing cooperatives" -- administrative mechanisms for pooling people together to help them purchase insurance. While the alliances also serve other administrative and consumer-education functions, they should not become additional layers of regulation and bureaucracy.

State Flexibility

Finally, Mr. Chairman, I'd like to issue a word of caution about the plan's provisions regarding the role of states. As you know, this proposal gives states a large amount of flexibility to design the health delivery and financing system within their borders. In addition, it encourages states that are already developing their own health reform plans to continue that effort.

While state flexibility is important, we must remember that the goal of this proposal is to reform our nation's health system for patients as well as for physicians. Toward that end, the federal government should set clear criteria and carefully monitor state actions to make sure that goal is achieved.

Conclusion

Mr. Chairman, we applaud the President's initiative. The time for reform is now. The status quo won't do for physicians or their patients. A new system that provides health security to all Americans, while allowing physicians to once again practice medicine free from red tape and interference is long overdue. We look forward to working with you and your colleagues as the legislation is developed. Thank you.

Mr. WAXMAN. Ms. Shinn?

STATEMENT OF LINDA SHINN

Ms. SHINN. Thank you, Mr. Chairman.

I am Linda Shinn, the executive director of the American Nurses Association. We also testify on behalf of the American Association of Nurse Anesthetists, the American Association of Critical Care Nurses, the American Association of Colleges of Nursing, the American Association of Spinal Cord Injury Nurses, the Association of operating Room Nurses, the Emergency Nurses Association, and the National Nurse Practitioner Coalition.

We are pleased to appear before the subcommittee as you begin to decide how, not whether, to reform our Nation's health care system, and we commend the members of both of these subcommittees for their leadership in advancing the debate in health care reform. We are also pleased that a number of members of this subcommittee have introduced or cosponsored bills that propose a variety of different approaches to the reform of the health care system. This will ensure that this issue is comprehensively discussed and that all options are thoroughly considered.

We too make a commitment to working with you. America's 2 million registered nurses deliver many essential health care services in the United States today in a variety of settings, in hospitals, in nursing homes, in schools, in home health agencies, in the workplace, in community health clinics, in private practice and in managed care settings.

Nurses know firsthand of the inequities and problems with our Nation's health care system. Because we are there 24 hours a day, 7 days a week, we know the system succeeds for some and fails shamefully for too many others.

Like the President and Mrs. Clinton, and many Members of this Congress, America's nurses believe that it is time to frame a bold new vision for health care. For most nurses believe that universal access to health care services is a principle that cannot be compromised.

For any health care reform plan to be successful, it is critical that it not only address access to health insurance, but access to health care services. Under the administration's proposal, the health care setting could be restructured and reoriented so that services would be available in schools, in workplaces, in community settings, as well as hospitals and providers' offices.

Consumer access to health services must be maximized. The cornerstone of any health care reform proposal is the guarantee, we believe, of a standard health benefit package.

We are pleased that the administration's plan places new emphasis on primary care and preventive services delivered not only by physicians, but also by nurses and qualified health care providers in convenient, accessible settings. Expanding the role of the nurse in a reformed health care delivery system is critical for increased preventive health services which have been the very center for nursing practice since the inception of our profession.

However, the ability of nurses to deliver these services has been continually hampered by a number of artificial barriers that serve to cut the consumer off from access to these services. These barriers include restrictive reimbursement policies based upon specialty or geographic location and various and numerous State restrictions on nursing practice.

The President's plan addresses this problem by preempting barriers to practice, by providing incentives for the States to adopt a Federal model for nursing practice statutes, and by including payment for services for advanced practice nurses. We believe it is important that these barriers be tackled and be removed.

In 1991, the Rural Nursing Incentive Act that allowed nurse practitioners and clinical nurse specialists who practice in rural areas to receive direct reimbursement under Medicare was enacted. It now needs to be expanded to cover the services of all nurse practitioners and clinical nurse specialists regardless of geographic location and practice setting.

This expansion of coverage does not provide for reimbursement of new services, but rather provides for reimbursement for existing services and allows greater access to those services to older Americans. In addition to the access problems covered by our senior citizens, many Medicaid recipients are also forced to forego essential health services because health care providers are not available to them.

Under the current law, the Medicaid program mandates the coverage and payment for nurse midwifery, certified pediatric nurse practitioners and certified family nurse practitioners, but it does not mandate the coverage for services provided by other advance practice nurses. The Medicaid program needs to directly reimburse nurses for these services so that Medicaid recipients will have access to them.

We are also concerned in this time of transition about critical work force issues which are raised by the specter of health care reform. Nurses are the single largest group of health care providers as you know, and it is estimated that many of us are going to be facing some retraining and redeployment needs, so we believe it is critical and that we attend to those needs in any kind of reform endeavor.

We commend your subcommittees for holding this hearing and look forward to working with you to bring a different set of health care services to the American people.

Mr. WAXMAN. Thank you.

[Testimony resumes on p. 446.]

[The prepared statement of Ms. Shinn follows:]

LINDA SHINN, MBA, RN, CAE
EXECUTIVE DIRECTOR (INTERIM)
AMERICAN NURSES ASSOCIATION

Mr.. Chairman, Madame Chairwoman and members of the Subcommittees, I am Linda Shinn, MBA, RN, CAE, Executive Director (Interim) of the American Nurses Association (ANA). Thank you for inviting us to testify today on health care reform proposal.

The American Nurses Association is the only full-service professional organization representing the nation's two million registered nurses including staff nurses, nurse practitioners, clinical nurse specialists, certified nurse midwives and certified registered nurse anesthetists. ANA advances the nursing profession by fostering high standards of nursing practice, promoting the economic and general welfare of nurses in the workplace, projecting a positive and realistic view of nursing, and by working closely with the U.S. Congress and regulatory agencies on health care issues affecting nurses and the public. ANA is proud to support President Clinton's health care reform proposal.

Access to high quality, affordable health care is of concern to millions of Americans -- not only to the over thirty seven million who are uninsured, but to the growing number of currently insured who fear that changing or losing their jobs will result in loss of coverage or that skyrocketing costs will make their dependent's coverage or their own out-of-pocket health care costs unaffordable.

We are also testifying on behalf of the:

* **American Association of Colleges of Nursing**, with over 450 members offering baccalaureate, master's, and doctoral nursing education;

* **American Association of Nurse Anesthetists (AANA)**, the professional society that represents over 24,000 certified registered nurse anesthetists (CRNAs), which is 96 percent of all nurse anesthetists who practice across the United States. AANA's Board has voted to support President Clinton's health care plan;

* **American Association of Spinal Cord Injury Nurses**, representing 1,500 members specializing in spinal cord injuries;

* **The Association of Operating Room Nurses, Inc.**, the professional organization of perioperative nurses dedicated to enhancing the professionalism of perioperative nurses, promoting standards of perioperative nursing practice to better serve the needs of society and providing a forum for interaction and exchange of ideas related to perioperative health care;

* **Emergency Nurses Association**, the voluntary membership association of over 21,000 professional nurses committed to the advancement of emergency nursing practice; and the

* **National Nurse Practitioner Coalition**, a group of nurse practitioner organizations who

advocate for universal access to basic health care and the removal of barriers to consumer access to nurse practitioner care.

Mr. Chairman and Madame Chairwoman, we commend both of you on your leadership on health care reform issues in the past years. We have been proud to work with both of you on many proposals addressing health care including increasing access to health care services for specific underserved populations in our nation. We also thank you for your attention to nursings' issues throughout your leadership with your respective Subcommittees.

America's two million registered nurses deliver many essential health care services in the United States today in a variety of settings -- hospitals, nursing homes, schools, home health agencies, the workplace, community health clinics, in private practice and in managed care settings. Nurses know firsthand of the inequities and problems with our nation's health care system. Because we are there -- twenty-four hours a day, seven days a week -- we know all too well how the system succeeds so masterfully for some, yet continues to fail shamefully for all too many others.

Nurses see people on a daily basis who are denied or delayed in obtaining appropriate care because they lack adequate health insurance or are unable to pay for care. These people often postpone seeking help until they appear in a hospital emergency department in an advanced stage of illness or with problems that could have been treated earlier in less costly settings or, more appropriately, prevented altogether with earlier treatment or prevention services.

Delayed access to needed care is associated with problems of increased morbidity and mortality as well as countless hours of lost productivity in the workplace. Infants and children, pregnant women, the frail elderly, people with persistent health problems, rural and inner city residents and minorities are disproportionately represented among these most vulnerable uninsured groups. Their complex and diverse needs are not met by the existing system.

Nursing is concerned by the failures in our current health care system. More than 37 million people have no health insurance and millions more are critically underinsured. Our health care systems are oriented toward expensive interventions to treat illness, rather than essential health services designed to promote and maintain health. As a nation, we have failed to develop appropriate ways to allocate available health care resources and services. Unfortunately, the burden of the reality of the failures of our health care system are disproportionately felt by vulnerable segments of our nation's population. This includes the very young, the very old, the poor, the illiterate and those who live in rural and frontier communities and low-income urban communities.

Like President and Mrs. Clinton, the members of these Subcommittees and many others, nursing believes that it is time to frame a bold new vision for reform -- one that keeps what works best in our current system, but casts aside institutions and policies that fail to meet present and future needs -- a plan that addresses the triad of problems that exist in the current system: **inequitable and limited access, soaring costs and inconsistencies in quality and appropriateness of care delivered.**

NURSING'S AGENDA FOR HEALTH CARE REFORM

For the last five years, nursing has worked to develop a plan which encompasses the profession's best vision of a health care system for the future. To date, in addition to ANA's state and territorial associations, more than 80 national nursing and health-related organizations have endorsed this proposal for health care reform, entitled **"Nursing's Agenda for Health Care Reform".**

Nursing defines the health care crisis in terms of the need to **restructure, reorient and decentralize** the health care system in order to **guarantee access to services, contain costs and ensure quality.** Fundamental restructuring must occur because patchwork approaches have failed. Health care reform must be comprehensive and not limited to addressing only one or two components of the problem. Nursing's proposal does not define the problem only in terms of the uninsured or underinsured; rather, it **addresses the health care needs of the entire nation.** It is nursing's belief that the system must emphasize and support health promotion and disease prevention and show compassion for those who need acute and long-term care.

"Nursing's Agenda for Health Care Reform" calls for building a new foundation for health care in America while preserving the best elements of the existing system. Influencing the direction of health care reform is a complex, demanding task. Nurses know, however, that in order to preserve the health and well-being of our country and its people we must make important, fundamental changes in how, where and to whom health care is delivered.

Today, America's two million registered nurses are united in urging that the nation's health care system be cured...and cured **now.** We must reshape and redirect the system away from inappropriate use of the expensive, technology-driven, hospital-based models we currently have. **A balance must be struck between high-tech treatment and prevention.** It is nursing's belief that the system must emphasize and support health promotion and disease prevention and show compassion for those who need acute and long-term care.

Among the basic components of "Nursing's Agenda for Health Care Reform" are the following:

*** universal access for all citizens and residents provided through a <u>restructured</u> health care system;**

*** a federally-defined standard package of health care services including preventive, pre-natal, well-child, mental health, acute and short duration long-term care services;**

*** guarantees that coverage is provided for the poor with a plan administered by the states in order to anticipate the health care needs and changing demographics of the population. Elimination and restrictions on co-payments and deductibles for those near or under the poverty level;**

*** an employer mandate to ensure that all employed persons have access to health insurance**

with a standard benefits package;

* **a shift in focus to provide a better balance among treatment of disease, health promotion and illness prevention** such as coverage for immunizations, prenatal care, and health screening which has proven effective in preventing costly and devastating disease (e.g., colorectal exams, pap smears, mammograms, and hypertension screening);

* **enhanced consumer access to services by delivering primary health care in community based settings.** The new system would facilitate utilization of the most cost-effective providers and therapeutic options in the most appropriate settings;

* **Steps to reduce health care costs,** such as:

- ensuring consumer access to a full range of qualified health care providers;

- providing early treatment and prevention services at convenient sites, such as schools, the workplace, and other familiar community settings;

- reducing defensive medicine and unnecessary practices;

- controlled growth of the health care system through planning and prudent resource allocation; and

- elimination of unnecessary bureaucracy and decreased administrative requirements through the use of uniform claim forms and electronic billing;

* **utilization of case management** for people with continuing health care problems to promote active participation in their care and reduce fragmentation of the health care system;

* **provision of long-term care services of short duration and in addition to a program of extended care in order to prevent personal impoverishment. This proposal will require more shared community responsibility for care.** It will prevent impoverishment due to extended long-term care needs;

* **insurance reforms** are required to ensure improved access to coverage, including community ratings, affordable premiums, reinsurance pools for catastrophic coverage and other proposals to assist the small group market;

* **access to services are ensured by no payment at the point of service and elimination of balance billing in all health plans.**

There are several key features of **"Nursing's Agenda for Health Care Reform"** that are very similar to provisions contained in President Clinton's health care plan, announced on September 22. We commend President and Mrs. Clinton, as well as members of the President's Task Force on Health Care Reform, for the time and effort they have devoted to this critical issue.

UNIVERSAL ACCESS

Like the Clinton Administration, nursing believes that universal access to health care services is a principle that cannot be compromised. The Clinton Administration proposal would ensure that health care would be available to everyone -- including those who are now uninsured, underinsured and those who are potentially uninsured.

For any health care reform plan to be successful, it is critical that it address not only access to health insurance, but also access to health care services. Under the Clinton Administration's proposal, the health care setting could be restructured and reoriented so that services would be available in schools, workplaces and community settings as well as in hospitals and providers' offices. Consumer access to health care services must be maximized. Consumer education must be prioritized to foster increased awareness and responsibility for personal health and self care and to provide a greater capacity for informed decision making in selective health care services. In addition, criteria for outcomes of care should reflect the joint perspective of both the health care consumer and the health care provider.

The plan's emphasis on preventive and primary care services is also crucial, because it means that consumers will have a relationship with a primary care provider including nurses, nurse practitioners, certified nurse midwives, etc., that begins when they are still well -- so that disease can be prevented whenever possible and so that the provider will be able to intervene earlier, to minimize the severity of illness.

We commend the Administration's plan for recognizing that there will be a greatly increased need for primary care providers in order to ensure access to care and for addressing this need in a comprehensive manner. The plan calls for increased funding for primary care providers -- including advanced practice nurses such as nurse practitioners, clinical nurse specialists and certified nurse midwives. It also calls for removing barriers to the practice of these advanced practice nurses so that consumers' access to these much-needed services is not restricted.

We applaud these moves because they will greatly assist in achieving the goal of universal access to care. The role of nurse providers is very important to the issues of access to high quality health care. The health care system will need a substantial increase in hours of care of these providers.

We are also extremely pleased to see that the Administration plan has addressed the need for increased access to services in rural areas by creating incentives, including financial incentives, for health care providers to serve in those areas. Again, nurse providers can play a key role in treating the newly insured populations under health reform.

As the members of these Subcommittees know, there is a growing trend in this country toward part-time and intermittent employment. Unfortunately, such employment status has often meant foregoing benefits, including health insurance benefits. Women comprise the majority of these part-time employees. Nurses have not been immune to this trend, and nursing associations are very concerned about it. Increasingly, nurses in both full-time and part-time employment are losing their employment benefits including health insurance. We know of registered nurses employed full-time at $10.00 per hour and with no health care benefits. Their salary does not permit purchase of individual insurance. Guaranteeing health insurance to all employees is something that is of great importance to nurses both as health professionals and as employees.

STANDARDS BENEFITS PACKAGE

A cornerstone of "**Nursing's Agenda for Health Care Reform**" has been the guarantee of a standard health benefits package. We are gratified that the Administration's proposal provides a guaranteed package of benefits, emphasizing a broad scope of quality health services, not just treatment of disease. It supports school-based clinics, enhanced services for underserved populations and health education. It includes such critical elements as home-based care and public health initiatives and also takes an important step toward addressing the growing need for better and more accessible long-term care services. In addition, the Administration's package includes such important preventive services as immunizations, screening and prenatal care. It places new emphasis on primary care and preventive services delivered not only by physicians, but also by nurses and other qualified health care providers in convenient, accessible settings.

By including services that are geared toward preventing and minimizing disease, the Administration's plan can save the health care system immense amounts of money and ensure a healthier population. One of the clearest examples of preventive care saving long term costs in the health care system is the provision of pre-natal care. Numerous studies have shown that receipt of adequate pre-natal care is associated with the improvements in pregnancy outcome, particularly a reduction in the risk of low birth weight infants. For example, California Department of Consumer Affairs has estimated that the State could save $66 million annually in neo-natal intensive care unit changes if all women received adequate prenatal care.

We urge the Committee to act to ensure that full and complete reproductive health services are available to women and that preventive screening services, such as mammograms and Pap smears, be available in intervals that are sufficient to detect disease in a timely fashion.

THE ROLE OF THE NURSE PROVIDER

The expanded role of nurses in a reformed health care delivery system, including advanced practice nurses such as nurse practitioners, is apparent throughout President Clinton's proposal. It is an important element of the plan's emphasis on preventive health services--services which have been at the center of nursing practice since the inception of the nursing profession. Nurses are key providers in acute care, school and community health clinics, in home care, hospice care and ambulatory care, all of which are part of the package of benefits to be available under the President's plan.

Nurses, including advanced practice nurses, are well-positioned to fill many of the current gaps in accessibility and availability of primary and preventive health care services. There are approximately 100,000 advanced practice nurses with advanced education and training in providing primary care services. As many as 300,000 additional nurses could be prepared to provide such services with additional training.

Nurses often provide care to those who have no access to the current health delivery system. For example, the Family Nurse Practitioner Program at the University of California - San Francisco has developed a health services program in an inner-city homeless shelter for families. A nurse practitioner is the only health care provider for these families. She diagnoses and treats episodic health problems and has demonstrated that, with regular return visits to the Shelter's Clinic, many of the problems are kept from worsening and requiring hospitalization.

A family nurse practitioner in Washington, Kansas directs a clinic serving the critically underserved, as defined by the Kansas Department of Health and Environment. The physician director of this clinic left in 1986, and the clinic subsequently lost its Federal funding. At this time, the clinic is being leased by a country hospital from a non-profit corporation and has contracted with the nurse practitioner to run the clinic which includes eight fully-equipped exam rooms. Since a physician is not on the premises, the advanced practice nurse needs to be eligible for direct reimbursement of her services. As she serves in a rural area, she became eligible for reimbursement under Medicare in 1991. She also works through the Kansas Blue Cross and Blue Shield office, the state Medicaid Bureau, and other private insurers to obtain reimbursement under each of their systems. Currently, in the town of Washington, Kansas, there is only one family physician and only three physicians in the entire county. The nurse run clinic is essential to providing the citizens of Washington, Kansas with health care services.

In Chicago, there is a program called the Beethoven Project. This program occupies 10 renovated apartments in a Chicago public housing project which has a high level of poverty and crime. Comprehensive services, such as primary health care, Head Start, and a full-time child care center in addition to drop-in counseling, psychological consultation and care management are provided by the nurse directors.

The Marriott Corporation has a nurse-managed program that administers a multifaceted approach to work site health care including primary, secondary and tertiary care. Marriott estimates that with the services of each nurse, the company saves $250,000 per year in health care costs and lost productivity. Occupational health nurses work as employee advocates handling worker's injuries and collaborating with physicians to make sure injured workers receive appropriate care as well as providing primary and preventive care to ensure workplace safety.

The Department of Labor is currently using registered nurses as case managers for workers compensation cases. The use of registered nurses has enabled the participating states to reduce case backlog and has facilitated earlier rehabilitation and return to work of the injured employees.

In Spencer, Iowa, a program entitled **"The Northwest Aging Association's Parish Nurse Project"** provides health education, resources and referral to elderly persons and facilitates implementation of volunteers and support groups. These interventions have provided assistance which has allowed 118 of the elderly in Spencer to remain in their homes -- a cost savings to both the families and the health care system.

Nursing centers with nurse practitioners in 17 nursing centers in southern Arizona provide health care to about 6,500 patients each year, including many traditionally underserved and at risk populations (e.g., especially senior citizens, Hispanics, and Native Americans). Another successful program in Arizona, entitled the Community Nursing Network, utilizes community health nurses for one day per week to set up health centers in churches, recreation centers, physicians' offices, and retirement communities. These registered nurses manage 25,000 visits each year, performing physicals, treating minor illnesses, and monitoring chronically-ill patients. These programs provide free care for those with no insurance coverage.

However, the ability of nurses to provide health care services has been continually hampered by a number of artificial barriers that serve to cut the consumer off from access to services provided by these competent and qualified health providers. These barriers include restrictive reimbursement policies by Federal and state programs and private insurers, and they also include irrational restrictions on nursing practice such as physician supervision requirements by laws and regulations at the state level. The laws regarding reimbursement for advanced practice nurses are complicated and convoluted as to which categories of advanced practice nurses may be reimbursed, in what geographic areas, who may be paid and whether or not collaboration with other health providers is required. The current laws are so confusing and complex for carriers, providers and consumers that they have become a barrier to access to these services in and of themselves.

We must guarantee that barriers to health care for the nation's elderly are removed.

ANA was pleased to have the opportunity to work closely with Members of this Committee, as well as with Members of the House Ways and Means and Senate Finance Committees, to achieve enactment of the "Rural Nursing Incentive Act". That provision, which was included in the Omnibus Budget Reconciliation Act of 1990 (Public Law 101-508) allows nurse practitioners and clinical nurse specialists who practice in rural areas to receive direct reimbursement under Medicare.

That law now needs to be expanded to cover the services of all nurse practitioners and clinical nurse specialists, regardless of geographic location and practice setting and regardless of whether they are associated with another health care provider. This expansion of coverage does not provide for reimbursement for new services, but rather provides for reimbursement for existing services in alternative cost-effective settings by non-physician providers. In addition, modeled after the bonus payment of physicians who work in health professional shortage areas (HPSAs), these practitioners would also be paid a bonus payment when they work in HPSAs. Extending bonus payments to non-physician providers has also been recommended by the Physician Payment Review Commission. By taking this action, these advanced practice nurses would provide essential services to meet the health care needs of those older Americans who currently have no access to affordable health care.

ANA has been working closely with Members of the House and Senate to achieve this objective. Legislation to provide direct Medicare reimbursement to nurse practitioners, clinical nurse specialists and certified nurse midwives has been introduced in the House by Reps. Ed

Towns (D-NY) and Bill Coyne (D-PA) [H.R. 2386] and in the Senate by Senators Charles Grassley (R-IA) and Kent Conrad (D-ND) [S. 833]. The Congressional Budget Office has recently estimated that if Medicare reimbursement were extended to nurse practitioners, clinical nurse specialists, and certified nurse midwives at 85 percent of the physician fee schedule, and that if that Medicare reimbursement was also provided to physician assistants, the cumulative cost would be only $117 million over a five-year period. That is a minuscule amount to expend to ensure that access to health care services would be available to individuals who might otherwise not be forced to forego those services.

Another example of payment inequities for nurses under the Medicare system is the lack of reimbursement for operating room nurses serving as assistants at surgery. The issues of Medicare reimbursement for registered nurses who assist at surgery has been an important issue for ANA and the Association of Operating Room Nurses since a provision was included in the Omnibus Budget Reconciliation Act of 1986 that permitted reimbursement for physician assistants who first assist at surgery. The ability of physician assistants to be reimbursed under Medicare has created employment disparity for nurses who provide the same service, but are not reimbursed under the law. Rep. Cardiss Collins (D-IL) has introduced legislation, H.R. 1618, to permit direct payment under Medicare Program for the services of registered nurses as assistants at surgery. We support this legislation.

In addition to the access problems confronted by our senior citizens, many Medicaid recipients are also being forced to forego essential health care services because health care providers are not available to them. In order to improve access to care under Medicaid, certain reforms in payment and coverage policy must be enacted by the Congress. At the present time, the Medicaid program mandates the coverage and payment of nurse midwifery, certified pediatric nurse practitioners and certified family nurse practitioners, but does not mandate the coverage of services furnished by other nurse practitioners, or by clinical nurse specialists and certified registered nurse anesthetists. The Medicaid program needs to directly reimburse for the services of these practitioners so that they may be utilized by Medicaid recipients.

Several states have changed their State Medicaid payment and coverage policies to encourage the use of these practitioners and have been able to increase access to care for vulnerable populations. For example, in New Hampshire it has been demonstrated when the services of nurse practitioners are covered by Medicaid, access to care for the underserved populations is improved. Many physicians have a limit on the number of Medicaid patients they will accept in their practice and refer additional Medicaid beneficiaries to nurse practitioners who see them in their own practice or through well-child and pre-natal clinics. Some nurse practitioners in New Hampshire have a caseload that is 90 percent Medicaid. The State's Medicaid payment policy also encourages the use of these practitioners. Since 1982, nurse practitioners have had their services covered by the Medicaid program at 100 percent of the physician rate. According to Charles Albano, Chief of the Bureau of Maternal and Child Health in New Hampshire, nurse practitioners are relied upon to provide the vast majority of services to low income women, 75 percent of whom are Medicaid recipients. Nurse practitioners are also used to staff the family planning clinics and the well-child services in the state.

Medicaid payment policy needs to be improved to increase access to care. Payments to nurses in advanced practice under the Medicaid program need to be based on the service and not on the type of provider. This policy in New Hampshire provides a positive incentive for pre-natal and well-child clinics to use nurse practitioners. Washington State has adopted a similar policy of payment based on the service.

Laws and regulations in many states place unnecessary restrictions on the practice of nurses, including advanced practice nurses, to provide services to patients, to provide routine care and medications, to bill insurance companies, to operate a private practice, to obtain clinical privileges or to admit patients to a hospital. For example, in Vancouver, Washington, one nurse practitioner provides health screening, immunizations and other services to over 2,000 poor children in five inner-city schools which she visits weekly in her mobile van. However, in other states, such as Illinois, this nurse practitioner could not perform these services, since State law prohibits her from being directly reimbursed by Medicaid.

Washington State specifically changed its Medicaid fee schedule to improve access to care. In 1989, the State Legislature added $200 - $300 to the obstetrical package to offset malpractice costs and to improve recruitment of providers. In 1990, the policy was established to pay all providers the same rate for the same services. This had a significant effect on recruiting nurse practitioners and certified nurse midwives. There is no nurse midwifery educational program in the State, and yet the improved competitive fees were instrumental in bringing these practitioners into the State to staff the clinics. In two years, the number of certified nurse midwives increased by 33 percent and there has been a limited turnover of certified nurse midwives, despite their serving a high risk population.

Representative Bill Richardson (D-NM) has introduced a bill (H.R. 1683) to improve access to the services of nurse practitioners and clinical nurse specialists by mandating the coverage and payment of all nurse practitioner and clinical nurse specialist services under the Medicaid program. An identical bill (S. 466) has been introduced in the Senate by Senator Tom Daschle (D-SD). The Congressional Budget Office recently estimated that the cost of enacting this proposal would be $46 million over a five-year period. That is a very small amount when compared to the value of increasing the access of Medicaid recipients to badly needed health care services.

Inconsistent state restrictions or prescriptive authority for advanced practice nurses are another barrier to health care and promote the costly use of an additional provider.

In addition to the general examples of barriers to practice just noted, there are three specific Medicare reimbursement barriers to practice that exist for certified registered nurse anesthetists (CRNAs). First, the current Medicare conditions of payment for anesthesiology services that anesthesiologists must meet in order to be paid for Medicare for medically directing a CRNA, restrict CRNAs from performing all the components of an anesthesia service that they are legally authorized to perform. For example, some anesthesiologists insist on performing the anesthesia induction on all patients themselves, then leaving the CRNA to finish the case.

Second, the current Medicare hospital condition of participation for anesthesia services and the Medicare ambulatory surgical center condition of participation for coverage for surgical services restrict CRNA practice by requiring physician supervision of CRNAs. Third, the current Medicare regulation on payment for the services of CRNAs states that if a CRNA and anesthesiologist work together on one case, the anesthesiologist may bill the case as if he/she personally performed it and receive 100 percent of the Medicare payment. No Medicare payment is typically made to CRNAs involved in such a case, even if the CRNA was the provider actually administering the anesthesia to the patient.

Nurse managed units within acute care settings are also both cost effective and provide quality care. For example, nurse managed units are proving to be very successful in managing patients being weaned from respirators. In addition, studies have documented the positive outcomes demonstrated by the use of neonatal nurse practitioners with low birthweight infants.

The President's plan would address the problem of artificial restrictions on nursing practice by preempting such barriers to practice, providing incentives for states to adopt a Federal model for nursing practice statutes, and by including payment for services of advanced practice nurses. It is our understanding that the Administration plans to shore up these provisions by ensuring that advanced practice nurses do not face exclusion or other discrimination by health plans and by extending Medicare coverage to the services of nurse practitioners and clinical nurse specialists in all settings.

Just as nurses throughout the United States have demonstrated their ability to provide high quality, cost effective and accessible health services, consumers have shown their widespread acceptance of these services and their willingness to continue receiving primary care services from nurses. A recent Gallup poll revealed that the vast majority of Americans (86 percent) are willing to receive everyday health care services from an advanced practice registered nurse that they now must go to a physician to receive. Only twelve (12 percent) percent said they would be "unwilling" to go to a registered nurse. Nurses are currently working with consumer-oriented organizations in order to promote shared principles of health care reform. We are confident that as the American public becomes more familiar with the primary care services that nurses can provide, and as more Americans have an opportunity to receive such care from nurses, that the "unwilling" category will decrease sharply. In fact, we believe that, based on the experiences of advanced practice nurses in HMO, clinic, and private practice settings, more and more Americans will identify nurses as their provider from whom they select to receive primary care services.

QUALITY ISSUES

As health care reform becomes a reality, hospitals and other health care institutions will experience increasing pressure to contain costs. As the focus of the health care delivery site shifts from acute-care institutions to community based care, there will be an increase of hospital mergers and closures of hospitals resulting from an oversupply of beds. It is anticipated that some hospitals will specialize and others will integrate services such as home health and nursing homes.

Nurses have had an opportunity to experience first-hand what many hospitals do when they face pressure to cut costs. In the last few years, nurses have grown increasingly alarmed at the wholesale reduction in quality of care that many hospitals have initiated in the name of cost-savings and cost-efficiency. Numbers of nurses have been cut and nurses have been laid off. In their place, hospitals have hired unlicensed, semi-skilled personnel, often trained by the hospitals themselves in brief training courses. While the use of unlicensed personnel to assist registered nurses is not new, hospitals in the last few years have greatly expanded the use of these personnel, both in numbers and in the range of functions they perform. This has happened at a time when, due to a number of factors, the severity of illness of the hospitalized patient population has increased significantly. As a result, registered nurses find themselves caring for and supervising care for ever-greater numbers of increasingly sick patients. This has meant a continual downgrading of care for patients, one which poses a real risk to their health and safety while hospitalized.

Many hospitals have openly stated--threatened, if you will--that they will increase the trend toward downward substitution if health care reform is enacted. We consider this not only a threat to the professional and economic security of nurses, but also to the patients we care for--patients who literally entrust their lives to the hospitals. We believe that hospitals must adhere to strict quality controls if patient care is to be protected. Hospitals should not be permitted to sacrifice patient care in the name of cost efficiency. We have received every indication that the Administration will work to institute mechanisms to protect and ensure safe, quality care both in the long run and in the period of transition to a reformed health care system. These mechanisms will include the development of patient outcome measures as well as, in the immediate period, criteria that monitor changes in hospital staffing and patient care delivery patterns to ensure that patient care is not compromised.

THE HEALTH CARE WORKFORCE

Nursing has been working with the Department of Labor and the White House on their workforce proposals in the health care reform plan. We commend the Department of Labor for developing an initiative that provides assistance to workers before they potentially become unemployed. Nursing supports their concept of developing a National Institute for Health Care Workforce Development in order to have a mechanism to analyze the workforce needs of a new health care system.

Critical workforce issue are raised by the health care reform plan and its effect on employment. Within the health care industry, there will be impacts based on the types of jobs individuals hold. Nurses are the single largest groups of health care providers. It is estimated that fully two-thirds of the nation's registered nurses will need to be retrained to appropriately staff a revised health system. Although we are optimistic that nurse displacement will be short term, it will be essential that a retraining and redeployment plan be designed to facilitate that transition. Nursing believes that the transition plan must include a series of interim quality protections that safeguard patient care and provide for re-training and re-deployment of health care personnel. The decision of hospitals and other institutions to significantly alter staffing levels , mix or re-ploy personnel should be guided by several basic principles:

* Advanced public disclosure of the intention to merge, close, or significantly redeploy personnel;

* Involvement of consumers and affected professional personnel in development and implementation of educational programs and other means for re-deployment;

* Evaluation and report to health care consumers;

* Analysis of the impact of the re-deployment on patient outcomes and other quality care indicators; and

* Assurance that re-deployment plans use professional personnel in accord with licensure laws, educational preparation and assessed competence.

In addition, a national transition plan for the health care workforce should contain, at a minimum:

* Retraining and relocation programs to prepare personnel to assume positions in primary health care, public health, and critical care across a variety of health care delivery settings;

* Use of conversion boards to assess the opportunity for the hospital or institution to be converted to some other use in order to keep the jobs in the community;

* Institution of training programs on "How To Start A Business" and access to small business loans in order to encourage nurses and other providers to establishment small community health care clinics to benefit their communities;

* Pre-notification to providers and the community of any hospital closure or merger;

* Continuation of health and pension benefits for health care personnel;

* Continuation of HIV disability coverage;

* Limits on discounting health care services to prevent cost shifting; and

* Annual public reports about the impact of major institutional changes in staffing levels, mix, or deployment on the quality of care delivered.

The situation of a re-focused health care workforce must be monitored very carefully throughout the transition period and into the enactment of health care reform. Should there be significant increases or changes in morbidity or mortality rates or increases in adverse occurrences (i.e., falls, infections, medication errors) or other indicators of change in the quality of care in hospitals, then more aggressive steps to ensure quality patient care will need to be enacted such as a decertification or fine system for hospitals not complying with quality standards.

We understand that the Administration's health care proposal contains many of these provisions to provide a workforce transition plan for health care personnel. Nursing cautions, however, that training opportunities envisioned for low skilled workers in the health care industry (clerical and administrative support positions) may inadvertently increase the pool of another group of low skilled workers (such as nurses' aides, nursing technicians, nursing assistants). Nursing is concerned that any emphasis on short-term and on-the-job training as well as the use of the term "higher value added health care jobs" without defining such jobs will increase the number of low skilled health care providers. This goal neither meets the health care needs of the nation, or is in the best interest of these workers, most of whom are women. Rather, increasing the pool of professional health care providers is critical.

Another issue associated with a decreasing demand for hospital based nurses is the possible decline in nursing wages. To minimize this downward pressure on wages, the current and future supply of nursing labor must be channeled away from settings with decreasing demand and into high growth areas. To maximize nurses' earnings and avoid serious imbalance in the supply and demand for nurses, a specific plan to systematically assess, manage and evaluate the recruitment, education and utilization of nurses is needed.

NURSING EDUCATION

Health care reform will require a refocusing of knowledge and skills for nursing faculty and future nurses. With greater emphasis on prevention and early intervention, as well as a decreased need for acute care nurses, nursing education will need to be re-focused on primary health care and the management of acute minor illness and complex chronic diseases. Skills in case management, discharge planning, supervision of health personnel, and financial planning will be essential. Fortunately, many nurses are skilled in these vital areas, but many more will be needed.

The trend that will occur in a health care reform environment which is of most significance to nurses is the shift in balance between episodic, high cost, specialty focused, hospital based tertiary care to primary and preventive care delivered in a range of ambulatory care settings by a variety of practitioners. This shift is already occurring, as witnessed by the rapid growth in home care and ambulatory care services.

Since World War II, the majority of nurses have been educated for and employed in hospitals. Significant educational efforts on both the part of individual nurses and the health system are now needed to focus on the delivery of primary health care services. The Administration has included several health provider education initiatives in their proposal. Under their plan, the Secretary of Health and Human Services will determine the estimated need of nurse workforce and advanced practice nurses needed to meet the current health care demands of the nation. This will be based on the workforce estimates developed by the National Council on Nurse Education and its allocated regional councils. To fund nurse education, new programs need to be established to increase the supply of nurses.

According to the National Sample Survey of Nurses (1988), there are approximately 125,000 registered nurses working in physician offices, freestanding clinics, ambulatory surgical centers, health maintenance organizations and other ambulatory care settings. In addition, there are approximately 11,000 registered nurses working in community/public health settings, 48,000 in school health, and another 22,000 in occupational health. With the appropriate funding support, this pool of generalist nurses could begin to rapidly increase the nation's supply of primary care providers.

Nursing commends the Clinton Administration for its increased focus on nurse education issues. It is clear that the United States health care system has an increasingly urgent need for primary care providers. Immediate funding must be made available to strengthen existing advanced practice nurse programs and to establish new programs to prepare the primary care providers so urgently needed.

The Administration's plan would shift the funding emphasis under Graduate Medical Education from specialty physicians to primary care physicians. Advanced practice nurses will be increasingly needed to fill the future gap created in this shift to primary care providers and in some specialty areas. For example, a reduction in the supply of physician anesthesiologists will require increased funding to educate a greater number of certified registered nurse anesthetists.

Nursing has specifically recommended that an amount equal to 10 percent of direct

Graduate Medical Education (GME) funds be pooled from all insurers and be used in a manner similar to that used in the GME program for physicians. These funds would be allocated to support the education and training of primary care nurses and specialty advanced practice nurses, such as certified registered anesthetists, who will be needed in greater numbers under the Administration's plan by allowing reimbursement of providers for faculty costs and student stipends through GME. This program would enable hospitals to maintain quality service and cost effectiveness within the constraints of the new system. This new program could be funded by a combination of Medicare contributions and a surcharge on health premiums. Because of the importance of advanced practice nurses to the delivery of care, a constant stream of dollars is needed to support the education and training of these providers on a basis similar and equal to resident physicians. Nursing believes that this fund must be in addition to the current Nurse Education Act program.

We applaud the Administration's proposal to also expand The Nurse Education Act for the purposes of retraining nurses to meet the new health care needs of the nation as well as expand the supply of nurses. Increases in the number of graduate programs which focus on primary care as well as increases in the capacity of current graduate funding programs will be necessary under a reformed health care system.

Funds are needed to develop retraining opportunities for nurses who are forced to leave the tertiary care workforce for community, primary and preventive care practice areas including post-master's certificate programs to enhance the primary care skills and abilities of clinical nurse specialists and other master's prepared nurses. BSN programs will need to be expanded to assist the diploma and associate degree nurses employed in acute care settings to rapidly obtain a BSN in order to enhance their community, public health and/or critical care knowledge and skills. In addition, hospitals will need assistance to provide continuing education to acute care nurses for acquisition of community care nursing skills. These BSN assistance programs and continuing educations programs are essential in order to prepare nurses to make the transition from hospital to community based nursing care.

In addition to preparing primary care providers and other nurses, it is also of importance to ensure that there is an adequate supply of nurse educators, both at the undergraduate and graduate levels of education. Existing nursing faculty may need additional training themselves in order to become nurse practitioner and other advanced practice nurse educators.

Nursing strongly supports the Administration's stated intention to increase the cultural diversity of the health care workforce by supporting programs aimed at under-represented ethnic, minority and/or disadvantaged persons. The proposal supports efforts to recruit and retain students to nursing and other professions and to increase the number of minority faculty and researchers in the health professions.

RESURGENCE OF THE PUBLIC HEALTH SYSTEM

Increased funding for public health programs at a state level is critical to the future health and well being of a diverse population. The Administration's proposal coordinates the delivery of personal health care services through state alliances with the delivery of public health services in order to reach the common goal of improving the health of the American population.

Nursing endorses the Administration's proposal to repair, strengthen and consolidate essential Federal, state, and local public health services. The plan's focus would help to restore the original mission of public health programs to engage in community prevention rather than direct delivery of health services. The plan would support such core public health activities as data collection; surveillance and monitoring; protection of the environment, housing, food, and water; and disease investigation and control.

We applaud the inclusion of a strong public information and education component to mobilize communities and motivate individuals to reduce risks to health. Nursing stands ready to lead community and individual efforts to reduce some of our deadliest and costliest health risks -- tobacco use, drug and alcohol abuse, sexual activity that increases the prevalence of HIV infection and other sexually transmitted diseases, inadequate or poor nutrition, physical inactivity, and the lack of childhood immunizations.

REMOVING BARRIERS TO PRACTICE

One of the key features of the Administration's proposal is the elimination of anti-competitive practices in the health care industry to ensure that health providers are treated equitably within the health system by removing barriers to practice. In discussing how this can best be achieved, nursing has stressed aggressive enforcement of anti-trust guidelines and a

77-929 O - 94 - 15

reiteration of their commitment to encouraging competition in the health care marketplace.

Nursing encourages this Committee to develop a new health system that will compel all business entities to treat all health providers in accordance with the legal scope of their practice and will review all actions taken by corporations working within a health plan, especially when they adversely impact upon one class of health professionals.

ADMINISTRATIVE SIMPLIFICATION AND COST SAVINGS

Nurses throughout the nation breathed a collective sigh of relief when the President outlined the need to simplify the mounting paperwork and other administrative requirements that burden our health care system. We know firsthand what a waste of professional time these requirements can represent. Too often, nurses are forced to take time away from patient care and devote it to filling out forms. It has been estimated that a staff nurse fills out an average of 19 forms per patient. Thus, we applaud the President's proposals to pare down and simplify paperwork and other wasteful administrative requirements.

However, we need to draw a distinction here between completion of insurance forms and other activities that serve little other than facilitating the flow of paperwork and bureaucracy, and documentation that does facilitate maintaining and improving quality and patient care standards. The Administration's proposal would emphasize data collection that is related to quality of care, development of outcomes criteria and other activities that are directly relevant to patient care. As health care professionals, we regard this as important and necessary. The distinction we make is between needless and endless paperwork and the collection of patient care information that leads to continuous improvement in the quality of care. We are more than happy to give up the former and opt for the latter.

Nursing also supports the greater use of community rating, eliminating pre-existing conditions as a way for insurance companies to reject higher-risk individuals and limiting an individual's out-of-pocket expenses following a catastrophic health event.

CONCLUSION

Mr. Chairman and Madame Chairwoman, we commend these Subcommittees for holding this hearing and for working so diligently to find solutions to the health care crisis. We appreciate this opportunity to share our views with you and look forward to continuing to work with you as comprehensive health care reform legislation is developed.

Thank you.

G:\grel\cmd\healthre\hcrtest.E&C
10-11-93

Mr. WAXMAN. Dr. Bristow?

STATEMENT OF LONNIE R. BRISTOW

Mr. BRISTOW. Thank you.

Madam Chairwoman, Mr. Chairman and members of the subcommittee, I am Lonnie Bristow, M.D., chair of the board of trustees of the American Medical Association. We are pleased to be here today to provide our views on the President's health system reform plan.

We too applaud President Clinton as well as the First Lady for taking the first necessary steps in bringing to an end the difficulties far too many of our patients have in finding affordable adequate health care coverage. The basic principles of the President's plan mirror what the AMA has been calling for in its own reform proposal, Health Access America, for the last 4 years.

Both plans seek to build on what already works well in health care and both would make certain that the health care system works fairly for all Americans. We also understand the need to produce a system that is disciplined and can provide a measure of quality upon which our patients can rely.

Our two plans also agree on the need for universal coverage, a national package of health benefits emphasizing preventive care, a requirement that all employers share in the responsibility of providing coverage that most employees in America have long enjoyed, while at the same time providing mechanisms to deal with the potential for dislocation among small employers and their employees.

Our two plans also agree on insurance reforms that will require insurers to insure risk rather than avoid it, a competitive environment where health care costs at all levels will have to be justified, and pluralism as a means of guaranteeing health care quality and access. We are pleased that in the various discussions we have had with the administration as it crafted this proposal many of the suggestions we offered were accepted.

In many other crucial aspects of the President's plan, however, we do not see the necessary level of physician participation on behalf of their patients that we discussed. We understand that modification is ongoing and we are encouraged that the President has signaled a willingness to negotiate specifics of the plan.

Yet right now, physicians have simply too many questions about how the plan will be implemented, about why the plan's effort to cut waste and spending does not go far enough in limiting liability costs through caps on non-economic damages and meaningful limits on attorneys' fees, about why physicians will not be given adequate exemptions from current antitrust restraints to allow them to protect their patients' interests in a health care market that will be dominated by large managed care entities under this plan, about why strict spending controls are called for when they have never been shown to work anywhere, about a National Health Board designed to regulate the system when a better approach might be to involve physicians and others in a participatory process to provide guidance to the health care system, and about health alliances that could add another level of regulatory authority to the system when all that is needed is an impartial entity that helps organize the way insurers and small employers come together in the marketplace, about the intent to nationalize medical education by dictating what careers students may pursue, something done nowhere else in any field in this Nation; and about why a whole new bureaucracy of oversight will be better than that now existing in the private sector.

Before physicians can say whether they oppose or support the President's plan, they need more detailed answers to these questions. Other health system reform plans have been and will continue to be offered from both sides of the aisle. None can be perfect and we should not expect them to be at this juncture, but on balance, the President deserves our congratulations for his unprecedented leadership in making at long last meaningful comprehensive health system reform a real possibility.

We also congratulate these subcommittees for quickly beginning the task of examining and shaping the President's plan. There is still much work to do, however, and at the end of this long process when all is said and done, physicians will judge the acceptability of any health system reform based on the answers to these questions.

Will patients have the freedom to obtain care from the physician and practice arrangement of their choice? Will their physicians have a corresponding freedom to choose the kind of practice arrangement that best allows them to apply their professional judgment? Will patients be able to receive necessary, effective and efficient care without restrictions on their physician's clinical judgment?

Patients and physicians deserve positive answers to these questions and the American Medical Association promises to work with the administration, the Congress and our patients to see that positive answers will be achieved.

Thank you.

Mr. WAXMAN. Thank you.

[Testimony resumes on p. 464.]

[The prepared statement of Dr. Bristow follows:]

STATEMENT

of the

AMERICAN MEDICAL ASSOCIATION

to the

Committee on Energy and Commerce

Subcommittees on Health and the Environment and

Commerce, Consumer Protection, and Competitiveness

U.S. House of Representatives

Physicians' View of the President's Health Plan

Presented by

Lonnie R. Bristow, MD

October 14, 1993

Mr. Chair and Members of the Committee:

My name is Lonnie R. Bristow, MD, Chair of the Board of Trustees of the American Medical Association (AMA).

On behalf of the AMA's 300,000 member physicians, I am pleased and honored to be able to share with you what I believe many individual physicians would say about the President's proposal for health system reform if they had this opportunity to be here and talk with you today.

The President's proposal is long awaited. Physicians know the limitations of the current system. They see the difficulties far too many Americans have finding affordable, adequate health care coverage. For the past four years, the AMA has been telling whomever would listen about the need for comprehensive reform and a way to achieve meaningful change through our own proposal, **Health Access America**. Before that, we helped organize an effort of leaders among physicians, a wide range of health care providers, academia, and both federal and state government to define the difficulties and solutions needed to address problems in the health care system -- called **Health Agenda for the American People** -- well before the problems of the health care system captured the public's attention as they have in the last several years.

We have long understood that problems with America's health care system had to be addressed, that the status quo was no longer sufficient. We applaud President Clinton for his resolve in addressing these problems, in taking the first necessary step to end the status quo. Likewise, we applaud the First Lady for her leadership in the difficult process of framing the President's proposal. It is encouraging to physicians that the President has signalled a willingness to negotiate details of the plan as long as such negotiation does not undermine the basic principles of reform. We look forward to such negotiations as the package proceeds through the Congress.

For these reasons alone, I can confidently say that the Administration, the Congress, the medical profession and others can move forward into a new era of health system reform.

Building Fairness into What Works

That confidence is fueled by how much we have found in President Clinton's proposal that is consistent with our own plan for health system reform. What we see as basic principles in the President's plan are our own basic principles. Most importantly, we share President Clinton's intended goal of building on what works well in the system now, not replacing it or tearing it down. We support the President's reliance on pluralism as a means of guaranteeing health care quality and access as well as his intent to create an environment where health care costs at all levels will have to be justified.

We also recognize that a strong theme in the President's proposal is enforcing fairness on a system that, for all the world-leading wonders in medical care it makes readily available to most Americans, cannot fairly ensure that all Americans have access to that same level of care. Every American can have adequate, affordable health care coverage if the rules of the system work the same for everyone. President Clinton's proposal would make a great leap in ensuring that they will:

- by making sure that all employers share in the responsibility of offering health care coverage that most employees in America have long enjoyed, while at the same time providing mechanisms to deal with the potential for dislocation among small employers and their employees;

- by defining at the national level a package of health care benefits including preventive care that will be available to all Americans;

- by requiring health insurers to insure risk, not avoid or limit it;

- by reconstructing federal tax incentives so that the self-employed are treated the same as large corporations, and ending federal tax dollar underwriting of health care benefits richer than the nationally defined benefit package; and

- by establishing reasonable cost-sharing requirements that will encourage individuals to assume a level of responsibility for the health care choices they make. We are also encouraged that the plan recognizes the need for liability reform to be part of health system reform.

These changes alone would bring about a resolution of many of the difficulties our patients now experience in the health care system. Even more is needed, though. Unfortunately, many of the directions taken in the President's proposal beyond these basic principles create in physicians serious reservations about the affect the proposal, if enacted as it stands today, would have on the ability of physicians to provide quality health care to their patients.

One Measure: The Physician-Patient Relationship

There is only one measure by which physicians will judge this proposal -- how will it effect the ability of a physician and his or her patient together to make whatever decisions are necessary about the patient's medical needs. When a physician sits in an examining room with a patient facing a difficult, often life-threatening moment of decision, the physician needs to know, without doubt, that a decision can be made solely in the best interests of that patient's health and well-being, nothing else. As the President's proposal stands now, far too much could come between the physician and patient at that moment of truth, making it difficult to make the best possible decisions on behalf of patients.

The combination of arbitrary global budgets, premium caps, and the cost-cutting that health plans will undertake could necessitate many of the same intrusive controls and second guessing of physician decisions that exist in many of today's tightly controlled insurance plans. Such interference is, has been, and continues to be inappropriate. It is inappropriate now when insurance companies arbitrarily second-guess physicians' clinical decisions in utilization review or force physicians to step out of the examining room to seek preauthorization for necessary care. It is likewise inappropriate when the threat of liability action forces physicians to order tests that would not be necessary in a less hostile environment.

Unless changes in the President's plan are made, these kinds of interference will not only continue, but will be increased with new levels of interference resulting from bureaucratic, centralized decisions about the availability and quality of health care being made far removed from the needs of a physician's individual patient. There are many positive aspects of the President's plan that could and should be carried out with little government involvement.

However, new bureaucratic entities are also envisioned at the federal, state, and corporate levels that have the danger of supplanting much of the medical profession's long-standing and well proven capability to set its own standards of clinical practice and professionalism. If that is the intent, physicians must wonder what role will be left to them in the new system.

Federal Interference

At the federal level, a national health board of seven individuals would have sole responsibility for establishing, administering, and disciplining the system proposed by the President. One of its key responsibilities would be to enforce global budgets on health care spending. If such budgets were instead targets, established with the help of physicians to be flexible guides to help identify specific cost difficulties in the health care system as well as specific solutions, taking into account changing demographics and specific health care needs across the population, the AMA could support them. Instead, the "targets" here are strict spending controls based solely on changes in the Consumer Price Index and enforced through the cost of insurance premiums, with potential assessments on providers.

Nowhere in the world, in any kind of system that delivers any service or good to anyone, have such spending controls ever worked. Their implementation does nothing to control the demand for services and often times increases that demand. Such controls result in arbitrary maldistribution of services that often falls far short of meeting consumers' needs. With health care in the United States, the result will be no different. Treatment plans on how to meet individual patient needs now made between a physician and a patient in the physician's examining room could be made instead in Washington, DC. Physicians cannot accept this limitation. We do not believe our patients will either when beneficial care is not promptly available. That is not the kind of reform the American people are expecting.

Physicians have the same kinds of concerns about the control the federal government will be taking over the supply of physicians under the President's proposal. By mandating medical schools to train fifty percent of their physicians in primary care and allocating medical residency slots through new national and regional graduate medical education councils, the federal government will essentially nationalize medical education in this country. While there is a need for more primary care physicians throughout the nation, the incentives to practice primary care included in the President's plan, along with changes in the health care marketplace that are already occurring, may well be enough to encourage and enable medical students to pursue primary care. The AMA has advocated for these same incentives for a long time. They should finally be given an opportunity to work.

State Interference

At the state level, health alliances, as proposed in the President's plan, will add still more to this bureaucratization of the health care system, providing another layer of decision-making that could undermine the physician-patient relationship. The AMA has watched with interest the development of the concept of health alliances in the managed competition proposals that have come before Congress. In a pure managed competition approach, health alliances -- or health insurance purchasing cooperatives -- would act simply as unbiased conduits between health insurance plans and consumers, acting to organize the market under rules that apply equally to all. There is a need for such entities to help small businesses organize their purchasing power in the insurance market. Such a system -- the Federal Employee Health Benefit Plan (FEHBP) -- provides health benefits to federal workers, members of Congress, and their dependents. With little bureaucracy, FEHBP empowers individuals to make rational insurance purchasing decisions based on their needs and desires. The American people deserve no less.

President Clinton's proposal for health alliances goes beyond this basic need, however, giving alliances what will amount to regulatory command and control authority, in concert with the national board, to enforce premium prices on insurance plans and exclude plans with higher premiums. Authority also is given to alliances to determine what kinds of health plans would be allowed to compete by limiting the number of fee-for-service plans under an alliance. This is not competition. We recognize the need to manage competition fairly, but this limitation is not fair and is not going to promote competition, which is the only way that cost-effectiveness and quality health care can be guaranteed. An open fee-for-service plan should be available in every area of the country.

The proposal for health alliances is also problematic in that it requires all employers with up to 5000 employees to purchase coverage through them. Such a high threshold will give alliances far too much market power in a state or region, choking off pluralism and competition in a market. It is truly small employers, those with less than 500 employees, that need government help in pooling their resources to buy insurance, not employers with thousands of employees. Government involvement should be limited to where there is a need, allowing competition to work where it is able. Allowing medium sized employers to maintain their own plans will provide an appropriate counterbalance to the power of the alliance and will provide freedom for an expanded number of plans in any particular geographic area.

Corporate Interference

Finally, physicians see the erosion of their professional decision-making role and their ability to represent the best interests of their patients in the overwhelming preference the plan gives to what will no doubt become large corporate managed health care entities. The AMA does not oppose managed care. We understand the current economic pressures that are already pushing more and more physicians into managed care arrangements. That is competition, for now. A health care reform plan should not, however, codify that marketplace phenomenon. If fee-for-service is truly noncompetitive, our patients should make that decision, not the federal government. Government action should at least be neutral, or, where there is a dominance in a market, should help balance the marketplace to encourage competition.

Instead, we see a proposal labeled fee-for-service that actually eliminates many of the elements of fee-for-service. Rather than giving physicians and patients the ability to choose how and where medical care is delivered, and how much the service should cost, the government will impose a price on services that all physicians choosing to practice outside large managed care entities will have to accept. It is doubtful whether many physicians will be able to make this choice outside of already underserved areas of the country where managed care corporations will not find it cost-effective to go. As a result, in a short time, managed care will have no competition in the marketplace. A physician will have little choice if she or he cannot agree to managed care decisions that limit her or his ability to meet patient's medical needs. Such a situation is unacceptable to physicians. The fee-for service option, as proposed by the President, combined with the global budget would limit patient freedom of choice to only an IPA/HMO type of fee-for service plan.

True fee-for-service, without arbitrary constraints, should be given an opportunity to fully compete in a new health system. Instead of price controls, a reimbursement system based on the RBRVS could be created, giving patients an opportunity to compare prices based on physicians' choices of conversion factors they individually want to apply. Then, patients would be given a true opportunity to choose -- not only from among physicians, but also health care delivery systems. Competitiveness among quality as well as costs will be assured.

Also needed are greatly expanded protections from anti-trust constraints for physicians to ban together and organize networks to compete with the accumulation of health care market power in large corporate entities. Physician organizations like the AMA should be allowed to represent physicians. Current restraints on such activities are already no longer valid, especially where individual physicians have little choice but to accept arrangements offered to them by dominant health insurance plans.

Physicians also must be given the opportunity to compete for patients in such markets, by requiring dominant managed care entities to allow physicians who meet credential requirements to provide care under a managed care arrangement. Large corporate entities should not be allowed to freeze otherwise qualified physicians out of providing needed care to their patients if those patients want to choose that physician.

Financing

Adding to physicians' concern over the President's proposal is the light brush that has been given to financing the plan. The key revenue source offered is a continued federal cutback in Medicare and Medicaid funding. Not only is this unacceptable to physicians and their patients who rely on these already underfunded programs, it is doubtful that this can be a reliable revenue source to fund the expansion of health care access hoped for in the proposal.

The AMA would support an increased "sin" tax on tobacco that the President has proposed. We would also support increased taxes on alcohol.

With some reservations, the administrative cost savings offered in the plan are laudable and necessary. But given the bureaucratization of health care at the federal, state, and corporate level provided in the plan, we also see increased administrative costs. For example, the National Board will have numerous sub-boards and commissions to oversee areas such as quality, benefits, and graduate medical education. Each will need to develop complex rules and regulations. A system that adds levels of management, not reduces them, can only be more expensive. The expensive duplication of oversight physicians and patients now experience under insurance company control will not lessen under a system dominated by large corporate health care entities. The new state and federal superstructure of control will only add to this burden. We simply do not see sufficient administrative cost savings in the President's proposal.

Where there are unnecessary costs in the system due to medical liability litigation and defensive medicine, the President's proposal takes too little action. To ensure that such high costs do not continue under a new system, initiatives similar to those taken by California under its MICRA liability reform law should be enacted. A $250,000 limit on noneconomic damages must be established if true cost savings are to be achieved, and limits on attorneys' fees significantly below the 33 1/3 percent limit proposed by the plan are needed. That is no limit at all, since this is the typical share of awards taken from their clients now.

Clearly, more work in determining financing is needed. Physicians and the American people need to know from where the actual financing of the President's plan will come.

Conclusion

The President and the First Lady should receive full credit for ensuring that health system reform has finally begun. Now, Congress has an unprecedented opportunity to enact legislation that will change forever the way health care is delivered in this nation. It is our goal to help ensure that change is for the positive, so that all Americans can receive the high quality, personal medical care that most Americans now receive from their physicians.

My comments today are general. It is my intent to provide an overview of our more basic concerns as the President's proposal applies to physicians' ability to continue to serve in their professional role of providing medical care to their patients, without constraint. In that, physicians have serious reservations. (A detailed response to the President's plan is attached.)

Many Congressional hearings will be held on these and many more specific issues over the next several months. I hope and trust that the AMA will have the opportunity to make more specific comments when the time is appropriate.

AMA's Analysis of the Clinton Plan

The President's Program	AMA's Response
Coverage All US citizens/legal residents must enroll in health insurance plans. Plans may be purchased through a state/regional health alliance. A large employer (more than 5000 employees) may provide coverage through its own alliance. Health security card entitles each to nationally defined comprehensive benefit package. Government employees, Medicaid beneficiaries, and retirees under age 65 also purchase through alliances. Medicare, military health care, VA, and Indian Health Service continue.	Purchasing cooperatives can be useful in helping small businesses pool their purchasing power to buy insurance. Large employers should remain outside of alliances to create true competition. As envisioned here, though, alliances have far too much market influence and must serve a regulatory role under the control of the national health board. For alliances to work, large employers must be defined at more than 500 employees, not 5000. It is truly small employers, not ones with thousands of employees, who now have problems buying insurance and could use alliances. By including large employers, alliances will monopolize markets, thereby reducing competition and consumer control of health care decisions. Also, the alliances are far too much under the control of the national health board to be effective, especially because of the budget caps they must enforce. Rather than helping improve the insurance market, alliances will serve as regulators, thereby bureaucratizing the health care system even more than it is now.
Employer Requirement All employers must pay 80% of weighted-avg plan premium for all employees, with pro-rata contribution for part-time employees under 30 hrs a week. But employer contribution is capped at 7.9% of payroll. Small employers (less than 50 employees) are capped between 3.5% and 6.5%, depending on employee avg annual wages. Corporate alliances: self-insured large employers (5,000+) and equally large union plans may self-fund, contract with health plan, or arrange coverage through alliance; but must generally meet same requirements as insured plans.	The AMA believes that the best way to achieve meaningful health reform is to build on the existing employer-based health insurance system. The inequities in the current system should be addressed without sacrificing the health care quality and access that most Americans enjoy. This goal can be achieved through an employer requirement with appropriate protections for small businesses. Likewise, it is critical for employers to contribute the same percentage of premium to whichever plan its employees choose, otherwise the system is biased toward managed care. The percent of payroll cap is too low for large business, discouraging them from establishing their own plans, therefore increasing monopsony buying power of the alliances
Employee/Individual Requirement Employees pay 20% of weighted avg-cost alliance health plan, depending on its cost. Self-employed and unemployed pay 100%, but anyone below 150% of poverty receives federal premium assistance from alliance. Undocumented aliens not eligible, but federal aid to institutions for their care continues. States must address migrant worker issues.	The federal government must increase, not reduce its funding and leadership in addressing undocumented individuals and migrant workers. Problems associated with providing them care go far beyond states' resources. Assistance should be provided for individuals and families with incomes under 200% of the poverty rate.
Nationally Defined Benefit Package Comprehensive medical; clinical preventive services based on periodicity schedule; hospice and home health; 30 days/episode and 60 days/yr inpatient mental health/substance abuse with 30 visits/yr psychotherapy; family planning;, pregnancy-related; hospice; outpatient prescription drugs; rehab; DME and prosthetic/orthotic devices; vision/hearing; preventive dental for children; health education.	The preventive benefit package is inadequate and does not appear to use most current data. Other benefits are not inconsistent with AMA's own recommendations for a standard benefit package. But much more detail is needed. Any national health board updating of this package should be subject to Congressional approval. Coverage for mental health/substance abuse should mirror medical care.

The President's Program	AMA's Response
Cost Sharing Health plans may offer 1 of 3 options: • Low cost sharing -- no deductible, $10 copay for outpatient services but none for inpatient, 40% coinsurance point-of-service option, $1500 individual/$3000 family out-of-pocket max, $5 copay for prescription • High cost sharing -- none for preventive; $200/$400 deductible, 20% coinsurance, and same out-of-pocket max for inpatient/outpatient; $250/yr deductible, 20% coinsurance, and same out-of-pocket max for drugs • Combination -- low cost sharing if preferred providers used and higher cost sharing with 20% coinsurance for out-of-network providers; same out-of-pocket max.	Under low cost sharing, 40% coinsurance for a point-of-service option is unacceptable, especially under a plan that will allow managed care plans to dominate the market. To help ensure the quality of managed care, patients must be given a reasonable opportunity to see physicians outside a plan. Further, managed care plans should be required to accept any physician who meets stated credentials and who agrees to provide services under an agreement with the plan and subject to plan capacity. Medical savings accounts (MSA) should be authorized to assist individuals and families in meeting out of pocket expenses including co-insurance and deductibles. Plan should authorize individuals to contract for any health services they want with their own after-tax funds.
National Health Board National board oversees the establishment and administration of the new system. President appoints 7 members to staggered 4-yr terms who then are federal employees and may not have health care assets; 1 must represent states. Duties include • implementing and enforcing national health spending budget • establishing state plan requirements, monitoring compliance • reviewing alliance plans submitted by states, with enforcement through HHS and Treasury • interpreting/updating benefit package • setting quality management/improvement system • commenting on breakthrough drug prices, but cannot control drug prices.	The AMA unequivocally opposes a national health spending budget and giving a national board responsibility for implementing and enforcing one. Such centralized decision-making and artificial spending have never worked anywhere and will quickly bring about difficulties in health care access and quality. A truly representative national commission may be able to help in setting goals for the health care system for expanding access, and in setting budget goals that take into account disease and demographic changes and changes in demand. But this proposal creates a new federal bureaucracy with price control authority. Also, it is unacceptable that no place has been reserved on the board for a physician or AMA representative.
State Responsibilities States • by 1/1/97, must establish at least 1 alliance and assure all eligible individuals enroll • certify health plans to participate in alliances • ensure the availability of a plan priced at or below weighted-avg premium • submit to National Health Board plans to regulate health plans, administer data collection and quality management/improvement • may establish a single-payor health care system complying with benefit package and cost sharing requirements, or a single-payor alliance for part of a state.	The AMA strongly opposes the establishment of a single-payor health care system, whether on a state or national level as part of national health system reform legislation. No centralized decision-making authority can control costs and ensure adequate access to quality services, especially in health care. When, for good reason, the national plan rejects a single payor system nationally, allowing a state to subject its residents to such an unreasonable approach is contradictory and makes little sense.

The President's Program	AMA's Response
Health Alliances Health alliances are meant to act as conduits between health plans and individual purchasers of health insurance coverage, contracting with health plans to provide the required benefit package and providing a simplified, uniform means for individuals to choose between plans. Alliances • must contract with a plan unless its premium exceeds the weighted-avg premium by more than 20%, its quality is poor, or it discriminates. • must use risk-adjustment mechanism to account for enrollment variations across plans • may be a nonprofit corporation or state agency, but nonprofit's board must equally consist of consumers and employers whose selection is determined by the state • must establish provider advisory boards • must enroll all eligible individuals and have annual open enrollment periods • may not bear insurance risk • must publish consumer info on cost, providers, access restrictions, and quality of plans. Alliances must offer at least 1 any-willing-provider **fee-for-service plan**, but may limit number to 3 through competitive bidding. National board may waive requirement if not viable or insufficient interest. After collective provider negotiations, alliance sets provider **fee schedule** for each fee-for-service plan, and **providers may not balance bill**. States may impose prospective budgeting on fee-for-service plans. Corporate alliances must also offer at least 1 fee-for-service plan.	The AMA is adamantly opposed to the plan's restrictions on fee-for-service. True fee-for-service gives individuals the freedom to choose health care services. By establishing a fee schedule and barring physicians and patients willing and able from agreeing to the cost of their medical care, true choice no longer will exist in the US health care system. Physicians and patients will find it difficult to use choice to guard against health care decision-making made at corporate and bureaucratic levels, thus diminishing the ability of physicians to advocate for their patients. If a health alliance acts as an impartial conduit between health plans and purchasers, acting to make it easier for individuals and small businesses to make insurance purchases and encouraging competitiveness between health plans, health alliances can help bring about needed fairness in the health insurance market. If an alliance cannot act fairly, true competitiveness cannot be assured. Alliances should be required to accept all fee-for-service plans offered, instead of limiting the number to 3. True freedom-of-choice for individuals to determine what kind of health care delivery best meets their needs is severely diminished. Plans should be encouraged to recognize the RBRVS for determining physician reimbursement using individual physician selected conversion factors. Plans should authorize individuals to contract for any health services they want with their own after-tax funds.
ERISA • Corporate alliances subject to new fiduciary/ enforcement requirements regarding national benefit package, plan info requirements, and uniform data, claims, electronic billing, and grievance procedures. • Self-funded plans must set benefit payment trust fund; beneficiaries receive special protection in bankruptcy if employer fails. • National guaranty fund established. • ERISA preemption of state laws modified to apply only to corporate alliances, allow nondiscriminatory taxes on them, allow state all-payor rate setting, allow states to include corporate alliances to reimburse essential community providers.	AMA has long supported ERISA reform. The plan proposes to address many of the problems identified by the AMA that have developed under ERISA, including protecting beneficiaries of self-insured plans from unfair coverage decisions and plan insolvency. Such changes have long been needed to ensure that all Americans are treated fairly by those who insure their health benefits, whether an employer or an insurance company. However, ERISA's preemption of state law should not be amended to authorize a state single payor system to apply to large employers or to allow varying reserve requirements from insured plans within the state.

The President's Program	AMA's Response
Health Plans • Health plans must accept all eligible individuals, have an open enrollment period, and may not cancel/reduce benefits even for enrollee nonpayment. Pre-existing condition limits and disease-specific exclusions are prohibited. • Each August, alliance negotiates premium rates with each plan and publishes rates. Employer/employee pay community rate. Alliance adjusts payments to plans based on risk, using formula set by national health board. Plans with high risk populations may reinsure. • Plans must provide alliance with extensive info on cost, quality, provider availability, UR, consumer rights, and plan responsibilities. • Plans must provide consumers info on risks, benefits, medical procedure costs, and advance directives. Grievance procedures and alternative dispute resolution required. • State laws protecting against managed care abuses are preempted. • State laws banning the corporate practice of medicine are preempted. • The ability of plans to own facilities or offer medical services is authorized. • Out-of-service-area emergency/urgent care required, paid on alliance's fee-for-service payment schedule. • A plan must have advisory boards of providers selected by providers, which must be consulted frequently and has access to plan information. • Loans are available for community-based plans.	The insurance reforms offered in the President's plan are important elements of health system reform. Setting premiums based on community rating and eliminating pre-existing condition exclusions have long been urged by the AMA. Health Plans should be required to create a committee of practicing physicians within the plans that is responsible for establishing clinical decision criteria. Exceptions to community rating should not be granted to large firms. Establishing a system of sharing uniform information about plans through the alliances will help consumers make informed insurance purchasing decisions. Nevertheless, provisions that would preempt laws that states have enacted to protect against abuses in managed care need to be eliminated. The President's plan, overall, gives such a strong encouragement to managed care that states need to be allowed to continue their authority to act when abuses occur. The plan should not override state corporate practice of medicine laws in states that currently prohibit such. Further, managed care plans should be required to accept any physician who meets stated credentials and who agrees to provide services under an agreement with the plan and subject to plan capacity.
Global Budgets/Price Controls The plan describes a national health care budget based on the weighted-avg premium for the guaranteed benefit package as a targeted **backstop** to market action. The **target** increase in premiums for 1996 is CPI + 1.5, CPI + 1 for 1997, CPI + 0.5 for 1998, and CPI for 1999 and beyond. A national per capita based premium is set by the national board, as is a system to adjust at alliance level for risk factors like age/demographics. Alliances then receive an avg premium from the national board. Plans submit bids to alliances either blind or with knowledge of the target. Alliances then submit their negotiated premiums to national board, which tells the alliance if its avg premiums is acceptable of not. If not, the alliance renegotiates. If the alliance exceeds its target, there is a 2-yr recoupment. Targets may not be adjusted, except by Congress. Corporate alliances use an equivalent target and are terminated if they miss target 2 out of 3 yrs.	The AMA staunchly opposes the setting of any national budget. Any decision-making in health care based mainly on economics and not on patient needs is not in the best interests of patients, and will lead to rationing that cannot address the difficulties and inequities in our current health care system. This issue will be a key area of concern and activity in the coming months as health system reform continues in Congress. The President's plan calls its spending limits "targets." The AMA believes that a participatory process that includes physicians might be useful to establish true goals that can be flexible and are based on patient needs. As written, though, these "targets" are stringent, arbitrary caps on spending. This is fully unacceptable.

The President's Program	AMA's Response
Administrative Simplification	
• National board must develop simplified forms. By January 1995, UB92 must be used for institutional services, standard health insurance claim form similar to HCFA 1500 for noninstitutional, HCFA 1500 for dentists, and universal drug claim form for pharmacies. • National board must set automated transaction and coding standards. Private payors must adopt electronic data interchange (EDI) standards by 1/1/95; federal programs ASAP after enactment. Providers, including medical groups of over 20, must automate within 6 months of standardization. States may deny payment to plans not using EDI. • Medicare simplification: contractors will be consolidated based on function, not area; balance billing for DME eliminated; national data file on Medicare beneficiaries created, and Medigap terminations take place as part of national data file; presumptive waiver of co-insurance with physician's acknowledgement; physicians input in carrier performance; Parts A and B claim processing integrated; attestation requirement eliminated except for hospital medical staff privileges; pre-approval for 10 surgical procedures eliminated; system changes more than once every 120 days prohibited; PROs must focus on patterns, not individual cases • The health security cards all individuals receive is like an automated teller machine card, to be used to access a national uniform health data set established by the national board. • Unique identifiers to be established for plans, practitioners, providers, and patients. • An information system is envisioned that will be able to collect data from all encounters, using a standard format with an emphasis on electronic records. Encounter data is to be transmitted to regional information network, to be used to set national info trends. A national data advisory committee for research is established.	AMA supports forward movement in electronic data management and administrative simplification to allow physicians and other health care professionals more time for patient care activities. These efforts are necessary to improve access and help contain health care costs, but it is critical that meaningful clinical management information systems be preserved. Through the development and maintenance of the AMA's CPT coding system, the medical profession has demonstrated its ability to create and administer an efficient procedure coding system in partnership with the government. CPT already is widely used and accepted by Medicare, Medicaid, and all major third-party payers. The national board should recognize the profession's contribution and be careful not to create new administrative burdens in the course of trying to simplify information systems. We are also concerned that, while private payors are given the responsibility for adopting EDI standards, a time limit is set for its adoption. We are confident that the private sector is developing and quickly integrating EDI without government involvement. No new unique identifiers should be created by the government. Physicians already are identified by Medicare/Medicaid UPIN numbers, and SPIN (Standard Prescriber Identification Number - an AMA/private sector initiative to create a unique identifier for claims processing and drug utilization review) is receiving a favorable response as a solution to the need for uniquely identifying prescribers. Accepted identifiers need not be duplicated. As with other EDI issues, assuring patient confidentiality will continue to be a goal of the AMA. There should be no micro-management of the information system at the national level. The costs of developing any information management systems should be kept to a minimum and not shifted. Confidentiality must be assured.
Quality	
• A national quality management program is set, to be overseen by a 15-member advisory council to the national board, consisting of consumers, plan reps, states, and public health and quality experts. National performance goals, minimum standards, research support, and a report on quality are required. Advisory council must set national program to develop practice guidelines, scientific standards, and priorities. • Program is "customer-focused," based on consumer satisfaction and outcomes. Plan info collected by alliances is to be used to compare plans. Program publishes results of all plans annually. Regional data centers created. States enforce standards. • National regulation preempts local regulation; intervention must focus on problems, with targeted reviews and randomly selected validation sites; demo program required by 1/1/96. • Medicare PROs continue until HHS determine they are no longer necessary. • NIH funding expanded for effectiveness and outcomes based on quality, with a program to evaluate reform and program to study how consumer choice and decision-making take place.	AMA recommended a comprehensive program that would recognize the profession's well-established accrediting and quality assurance programs. The AMA is deeply concerned that physicians have not been included specifically in the advisory council that will be responsible for so many initiatives in quality, especially the establishment of practice parameters. We will work to ensure that such efforts continue to be led by the profession. We

Mr. WAXMAN. Dr. Ebert?

STATEMENT OF PAUL A. EBERT

Mr. EBERT. Thank you very much, Mr. Chairman.

I am pleased to make comments on behalf of the American College of Surgeons and to compliment the President and to say that we agree with the main goals of the plan and certainly support these objectives. We have certain problems looking at the President's plan when it calls for a major restructuring of the health care system through creation of what seems to be a fairly new and highly bureaucratic scheme.

All sorts of new boards, corporations, advisory councils, sometimes quasi-governmental alliances, would probably be created throughout the country to carry out activities such as setting and enforcing budgets, implementing regulations, governing the content of health plans, negotiating payments, managing the postgraduate training and education of physicians, and collecting and disseminating vast amounts of data on the health care services.

Other colleagues expressed the problems of the practicing physician as the practicing surgeon with existing health care administration complexities. I think we would all feel much more relieved so to speak if we had some assurances that we could handle some of the complicating problems that exist and bother practicing surgeons today rather than looking forward to some form of a really major restructuring of the health care system that in our view does seem to put in place so-called reinventing government at a time when we were somewhat hopeful that people might be able to reduce its influence.

The College does not take issue with the interest of the policymakers to meet the primary care needs of all Americans. However, we do believe that some elements of this reform plan seek to achieve that goal in ways that could create potential barriers to the availability of surgical and other high technical health care services.

We would hope the Congress would consider carefully the wisdom of trying to finance so much of the reform plan from reduced or redistributed Medicare and Medicaid funds. Most individuals know today that if their practice were totally limited to Medicaid and Medicare patients in our current system they would have difficulty as well as any managed care organization to make a profit or at least stay in business if that was their only source of patient materials.

The College supports the continuing ability of individuals and families to meet health care needs through a wide variety of arrangements. We would be very concerned if the President's interest in a so-called, only managed competition approach to reform effectively limited choice to this only one type of health plan which might in that case most logically be some type of health maintenance organization.

We are pleased to see that under the administration's plan and most of the Medicaid recipients have the same opportunity as other Americans to make a choice in their health benefit arrangements. However, we are somewhat concerned that Medicaid patients who have financial resources that are by definition already limited, in reality many of these individuals could be denied real opportunities to enroll in certain plans that would be available only to those with greater financial resources. Thus I think that some of the specifics of this type of proposal we hope will be looked at so that all Medicaid recipients would have the freedom of choice and could enjoy a full range of benefits.

We understand the importance of including provisions in a reform program that will promote the goal of protecting universal health benefits in cost-effective ways. However, we believe that various incentives should be used instead of regulation to contain costs.

We have supported in the past incentives that involved some type of performance based methods. We also believe that the marketplace pressures are having a significant effect and probably much of the legislation that was put in place several years ago is just now starting to be felt.

For example, the College has been a strong supporter of the policy devices such as expenditure targets in Medicare volume performance because they have the opportunity involving physicians and physician organizations in the effort to address the annual growth and spending for the services which they provide. However, in the very early proposal, the President's approach to budgeting is not a performance-based method that involves physicians and other health care providers.

It calls for imposing arbitrary limits on the rates of increase in health spending at a national level for each regional alliance. Moreover, the budget allocations to the alliances would be established by this already mentioned seven unelected individuals who would comprise a National Health Board. Obviously we look forward to being able to further discussions as the plan is brought forward in more detail.

Thank you, Mr. Chairman.

[The prepared statement of Dr. Ebert follows:]

STATEMENT

of the

AMERICAN COLLEGE OF SURGEONS

to the

Subcommittee on Health and the Environment
and
Subcommittee on Commerce, Consumer Protection, and Competitiveness
Committee on Energy and Commerce
U.S. House of Representatives

presented by

Paul A. Ebert, MD, FACS
Director

RE: Health Care Revision

October 14, 1993

Chairman Waxman, Chairwoman Collins, and members of the subcommittees, I am Paul A. Ebert, MD, FACS, Director of the American College of Surgeons. On behalf of the more than 60,000 Fellows of the College, I am pleased to have this opportunity to offer comments on the President's health system reform proposal. Of course, like you, we have only been able to study a draft of the reform plan. We hope to frame our views on the various elements of the proposal more clearly when additional details are made available and all of us have an opportunity to examine it more thoroughly.

The College certainly commends the President for his leadership in proposing steps to bring about reforms to the nation's health care system. We support his call for achieving universal access to health care and for making needed reforms in the insurance marketplace.

We also welcome his interest in malpractice reform and administrative simplification, which, in our view, are long overdue. Nevertheless, there are several aspects of the President's plan that are of significant concern to us.

Reorganizing the Health Care System. The President's plan seems to call for a major restructuring of the health care system through the creation of a new and highly bureaucratic scheme. All sorts of new boards, corporations, advisory councils, and other quasi-governmental alliances would be created throughout the country, to carry out activities such as: setting and enforcing global budgets; implementing regulations governing the content of health plans; negotiating fees; managing the post-graduate training of physicians; collecting and disseminating vast amounts of data on health care services and financing; reviewing quality of care; collecting premiums, and so on.

At a time when we should be streamlining our system and reducing the bureaucratic and overhead burdens that drain funds that could be used to provide health care services, we find this very disturbing and fraught with the potential of seriously undermining the public's expectations about our ability to proceed along the path to reform.

The President recently called for "reinventing" government -- for enhancing the efficiency and responsiveness of federal agencies and programs by downsizing and consolidating the extensive federal organization that has evolved to meet the needs of the American people. We believe that the bureaucratic scheme set forth in the President's health reform plan needs to be examined carefully in light of this government reform initiative. Certainly, better ways can be found to achieve the goals of health system reform without resorting to a new and complex regulatory scheme that is so heavily dependent on decisions being made in Washington by a few federal policymakers.

Financing Health Reform. We realize that health system reform will require that new financial resources be invested to achieve the goals of universal access and coverage. However, the College believes the Administration has unrealistic expectations about financing the reform effort through very deep reductions in the Medicare and Medicaid programs, largely through significantly decreased payments to those who now provide health care services to elderly, disabled, and low-income Americans.

We are also concerned that the proposed premium caps could quickly lead many health plans to resort to health care rationing, or face the risk of failing altogether. In fact, it seems likely that adopting health system reforms will stimulate the overall demand for health care services. Yet, the President's financing plan would respond to any increases in consumer demand through further sharp reductions in Medicare and Medicaid, and by imposing premium controls in the private sector.

The Fellows of the College are also very much disturbed by an apparent attempt in the President's plan to address certain "primary care" objectives *at the expense* of other services. For example, it can hardly be considered fair for the Administration to propose paying surgical services less than justified under Medicare's resource-based payment methodology in order to pay more for primary care services than is justified under that same resource-based approach. We understood that this subcommittee and the Congress adopted the resource-based payment system in an effort to establish payment amounts that accurately reflect the work and resources involved in providing physicians' services, adjusted by performance-based volume considerations. In our view, the President's plan would essentially make a sham out of these purported efforts to rationalize the Medicare physician payment system.

Similarly, we think it is inequitable, and even rather odd, for the President to recommend eliminating the 10 percent Medicare payment incentive for surgical and most other physicians' services in *urban* health professional shortage areas in order to double the payment bonus for primary care services that are provided in rural and urban shortage areas.

The College does not take issue with the interests of policymakers to meet the primary care needs of all Americans. However, we do believe that some elements of the President's reform plan seek to achieve that goal in ways that could create potential barriers to the availability of surgical and other kinds of health care services. We hope that Congress will consider carefully the wisdom of trying to finance so much of the reform effort from reduced or redistributed Medicare and Medicaid funds, and from hoped-for savings under an untested and undesirable national premium control program.

Patient Choice. We applaud features in the President's plan that would provide Americans with a choice of at least three different types of health plans, including plans that will allow participants the option of consulting any health care provider, subject to reasonable plan requirements. The American College of Surgeons supports the continuing ability of individuals and families to meet their health care needs through a variety of arrangements. Indeed, we would be very concerned if the President's interest in a so-called managed competition approach to reform effectively limited choice to only one type of health plan, such as a health maintenance organization.

The College believes, however, that more must be known about the design of the health plan options under the President's proposal before decisionmakers can determine if Americans will, in fact, be presented with a reasonable choice of affordable health benefit arrangements, including plans that do not require individuals to seek care through gatekeeper mechanisms.

For example, in the case of the so-called high cost sharing option, which is presumed by the Administration to include plans that do not employ gatekeepers, alliances or states would be expected to negotiate fee schedules and other payment methods for the services provided under those plans. However, if those fees and payments are unreasonably low, as they are now under the Medicare and Medicaid programs, true freedom of choice in selecting a plan may not exist in some areas, or perhaps exist on paper only. Thus, the College is not convinced that real freedom of choice will be achieved only through defining the benefit and patient cost sharing features of the different options, as the President's plan suggests.

We are pleased to see that, under the Administration's plan, most Medicaid recipients will have the same opportunities as other Americans to make a choice in their health benefit arrangements from among the plans participating in the regional alliances. However, as we see it, these individuals may still have some of their options effectively constrained by the fact that they can only choose a plan that costs the same as, or less than, the weighted average local premium, unless they make an additional payment. Medicaid patients have financial resources that are, by definition, already limited. In reality then, these individuals could be denied real opportunities to enroll in certain plans that would be available to those who have greater financial resources. We hope that any such restrictions on the choices available to Medicaid recipients will not be applied in order that they, too, may enjoy the full range of benefit arrangements offered under health system reform.

Global Budgeting. The College has major concerns regarding the President's proposed global budgeting scheme, which, in our view, concentrates far too much regulatory authority in the hands of government and alliance officials. Under the President's plan, the federal government is responsible for enforcing the health care budget. Based on proposed premiums, the National Health Board would calculate the anticipated weighted average premium for every alliance throughout the United States. If an alliance's weighted premium exceeded its per capita target, "assessments" would be imposed in health plans with premium increases that exceed the alliance's premium target. Moreover, the same assessments could be passed along directly by the plans to the health care providers.

The College understands the importance of including provisions in a reform program that will promote the goal of protecting universal health benefits in cost-effective ways. However, we believe that various incentives should be used instead of regulation to contain costs. These incentives could include marketplace pressures and performance-based methods that make both patients and providers aware of the costs of medical care. For example, the American College of Surgeons has been a strong supporter of policy devices such as expenditure targets, or Medicare volume performance standards, that actually involve physicians and physicians' organizations in the effort to address the annual growth in spending for the services they provide.

However, the President's approach to budgeting is not a performance-based method that involves physicians and other health care providers. Instead, it calls for imposing arbitrary limits on the rates of increase in health spending at the national level and for each regional alliance. Moreover, the budget allocations to the alliances would be established by just the seven unelected individuals who comprise the National Health Board.

We believe strongly that the decisions about how much should be spent on health care in the future in all districts and states represented by Congress should not be left in the hands of these few individuals. Congress must assume a much more direct role in allocating health care resources, if the President's global budgeting mechanism is given any serious consideration. We doubt that the extraordinary diversity in the needs and desires of the American people for affordable, quality health care can be addressed through the rigid kinds of budget controls that are currently outlined in the descriptions we have seen of the Administration's proposal.

Physician Workforce/Graduate Medical Education. Finally, as you know, the College believes that Congress should consider graduate medical education financing and physician workforce issues in conjunction with any long-range health reform plan. We do think it is reasonable to consider a reduction in the total number of residency positions currently available, and to reconsider the rationale for maintaining such a large number of post-graduate positions that are now filled by international medical graduates. The College believes that establishing specific numerical limits on the number of physicians to be trained may be an effective way for policymakers to determine the future mix and numbers of medical and surgical specialists. In general, the President's reform plan proposes to manage the number of post-graduate training positions and to provide funding directly to the training programs.

The College has taken no position about the precise physician-to-population ratios that would best meet the nation's physician workforce needs, nor have we determined the most appropriate mix of physicians among the medical and surgical specialties. In previous testimony before this committee, we have urged that these goals be established after a more careful assessment is made of the potential implications that health system reform may have on the ways in which medical and surgical services are organized.

However, we are troubled by a provision in the President's plan that would require the Secretary of Health and Human Services to appoint 10 regional councils to allocate training slots among individual residency programs. These government-controlled councils would consist not only of representatives of academic institutions that train physicians in these regions, but also representatives of regional health alliances, health plans, consumers, and others.

Instead, the College believes that, if the Secretary establishes national residency goals (after obtaining any advice she feels necessary), the existing structure of the Residency Review Committees should be given the responsibility for establishing the program criteria that would work best to implement the national physician supply targets. We also believe that the President's proposals for graduate medical education financing should explicitly include a policy of adequate government funding for all residencies through the entire course of the training period. If we commit ourselves to establishing the number of physicians we want to train, it seems only reasonable to support that training for the full residency period.

Again, the College is pleased to have this opportunity to share some of its thoughts on the initial draft of the President's health reform proposal. Obviously, we have commented on only a few items in this proposal, and will undoubtedly be expressing opinions on other elements of the plan as more details are known.

I would be happy to answer any questions you or members of the subcommittees may have.

Mr. WAXMAN. We are being summoned to the Floor for a quorum. That was the second bell. I am willing to miss the quorum although I do want to attend the vote afterwards.

Let's do this: Why don't we start the questioning and we will see how far we can get. If members want to run and do the quorum and come right back, we will recognize them when they return.

Mr. Bliley?

Mr. BLILEY. Thank you, Mr. Chairman.

I have another chart and I ask unanimous consent to distribute it to all members of the committee.

There are many ways to approach the complexities and strange mysteries of the administration's financing schemes. Let's see if this chart to your left can help shed some light on these mysteries for you the providers who are the key to health care reform.

The physician in the middle of the chart being ripped apart represents the U.S. health care system under the administration's plan. You can see it is being pulled apart by three contradictory forces.

First let's look into the reduction in national health care expenditures projected under the administration's plan. On the last page of the September 7 draft, there is a chart which summarizes total national health care expenditures. It compares the CBO current services baseline for health expenditures without reform versus health care expenditures under the Clinton reform proposal.

This chart shows a $227 billion cut in national health expenditures for fiscal year 1998 to 2000 under the Clinton plan. It also shows these cuts from the CBO baseline rapidly accelerating in 1999 and beyond. So simply put, on one side, we have $227 billion fewer in the health care system for these several years.

Now let's look on the right side at the new entitlements which will be fully phased in by 1998. Approximately 37 million individuals will be newly covered under the basic benefits package. According to the administration's analysis, two-thirds of all Americans will have a benefits package as good or better than the plans on the market today.

There will be a new $72 billion Medicare drug benefit. There will be a new $80 billion long-term care benefit, and there will be a $30 billion early retiree benefit for those over 55, but not yet eligible for Medicare. Last but not least—my personal favorite—$91 billion in budget reduction.

Now let's recap. The administration's plan is cutting $227 billion in national health expenditures while it is simultaneously creating five large entitlements and also produces enough additional savings to reduce the Federal budget deficit by $91 billion at the same time. I personally think the likely result will be that the world's foremost health care system will be torn apart.

Last week we asked the Secretary of HHS for an explanation of this and she could not give one. Then I remember what Senator Moynihan said about the plan's financing; that it was built on fantasy.

Let me ask the panel members if they can shed any light on how the administration can accomplish this feat. I would like Dr. Bristow and Dr. Ebert to comment on my fee-for-service chart. [See p. 394.]

Mr. BRISTOW. I will be happy to start off, Congressman Bliley.

I would like to say that the same concerns that you have identified in terms of the financing are the concerns shared by, I am certain, most of us at this table. Certainly the American Medical Association is anxious to see the final figures and the final proposal so that they can be carefully checked as to their validity.

In accordance with your request, the chart concerning fee-for-service resembles what I would call a depiction of the incredible shrinking man as fee-for-service gets smaller and smaller and seems to be an endangered species unless the further clarification that we receive from the administration with the final proposal dispels some of the obvious concerns you have identified, not the least of which you have left out one of the toll stations, anyone who goes for the fee-for-service option first has to pay 20 percent of the premium and 20 percent of the co-pay as a co-pay after that. It creates a very sizable hurdle for anyone to choose fee-for-service.

Mr. BLILEY. Dr. Ebert, do you agree with that?

Mr. EBERT. I do. I think that your comments on the fee-for-service plan, we would call it a pay-for-service plan—if these payments were somewhat related to the magnitude of current Medicare and Medicaid payments and a doctor was limited only to one type of system, we think it would be very difficult to maintain or even have the existence of this particular type of system.

Mr. BLILEY. My time has expired.

Dr. Cleaveland and Ms. Shinn, do you agree generally with Drs. Bristow and Ebert?

Mr. CLEAVELAND. We have heard arguments on how much waste and administrative fat is in the system. It is enormous. I think there is a lot of money to be saved out there.

I don't totally agree. This is a fascinating presentation. I wish we had an hour and a blackboard because I think each can learn something from the other. The 237 million new insureds are getting care, but others are paying for it.

I agree that there are maybe some pie-in-the-sky benefits here, but the drug benefit for instance I think is realistic and doable. I don't think these are impossible numbers, so I respectfully disagree.

Ms. SHINN. I would just add that we should not underestimate the use of registered nurses in helping contain the cost of our health care system.

Mr. BLILEY. Thank you, Mr. Chairman.

Mr. WAXMAN. We will have to break now to respond to these votes on the Floor. There is a quorum call to be followed by a 5-minute vote so we will come back in 10 to 15 minutes and resume questions.

[Brief recess.]

Mr. WAXMAN. The committee will come back to order. I want to recognize Mr. Brown.

Mr. BROWN. Dr. Bristow, you mentioned in your testimony, which I am trying to find after this little break, on I believe the third page of your testimony, somewhere in the testimony, you mentioned that the preventive package isn't adequate in the Clinton plan and does not appear to use the most current data. Would you tell us precisely where the Clinton package is inadequate in terms of care, what has been left out, what you recommend should be included?

Mr. BRISTOW. We would be happy to subsequently provide you with detailed recommendations for a preventive package. The comments addressed to the Clinton proposal relate to the fact that all the recommendations in the proposal are not identical with the recommendations of those most experienced and most expert in preventive medicine such as the recommendations that might be put forward by the American Cancer Society, for example.

If we have said that the Clinton proposal is defective, that may be too harsh a word. I think you can decide how much preventive medicine you wish to have in a package and how much you wish to pay for and then if individuals decide that they want more and can perhaps afford that they can perhaps get more. But certainly the proposal as written and released a few weeks ago does not contain all of the recommendations that would be offered by those most expert in preventive medicine.

We will be happy to provide you with a more detailed list of that after this testimony today.

Mr. BROWN. I would appreciate that, if you would provide that to my office in writing. Thank you.

Ms. Shinn, you mentioned a nurse-managed program that administers a multifaceted approach to work site health care, including primary, secondary, and tertiary care. I am interested in the wellness work site issue and providing appropriate places for employers to develop such programs.

Would you elaborate on the operation, its cost to the company, its response to employees? Give me some more thoughts about that, if you would.

Ms. SHINN. I will also be sure that you get a recent publication that the American Nurses Foundation published on that very subject.

Let me give you an example of the Marriott Corporation. Marriott Corporation estimates that they are saving in employee health care costs per year around $250,000 by virtue of a variety of approaches that they use at the work site and within their corporate headquarters using both the occupational health nurse and the nurse practitioner to do a variety of things—to respond to accidents or injuries on the job, to respond to some health care teaching needs that employees generally always have, to keep people's immunizations up to date, to do teaching, and to provide some of those counseling services that are often needed when people have tough times.

That is just one example of a corporation who is making a broad use of nurses and are finding the cost savings well worth it.

[The information follows:]

MARRIOTT'S COMPREHENSIVE DELIVERY AND COST CONTAINMENT PROGRAM

Hospitality giant Marriott illustrates a multifaceted approach to work site health care. Starting from the top down with its nurse-managed program, Marriott incorporates primary, secondary and tertiary care. The intent is to improve employees' health, return employees to work and provide employee assistance, while managing disability and worker injuries.

Nurses in casualty claims offices take charge of bill auditing programs, utilization review and negotiation for equipment and services. In all six regional casualty claims offices, nurse review specialists set up physician panels and act as medical advisors and conduct education programs for claims adjustors. They also manage referrals to rehabilitation and physical therapists, negotiate MRI costs and audit functions to hold the line on costs.

"For each nurse, we save $250,000 a year," says Rachel Ebert, COHN, director of Occupational Health Services for Marriott. "There's an awful lot you can't measure so that's a very conservative estimate."

Nurse C.A.R.E. managers serve as employee advocates, working autonomously to handle worker's injuries and coordinating action and response activities. Marriott has three nurse C.A.R.E. managers, certified as occupational health nurses, and plans to add four more in 1993. These nurses coordinate among employees, managers and the claims office and collaborate with physicians to make sure injured workers receive appropriate care and return to work quickly.

"The number of litigated cases has been reduced 30 to 50 percent," Ebert says. The program also decreases corporate losses due to injuries. Each of the three nursing centers saves Marriott $260,000 to $270,000, Ebert says, representing a 4 to 1 return on investment.

Nurses on hotel properties serve as associate health managers. Fifteen occupational health nurses work on-site at hotels, providing primary and preventive care and ensuring work safety for employees. They manage worker's compensation and OSHA on properties. Plans are in place to add disability management and wellness programs, also.

"Non-work-related absences have been reduced 30 percent when nurses are situated in hotels," Ebert claims. "Many employees come to work to get advice on how to care for their personal illnesses or injuries."

The cost savings are harder to quantify in this program, Ebert says, but probably represent a 3 to 1 return on investment. In terms of managing injury followup, Ebert estimates a 20 to 30 percent cost savings due to reduced medical bills.

A nurse practitioner in a freestanding clinic serves 2,000 hotel employees in the Phoenix area. Initiated in April 1992, the nurse practitioner treats injuries, follows patients, conducts wellness programs, counsels employees, sutures, and writes prescriptions.

THE BOTTOM LINE—Each nurse saves money for the company and, more importantly, takes care of the employees by providing the right care at the right time.

Mr. BROWN. Under the Clinton health plan, the employees and the companies in the health alliance can't do it quite the same way as a self-insured company make Marriott might do today or a company that is not self-insured, but gets direct benefits because of the incentives. How do we go about getting health alliances to do some of the things that Marriott does?

Ms. SHINN. We have to demand that our payers, whoever they are, whether independent payers, whether they are government payers, we are going to have to be willing to pay for preventive services so that we can experience these cost savings on down the line. Now we pay generally when we are in trouble, when people have an accident or when people are ill or when people come to the emergency room. That is another whole set of scenarios related to uncompensated care.

We are going to have to be willing to pay for preventive services, which is not very attractive. One of the things we see in the Clinton plan is some interest in doing that.

Mr. BROWN. Thank you, Mr. Chairman.

Mr. WAXMAN. Thank you, Mr. Brown.

Mr. McMillan?

Mr. MCMILLAN. Thank you, Mr. Chairman.

One general question to any of you. This really gets at the heart of the President's proposal, which is—we probably don't disagree on the problems, most of us. But it seems to me what has been set up here is an extraordinary concentration of decision-making. You in effect have one national board that can set the price.

They may say that global budgeting is an option, but you and I know that the costs aren't necessarily going to control themselves, and it is going to be found very quickly necessary to capitate the system and that capitates every regional alliance and those regional alliances would include over 88 percent of the population.

Medicare would remain outside of that and out of control, but the only ones that would be excluded would be corporate alliances and they are only about 12 percent of the work force. A lot of them are going to probably forgo their own plans. So everybody will flow into concentrated decision-making and I think that is going to also mean less and less competition.

I think insurers are going to find that they have to combine to meet the standards that will be imposed from the top down. HMO's will continue to consolidate in order to try to achieve cost savings.

I guess I want to ask each of you if you essentially agree with that and do you think it will work?

Mr. CLEAVELAND. Let me respond first. If the National Health Board operated in a vacuum it could be a very dangerous board with a tremendous concentration of power. If on the other hand it had tentacles that extended through every State and through every alliance where there was a constant feed-in of clinical guidelines of what is best, most economical, most humane, I think it can work.

If it is seen as a board of directors of a vast enterprise, that takes into account quality and economy of care—a personal vignette here. My father is very ill at this time. He could stay in a hospital and that would be appropriate care, at $2,000 a day. He has a physician who very kindly arranged for him to stay at home with wonderful home health care at about $200 a day, both very appropriate, one with tremendous savings and the tremendous savings in this case go along with a much more humane form of treatment.

I am very optimistic about what the board could do, sir.

Mr. MCMILLAN. I don't disagree. I just went through a terminal illness with my mother and we had to face the same questions, but I am not sure that decision should be determined by a seven-person board. I think the system should be able to respond to that and make intelligent choices.

Mr. BRISTOW. I think you have put your finger on a great concern on the part of many physicians across the country, and that is a global budget has never worked when it is applied to a single segment of society. It is fine if you apply it to the entire Nation as in wartime, but if you single out one portion of the society and apply a fixed budget to it, it has never worked before.

It has been tried under President Nixon. It has been tried under President Carter, and it has failed because if you take a single segment in that fashion, you create stresses that are very, very abnormal that result in either rationing or a black market approach to whatever that service or commodity is that has been isolated in that fashion. I think you have put your finger on one of our major concerns.

We are also concerned that there is a strong flavor of capitation to this and that creates perverse incentives for those who are physicians and hospitals trying to serve the public of the United

States. We have a great deal of concern about that and I am pleased that you are planning to examine that issue.

Mr. McMILLAN. Does anyone else care to respond?

Mr. EBERT. You raised a question is there going to be competition in future years after a plan is put in place? If the plan mirrors the proposal, we believe that competition as an issue will diminish very quickly. I wish we had more experience in the Oregon scenario, for instance, because one would like to know how far down the list someone might go each year if funds are limited or restricted.

Mr. McMILLAN. A lot of attention has been given to the issue of primary care and I think we agree about the need to enhance that access to primary care, the role of primary care in the community, but I have a lot of other specialties, particularly OB-GYN and my family experience has been true. My wife is 50—I shouldn't say this—I will understate it. She is 50. Her OB-GYN has always been her primary care physician.

I would expect there are other specialties that aren't defined in regulations as primary care that perform primary care. Is there a way in what we do here whereby primary care can be compensated for or the incentives put in place that is based on the procedure not on what a physician calls themselves? Is that possible?

Mr. CLEAVELAND. That is tough. You have exposed the limitation of labels. I know in my community some obstetrician-gynecologists who provide wonderful primary care perhaps to a point. Where the heart would come in, they would back off.

I know of cardiologists who do the same. We have to come up with a concept of a valuation and management way to look at practices to see the extent to which anyone regardless of their label has this ability and training and experience to do broad evaluation and management services. But you have exposed a real problem in the artificial barriers we set up with our labels.

Mr. McMILLAN. You get the importance of practice guidelines which are essential to a lot of things, reimbursement rates, malpractice, et cetera.

Thank you very much.

Mr. WAXMAN. Thank you. I sense a difference in the views of this panel with respect to the President's reliance on limiting annual increases in health plan premiums.

Ms. Shinn, you and Dr. Cleaveland both seem to feel that this approach combined with incentives for health plans to compete on price and quality is an acceptable cost containment strategy, one that provides a credible assurance for those who pay for benefits that cost increases will be limited.

On the other hand, Dr. Bristow and Dr. Ebert, you seem to be in opposition to this approach. Dr. Bristow, you have argued that such budgeting efforts have never worked in any system including presumably in those budgeted health systems operated by virtually all of our international competitors.

On Tuesday we heard from a lot of folks who are spending money on health care, the business community, and while they had some disagreements they were united in their support of the President's proposed cap on premium increases. Without explicit across-the-board cost controls, they have no real assurance that health costs will be predictable and affordable. This is the kind of situation we are in as we try to deal with these different competing forces.

My question is, Ms. Shinn, how is it that you and Dr. Cleaveland can live with this while your colleagues on the panel have rejected this approach outright?

Ms. SHINN. Well, I can't speak for my colleagues on the panel, but I can say that the approach that we see embodied in the plan is a bit of a different one than we have historically had in this country. When you try to focus on prevention for a change, when you look at utilizing a broad array of providers, when you look at delivering services in a variety of settings, in schools and offices and homes, when you look at some of the administrative simplification that is called for, we think that some of those things can begin to make a big dent in some of the costs that we are experiencing and begin to help us contain some of those costs.

Mr. WAXMAN. So with those changes you think a limit on increases in health plan premiums could work?

Ms. SHINN. I think we should give it a try.

Mr. CLEAVELAND. I agree. Let me take MRI's of the head. There was a time if a patient came to me with a headache, we would observe the headache treatment, we would try a simple means of treatment. Now that patient comes in and virtually demands on the first interview a $1,500 MRI scan.

We are choking on our own technology and just because a test is available we figure it has to be done on every occasion.

Mr. WAXMAN. Do you think better management of the use of our health resources could mean that we could set up a health care premium level and live within that level?

Mr. CLEAVELAND. Absolutely.

Mr. WAXMAN. Dr. Bristow?

Mr. BRISTOW. One has to keep in mind that if you set a finite limit of cash flow going into the system without limiting the expenses of that system, like tongue depressors continue to go up, rents go up, costs of personnel go up, energy costs go up for those that are operating within that system, then you fail to realize that there has to be a give on either access or quality if you hold those costs in that fashion while expenses continue to go up.

A classic illustration was in this morning's paper. I read where in my home State of California, a large purchasing entity known as CALPERS has informed those providers that have contracted with it that although last year you kept your increase to less than 2 percent of the premium, next year they are demanding a 5 percent reduction below what they are paying now.

If you think those providers are going to give up the contract with CALPERS, you have another think coming. They will but somehow they will have to cut back on quality or access. That is exactly what will happen, and I don't think the American public should be fooled about that.

Mr. EBERT. I would like to make two comments. One, there is no way you can not support the issue of prevention as far as education and care. On the other hand, anyone that thinks we are going to get instantaneous savings from prevention, unless a new miracle comes along, a vaccine for HIV, then you can eliminate a large cost segment. Most prevention that increases life-span does not decrease the existence of aging diseases.

Mr. WAXMAN. We want to prevent the kind of cost increases we have had in the health care system that we can't afford.

Mr. EBERT. I don't disagree with that. We think it would be wonderful if you didn't have to do that MRI scan, but I think you are going to have to correct the malpractice laws if you believe that we are going to be able to limit those type of events. You go to Holland and have a bump on the head and they wouldn't consider it, but also they don't get sued either.

Mr. WAXMAN. Mr. Brown, you had another question. I will recognize you.

Mr. BROWN. Dr. Bristow, you had said that the AMA, you expressed the opposition of the AMA to a single-payer system at the State level. I have met with a lot of doctors, a lot of local medical societies in my district about these issues, and the two things come up over and over is they want a guarantee under the health plan physician choice and hospital choice, particularly physician choice, and they particularly complain about insurance companies peering over there shoulder.

At the same time, I hear more and more local physicians saying that single-payer is becoming a not unattractive option in what we need to at least look at. Why is the AMA considering the issue of choice, the issue of insurance companies peering over their shoulders? Why is the AMA continuing to so adamantly oppose single-payer?

Mr. BRISTOW. Because single-payer has a siren-like quality to it, but you must remember that a single-payer system is to confine patients to the choices available within that system. You will often hear an advocate of single-payer saying a patient can choose any doctor they wish to.

Yes, they can choose any doctor they wish to in that system. That is like taking a very large HMO and saying you belong to that HMO. You can choose any doctor within the HMO. You are still locked within the system and in order to get a different type or quality of care, you must leave that system.

With a single-payer system, it means you must leave that geographic area and what happens with a single-payer system is you limit choice. It is antithetical to true choice. You are simply allowed to choose between individual providers who are all caught within the same system and whatever limitations that system may have.

What sort of limitations? A single-payer system traditionally is equated with the government acting as a single-payer. That means the government's priorities in defense, agriculture, et cetera, will determine what sort of health services are available to its citizens because they will have equal priority with the expenditures for health that are made available.

Mr. BROWN. But if my State of Ohio chooses single-payer, I don't think that is very restrictive of patient choice. There aren't a lot of times when very many Ohioans, if they had the financial wherewithal, choose to leave the State to get medical care. We are not talking about a HMO in a small community. We are talking about a State deciding we would like single-payer or for that matter the

U.S. government deciding that we will go to a Canadian single-payer system.

I don't think that restricts—there are arguments against single-payer. I don't think you have made one yet, Dr. Bristow.

Mr. BRISTOW. Let me try again. I am saying that if Ohio were to do that, then Ohio would become one large HMO. Whatever is the dictate of the system within that geographic confine, it becomes one large, in this instance, HMO. That is exactly what has happened in Canada and what happens there is the citizens of Canada, when they want to leave the system, they have to leave the country.

Mr. WAXMAN. Will the gentleman yield?

That doesn't follow. As I understand it, in Canada you can go to any doctor you want. You can go to a specialist. You can go to a primary care doctor. You can choose the physician you want for any particular service. Doctors however work within an overall budget. If we didn't have an overall budget but we had managed competition and all the incentives for people to get into HMO's or other systems like that, you would have a bunch of gatekeepers telling people they cannot go to certain physicians because they may be specialists and therefore more likely than not to require the services that they provide.

So you can have a single-payer system with a lot of choice and you can have a system that is not a single-payer system with very little choice. Do you agree with that?

Mr. BRISTOW. You can have a single-payer system that has a lot of choices of the individual components within that system. In Canada when the budgetary limits are reached, those who need services either have to wait for them or they have to leave the country. Certainly they can choose any doctor they want to within the country, but they go to a different doctor and they still have two witnesses for those services.

Mr. WAXMAN. Can we give everybody in this country everything they want, exactly when they want it? Isn't there a limit to how much money we can spend? Don't we have to make some judgments, meaning that somebody would have to wait a while for some service or are some procedures really not that beneficial?

Mr. BRISTOW. I totally agree with you, Mr. Waxman, in terms of that statement. Let me clarify, we are not talking about a profligate system, we are not talking about being opposed to cost savings. We are simply suggesting that there are other ways of accomplishing the same goals which we think will work at least as well and will preserve choice. That is the only difference that we are having.

We are saying let's choose alternative routes that would reawaken market forces. We are the first ones to say market forces are not well functioning in our system as it is now. We think that can be corrected in other ways.

Mr. WAXMAN. You have exceeded your time.

Mr. BROWN. Whatever you say, Mr. Chairman.

Mr. WAXMAN. Mr. Greenwood?

Mr. GREENWOOD. Thank you, Mr. Chairman.

In our recent hearing with Secretary Shalala, there was concern expressed over the increased bureaucracy, and particularly the role of the National Health Board which will be charged with the responsibility of determining the amount of health expenditures in this country. Secretary Shalala responded that this should not be a serious concern. She characterized the National Health Board as a: "minor oversight group with some functions."

The question is, is this your view and understanding of the role of the board? Somewhere between her characterization of the National Health Board as a minor oversight group, and mine as a 25-story building, may be the truth. I am curious. Let me start with Dr. Bristow as to your response to that question.

Mr. BRISTOW. We believe that the National Health Board as described in the draft document a few weeks ago would constitute an agency with an enormous amount of power over the lives of Americans. There is a role that we believe would be fitting and proper for a national board, and that would be to help to define what is a basic benefit package.

We think that is essential to have in this Nation, a standard benefit package for comparability, and we believe that it can also be of great value in defining quality expectations that should be available to every citizen, but we have enormous concern about the ability of a group, albeit based in Washington, D.C., to determine what every American should be allowed to spend for a product or service that they consider to be of great value.

Mr. GREENWOOD. Dr. Ebert.

Mr. EBERT. I would agree. We would like to know what you think of it because we haven't really been able to get a true definition of it. I could see it being either direction. I think we are very concerned that all the health care decisions be put into a board that may have very little medical input into it. It would seem to us that it is more of a financial structure board rather than a medical care or definition of how far medical care can be extended with a particular patient, so I don't know. I would be more comfortable if you told us you were going to guarantee that all the funding they recommended would be approved by Congress, but I don't see Congress giving up that responsibility.

Mr. GREENWOOD. Well, we are not quite sure what to make of it ourselves yet, either. I think some of us use as a reference the fact that anything that is created by this Congress is a thing that grows rapidly. Let me ask one more question in the time that remains, and pose it to any or all of you. That is, how do you feel about testifying about a bill you haven't seen yet? Will you feel that you have had due process if you aren't invited to come back and speak after you have had an opportunity to actually receive the legislation, digest it, analyze it and comment upon it?

Mr. CLEAVELAND. This is like a game of "Jeopardy" in who can get to the button first. The way I view the proposal that is before us is we have been given a map, a strategic map of what the targets are, and it is up to the ladies and gentlemen of the House and Senate. It is up to the professions, the provider professions, the consumer groups to design the airplane that flies to these targets. I am very reassured that we can testify so early in the process and share our common viewpoints.

I have learned a lot just from the questions that have come this morning, and I would anticipate that we would have the opportunity to comment in an ongoing fashion. I think it is highly appropriate that we can comment so early in the design of our airplane.

Mr. GREENWOOD. This is like a game of "Jeopardy" in more ways than one.

Ms. SHINN. I would just say, Mr. Greenwood, that we have been energized by participating in 3 hearings in 10 days. We notice in this morning's Post that the legislation has now reached about 1,600 pages, so after we have the opportunity to take a look at it I think we will be back to persuade you in any way we can whether it is in a public hearing format or just talking face to face, and we welcome the opportunity to testify again, and we are very pleased to have been asked to do so today.

Mr. BRISTOW. I would say that it is extraordinarily difficult to try to provide testimony on a document which does not exist at this point in time. I was always warned by my mother to never buy a pig in a poke, and that is why the AMA at this point is neither able to endorse nor oppose the President's proposal in its entirety.

There are obviously many things that are good in terms of the goals that have been identified. We have identified a number of areas of concern today that we have, and we would be delighted to be able to return and to express comments and opinions once there is something firm in front of us.

Mr. EBERT. I think surgeons are usually asked to make clean-cut decisions and incisions, so I would have to say it is always simpler for us once we have seen a more firmly defined program, and we feel the same way. We hope we have a chance to comment in the future.

Mr. GREENWOOD. I am going to yield to my colleague here, but I also wanted to just add that after we finish playing "Jeopardy"——

Mrs. COLLINS [presiding]. The time of the gentleman has expired.

Mr. GREENWOOD. We are going to play "You Bet Your Life."

Mrs. COLLINS. The time of the gentleman has expired. There is much concern over the possibility that utilization review and preauthorization procedures with powerful health plans would limit the flexibility of providers to treat their patients as they see fit. Therefore, my question to each of you, or whoever wants to answer, would be what protections against this occurrence would you recommend? Start with you, Dr. Cleaveland.

Mr. CLEAVELAND. Madam Chairwoman, the problem right now is that we are beaten to death by dozens of different utilization review plans which seem to have no basis in fact. They seem to be based more on the whims of particular companies. I would love to see a system in which utilization review and quality assurance could be unified under one predictable set of guidelines to which providers and patients and all of us had access to the guidelines so that we could respond to these.

There is a system right now in the utilization review field that rivals complete chaos, so I would welcome a consolidation of these functions, but with public standards to which we could all adhere.

Mrs. COLLINS. Thank you.

Ms. SHINN. We have had the opportunity over the last several months to participate in the development of various guidelines, and we think that continued process is supported in the plan, so we will we think that continued process is supported in the plan, so we will at least have some road map to follow as we talk about interventions and who is most appropriate to intervene.

I think the other thing we are excited about in the plan is the whole issue of access to a broad array of providers, so I think that should be somewhat assistive in the whole utilization picture.

Mrs. COLLINS. Dr. Bristow.

Mr. BRISTOW. Thank you, Congresswoman. The whole idea of utilization review being conducted from a black box has been a great concern of the profession for sometime. We are pleased to see that during the last 12 months there has been a movement away from that, a desire on the part of government to reveal what are the criteria that it uses in assessing the quality of care that physicians render.

The vast majority of physicians are interested, committed to providing the best quality of care they can for their patients, and they simply need to be told what are the rules, what are the guidelines. The development of outcome studies, the continued development of practice parameters, we believe, will be very helpful in allowing an assessment of the care that is being given to be much more objective than it has been up until now.

We look forward to the further development of those sort of tools. Right now they are still in a stage of infancy as far as their development and the ability that we would have to use those tools, but I think one of the positive things about the Clinton proposal is that it is supportive of further development of that thrust.

Mr. EBERT. Congresswoman, you mentioned preauthorization and utilization review. I would say these are the two issues probably on this panel that the surgeons have been—have lived with the longest and been plagued with for more times than we would like to admit. We would love to see someone take a serious look at preauthorization, for instance, and even utilization review of in-hospital services.

Most of the time these have proven to be very ineffective and to be unnecessary, but the burden put on the profession is unbelievable. If there is some type of fee for service or payment related to what you do in the new proposal, then the denial of payment issue that we currently live with is unbelievable, and it is easy to see that if someone has appendicitis in the middle of the night on a particular carrier, you can't get to the carrier because they are only open from 8 to 5 and then the line is usually busy because there is one. You usually go ahead and treat the patient, oftentimes when you go back on Monday and try to get approval, you usually find that, no, it wasn't necessary and wasn't indicated, and when people use the word "practice" guidelines, that is almost like using single payer. You have got to define what you are talking about.

Are we talking about clinical guidelines for particular disease entities? Are we talking about guidelines that allow you to get a service within a particular health plan, and we would applaud any efforts that were made to decrease some of the burden that goes with these particular issues.

Mrs. COLLINS. Thank you very much. We have a vote on the Floor.

Mr. Waxman has gone to vote, and I have to do the same thing; so we are going to recess for 10 minutes. The subcommittee is recessed for 10 minutes.

[Brief recess.]

Mr. WAXMAN. The meeting will come back to order. I want to call on Congressman Towns for his questions.

Mr. TOWNS. Thank you very much, Mr. Chairman. Also let me thank the witnesses because I think this is a very important subject. I think that we need as much information as we can get to be able to move forward comfortably, but I do have some concerns. I am getting calls and letters from black physicians in particular. They are concerned about being shut out of the managed care plan, so how do we prevent "cherry picking" of doctors by the managed care plans established by these alliances? How can we protect minority physicians?

Mr. CLEAVELAND. If I may respond, Congressman Towns, that is a very real concern of mine in Tennessee where we have quite a battle going as our health care is reorganized under a program called TennCare, about exclusion of physicians from plans based on very arbitrary criteria. I think this is an area where on a national legislative basis that ground rules for participation in the provider networks has to be guaranteed so that you simply do not pick your physicians on the basis of zip codes or some other completely arbitrary standard.

I very, very much share the concern of the physicians who have phoned your office.

Mr. BRISTOW. Mr. Towns, if I may, this is an area of great concern to the American Medical Association. We have proposed three areas of relief that we think would be very helpful there. The first is it is terribly important that to the extent that a given health plan has the capacity to take in additional providers that they allow any willing, competent provider. When I say willing, I mean willing to abide by all of the proscriptions and guidelines and rules of that health plan.

As long as they are competent and are willing to go by the rules that have been set up by that health plan and fit within the capacity requirements of the health plan, if the health plan says we don't need any more people, obviously that is a different matter, and there should be a showing of cause if an individual is rejected from being a member of that presumably open health plan.

The second thing that is terribly important is physicians need the right to be able to negotiate in a meaningful fashion something that approaches parity with the entity that they are negotiating with, with the health plan.

The third thing that is very important is that there should be sufficient antitrust relief to allow physicians to collectively participate in those negotiations that I was speaking of before, but if those things can be done, I think it will go a long ways towards improving the plight of minority—I know what the third was. That is the Clinton proposal at this time indicates it wishes to do away, preempt those State laws that govern the corporate practice of medicine.

The corporate practice of medicine is of great concern because a business has a bottom line mentality and therefore would have a tendency to not take into account the professional needs of a given community, and we believe that that is an area of great concern if, as has been proposed in the draft document, an attempt was made to preempt those State laws against the corporate practice of law, of medicine, sorry.

Mr. TOWNS. Thank you very much. I have no further questions, Mr. Chairman.

Mr. WAXMAN. Did you have—Mr. McMillan, do you want to be recognized? I am going to recognize you for 3 minutes, then we are going to move on.

Mr. MCMILLAN. Thank you. I have really just a short question.

Mr. WAXMAN. You can take less than 3 minutes, but I want to recognize you for 3 minutes.

Mr. MCMILLAN. I will try, but the answers may be longer. I am one who offered a malpractice reform bill which is essentially contained within the Republican proposal in the House. Mostly it is an amendment adopted in the Cooper bill. It is a very good piece of legislation in my judgment, well drawn.

I believe, Dr. Cleaveland, in your written testimony you indicated that the administration's plan was weak in its malpractice proposal. I am not sure we have seen it all, but basically I think it is a pilot program, and while it may include some suggestive language on alternative dispute resolution, it doesn't really have any teeth in it. There are good alternatives out there that require alternative dispute resolution that put limits on noneconomic damages that only allow resort to the courts on appeal from an alternative dispute resolution process and that even go so far as to require that the loser in litigation pay the costs, and that is out there, and I would simply like you to draw that to everyone's attention and ask any of you, if you will, to comment on it because I think there is some good things there, and no one is out to get lawyers. I am certainly not.

In fact, I would vote just to pay all their legal fees and get them out of the way, and the damages aren't all that great, but the response of the system to it as a part of unnecessary procedures, and I am not going to attribute it all to malpractice, but—or the threat of litigation, but certainly that is interwoven into the whole pattern of unnecessary procedures that Dr. Koop himself estimates as being as much as 25 percent of total diagnostic and therapeutic costs, so I would simply like to, I guess, ask you have you looked at the alternative proposals that are in the Republican alternative and in the Cooper bill and would you tend to favor those over the administration proposal?

Mr. CLEAVELAND. Yes, very definitely because they are clearly delineated and they would greatly help undo the mischief of the present malpractice system. They are very strong, well done pieces of legislation, and I hope that they continue to progress through the process.

Ms. SHINN. I would say, Mr. McMillan, that we are looking at those. I think we have to continue to keep in mind that this society wants a guaranteed result for everything, and so there is a real balance to be struck between compensation for legitimate injury, protection of the provider, and at the same time realistic expectations.

Mr. BRISTOW. Let me say that as I have read those they seem to very closely mirror the MICRA law changes that occurred in California a number of years ago. During the last 10 years let me tell you what MICRA has done. During the last 10 years as an internist I paid $5,000 a year for standard liability insurance coverage 10 years ago.

My counterpart in lower New York State was paying $5,000 10 years ago. Today my counterpart pays $18,000 for the same coverage. I pay $5,500 a year. That is what MICRA does, that is what those tort reform proposals will do for the Nation as a whole. They are of great importance if we are serious about trying to reduce costs to their essential minimum.

Mr. EBERT. I would like to second that. I spent most of my practicing life in San Francisco, and my premiums were a little higher than Dr. Bristow's because of the field I was in or maybe I was just worse, but they certainly have decreased in amounts over the 15-year period since 1975 when the legislation was introduced. Just two comments.

Surgeons have given up essentially that Congress will ever be able to enact legislation on a national level on this issue. Now, maybe we are naive and maybe we will be proven incorrect. However, we do suggest that there are incentives you could use from Congress to try to encourage States to pass similar-type legislation. Michigan and Louisiana recently passed fairly reasonable legislation on malpractice, and each year a few more join in, but it still is a problem.

The other thing is that your Office of Technology Assessment now is doing a study, and we participated in it, to try to find out that question as to whether it is 20 percent, 10 percent or whatever on a series—we have taken head injuries and some of the others—as how much money could be saved and hopefully that would give some indication, but I would certainly encourage any way you could get the California system in place, the country would benefit on this particular issue.

Mr. MCMILLAN. Thank you.

Mr. WAXMAN. Before you leave, I just want to get you on record. A couple of days ago we had small businesses and large businesses, some were for the mandate, others were against the mandate, but all of them were for limits on premium increases. You have differences on whether we ought to have limits on premium increases. Do you all agree that we ought to have a mandate on businesses so that we have universal coverage?

Mr. CLEAVELAND. Yes.

Ms. SHINN. Yes.

Mr. BRISTOW. Yes.

Mr. WAXMAN. So all of you do agree on that point. I want to thank you very much for your presentation. We will look forward to talking further with you and working with you on this important issue.

Our last panel today brings together three organizations that represent hospitals. Michael Pugh is the president and CEO of Parkview Episcopal Medical Center in Pueblo, Colo. Mr. Pugh is testifying on behalf of the American Hospital Association. Sister Bernice Coreil is the vice president for system integration of the

Daughters of Charity National Health System in St. Louis. She is testifying on behalf of the Catholic Health Association, and Michael D. Bromberg, who is executive director of the Federation of American Health Systems.

I want to welcome you to our hearing today. Your prepared statements will be in the record in full. What we would like to ask each of you is to limit the presentation to no more than 5 minutes. Mr. Pugh, why don't we start with you.

STATEMENTS OF MICHAEL PUGH, PRESIDENT, PARKVIEW EPISCOPAL MEDICAL CENTER, ON BEHALF OF AMERICAN HOSPITAL ASSOCIATION; SISTER BERNICE COREIL, ON BEHALF OF CATHOLIC HEALTH ASSOCIATION OF THE UNITED STATES; AND MICHAEL D. BROMBERG, EXECUTIVE DIRECTOR, FEDERATION OF AMERICAN HEALTH SYSTEMS

Mr. PUGH. Thank you, Mr. Chairman and Madam Chairwoman. It is a pleasure to be here today representing the American Hospital Association as we work together to move health care reform forward.

On behalf of my hospital, Parkview Episcopal, I would like to thank you and your fellow committee members for the work done in past sessions on the Medicaid disproportionate share issues. Without the DISH payments Parkview's ability to deliver quality care to the people of southern Colorado would be severely compromised. We thank you for your leadership in this area. I am going to limit my remarks to some of the big issues that the President's plan presents and hope we have the opportunity to come back later to talk about the details.

As a member of the AHA board, I have had the opportunity to be involved with developing the AHA vision for health care reform. We are very pleased that the President's plan shares so much common ground with our vision for reform. Hospitals have called for improving the health of the population, universal access to health insurance, a more integrated health delivery system, economic discipline to get a handle on costs, and public accountability. All of these are elements of the President's plan and fit our vision of health care reform.

We stand squarely behind the President's insistence on achieving universal access to insurance through the workplace. Without universal access we will not achieve health care reform. The President's plan also begins to create a new environment for health care delivery, for hospitals, doctors, and other providers. The accountable health plans proposed by the President are close cousins to the AHA-proposed community care networks. We had hoped that they would look more like twins instead of cousins, but we think we can build on the President's proposal to build a delivery system that allows all of us in health care to do what we do best—keeping people healthy and taking care of them when they do get sick.

As you well know, the issue of health care reform is exceedingly complex. Any comprehensive plan for reform is going to have some flaws. I would like to point out several areas of possible concern and some recommendations on what might be done to improve the President's plan.

First, the proposed Medicare caps on spending to squeeze $124 billion out of the Medicare system by the year 2000 should not be mistaken for health care reform. Nothing in the President's plan calls for any change in the way Medicare is financed or delivered except for an expansion of benefits. We are not opposed to expanding benefits and recognize that a prescription drug benefit may help to improve the health status of the elderly, but payment for this new benefit should not come out of reductions in Medicare payments to other providers.

This, coupled with the fact that the President's plan for services to the Medicare population continues to be paid on a per unit basis, amounts to business as usual for Medicare and a real disincentive for cost control for the whole system. One alternative is to keep the $91 billion proposed in the President's plan and tagged for deficit reduction in the health care pot where it belongs, and to truly reform the system, including the Medicare population, which is about 40 percent of hospital dollars and one-third of hospital patients which are from the Medicare program, you need to include them.

It makes absolutely no sense to split hospital patients into two groups with conflicting payment and delivery incentives. We are also very concerned about the effort to cap spending on the private side through global budgets. We agree on the need to slow health spending growth, but establishing a rigid formula to slow growth as proposed by the President's plan literally puts the system on cruise control and takes the hands off the steering wheel while we try to navigate health care through new uncharted territory. We think that a key part of the job of the independent commission is to try to match health care spending with the needs and available resources in a very public and open process instead of a global budgeting system running on autopilot steered by unrealistic and rigid formulas.

Health system costs can only be controlled if we change the way we operate at the community level in the delivery of care. The President's plan would employ the use of capitated payments to providers, a concept we support. Changing the incentives in health care delivery is absolutely key to cost control. We need to move from a sick care system where the incentives are to compete for more care to a health care system where the incentives are to collaborate and keep people well, and when they are sick to make them well in the most rapid and cost-effective manner possible.

In order to achieve a change in the delivery system, we believe there is a need for some change in the way the President's health plans are defined and structured. There must be better safeguards to prevent these plans from being simply fly-by-night insurance schemes. We propose minimum Federal guidelines for health plans to ensure that they are locally governed and accountable to the people they serve. These are the key issues for America's hospitals.

We pledge to play a constructive role in the process of health care reform and to support reform elements we believe build the right foundation for the future, and we seek agreement in the areas we feel are not solidly grounded. We will look forward to working with the committee to make these changes part of the plan and sincerely hope to be standing with you in the rose garden next year to witness the signing of a bipartisan comprehensive health care reform bill.

Thank you and I look forward to your questions.

[Testimony resumes on p. 503.]

[The prepared statement of Mr. Pugh follows:]

American Hospital Association

AHA

Capitol Place, Building #3
50 F Street, N.W.
Suite 1100
Washington, D.C. 20001
Telephone 202.638-1100
FAX NO. 202.626-2345

Statement
of the
American Hospital Association
before the
Subcommittee on Health
and the Environment
and the
Subcommittee on Commerce, Consumer Protection,
and Competitiveness
of the
Energy and Commerce Committee
United States House of Representatives
on
President Clinton's Health Care Reform Proposal

October 14, 1993

I am Michael Pugh, President and Chief Executive Officer of Parkview Episcopal Medical Center, Pueblo, Colorado. I am here as a member of the Board of Trustees of the American Hospital Association, representing 5,000 hospitals and health care organizations across America. It is a pleasure to be here today in the cause of moving health care reform forward. Members of the subcommittees have been true pioneers in the effort to extend and improve health coverage for the nation, and I know you share the American Hospital Association's excitement about the real opportunity for achieving that goal that the current environment provides us.

AHA salutes President Clinton and the First Lady for their significant work in nurturing the current reform climate. America's hospitals, through AHA, have worked for more than two years to shape our own blueprint for health care reform: we are very pleased that the President's plan shares many of our building blocks. In a nutshell, AHA's reform objectives include:

1. Universal access in a reasonable time period financed in a pluralistic manner;
2. Redeveloping health care delivery into an integrated and coordinated system able to address the needs of the population;
3. Economic discipline based on clear incentives rather than micromanagement;
4. Balancing promised benefits with adequate financing;
5. Public accountability for the clinical effectiveness and economic efficiency of health plans;
6. Antitrust and malpractice reform.

Areas of Agreement With Clinton Plan

Universal Access

You will notice that "universal access" is at the top of the list. We share the President's belief that any reform plan must move us as quickly as possible to health coverage for all. This is a non-negotiable item for us, not only because it is the morally right thing to do, but also because without universal coverage health care reform simply doesn't work -- without it, you will still have a system with providers continuing to shift costs from the uninsured to the privately insured, undermining our goal of moderating rising health costs.

Health Care Delivery Reform

The other basic building block we share with the Clinton proposal is its boldness in calling for a fundamentally restructured health care delivery system. In the Clinton proposal, health plans would offer a guaranteed national benefit package to consumers, without regard to pre-existing conditions. The plans would receive a fixed, per-person annual payment, providing the financial resources for preventive care that our current system so sorely lacks.

The Clinton proposal's "health plans" provide the structure to accommodate AHA's own approach to restructuring the delivery system through community care networks℠ -- cooperating groups of local providers paid on a capitated, or per-person, basis. This approach provides the economic incentives for providers to work together, eliminating expensive duplication of services and technology, and for establishing a seamless system of care that works better for patients.

Independent Commission

We also like the fact that the Clinton proposal establishes a framework for a national independent commission that would interpret and update the guaranteed national benefit package to be offered to consumers.

Medicaid

While the specific details of the President's Medicaid proposal remain to be filled in, we are encouraged by the President's goal of rapidly integrating Medicaid acute care services into the new health care system.

Antitrust

We endorse the proposal's movement toward more clearly spelling out antitrust guidelines. The current antitrust climate is murky. Hospitals that want to merge or share technology are sometimes discouraged from doing so out of fear of challenge by federal enforcement agencies, state attorneys general, and private parties. This chilling effect undermines our shared goal of achieving greater efficiency in health care delivery.

The six policy statements recently issued by the Department of Justice and the Federal Trade Commission -- particularly the expedited review process -- are an important first step in putting hospitals on firmer ground. AHA looks forward to working with the agencies and Congress to develop additional workable guidelines.

Suggested Improvements in the Clinton Plan

While we have more agreement than disagreement with the Clinton proposal -- more common ground than battleground -- we would like to share with you our areas of significant concern, and offer our view of how these areas can be improved.

Medicare

First, under the Clinton proposal Medicare spending growth is capped so that $124 billion is squeezed out of the program by the year 2000. These changes are not intended to fix what's wrong with the Medicare program. Instead, their purpose is to fund prescription drug and long-term care benefits for the elderly. While we are supportive of these benefits, we can't support underpaying hospitals in order to finance them.

The solution? The Clinton plan calls for using reform savings and taxes to reduce the deficit by $91 billion. We believe those savings should be left in the health care reform effort where they can reduce the need for arbitrary cuts. First of all, providing universal access to health coverage is going to require additional resources -- this is not the time to arbitrarily take resources from the system. Second, the process of reconfiguring hospitals and other provider services into more efficient cooperative arrangements also takes both human and financial resources. For example, we know from experience that laying out a solid plan for merging services between two hospitals, or between a hospital and physician group, can take a year or more. Hospitals must have the resources that allow them to do this -- resources that could be freed up through the greater efficiencies and lower administrative costs that are the bounty of reform. But our fear is that a too-constrained financial environment at the outset could prevent reform from getting off the ground.

The infrastructure investments we all endorse in order to reduce administrative costs -- electronic billing, computerized patient records, new information systems -- also require front-end dollars before they can be put in place. Our ability to get beyond the traditional hospital acute care role that will be necessary under reform is also jeopardized by excessive spending reductions. For example, consumer education, wellness, and outreach programs -- not funded by the current system -- are among the most vulnerable programs when finances are squeezed.

Global Spending Caps

A similar disconnect of actual needs from resources happens on the private side in the Clinton proposal, where spending growth is capped by tying it to the Consumer Price Index (CPI). But the CPI has no real link to the actual costs of providing care; health care has its own set of input costs that aren't reflected in the CPI -- labor costs that are driven up by health care personnel shortages and the steeply rising cost of new medical technology, for example.

We agree on the need to slow health spending growth. But to try to do it through a rigid formula amounts to putting the system on cruise control, taking one's hands off the steering wheel, and hoping for the best. That is not a responsible way to navigate the uncharted territory of health reform. Why? Because it doesn't allow us to adjust course to accommodate unforeseen circumstances. The slowness of the economy in coming out of the recession, previously unknown crises such as the AIDs epidemic -- all caution that we keep our hands firmly *on* the steering wheel. And the way we do that is to match health needs with available resources in an on-going, open and public way. In our view, that should be the job of the independent national commission.

Medicaid

While AHA supports the goal of integrating Medicaid services into a reformed health system, we believe any plan to do so must have an adequate funding mechanism that enables providers to deliver quality health care to all individuals, regardless of the source of their health care premiums. Payments to regional health alliances and, in turn, to health networks, must be adequate to cover the cost of delivering promised services and include the establishment of adequate risk adjustments for this population.

The proposal to phase out the Medicaid Disproportionate Share Hospital (DSH) payment program deserves careful attention. The program's historical purpose was to compensate hospitals for the higher costs of treating low-income patients, and to assist financially distressed hospitals serving large numbers of low-income patients to assures those patients access to needed care. The necessity of a DSH payment may diminish as health care coverage through universal access increases. But as states move their Medicaid populations into the new health care system, any plan to phase out Medicaid DSH payments must provide the necessary assistance to hospitals until all low-income individuals are fully integrated into the new heath care system.

Structure of Health Plans

We also have concerns about the structure of the Clinton health plans. While they have shared characteristics with our vision of integrating care through community care networks, they are by no means identical. The health plans must have a better-defined role set out at the national level, and more accountability built in at the local level. We have real concerns that as currently defined they could harbor fly-by-night insurance schemes. The way to address these concerns is to make sure health plans are under local governance, are targeted toward meeting local needs, and have a local accountability mechanism.

Public Health Initiatives

The President's reform plan allows for the designation of essential community providers to assure access and continuity of care in underserved areas during the first five years of reform. This provision will require health plans to contract with and reimburse established "essential community providers" in underserved areas. AHA believes hospitals should be included in the list of health care professionals and institutions eligible for designation as "essential community providers" by the Department of Health and Human Services. This will help essential community hospitals make the transition to the new health system without interrupting communities' access to necessary health services.

Conclusion

There are many other aspects of the Clinton plan -- some of which require further clarification -- that we are currently reviewing. These include: the size and role of the alliances; the process for seeking state waivers; payments for the training of physicians and other allied health professionals; the treatment of illegal aliens; and the role of providers in underserved areas, both rural and inner-city. We will continue to study these issues and look forward to working with you to find the best way to include them in comprehensive reform.

So yes, there is work to be done in examining these issues and other areas of concern. We need to work together to identify options and compromises. But it's not an impossible job. We have been given a strong start by the President and the First Lady in putting forth a serious reform initiative. Much work has already been done in Congress as well, including efforts by this subcommittee. And a spirit of bi-partisanship is emerging.

For those of us who see a broken health care system and want to fix it, it's a truly exciting time -- even an historic time -- for health policymakers and providers. We sense a rare opportunity, an opportunity that may not come again for a long time, to reshape our health care system to make it work better for all of us.

Hospitals pledge to play a constructive role in that process -- to work hard to support reform elements we believe build the right foundation, and to find agreement in those areas we now feel are not solidly grounded. As the American Hospital Association serves in that role, we don't see ourselves as advocates for the President's plan, the Conservative Democratic plan, the Senate Republican plan, for business or for labor. We see ourselves as advocates for the workable, the truly better -- in short, for good public policy.

Legislation that captures these qualities is likely to be drawn from positions all along the political spectrum. As politicians skilled in the art of compromise, I know you recognize that truth as well. The American Hospital Association looks forward to working with you to reach our shared goal of better health care for all Americans.

Mrs. COLLINS [presiding]. Thank you. Sister Coreil.

STATEMENT OF SISTER BERNICE COREIL

Sister COREIL. Thank you. My name is Sister Bernice Coreil, and I want to focus my remarks today primarily on three ways in which the Catholic Health Association of the United States, CHA, believes the Clinton proposal must be strengthened. Before I do that, however, I want to state that CHA believes that President Clinton's proposal is headed essentially in the right direction.

We are in basic agreement with many of the components of his plan. Two years ago CHA developed its own proposal for systemic health care reform, and the two plans contained striking similarities. Primary among the plans' similar components is universal coverage achieved in a timely fashion. That, indeed, is the linchpin of reform.

The CHA urges the members of this subcommittee and these subcommittees to hold fast to the goal of universal coverage and the seven other components I addressed more fully in my written statement. Now, let me turn to the three recommendations CHA believes can and must strengthen the President's proposal.

First, his plan needs a much sharper focus on reforming the health care delivery system. CHA believes that delivery system reform is absolutely necessary to achieve the kind of fundamental reform needed to serve people better. This reform can be achieved by merging the insurance and delivery functions in the form of integrated networks that provide a coordinated continuum of care to enrolled populations.

Second, incorporating Medicare into the overall reform system through a schedules transition process. Third, fully integrating long-term care with acute care under a specified timetable and, fourth, creating a more realistic time frame for reducing the rate of growth in both public and private health care spending.

Second, the President's plan needs to employ a more informed and realistic process for setting the global budget. CHA's reform proposal calls for a bottoms up, top down national budget setting process that would incorporate critical information on population needs and local systems efficiencies over time.

In contrast, the President's plan calls for a top-down only approach to a national budget as defined by a formula-driven rate of increase. In CHA's view this approach misses an important opportunity to make health care expenditures not only more predictable and reasonable, but also more consistent with changing health care needs, system capacity, and the public's own view with regard to the trade-offs between health care and other important social goals. We urge you to retain a global budget, but to use an informed process to determine the annual amount.

Third, the President's proposal may need to incorporate safeguards to preserve the professional ethos in health care and protect against an excessively commercialized system. Most politically viable reform proposals, including the President's, would rely heavily on market forces to control health care costs and improve the quality of care. Most analysts believe that shielding the clinician and patient from the economic consequences of their actions has led to an inefficiency and high cost that is no longer economically or politically sustainable and CHA agrees with this assessment. However, the implications of shifting financial risk to providers in the context of an all-out price competition have not been carefully examined.

It is quite possible that intense competition in some health care markets will unleash commercial influences that will overwhelm the patient-first ethic in American medicine, threatening patient care and undermining the long-term stability of a community's health care resources.

At least two questions need to be addressed in this regard. How will patients fare when the costs of the treatment they need could make their provider less competitive or less profitable; and second, will health plans owned by commercial interests beholden to distant shareholders abandon communities when their profits are squeezed? These are critically important questions that have not received enough attention.

We intend to examine the President's legislation on this issue to develop specific recommendations, and we hope we can work with you to ensure a new health care system that is responsive to patients and the communities they serve.

Mr. WAXMAN. Thank you very much for your testimony.

[Testimony resumes on p. 521.]

[The prepared statement of Sister Coreil follows:]

STATEMENT OF SISTER BERNICE COREIL

Good morning, ladies and gentlemen of the Health and Environment subcommittee and the subcommittee on Commerce, Protection and Competitiveness. Chairman Waxman and Chairman Collins, I am honored to appear before this joint hearing as you begin to determine how - not whether - to reform our nation's healthcare system.

My name is Sister Bernice Coreil. I am Chairperson of the Leadership Task Force on National Health Policy Reform of the Catholic Health Association (CHA). CHA represents more than 1,200 healthcare facilities and organizations that make up the nation's largest group of not-for-profit healthcare institutions under a single sponsor.

I am also Senior Vice President for System Integration of the Daughters of Charity National Health System in St. Louis. The system is the largest not-for-profit hospital system in the United States with 60 healthcare facilities and more than 16,000 beds in 18 states and the District of Columbia.

CHA shares President Clinton's belief that universal healthcare coverage is and must remain a non-negotiable item throughout the coming debate on healthcare reform. It is, in fact, the linchpin of reform. Since 1986, CHA has been a consistent advocate for universal coverage in a redesigned healthcare system. In our testimony today, we will, first, state our basic agreement with many of the components of President Clinton's proposal and indicate that we believe his proposal is headed in essentially the right direction. Second, we will make a number of recommendations that we believe are necessary to strengthen the proposal. Finally, we will pledge ourselves to work with the White House and the Congress to do everything we can to make meaningful healthcare reform a reality in 1994.

A. THE NEED FOR VALUES-BASED REFORM

Two years ago the Catholic Health Association developed its own proposal for healthcare reform.* This comprehensive plan describes our vision for a healthy America. You can imagine how pleased we were to hear Mrs. Clinton cite our plan as a model for the Administration's own reform proposal in her recent testimony on Capitol Hill.

Like the President, we believe that healthcare reform is essentially a debate about values. Accordingly, our proposal is anchored in the following set of core values. We believe that:

- healthcare is an essential social good, a service to persons in need which should never be reduced to a mere commodity exchanged for profit;
- human dignity requires that all persons be guaranteed a right to a uniform, comprehensive package of healthcare services;
- our nation's excessive focus on individual and institutional self-interest must be balanced by a recognition of the common good;
- our healthcare system must be reorganized so that it can better manage healthcare resources and better control the growth in healthcare spending;
- we must re-establish the principle that the well and the wealthy have a responsibility to care for the poor and the sick; and,

---

* *Setting Relationships Right: A Proposal For Systemic Healthcare Reform*, The Catholic Health Association of the United States

- a reformed healthcare system must promote simplicity by placing responsibility at the most appropriate levels of organization.

CHA is encouraged that President Clinton's reform proposal is based on a similar set of principles. As the President's proposal notes, these values "reflect fundamental national beliefs about community, equality, justice and liberty" and they anchor healthcare reform in our nation's "shared moral traditions."

B. THE NEED FOR SYSTEMIC HEALTHCARE REFORM

Today, millions of working Americans, their families, and others cannot afford or otherwise obtain healthcare insurance, and are often excluded from the benefits of our nation's healthcare system. Hundreds of thousands go without needed care or become impoverished when they have to pay their medical bills. And large numbers die prematurely for lack of care. Paradoxically, all of this is happening at a time when national healthcare expenditures are escalating rapidly, seemingly without control, and are consuming increasing portions of the nation's wealth. These problems have been exacerbated by the abandonment of community rating in private health insurance and employers' growing resistance to cost shifting. Together these developments are undermining our nation's voluntary social safety net in healthcare and are making it more difficult for many of our non-for-profit healthcare institutions to meet their historic missions of community service.

Meanwhile, the healthcare delivery system is fragmented and lacks economic discipline. It is increasingly burdened by a broad range of private and public rules on prices, volume, and methods of treatment that make American healthcare providers

77-929 O - 94 - 17

among the most regulated in the world.

Ladies and gentlemen, we have reached the point in healthcare when one thing is certain: if Congress fails to act forcefully, comprehensively, and soon, things will only get worse. We no longer have the luxury of ignoring the problem and hoping that, somehow, someday, it will simply fix itself. Similarly, partial or incremental approaches are no longer an option. The underlying problems are systemic in character and, as the President has recognized, can only be addressed through comprehensive change.

C. COMPONENTS OF THE CLINTON PROPOSAL SUPPORTED BY CHA

Now let me turn to the specifics of the President's proposal. CHA calls on the members of these subcommittees to hold fast to several critical components of the President's approach to reform.

1. **We urge you to hold fast to universal coverage.** For both moral and pragmatic reasons, we ask you not to compromise either on the principle of universal coverage or the speed with which it is accomplished under the Clinton proposal. The moral reasons should be clear to everyone. We should no longer tolerate being the only Western industrialized nation that leaves millions of people without healthcare coverage. Research has shown repeatedly that the 37 million uninsured in this nation are more likely to forego or postpone care than their insured counterparts.

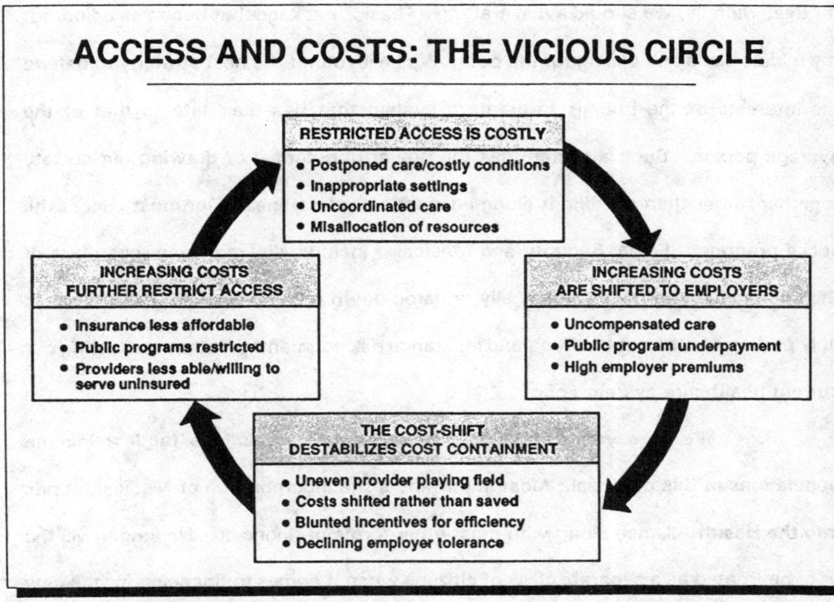

Catholic Health Association of the United States

The pragmatic reasons for universal coverage are equally compelling. Anything less than universal coverage creates a vicious circle whereby the uninsured are more likely to receive care in costly settings like the emergency room, and for conditions that have grown more severe with time. The resulting high cost of this care is then shifted to employers who in turn find insurance coverage for their workers increasingly unaffordable. We must break this vicious circle if there is to be any hope of controlling health expenditures in this nation.

2. **We urge you to <u>hold fast</u> to the guaranteed national benefit package** included in the Clinton proposal. Again there are both moral and pragmatic reasons

for this. Morally, we should avoid crafting a "basic" package that becomes a floor for the middle class and ceiling for the poor. We believe that the best strategy to defend the interests of the poor is to create a system that ties their fate to that of the average person. Such a system has the powerful potential of drawing our society together rather than dividing it along economic or class lines. Our most successful social programs, Social Security and Medicare, include all Americans regardless of their economic status. Pragmatically, a pared down uniform benefit package would only perpetuate the cost shifting and insurance risk segmentation that are tearing our current healthcare system apart.

3. **We urge you to hold fast to the many protections for low income populations** in this proposal. Most important is the incorporation of Medicaid funds into the Health Alliance along with most other forms of financing. No longer will the poor be treated as a separate class of citizens when it comes to financing for the new system, because premium payments to plans for former Medicaid recipients, other low income populations, and everybody else in the Health Alliances will be indistinguishable. The fate of the poor will be tied to the fate of the middle class. This is the right and moral thing to do. It also contributes substantially to system stability over time because it ends the cost shift from Medicaid to the private sector, reduces the exposure of Medicaid financing as a singular "easy" target for budget cutting, and eliminates financial obstacles to serve the poor. Finally, it eliminates the current disincentive to leave welfare since the poor would no longer face the prospect of losing their health insurance when they take a job.

4. **We urge you to <u>hold fast</u> to provisions for continuous, uninterrupted coverage of consumers.** As in our own proposal, President Clinton largely ends the link between employment and health insurance coverage. Both the employed and the non-employed under his plan can select from among any certified health plan in their community. No longer is a person's choice restricted to the one or two health plans selected by his or her employer, and when a person changes jobs or becomes temporarily unemployed, he or she can stay with the same health plan and the same family physician. This is important both because it is the humane and dignified thing to, and because a continuous, uninterrupted relationship with one's physician is critical to the goal of keeping people healthy.

5. **We urge you to <u>hold fast</u> to the high degree of consumer choice** embodied in the President's plan. The main reason there is so much choice in his plan is not because of the so-called "fee-for-service" option, but because the link between employment and health care coverage is severed. Even without the fee-for-service option, a family could select any certified plan in the community, which means they could go to the health plan that has their family physician as a practitioner. This is simply not possible for many working families today who often find they must abandon their family physician as they change jobs.

6. **We urge you to <u>hold fast</u> to overall expenditure control** in the President's proposal. CHA has long been on record in favor of a global budget. Morally, this is a question of responsible stewardship. As a nation we can no longer allow unpredictable and uncontrollable health spending increases to squeeze out other

important social needs (e.g. education), enlarge the deficit, and weaken the international competitiveness of many U.S. companies. Pragmatically, we all know that the rate of increase in healthcare spending is unsustainable and there is no guarantee that "managed competition" by itself will work without an expenditure backstop.

7. **We urge you to hold fast to the more equitable financing inherent in the Clinton proposal.** Everyone is asked to share the burden in this plan and "free riders" are no longer allowed to shift their health care costs to those who have been willing to pay. The employer mandate is critical to this approach because it ends the destabilizing cost shift from one employer to the next, and because it reinforces the notion that we are all in this together. Please don't retreat on the employer mandate.

8. **Finally, we urge you to hold fast to the high size threshold for firms that use the Health Alliances.** Under the President's plan, all firms with fewer than 5,000 employees pay standardized premiums to the Health Alliance which then negotiate with health plans on behalf of all workers. To lower this threshold and allow substantial numbers of employers to continue negotiating separately with health plans outside the Health Alliance would be a mistake. We carefully considered letting employers have this option when we developed our own reform proposal, but we found that it would have the potential to:

- **perpetuate the cost shift** as different premium levels are negotiated inside and outside the health alliance;
- **constrain consumer choice** as families might be limited to the health plans selected by their employer rather than all health plans in a community;

- **disrupt continuous relationships with physicians** as many consumers are forced to change plans when their employment status changes;
- **segregate lower and higher income populations** as the health alliances would serve predominately small, low wage firms and the former Medicaid populations;
- **reinforce risk segmentation** as health plans could continue to find ways (even with insurance market reforms) to selectively market to firms with younger, healthier populations; and
- **increase administrative costs** associated with continued employer involvement, multiple health plan contracts, and turnover among plans by consumers.

Please don't retreat on the high employer threshold for participation in the Health Alliances.

D. STRENGTHENING THE CLINTON PROPOSAL

Allow me to share with you five ways in which the Catholic Health Association believes the Clinton proposal must be strengthened.

1. Sharper Focus on Delivery Reform

First, the proposal needs a much sharper focus on reform of the healthcare **delivery system.** As it now stands, the proposal deals extensively with coverage, access, financing, and expenditure control, but says very little about how the healthcare delivery system can and should be reoriented to achieve both lower costs and clinically effective healthcare.

CHA's healthcare reform proposal starts with delivery reform as the way to make healthcare better coordinated, less costly, and more responsive to needs of people and communities. At the heart of our plan is the person-centered, community-based Integrated Delivery Network or IDN. The IDN is a set of providers organized to assume financial risk for a full continuum of healthcare services. Providers are linked together through a series of contractual or ownership arrangements. These networks receive a risk-adjusted, capitated payment and are held accountable for improving or maintaining the health status of their enrolled populations. In the CHA vision, consumers participate in network decision-making and choose among competing networks based on quality and service.

We believe that the kind of delivery reform embodied in these networks is essential for true, long term cost control in a reformed system. This is because the incentives in a capitated network are realigned to encourage primary and preventive care, less unnecessary care, better coordinated care, services in less costly settings, more appropriate capacity levels, and a more rational use of high technology services. Without delivery reform, however, insurers will be encouraged to rely on *a la carte* discounting, rate setting, externally imposed utilization controls, and micromanagement of providers in order to get the "quick" savings they need to live within premium caps. Some of these devices may, in fact, be appropriate. But to rely on them solely is a mistake. We believe that the insurance function should be merged with the delivery function in the form of integrated networks and that the focus should be on more efficient methods of organizing care, not simply clamping down arbitrarily on payments and utilization.

I want to emphasize that the Clinton proposal does include new incentives for delivery reform. As you know, consumers in the President's proposal are given financial incentives to select cost-effective health plans, and the plans will often have to organize themselves to operate within annual premium limits. The President also stresses primary and preventive care in his guaranteed national benefit package.

But there are also several elements of the Clinton proposal that will impede or hinder delivery reform.

- **First, there is little emphasis on the need for clinical and financial integration of care in the form of community-based, person-centered networks.** Rather, the proposal assumes and even encourages significant reliance on insurance companies to form and administer plans. This, in itself, is not a problem as long as the insurers act as partners with providers to create truly integrated community-based networks. It does become a problem, however, if insurers act as distant regulators who seek savings simply through discounts and formula-driven utilization controls, as many do today. This kind of arrangement may bring "quick" savings to the system and substantial profits for insurers, but it will not result in better coordinated or more efficient care. Nor will it ensure accountability to local communities.

- **Second, Medicare is left outside the new financing arrangements.** While the Health Alliances may encourage more integrated systems of care through annual per person payments, Medicare will perpetuate the opposite incentive by paying providers on a procedure-by-procedure basis. Thus providers will continue to face the mixed and counterproductive financial incentives that plague our current system. We can understand why Medicare may not be immediately folded into the Health Alliances, but we urge you to consider a fixed schedule and transition plan for bringing in Medicare to ensure consistent, stable incentives.

- **Third, the President's plan fails to fully integrate long term care with acute care.** We support the President in his expansion of long term care services to the disabled and elderly, but once again, sustainable cost savings will occur only if integrated networks can manage the full continuum of healthcare services, thereby allowing them to make patient-specific decisions about the most appropriate, most humane, and least costly patient care settings. Admittedly, local healthcare systems are not yet prepared to accept capitated payments for the full array of acute and long term care services, but reform should move the system in that direction through a target date and transition plan. Otherwise, we will perpetuate an artificial and costly bifurcation in what should be a seamless continuum of care for people in all stages of life.

- **Finally, delivery reform will be hindered because expenditures in the Clinton proposal are compressed unevenly and unrealistically fast.** As I said earlier, CHA fully supports the need to bring both private and public healthcare costs under control through a global budget. But the current draft of the Clinton proposal calls for a faster compression for the two major public programs: Medicare and Medicaid. This will result in greater cost shifting between the public and the private sector, and could ultimately lead to severe access problems for the elderly. More importantly, total spending is brought down at an implausibly rapid rate that may well encourage "quick and easy" payment and utilization controls, but certainly will not allow time for the development of efficient, community-based healthcare networks. The reduction in spending increases envisioned in the Clinton plan may not be too much, but it is certainly too fast for effective delivery reform.

2. Process for Setting the Global Budget

Our second recommendation for strengthening the President's proposal is to employ a more informed and realistic process for setting the global budget. Our reform proposal calls for a "bottom up/top down" national budget-setting process that would incorporate critical information on population needs and local system efficiencies over time. Our plan likewise outlines a series of "checks and balances" that would help ensure direct and explicit accountability to voters for each year's global budget. For example, the National Health Board in our proposal uses data from local Health Alliances to recommend an explicit and visible national budget amount to Congress which must then act on with an "up or down" vote.

In contrast, the President's plan calls for a "top down only" approach to a national budget as defined by a formula-driven rate of increase. In CHA's view, this approach misses an important opportunity to make healthcare expenditures not only more predictable and reasonable, but also more consistent with changing health needs, system capacity, and the public's own view with regard to the tradeoffs between healthcare and other important social goals.

We urge you to retain a global budget, but to use an informed process to determine the annual allowable increase in national healthcare expenditures.

3. Abortion

CHA strongly opposes on both moral and political grounds the inclusion of abortion in the guaranteed national benefit package provided under healthcare reform. While abortion is currently legal it is strongly opposed by millions of employers and taxpayers. This government should not compel them to pay for abortions. We believe that this position is shared by many members of the House and Senate. We are therefore hopeful that when Congress decides this issue it will come down in favor of keeping healthcare reform and legal abortion separate and distinct issues.

4. Conscience Clause

CHA firmly supports the inclusion of a strong conscience clause provision for individuals, institutions and employers in healthcare reform legislation. The President has stated his intention to include conscience clauses in his legislation. CHA will be working with the White House and Congress to ensure that the protection is adequate.

5. Maintaining the Professional Ethos in American Medicine

Most politically viable healthcare reform plans (including the President's proposal) rely heavily on market forces to control healthcare costs and improve the quality of care. They accomplish this by shifting most of the financial risk in healthcare from the purchasers of care (government and employers) to those who are providing the care, hospitals and doctors. The latter would be organized into accountable health plans that would compete with one another on price and quality for market share. Inefficient plans and/or low quality plans would either improve or fail and leave the market. In certain areas of the United States economic forces already are forcing local healthcare systems to reorganize themselves along these lines.

While it is hoped that these developments will result in lower cost/higher quality healthcare, it is important to recognize that they represent a profound shift from existing practice. During the past fifty years, healthcare providers have been largely shielded from financial risk and enabled thereby to treat their patients without regard to the economic consequences for the patient, themselves or society. This separation of financial accountability from clinical autonomy has helped to preserve a strong professional "patient-first" ethic in American medicine. While some patients are occasionally overtreated, few <u>insured</u> patients are ever systematically undertreated.

Furthermore, most U.S. communities are able to develop and sustain reasonably good-to-high quality healthcare services. Nevertheless, most analysts believe that shielding the clinician and patient from the economic consequences of their actions has led to a level of inefficiency and high costs that is no longer economically or politically sustainable. CHA agrees with this assessment.

However, the implications of shifting financial risk to providers in the context of all-out price competition have not been carefully examined. It is quite possible that intense competition in some healthcare markets will unleash commercial influences that will overwhelm the professional ethos in American medicine, threatening patient care and undermining the long term stability of a community's healthcare resources.

At least two questions need to be addressed in this regard:

- How will patients fare when the treatment they need could make their provider less competitive in a market, less profitable, or even force the provider into bankruptcy?

- Will health plans owned by commercial interests beholden to distant shareholders abandon communities when their profits are squeezed (as they will be) and a higher return on investment can be achieved elsewhere in the economy?

These are critically important questions that have not received enough attention. We know from the savings and loan debacle that when economic incentives change and systems of accountability are relaxed, individuals and society can be unintentionally saddled with very high costs.

We urge you to strengthen the President's proposal wherever possible to preserve the professional ethos in healthcare and protect against an excessively commercialized system. We intend to examine the President's legislation carefully on this issue to develop specific recommendations, and hope that we will have future opportunities to work with you to ensure a new health system that is sufficiently responsive to patients and communities even as it saves costs.

E. THE MEASURE OF SUCCESS

Finally, we conclude our testimony by returning to the point at which President Clinton opened this historic healthcare debate: a clear focus on values. Values are the beacons which guide us, especially in stormy times when our sense of direction can become distorted. But values also provide us with the criteria by which we can measure our progress. How should we measure it in this debate? By one very simple standard: the availability of persons throughout America's future healthcare system who are motivated to help others.

However impressive governmental programs, universal coverage, fee schedules, "market opportunities," corporations and institutions may be, successful healthcare reform will come down to people caring for people. When we are sick and in need, it is the very small events in each of our lives that make the difference. At such times we ask, "Is someone there when I call? Do they make me feel like a human person? Can I maintain my dignity and self-respect?" These are the issues by which future generations of Americans, their families and communities will judge the success of what we are beginning today. They are the issues we must keep in front of us throughout this debate. It is what the American people expect of us and what we owe to them.

Mr. WAXMAN. Mr. Bromberg.

STATEMENT OF MICHAEL D. BROMBERG

Mr. BROMBERG. Thank you, Mr. Chairman. It is a pleasure to be the last witness in a long day, so I will try to be brief. We are very excited about the leadership of President Clinton and Mrs. Clinton and very excited about the fact that there is hope for passing a meaningful health reform bill, but there are about four areas I would like to mention where we have grave concern.

All four of those areas or at least three-and-a-half of them we think are better served by the Cooper bill which we have endorsed, and the four areas basically are, number one, the absence of any economic incentive for all the stakeholders to act as prudent buyers and to make prudent choices.

Unless something is done about capping the tax free, unlimited, open-ended ability of employers to deduct and employees to exclude from their income, there is no motivation for them to make the correct choices when faced with multiple plans. We think that, in fact, if there was any one thing you could do to contain costs in the system and if you could only do one thing, that would be the thing to do.

I think a lot of the things we also support, like networks and purchasing alliances, et cetera, would happen automatically if you made that one change. The second one is obviously the Draconian Medicare-Medicaid cuts in this bill.

I just leave you with the thought that hospitals have only three choices if we get underfinanced in our payments. Those three choices are cut jobs, cut services or cut wages. There is really nothing else we can do, and I think we need to go into that issue in a little more depth later.

Third, the third area is the issue, and I will combine the third and fourth, the regulatory nature and size of these purchasing alliances makes them look an awful lot like government agencies that have too much power, in our opinion, and second, the global budgets and price controls which they wield. When put together those are other areas which lead us to believe the Cooper bill is a much better place to begin because it does address those problems.

I want to give one or two examples, if I may. One is I think if you look at this bill you can look at it as a $1 trillion appropriation bill, in effect, or like a $1 trillion appropriation bill because really what this bill does, it says that let the taxpayers of America trust the Congress and the government to manage a trillion dollars, one seventh of the economy, politicize it, give some more to some districts, some to others, reward some States, penalize others, and play with this pot of money the way you are now playing with the Medicare pot of money. That to me is a little bit frightening and needs to be looked at.

The second illustration I will give you is one which goes like this, let's say all of us in this room belong to a purchasing co-op, hopefully one that is smaller than the one in the Clinton bill, but we all belong to one, and we all go down there to buy our insurance. The second year we go back, there are five plans on the table, they sell for 1-, 2-, 3-, 4-, and $5,000 respectively. The weighted average premium is three, and all five insurance plans, whether they are hospital-based or Blue Cross or commercial-based, hold a press conference and say as good public citizens we are going to freeze our premiums, freeze them. We don't want the CPI. We are going to be really good citizens.

Now, the problem with that is that if some of us choose plan four instead of plan three, we have now triggered off an incredible number of sanctions. We have broken the global budget, and the sanctions we have triggered, aside from price controls, taxes, and a few other things, is that the alliance will then be authorized to withhold, freeze enrollment in plans four and five because they are above average in cost.

Now, the word "choice" is one the pollsters say everybody needs to use, and I praise the Clinton bill for increasing choice on the one hand, but on the other hand it decreases it. On the one hand, I am a small employer. I now tell my employees this is your insurance, good luck. Under the Clinton plan they will go down to this co-op and have 10 choices, I hope. That is terrific. That is increased choice.

On the other hand, we have empowered them to make the choice, and if government, Big Brother, Big Sister maybe, doesn't like the choice, they penalize the consumer. You didn't choose the plan the government thought was best for you; you chose one that was more expensive.

Now, they chose that plan with their own money, not a dime of Medicare money, not a dime of Medicaid money, no tax subsidy, nothing. I am not sure that is constitutional, and I think you ought to look at the constitutionality of it, but I know it is not good public policy. We are not at war. We don't have an item in short supply.

I don't know how government can tell a consumer that they can't with their own money buy a plan that is more than 3 percent above the weighted average premium or anything that exists. If I have one request to the committee it would be read page 98 of this leaked document that we are testifying on. Just read it and ask yourself whether you could go home to your districts and tell the people you voted for page 98. I honestly think when you read it you will have an answer that I would trust.

Let me just close by saying we do want to work with you and the administration. We desperately need health reform, and I hope we get a good bill. Thank you.

[Testimony resumes on p. 536.]

[The prepared statement of Mr. Bromberg follows:]

STATEMENT OF
MICHAEL D. BROMBERG, EXECUTIVE DIRECTOR
FEDERATION OF AMERICAN HEALTH SYSTEMS

Madam Chairwoman, Mr. Chairman and Members of the Subcommittees, my name is Michael D. Bromberg and I am Executive Director of the Federation of American Health Systems. Our association represents more than 1,400 hospitals, health systems and managed care plans. Investor-owned management companies also manage under contract more than 300 non-profit hospitals.

We appreciate the opportunity to appear before you to discuss the important issue of health care reform. Members of these subcommittees have played an important role in the long debate on how to improve our nation's health care system and have helped move the issue to its rightful place at the top of our nation's priorities.

We applaud the leadership shown by President Clinton and the work done by the First Lady and the health reform task force in developing a health plan that seeks to provide health care coverage for all Americans. We support many components of the plan but we object strongly to provisions imposing a global budget, price controls on premiums, creating regulatory health alliances rather than purchasing cooperatives which act as brokers and draconian reductions in Medicare and Medicaid reimbursement.

PRINCIPLES OF REFORM

The Federation believes that health care coverage should be universal and should be financed on ability to pay. Any health reform proposal should reform Medicare and Medicaid by purchasing coverage in health plans instead of services and create new tax to extend employment-based health coverage to all full-time workers.

The Federation has long favored health reform which eliminates the perverse incentives in our tax code. Congress needs to replace the current rewards for volume with rewards for cost effectiveness.

We strongly believe that only a competitive bidding system will contain health care costs without destroying the quality of health care Americans expect and deserve. This can be achieved by limiting the amount of health insurance premiums tax employers and employees may deduct or exclude from taxable income. This one change would do more to foster cost containment than any other regulatory or market-based reform. It would change the behavior of all the stakeholders by offering positive economic incentives for organizing and purchasing cost effective health plans.

Health insurance is the only fringe benefit which is not capped and a small fraction of the approximately $60 billion in lost revenue from the tax exclusion could subsidize care for the neediest segment of our population. Lower income employees could be exempted from such a change in the tax code to assure a fair and equitable redistribution of the tax subsidy for private insurance.

We can also achieve a more efficient health system by: eliminating the current state-level regulatory barriers that impede the development of managed care plans; eliminating state-mandated benefits above the basic benefit package; privatizing Medicare and Medicaid by converting them to programs that buy health coverage instead of health services; accelerating the development and use of "best practice" treatment standards; and eliminating the high cost of defensive medicine by capping malpractice awards for non-economic damages and establishing an arbitration system.

Clearly, we have much in common with the proposal put forward by President Clinton. His plan establishes a minimum benefit package and allows Medicaid recipients to participate in the private insurance market so that they will have the same access to health providers as any other privately insured individual. The plan offers Medicare beneficiaries the opportunity to continue their private coverage when they reach eligibility for Medicare.

It calls for insurance reforms to assure all Americans access to coverage, regardless of their health status. The plan also overrides state barriers to the growth of managed care. While not including what most consider a critical component of malpractice reform, capping non-economic rewards, the President's health reform proposal does address some malpractice issues, such as contingency fees, alternative dispute resolution and periodic payments. The President's proposal also creates purchasing alliances to receive competitive bids from integrated health plans.

Much of the Clinton plan is bold and innovative. However, the obsession with deficit reduction threatens to override the opportunity for structural reforms to prove a market-oriented approach can work to contain costs. The President's plan calls for unprecedented and unrealistic reductions in spending for the Medicare and Medicaid programs. Congress, after much debate, recently passed a budget reducing Medicare spending by the largest amount in the history of the program: $56 billion over the next five years. The Administration's plan calls for more than twice that amount, $124 billion, in additional reductions. Medicaid funding would be reduced by $114 billion.

Access to universal coverage should be financed through a broad-based mechanism, not by deep cuts to providers of health care to the poor, elderly and disabled. Hospitals are labor intensive institutions which will not be able to absorb such massive underfunding of these Federal programs without reducing services and eliminating jobs or cost of living wage increases for our employees.

GLOBAL BUDGETS

The President's plan includes a global budget enforced through limits on annual increases in insurance premiums. The global budget would be apportioned on a state-by-state basis. The global budgets would drive down the growth in all health expenditures, both public and private, to equal the consumer price index increase plus population growth.

We strongly oppose a global budget or price controls. When price controls "work" they do so by rationing access to care and further limiting access to expensive new technology. A global budget would mean reducing care for all Americans to the lowest common denominator as shown by the impact of expenditure caps tried in Canada and several European nations.

A global budget would also have a detrimental effect on many states because a cap rewards high-cost states. For example, because the current per capita health spending in South Carolina is 56 percent as high as Massachusetts , a Federal cap based on historical spending would allow South Carolina 44 percent fewer dollars per resident annually than Massachusetts. Over the first five years of a seven percent global cap, Massachusetts could spend $8,258 more per person than South Carolina.

As you can see, global budgets freeze the current system's inefficiencies in place, they make no pretense about reform and they do not address any of the underlying reasons for rising costs, such as the unrestrained demand for unlimited health care services. Global budgets further undermine any effort to stimulate competition among health plans.

Giving government the power to budget private health expenditures makes this plan a trillion dollar appropriations bill and that in our view is too much government intrusion into personal health care decisions.

PREMIUM CAPS

The task force and the President rejected across-the-board price controls, but included price controls on insurance premiums. Such premium caps would drastically undermine efforts to organize delivery networks envisioned by the President. Unless modified by Congress, price controls on premiums will become an obstacle to driving down costs because price ceilings will immediately become the floors. Insurers would not be likely to set their premiums very low when their future pricing options are limited by government caps.

Premium caps will also inhibit the growth of new and innovative health plans, that will require large amounts of risk capital to develop health services delivery networks, whether they be formed by insurers, employers or providers.

MANAGED COMPETITION

The Federation has endorsed the managed competition concepts contained in the "Managed Competition Act" introduced by

Representative Jim Cooper (D-TN) and more than 45 other cosponsors. Similar legislation will be sponsored by Senator John Breaux (D-LA) and others in the Senate. These bipartisan measures rely on the creation of large purchasing pools for small employers and individuals to buy coverage at reduced costs from accountable health plans which submit competitive bids to purchasing cooperatives.

The Managed Competition Act shares many features of the President's plan. Several provide for universal access to health insurance through: establishing a standardized benefits package to be offered by health plans; subsidies for individuals' purchase of coverage based on their income; requiring health plans to offer coverage to everyone; and prohibiting insurers from denying coverage for pre-existing medical conditions.

Both plans include features making health insurance more affordable and enhancing the quality and efficiency of care. These include: establishing regional purchasing groups through which individuals and small businesses purchase coverage; preempting state anti-managed care laws; requiring health plans and providers to report on the quality of their health care and outcomes and enrollee satisfaction; and promoting administrative simplification.

There are significant differences between the President's plan and the Managed Competition Act. The President's plan imposes a global budget on private sector health care spending, enforced with premium caps on managed care plans and provider price controls for fee-for-service plans. The Managed Competition Act does not rely on this arbitrary regulatory approach.

The nature of purchasing cooperatives described in the two plans also differs drastically. Health plan purchasing cooperatives under the Managed Competition Act are non-regulatory bodies -- essentially brokers -- which offer their members a choice of all health plans in the area.

States determine the employer size for participating in the purchasing cooperative, but it must be between 100 and 500 employees. The Clinton plan's Health Alliances are state regulatory agencies that can limit plan choices and require that all employers with fewer than 5,000 employees must purchase insurance through the alliance.

The Managed Competition Act caps the employer deductibility of health benefits at the cost of the lowest-priced, qualified plan offering the standard benefits package. As mentioned earlier, the Federation believes the tax cap provides the most effective cost containment tool. It involves all the parties contributing to health care expenditures: consumers, employers, providers and insurers.

The Clinton plan sets no limit on tax deductibility for the standard benefit package, regardless of cost, if purchased through the alliance. Supplemental benefits paid for by an employer would be considered taxable income to employees. However, for collective bargaining agreements currently in effect, the loss of the employees' tax exclusion would not occur for ten years.

The Clinton plan contains an employer mandate requiring employers to pay 80 percent of their employees' health premiums. The Managed Competition Act would not require employers to pay for employees' health costs. We believe Congress should immediately provide coverage for those who cannot afford it based on their income, and postpone any decision on an employer mandate. Imposing such a mandate would have a detrimental effect on jobs at a time when the health sector also will be undergoing major restructuring.

Finally, the Managed Competition Act provides for caps on non-economic damages in malpractice awards. The Clinton plan would only limit contingency fees.

SECURITY AND CHOICE

The President has listed six criteria essential for meaningful health reform. The first is security. We applaud the Administration's proposal to assure Americans that their health coverage will always be there. But we are concerned about security against losing the quality of the care received.

Choice is another criteria mentioned by the President. Parts of his plan result in increased choice. An example is that employees will be able to choose from a variety of plans instead of accepting the single choice of their employer.

However, other parts of the plan restrict choice. An example is the regulatory authority granted to alliances to freeze enrollment in plans where global budgets are exceeded. Choice can be restricted when the growth in the weighted average premium in an alliance rises faster than inflation. For example, if all plan premiums in an alliance grow at the rate of inflation, but some individuals elect to switch to a higher cost plan, the growth in the weighted average premium in that alliance would exceed inflation. In this case, consumers who want to switch to higher cost plans can be penalized by having their choice denied by the alliances, even when the desired plan did not increase its premiums from the previous year.

This raises serious constitutional and policy questions about whether government can cap private spending decisions by consumers which involve no government funds and there exists no national emergency nor shortage of supply.

BASIS FOR CONSENSUS

The concept of managed competition already enjoys the endorsement of an unprecedented number of diverse groups in the private sector. Managed competition also has strong bipartisan support in the Congress, a necessary element for avoiding gridlock on the important issue of health care reform. With the exception of global budgeting and price controls, the government and the private sector have never been closer to a compromise on health care reform.

The managed care revolution has been under way for a decade. Indemnity insurance is giving way to a new system which restrains excessive treatment. There has been little talk about rationing during this debate, but rationing of health care is a central issue.

If we define rationing as withholding care, we see clearly the differences in the two approaches. Managed care does not withhold needed care; it manages care to restrain unneeded services. Price controls and global budgets limit care without regard to medical necessity. President Clinton wants to try both at the same time. But that would doom managed care by putting controls ahead of case management, budgets ahead of needed care and regulators ahead of patients.

We have before us a historic opportunity. Our industry stands ready to help President Clinton use his leadership and consensus-building skills to implement a national health reform policy that builds on the best features of our American health care system.

Mr. WAXMAN. Thank you very much. I want to recognize Mr. McMillan to proceed with questions first.

Mr. MCMILLAN. Thank you for accommodating my schedule, Mr. Chairman. Just to refer to the comments a little bit of Mr. Bromberg, I don't think Governors would be allowed to operate seven alliances, so all governmental employees will have to become part of regional alliances, and I presume that means Members of Congress would have to be a part of a regional alliance which presumably will be the District of Columbia. I don't know what I will do when I go home. This thing really does get complicated, cross-jurisdictions and so forth.

I think we all should read page 98 or the probably 400 or 500 pages that it will take to define page 98 when the full bill comes out. I want to touch with all of you a little bit on the issue of antitrust.

We think we have got some good antitrust provisions in alternative legislation that has been put forth and the administration proposes, I think, to approach this experimentally as a pilot program when, in fact, you and I know that out there in the system today is enormous pressure because of the downward pressure on cost to create accommodations not in the interest of restraining trade, but in the interest of providing better coordinated services.

I know it is happening in my community between central city hospitals and rural hospitals, and it really makes good sense, so we have introduced, I introduced antitrust legislation which has become part of the House Republican alternative, but recently I think the FTC and DOJ have issued some antitrust guidelines.

Are you familiar with those guidelines that have been issued by those two departments? Do you see them as being adequate to eliminate what I would classify as a chilling effect on constructive combinations simply because of the potential for litigation and the high probability that your legal fees may exceed your potential savings through the combination?

Would you care to comment on those two guideline statements that have been recently issued.

Mr. PUGH. We appreciate your leadership on the issue of the antitrust. At the AHA, the guidelines, and I am familiar with them for a couple of reasons, the guidelines are a start. They certainly help some very specific situations, but they do not, in our opinion, go far enough to deal with these issues of collaboration, formation of networks and new physician entities, and from personal experience we are currently before the FTC in Pueblo, Colo., right now with a proposed consolidation of two hospitals in the community to form a single entity.

It is the community's desire. We have 350 letters of support, all of our elected officials. We have only one payer that is in opposition. All other payers are in support, and yet we appear to be embroiled in an FTC process that may be long and costly. When we realize it is the only way we can save for our community $10 million a year in operating expenses, so I think there needs to be some more movement in terms of antitrust stock in terms of how we can allow some of these things to happen when it is in the best interests of the community.

Mr. McMILLAN. Do you have any estimate as to what your legal fees will be to prove your point to achieve $10 million worth of savings a year?

Mr. PUGH. If we end up in litigation, I have been told the sky is the limit, and I think the ceiling is about, the cloud ceiling is about $3 million. We are hoping to get out of this in under a million dollars in legal fees.

Mr. McMILLAN. It seems to me we could define government's objectives more clearly than that, doesn't it?

Mr. PUGH. It would seem to me also.

Mr. McMILLAN. Would anyone else care to respond to that question?

Sister COREIL. I would agree with Mr. Pugh. I think that the regulations that came out, at least the guidelines, more or less just reinforce what was already there with a little bit of encouragement for us, but it doesn't go far enough for the things we need to do if we really want to make an integrated delivery network to serve people's needs.

Mr. McMILLAN. In my community, the largest hospital, which is a public authority, it is close to 1,200 beds, is creating a joint venture with the largely Catholic institution Mercy Hospital, and I haven't talked to them, but I would expect that under existing law they have decided that they are going to assume the risk of the legal fees because the packaging and the training is so enormous.

Sister COREIL. There is so much time tied up in it, if it could be done expeditiously.

Mr. BROMBERG. If I could just add to that. No disagreement, and I support some of the stuff you have drafted along these lines, but just one caveat. I think it is really important to make sure we don't go too far down this road. I think antitrust enforcement, especially at the plan level, is going to be the only way we assure consumers that they are going to have a choice.

We have got to guard against boycotts and restraints of trade. For example, if all the doctors or hospitals in some community get in a room and decide they are not going to contract with any HMO's, we have seen some of that. I would much rather people, when they go down to the alliance, have 10 choices or 5 and not only 1 or 2 or 3. The word "collaboration" is fine, and, yes, hospitals should set up networks and we need a little bit more guidance from the FTC and Justice, but, boy, I hope they are vigilant in watching against boycotts and restraints, because that could really hurt consumers.

Mr. McMILLAN. I would agree.

Mr. WAXMAN. The gentleman's time has expired.

If he would just yield to me the time he doesn't have to follow up on the question. You think there ought not to be restraints.

Mr. McMILLAN. I have no more time, Mr. Chairman.

Mr. WAXMAN. By unanimous consent the gentleman is given an additional minute to yield to me.

Do you think we ought to also say that all hospitals ought to take Medicaid patients?

Mr. BROMBERG. I don't think that will be a problem.

Mr. WAXMAN. You don't want the hospitals to get together and say don't refuse to contract with HMO's, but how about hospitals getting together and refusing to take Medicaid patients?

Mr. BROMBERG. I think the best part of this legislation that is going to be proposed by the President, if I had to pick one of the sections in it, it is the section that takes the Medicaid program, and instead of buying people services as if they are on welfare and paying for each service individually, gives them first class, same private insurance as a millionaire down the road, and as a result of that, I don't think you will have to worry.

Mr. WAXMAN. Maybe.

Mr. BROMBERG. So does the Cooper bill.

Mr. WAXMAN. But I am just wondering, when you are talking against restraints by institutions for discrimination purposes, I would like to know, maybe you can furnish for the record how many of your institutions in your organization take Medicaid. If I were to guess, I would guess it would be quite few.

Mr. BROMBERG. I think the State of California is probably our highest Medicaid load in the country. Nationally it is 8 percent. In California it has got to be much, much higher. The problem with our institutions is many of them are in the South in States who have Governors and legislators who are too cheap to fund the Medicaid program, maybe in Texas and Florida, for example, if you make $2,000 a year you are too rich for Medicaid. Whereas in your State if you make $12,000 you are in it, and most of our hospitals are in those three States in the sun belt, but I think we take our share of Medicaid.

Mr. WAXMAN. We will see if we can get a system where everybody is brought in mainstream and then hospitals and institutions that provide care will be fair to all of them.

Mr. MCMILLAN. If the gentleman would yield.

Mr. WAXMAN. Your minute is up.

Mr. MCMILLAN. No, the institution, Carolinas Medical Center that I mentioned was creating a joint venture with Mercy Hospital is also in the process of setting up an HMO primarily to give to Medicaid, under North Carolina's limited Medicaid program, and under whatever is done, whether it is a Republican alternative, the Cooper bill, or the President's, Medicaid is going to be more fully funded, and an HMO is a logical way to deal with it.

Mr. WAXMAN. Ms. Collins.

Mrs. COLLINS. Health insurance redlining can take a number of forms, and one form is a refusal to contract with certain providers or a provider located in certain neighborhoods to discourage certain groups of people from enrolling with that insurer. In fact I recently heard that some providers, including a paramedical company, a laboratory, and physical therapists have had some difficulties in contracting with insurance companies already. So my question to you, Sister Coreil, would be perhaps what is your recommendation for more effectively preventing these kinds of practices?

Sister COREIL. Congresswoman Collins, I believe that if we go into a true integrated delivery network and we take away the price competition—I am against price competition, I think we should compete on service and quality—that people will have access to a full spectrum of care, and it doesn't matter whether we are black or white or we are rich or poor. I mean we will all have the same, so I think the key is in the delivery reform. We must reform the delivery system so that the incentives are in the right place, so that people can have access to what they need.

Mrs. COLLINS. Mr. Pugh, the President's proposal makes mandatory the inclusion among each health care plan's providers network of clinics and health centers in medically underserved areas for the first 5 years of the program. Will inclusion of these "essential providers", in your view, provide a sufficient degree of service to these communities or do you think more is needed? Second, do you think the 5-year phaseout is appropriate?

Mr. PUGH. I think the inclusion of essential providers recognizes some of the problems that you were alluding to in the inner city areas as well as in the rural areas. I think it also allows, then, for these integrated delivery systems that the Sister refers to or community care networks or restructured health care delivery systems to get off the ground and be functional and, hopefully, after 5 years the issue of essential providers will be eliminated.

I don't know. It is one of those what-ifs in the plan that we are just not sure of how exactly it will play out.

Mrs. COLLINS. Do you think 5 years will be long enough?

Mr. PUGH. I don't know.

Mrs. COLLINS. Sister? Do you think 5 years might be long enough?

Sister COREIL. We hope it is. I am not sure. It is true when we are dealing with things that we haven't dealt with before, if we get enough support in the beginning I think, yes, it is.

Mrs. COLLINS. One of the responsibilities of the National Health Board would be to establish basic quality standards and practice guidelines. If a patient had an unusual case, would their treatment be limited to what is in that guideline? Also if the physician in good faith deviates somewhat from that standard or guideline and the treatment is ultimately ineffective, will that substantiate a case for medical malpractice in your views? Either of you can answer. Mr. Pugh.

Mr. PUGH. We have had some experience at Parkview in developing guidelines, protocols, trying to integrate the physician ordering and nursing delivery altogether. We found that we can generally get about 80 percent agreement on the elements of that, but there is still 20 percent that is unknown, and I think that just guidelines are simply road maps. They are not precise formulas for exactly how care ought to be delivered, so I am not too concerned about the unusual patient being given inappropriate care because of the guideline.

There is an argument about the guidelines being some basis for protection during malpractice, for malpractice suits, and then there is some discussion on the other side if you don't do what the guideline says you expose yourself. I am not sure that those, either of those would be big issues if some of the other malpractice reforms that the previous panel testified to take place.

Mrs. COLLINS. Thank you. I have no further questions.

Mr. WAXMAN. Thank you, Mrs. Collins.

Mr. Brown, do you want to ask a quick question in the few minutes we have remaining?

77-929 O - 94 - 18

Mr. BROWN. Mr. Pugh, you talked in your testimony that one of the first things to go, you said oftentimes when costs are squeezed, are wellness programs, consumer education, outreach and community health kind of education, programs like that. How do we ensure that these programs continue to exist? What can we do from here to sort of guarantee that in times like this?

Mr. Pugh.

Mr. PUGH. I think it is what the Sister referred to in her testimony also about the restructuring of the health care system so that the incentives become to keep people well. Right now you have to understand we have a sick care system where the incentives are to treat people when they are sick. That is the only way money flows into the system, but if we move to these networks and capitated plans, all of a sudden the providers have incentive to keep people well, and so I think we will see more money put into early disease identification programs, stop smoking programs, wellness programs, et cetera, as these networks evolve, and they will become really true health maintenance organizations.

I think we have had HMO's as a name, but they haven't functioned that way because they have still been pretty much, the incentives have been for service delivery. I think we have to move towards incentives for health care.

Mr. BROWN. Sister, would you comment, too, briefly.

Sister COREIL. I agree with Mr. Pugh. I think we have to look at—our hospitals in the past have been our revenue centers. That is how we got money to do the things we do, and now we are going to look at our hospitals as a cost center, so it is not going to be what can we do to fill empty beds when we are overcapacitated in that area, but how can we keep them empty and get people so they don't have to use them, so I agree that the restructuring is the key. It is the linchpin to any type of reform. We must change the delivery system. We are fragmented, we have a lot of waste in it.

Mr. BROMBERG. I would just add to that, not to harp on it again, but the more choice there is, the more it is likely to happen. Capitation, the last question it is interesting, the last question about underutilization, you have to have quality standards to make sure that enough care is given. With respect to your question in order to make sure that enough preventive care is given, I think the incentive of capitation will do it provided there are several choices around, but if you get to a monopoly situation where there is only one or two, you may lose some of that, but capitation is the short answer.

Mr. BROWN. Thank you, Mr. Chairman.

Mr. WAXMAN. I want to thank you for your presentation to us. If you would permit, some of the members didn't get a chance to ask questions, myself included, and we may well submit some questions in writing to you, and we would like you to respond in writing. Thank you.

With that, that concludes our hearing for today. We stand adjourned.

[Whereupon, at 3:14 p.m., the subcommittee was adjourned, to reconvene at the call of the Chair.]

HEALTH CARE REFORM

Executive Agency Testimony: Impact on the Economy

THURSDAY, OCTOBER 28, 1993

HOUSE OF REPRESENTATIVES, COMMITTEE ON ENERGY AND COMMERCE, SUBCOMMITTEE ON HEALTH AND THE ENVIRONMENT, AND THE SUBCOMMITTEE ON COMMERCE, CONSUMER PROTECTION, AND COMPETITIVENESS,

Washington, DC.

The subcommittees met, pursuant to notice, at 10 a.m., in room 2123, Rayburn House Office Building, Hon. Henry A. Waxman, chairman, Subcommitte on Health and the Environment, and Hon. Cardiss Collins, chairwoman, Subcommittee on Commerce, Consumer Protection, and Competitiveness, presiding.

Mr. WAXMAN. The meeting of the two subcommittees will come to order.

Yesterday, President Clinton transmitted his health care reform legislation to the Congress. I am cosponsoring the President's plan to indicate my strong support for his efforts to enact health care reform which will guarantee universal coverage for comprehensive benefits to every American. Now we have the opportunity to begin a full debate on the details of the plan, keeping in mind the President's admonition that, when we are done, universal, affordable coverage is a reality for all.

Today, we begin this process by focusing on the impact of this plan on our economy. As we know, all of our international competitors have achieved universal coverage and have done so for far less of an investment than what we are spending on our broken system. The President has correctly observed that we cannot have national healthy economy if our work force lacks the security of a guaranteed health benefits. Moreover, we cannot sustain economic growth if workers and employers face a never-ending spiral of health care increases.

At the same time, we must take care and fairly distribute the responsibility for financing health coverage. Low-wage workers and those outside the workforce must be assisted with the purchase of coverage, and those who do not offer it must have help. The President's plan offers that help in two ways, by providing Federal subsidies to small firms and low-wage workers and the unemployed and by holding out the promise of more predictable and reasonable increases in health costs.

Our distinguished witnesses this morning are especially well qualified to address the economic implications of the President's plan. It is a privilege to have with us the Secretary of the Treasury, Mr. Bentsen; the Secretary of Labor, Mr. Reich; and the Administrator of the Small Business Administration, Mr. Bowles.

Before calling on our witnesses, I would like to recognize my cochair for this hearing, Congresswoman Collins for an opening statement.

Mrs. COLLINS. Good morning. I would also like to welcome everyone to today's joint hearing of our two subcommittees on President Clinton's health reform plan. I am pleased to be cochairing with my friend and colleague, Chairman Waxman.

We are delighted to welcome Secretary Bentsen, Secretary Reich and the Administrator of the Small Business Administration, Mr. Bowles, to testify before us today. It is an event made even more significant by yesterday's transmittal to Congress by the President of his health care reform legislation.

The process of consultation with Congress has been a worthy one. I appreciate the opportunities we have been given for input into the formulation of the President's package, which I wholeheartedly cosponsor. Now we begin to examine the specifics of the proposal.

All of us in Congress share the President's goal of providing health security for all Americans. We have a great deal of work ahead of us, and if we are to meet our goal of enacting legislation in this Congress, I am prepared to do my part. I believe that my colleagues are prepared to do theirs, as well.

Our witnesses today are prepared to discuss some of the key economic questions surrounding the President's health care reform proposal. These questions include how the plan will be financed and whether the financing will be adequate, whether the plan will affect jobs, wages and small businesses, and how they will do.

I hope our witnesses will also address one other important question. That question is, what would be the economic consequences if we fail to reform our health delivery system?

With so much ground to cover, I would like to conclude my opening remarks now, Mr. Chairman, in order to take full advantage of the time we have for our witnesses. I yield back the balance of my time.

Mr. WAXMAN. Thank you very much, Mrs. Collins.

Mr. Bliley.

Mr. BLILEY. Thank you, Mr. Chairman. First, I, too, would like to welcome our distinguished guests at today's hearing, Secretary Bentsen, Secretary Reich and SBA Administrator Bowles. Today's hearing will look at some of the critical budgetary, fiscal and economic assumptions underlying the President's proposal. Because the administration's health care proposal will have the Federal Government reallocate hundreds of billions of dollars and create new massive Federal health care entitlements, it is important that we examine the fiscal and budgetary assumptions and numbers in great detail.

Since I am not aware of one independent health care expert or economist who has found the administration's current financing and cost containment proposals credible, it is imperative that the quantitative documentation be made public so that the Congress can determine the validity of the analysis.

I would again like to remind my colleagues that the first question I asked Mrs. Clinton at our September 28 hearing was regarding her willingness to make available to the committee the task force's quantitative work product.

Let me quote Mrs. Clinton's response: "We will be happy to share with you all of our data that you requested, all of our calculations and economic models."

Well, now it is 1 month later, and we are still waiting. The committee has still not received even one page of analysis from the administration.

One set of issues we want to explore today with our distinguished witnesses is the following group of interrelated questions: What is a Federal tax? What is a Federal activity? When should Federal programs appear on the Federal budget?

Yesterday, during a Republican leadership press conference concerning the Clinton health reform plan, I explored these issues in depth and will do so again today. These are critical issues because the administration wants to uphold the pretense that a federally mandated tax payment based on a percentage of payroll is not a tax, but a private transaction. I strongly disagree, and we will be exploring this issue shortly with the witnesses.

Also, yesterday, the Minority Leader Bob Michel asked the Rules Committee to make in order a continuing resolution that would provide a very simple and common sense scorekeeping rule for CBO, OMB and the Joint Tax Committee for any change in law. This one-page amendment would do more to shed the glow of budgetary honesty on this 1,350-page bill, that I can hardly lift from the desk, than Ira Magaziner and his 500-member task force, the White House Health Care Reform War Room, or any other "political spinners" and public relations experts. It simply directs the scorekeeping agencies to consider any obligation, payroll tax, assessment, premium or fee required of employers or any other individual which is paid to an entity under the requirement of the sovereign power of Federal law shall be treated as a Federal receipt, and any related expenditure made by such entity pursuant to Federal law shall be treated as a Federal outlay.

This amendment was not made in order, and today the Minority will oppose the rule on the CR during Floor debate. I can assure everyone, this is not the last time this committee will see this amendment, which is simply calling for honest and credible scoring.

Mr. Chairman, I ask unanimous consent to include the rest of my statement in the record.

Mr. WAXMAN. Without objection.

[The opening statement of Mr. Bliley follows:]

STATEMENT OF THE HONORABLE THOMAS J. BLILEY, JR.

MR. CHAIRMAN, FIRST I WOULD LIKE TO WELCOME OUR DISTINGUISHED GUESTS TO TODAY HEARING, SECRETARY BENTSEN, SECRETARY REICH, AND SBA ADMINISTRATOR, MR. BOWLES. TODAY'S HEARING WILL LOOK AT SOME OF THE CRITICAL BUDGETARY, FISCAL, AND ECONOMIC ASSUMPTIONS UNDERLYING THE ADMINISTRATION'S PROPOSAL. BECAUSE THE ADMINISTRATION'S HEALTH CARE PROPOSAL WILL HAVE THE FEDERAL GOVERNMENT RE-ALLOCATE HUNDREDS OF BILLIONS OF DOLLARS AND CREATE NEW MASSIVE FEDERAL HEALTH CARE ENTITLEMENTS, IT IS IMPORTANT THAT WE EXAMINE THE FISCAL AND BUDGETARY ASSUMPTIONS AND NUMBERS IN GREAT DETAIL.

SINCE I AM NOT AWARE OF ONE INDEPENDENT HEALTH CARE EXPERT OR ECONOMIST WHO HAS FOUND THE ADMINISTRATION'S CURRENT FINANCING AND COST CONTAINMENT PROPOSALS CREDIBLE, IT IS IMPERATIVE THAT THE QUANTITATIVE DOCUMENTATION BE MADE PUBLIC SO THAT CONGRESS AND THE PUBLIC CAN DETERMINE THE VALIDITY OF THE ANALYSIS. I WOULD AGAIN LIKE TO REMIND MY COLLEAGUES THAT THE FIRST QUESTION I ASKED MRS. CLINTON AT OUR SEPTEMBER 28TH HEARING WAS REGARDING HER WILLINGNESS TO MAKE AVAILABLE TO THE COMMITTEE THE TASK FORCE'S QUANTITATIVE WORK PRODUCT.

LET ME QUOTE MRS. CLINTON'S RESPONSE: "WE WILL BE HAPPY TO SHARE WITH YOU ALL OF OUR DATA THAT YOU REQUESTED, ALL OF OUR CALCULATIONS, OUR ECONOMIC MODELS, ET. CETERA."

WELL, NOW IT IS ONE MONTH LATER, AND WE ARE STILL WAITING. THE COMMITTEE HAS STILL NOT RECEIVED EVEN ONE PAGE OF ANALYSIS FROM THE ADMINISTRATION.

ONE SET OF ISSUES THAT WE WANT TO EXPLORE TODAY WITH OUR DISTINGUISHED WITNESSES IS THE FOLLOWING GROUP OF INTERRELATED QUESTIONS: WHAT IS A FEDERAL TAX?; WHAT IS A FEDERAL ACTIVITY?; AND WHEN SHOULD FEDERAL PROGRAMS APPEAR ON THE FEDERAL BUDGET?

YESTERDAY, DURING A REPUBLICAN LEADERSHIP PRESS CONFERENCE CONCERNING THE CLINTON HEALTH REFORM PLAN, I EXPLORED THESE ISSUES IN DEPTH, AND WILL DO SO AGAIN TODAY. THESE ARE CRITICAL ISSUES, BECAUSE THE ADMINISTRATION WANTS TO UPHOLD THE PRETENSE THAT A FEDERALLY MANDATED TAX PAYMENT BASED ON A PERCENTAGE OF PAYROLL IS NOT A TAX, BUT A PRIVATE TRANSACTION. I STRONGLY DISAGREE, AND WE WILL BE EXPLORING THIS ISSUE SHORTLY WITH THE WITNESSES.

ALSO, YESTERDAY, THE MINORITY LEADER BOB MICHEL ASKED THE RULES COMMITTEE TO MAKE IN ORDER AN AMENDMENT TO THE CONTINUING RESOLUTION (CR) THAT WOULD PROVIDE A VERY SIMPLE AND COMMON SENSE SCORE-KEEPING RULE FOR CBO, OMB, AND THE JOINT TAX COMMITTEE FOR ANY CHANGE IN LAW. THIS ONE PAGE AMENDMENT WOULD DO MORE TO SHED THE GLOW OF BUDGETARY HONESTY ON THIS 1350 PAGE BILL, THEN IRA MAGAZINER AND HIS 500 MEMBER TASK FORCE, THE WHITE HOUSE HEALTH CARE REFORM WAR ROOM, OR ANY OTHER "POLITICAL SPINNERS" AND PUBLIC RELATIONS EXPERTS. IT SIMPLY DIRECTS THE SCORE-KEEPING AGENCIES TO CONSIDER ANY OBLIGATION, PAYROLL TAX, ASSESSMENT, PREMIUM OR FEE REQUIRED OF EMPLOYERS OR OF ANY OTHER INDIVIDUAL WHICH IS PAID TO AN ENTITY UNDER THE REQUIREMENT OF THE SOVEREIGN POWER OF FEDERAL LAW SHALL BE TREATED AS A FEDERAL RECEIPT, AND ANY RELATED EXPENDITURE MADE BY SUCH ENTITY PURSUANT TO FEDERAL LAW SHALL BE

TREATED AS A FEDERAL OUTLAY. THIS AMENDMENT WAS NOT MADE IN ORDER, AND TODAY THE MINORITY IS GOING TO OPPOSE THE RULE ON THE C.R. DURING FLOOR DEBATE. I CAN ASSURE EVERYONE THIS IS NOT THE LAST TIME THIS COMMITTEE WILL SEE THIS AMENDMENT, WHICH SIMPLY IS CALLING FOR HONEST AND CREDIBLE SCORING.

DURING THE PAST DECADE, THE FEDERAL BUDGET AND THE BUDGET PROCESS HAS DRIVEN FEDERAL HEALTH CARE POLICY. THROUGH OUR INNUMERABLE RECONCILIATION BILLS, DRAMATIC AND OFTEN CONTRADICTORY CHANGES HAVE BEEN MADE IN THE MEDICARE AND MEDICAID PROGRAMS. AT THE SAME TIME, MANY BUDGET EXPERTS HAVE POINTED OUT THAT THE PRIMARY COST DRIVER OF THE FEDERAL BUDGET HAS BEEN THE ANNUAL DOUBLE DIGIT GROWTH RATES IN MEDICAID AND MEDICARE.

THE ADMINISTRATION'S BILL CREATES A NUMBER OF NEW FEDERAL HEALTH CARE ENTITLEMENTS WHICH IT SIMULTANEOUSLY PAYS FOR BY DRACONIAN CUTS IN MEDICARE AND MEDICAID--TO THE TUNE OF $124 BILLION IN MEDICARE CUTS AND $65 BILLION IN MEDICAID CUTS. FOR THE CLINTON ADMINISTRATION TO EVEN THEORETICALLY FINANCE THESE NEW ENTITLEMENTS, ALL OF THESE SAVINGS MUST MATERIALIZE DURING THE 5 YEAR BUDGET SCORING PERIOD. TO REALIZE THE IMPOSSIBILITY OF THIS TASK, ALL WE HAVE TO DO IS LOOK BACK AT PAST RECONCILIATIONS WHERE WE CUT JUST A FRACTION OF THE $189 BILLION THAT THE ADMINISTRATION CLAIMS IS POSSIBLE. DURING THIS HEARING THE MINORITY IS GOING TO EXPLORE WITH THE WITNESSES THE CBO MEDICARE AND MEDICAID BASELINES BEGINNING FROM OBRA 1990 TO DETERMINE IF ENTITLEMENT SAVINGS ACTUALLY EVER MATERIALIZED FROM PAST RECONCILIATION CUTS. LET ME FOREWARN THE SQUEAMISH, IN THE SPIRIT OF HALLOWEEN, THAT ANNUAL "TECHNICAL CHANGES" TO THE CBO MEDICARE/MEDICAID BASELINES ARE A TERRIFYING SIGHT. THE ADDITIONAL BILLIONS THAT ARE ADDED TO THE CBO BASELINE ANNUALLY WOULD EASILY FINANCE THE BUDGETS OF MOST

MEDIUM SIZED COUNTRIES.

FINALLY, WE ARE GOING TO EXPLORE WITH THE WITNESSES THE SERIES OF BUDGET ESTIMATES THAT WERE MADE THE LAST TIME WE ENACTED LEGISLATION THAT CREATED NEW HEALTH CARE BENEFITS FOR THE ELDERLY-THE MEDICARE CATASTROPHIC COVERAGE ACT (MCCA). AS MOST OF US REMEMBER THAT LEGISLATION LASTED JUST ONE YEAR BEFORE IT WAS REPEALED. WHAT MANY OF US HAVE FORGOTTEN IS THAT ONE OF THE FINAL NAILS IN THE COFFIN OF THE CATASTROPHIC COVERAGE ACT WAS THE CBO RE-ESTIMATES THAT ADDED OVER 18 BILLION DOLLARS TO THE ORIGINAL $30 BILLION ESTIMATE.

THANK YOU.

h:TAX.STA

WHY THE CLINTON PAYROLL TAX SHOULD BE ON-BUDGET

SECRETARY BENTSEN, AS YOU KNOW, THE BUDGET IS THE PROCESS BY WHICH CONGRESS AND THE PRESIDENT ALLOCATE SCARCE RESOURCES AMONG COMPETING PUBLIC PRIORITIES. THE ADMINISTRATION'S HEALTH CARE PROPOSAL WILL HAVE THE FEDERAL GOVERNMENT RE-ALLOCATING HUNDREDS OF BILLIONS OF DOLLARS, OR APPROXIMATELY 14% OF THE ECONOMY. IF ALLOWED TO DO SO OFF-BUDGET, CONGRESS AND THE PUBLIC WILL BE DEPRIVED OF THE ESSENTIAL MEASUREMENT OF THE FISCAL AND ECONOMIC IMPACT OF THESE POLICY DECISIONS.

THIS IS A CRITICAL ISSUE, BECAUSE THE ADMINISTRATION'S REFORM PROPOSAL CALLS THE EMPLOYER'S PAYROLL TAX A NON-FEDERAL PRIVATE TRANSACTION. ALTHOUGH UNIVERSAL COVERAGE IS POPULAR, TAXES ARE NOT, AND SO THE ADMINISTRATION IS ATTEMPTING TO CHARACTERIZE A MANDATORY TAX AND A LARGE FEDERAL REGULATORY ACTIVITY AS PRIVATE TRANSACTIONS.

I STRONGLY DISAGREE. WHEN LEGISLATION INVOKES THE SOVEREIGN POWER OF THE GOVERNMENT TO COMPEL THE PAYMENT OF FUNDS, DEFINES A CLASS OF BENEFICIARIES, GUARANTEES SPECIFIC BENEFITS, AND ESTABLISHES A FEDERAL REGULATORY APPARATUS, THAT LEGISLATION HAS CREATED A FEDERAL ACTIVITY FINANCED BY A FEDERAL TAX.

BUT RATHER THAN DEBATE WHAT IS A TAX OR A FEDERAL ACTIVITY, LETS LOOK AT LEGISLATION ENACTED LAST YEAR UNDER SENATOR ROCKEFELLER'S LEADERSHIP IN THE SENATE FINANCE COMMITTEE, WHEN YOU WERE THE CHAIRMAN. THE LAW IS THE UNITED MINE WORKERS OF AMERICA

(UMWA) HEALTH BENEFIT PLAN, WHICH ADDRESSES THE FINANCING OF HEALTH BENEFITS FOR UMWA RETIRED COAL WORKERS.

TO HELP COMPARE THE STRUCTURE OF THE UMWA HEALTH BENEFIT PLAN THE ALLIANCE STRUCTURE UNDER THE PRESIDENT'S BILL WE WILL USE THESE TWO CHARTS. FIRST, THE LAW MANDATES THAT COAL OPERATORS MAKE MANDATORY, ANNUAL PREMIUM CONTRIBUTIONS TO THE COMBINED BENEFIT FUND, WHICH IS SPECIFICALLY CHARACTERIZED AS A PRIVATE PLAN. NO PREMIUM CONTRIBUTIONS ARE EVER TRANSFERRED TO THE FEDERAL GOVERNMENT. THE COMBINED FUND IS MANAGED BY A BOARD OF TRUSTEES MADE UP EXCLUSIVELY OF PRIVATE INDIVIDUALS. THE CLASS OF ELIGIBLE INDIVIDUALS IS SPECIFIED IN STATUTE. THE HEALTH CARE BENEFITS ARE SPECIFIED IN STATUTE. THE FIRST YEAR PREMIUM IS SET IN STATUTE, AND THE LAW AUTHORIZES THE SECRETARY OF HHS TO INDEX THE PREMIUM BY THE MEDICAL COMPONENT OF THE CPI.

NOW LET'S LOOK BRIEFLY AT THE STRUCTURAL OUTLINES OF THE ADMINISTRATION'S HEALTH CARE PLAN. WE HAVE FEDERALLY MANDATED PREMIUM PAYMENTS BASED ON PERCENTAGE OF PAYROLL. ADDITIONALLY, WE HAVE FEDERAL AND STATE MEDICAID AND SUBSIDY PAYMENTS TO THE ALLIANCE. THE ALLIANCE IS MANAGED BY A STATE AGENCY OR NON-PROFIT CORPORATION. THE CLASS OF ELIGIBLE INDIVIDUALS WILL BE SPECIFIED IN STATUTE. THE HEALTH CARE BENEFITS WILL BE SPECIFIED IN STATUTE. THE BILL WILL SET A METHOD TO DETERMINE THE FIRST YEAR PREMIUM, AND PREMIUMS ARE INDEXED BY A CONSUMER PRICE INDEX CAP.

NOW, IN THEIR KEY STRUCTURAL ELEMENTS, THE UMWA COMBINED BENEFIT FUND AND THE ADMINISTRATION'S HEALTH REFORM PROPOSAL ARE INDISTINGUISHABLE. BOTH BILLS ATTEMPT TO CHARACTERIZE THE PREMIUM CONTRIBUTIONS AS A PRIVATE TRANSACTION. BOTH HAVE THE TRANSFER OF MONIES TO THE ALLIANCE RATHER THAN TO THE FEDERAL GOVERNMENT. BOTH

KEEP FEDERAL OFFICIALS OFF BOARDS OF TRUSTEES.

SINCE THE COMBINED BENEFIT FUND WAS ENACTED LAST YEAR, THERE IS ONE MAJOR DIFFERENCE--WE DO KNOW HOW BOTH CBO AND OMB CHARACTERIZED IT. AND BOTH CBO AND OMB DETERMINED THAT SINCE THE STATUTE INVOKED THE SOVEREIGN POWER OF THE FEDERAL GOVERNMENT TO COMPEL PAYMENTS FROM COAL OPERATORS, AND SINCE THE STATUTE DEFINES BENEFITS, THE CLASS OF BENEFICIARIES, AND THE PREMIUM LEVELS, IT IS A FEDERAL TAX WITH BOTH REVENUES AND EXPENDITURES ON-BUDGET. THIS APPEARS ON P.1153 OF THE APPENDIX OF THE BUDGET OF THE UNITED STATES GOVERNMENT, FISCAL YEAR 1994. THE CONGRESSIONAL BUDGET OFFICE ALSO CHARACTERIZES THE COMBINED BENEFIT FUND AS A TAX, WITH BOTH REVENUES AND EXPENDITURES ON-BUDGET.

CLEARLY, THE CONGRESSIONAL BUDGET OFFICE AND OMB WILL HAVE NO CHOICE BUT TO CHARACTERIZE THE ADMINISTRATION'S PAYROLL TAX AND BUREAUCRACY AS TAXES AND AN ON-BUDGET FEDERAL ACTIVITY. TO CHARACTERIZE THE ADMINISTRATION'S PROPOSAL AS OFF-BUDGET WOULD UPHOLD A PRETENSE THAT WOULD LEAD TO A SERIOUS EROSION OF FISCAL DISCIPLINE IMPOSED BY THE BUDGET AND THE BUDGET PROCESS.

SECRETARY BENTSEN, CAN YOU DISTINGUISH ANY DIFFERENCE BETWEEN THE FINANCING AND OPERATIONAL PROCESSES OF THE COAL MINER'S FUND AND THE PRESIDENT'S PROPOSAL? IF THE UMWA HEALTH BENEFITS FUND IS ON-BUDGET AS A TAX, HOW CAN THE EMPLOYER PAYROLL TAX IN THE PRESIDENT'S PLAN NOT BE INCLUDED IN THE FEDERAL BUDGET AS A TAX?
H:TAX.QUE

Mr. WAXMAN. Mr. Stearns, Ranking Republican Member of Mrs. Collins' subcommittee.

Mr. STEARNS. Thank you.

I want to welcome our distinguished panel, Secretary Bentsen, Secretary Reich and Administrator Bowles.

I think we all recognize the importance of health care. I think this will be a very important hearing for all of us. We are concerned about the future.

President Clinton spoke yesterday about the importance of preserving consumer choice. I think that is a word we are working hard to incorporate.

The Republicans, the Minority, are in complete agreement on this point. However, I am concerned that the ultimate result under the President's plan will leave the consumer with no choice; and we will bring this out in the questioning.

As the Ranking Republican on the Commerce Subcommittee, I have learned that in order for insurers to remain solvent, their premiums must cover their risks and resulting claims. This basic principle has been underscored time and time again during the years of hearings that this committee has held on insurance solvency.

The primary cost control mechanism in the President's plan is a combination of mandated premium caps and global budgets, effectively limiting insurance premium growth to 1 percent over inflation. Even accepting Mrs. Clinton's claim of a $200 billion one-time savings, it is difficult to believe that insurers can limit premium growth to the CPI plus population growth and still remain solvent, especially when neither Canada nor Great Britain have been able to accomplish this feat.

What happens if a health care plan cannot keep its premiums at or below the nationally mandated cap? Under the President's program, health plans basically have three options: one, negotiate lower doctor and hospital fees; two, find new administrative efficiencies; three, tighten control over utilization, which frankly is just a fancy way of saying rationing care.

Even if insurers were able to accomplish these savings, they could still be faced with too many bad risks with insufficient risk adjustment, alliance-mandated increases in fee-for-services rates or rapid changes in environmental or health conditions which increase costs. All of these things, alone or in combination, work to upset the basic balance of risk and premium, the balance on which every insurance company rests.

Currently, States are responsible for monitoring the solvency of insurance companies and regulating the premiums that insurers can charge. These two areas of regulation are closely related and rightly so. We have seen that when rate-making and solvency are separated, insurance companies go under.

My concern is that the President's plan separates these from each other at the outset and all that Americans can look forward to are a shrinking number of profitable health insurers and dwindling choices for consumers.

Mr. Chairman, I look forward to hearing our witnesses' comments.

Mr. WAXMAN. Thank you. Let me ask unanimous consent that all members have an opportunity to insert a statement at this point in the record. I would like to urge the Chair and the Ranking Members of the two subcommittees to take advantage of inserting your statements in the record.

Under the rules, members are entitled, if they wish, to take 3 minutes. I will accord that right to any member that insists upon it. I thank my colleagues.

We are privileged to have with us this morning the leading economic policy-makers for the Clinton administration, Secretary Bentsen, Secretary Reich, and Administrator Bowles.

The President is especially fortunate to have the benefit of Secretary Bentsen's counsel. I had an opportunity to work with Lloyd Bentsen during his years as chairman of the Senate Finance Committee. We were able to expand health care security for children with special needs. I came to know him as a honorable, skillful and tenacious negotiator, and the administration will certainly need such skills to move its proposal through the Congress.

Gentlemen, we welcome you to the subcommittee. Your written statements will be inserted in the record in full.

Secretary Bentsen, why don't we start with you.

STATEMENTS OF HON. LLOYD M. BENTSEN, JR., SECRETARY OF THE TREASURY; HON. ROBERT B. REICH, SECRETARY OF LABOR; AND HON. ERSKINE B. BOWLES, ADMINISTRATOR, SMALL BUSINESS ADMINISTATION

Secretary BENTSEN. Thank you very much, Chairman Waxman, Chairwoman Collins and members of this committee for the opportunity to discuss the President's health care program. I will give you a summary statement with your permission and put my full statement in the record.

Many of you and I have worked together over the years on health care issues and have worked on some of the same problems which we are addressing in the President's proposal.

I would say, Chairman Waxman, that the things we did to expand coverage of Medicaid—prenatal care and neonatal coverage for children to ensure that they were born with sound minds and bodies to the extent possible—I can understand the enthusiasm that the Governors now have for additional Federal funding that is envisioned under the President's plan.

Reform of the health care system is obviously one of the President's highest priorities and an integral part of the administration's economic strategy. With the first step, the deficit reduction plan, we renewed the basis for economic growth and rising wages in America.

But recovery itself will not ensure a higher standard of living for Americans. For too long now, rising health care costs have been a drag on wages and profits, not to mention being a major contributor to the Federal deficit.

So now we must turn to health care reform. Let me assure you that, from an economic standpoint, failing to act is just not an option. When employers pay their workers more, but health care costs go up far more, workers' paychecks just don't increase as they should. The average worker today would be earning at least $1,000 more a year if health insurance costs had not risen faster than wages in the last 15 years. If nothing is done, 120 percent, every bit and more, of projected wage increases in the coming decade will be consumed by increasing health care costs.

You talk about going backwards. This country spends 14 percent of its gross domestic product on health care costs, 50 percent more than in the G-7 countries, our major competitors. If nothing is done, health care costs are projected to consume more than 19 percent of the GDP by the year 2000, while our competitors stay under 10 percent.

For all this extra spending, health coverage in this country is no better than that of our major trading partners. In many areas, it is worse.

We are spending more money and not offering Americans health security. The President's health security plan addresses the fundamental problems with the current system, the cost and the real tragedy of Americans who do not have coverage under the present plan. More than 37 million Americans have no health insurance coverage and almost 10 million of those are children. Another 22 million Americans are underinsured.

This lack of universal coverage affects all of us. Every time that someone without insurance is treated in an emergency room, each of us with insurance foots the bill. Estimates show that corporate premiums are 10 percent higher than they need be in order to pay for uncompensated care. I can think of just two hospitals in Texas where last year they provided over $80 million worth of uncompensated care. That means unpaid bills. That means the cost of the bed goes up. That means the physician's cost, the anesthesiologist's, all increase; and we pay for it.

I think universal coverage is critical to getting costs under control. My desk mate in the Senate for years was Lawton Chiles. I remember when Lawton was the chairman of the Budget Committee in the Senate. He was convinced it was necessary to get control of health care costs first, before extending coverage to everyone.

He left the Senate and became Governor of Florida. In less than a year, he was before the Senate Finance Committee telling us he had changed his mind; universal coverage was absolutely necessary in order to control costs so that businesses and people do not become the victims of cost-shifting, paying higher premiums to cover care for those who have no coverage.

The health security plan addresses the coverage issue. It will provide security to all Americans and shift resources to more productive uses. Many businesses will see their costs fall and others will be able to offer insurance for the first time. Slower cost growth will let employers enjoy real pay increases and universal coverage will ensure that workers no longer have to fear losing their health insurance if they change jobs or if they want to start their own businesses.

The key to making this plan effective is to build on the existing system of insuring individuals; just as they do today, the employers and individuals will pay premiums to cover the bulk of health coverage costs. Additional Federal support will be required to cover the costs of discounts to businesses and individuals eligible for reduced premiums, as well as the cost of the new drug benefit and long-term care benefits.

Funding for these subsidies and program improvements will come largely from slowing the rate of growth in Medicare and Medicaid, a 75-cent increase in the tax on a pack of cigarettes and an assessment on large companies that choose to establish their own corporate alliances.

The Treasury Department has been responsible for estimating the new sources of revenue for this program, so I would liked to talk to you a minute about some of the major provisions.

First, there are three points I want to emphasize:

One, the President's plan is a comprehensive proposal that spells out exactly how it will be financed and lays out the specifics of the benefit plan. That is the fiscally responsible way to do it.

To put our numbers together, we have consulted with the Nation's best actuaries and health care economists. I feel confident that we have approached the estimating process in a very responsible way.

Two, we have protected both the private sector and the public sector from cost overruns by insisting on accountability.

Three, this plan will be phased in, which allows sufficient time to make adjustments should we find that modifications are needed.

Let me offer some specifics. On the tax side of the plan, several provisions would accomplish the goals of this committee. We propose increasing the excise tax on cigarettes by 75 cents to 99 cents per pack.

We also propose raising the Federal excise tax on all other tobacco products. These changes will promote better health, not just among adults, but very importantly, among our children. Like many of you on this committee, I am very concerned about the increase in the use of tobacco products among our youngest children.

The Clinton plan will provide the funds needed to continue Federal support of critical health research by assessing larger employers who opt to form their own health alliances. That is something that a number of us have worked on over the years to ensure that we remain preeminent in medical research and clinical science. In addition to those steps, we want to help the self-employed better afford their contribution to health coverage by increasing their tax deduction from 25 to 100 percent. How many times have some of us proposed this change?

In addition, we want to be sure that our rural residents and those who live in certain urban areas have adequate access to quality health care. This plan provides for that. It encourages doctors and nurses to locate in underserved areas.

I think the administration has offered a very bold and comprehensive plan. It can make our businesses more competitive, and over the long term I believe it will help in job creation. Beyond that, it accomplishes what many of us tried to do in the last Congress and more, much more.

I have been waiting a long time for a President willing to take the lead on this issue. I am proud to be part of an administration tackling this country's health care problem. This is a problem that can cripple our economy if we don't act, and it makes us less competitive.

President Clinton is committed to universal coverage, comprehensive benefits, and lifetime coverage. He is intent on seeing that the quality of health care improves and that consumers have a choice of plans. He wants to reduce the paperwork burden. He is intent on financing the health security plan in a responsible manner with minimum government regulation. Those are important principles.

There are a number of ideas out there, but few meet all of those tests— particularly, universality, comprehensive benefits defined from the outset, and responsible financing.

The President wants a bipartisan solution to this problem. A number of the provisions that you see in our package have been offered in the past by Republicans and Democrats who want to work to see that it is not a partisan issue.

The President looks forward to working with the members of this committee and others in the Congress to pass a comprehensive and lasting reform of our health care system.

Mr. WAXMAN. Thank you, Secretary Bentsen.

[The prepared statement of Secretary Bentsen follows:]

RECORD TESTIMONY OF TREASURY SECRETARY LLOYD BENTSEN BEFORE THE SUBCOMMITTEE ON HEALTH AND THE ENVIRONMENT AND THE SUBCOMMITTEE ON COMMERCE, CONSUMER PROTECTION AND COMPETITIVENESS

Thank you, Chairman Dingell, Chairwoman Collins and Chairman Waxman for the opportunity to come before you today to discuss the President's health reform plan.

As you know, this is an issue which holds great interest for me, and one on which we worked closely with one another over the years when I served in the Senate.

Reform of the health care system is one of the President's highest priorities and an integral part of his economic strategy.

From the beginning, this administration has been dedicated to raising the standard of living in this country for us and for our children. Over the long term the only way to ensure higher standards of living is to have faster wage growth.

Faster wage growth requires investment in plant and equipment. But when this administration took office, the country's debt and deficits were growing faster than the economy. This was driving up interest rates and creating a climate that was hostile to business planning and investment.

The first thing we had to do was get our deficit headed down. Our budget plan and its $500 billion in deficit reduction has provided the basis for economic growth and rising wages. As soon as the critical elements of the plan emerged last winter, interest rates began to fall and they have been falling ever since. They're the lowest they've been in 20 years. In response, the interest sensitive sectors of our economy have taken off and we are well on our way to a healthy and steady, investment-led recovery.

An economic recovery by itself, however, will not ensure higher standards of living. For too long now, rising health care costs have been a drag on wages and profits -- not to mention being a major contributor to the federal deficit. So now we turn to health care reform. Let me assure you, from an economic standpoint, failing to act is not an option.

LMB-467

When employers pay their workers more, but health care costs rise also, workers' payslips don't go up as they should. The average worker today would be earning at least $1,000 more a year if health insurance costs had not risen faster than wages for the last 15 years. If nothing is done, 120 percent -- every bit and more of projected wage increases in the coming decade -- will be consumed by health care costs. Talk about going backwards!

As a nation, we spend 14 percent of GDP on health care. No other developed country spends near that. Japan and Germany are down around 9 percent. If nothing is done, health care will consume more than 19 percent of GDP by the year 2000, while our competitors remain under 10 percent.

Maybe spending all this money would be worth it, if we saw good results. But other countries have longer life expectancy and lower rates of infant mortality. They spend less and they cover everyone. We're spending more money and not providing all Americans the security they need.

The Health Security plan addresses the fundamental problems with the current system. The current system costs too much, and the real tragedy is that too many people have inadequate coverage or lack coverage altogether. More than 37 million Americans have no health coverage, and nearly 10 million are children. Another 22 million more are underinsured.

This lack of universal coverage is not a problem just for the uninsured. Every time someone without insurance shows up at the emergency room and is treated, every one of us who has insurance foots the bill. Estimates show that many corporate insurance premiums are 10 percent higher than they need be in order to pay for uncompensated care.

Universal coverage is critical to getting costs under control. I remember when Lawton Chiles was chairman of the Budget Committee in the Senate. He was convinced that it was necessary to control health care costs first <u>before</u> extending coverage to everyone. Lawton left the Senate and became governor of Florida. Within less than a year he was telling the Finance Committee that he had changed his mind. Universal coverage was absolutely necessary <u>in order</u> to control costs so that business and people do not become the victims of cost shifting -- paying higher premiums to cover the cost of care for those who have no coverage.

The Health Security plan addresses the coverage issue. It will provide security to Americans and shift resources to more productive uses. Many businesses will see their costs fall, and others will be able to offer insurance for the first time.

Slower cost growth will allow workers to enjoy faster growth in real wages, and universal coverage will ensure that workers no longer have to fear losing their health insurance coverage if they change jobs or want to start their own businesses.

To avoid major disruptions, the new system will be financed primarily like the current system. Creating a broad, single-payer program would have been too disruptive and transferred too large a role to the federal government. The key to making this plan effective is to build on the system of insuring individuals through their employers. Most businesses already cover their workers; even two-thirds of small businesses already provide health insurance. Just as they do today, employer and individual health insurance premiums will pay for the bulk of health coverage.

Employers will be required to pay 80 percent of the average premium. However, the plan limits the percentage of payroll that would be devoted to health care premiums to 7.9 percent for large firms, and provides discounts for small low-wage firms and individuals of modest means. Unless they qualify for a discounted premium, individuals will be asked to contribute the balance of the total premium cost.

Additional federal support will be required to cover the costs of these discounts, as well as the cost of the new Medicare drug benefit and long-term care benefit. Revenues for these outlays will come from slowing the growth in Medicare and Medicaid, a 75-cent increase in the tax on a pack of cigarettes, an assessment on large companies that choose to establish corporate alliances, and increased revenues as compensation shifts from non-taxable health care benefits to taxable wages and profits.

The Treasury Department has been responsible for estimating the new sources of revenues for the program, so I would like to talk to you for a minute about the major provisions.

First, however, there are three points I want to emphasize. One, the president's plan is the only comprehensive proposal that spells out exactly how it will be financed. Laying out the specifics of the benefits package is the only fiscally responsible thing to do. To put those numbers together, we consulted with some of the nation's most respected actuaries and health economists. I feel confident that we have approached the estimating process in a very responsible way.

Second, we have protected both the private sector and the public sector from cost overruns by insisting on accountability.

And third, this plan will be phased in, which allows sufficient time to make adjustments should we find that modifications are needed.

Now, as to some specifics.

As you know, our plan includes a proposal to increase the tax on tobacco products. Specifically, the excise tax on cigarettes would be increased by 75 cents per pack -- raising the federal tax from the current level of 24 cents to just under a dollar a pack. The administration also proposes to increase the federal excise tax rates on all other tobacco products.

This will both promote better health -- not just among adults but very importantly among our children. I am particularly concerned about the dramatic increase in the use of tobacco products by adolescents.

The increased tobacco taxes will provide much of the revenue we need to fund this plan.

Although we know it will promote better health, I want to elaborate briefly on this point. This is an entirely appropriate way to finance health care for several reasons.

First, tobacco consumption is the leading preventable cause of death and disease in the United States. As members of this committee know, it accounts for about half a million deaths a year and billions of dollars in health care costs.

Second, since the president's health care plan does not generally allow differential health insurance premiums for smokers and non-smokers, the fact of the matter is non-smokers will bear some of the increased health costs of smokers.

Studies by the Department of Health and Human Services, as well as the Canadian experience, demonstrate that raising tobacco taxes can successfully discourage the use of tobacco products by the young. This is particularly true for the proposed increase in taxes on smokeless tobacco. Studies have shown that nearly 20 percent of high school students use this type of tobacco, and it presently is taxed at a disproportionally low rate in comparison to cigarettes.

In addition, the Clinton plan will support critical health research with a payroll assessment on large employers who opt to form their own health alliance. Employers who are in the regional health alliances will also contribute to the cost of medical education and research. It is a fair and straightforward way to allow corporate alliance employers and employees to contribute to the health research and specialized care from which they also benefit.

Let me remind you, small expenditures in research have paid billions of dollars in dividends. This money, among other things, will go for added research into such areas as heart disease, cancer, AIDS, Alzheimer's disease and others. It also will be used for studies that give American health consumers important information about the quality and cost of health care.

I would also note that we anticipate that revenue impact of the general reform proposals in the health plan would result in a $23 billion increase in tax revenues. This results largely from increased competition and greater cost consciousness and other cost containment measures which are expected to lead over time to lower health insurance costs. It is assumed that the lower per-employee costs of tax-preferred employer-provided health insurance will lead employers to increase taxable wages, which in turn will generate more income and payroll taxes, despite the increased numbers of workers covered.

There are other tax provisions in the president's health plan that will accomplish many of the goals of this committee.

For example, the individual income tax health insurance deductions for self-employed taxpayers will be increased to 100 percent of the costs of the comprehensive benefit package. A self-employed taxpayer could claim the full deduction once the state of residence establishes a regional alliance. The 25 percent health insurance deduction for self-employed workers will continue in force until the 100 percent deduction is applicable.

In addition, I know that many of you here are very interested in making certain our rural residents, and those who live in some urban areas, have adequate access to quality health care. This plan provides for that. It encourages doctors and nurses to locate in underserved areas. The plan's initiatives work well with the expanded National Health Service Corps and Community Health Center initiatives. It will have at least 3,000 primary care practitioners in rural areas by the end of the decade, and increase the number of minority physicians, nurses and other health professionals.

Specifically, we propose two tax incentives to encourage adequate medical care in all areas of the country. A physician who works full-time for at least two years in an area designated as being short of health professionals can receive a tax credit of up to $1,000 per month for up to 60 months. Certified nurse-midwives, nurse practitioners, and physician assistants who work in health professional shortage areas can receive a tax credit up to $500 per month for up to the same period. In addition, for physicians who work in areas designated as being short of health professionals, the section 179 expensing limit will be increased by $10,000 for medical equipment.

There are other ways the tax system will be used to achieve other objectives of the health plan. For example, it will expand and improve long-term care options, stressing home and community-based services and the improvement of private long-term care insurance.

The plan proposes to modify the current tax treatment of long-term care expenses and insurance. Qualified long-term care expenses incurred by certain incapacitated individuals will be treated as deductible medical expenses, and taxpayers will be able to exclude up to $150 a day from taxable income for benefits paid under qualified long-term care policies. In addition, employers could deduct the premiums paid for these policies, and employees will also be able to exclude the value of this employer-provided coverage from taxable income.

But the non-tax aspects of the president's health plan on long-term health insurance markets are equally important. Under the plan, the Secretary of Health and Human Services has regulatory authority to establish uniform standards for the provision of private long-term care insurance. This authority will be exercised in consultation with a newly-established National Long-Term Care Insurance Advisory Council, appointed by the HHS Secretary. Federal regulations will provide standardized formats and terminology for long-term care insurance policies, require insurers to provide customers with information on the range of public and private long-term care coverage available, and establish other requirements to promote consumer understanding, make it easy to compare benefits, and regulate sales practices, insurance coverage, premium rates and increases, and conditions for payment of benefits.

CONCLUSION

The administration has offered a bold and comprehensive plan. By holding down health care costs, it can make our businesses more competitive and could lead to lower prices. It also can, over the long run, create jobs.

But beyond that, it accomplishes everything many of us tried to do in the last session, and much more. You may recall that last year we worked together to fashion four bills that, taken together, would have made important but incremental progress in extending health coverage to low income families. I helped develop those bills because at the time it was as far as I thought we could go in achieving some reform of the health care system. Things have changed.

I've been waiting a long time for a president willing to take the lead on this issue. I'm proud to be a part of an administration tackling this country's health care problem. It's a problem that can cripple our economy if we don't act.

President Clinton is committed to universal coverage and comprehensive benefits, with lifetime coverage, and coverage and cost protections for every American. He is committed to choice in health care.

Furthermore, President Clinton is intent on seeing that the quality of health care improves. He wants to reduce the paperwork burden for individuals and employers. He wants to make everyone responsible for health care. And, he is intent on financing the Health Security plan in a responsible manner. This plan does all of that with minimal government intrusion.

These are important principles. There are a number of ideas out there, but few meet all those tests -- particularly universality, comprehensive benefits defined from the outset, and responsible financing. Some would, for instance, attack the problem by only changing insurance requirements, but that approach leaves health care consumers without sufficient leverage in the marketplace.

The president wants a bipartisan solution to this problem. It is an American issue, not a partisan one. The president looks forward to working with the members of this Committee, and others in Congress, to enact a comprehensive and lasting reform of our health care system.

Thank you.

-30-

Mr. WAXMAN. Secretary Reich.

STATEMENT OF HON. ROBERT B. REICH

Secretary REICH. Thank you. With your permission, I will submit my formal remarks for the record and summarize them.

There is an intimate connection between jobs and health care in this country right now. The President's plan builds on that connection. We felt it was burdensome and inappropriate to go and create something entirely new.

Of families with health insurance, 90 percent now get it through their work. Of those without health insurance, about a third have a full-time worker in the family working full-time and working year-round. But that intimate connection between work and health care, without universal coverage and without some attempt to get control over those health care costs, creates and has created some enormous problems for American workers and enormous problems for American companies.

I want to outline very briefly four issues with regard to jobs and health care on which we need to keep our attention focused and which this plan deals with:

Issue 1: American competitiveness. Competitiveness, we have all been talking about it for years. It is a word that has gone directly from obscurity almost to meaninglessness without any intervening period of coherence.

I think when most of us talk about competitiveness, we are talking about the ability of American firms to compete internationally and the ability of American workers and American products to compete on their own.

What has happened is that the rise in health care costs—and they continue to rise far, far beyond inflation—has crippled American business. It has made it more difficult for American businesses to compete. We have the most expensive per-person health care system in the world. American auto producers are spending $1,100 per car sold on health care versus many of our competitors who are producing cars with a health care component of $500 or $600.

American companies are spending $200 billion on health care. If we got some control over spiralling health care costs, American companies would be able to invest more, create more jobs and create better jobs.

The extraordinary increase in health care costs, in other words, is not just a problem for Medicare, Medicaid, for the Federal budget; it is an enormous problem for American businesses. We need to get control over that problem.

The plan lowers aggregate business spending by the end of the decade, we estimate by $10 billion a year. That means more sales, more dollars, more jobs and more investment. Small businesses will be helped in particular.

Director Bowles will get into more specifics on this, but let me say, in outline, right now most employees of small businesses are insured. They get that insurance through their employer. But small businesses face a much higher administrative cost than large businesses, and small businesses are not able to exert the bargaining power with providers that large companies can exert.

As a result, small businesses' costs are 35 to 40 percent higher per employee than large businesses with regard to health care.

Moreover, getting some control over these costs, allowing small businesses to pool their bargaining power in health alliances, allows small businesses to compete effectively with large businesses.

By the way, small businesses do want to provide health care coverage, even those that don't. Why? Because by providing health care coverage they can compete with other businesses to get good employees. That is a tremendous attraction. How can you get the best employees if you are not providing health care?

Small businesses—many of them want to provide it who are not now providing it. Most employees of small businesses do get it already; those who do not get it in small businesses would like to, but they cannot afford it.

This proposal makes insurance affordable for small business. It also places a cap on premiums. Many small businesses, particularly those that employ a large number of minimum wage workers, would only be paying up to 3.5 percent of their payroll. That is a tremendous benefit to small businesses.

Second, let me point out the effects of this plan on labor mobility. There are misallocations right now in the labor markets. One misallocation is called, colloquially, "job lock."

The problem is that a lot of people who are capable of moving on to a better job, want to move on to a better job, but they are often unwilling or often scared to leave their present employer for fear that they will lose their health insurance. They are not sure the next employer will give them the same health insurance.

Forty percent of insurers do not provide insurance to employees with a preexisting condition. If you have a preexisting condition, it is not at all clear that you can move to the next employer. There is a great deal of fear out there with regard to job mobility.

There are estimates that up to 30 percent of employees right now would like to move to a better job, but cannot and will not because of job lock.

Another issue with regard to labor mobility has to do with welfare lock. Estimates are, from 16 to 25 percent of the current welfare population would like to get off welfare, could get off welfare. They are there because they are afraid of losing their Medicaid, they are worried about losing their medical insurance. If I get off welfare, what will happen to me and my family with regard to medical care?

Again, this plan eliminates job lock and it eliminates welfare lock. It enables the labor market to move more smoothly. It allows people to move to places where they can get jobs and get better jobs.

Disability lock might be a third colloquialism. Many people with disabilities also are afraid to switch jobs. Some can't get jobs in the first place because the employers will not provide health insurance, because insurance companies will not provide the insurance to people with disabilities.

We have seen a shift to part-time employees and temporary employees. Many employers are shifting to part-time and temporary workers because they cannot afford the same kind of health insurance that they are providing their full-time workers. That kind of shift is not necessarily good for the employees or the employers. Both would rather not make that shift, but in many circumstances, they feel they have to because of the cost of medical care as it is now constructed.

Finally, the plan would make it easier for employees to take early retirement, but are afraid now that if they leave their business they will lose their health care.

We estimate 350,000 to about 600,000 employees would take early retirement between the ages of 55 and 65, opening up all kinds of job opportunities for younger people. Under this plan, they will have health insurance.

A third effect has to do with occupational shifts. One of the purposes of this plan is to reduce the size of the paper health care sector. Let me put it delicately—that is the sector that is involved in administrative paper pushing, putting data into computers, taking data out of computers, monitoring claims.

We would expect a reduction in the paper health care sector, but an increase in employment in the primary health care sector, the actual people who are providing health care. It is not just high-tech, good, health care jobs; it is also relatively low-tech jobs, such as home health care.

A lot of studies show it is much more efficient to provide health care for many people at home rather than at the hospital. We expect a substantial increase in the demand for home health care workers when we get the incentives correct, so hospitals and insurance companies simply don't add gold plating, keep people in hospitals who don't have to stay in hospitals.

Number four, let me say a word about the effects on employment among minimum wage workers. There has been some misinformation about this. Let me try to clear the air.

With the offsetting subsidies in this plan, employers would not be spending more than 35 cents an hour, and minimum wage employees would cost employers around 15 cents an hour in small firms. Now, 15 to 35 cents as an addition to the minimum wage of $4.25 would not have negative employment effects. It would not cause job loss.

There have been a number of studies. In 1990 and 1991, as this committee knows, the minimum wage was increased by far more than 7.9 percent, which is the maximum we are talking about here, with no negative employment effects. Study after study has shown that those minimum wages, 1990 and 1991 minimum wage increases, had no negative employment effects. In fact, to some extent, they induced more employment because people came into the market who would not otherwise want to come into the labor market.

I should add that the current minimum wage of $4.25 an hour is almost 25 percent below what it was two decades ago adjusted for inflation.

Two weeks ago, after reviewing all relevant studies, I concluded that the minimum wage could be increased moderately with no loss of employment. But I also noted at the time that I would be making a recommendation to the President on a minimum wage increase only after taking into account any added costs to employers of providing universal health coverage so that we make absolutely certain that there is no negative employment effect.

In conclusion, let me just say that although we don't have any model large enough to predict precisely what the employment effects are for one-seventh of the economy, our judgment is that the employment effects, taking all those positives and all of those potential negatives into account, would be negligible, about plus or minus one-half a percentage point on total aggregate employment.

But there will be, as I said, tremendous improvements in allocative efficiency in terms of labor mobility, in terms of American competitiveness and also in terms of new work in the primary care instead of the paper health care professions.

Thank you.

Mr. WAXMAN. Thank you very much, Mr. Reich.

[The prepared statement of Secretary Reich follows:]

**STATEMENT OF ROBERT B. REICH
SECRETARY OF LABOR
BEFORE THE
HOUSE ENERGY AND COMMERCE COMMITTEE
SUBCOMMITTEES ON
ENERGY AND POWER
AND
HEALTH AND THE ENVIRONMENT
OCTOBER 28, 1993**

HEALTH CARE REFORM

Mr. Chairmen, Members of the Committee. Thank you for giving me the opportunity to discuss the Administration's health care reform plan. These hearings demonstrate your commitment to a thorough exploration of an issue which is of profound importance to the Nation.

In the past month, President Clinton and the First Lady have each made historic appearances before Congress. They described for you a comprehensive plan for providing all Americans with health care coverage. This plan is based on six principles: security, simplicity, savings, choice, quality, and responsibility. Yesterday, the President and the First Lady returned to deliver the goods--the Administration's draft legislation.

Rather than repeat their descriptions of the principles and structure of the plan, today I will focus on the urgent need for health care reform and the substantial benefits it will bring for workers, business, and the economy.

The Cost of Doing Nothing

Even before the Administration's plan was unveiled, special interest groups, lobbyists, and sentries of the status quo were out in full force. Foremost among their dire predictions has been the complaint that we can't possibly afford to provide real health security for all Americans.

Mr. Chairmen, Members of the Committee, if there is one point we must agree upon, it's that we can't afford <u>not</u> to reform this badly broken health care system. Exploding health care costs are choking our economic competitiveness and robbing American workers of the fruits of their labor. Fundamental change is needed to ensure our future prosperity and security.

Americans will spend over $900 billion on health care this year. Next year, this amount will rise to nearly a trillion dollars. Since 1980, the nation's health costs have nearly quadrupled, growing at 2-3 times the rate of inflation. Health care's share of the gross domestic product (GDP) has risen from 9% to 14% during this period. If medical costs continue growing at this pace, health expenditures will be over 19% of GDP by the year 2000 and will swallow up 40% of all the real per capita GDP growth we will achieve from 1993-96. No other advanced industrialized nation spends more than 10% of GDP on health care.

These soaring costs are a function, in part, of a bloated and inefficient administrative structure. Over $45 billion of health care expenditures went for administrative expenses in 1992. And no wonder. Doctors, nurses, and hospital administrators must contend with 1500 different claims forms, most of which must be filled out by hand and submitted to more than 1000 different health insurers. We have heard endless horror stories about physicians and nurses spending hundreds of hours each year on paperwork instead of patient care. And on top of all this, fraud and abuse may account for up to 10% of U.S. health care costs.

Every dollar our society unnecessarily spends on health care is a dollar we can't spend on education, training, infrastructure, environmental protection, and other important needs. For American families, every dollar unnecessarily spent on health care is a dollar that can't be spent on food, clothes, transportation, household goods, tuition, or other expenditures that improve the quality of life.

Business currently spends over $200 billion on health care. Real business spending on health care per employee has risen by 200% since 1970. For business, every dollar unnecessarily spent on health care is a dollar that cannot be invested in wages, capital improvements, marketing, workforce development, or R&D. Remarkably, business health care expenditures now nearly equal after-tax profits.

These exploding health care costs are putting American companies at a competitive disadvantage in the world marketplace. For instance, health care costs add $1100 to the cost of an American car -- double the burden carried by Japanese imports. This disparity will continue to widen as heavy corporate obligations for retiree health care come due.

Health care costs are so high partly because $25 billion in costs for uncompensated care are shifted to companies that do provide insurance. Many people who cannot afford insurance wait until they are acutely ill to seek emergency room health care. Since these people cannot afford to pay for this expensive treatment, these costs show up in the rapidly rising price of premiums charged companies providing health care coverage.

As the President said in his address last month, rising health care costs are a special nightmare for small business, an important source of entrepreneurship and job creation in this country.

Health care premiums for small businesses are up to 35% higher than for large corporations. Even so, a majority of workers in businesses with fewer than 100 employees are offered health insurance by their employer. Small firms that provide insurance are at a competitive disadvantage with respect to both large firms and small businesses that do not provide coverage. To add insult to injury, the cost of premiums for companies that do insure is high in part because they are subsidizing the health care costs of their competitors' uninsured employees.

Rising workers' compensation medical costs are further increasing the health care burden on American firms, both small and large. Between 1980 and 1985, workers' compensation medical costs grew more than 1.5 times faster than medical costs generally. In 1991, medical payments reached $16.8 billion or about 40% of total workers' compensation benefits.

American workers spend $55 billion a year on premiums and out-of-pocket costs. In addition, the excessive cost of health insurance translates into lost wages or reductions in other forms of compensation. It is estimated that the average worker today would be earning $1000 more per year if the cost of health insurance had not outpaced wages over the past 15 years. If the cost of health insurance continues at the current pace, by the year 2000, workers may lose another $650 in annual wages. The Brookings Institute has estimated that rising health care costs have consumed 58% of workers' potential wage increases since 1980, and, unchecked, would soon consume 100%.

Workers are being asked to pay an increasing share of their health care costs. Health benefits were a key issue in more than one-half of the major strikes in 1990. In four-fifths of the strikes where health benefits were a major concern, employers' attempts to increase their employees' share of costs were at issue. Contract settlements have increasingly shifted health benefit costs to the workers.

Skyrocketing health care costs are only part of the problem for American workers. Of the 37 million uninsured in this country, a majority are workers and their families. Millions more American workers are, as the President said, just a pink slip away from losing their insurance. The tragedy of job loss is compounded by loss of health insurance. Surveys show that up to 30% of workers are locked into their current jobs because they fear their new employer may not offer insurance, or because someone in their family has a preexisting condition that would not be covered if they switched jobs.

Concerns about health insurance also contribute to "welfare lock." Studies show that a substantial number of non-working welfare recipients would be more likely to work if they could be assured of continuous health care coverage.

Among part-time workers, only 28% of those who work in large firms, and 6% of those who work in small firms, participate in health care plans at least partially supported by employers. Temporary workers have an even harder time qualifying for medical benefits.

The Remedy: The Clinton Plan

Let me move to the specific job effects of President Clinton's health care reform plan. The benefits of the plan can be best understood by analyzing the job consequences under the following four-point framework:

1. Competitiveness -- Lifting the extraordinary burden of health care costs from American companies will increase their competitiveness, resulting in higher profits, more investment, higher wages, and more jobs.

2. Worker Mobility -- Enabling people to keep their health insurance when they find a better job or leave welfare to join the job market will end job lock and welfare lock. Guaranteed coverage will also free individuals to join or start new businesses.

3. New Jobs -- Universal coverage will increase the demand for health care services and therefore expand the number of health-related jobs. For instance, dramatic growth in the use of home health care services will result in a significant increase in number of people needed to care for people at home.

4. Low Wage Workers -- The Clinton plan is designed to minimize any potential adverse employment effects on low-wage workers.

1. Competitiveness

Soaring health care costs are weighing down the competitiveness of American firms. The cost per product for health care in the United States is apt to be much higher than the health care cost per product manufactured in other countries. That makes our businesses less competitive, and less successful in the marketplace. When we get health care costs under control, we are making American industry more competitive.

Under the Administration's reform plan, no firm that participates in a regional alliance will pay more than 7.9% of its total payroll for the guaranteed comprehensive health benefits. This cap will lower costs for most large corporations, making it easier for them to hire future workers, give wage increases to existing workers, and invest in training, capital, equipment, and

R&D. They can also lower prices to increase competitiveness. Firms with older workforces will benefit from community rating and a reduction in the cost of fulfilling their obligations to early retirees. Firms will benefit from less-protracted labor-management disputes as the issue of providing guaranteed health care benefits is removed as a source of controversy. These effects will provide a much needed shot in the arm for manufacturing firms, which have borne more than their fair share of the nation's uncompensated health care costs.

The small businesses that are currently providing health insurance have a special stake in reform. While it is true that small businesses that now fail to insure their workers will pay more under the new system (since they pay nothing now), small businesses currently providing insurance will be much better off. Here are some of the ways:

- Small businesses that join together into regional alliances will be able to realize the same administrative efficiencies and cost advantages that large firms already enjoy.
- Firms with fewer than 75 workers and low wages will be eligible for discounts. Many small firms will pay as little as 3.5% of total payroll on health insurance.
- The Clinton plan will eliminate the free-rider problem and level the competitive playing field between businesses that currently provide insurance and those that don't. Firms will compete on the basis of the quality of their products and services, not on the ability to avoid health care costs.
- Small businesses are likely to experience less employee turnover once they are able to provide workers with good health insurance.
- Administrative costs for small business should decline significantly. Small firms currently pay as much as 40% of their health insurance expenditures on administrative activities. The President's plan will eliminate most of these administrative burdens.

These reforms will allow small businesses to better compete with large firms and will enhance their ability to generate jobs and pay higher wages.

The partial integration of workers' compensation medical costs into the new system will help lessen the burden that these costs impose on American industry. Under the President's plan, workers who are injured on the job will receive care through their regular health plan, and the doctor they have chosen. Employers will

77-929 O - 94 - 19

continue to buy separate insurance through workers' compensation insurance carriers on an experienced-rated basis. Regional alliances will set fee schedules for workers' compensation cases.

This policy will ensure that the cost savings of health care reform are passed on to the workers' compensation system, while preserving the employer's incentive to maintain a safe and healthful workplace. It also will eliminate wasteful disputes over which provider will treat a work-related injury. And the fee schedule will prevent providers from charging exorbitant fees for workers' compensation cases.

Large and small businesses alike will benefit from the plan's increased-emphasis on preventive care. This will result in fewer lost work days and a healthier, more productive workforce.

2. *Enhanced Mobility and Other Benefits for Workers*

The reform plan will provide substantial benefits to workers. First, the guarantee of comprehensive coverage will eliminate job lock, welfare lock, and other limitations on the mobility of workers in and out of the workforce. As the President said, if you switch jobs or lose your job, you're covered. If you're laid off, you're covered. If you have a preexisting condition, you're covered. If you're on Medicaid and you get a job, you're covered. If you decide to retire early, you're covered. If you are a part-time or temporary worker, you're covered. If you leave your job to start a new business, you're covered.

As a consequence, people will no longer feel they cannot get a better job because they fear that if they leave their present job, they will lose their health insurance. People on welfare will no longer feel that they cannot join the workforce, because they are afraid of losing their health insurance. Individuals who would like to start or join a small business will not be prevented by fear of losing their own health insurance or by the prohibitive costs and burdens of providing their employees with health insurance.

Second, by putting the brakes on health care inflation, the President's plan will allow workers to pay lower premiums, earn a higher income, and enjoy a better standard of living.

Third, the President's plan will guarantee workers a choice of plans, both in the regional and corporate alliances. Only 29% of companies with fewer than 500 employees currently offer any choice of plans. Under the new system, workers, not employers, will choose the plan that suits them best. They will have at least three categories of choices in the reformed system: an HMO, a PPO (preferred provider organization), and a fee-for-service plan.

And, in most cases, there will be several plans to choose from in each of these categories.

Fourth, by requiring all employers to contribute to their employees' health care coverage, the plan also eliminates the incentive to hire people based on their health insurance status rather than their productivity and qualifications. And firms will no longer have an incentive to hire part-time and temporary workers simply to avoid paying health care benefits.

3. The Reform Plan Will Create New Jobs and Occupational Shifts

Because the vast majority of large firms will pay less for health insurance, they will have more funds available for better wage increases, hiring new workers, and investment. Each of these results will stimulate the economy and increase employment. In addition, small businesses that already provide insurance will see lower costs under the reform plan, and will not face the uncertainty of unbridled rising costs. As a result, these firms also will be able to create more jobs and pay higher wages.

Increased demand for health care resulting from universal coverage will likely lead to short-term increases in employment in the health care industry. Thousands more nurses, physician's assistants, home health aides, and other non-physician health providers will be required to directly or indirectly support the health care system during the first few years.

Undoubtedly, the purpose of much of the reform plan is to reduce paperwork. We have seen an extraordinary increase in what may be called the "paper health care industry." A lot of people put data into computers and take data out of computers, monitor forms and process paper. These jobs would not grow as fast; in fact, many of these jobs may be eliminated.

The plan will contain a workforce development proposal to ensure an adequate supply and mix of health care workers in the new system. This program will also create new training and employment opportunities for workers in the health and insurance industries, offering them a chance to move to higher-wage, higher-skilled health care provider positions or to switch from one field to another.

4. Impact on Minimum Wage and Lower Skilled Workers

It is true that health care reform potentially places the greatest pressure on low wage workers in firms that do not now provide health insurance. The President's proposal contains a system of discounts that is specifically designed to alleviate this pressure. The plan limits the amount companies will pay to 7.9% of payroll for all businesses purchasing insurance through the regional alliances. This amounts to less than 35 cents per hour for a minimum wage worker. These lower paid workers are heavily concentrated in the smaller, low wage firms that will be eligible for additional subsidies under the reform plan. Many of these employers will pay as little as 3.5% of payroll, which amounts to only 15 cents per hour at the minimum wage.

Some have argued that even these minimal additional costs will cause job losses. The evidence simply does not support this view. These levels of cost increases would not even bring the current cost of minimum wage labor up to the real levels of the mid-1980's. Analyses of recent and prior increases in the minimum wage do not support the contentions of job losses that the critics have put forth. In both 1990 and 1991, the minimum wage was increased by far more than 7.9 per cent. Despite dire predictions of job losses by the same groups now making similar claims about health care reform, analyses of the effects of these increases on employment concluded that the impact was minimal and in some cases led to greater employment. Analyses of the history of changes in minimum wage laws have reached similar conclusions.

In any case, any worker who loses his or her job during the health care reform transition period will be eligible for enhanced retraining and employment services through a comprehensive dislocated workers program which the Administration will be developing in coordination with many of you. Workers will be eligible for services under this program regardless of the cause of their displacement.

Conclusion

In short, we cannot afford not to reform our current health care system. If we don't get costs under control and provide true health care security, many more jobs will be lost in the long-term as American businesses of all sizes are forced to spend an increasing share of their payroll on health care, eroding their competitive advantage in the world marketplace.

Even when change is in the best interest of all Americans, there is a natural fear of stepping beyond the status quo. I am convinced that many concerns about the President's plan have little to do with health care reform per se, and much to do with the pervasive anxieties arising from economic and social changes that are already affecting Americans. We cannot let these anxieties paralyze us and prevent necessary reforms. Our health and the health of our economy depends on our ability to provide health care security at an affordable price for all Americans.

I look forward to working closely with the members of this Committee in our efforts to improve the lives of American workers land their families.

Mr. WAXMAN. Mr. Bowles.

STATEMENT OF HON. ERSKINE B. BOWLES

Mr. BOWLES. Chairman Waxman, Chairwoman Collins, thank you for inviting me. Let me ask that my statement be made a part of the record, and I will speak to you from notes.

I think Secretary Reich and Secretary Bentsen have talked about the big-picture effect. I would like to talk to you about the effect of health care on small businesses.

I have had a chance to now go around the country. I have been holding a series of town hall meetings, and I have now had a chance to meet with literally thousands of small businesses. I have heard the same thing over and over again. My impression is that we cannot devise a health care system that is more anti-small business than the present current health care system that we have in this country.

Today, small businesses are experiencing average annual—I want to stress "annual"—increases in the cost of health care of 20 to 50 percent a year. Small businesses today are paying three times as much for the same insurance big business buys, and the rate of increase is 50 percent higher than the rate of increase for big businesses.

What are we able to buy for these literally skyrocketing increases in the cost of health care? Almost nothing. We are able to buy a bare-bones package or something that has such a huge deductible that it will only cover catastrophic events.

We are also subjected to almost every single abuse in the health care system, everything from occupational redlining to exclusions for preexisting conditions.

Prior to coming with the administration, one of the jobs I had was serving as president of the Juvenile Diabetes Foundation. My oldest son is a diabetic. I had a chance to meet with many parents of diabetic kids. A number worked for major corporations, who would have liked to have left that major corporation and started a small business but could not because they were locked in, because they had a preexisting condition.

I know as a former owner of a small business that when you go out to get insurance and the insurance company comes in and says, sure, we will offer you a great plan, but you have to exclude all these people who have preexisting conditions, they give up a pretty good rate. A year later when those people come on the payroll and come in the plan, the rates go so high that the insurance is something you cannot afford.

Those are not the only problems small business faces today. One of the things I have heard small business people talk about over and over again is something that I term almost the "hassle factor." The small business person doesn't have any power in trying to sit down and negotiate—and calling it a "negotiation" is almost a joke—with the insurance companies.

They have all the power in the market place today, it is all in the hands of the providers. They have changed the terms and conditions. They have a different set of accounting rules. We, the small business people, when we try to sit down to negotiate with them, we have to take time away from our customers and from managing our businesses. We don't have benefits departments, so we really don't have any power to negotiate with the insurance company.

In addition, when you talk to the self-employed, the self-employed, as Secretary Bentsen said, are treated totally unfairly under the present system. The self-employed get to deduct 25 percent of the cost of their health care and everybody else gets to deduct 100 percent. That is not fair.

Worker's Compensation. The only item on my income statement that grew at a faster rate than health care was Worker's Compensation. So today small businesses have the worst of all worlds. We have skyrocketing increases in the cost of our health care and we are subjected to every abuse in the system.

I come from the private sector, and I believe in the private sector. We have done everything we could to hold down the cost of health care. We have tried switching programs, we have tried managed programs, we have tried self-insurance, we have tried reducing benefits, and we have tried passing along a bigger share of the costs to our employees. Nothing helps. The cost of health care continues to rise; it rises at 25 to 50 percent a year for small businesses.

I am here to tell you that my opinion is that there is no solution to this health care mess this country is in without universal coverage. You can believe those 37 million people that Secretary Bentsen mentioned a minute ago get coverage. They get it at the emergency room of the hospital at four or five times the cost that they would pay in the doctor's office. Who pays for that? The small business people do. That is why our costs increase at a 20 to 50 percent annual rate.

When the President tried to attack these issues head on in this plan, first of all, what this plan does is, it forms alliances. What these alliances are are buying groups, and what these buying groups cause to happen is they shift the power of the marketplace. They change the supply and demand equation from favoring the provider and the insurer to favoring the consumer. That is important for us. That shifts the power in favor of the consumer and the small business person.

The second thing we worked on was simplification, taking cost out of the system going to things like standardized forms, uniform bill, electronic claims processing.

Today, in the average doctor's office a nurse—a nurse—spends 50 percent of her time filling out forms; the average is 19 forms per patient, per day, in an average hospital. As Congressman McMillan knows, I served on the Charlotte-Mechlenberg Hospital Authority. At a hospital, 25 cents out of every dollar we spend today is spent on administrative costs. That doesn't buy a nickel's worth of health care. Ten cents out of every dollar we spend today goes to fraud and abuse; that is $80 billion. We can take cost out of this system.

The President wanted to be sure that this plan was good for small business. This plan offers small business exactly what they said they wanted. It offers absolutely rock solid, comprehensive, real insurance. It is not some bare-bones plan or a plan that just offers catastrophic coverage, but real insurance.

The third thing is, he made it affordable. That is why the caps and subsidies that Secretary Bentsen and Secretary Reich talked about are in there. Those subsidies are in there to hold down the cost of health care for small business, to make it affordable.

But if they are right and if that is true, that small business will be able to supply its workers with rock solid, comprehensive, real insurance at a cost of less than $1 a day per employee.

The fourth thing this plan does is, it has the mechanisms built into it to hold down the cost of health care so it doesn't grow at 20 to 50 percent a year.

The fifth thing it does is, it outlaws the abuses—no more exclusions for preexisting conditions.

The sixth thing it does is, the hassle factor is gone. We now have some power of the marketplace on our side. We have the alliances to negotiate on our behalf in order to bring down the cost of health care. I truly believe that if the small business people don't get scared off by the rhetoric of people talking about the "M" word, about mandates, I believe if they look at this plan and lay this plan side by side, by the ones they currently have, the vast majority will see that they get better coverage at lower costs.

Not everybody wins under this plan; that doesn't happen. But the vast majority will have better coverage at lower costs. For the small businesses that don't have health care, what they have said they want is to be able to provide health care, but they cannot. They say the reasons they can't is because today: A, they cannot afford it; B, what they can buy just isn't worth buying; and C, if they can afford it today, they cannot afford it tomorrow because the costs will go up 20 to 50 percent a year.

We have met those problems head on and I think this will be good for small business. Thank you.

[The prepared statement of Mr. Bowles follows:]

U.S. SMALL BUSINESS ADMINISTRATION
WASHINGTON, D.C. 20416

STATEMENT OF ERSKINE B. BOWLES

ADMINISTRATOR

U.S. SMALL BUSINESS ADMINISTRATION

BEFORE THE

HOUSE ENERGY AND COMMERCE COMMITTEE

OCTOBER 28, 1993

HEALTH CARE REFORM

Mr. Chairman, I am pleased to testify today on the economic effects of the Health Security Act on our nation's small businesses. I want you to know up front that I am excited about this plan and I am excited about what it can do for small business. For the first time ever, small business will be able to buy rock solid, comprehensive insurance at an affordable rate. I believe this plan will be good for small business and it will create jobs.

I am also concerned by what could happen to our country and to small business if we don't enact comprehensive health care reform and do it now.

RISING HEALTH COSTS: THE BIG PICTURE

Mr. Chairman, the statistics reflecting the current health care system are frightening. Every month, two million people lose their health care coverage. During the next two years, one out of four Americans will be without health care for some period of time. There are 37 million Americans without insurance today, and another 22 million who are underinsured.

The rising costs of health care are out of control. The U.S. now spends more per capita on health care than any other country in the world; more than double what Japan spends and 40% more than Canada, which is the country that devotes the second largest amount of its income to health care.

Twenty-five years ago, health care consumed 5.9% of GDP. In 1992, that number topped 14% to reach a staggering total of $840 billion. By the year 2000 we will see health care spending top $1.6 trillion and cost more than 19% of GDP if this trend continues. If we do nothing, health care costs will consume about two-thirds of the increase of GDP in the rest of this decade. This is simply unacceptable. Clearly, from a macro economic viewpoint, we have a serious problem in this country with our health care costs.

SKYROCKETING HEALTH CARE COSTS HURT SMALL BUSINESS

Small business is faced with the worst of all worlds with respect to rising health care costs. The two-thirds of small businesses that are still able to afford to provide their employees with health care coverage are experiencing skyrocketing cost increases. Health care costs have increased for small business at a rate of 20% to 50% a year. Small businesses pay 35% more for the same insurance than do big businesses, and the rate of increase in the cost of health care for small businesses is 50% higher than the rate of increase for big businesses. Unfortunately, the smaller the company, the more disproportionate are the costs they pay for health insurance.

ABUSES OF CURRENT SYSTEM DISADVANTAGE SMALL BUSINESS

Not only have small businesses experienced skyrocketing increases in the cost of health care, they also have been subjected to every one of the most blatant abuses that occur within the health care system. These abuses include such practices as occupational redlining, whereby insurers will simply refuse to cover entire industries perceived to be too high a risk. These industries often include such basic businesses as automobile dealerships, florists, grocery stores, barber and beauty shops, construction companies, and trucking firms.

Some insurance companies also engage in price baiting and gouging, by offering discounted rates for the first year of coverage, to be followed by much higher rates in the next year when pre-existing condition exclusions expire. Many insurance companies refuse to renew insurance policies if one of the employees of a small business gets sick and really needs insurance. When this happens, the insurer may either pull the policy or jack up the cost to an unaffordable level.

OTHER WAYS THE CURRENT SYSTEM PENALIZES SMALL BUSINESS

Unlike large firms, small business owners generally don't have a benefits department. The small business owner or a valued employee must perform all the functions of such a department. As a result, the small business owner not only loses valuable time away from his business, but he also is at a disadvantage when trying to negotiate the purchase of a benefit for his employees that is extraordinarily complicated to understand and is constantly changing.

A self-employed individual also operates at a disadvantage because of the inequitable tax policies for the self-employed. A self-employed individual is only allowed to deduct as a business expense up to 25% of the cost of health care coverage. All other businesses are able to deduct the full amount they pay for coverage. This is clearly unfair to the self-employed and almost, by definition, increases their cost of insurance for their families.

Workers compensation has also become a bigger burden to small business owners. Increasing at an even faster rate than the rest of the health care system, workers compensation medical costs grew more than one and a half times as fast as medical costs between 1980 and 1985.

Clearly, small businesses have a large stake in solving the health care crisis in this country.

SOLUTION: UNIVERSAL COVERAGE

Today, together with individuals, three major groups finance the cost of health care in this country:

1. The government;

2. Self-insured companies -- generally big corporations; and

3. Businesses which insure through traditional insurance companies -- generally small businesses.

These groups finance virtually all of the nation's health care spending. When one of these groups pays less, the others must pay more to cover the cost.

Large, self-insured plans frequently have a great deal of clout in a given area and can negotiate with providers to reduce the impact of this cost shift on them. Small employers, however, have no ability to reduce this cost shift and must bear its full brunt.

This same cost shifting scenario also occurs when providers deliver uncompensated care, primarily to the uninsured. Make no mistake about it, the uninsured are provided health care in this country. They simply get it at the emergency room at four or five times the cost it would be at the doctor's office. And because there is no insurance coverage, someone has to pay for this treatment. Today much of the cost of the uninsured is shifted to

small business. Clearly, no part of the business community is hit harder by the high cost of the uninsured than small business.

A solution that doesn't offer universal coverage for all Americans is simply no solution. Unless the 37 million uninsured Americans are provided insurance, we will continue to have the cost shifting that has gone on in the past. Unfortunately, the sector of the economy that will bear a big portion of this cost shift will be the small businesses that are currently paying as much as 35% more for the same insurance that big business pays today.

HOW THE HEALTH SECURITY ACT WORKS FOR SMALL BUSINESS

The Health Security Act provides small business with comprehensive insurance coverage at an affordable rate. The President worked hard to give small business comprehensive and affordable insurance that couldn't be just taken away.

The Health Security Act will control the skyrocketing cost of health insurance by increasing competition in health care, reducing administrative costs, and imposing discipline on the system by giving small businesses and consumers buying clout. The Act shifts the power of the marketplace to benefit the consumer.

The Act simplifies the health care system and eliminates waste. The plan reduces administrative costs through standardized forms, uniform billing, electronic claims submission, creating a uniform benefits package, and malpractice reform.

The Act also reduces the enormous burden of paperwork and administration that currently falls on small business. The cost of administering coverage in small companies declines because they purchase through health alliances that exercise market power reserved only for large employers in today's system.

The Health Security Act will give small business what it needs by offering:

1. **Rock solid, comprehensive insurance coverage -- not a bare bones plan or just catastrophic coverage, but real insurance. The Act will provide subsidies to businesses with 75 or fewer workers if their wages average less than $24,000.**

2. **Affordable coverage with discounts to hold down the cost of health insurance for small businesses. National Small Business United estimates that the average small business that currently provides its employees insurance has a payroll of $15,600. If that is the case, then these small businesses will see their annual insurance cost fall to only $827 per employee. That's about $2.25 a day per employee, representing a significant savings for that average small business currently purchasing insurance.**

3. Health care costs that are under control to ensure that the cost of health care will increase by approximately the rate of growth of wages, as opposed to current skyrocketing costs.

4. Elimination of abuses of the current health care system. If one worker in a small business or his or her dependent becomes seriously ill, the business will no longer see their rates jacked up beyond belief or lose coverage for the sick employee or dependent.

5. Full, 100 percent tax deductibility of coverage for the self-employed instead of the current 25% deductibility.

6. Choice to employees to choose their own health plan, something that most employees don't have today.

7. Finally, the plan removes the hassle that small businesses must now undergo in dealing with insurance companies and frees up valuable time for the small business owner to manage and grow his or her business.

Mr. Chairman, I am confident that when small business owners who provide insurance compare the Health Security Act to their current plan, the vast majority of them will see both a decrease in cost and better coverage. Small business owners who have wanted to offer their employees insurance but couldn't afford it will see a comprehensive plan that they can afford. And those very small businesses that pay low wages are going to be able to offer their employees rock-solid, comprehensive insurance coverage that will cost the small business owner as little as $1.00 to $2.00 a day per employee.

Clearly, not every small business will pay less under the Health Security Act, but the vast majority will. Those small businesses that have been scared off by the constantly escalating cost of health insurance and the relatively poor coverage will see a plan that they can afford to offer.

In summary, Mr. Chairman, I am convinced that small business owners, when they examine the facts, will realize the value of the Health Security Act. They will understand that the Act is good for small business.

Thank you.

Mr. WAXMAN. I thank each of you for your testimony. I want to call on the members of the subcommittees to pursue questions under the 5-minute rule. Let me start.

We learned recently that the President's proposal includes a cap on the funds that provide subsidies for small firms, low-wage workers and retirees. While the administration has made it clear that its estimates of the subsidy costs are conservative, we understand there is an allowance of about 15 percent above what these costs are estimated to be. Nevertheless, there is a lot of concern that the estimates may be off and that the subsidies for one or more of the health alliances may not be adequate.

Can you describe for us what happens if the Federal subsidy cap is hit, what is the impact on the employers and workers in those alliances which need more subsidy dollars in order to guarantee the bill's basic benefits package? Will they be left holding the bag?

Secretary BENTSEN. Mr. Chairman, what we have done is, first we set up a global budget to try to see that this did not result.

Second, we made a conservative estimate as to what the cost of these discounts would be. Then to be certain, if those things were wrong, we would put a cap on that entitlement. If all of those things are to no avail and if that cap is threatened, what you would have is a report that was taking place continuously to show what the costs were. If it was in danger of reaching that cap, you could have some prior notice of it insofar as planning.

We saw that same type of thing in Social Security in the early 1980's, and we ended up with the Greenspan Commission report and Congress acting expeditiously. The President would advise the Congress of his recommendations to take care of any shortfall.

Mr. WAXMAN. In other words, you think the Congress would have to take care of it?

Secretary BENTSEN. That is correct.

Mr. WAXMAN. If the Congress did not take care of it, what would be the impact on the alliances if they did not get the subsidy dollars.

Secretary BENTSEN. I will tell you as a former Member of this Congress for 22 years that I don't look on that as a real possibility. Congress would face up to that responsibility.

Mr. WAXMAN. Let me mention to you that we held a hearing a couple of weeks ago. The President's plan would control the health care costs by limiting the rate of increases in health care premiums.

When we had our hearing, the Health Insurance Association of American said that these premium increases limitations are price controls that would "entail extensive government rationing."

The Council for Affordable Health Insurance told us at that hearing, and I quote, "Governmentally mandated behavioral controls in health care will assuredly lead to popular resistance like we have never seen before in this country."

Senator Bentsen, as a former insurance executive, you know a great deal about this business. Mr. Reich, as an economist, you recognize price controls when you see them; and neither of you looks like an instigator of popular uprising.

Do you gentleman believe that the premium limits that the President has proposed are price controls and that they will lead to extensive government rationing, resulting in popular resistance like we have never seen in this country?

Secretary BENTSEN. First, let me say that I think what we would see would be competition among those companies in the industry. I think that that will be the discipline. I have great confidence in the private sector.

As you state, I was a businessman for quite a number of years. I would rather rely on private sector competition, and I think that would be the discipline that takes effect under the administration plan.

Mr. WAXMAN. Mr. Reich?

Secretary REICH. Let me say that, right now, all of the incentives in health care are toward having more and more gold plating. There are very few incentives, if any, which are operating on insurance companies or on providers to minimize costs.

This plan turns the incentives around because health alliances will be shopping. They will be getting bids. There is a requirement that if an alliance's average premium exceeds its budget, an assessment is imposed on each plan whose premium rate of increase exceeds the budget target.

The primary vehicle here is competition. That is why the name, "managed competition," managed in terms of premium caps, other Federal guidelines, competition in terms of getting health care providers' to compete on the basis not just of quality, but also of costs. We will do nothing to compromise the quality, but the cost is out of control.

Mr. WAXMAN. Thank you.

Mrs. Collins.

Mrs. COLLINS. Secretary Bentsen, although the President's plan exempts people whose income places them at or below 150 percent of the poverty line from contributing to the premiums, it would require contributions from those whose income is just barely above that 150 percent of poverty.

So my question is, how was this threshold chosen, first of all; and second, do you agree that it is asking too much of people whose incomes are just above that threshold, including perhaps food stamp recipients, to be paying hundreds of dollars for health care each year?

Secretary BENTSEN. Chairwoman Collins, it is my belief and I think, the President's belief, that everyone who can should pay part of the cost of health care, that that is an incentive or discipline to make everyone understand what it means to have increased benefits and what the cost of those benefits will be.

Now insofar as low-income people, what has been done, is to create substantial discounts or subsidies. As you get cross-subsidizing for low-income people, you will help them afford their coverage.

Mrs. COLLINS. Although the President's package encourages the purchase of private long-term care insurance by providing for the first time a tax deduction on premiums paid toward that insurance, some critics have expressed concern in recent years that purchase of this insurance should not be broadly encouraged since it is only appropriate for very wealthy Americans.

The critics have also suggested that Federal tax benefits for the purchase of long-term care insurance is inappropriate because it subsidizes these very wealthy folks while doing nothing for other Americans.

I would like to know how you respond to these critics.

Secretary BENTSEN. In that instance, we have proposed a tax deduction for long-term care insurance, but we have tied it to a standard-package so that there will not be excess benefits paid on a tax favored basis. But it will also, I think, encourage insurance companies to be competitive in offering policies.

Mrs. COLLINS. Secretary Reich, if the Cooper bill, with its voluntary approach toward employee participation, were to become law, would you tell us how employees of businesses that choose not to participate would be covered and also whether those employees or groups of people would be uninsured if that were the case?

Wouldn't that be continuing the cycle of cost-shifting to those who do have the insurance, and if that is the case, wouldn't health insurance costs continue to spiral upward?

Secretary REICH. Yes. In the present circumstances, somebody who is unemployed and who has no income does get health care, but gets the care usually very late in the process after things have deteriorated—it is emergency health care; it is extremely expensive health care; it is paid for ultimately by insurers and providers, ultimately by businesses and individuals who do have health insurance—that is estimated to be about $25 or $30 billion a year or more.

Under the Clinton plan, everyone would be taken care of. The emphasis would be on prevention. Even people who do not have a job or families where there is an employed member would be protected, and they would have every incentive, through the health alliances, to get protection and preventive service before health care problems mounted.

In other words, the plan not only avoids the cost-shifting that occurs right now, but it also places a much greater emphasis on prevention for the entire population; which is much cheaper than waiting for problems to get so bad that you have to use the emergency room where you really are often dealing with catastrophic problems.

Mrs. COLLINS. Thank you.

Mr. WAXMAN. Thank you, Mrs. Collins.

The gentlemen from Virginia, Mr. Bliley.

Mr. BLILEY. Thank you, Mr. Chairman.

Secretary Bentsen, as you know also, budget is the process by which Congress and the President allocate scarce resources among competing priorities.

The administration's health care proposal will have the Federal Government reallocating hundreds of billions of dollars, or approximately 14 percent of the economy. If allowed to do so, off budget, Congress and the public will be deprived of essential measurements of the fiscal economic impact of the policy decisions.

This is a critical issue, because the administration's reform proposal calls the employer's payroll tax a non-Federal private transaction. Although universal coverage is popular, taxes are not. I am quite aware of that. So the administration, it appears to me, is attempting to characterize a mandatory tax in a large Federal regulatory activity as a private transaction. I strongly disagree.

When legislation invokes the sovereign power of the government to compel the payment of funds, defines the class of beneficiaries, guarantees specifically benefits and establishes a Federal regulatory apparatus, that legislation has created a Federal activity financed by a Federal tax.

Rather than debate what is and what is not a tax, all we have to do is look at the legislation passed last year when you were chairman of the Senate Finance Committee. The law is—the United Mine Workers of America health benefits plan, which addresses the financing of health benefits for United Mine Workers of America retired coal workers, if you look at them both, side by side, as you have before you—and I assume the members of the committee now have it—you will see that, what happened with the United Mine Workers bill.

[The charts follow:]

United Coal Miner "Orphan Retiree" Health Benefits

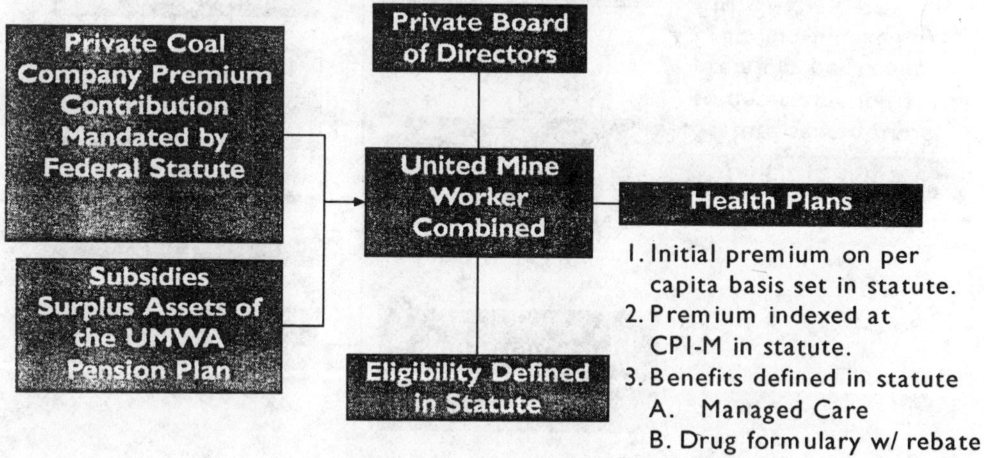

Alliance Structure -- Administration Plan

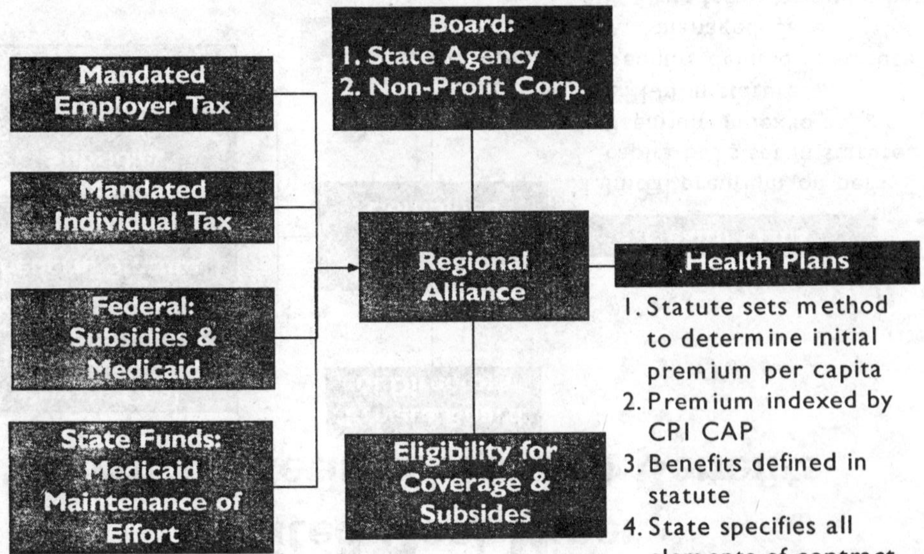

1. Statute sets method to determine initial premium per capita
2. Premium indexed by CPI CAP
3. Benefits defined in statute
4. State specifies all elements of contract, solvency, enrollment, marketing, reinsurance, etc.

Mr. BLILEY. They mandated that the coal operators contribute a premium for the benefits. They set up a private board of directors. They defined the beneficiaries and they had defined what the benefits were to be.

Now, you look at the alliance structure in the administration plan and you have a mandated employer tax, a mandated individual tax, Federal subsidies in Medicaid, State funds in Medicaid, maintenance efforts. You have a regional alliance. You have a board appointed by the President. You name who is eligible and you define the benefits.

Now, structurally, Senator Bentsen—I still want to call you Senator, you always will be—Mr. Secretary, would you tell me what the difference is?

Secretary BENTSEN. I have been dealing with that concern for years. Sometimes the line between premiums and taxes is not really clear.

Let me tell you what we are doing in this instance. I think in this instance it can be fairly characterized as a premium.

Mr. BLILEY. Didn't we start that way last year?

Secretary BENTSEN. If I might, let me say that what we are talking about in this instance, are premiums which are paid to the regional alliance and which then flow through the plan to provide insurance coverage for the workers. The premiums don't come to the Federal or the State government for that matter.

I think that when most people think of taxes, they think of something paid to government. Now, when you talk about something that is being mandated on these employers, that mandate is similar to what the government does when we require employers to pay a minimum wage.

Mr. BLILEY. But I——

Secretary BENTSEN. Congressman, I did not interrupt you. Let me make my point.

Mr. BLILEY. My time is limited.

Secretary BENTSEN. Go ahead.

Mr. BLILEY. This is exactly what happened with the coal miner. However, CBO and OMB said that because of the sovereign power of the government mandates this, because you define the benefits, because you name the beneficiaries, that it is a Federal activity and it is included on page 1153 of this document, the Federal Budget for 1994.

Now, if they come back, they must say that this is the same thing. That is what I am saying.

I realize that the administration would like not to have it on the budget. But the fact is, it should be there or we are going to have a serious problem. I believe that it must be there.

Secretary BENTSEN. I must say to you, I respect your point of view, but I think the retired coal miners' case was very much a special case. I think OMB has looked at that issue and has concluded to the contrary.

Workers negotiated for those benefits through collective bargaining. They earned the retiree health care that they were promised.

Let me further state that what we are talking about here, the amount of premium that is paid by the employer for any employee is directly related to the services that they will be receiving, in return, from the employees. That is not necessarily the case at all on a tax. So I think there is a clear difference here.

Mr. BLILEY. With all due respect, Mr. Secretary, CBO looked at it and they concluded otherwise. That is why it is in the budget.

Mr. WAXMAN. Thank you, Mr. Bliley.

Mr. Stearns.

Mr. STEARNS. Thank you, Mr. Chairman. I want to continue along with the questioning my colleague from Virginia talked about.

Mr. Bowles talked about the "M" word, mandate. We have not mentioned the "T" word, which is taxes. There are two others things we should be concerned about, the "I" word, which is insolvency; and the "B" word, which would eventually, of course, be bankruptcy, I think, in terms of mandates; and taxes are going to cause insolvency and are going to cause bankruptcy. So I have almost put those four together, MTIB, as an acronym meaning mandates, taxes, insolvency and bankruptcy.

Mr. Bowles knows from a small business standpoint how these affect small companies. My question to Secretary Bentsen is—just yes or no, and then I want to ask my question—the 7.9 percent on employers, the mandated, is that considered a tax, yes or no?

Secretary BENTSEN. 7.9 percent?

Mr. STEARNS. Just yes or no, and I would like to reclaim my time.

Secretary BENTSEN. No, no, no. You cannot do that to me. I have been in this business too long. I have given you an extensive answer on that.

Mr. STEARNS. No, no. Reclaiming my time, Mr. Chairman.

If you don't answer yes or no, then I can't get into my argument.

Secretary BENTSEN. Why don't you give me your argument anyway?

Mr. STERNS. As a small business person, you pay the FUTA tax, which is the Federal unemployment tax you pay to the State and you pay it to the Federal Government. In some States, you pay it all to the State, but in others you pay it separately.

My question is, aren't State unemployment insurance funds listed on the budget as a Federal revenue and outlay? If you turn to page 788 of the appendix to the budget of the United States Government—and it is right here—in all 50 States, unemployment insurance accounts are on budget. All of the State tax moneys are shown on the Federal budget as revenues and all expenditures are shown as Federal outlays.

Why is this so? Because the activities—is it defined as a mandatory obligation under the Federal Government.

Secretary Bentsen, if State unemployment trust funds are listed on the Federal budget because of the Federal FUTA tax mandate, doesn't it logically follow that the President's 7.9 percent payroll tax and alliance health care expenditures which will be mandated in Federal law should also be on budget?

Secretary BENTSEN. Once again, I tried to point out to you the differences here between what I think a premium is and what a tax is. I think this is clearly falling into the position of being a premium and it is properly treated.

Getting back to the point again, FUTA taxes are paid to the government, for example, and in this instance, we are talking about a situation where insurance premiums go to the alliances and they in turn pay for services. Many times, I don't feel the taxes I pay necessarily correlate to the services I get out of this government. That is quite a difference.

Mr. STEARNS. This goes to the concern of insolvency and bankruptcy. With a cap that limits premiums collected and an open-ended obligation to provide mandated benefits, many plans will be either forced to withdraw from the market, or worse, become insolvent.

In the event of a plan's bankruptcy, the State may assess other plans in the alliance up to 2 percent of their premiums. Won't the additional assessment of even 2 percent push other plans into bankruptcy given the tight margins resulting from premium caps?

Secretary BENTSEN. I would not anticipate that happening. There are other things that can be accomplished too. There can be a reduction in benefits taking place. You can get into a situation where you will get an extension and a delay in the benefits being applied. We have already set up the system to bring that about.

I think, too, that managed competition is going to take care of this, I believe in the private sector.

Mr. STEARNS. Secretary Reich?

Secretary REICH. Congressman, if I could have an opportunity to return to the definitional question you raised, I think it is critically important here to understand that most employers right now are paying health insurance. The American private sector is bearing the burden of over $200 billion a year.

Under this plan, we are going to reduce that burden. So the analogy simply does not hold.

Before 1935, before unemployment insurance, for example, you did not have the majority of employers paying unemployment insurance. You did not have unemployment insurance costs skyrocketing as they are now for the public and private sector. There is simply no relationship between the two, just like we require workers to have a healthy and safe workplace, most employers already do.

We are, under this plan, going to require all employers, to provide 80 percent of the average cost of the premiums. But again, understand the context; these costs are rising so fast as to make American businesses uncompetitive.

Mr. WAXMAN. Thank you.

Mr. Wyden.

Mr. WYDEN. Thank you. Let me commend all three of you for an excellent presentation. It seems to me what you have done is made the case that over the last decade medical costs have essentially been a wrecking ball pounding away at our economy and you have laid the case for reform.

Let me start with you, Secretary Bentsen, on the issue of assistance for the low income and the small businesses and early retirees. I share a number of Chairman Waxman's concerns. Let me ask you about a specified way it might be addressed.

What would you think about the idea with respect to the low income and the assistance for the vulnerable groups of devising a mechanism whereby congressional budget decisions affecting this assistance would be legally tied to other budget decisions that affect well-off Americans with lots of bargaining power?

That way we wouldn't just say, well, Congress will do the right thing. Because I think a lot of Americans are skeptical about that. But we would force the trade-off right within the budget so that if assistance for low income, in effect, was to be altered, there would have to be some sort of trade-off in terms of the politically powerful.

There are a number of areas to look at, tax deductibility where there are a lot of well-off Americans who receive those benefits. There are a lot of things we can look at, but I am asking you about the mechanism as a fairer way to deal with what Chairman Waxman talks about as a very understandable concern.

Secretary BENTSEN. Let me state that what we just passed in the budget was a tax increase on those most fortunate in our economy. It was a material tax increase, and that was to address certain needs of the less fortunate—that is to help us improve and expand the earned income tax credit, and to help us increase the amount of food stamps available to families.

We have done a substantial amount of income transfer to try to assist low-income families.

Mr. WYDEN. Mr. Secretary, with all due respect, I am not talking about income transfer. I am talking about spending reductions that would affect politically powerful people if, in fact, the systems for the low income are going to be reduced.

Secretary BENTSEN. With all due respect, I answered that I think we have moved and we have moved rather aggressively, and I think justifiably, in both reducing the budget deficit and, in turn, doing some things to try to help low-income people.

I think, with the income transfers that are already taking place in the system, that in effect the very minimal amount that they will have to pay for these benefits will not undercut that income transfer.

So I think we have gone a long way to address that concern.

Mr. WYDEN. I know that you do, Mr. Secretary. I just don't share your confidence that the Congress will do the right thing in terms of ensuring a fair shake for the poor.

I am interested in working with the administration on developing a formal mechanism within the budget, so that if assistance to low-income people is in some way reduced, that the politically powerful are going to be nicked a bit, too.

Secretary BENTSEN. We will be delighted to consider your proposal. I know your record. I know your concern and your responsibility.

Mr. WYDEN. That is very fair. I appreciate it.

Secretary Reich, at this very moment, my State, the State of Oregon, has a very bold plan to give health benefits to about 300,000 uninsured workers. We can do it about a year before the President's plan.

I think there are some other States in the same sort of boat as well. The key for us to do it is to get an ERISA waiver. I am about to introduce legislation to give Oregon an ERISA waiver. Can we count on your support?

Secretary REICH. I will have to look closely and carefully at your legislation before we support an ERISA waiver. We are not planning on providing any waivers before or after the plan.

Again, when you provide an ERISA waiver, remember what you are doing. We are talking about ERISA, which is designed to protect the pension and benefits of workers. That is a national statute which provides national minimum standards.

I am happy to look at what you come up with, but there is an extremely high burden of proof.

Mr. WYDEN. My time is up. I am going to try to make my legislation dovetail as closely as possible to your ERISA proposal. I want to see the uninsured workers get help as soon as possible. My State and others have gone a long way and can do it earlier.

Secretary REICH. Let me say quickly that the Clinton plan is designed to provide States with as much flexibility as possible without losing the fundamental principles of controlling costs and also providing these benefits to everyone who needs them.

Mr. WAXMAN. Thank you, Mr. Wyden. Mr. Bilirakis.

Mr. BILIRAKIS. Thank you, Mr. Chairman. I wish to join you and the rest of our panel in welcoming Secretary Bentsen and the other members of the panel.

I also would say the word "consensus" is used. You probably would agree with me, Mr. Secretary, that there is consensus in the entire Congress on both sides of the aisle that something needs to be done in terms of health delivery.

I certainly commend the administration for moving forward in that regard. It is a tough row to hoe. The President himself admits it.

During your testimony and the testimony of the others, you have mentioned "sub-issues," which I call, clearly, "consensus issues." They are in virtually every piece of legislation that has been introduced this Congress and also in the President's plan. I am referring to health insurance portability.

Secretary Reich talked about job lock. There is so much of that taking place. There are many people who cannot pick up health insurance because of preexisting conditions. I am talking about antitrust. That was not mentioned, but the opportunity for facilities to share resources, streamlining the system was mentioned—electronic billing and things of that nature.

In the President's plan, particularly title V, subtitle B, part 3, calls for the development of standard health care benefit forms. Add that to the streamlining and electronic bill. We are talking about streamlining the system. We are talking about saving dollars now.

Subtitle D has to do with medical malpractice and proposes action on liability reform. There are differences on what we mean by liability reform, but at the same time, I believe there is a consensus that something needs to be done.

Subtitle E on fraud and abuse establishes a program.

Since there is consensus, if these issues were given force of law now, we would start saving money now, we would start helping people now. There are so many people falling through the cracks now. They can't wait for the all-or-nothing approach. We need to help them out.

What is wrong with Congress and the White House going forward with these provisions now, along with the insurance portability I mentioned, the sub-issues that are currently in the President's plan, adding to it again a very, very important issue, insurance portability?

Secretary BENTSEN. Congressman, that is where I was last year.

Mr. BILIRAKIS. You were on the right course.

Secretary BENTSEN. But let me tell you, that was not enough, and the only reason I didn't go all the way was because I didn't think we could exact reform with universal coverage.

But I don't think you can get control of health care costs, I don't think you can cut down the shifting of those costs until you achieve universal coverage.

Mr. BILIRAKIS. But we start helping people now, sir. You may be right about the costs. You referred to Governor Chiles from my State of Florida. I don't disagree. But there are so many people out there now.

A lady approached me last Saturday. Her son was married, with four children, and full disability; because of that, he lost his health insurance. He has to wait 2 years before Medicare can pick him up.

Secretary BENTSEN. I have a grandchild who is a Down's syndrome child. I know what health care costs can be. All of us can relate to families or close friends with those kinds of problems, but you cannot get control of the shift that takes place unless you go to universal coverage. I think these are the things that we need to take. We are under pressure to resolve health care issues comprehensively, hopefully once and for all. I think it has to be done.

I look at these kids that are bought to the emergency room. They look for the gunshot wound or the stab, and it is not there, they say let's put that child aside while we take care of this next ambulance that comes in with a trauma victim. When they finally get to that child who was not taken to the doctor earlier because the family could not pay for it, and they waited until the child was too sick, it is much more expensive to take care of that situation in an emergency room setting. I think that those types of cases and the uncompensated care affect the incredible increase in costs that is taking place. I think we have to hold the President's package together to be able to get that truly addressed.

Mr. WAXMAN. Thank you, Mr. Bilirakis.

Mr. Rowland.

Mr. ROWLAND. Thank you. Let me follow up on what the gentleman from Florida was talking about. You mentioned cost-shifting and the fact that we do need universal coverage in order to bring the cost of health care under control. If it was possible to put in place some kind of system that would cover those people who were uninsured and underinsured, to be sure that there was universal coverage and to stop that cost-shifting, would you be receptive to considering a system like that?

Secretary BENTSEN. I would be delighted to look at it. I don't know how you can structure that one. We have looked at the problem and concluded that we need comprehensive reform.

Mr. ROWLAND. I am inclined to believe that we should do some demonstration projects in our country, networking community health centers, which now do an excellent job—and there are now more than 7,800 community health centers in our country to provide acute outpatient care for individuals; I can give you examples of that—and to bring money that now comes from the Medicaid program to these health centers. You know there is a great deal of abuse in that system.

You mentioned people going to emergency rooms, and it costs four times the amount that it would cost if they went, for example, to a community health center to get their care; the amount that could be saved in doing that, that could provide care for those underinsured or uninsured.

And the same way for inpatient care on an acute basis, to work with a system where community health centers and the hospitals work together, building from the community level up to provide care for those people and stop that cost-shifting, to do some demonstration projects to see whether or not that would work.

Would you be receptive to looking at something like that?

Secretary BENTSEN. Dr. Rowland, because of your experience and background, obviously I would be delighted to look at it. I must tell you, that approach is one we are using in south Texas, and it is working pretty well.

Mr. ROWLAND. It is working quite well in the State of Georgia. I am pleased to see that you would be receptive to looking at something like that.

I have another question, if I may. Are there any industrialized nations where employers provide benefits for their employees in part? Are there any others in the world, industrialized nations that do that, other than the United States?

Secretary BENTSEN. I have talked to Theo Waigel about that one, the Finance Minister of Germany. We sent some of the Senate Finance Committee staff over there last year.

Mr. ROWLAND. It is not to the extent we have it here in our country.

Secretary REICH. I think you are correct. Employers in several other industrialized countries do contribute to the cost, but again we are starting from an entirely different place. We are beginning right now.

Our system is employer based for the most part right now. Our judgment is that we have should start from where we are right now, that it is easiest for individuals and easiest for employers, to build on the system.

Mr. ROWLAND. I understand, but might that not be a flaw in our system, and we are starting from a point where the base is already flawed?

Secretary REICH. Our judgment is that it would be an almost Herculean task to create, from out of nothing, an entirely new system that was not employer based. You have to start from where employers and employees are most comfortable. It is difficult to start a system that is not premised on what you have.

Our premise has been that you can improve upon the present system through the principles we have been emphasizing, competition, cost control, and universal coverage. Through this approach, we avoid all the distortions—job lock, welfare lock and all the other things we have been talking about. You can do that. And I think we have.

Mr. WAXMAN. Thank you, Mr. Rowland.

Mr. Greenwood.

Mr. GREENWOOD. Thank you, Mr. Chairman. I would like to direct my question to Secretary Reich. As we have heard this morning, there is concern about whether or not the employer contribution is or is not a tax and whether or not it should be classified as such for the purposes of the Federal Government.

Over the past several weeks, and again this morning, the administration has made the argument that these mandated contributions do not represent a new Federal payroll tax, but are merely premiums payments for health insurance that should be treated as off-budget spending, similar to current employer-employee payments for health insurance.

In a recent article discussing whether these contributions were a tax in the National Journal, Walter Zellman of the White House staff was quoted as follows: "I think when people think about health insurance premiums, they think about buying a premium for themselves. When they think about taxes, they think about putting money in a big pot; when the money is redistributed, they may get more or less than they put in."

I would like you to walk with me through this chart, which I think you have before you, to illustrate how the Clinton plan would work. This is taken from an example described on page 223 of the September 7, 1993, working group draft using an 80 percent employer contribution, an average $4,200 family average premium and an average of 1.5 workers per family in a health alliance.

Family 1 has two workers and is enrolled in Plan A, where the premium is $4,200. Family 2 has one worker and is enrolled in the same plan with the same premium.

Let's walk through the premium for Family 1. The 80 percent share of the premium that each of the employers of both the husband and wife in Family 1 is obligated to pay is $2,240, bringing the combined employer contribution for Family 1 to $4,480. Family 1 is then required to pay its 20 percent share of the premium which is $840. In total the amount of money paid toward the premium for Family 1 is $5,320.

Now let's look at Family 2 which is enrolled in the exact same plan. In this case, the husband, who prefers staying at home to working, stays home and the wife works. Under the Clinton plan, the wife's employer pays 80 percent of the cost of the premium that comes to $2,240. Family 2 contributes the same 20 percent share as Family 1, $840. The total sum paid on behalf of Family 2 is $3,080. This is $2,240 less for the same plan as Family 1.

In essence, Family 1 with two workers is subsidizing Family 2 because one of the spouses doesn't care to work.

Do you agree to the characterization of a tax by Mr. Zellman or, as an economist, do you believe that this element of the Clinton plan represents cross-subsidization?

[The chart referred to follows:]

PREMIUM CROSS-SUBSIDIZATION IN THE CLINTON PLAN

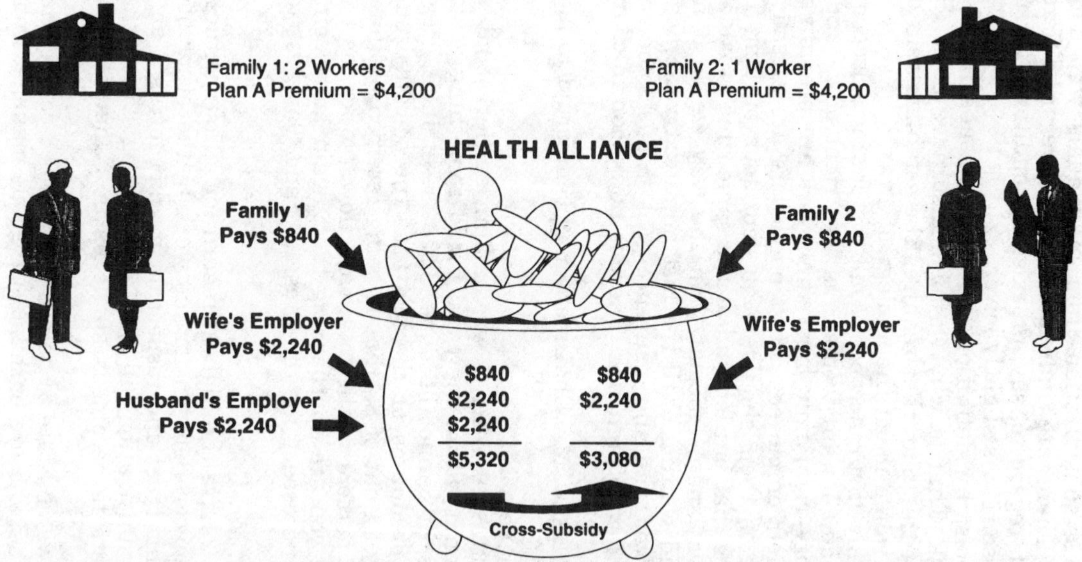

"I think when people think about buying health insurance premiums, they think about buying a premium for themselves. **When they think about taxes, they think about putting money into a big pot, and when that money is redistributed, they may get more or less than they pay in."** Walter Zelman, *National Journal,* 10/9/93, page 2415.

Estimated employer premium contributions are based on an illustrative example as described on page 223 of the 9/7/93 Working Group Draft using an 80% employer contribution toward an average $4,200 family premium and an average of 1.5 workers per family in a health alliance.

Secretary REICH. Every insurance pool in the private sector, involves some cross-subsidization from individuals who don't need the insurance. There are individuals who are in different circumstances with regard to, say, preexisting conditions versus other individuals whose risk is slightly lower.

Insurance pools, by definition, entail cross-subsidies from low risk to high risk. That is why we have insurance pools. So there is nothing about this plan that requires the establishment of insurance pools that would merit the analogy of a tax.

Presumably any insurance pool could be characterized as a tax.

The second point I want to make is that right now—and I want to emphasis this—right now most employers are providing health insurance to their employees. Most employers are already undergoing and have on their shoulders an enormous burden. The purpose is to reduce that burden and at the same time provide universal care in a way more efficient than the way we do it by emergency rooms and waiting until the last minute. So the health care costs will be lower, and any insurance pool entails some cross-subsidization from low to high risk. There is no reason to characterize this as a tax.

Secretary BENTSEN. Mr. Chairman, may I interrupt to modify my statement.

Mr. WAXMAN. Yes.

Secretary BENTSEN. When I was talking earlier about what we could do to remain within the caps, I said something about reduction of benefits. It cannot be done. That is set in the legislation. You can raise premiums or the fact that the so-called subsidy or discount is only $1 out of $5 that is being received by the alliance, so it is only 20 percent of the total cash flow. Notice, as I was saying, as you see you are approaching that, again and begin to take what action is necessary for the President and Congress to correct it.

Mr. WAXMAN. Mr. Cooper.

Mr. COOPER. I have the highest regard for all our witnesses, and particularly Senator Bentsen for his work in the other body. I always admired his trust and respect for market forces. I am worried that in the administration bill that we have legislation that would permit any State to become a single payer Canadian health care State.

It really allows no State to be a true managed-competition State. Since those of us who are enthusiastic about managed competition feel that certain elements such as our tax cap are an indispensable part of real managed competition. That is the aspect of the President's plans that worries me, if we Balkanize our health system with several States choosing single payer options.

No one ran for President in the last election or previous elections championing single payer. The global budget is not a backstop. It will kick in 2 years before universal coverage. Health providers will be trying to please the bureaucrats that are trying to set up the budgets. Those two aspects of the administration plan worry me greatly because they do not seem to allow competitive forces, in some cases, to exist or flourish.

We want to work with the administration to figure out ways we can improve the competition that is in the plan, so we can have more market-based reform and less big government.

Secretary Reich mentioned it would be a Herculean task to move away from our system. I would say the administration is already moving away from an employer-based system because if you are covering the uninsured, the employer alone will not do it; 30 percent of the uninsured have no contact with the work force whatsoever.

So you will have to add a mandate for reaching people outside the work force. We have very little evidence of how you would do that.

We want to work with the administration and figure out answers to these complex questions, but we have a hard time right now understanding how this can be achieved.

Secretary BENTSEN. I know your deep interest in this and all the work that you have done on it. I was looking at all five plans and the number of things we shared in that regard. That helps move all of this debate along. But I must tell you that we put together the people with experience, the best expertise we think we can find. We have tried to have a cushion in that subsidy budget so that in effect it will not be hit by substantial competitiveness in the managed competition approach to this issue.

I have that kind of confidence in the private sector. I think we can have that competition and not hit the subsidy cap. I and others felt strongly that we wanted a further safeguard, and the President agreed, and so there is a cap on the entitlement. We have tried to be sure this program is not something open ended and a blank check. We don't have all the answers. In some of these issues, what we have done was look to the best resources we can to give what we thought was an objective study and understanding of the cost of this proposal and still accomplish the objectives.

Secretary REICH. With regard to the unemployed and the building of a system, undoubtedly if we are going to move to a system that deals with those who are not now covered we have to create something new. The question is, do you start from a base structure that you already have or do you embark on an entirely new building.

My judgment is that we need to improve upon what we have. We have to provide coverage to the uninsured.

By the way, the unemployed would still be in health alliances. In terms of their residence, they would still be in health alliances. If they move from job to job, they would keep their health coverage and stay in the same health alliance if they remained in the same area.

Competition would be allowed to work from day one. This is an extremely important point. Our notion and expectation is that competition will keep costs below the premium caps.

With regard to premium caps, we regard that as an insurance policy. We need premium caps as a fall-back. We owe this to the American people. But our perception is that competition, working through health alliances and working through the bargaining leverage that health alliances will have in getting bids from individual providers, will be the driving force in keeping health care costs under control.

Mr. WAXMAN. Thank you, Mr. Cooper.

Mr. McMillan.

Mr. MCMILLAN. Thank you, Mr. Chairman. Let me add my welcome to all of you for whom I have enormous respect. I would like to extend my welcome to my friend Erskine Bowles, a fellow Panther fan.

Few of us disagree with the goals that you stated, or the identification of the problems you pointed out. I am hopeful that ultimately, through a bipartisan effort, we will reach a kind of accommodation that will produce a very common sense solution to the issue of universal health care.

Where we disagree perhaps is on the means. I think the gentleman from Tennessee touched upon at least one of these proposed solutions. I think the dynamics of the structure that the President proposed will inevitably lead to less and less competition, and consolidation among insurers and alliances providers so there won't be true competition under a capitated system, resulting in consolidation into a very few alliances.

With 88 percent of the work force being forced into regional alliances automatically, and those employers in excess of 5,000 which currently constitute 12 percent of the work force, many will opt into the alliance system. I don't think that consolidation maximizes the private sector response. I think there are some good, responsible alternatives to deal with this that would not disrupt the goals that you seek to achieve.

What I really wanted to focus on today, because I think it is really important is the financial ramifications of what the President is proposing, as well as the alternatives. All of us know well, Mr. Secretary, that the principal problem in the budget today is uncontrolled entitlement programs. If we had the control on the entitlement programs that we have on the balance of the budget, we would not have to have a debate on the budget. Had that been in place, we would have probably taken action to remedy that.

So I think going into something as complicated as health care reform, we need to be darn sure we don't repeat the same mistakes.

I think it is very important that we get that out and as quickly as possible. I have one chart over here which I will just throw up which illustrates my point.

[The chart referred to follows:]

Medicare Catastrophic Coverage Act, and its Repeal

	Outlays 1989-1993		*Difference*	
	*June 1988 Estimate**	*August 1989 Estimate***	*$*	*%*
Prescription Drugs	$5.70	$11.80	$6.1 billion	207%
Skilled Nursing Facilities	2.10	13.50	$11.4 billion	643%
HI (Non-SMF)	7.40	7.80		
SMI (Part B)	14.90	15.20		
Total	30.10	48.30	$18.2 billion	

All amounts in $billions.

*Official CBO cost estimate when Medicare Catastrophic Coverage Act (MCCA) enacted

**Aug. 1989 CBO memo on reestimating MCCA prepared for Senate Finance Committee

Mr. McMILLAN. This chart deals with the catastrophic coverage debate which we had a few years ago and quickly repealed. I don't need to redebate this, but many of the same things we will be addressing in health care reform are included in this last debate.

When the first estimates were made in June 1998, the total cost estimate was roughly $30 billion. Twelve months later, the cost estimates on the same program had risen to an astounding $48 billion. I just think that is an illustration of the importance of good, solid, reliable estimates.

Secretary Bentsen mentioned that the best experts and the best analysts have been pulled together to come up with those costs. I feel certain that as responsible and experienced as each of you are, that you would not be behind the plan if you were not satisfied with that. The only trouble is that the administration has not bothered to share the plan with the rest of us. I think it is extremely important to do this now. We have seen shifting numbers. For example, in Medicare, as I understand it, your savings estimates are $124 billion over 7 years.

Yet your plan—and this is changing or has changed—does not reduce benefits but expands benefits dramatically to the tune of over $131 billion over the same period of time. This is absurd. There is not a clarification here. There is no definition of what it will cost to fund uninsured individuals.

There is no definition of the cost of an expanded Medicaid to bring coverage up to 150 percent of the level of poverty. There is no statement of the amount it will take to subsidize the insurance plans of business, regardless of whether you call this a tax or don't call it a tax.

I believe the American people are entitled to know, however, the additional cost that is going to be mandated upon them even if paid into a insurance alliance to cross-subsidize the cost of others in that insurance pool. If I could just mention a couple more.

Mr. WAXMAN. Mr. McMillan, your time has expired.

Mr. McMILLAN. Let me just say that I bring those up to identify them because I don't think those costs are identified in the plan. I would hope and ask the question when we will be able to see numbers that very specifically define the sources and uses of funds you propose in the health security act proposal?

Secretary BENTSEN. Let me make one point. You referred to Medicare catastrophic, which I remember with great pain. But let me state in that one, we did not include the limits on subsidy spending, so we sure are not making that mistake this time. We tried to anticipate and understand and benefit from our experience in the past.

I think you made a very legitimate point. All I can tell you is that I am totally convinced that you are not looking at tilted numbers and that we, that is OMB, HCFA, and Treasury have estimated and reestimated.

One of the reasons I was delayed in coming up here, asked to be delayed, was that I wanted to be sure of the numbers and I wanted to be sure we finished our internal estimating process.

Mr. McMILLAN. That is the way, but when are we going to see them?

Secretary BENTSEN. I assume we are in the process of giving you numbers now. That is part of what our testimony is about.

Mr. WAXMAN. Thank you, Mr. McMillan.

Mr. Slattery.

Mr. SLATTERY. First of all, Mr. Chairman, let me join my colleagues in expressing my gratitude to all of you today and certainly for the President in providing this country with urgently needed leadership in a most complex problem. I appreciate your courage and his courage in telling the American public in effect, we have a plan. It might not be a perfect plan. But you have led and you are challenging others to come forward and try to improve upon it. I think that is the role of leadership.

I appreciate the fact that you all have done that. Let me share with you several philosophical concerns that I have and then a question.

I am very troubled by what effect this whole proposal is ultimately going to have on your deficit. When I look at the deficit, and I have struggled with this for the better part of the last decade with you and several others, Secretary Bentsen.

What that deficit really is is the difference between what politicians have promised the people of this country and what the people are willing to pay for. That is really what the deficit is. There is a collosal problem with frustrated expectations in this country. People thinking they are overtaxed and people thinking they are not getting the government services they are paying for when in reality they are getting $300 billion of services from the Federal Government that their kids and grandkids are paying for.

One point that I feel extremely strong about, in fact I am not going to compromise on, and that is that we do in fact have in place a system and a method that will enable us to pay for our health care. We should not borrow one bloody dime from our kids and grandkids to pay for our health care costs in this country. I will be looking at all these plans and looking at it from the stand point of how much are these benefits going to cost.

Historically, we have always underestimated the cost of benefits and we have always overestimated savings. This is something that is extremely troubling to me. I hope that as we move forward with this debate, that we don't overpromise to the American public. That is the most important single thing that we have to avoid doing. Let's be candid with the American public.

We should tell them, first, we are not going to solve this problem. We are not going to solve this problem. Why do I say that? There is one simple reason. It is because we are all going to die. I hate to be so blunt, but it is the truth. We ought to tell the American people that what we are trying to do is to restructure this system so we can enjoy life maybe a little longer.

We need to set the parameters of the debate. One of the questions that I have is that when I look at this global budgeting idea, and I am very skeptical about it simply because I have no confidence in this institution's ability to say no. And that is based on 10 years' of experience here. Any suggestion that this institution is going to say no to a demand to raise the global budget so that we can spend more on health care to keep our hospitals open or whatever is absolute nonsense. This institution isn't going to say no. We have no evidence of that. And I don't believe it will in the future.

I want to know specifically where the $124 billion in Medicare cuts are coming from. I have not yet found that information. That is one of the linchpins in this whole thing because if we cannot find the $124 billion in Medicare cuts then we are in to redesigning this whole plan from the standpoint of the benefit package.

I don't have to remind you how bloody difficult it was to find $56 billion dollars here a few months ago with the deficit reduction plan. I am looking at this from the standpoint of how this affects rural America, and I need the details of where this $124 million is coming from.

Secretary BENTSEN. I think that is a very legitimate question. Let me state that HCFA is sending up a list of 25 specific proposals. Congressman, I want to get more numbers and more detail and I will get that to you.

Mr. SLATTERY. So the answer to the question is, we don't have the specifics yet on where this $124 billion is coming from?

Secretary BENTSEN. I understand the proposals are in the bill. HCFA has listed them and they are there.

Mr. SLATTERY. I have not seen the numbers attributed to the specific programmatic changes. That is what I hope I will have an opportunity to see.

One last question.

Secretary BENTSEN. We will get you those tables.

Mr. SLATTERY. When I deal with this question of cost containment, it seems like you have the global budget idea, fee schedule ideas or something else, managed competition. Have you all really looked at and explored the possibility of giving the States the lead role to play in cost containment. The States would have a big incentive in dealing with costs to make their locality more attractive for business expansion.

When I look at this system, I do not see the kind of mechanism that really creates the tension that is going to be needed to contain costs. I like the ideas of entitlement caps because it does create tensions among all the competing interest groups. I was curious if you looked at that idea.

Mr. WAXMAN. The gentleman's time has expired.

Secretary REICH. One of the premises we began with here was that we wanted to get the private sector as actively engaged as possible. We wanted to set up the health alliances on an independent basis, get the forces of competition moving.

If a State wanted to set up its own system, we wanted to provide maximum flexibility. Only the cost controls we wanted to rely on the private sector and private sector institutions.

Again, we don't want to shut off the tap of experimentation but the only way we are going to really get those costs under control is through private market competition. These health alliances are private institutions and will be set up in order to take these bids and conduct market competition.

To put the matter another way, the public sector's responsibility here is to construct a market not to substitute for the market.

Mr. WAXMAN. Thank you Mr. Slattery.

Mr. Hastert.

Mr. HASTERT. Thank you, Mr. Chairman.

I want to welcome all of you gentleman here, and Secretary Bentsen especially, because I have watched your actions in working on health care reform over the last few years.

I think you can agree that health care has to be a bipartisan issue. There is no one way to keep it. I don't think anyone disputes that point. We believe in health security, too. We need to do away with preexisting condition limitations. Portability of health care is absolutely necessary.

There are good ways to cut skyrocketing costs.

I remember your bill, Mr. Secretary, last year, you looked at that small market and you proposed great, pragmatic, common sense legislation where you started to pool the markets and address the problems confronting small businesses. Hopefully, we do not abandon those ideas that are good.

The real issue, I think, in contention here is access. Do you turn one seventh of the economy on its ear to expand access or do you do it in a more common sense and pragmatic way? There are gentlemen on the other side of this dias that are working on that as well as we are.

One of the things that you said intrigued me. You talked about how Congress would face up to the challenge if that shortfall would result from global budgets and caps on entitlements and premiums. You said it was your intent of that comment that Congress would have to face up to the shortfall by increasing taxes and increasing the deficit?

Secretary BENTSEN. I think what you saw in that situation was the Greenspan Commission on Social Security. Frankly, I would expect that, if necessary, they would again take that kind of responsible action to try to bring that about. I don't think I can specify what they do.

Mr. HASTERT. But those would be part of the alternatives that we would have to look at.

Secretary BENTSEN. To increase the deficit? That is my bad ear. I don't hear very well in that ear.

Mr. HASTERT. We are looking for your leadership later on, maybe suggesting things that we would have to do if the premiums were not enough to guarantee the services. I have a question and it has been plaguing me ever since we have been working on it.

Let's say there is a business, a national newspaper, and it has 2,000 employees spread out across 20 States in this country—presumably in 20 different cities and thus, they'd be dealing with different health care alliances, rather than the one insurance company that they currently deal with.

Am I correct in understanding that this proposal would require this newspaper or this national company to deal with 20 different regional alliances with different health plans and with different required employee costs? In a sense, each of those employees in different areas would have a different type of health plan.

Secretary BENTSEN. I think it would, but those companies are having to deal with all those States now.

Mr. HASTERT. I think a national company would have insurance in its home base. They work that way and spend it.

Secretary BENTSEN. When you have 5,000, they are self-contained.

Mr. HASTERT. Thank you. I yield back the time.

Mr. WYDEN [presiding]. I guess I get to ask a question by default. Let me ask you about another area where it seems to me we could give the poor a fair shake. We talked about this with your staff. It is establishing an enforceable standard relating to community service for the health care institutions that qualify for a nonprofit tax status.

This has been an area of concern for our committee because we found that a lot of these so-called nonprofit programs get this huge Federal tax break and don't seem to want to give a lot of care to poor people.

I and others have been interested in developing a Federal and enforceable standard so that if the taxpayers are going to continue to give out billions of dollars as far as I can count in the administration's proposal, there is no change in that tax status, we can wring more value out in terms of indigent care for the poor. I would be interested in your reaction to that.

Secretary BENTSEN. Well, one of the things we would achieve in this plan, there would be no one who would be uninsured. That tax break is important to many of our urban hospitals given the number of poor persons that they had to handle. But we think we take care of that when you have no uninsured any more.

Mr. WYDEN. Maybe I am reading the proposal wrong. Is the nonprofit tax break that is given to hospitals and these providers nationwide, has that changed in the administration's proposal?

Secretary BENTSEN. Yes, it has changed. The current law requires a tax exempt hospital or other provider to promote the health of a class of persons broad enough to benefit the community. Under the administration's plan, in addition to meeting this community benefit test, a hospital or other provider will be required to assess the health needs of this community and develop a plan to meet those needs, hopefully, some of the concerns that you are talking about and we want your input. We will have to plan development process at least annually with the participation of community representatives.

Mr. WYDEN. That certainly sounds like something that indicates the administration wants to work on this. I would just like to see us flesh that out because we are talking about billions of dollars, and particularly with the limit on the subsidies, I think it will be another way to help the poor.

Secretary Reich, one of our colleagues, Mike Synar of Oklahoma, was interested in exploring with you the effects of the President's proposal on productivity and labor mobility. He could not come today. I will ask it for him.

Secretary REICH. On productivity our judgment is that the proposal would increase productivity substantially because American businesses are spending $220 billion a year on health care. That is a tremendous drain on productivity and competitiveness. It is not directly related to productivity.

To the extent that those costs can be contained and controlled, the American business has more money to invest in worker retraining, new machinery and equipment, hiring new people, providing better salaries and benefits.

So containment of that trend, and remember, we are talking about a trend of increasing costs. American businesses, adjusted for inflation, have suffered the burden of increased health care costs of 200 percent since 1970. That trend seems to be up at a tremendous angle. That will reduce the burden, and American companies will be more productive and competitive.

In terms of labor mobility, let me stress the 6 lock, welfare lock and the disability lock. These obstacles prevent people from even getting into the work force because of the difficulties of negotiating health care. All of those would be removed.

Now I didn't mention one thing before that might be particularly pertinent to this question. That is that labor-management relations in recent years, particularly with organized labor, has run aground repeatedly on the shoals of health care.

Over the last couple of years, half the strikes in this country have been over health care benefits. When we get that off the table, we improve labor-management relations as well.

Mr. WYDEN. Mr. Klug.

Mr. KLUG. Let me say that I, like Jim Cooper who asked questions earlier, also have deep concerns about the employer mandate. There was a study released last week that said in Hawaii, which has an employer mandate, the rate of uninsured was 6.8 percent. In my State of Wisconsin, the rate for uninsured was 7.1 percent. So there is really not any clear evidence, at least from my perspective, that an employer mandate necessarily solves the problem completely.

Let me ask about two additional benefits in the President's proposal which I also have grave concerns about in terms of new entitlement programs.

Secretary Reich, the first one, is the administration proposal to have the Federal Government assume liability for early retirees. Doesn't that become an open invitation for more American companies to offer early retirement plans? If I am the president of General Motors, that may be a great deal. I am not sure that is a great deal for the American taxpayer.

Secretary REICH. It is in the sense that many people would like to take early retirement and many companies would like to offer it but they cannot do so because of cost implications. With more people retiring early, we create more options for jobs for younger people coming up through the ranks.

Remember, individuals will have to bear part of the cost, 20 percent, and the Federal Government bears 80 percent of the costs. While it does provide some incentives for early retirement, the strongest incentive actually comes from the existence of universal coverage.

Most of the individuals who will be induced to retire early would be eligible for discounted interest premiums if they chose to retire early even without the early retiree benefit.

I should say also that there is, in the current proposal, a requirement that companies offering early retirement pay back to the Federal Government a part of those costs. So it is not simply an 80 percent share across the board.

Mr. KLUG. What do your projections say in terms of who may take advantage of this early out? I mean, how many people will we see retire early as a result of it with the corresponding Federal liability?

Secretary REICH. Our projections are that at any given time, once this plan is fully in place, 350,000 or 600,000 more people than now would be taking early retirement, would be retiring between the age of 55 and 65. The plan does take into account the additional costs that those 350,000 to 600,000 would entail.

Mr. KLUG. What incentive is there? Why is this a good deal for the Federal Government to underwrite the problems of the automakers.

Secretary BENTSEN. That is for people who have independent income—so called unearned income or total income. When they get up to a point of $130,000 per couple, they would end up paying the 80 percent. So that takes care of your concern, which would have been mine, too.

Mr. KLUG. That dovetails with my second question, which is a subsidy for the elderly to buy prescription over the age of 65 without any kind of tough means testing. Again, at a time when we are wrestling with the same budget problems that you are, please explain to me why we should be subsidizing Ross Perot's high blood pressure medicine or Lee Iacocca's antibiotic. I don't quite see what the public policy advantages are to doing that. That is a great political deal for AARP, but I am not sure about the taxpayers.

Secretary BENTSEN. Another point on Medicare Part B addresses some of your concern there. Where now it is heavily subsidized and the beneficiary pays just 25 percent of it, it would go up to 75 percent for people of means; they would have to pay that additional amount of that subsidy.

Mr. KLUG. And that doesn't cause you any concern, given the problems we already have in this country with entitlement programs.

Secretary BENTSEN. Well, it gives me some comfort that we have proposed a means related premium.

Secretary REICH. I was just informed that there would be the assessment on the companies in early retirement, it would be 50 percent of what they would have been paying for a 3-year period, so there is that cash back for the Federal Government.

Mr. KLUG. Thank you. My concern was why we gave the breakdown of 50 percent in the first case.

Thank you.

Mrs. COLLINS [presiding]. I would like to return to long-term care insurance very briefly. Some critics have expressed concern over giving tax benefits for the purchase of long-term care insurance because the product is aimed toward wealthier Americans and it would subsidize them while doing nothing for other Americans.

Now, do you believe the President's bill is judicious in the choice to award these tax benefits to those who are already wealthy?

Secretary BENTSEN. We are talking about a limited package insofar as long-term care is concerned, and we are trying to assist that. I must say, as I stated earlier, that as you look to that, we have addressed a number of these things in means testing. I just addressed the one on Part B and what we have done there in increasing that for cost to those people of means. Instead of paying 25 percent of the subsidy, they are now going to pay as much as 75 percent of that subsidy. That is the difference that is taking place.

Insofar as people taking early retirement who have additional means, on that one we went up to $125,000 for a couple, that they would pay the full 80 percent. So we are addressing a lot of that.

Mrs. COLLINS. Mr. Secretary, if it is possible, could you just give me a yes or no answer, do you believe the President's bill is judicious and does it award these wealthy Americans tax benefits when those who are not as wealthy don't have any benefits like that?

Secretary BENTSEN. Would you state that again?

Mrs. COLLINS. Do you believe this bill is fair when you are going to give tax deductions to very wealthy Americans and not to Americans who are not wealthy?

Secretary BENTSEN. You know this yes or no stuff——

Mrs. COLLINS. The reason I am asking is because you did not really answer my question.

Secretary BENTSEN. I will answer it in full.

Mrs. COLLINS. You did not answer the first time. The second time I am trying to get a specific answer. I want you to understand and give me your answer.

Secretary BENTSEN. Long-term care insurance will be available to all Americans.

Mrs. COLLINS. How about tax deductions for wealthy Americans?

Secretary BENTSEN. We have materially limited tax deductions in this package for wealthier Americans.

Mrs. COLLINS. End of answer?

Secretary BENTSEN. Yes.

Mrs. COLLINS. Mr. Brown.

Mr. BROWN. I applaud the administration's efforts in this bill, especially with regard to preventive care. I think when Mrs. Clinton came here to this committee back in about February, she really talked about much of the theme of the plan will be preventive care.

This question is either for Secretary Reich or Administrator Bowles. It may fall short with those employers of under 5,000 that will be put into the health alliances, those employers doing a particularly good job with wellness programs, everything from bringing a physician in to doing certain kinds of testing, to having fitness centers and aggressive anti-smoking campaigns, all the kinds of things employers might be doing now in a business of 300 or 400 or 500 or 600 or 2,000 whatever employees.

Is there any plan—I cannot see it looking through the bill from yesterday—is there any effort on your part to build into the premium structure some kind of incentive in addition to the incentives already in terms of productivity of workers that they are well and coming to work and less absenteeism and that.

Is there any incentive built into the plan to encourage the employers who are now doing that to continue doing that once they are put into the larger health alliances?

Secretary REICH. There are incentives for the employers to take every step toward prevention. Moreover, health alliances will encourage providers to take every step toward prevention. Those are the two major pressure points with regard to prevention.

Several questions have come up about tax incentives and the tax breaks for wealthier people. This plan provides major subsidies depending upon your income. The poorer you are, the more of a subsidy you have. The subsidies are means tested. That is a core element of the plan.

Mr. BROWN. I have a couple of more questions following up on my earlier question. Secretary Reich, can you build something into the premium structure for those incentives so it is also done on the employer level?

Secretary REICH. We would be interested in hearing about that.

Mr. BOWLES. That is something we heard from a number of businesses trying to hold down on the cost of health care and that is one of the things we have under discussion now.

Mr. BROWN. How about down the road, if the tax system changes. What about any kinds of programs that an employer does again for preventative care and wellness, bringing doctors in for various kinds of testing programs and wellness programs. Is there any provision of the bill that would exempt them from being a taxable benefit?

Are they going to be taxed on that additional benefit that they have because the bill certainly provides for that taxable, if you will, of the benefits or other kinds of benefits.

Secretary REICH. Let me say two things: Number one, for 10 years, employers can provide additional benefits in the package of health benefits over and above the benefits that are tax free. It is at the 10-year mark where it is reduced to the basic package.

I also want to emphasize that quite apart from all of the other incentives built in at the health alliance stage and also with regard to providers, given their bidding process, there is inevitably an incentive for employers to have healthy employees, to be sure their employees are alert and fully prepared to put in a productive day of work.

I think it is an interesting proposal that you raise with regard to specific benefits that are geared toward improving employee's health and, again, we would be interested in discussing it with you.

Mr. BROWN. Since Secretary Reich took some of my time answering questions——

Mr. WAXMAN. Don't ask. Don't ask me.

Mr. BROWN. I am new around here. Sorry, I can't catch on to that. Surely there are for productivity reasons for an employer and humane reasons incentives now for wellness programs, but there is also an incentive now for an wellness program in terms of lowering the cost of health care premiums. Those are probably never effective.

So do we want to take away any of programs, which is what the plan will do, if we don't address the taxable income 10 years from now and the premium structure on joining health plans now? I would advocate not to take any of that away but find a way. I will be happy to work with any of you in finding a way we can do that now.

Mr. WAXMAN. Mr. Hall.

Mr. HALL. I want to thank the gentlemen for their time and the many gifts they have given to this country in the form of public service. Lloyd Bentsen being from Texas, you would understand my saying I would follow him up any hill, but that is what most Texans say about Lloyd Bentsen. We are Lloyd Bentsen people down there. Thank you for the many, many years of service we have had together.

I might be like the gentleman from New York and use up all my time with my question. You remember the late Senator Tom Connally came through our State in a whistle-stop. He had 10.5 minutes and at 9 minutes, the mayor was still introducing him.

Secretary BENTSEN. I saw Bob Pogue do that to Harry Truman.

Mr. HALL. If the kind chairman does not extend me a little time or cut me some slack, I will get the answers later. I hope it will work. I am a sponsor of a plan. I think it is very laudatory to even dream of flat coverage for everyone because, like you, and like all of us, I have someone in my family that cannot be covered. I think it is a great plan.

We are in the glean years of this health program because we are telling everybody how good it is. Also the moment of truth started yesterday when they filed the bill and we got the bill and began to read it and ask questions about it. Today was to be on what is it going to cost, who pays, and what does it do to the deficit. I know those questions are important to you, or more so, than they are to any of us individually.

I heard Mr. Bowles say not everybody wins, but I did not ask the question who loses. I guess the question is: Who believes they are the losers?

Let me read you an excerpt from letters that I have received that show you how people are thinking and writing to us. These are questions we, who are trying to be supportive, have to answer. From the H&H Farms in Emory, Tex.: "I cannot afford to purchase health insurance for my employees. At present, I employ six full-time, permanent employees. And in the spring, the number increases with temporary, part-time labor. I feel the wages and the working conditions here are good. Otherwise, these employees would not continue to work for me. Each has indicated to me that they prefer this to having a wage decrease that would enable me to furnish them health coverage. They want the security of food on the table. They will take their chance with health provisions."

Another with 32 members, the Reddick Enterprises of Denison, Tex. It employs 32 people. It goes on to say, "mandated Federal health care will break thousands of small businessmen, completely destroy most part-time jobs, and substantially reduce wages for most American workers." From Terrell, Tex., the Worth Home & Auto, Western Auto. "As the owner of a small business, I am opposed to any health care legislation that mandates that I purchase health insurance for myself or my employees or pay additional taxes to cover the population as a whole."

Elliott's Dry Good Hardware Store, a husband and wife and two employees. He has operated it for 48 years. He says, "I am opposed to any health care legislation that mandates that I purchase health insurance for myself or my employees or pay additional taxes to cover the population as a whole. I think that a government mandated plan could put me and a lot of others like me out of business."

The Cannon Steel Erection, Inc., from Tyler, Tex.: "Although I agree that we need reform in our health care system, we need to fix our governmental system first. Let's fix the deficit and the Social Security and Medicare. Let's fix the drug problems and the increasing violence and a long list of other things that the government has tried to fix. Then if government is successful at fixing these things, then and only then should they fix our health care system."

Those letters and many others like them deserve an answer and as time goes along, I hope we will receive an answer that will be acceptable to them. Your work is cut out for you.

A recent Washington Post article reported that when Congress first enacted Medicare legislation in 1965 to expand health care, the government predicted annual costs of $9 billion by 1990. It was $106 billion in 1990. Medicaid suggested a budget of about $1 billion. Last year, Medicaid was $76 billion.

What do I tell people who ask me now, "how can I trust the government to handle this program in a financially responsible position?" I get the chance to eat lunch with you, Lloyd, a little later today. Perhaps you can answer them then. I thank you for your time.

Secretary BENTSEN. I will tell you, I appreciate that very much, particularly from a man with such a long career of distinguished service.

Mr. Chairman, there are winners and losers. For employers that have provided no health benefits, they have an additional cost. But insofar as taking care of those that come in and do uncompensated care, we will achieve more fairness in the system. That is what we are trying to bring about.

If you are talking about a very major company with a lot of low-income workers that it does not cover, then they will pay more. If you are talking about small businesses that have health insurance at the present time for their workers and have a reasonable package, they are going to have a cost reduction. It helps in that regard. Their businesses will not be subject to red lining. They are not going to have an insurer come in and say you have 25 people, I will take them but I won't take her because she has a heart condition. Even though she is the one who probably needs it the most. Those kinds of things are going to be taken care of.

Mr. BOWLES. There is no question I have received a number of letters like those. I have been back to them and found out what they are paying for health care now and what kinds of health care benefits they are able to provide their families and employees.

Doing the arithmetic, we have found the vast majority under the American health care plan will be able to provide better coverage at lower costs when they see the reality of it. Under every circumstance we have seen, whether it is our surveys or NFIB surveys or any other trade group surveys, we found that health care is the number one concern of small business. Every small business wants to provide health care.

What the problem has been is that today it costs too much. The benefits they are able to provide are just not worth it and the costs increase so much that if they truly cannot afford it today, they cannot afford it tomorrow. We have to get this health care mess under control.

Mr. HALL. I certainly join you in hoping that the numbers will fit when volume moves in and the savings take place and maybe we will have a favorable answer for those folks. I thank you for your time.

Mr. WAXMAN. Thank you, Mr. Hall. I know the witnesses have been very generous in their time, but they have other appointments.

[The following letters were submitted.]

WHOLESALE SEASONAL BEDDING PLANTS
SPECIALIZING IN QUALITY

H & H FARMS

RT. 3 BOX 438
EMORY, TEXAS 75440
(214) 473-2717

272552.A

October 20, 1993

The Honorable Ralph Hall
United States House of Representatives
Washington, DC 20515

Dear Representative Ralph Hall:

With utmost respect for you; and, your excellent record of listening and responding to your constituents, I am encouraged to write this letter.

As a small business owner, I can not afford to furnish health coverage for my employees.

At present, I employee six full-time, permanent employees. In the spring the number increases with temporary, part-time labor. I feel the wages and the working conditions here are good, otherwise, these employees would not continue to work for me. Each has indicated to me they prefer this to having a wage decrease that would enable me to furnish them health coverage. They want the security of food on the table.... they will take their chance with health provision.

My business is built on quality and service. The rising taxes already make it a struggle to remain competitive in the greenhouse industry. I have worked too hard and long for what I have, therefore, I will shut down before I allow this situation to take me down. I do not believe I am the only one that this would put out of business.

Based on the free enterprise system, and my personal experience, one gets out of life what one puts into it....it can not be given to you! We already have socialized medicine with our county hospital and current welfare system.

Please take this into consideration when making the decision to enforce this upon us.

Sincerely,

Merle Hutchings

Merle Hutchings

HC 275479.A

CCTP (SINCE 1970) A Division of REDDICK ENTERPRISES ★ Cable: REDENTCO
P.O. BOX 314 ★ DENISON, TEXAS 75020-3194 ★ PHONE: (903) 463-1366 ★ FAX: 903-463-7734

October 3, 1993

Congressman Ralph Hall
236 Cannon HOB
Washington, DC 20515-4304

Dear Ralph:

As an employer of 32 people, I am writing in opposition to any type ~~of national or mandated~~ employer paid health care. We already offer it to most of our permanent employees, but we can't afford the type of mandated care the Clintons are promoting.

During the time you incorrectly describe as being "bad", we were able to triple our business and create 24 brand new jobs! During this time, we and our employees paid a lot of income and social security taxes so that a bunch of lazy, do-nothings and illegal alien wouldn't have to work. Furthermore, because of the good business climate that Presidents Reagan and Bush created, we were able to more than double the average wage we pay our employees. During this time, we also added an incentive plan that now pays over $1.50 per hour per employee, health care coverage, sick pay, longer vacations, and an improved work place. How can Clinton describe this as being bad????

My wife and I both work very, very hard running our business and raising our children and I bitterly resent Clinton's & Gore's accusations that people such as us "profited unfairly". We've re-invested almost every dime we've made during the last 20 years and I think we earned every penny we've made. I normally work 12 to 16 hours 6 or 7 days every week and have a large investment in a building, equipment, and merchandise, (along with a big risk and lots of worrying!), so why shouldn't I make more than some guy that works 8 hours and goes home?

We had planned to establish a 401K retirement plan for our employees this year and were going to expand by tripling the size of our warehouse and office facilities. However, due to the new income taxes and the threat of mandated health care, and the threat of even more federal government intervention in our lives, we've had to shelve these plans. This means that we will not be able to hire the additional employees this expansion would have warranted.

The Clintons' health care plan will provide far worse quality, much higher prices, and rationed care. Witness the deterioration of our public schools thanks to federal mandates and intervention, not to mention that religion has been virtually scrubbed out of them. The same thing will happen to our hospitals - I know, because I've seen it firsthand. My wife is Comanche Indian and was subjected to the

Letter of 10/3/93, Page 2:

lousy U.S. Public Health Service Indian Hospitals in Oklahoma and her uncle was a WWII veteran and received horrendous treatment at the VA hospital in Oklahoma City. One of our employees is a Vietnam veteran and he could hardly even get into the VA hospital in Dallas, so he just gave up! You could also compare it to most of the other bloated, out of control federal agencies and programs such as the Department of Agriculture and the Post Office.

Mandated federal health care will break thousands of small businessmen, completely destroy most part-time jobs, and substantially reduce wages for most American workers. To remain in business, we will have to cut wages, eliminate all part-time jobs, increase our work week, process more goods overseas (thus eliminating several jobs we now do here in the U.S.) and eliminate some other benefits. And then it is not certain that this would be enough, based on the preliminary cost figures I've seen.

You need to work even harder now to CUT SPENDING, CUT TAXES, AND GET THE FEDERAL GOVERNMENT OUT OF OUR LIVES!

I look forward to hearing from you soon.

Very truly yours,

J. Rex Reddick

JRR:go

12J474.A

XC

WORTH HOME & AUTO
WESTERN AUTO - TRUE VALUE HARDWARE
1405-7 W MOORE
TERRELL, TX 75160
October 6, 1993

The Honorable RALPH M. HALL
United States House of Representatives
2236 RAYBURN HOUSE OFFICE BUILDING
WASHINGTON, D.C. 20515

Dear Representative Hall:

I have owned and operated a Home & Auto store in Terrell, Tx for 32 years. I am writing because I am concerned about the health care legislation that Congress will consider soon and I am also concerned about my own health care plan.

As the owner of a small business, I am opposed to any health care legislation that mandates that I purchase health insurance for myself or my employees or pay additional taxes to cover the population as a whole. I think that a government mandated plan will be too expensive for me to afford and could put me and lots of others like me out of business. I also think it is important that health care legislation gives businesses like mine the most flexibility possible in terms of who I can buy health insurance from and what types of benefits I have to buy. This is particularly important in rural and non-metropolitan areas where choices are inherently limited.

KEEP THE GOVERNMENT OUT OF HEALTH CARE PLANS AS THEY HAVE PROVEN THAT GOVERNMENT CANNOT OPERATE EFFICIENTLY OR WITHOUT ADDITIONAL COSTS.

I URGE YOU TO VOTE AGAINST LEGISLATION WHICH HAS THE POTENTIAL TO PUT ME OUT OF BUSINESS AND WHICH WILL MOST CERTAINLY INCREASE UNEMPLOYMENT AND SLOW ECONOMIC RECOVERY.

Sincerely,

WORTH HOME & AUTO

James Farnsworth

James Farnsworth, Owner

ELLIOTT'S
THE HARDWARE STORE
THAT HAS HARDWARE

October 13, 1993

The Honorable Ralph M. Hall
United States House of Representatives
2236 Rayburn House of Representatives Office Building
Washington, D.C. 20510

Dear Representative Hall,

I have owned and operated a True Value Hardware store in Dallas, Texas for 48 years. I am writing because I am concerned about health care legislation that Congress will consider soon and I am also concerned about my own health care plan.

As the owner of a small business, I am opposed to any health care legislation that mandates that I purchase health insurance for myself or my employees or pay additional taxes to cover the population as a whole. I think that a government mandated plan will be too expensive for me to afford and could put me, and lots of others like me, out of business. I also think it is important that health care legislation gives business like mine the most flexibility possible in terms of who I can buy health insurance from and what types of benefits I have to buy. This is particularly important in rural areas where choices are inherently limited.

I urge you to vote against legislation which has the potential to put me out of business and which will most certainly increase unemployment and slow economic recovery.

Sincerely,

Gary C Farber

Gary Farber

138084.A

CANNON STEEL ERECTION, INC.
1201 EAST ERWIN STREET
TYLER, TEXAS 75702
Telephone: 903-593-9913
Fax: 903-592-9744

The Honorable Bill Clinton
President of the United States
The White House
1600 Pennsylvania Avenue
Washington, D.C. 20500

Dear Sir:

I would like to take a few minutes of your time to introduce myself and share my thoughts and opinions on government health care.

I am owner of a small successful business in the East Texas area and employ 15 to 25 employees on the average. For an one man operation this is a handful. What I do not need is more paperwork and responsibility put on my shoulders by the President. How can anyone possibly believe that the government would have the ability or expertise to make this program work.

The reality of the situation is that we are being railroaded into something that we as taxpayers and citizens of a free country can't afford financially or as a free people. Government is being very successful in gaining more and more control over our daily lives and pocket books. This is a terrible but true picture of what is happening in America today.

Although I agree that we need reform in our health care system, we need to fix our governmental system first. Let's "fix" the deficit and the social security & medicare. Let's fix the drug problems and the increasing violence and a long list of other things that the government has tried to "fix". Then if government is successful at fixing these things, then and only then should they "fix" our health care system.

Sincerely,

David E. Cannon

DEC:ml
cc: Hon. Phil Gramm
Hon. Ralph Hall

Mr. WAXMAN. To conclude today, I will call on Mr. Bliley.

Mr. BLILEY. Mr. Chairman, I would like to ask unanimous consent that we keep the record open and perhaps the questions that could not be answered today we can have them answered in writing.

Mr. WAXMAN. Without objection we will take questions in writing and ask the witnesses to respond to those.

Mr. BLILEY. Every time President Clinton makes a speech about his health care plan or the administration puts out a paper on the plan we hear over and over again about six goals.

One of those principles is choice. I agree that guaranteeing choice is a fundamental principle and that we should not pass a plan that doesn't provide. Choice. Clearly the administration believes that the September 7 draft places undue restrictions on choice, particularly with regard to fee-for-service plans.

In the draft the alliance was given the authority to limit the number of fee-for-service plans to three and that restriction appears to have been dropped. But I continue to have serious doubts the extent of choice provided in the Clinton plan, particularly choice of more expensive fee-for-service plans that allow freedom to choice any doctor.

When you look at how the plan actually operates, you realize that choice is very limited. For example, let's look at how the alliance is operating.

[The charts referred to follow:]

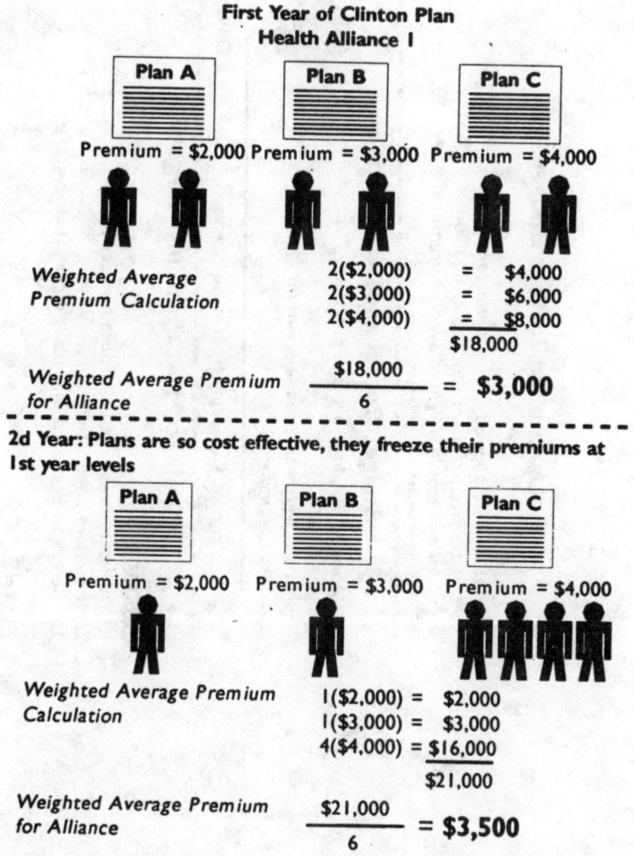
First Year of Clinton Plan
Health Alliance I
Plan A
Plan B
Plan C
Premium = $2,000
Premium = $3,000
Premium = $4,000
Weighted Average Premium Calculation
2($2,000) = $4,000
2($3,000) = $6,000
2($4,000) = $8,000
$18,000
Weighted Average Premium for Alliance
$18,000 / 6 = $3,000
2d Year: Plans are so cost effective, they freeze their premiums at 1st year levels
Plan A
Plan B
Plan C
Premium = $2,000
Premium = $3,000
Premium = $4,000
Weighted Average Premium Calculation
1($2,000) = $2,000
1($3,000) = $3,000
4($4,000) = $16,000
$21,000
Weighted Average Premium for Alliance
$21,000 / 6 = $3,500

Update for 2d Year Budget

Alliance: *Update allowed for premium cap* = 5.2%
Update premium = (5.2%)($3,000) = $151
Permissable weighted average premium = $3,151
(Premium cap from 9/7/93 draft)

Budget Compliance Calculation

Allowed weighted average premium per person = $3,151

Actual weighted average premium based on individual choice = $3,500

Amount Exceeding Budget, per person = $349

Tools to Meet Premium Targets

Alliance

1. An assessment can be imposed on each plan
2. Premium negotiations
3. Refuse to negotiate with plans higher than average

State

1. Limit enrollments in high cost plans by:
   * Freezing enrollment in higher cost plan -- Alliance develops a lottery to reassign individuals
   * Surcharging higher-cost plans
2. Rate setting for doctors and hospitals
3. Limiting new health care technologies & innovations through plans

Federal Government

The National Board notifies Secretary of HHS and the Federal Government takes over Alliance.

Mr. BLILEY. If we start at the top of the chart we see how the weighted average premium is determined in year one of the Clinton plan. Plan A has a premium of $2,000 and two individuals have selected that plan.

Plan B has a premium of $3,000 and two individuals have selected that plan. Plan C has a premium of $4,000 and again two individuals have selected that plan. Let's also remember that the Clinton plan mandates Federal subsidy levels so that Medicaid recipients the lower income and the unemployed will been forced to choose the lower priced plan.

The weighted average premium is determined by multiplying the number of individuals by the premium amount to arrive at the total amount of premiums paid to each plan. An example is to add two times two is four. The totals are added to get the total amount of premiums paid to all plans, in this case, $18,000. This number is then divided by the total number of individuals in all the plans and the calculation comes out to a weighted average of $3,000.

Let's assume as in the bottom half of that chart that a miracle occurs that the plans are so efficient that they don't raise their premiums a cent. However, some of the people in plans A and B decide they are willing to pay more and want to to move into the higher cost plan. One individual from plan A, one individual from plan B moving into C, the weighted average automatically increases to $3,500.

Well, as we can see from the second chart, this is simply unacceptable. You see under the Clinton plan premiums are only allowed to grow at 5.2 percent in the second year of the plan. Five point two percent of $3,000 is $151 which means that the weighted average premium in year 1 can be no more than $3,151.

We have a problem because the weighted average premium achieved only by individuals choosing different plans is $3,500.

The alliance must now take steps to reduce the level of spending in the system. Another one of my colleagues will explore in more detail the tools available, but I want to emphasize that it is at this point that choice goes out the window.

This point was clearly enunciated in one of our earlier hearings by Michael Brumberg, executive director of Federal American Health Systems. He states that on the one hand the Clinton plan has increased choice for individuals but on the other hand, we have empowered them to make the choice, and if government doesn't like the choice, they penalize the consumer.

You did not choose the plan that government thought was best for you. You chose the one that was more expensive, he goes on to say. Now, they chose that plan with their own money, not a dime of Medicare or Medicaid money, no tax subsidy, nothing.

Now I am not aware of any other program where the Federal Government can tell me how to spend my money. Where is the choice of that?

Secretary Reich, will you please explain how an individual still retains choice.

Secretary REICH. Yes, Congressman. It is important to note that right now, large numbers of employees who have their health insurance from their employer have little or no choice.

This plan codifies the requirement that there in fact be choice, that every employer does provide a range of choices.

Let me just make one more point. Alliances can put caps on the number of people that can enroll in high-cost plans. That is permissible under this arrangement. But individuals who are not able to enroll in a high-cost plan could still buy supplemental insurance so that the particular calculation you made is simply not going to be a problem for alliances that are controlling their costs the way they should be controlling their costs.

Mr. BLILEY. Thank you. But you confirmed that my charts are correct because you say that they can cap and say that no more people can take the higher cost plan. And then you say they can get the choice if they buy supplemental insurance. So, in other words, they have to pay a lot more for it if they are going to have the choice.

Secretary REICH. That is right. Alliances can put caps on the number of people that can enroll in high-cost plans. But again, let me emphasize, individuals that are not able to enroll in a high cost plan could still buy supplemental insurance.

I want to emphasize something that Secretary Bentsen and Administrator Bowles have been emphasizing along with me—the whole point here is to get some control through market forces over this health care budget that is raging out of control and at the same time cover everyone and do it in an equitable way.

We feel that although there will be pressure put on health alliances to maintain their budgets, that is good pressure, not bad pressure. That is exactly what we want.

We will also be putting pressure on the health alliances to put pressure on health providers. That is good pressure, not bad pressure. That is pressure that we are talking about in terms of making the market work better and having the government create a health market that works better than now because right now there are very few incentives in the direction of cutting costs.

Mr. WAXMAN. Thank you very much, Mr. Bliley. Gentlemen, I want to commend you for your testimony, your willingness to answer these questions. We want to work with you.

Mr. BLILEY. I want to say this has been one of the best hearings that we have had.

[Whereupon, at 12:50 p.m., the subcommittees were adjourned, to reconvene at the call of the Chair.]

[The following correspondence was submitted for the record:]

ONE HUNDRED THIRD CONGRESS

CARDISS COLLINS ILLINOIS CHAIRWOMAN

EDOLPHUS TOWNS NEW YORK
JIM SLATTERY KANSAS
J ROY ROWLAND GEORGIA
THOMAS J MANTON NEW YORK
RICHARD H LEHMAN CALIFORNIA
FRANK PALLONE JR NEW JERSEY
JOHN D DINGELL MICHIGAN
(EX OFFICIO)

CLIFF STEARNS FLORIDA
ALEX McMILLAN NORTH CAROLINA
BILL PAXON NEW YORK
JAMES C GREENWOOD PENNSYLVANIA
CARLOS J MOORHEAD CALIFORNIA
(EX OFFICIO)

ROOM H2-151
FORD HOUSE OFFICE BUILDING
PHONE (202) 226-3160

DAVID SCHOOLER
STAFF DIRECTOR/CHIEF COUNSEL

U.S. House of Representatives
Committee on Energy and Commerce

SUBCOMMITTEE ON COMMERCE,
CONSUMER PROTECTION, AND COMPETITIVENESS

Washington, DC 20515-6120

November 3, 1993

The Honorable Lloyd M. Bentsen, Jr.
Secretary
U.S. Department of the Treasury
15th and Pennsylvania Avenue NW
Washington, D.C. 20220

Dear Secretary Bentsen:

Thank you for your appearance before our subcommittee. In order to clarify your answer to my question concerning tax benefits for long term care insurance, please provide the answers to the following questions, no later than November 17, 1993.

1) What is the estimated annual cost to the Treasury of the tax treatment of long term care insurance contained in the President's proposal?

2) In the calculation of the answer to the above question, what is (a) the assumed number of individuals receiving the tax benefit; (b) the assumed average annual premium paid; (c) the assumed average tax benefit per individual; and (d) the average annual income of individuals receiving such benefit?

In addition, if you have other information concerning your assumptions about the income of individuals who will benefit from the tax provisions, please provide it along with your answers.

Sincerely,

Cardiss Collins

CARDISS COLLINS
Chairwoman

CC:ds

DEPARTMENT OF THE TREASURY
WASHINGTON

ASSISTANT SECRETARY

November 30, 1993

The Honorable Cardiss Collins
Chairwoman
Subcommittee on Commerce, Consumer Protection, and Competitiveness
Committee on Energy and Commerce
U.S. House of Representatives
Washington, D.C. 20515-1307

Dear Madam Chairwoman:

Thank you for your follow-up letter to Secretary Bentsen concerning his appearance before your subcommittee.

In your letter, you ask about Treasury's revenue estimates for the Administration's health care proposals dealing with long-term health care insurance premiums. The Administration's health care package contained two such proposals. First, Treasury estimates that the proposal to allow a medical deduction for individually-purchased long-term care insurance policy premiums will cost $.7 billion over the 1995-2000 period. Second, Treasury estimates that the proposal to allow an individual to exclude from taxable income any employer-paid long-term care policy premiums will cost $.3 billion over the 1995-2000 period.

In calculating these estimates, Treasury relied on information provided by the Department of Health and Human Services (HHS). You should contact HHS for release of this information.

We hope this information is helpful. Please let us know if we can be of further assistance in this matter.

Sincerely,

Michael B. Levy
Assistant Secretary
(Legislative Affairs)

ONE HUNDRED THIRD CONGRESS

CARDISS COLLINS, ILLINOIS, CHAIRWOMAN

EDOLPHUS TOWNS, NEW YORK
JIM SLATTERY, KANSAS
J. ROY ROWLAND, GEORGIA
THOMAS J. MANTON, NEW YORK
RICHARD H. LEHMAN, CALIFORNIA
FRANK PALLONE, JR., NEW JERSEY
JOHN D. DINGELL, MICHIGAN
(EX OFFICIO)

CLIFF STEARNS, FLORIDA
ALEX McMILLAN, NORTH CAROLINA
BILL PAXON, NEW YORK
JAMES C. GREENWOOD, PENNSYLVANIA
CARLOS J. MOORHEAD, CALIFORNIA
(EX OFFICIO)

ROOM H2-151
FORD HOUSE OFFICE BUILDING
PHONE (202) 226-3160

DAVID SCHOOLER
STAFF DIRECTOR/CHIEF COUNSEL

U.S. House of Representatives
Committee on Energy and Commerce

SUBCOMMITTEE ON COMMERCE,
CONSUMER PROTECTION, AND COMPETITIVENESS

Washington, DC 20515-6120

December 7, 1993

The Honorable Lloyd M. Bentsen, Jr.
Secretary
U.S. Department of the Treasury
15th and Pennsylvania Avenue, N.W.
Washington, D.C. 20220

Dear Secretary Bentsen:

Thank you for your recent response to my November 3, 1993 letter, in which I requested additional information on the long-term care insurance tax benefits contained in the Health Security Act. (A copy of the November 3rd letter is attached.) Although you provided an answer to the first question contained in the letter, the second question was unanswered. Please respond to the second part of my request no later than December 21, 1993, so that it may be included as part of the hearing record.

Sincerely,

Cardiss Collins
CARDISS COLLINS
Chairwoman

CC:brk
Enclosure

DEPARTMENT OF THE TREASURY
WASHINGTON, D.C.

SECRETARY OF THE TREASURY

January 11, 1994

The Honorable Cardiss Collins
U.S. House of Representatives
Washington, D.C. 20515

Dear Mr. Collins:

Thank you for your letter of December 7 requesting additional information regarding the tax treatment of long-term care insurance under the Administration's proposed health care reform plan. Since we relied heavily on analyses prepared by the Department of Health and Human Services (HHS) of the anticipated future purchases of such insurance for our revenue estimates (which we sent you earlier), we suggested that you contact HHS for the answers to your remaining questions. I understand that you have sent a letter requesting this information to the Secretary of Health and Human Services, and that HHS is preparing a response to your questions.

Thank you again for writing.

Sincerely,

Lloyd Bentsen

ONE HUNDRED THIRD CONGRESS

CARDISS COLLINS, ILLINOIS, CHAIRWOMAN

EDOLPHUS TOWNS, NEW YORK
JIM SLATTERY, KANSAS
J. ROY ROWLAND, GEORGIA
THOMAS J. MANTON, NEW YORK
RICHARD H. LEHMAN, CALIFORNIA
FRANK PALLONE, JR., NEW JERSEY
JOHN D. DINGELL, MICHIGAN
(EX OFFICIO)

CLIFF STEARNS, FLORIDA
ALEX McMILLAN, NORTH CAROLINA
BILL PAXON, NEW YORK
JAMES C. GREENWOOD, PENNSYLVANIA
CARLOS J. MOORHEAD, CALIFORNIA
(EX OFFICIO)

ROOM H2-151
FORD HOUSE OFFICE BUILDING
PHONE (202) 226-3160

DAVID SCHOOLER
STAFF DIRECTOR/CHIEF COUNSEL

U.S. House of Representatives
Committee on Energy and Commerce

SUBCOMMITTEE ON COMMERCE,
CONSUMER PROTECTION, AND COMPETITIVENESS

Washington, DC 20515-6120

December 7, 1993

The Honorable Donna Shalala
Secretary
U.S. Department of Health and
Human Services
Hubert Humphrey Building
200 Independence Ave., S.W.
Washington, D.C. 20201

Dear Secretary Shalala:

Secretary of the Treasury Lloyd Bentsen recently sent a response to my November 3rd letter to him, a copy of each of which are attached, requesting additional information on the long-term care insurance tax benefits contained in the Health Security Act. Although he provided an answer to the first question contained in the letter, the second question was unanswered. He also indicated that your Department would be the appropriate office to contact for information that was used in the calculation of the Treasury Department's figures and he suggested that we seek that information from you. Please provide any information pertinent to my original request no later than December 21, 1993, so that it may be included as part of the hearing record.

Sincerely,

Cardiss Collins

CARDISS COLLINS
Chairwoman

CC:brk
Enclosures

DEPARTMENT OF HEALTH & HUMAN SERVICES

Office of the Assistant Secretary
for Legislation

Washington, D.C. 20201

The Honorable Cardiss Collins
Chairwoman
Subcommittee on Commerce, Consumer Protection,
and Competitiveness
Committee on Energy and Commerce
U.S. House of Representatives
Washington, D.C. 20515-1307

Dear Madam Chairwoman:

On November 30, 1993, the Department of the Treasury responded to your letter concerning questions related to tax benefits for long-term care insurance. I appreciate your interest in the Administration's long-term care proposals and would like to provide you with the additional information you requested.

The Administration's health care package contains two proposals related to long-term care insurance premiums. The first would allow individuals to deduct the cost of qualified long-term care insurance policies to the extent that total medical expenses exceed 7.5 percent of a taxpayer's adjusted gross income. The Treasury Department estimates that this provision would cost $0.7 billion over the 1995 to 2000 period.

The estimate of $0.7 billion is based on an estimate that approximately 300,000 persons would purchase qualified policies (either individually or through employer-sponsored group plans) in 1996, increasing to 930,000 by 2000, <u>and</u> would be able to deduct the costs of these policies for tax purposes.

The estimate of 930,000 purchasers is based on the assumption that approximately 10 percent of the estimated 9.3 million purchasers in the year 2000 would qualify for the tax deduction for medical expenses in excess of 7.5 percent of adjusted gross income. The estimate of 9.3 million purchasers in the year 2000 is from the Department of Health and Human Services using the Brookings-ICF Long-Term Care Financing Model. The estimate that approximately 10 percent of individuals who purchase long-term care insurance would qualify for the tax deduction is from the Treasury Department.

Treasury estimates that the average tax benefit per taxpayer who can deduct qualified long-term care policy costs in the year 2000 would be approximately $250. We note that DHHS estimates that the average annual cost of a policy in the year 2000 is estimated to be approximately $1,230.

Page 2 - The Honorable Cardiss Collins

The second provision related to long-term care insurance premiums included in the Health Security Act allows employers to exclude from an employee's taxable income payments on behalf of employees for qualified long-term care insurance policies. The Treasury Department estimates that this provision would cost $0.3 billion over the 1995 to 2000 period. Treasury estimates that approximately 400,000 individuals would have at least part of their qualified long-term health care premiums paid for by their employer. Treasury estimates that the average tax benefit per taxpayer who can exclude employer-paid qualified long-term care policy costs from taxable income in the year 2000 would be approximately $300.

The Health Security Act also allows individuals to exclude from income the benefits paid by long-term care insurance policies. The Treasury estimates that this provision would cost $0.6 billion over the 1995 to 2000 period.

In addition, the effective tax rate for the medical expense deduction taken by those who purchase qualified policies implies an average taxable income for those receiving tax benefits of approximately $37,000 for single persons and $61,000 for married persons in 1993 dollars (approximately $47,000 and $78,000 in 2000). Of course, average gross income would be higher than average taxable income.

We hope this information is helpful. Please let us know if we can be of further assistance in this matter.

Sincerely,

Jerry Klepner
Assistant Secretary
for Legislation

77-929 O - 94 (640)

ISBN 0-16-044158-7
90000
9 780160 441585